AUTOGRAPHS AND MANUSCRIPTS: A COLLECTOR'S MANUAL

AUTOGRAPHS AND MANUSCRIPTS: A COLLECTOR'S MANUAL

EDMUND BERKELEY, JR.
Editor

HERBERT E. KLINGELHOFER AND KENNETH W. RENDELL
Coeditors

Sponsored by
THE MANUSCRIPT SOCIETY

CHARLES SCRIBNER'S SONS
New York

Library of Congress Cataloging in Publication Data:
Main entry under title:
Autographs and manuscripts: a collector's manual.

Bibliography: p.
Includes index.
1. Autographs—Collectors and collecting. 2. Manuscripts—Collectors and collecting. I. Berkeley, Edmund, 1937— II. Klingelhofer, Herbert E. III. Rendell, Kenneth W. IV. Manuscript Society.
Z41.A92 929.8 78-8177
ISBN 0-684-15622-9

This book published simultaneously in the United States of America and in Canada—

Any correspondence or queries regarding the information contained in this book may be addressed to The Executive Secretary, The Manuscript Society, 1206 North Stoneman Avenue, #15, Alhambra, California 91801.

1 3 5 7 9 11 13 15 17 19 V/C 20 18 16 14 12 10 8 6 4 2

Printed in the United States of America

THE MANUSCRIPT SOCIETY

respectfully and affectionately dedicates
this book to

HERBERT E. KLINGELHOFER

whose tenacity and purpose made it possible.

CONTENTS

Editor's Foreword
Edmund Berkeley, Jr. — *xi*
Introduction
Clifton Waller Barrett — *xv*

SECTION I:
FUNDAMENTALS

The Development of Writing
Diana J. Rendell — 3
Writing Instruments and Materials
Edmund Berkeley, Jr. — 28
The History of Autograph Collecting
Joseph E. Fields — 40

SECTION II:
RUDIMENTS OF AUTOGRAPH COLLECTING

The Language of Autograph Collecting
Edmund Berkeley, Jr. — 53
Who Collects Autographs and Manuscripts, and Why: The Philosophy of Collecting
Kenneth W. Rendell — 63
Acquiring Autographs and Manuscripts
Herbert E. Klingelhofer — 66
The Detection of Forgeries
Kenneth W. Rendell — 73

Famous Forgers: Their Successes and Downfalls
Kenneth W. Rendell 92
The Autopen and the Signa-Signer
H. Keith Thompson 100
Hidden Signatures
Herbert E. Klingelhofer 106
Confused Identities
Joseph E. Fields 111
Changing Handwriting
Edmund Berkeley, Jr. 117
John Adams—His Handwriting
Gordon T. Banks 120
Fair Copies and Working Copies
Robert L. Volz 126
Organizing and Displaying Your Collection
David Herr Coblentz 134
Nothing Is Forever: Preservation, Repairs, and Your Responsibility
Robert C. Wiest 142
Your Manuscripts and the Scholarly World
Carolyn Hoover Sung 156
Legal Ramifications of Manuscript Collecting
Leslie J. Schreyer 170
Values
Mary A. Benjamin 178
The Market for Autographs: The European Scene
Michel Castaing 189
Ethics
John F. Reed 191

SECTION III: SOME AREAS IN WHICH TO COLLECT

Specialized Collecting
Richard Maass 203
Autographs of American Presidents
Christopher C. Jaeckel 211
American Literary Autographs
Michael Papantonio 258
English Literary Autographs
Roy L. Davids 270

French Literary Autographs
Walter G. Langlois 289
European and World Literatures
Henry Strutz 304
American Colonial and Revolutionary Autographs
John C. Dann 332
Autographs of the American Civil War
Charles F. Cooney 343
British Historical Autographs
John Wilson 347
European Historical Autographs
Members of the Editorial Board 361
Musical Autographs and Manuscripts
Irving Lowens 377
Collecting Scientific and Medical Autographs
Rudolf F. Kallir 392
Collecting the Documents of Art
Thomas B. Brumbaugh 405
Religious Manuscripts
James Kritzeck 425
Autographs and Manuscripts of Exploration and Travel
John Parker 440
Autographs and Manuscripts of Radicals and Reformers
Walter Goldwater 454
British Theater and Dance
C. A. Kyrle Fletcher 459
American Theater
Franklyn Lenthall 472
Justices of the Supreme Court of the United States
Gerhard A. Gesell 489

SECTION IV:

Bibliography 497
Notes About the Contributors 511
Glossary 518
Index 525

EDITOR'S FOREWORD

AUTOGRAPH COLLECTING IS almost as old as writing itself. Man has always been interested in the writing of other persons, perhaps because preserving a piece of their writing is a way of preserving a bit of the persons themselves. For thousands of years, autograph collecting had only a limited appeal because comparatively few persons learned to read and write; autograph collecting has no appeal to the illiterate. With the spread of general education in the mid-nineteenth century, the interest in autograph collecting grew rapidly.

The increasing popularity of the hobby, and the availability of relatively inexpensive printing in the nineteenth century, brought onto the market a number of books on the collecting of autographs written by collectors and dealers. Many were little more than reminiscences, but most contained a few bits of useful advice. To accumulate a useful store of knowledge about autograph and manuscript collecting, one had to acquire a good many books, gleaning from them a fact here and another there. Acquiring the books proved difficult, for many were printed in limited editions and others were not kept in print for long. The twentieth century brought no improvement in this situation until after World War II, and the novice collector found it difficult to acquire knowledge about his avocation unless he was lucky enough to be introduced to it by a friendly and experienced collector, or a dealer, who lived close by.

From the early days of the Manuscript Society, which was founded in 1948, it was the dream of a number of its members that the society would, one day, publish a comprehensive manual about autograph collecting. Such a manual would do a great deal, they believed, to promote the aims of the society, which are printed on its letterhead: ". . . to foster the greater use of original source manuscript material in the study, teaching and writing of history . . . to facilitate the exchange of information and knowledge among researchers, scholars and collectors . . . to encourage the meeting of collectors and stimulate and aid them in their various collecting specialities." It has taken many years to realize this dream.

In the fall of 1972, the board of directors of the society, headed by its president, Herbert E. Klingelhofer, decided to undertake the autograph book project; they demonstrated the commitment to it by appropriating a substantial sum toward the expenses. The directors appointed a committee headed by Gordon T. Banks to oversee the preparation of the book, and empowered the committee to engage an editor. Joseph E. Fields, John M. Jennings, and Herbert Klingelhofer have served on the book committee from its inception. Regrettably, Mr. Banks's health and his many commitments did not permit him to remain on the committee after the first year; Herbert Klingelhofer replaced him as chairman, and Kenneth W. Rendell was appointed to the committee.

The book was conceived from the beginning as a reference book. It was to be a cooperative project with articles on the various aspects of collecting, and on types of collections, each article to be contributed by an expert in that area. After the editor was chosen, the book committee met with him and a general plan for the book was evolved from the initial conceptions. It was to contain a lengthy section giving collectors information about the fundamentals of autograph collecting, its language, and procedures. A second section was to include articles on collecting autographs in various fields and areas of specialization. Finally, the committee and the editor agreed that the book should contain an extensive bibliography and a glossary. This general plan has been followed, and these elements make up this book.

The committee knew that the book could not include articles about every area of collecting, because there are almost as many areas of specialization as there are collectors. It decided that the book should include articles on some of the old and standard areas, and some on areas that would not be as obvious. In every instance the authors were to be asked to describe the appeal of this specialization, to note what material was available and could be obtained, to note what was unobtainable, and to suggest some new approaches or new subspecialties. A long and tedious process of locating knowledgeable persons who were willing to write for the book began in 1973.

This book exists because thirty-three persons very generously agreed to contribute their time and effort to the writing of articles for it. A number wrote two pieces; two authors wrote three each. The society is especially grateful to the contributors whose names appear in the "Notes About the Contributors" section and at the beginnings of their articles. Their essays have far surpassed our hopes for the book.

The prices of autographs are mentioned in many articles. The committee was concerned about using them, for it feared that readers would forget that these prices were accurate only at the time the particular article was written, and might not be at the time of reading. Prices have been included because the committee believed they are valuable as a means of comparison within the articles in which they appear, and because it felt that collectors would find it instructive to know what prices were in 1974–1976, when most of these articles were prepared.

Lists of suppliers, conservators, autograph dealers, and appraisers have not been included in this book. It is impossible to assemble an accurate list of autograph dealers. The number who handle autographs and manuscripts exclusively is limited, but many dealers in other collectibles also handle some autographs; there are literally hundreds of dealers who sell autographs. By examining copies of the various autograph journals listed in the bibliography, the names of dealers may be found in their advertisements. The best source of information about suppliers, conservators, and appraisers is a dealer, or a professional in an institution near the concerned collector. Other collectors also will be able to make recommendations. The Society of American Archivists maintains a list of archives and manuscript appraisers; it is free upon request, but a self-addressed, stamped, business-size envelope is appreciated.

The editor wishes to express his sincere appreciation to the members of the book committee for their dedication and generous assistance to him. The preparation of the book has been a long and drawn-out process, but the committee members have borne the strain with equanimity and good humor. My particular thanks go to Dr. Klingelhofer, who has been both a tower of strength and a font of information that have enabled me to overcome a number of problems. My wife and my children have been most understanding of my disappearing into the study every evening, and reasonably tolerant of the typing at late hours; I could not have completed this work without their support and forbearance.

Edmund Berkeley, Jr.
Charlottesville, Virginia
May 15, 1977

INTRODUCTION

THE COLLECTING OF MANUSCRIPTS is a pursuit that has been honored throughout the history of the recorded word. This, of course, includes the symbols of transmitted ideas, such as engraved tablets, hieroglyphics, and other evidences of languages, some of which have never been deciphered. Cuneiform impressions, the Rosetta stone, and the Aztec calendar are examples of records the preservation of which has added much to our knowledge of vanished civilizations. While the work of philologists, historians, and paleographers has been of vital importance in unveiling the secrets of the past, the activities of the collector have played an important part in the unearthing and safeguarding of these cultural treasures.

The collector of today, therefore, has a powerful motivating and sustaining force in the record of the labors of his predecessors, and one that helps to keep his collecting proclivities alive and active even in the face of discouragements and disappointments. No one has ever evolved a tenable theory as to what makes a collector do what he does. Although such individuals have existed through the ages, their creation and emergence has never been satisfactorily explained. Perhaps the simple statement "Collectors are born, not made" covers the case best. In any event, it might be well to put aside theorizing on the origins of this happy breed and concentrate on their activities. It may be that in doing so we can shed some light on their methods and achievements and, if we are lucky, establish some useful guidelines for collectors, both old and new.

Naturally, collectors vary in the intensity with which they pursue their activities. Some dabble intermittently in things that strike their fancies. Others devote lifetimes to the gathering of material in which they are interested. It is the latter class of collectors, to which we can apply the term "serious," with which we are particularly concerned.

The fields in which a collector of manuscripts can engage himself are almost unlimited. Such broad areas as science, art, history, and literature have endless subdivisions. One can pursue the letters and papers of a single individual, as evidenced by the renowned collection of Horace Walpole assembled by Wilmarth Lewis of Farmington, Connecticut. Conversely, significant collections can be made in the American Revolution period, as has been done at the Clements Library in Ann Arbor, Michigan, or the Bolshevik Revolution in Russia, at Columbia University. Perhaps the most alluring task is to gather a glittering assemblage of high spots, such as can be found at the Pierpont Morgan Library in New York or the Huntington Library in San Marino, California. Here it should be noted that few collectors have the enormous resources of a Morgan or a Huntington to gather the treasures of centuries in such profusion and in such superb examples.

Therefore, we should perhaps address ourselves to the hopes and achievements of collectors with less opulent resources. There will be no surprise to the seasoned practitioners in the statement that significant and valuable collections have been made, and will continue to be made, by individuals in this less-exalted financial category. There are numerous examples of such achievements in the single-author collection. The collection of Walt Whitman formed by Charles E. Feinberg, now at the Library of Congress; the William Faulkner and the Robert Frost collections at the University of Virginia; and the superb holdings of Petrarch at Cornell are only a few of many cases in point. Of course, there is no reason why a collector should confine himself to the work of a single author, artist, composer, soldier, scientist, or statesman. One can select from an infinite variety of subjects or periods.

One piece of advice that might be given to a collector is to concentrate. This need not be as limiting as it sounds. Concentration can be focused on a single outstanding figure, or it may include his contemporaries or cover his intellectual, social, or political background. In general terms, it might seek to encompass a cultural movement, a scientific development, or a historical period. The important thing is that the collection have a definite perspective or theme—or, if you please, an architectural form. Even a rather imposing collection of high spots loses luster in comparison with a gathering of material that thoroughly documents or illuminates a certain subject, a life, the activities of a group, or an important event. In these cases the material gains in value by its unity, the whole being worth more than the sum of its parts.

Once the collector has carved out his territory, so to speak, the question arises as to the kind of manuscript material he should seek. I believe that most dealers and collectors would agree that the cut signature is the least attractive kind of item. From there one can go upward to the perfunctory letter, the signed printed document, the significant letter, the run of interesting and revealing correspondence, the notebook, and the diary, until we reach the greatest desideratum, the original manuscript of an important work. In listing desirable material we should not forget the printed book that contains a presentation inscription or notes by the author.

In seeking material the collector naturally must establish a modus operandi. The places where desirable manuscripts may be discovered are innumerable. The family, friends, and associates of the writer are, of course, natural sources. The auction market provides many opportunities. Purchase of existing collections is a means of fleshing out or enriching new collections. Even the discovery of sensational items in attics and basements, although greatly exaggerated as to frequency and value of the material found, cannot be discounted. However, the opportunities for a collector to strike pay dirt in these various sources are limited by his pertinacity and the time and energy he can devote to the pursuit. Here is where the dealer comes in. There are a number of established manuscript dealers in the United States and abroad. In recent years the ranks of these practitioners have been considerably enlarged. This has naturally resulted in an intensification of the search for new material. In my opinion, it behooves the serious collector to establish relations with the leading dealers in his field. The criteria for the judging of dealers should, of course, include integrity, experience, and knowledge. The best method of employing their services is an individual matter; but a careful reading and a comparison of their catalogs provides a good guide to the variety of material offered, the dependability of the descriptions, and the fairness of the prices asked.

In any event, I believe the patronage of reputable dealers is an important—indeed, essential—requirement for the assembling of a good manuscript collection. Transactions with dealers need not be confined to purchases from their catalogs or visits to their offices for that purpose. Their advice can be sought in various ways, and their expertise can be of considerable assistance in determining values or in making formal appraisals. They can also render important service in the auction room. It is my firm opinion that purchases at auctions should be made only through a dealer. It is true that the collector must pay a commission for this service; but it is well worth the cost in return for the advice received as to the authenticity, relative scarcity, and range of prices. Thirty-eight years of collecting have confirmed my conviction that employing dealers at auctions is a beneficial practice.

One rather self-evident piece of advice I venture to offer collectors is to lose no opportunity to increase their knowledge in their particular field of interest. Aside from dealers, there is much to be learned from other experts. These include librarians and curators of manuscripts at various institutions. Here one finds individuals who have devoted many years to the gathering and study of this type of material. They generally are not only knowledgeable, but also agreeable and sympathetic. Naturally, an extra warmth of welcome can be expected if they harbor hopes of some day acquiring desirable manuscripts for their own institution. There are also other kinds of experts, such as historians, biographers, and specialized scholars, who can provide much important and useful information. Consulting these authorities can likewise be rewarding and pleasant.

Among the lasting benefits of collecting are the acquaintanceships and the friendships that are made along the way. I have derived much enjoyment and stimulation from these associations; and I can add that my identification with a legion of collectors, dealers, librarians, scholars, and others engaged in these endeavors has left me with a host of happy memories.

There is one more aspect of collecting that is of transcendent importance because it has exercised through the years one of the most potent influences on the collector himself. It can only be described by the somewhat hackneyed expression "the thrill of the chase." One of the happiest experiences a collector can have is the acquisition of something that has long eluded him. Indeed, occurrences of this kind are what keep him interested and active. One can imagine the joy of a collector of the Signers of the Declaration of Independence who completes his list with a document signed by Button Gwinnett. Or, how about a run of letters from Sally Fairfax to George Washington? What would one give for a letter from Thomas Jefferson to Napoleon, thanking him for his services in making possible the Louisiana Purchase? As a collector of American literature, I can dream about the emergence of the long-lost manuscript of *Moby Dick.* But, to go from the sublime to the obscure, I would experience considerable excitement if I could acquire a manuscript of Sarah Sayward Barrell Keating Wood, Maine's first fiction writer, author of three novels and a book of tales. Her most remarkable title is *Julia and the Illuminated Baron,* published in 1800. We have, at the University of Virginia Library, all of her books but not one line of her handwriting.

I conclude by wishing all of my fellow collectors happy hunting and by expressing the hope that during the years to come they will discover much new and exciting material bearing on the American scene and the great men and women who made it possible.

Clifton Waller Barrett
July 1975

AUTOGRAPHS AND MANUSCRIPTS: A COLLECTOR'S MANUAL

SECTION I

FUNDAMENTALS

THE DEVELOPMENT OF WRITING

DIANA J. RENDELL

WITHOUT WRITING there can be no culture, no communicable intelligence. Its importance cannot be overstated, though it is so basic and fundamental, its existence so accepted and understood, that it is, in fact, rarely understood at all. The history of the development of writing is extremely complex. Writing systems developed in various geographical areas, most of them interrelated, and have overlapping geographical and chronological boundaries.

Three writing systems are considered in this article in relative detail: Egyptian, Sumerian-Babylonian-Assyrian, and Greek. The first two were selected because of their importance and also because they are widely collected. Ancient writings, on papyrus and other materials, as well as examples impressed in clay tablets and carved in stone, can be obtained from two dealers who specialize in ancient writings. The prices of these early representations of the beginnings of civilization are quite modest and the quality of the items available is surprisingly fine.

The third script system, the Greek, is also collected in its ancient forms; this system is, moreover, of prime importance because most of the writing systems of the Western civilizations evolved from it.

The initial efforts toward writing began with the use of objects and graphic representations of objects that were static expressions. They did not represent a complete thought process, but only a specific piece of information.

Among the objects first used to record information were knotted cords, tallies or notched sticks, and wampum belts. These have continued in use until relatively recent times and are infrequently encountered in the collecting field. Knotted cords were employed by many peoples, most notably the ancient Inca, who designated specific officials, the *quipu camayocuna,* to read the *quipu,* as these knotted cords were called.

A *quipu* usually consisted of a thick main cord to which were attached thinner strings that differed in color and that were knotted in various ways. The order and length of the cords, as well as the color and knots, recorded specific data.

Indians in Los Angeles used notched sticks to record daily work, and it was the custom of the Maoris in New Zealand to register genealogical information on sticks called *rakau whakapapa.* Each notch represented a person, with a gap indicating the extinction of the male line. Tallies recorded debts; they were split lengthwise, and the creditor and the debtor each took half. The accuracy of the debt claimed was proved by matching the halves.

The Iroquois and Algonquian Indians of North America used wampum belts made up of four or more strings to which were attached small oval disks made from shells. The particular color of the shells communicated specific statements: dark colors represented unpleasant events, black or violet was utilized for danger or to express hostility, white conveyed peace and happiness, and red was a statement of war. The interweaving of colored figures into the belt made it a declaration of war or a peace treaty when it was sent to other tribes.

The first pictographic writings recorded single images by depicting specific objects. Rock drawings (called petroglyphs when carved, petrograms when painted) date from the late Paleolithic period (20,000–10,000 B.C.). These paintings are generally believed to be glimpses of the most primitive beginnings of decorative art or representations of religious beliefs. Proprietary marks are also an early form of graphic statement. These include pottery marks and, most commonly, markings on animals to identify their owners. Such markings have continued down to the present day in various forms.

The early petroglyphs and petrograms evolved into a more advanced picture writing that did not record single, disconnected images but represented the sequential stages or ideas of a simple narrative. These ideas are communicated through a series of pictures that can be expressed orally in any language because they represent ideas, not sounds. Pictography was used by many early peoples, including those of Egypt, Mesopotamia, Phoenicia, Crete, Spain, and China.

A more advanced form of picture writing is ideographic writing, the first step in rendering a script capable of conveying abstractions and multiple associations. It can illustrate a form that simply represents the thing drawn, or it can convey a concept and its underlying ideas. In simple pictography a circle might represent the sun, while in ideographic writing it might represent heat, light, day, or a religious concept of a god associated with the sun. There is no attempt to represent nature faithfully, only to convey an idea. The head of an animal therefore serves to convey the idea of the whole, and certain pictures are so simplified that they become symbols for various concepts rather than pictorial representations of the concept.

The earliest writings of the ancient Egyptians, Mesopotamians, Cretans, and Hittites, while undoubtedly ideographic at first, evolved into systems that combined elements of pure ideographic writing and pure phonetic writing in which each symbol represented a sound. The picture or symbol evolved from the object alone to a representation of a concept, to the expression of both the concept and a sound.

The evolution from an optical form of communicating to an acoustical system resulted in phonetic scripts in which a direct relationship has been established between the written and spoken language. Phonetic writing is the graphic counterpart of speech, and there need be no connection between the external form of the symbol and the sound it represents. This newly developed system became more complex because of homonyms. A symbol that formerly applied to only one meaning was now used to represent all of the meanings that had the same sound. Thus the Sumerian sign , meaning "mountain," came to represent the meaning "earth" because their sound value was identical.

Syllabic writing developed from phonetic by combining two symbols representing sounds to represent a new word. The Sumerian sign for "name," , was employed for its sound value, *mu,* in combination with other symbols. This system was less cumbersome and more precise than ideograms, but required a very considerable number of signs to represent all of the possible syllabic sounds in a language in which syllables contain more than one or two consonants. For example, the word "family" is simply represented syllabically, fam-i-ly; but the word "strength" is much more complex, se-te-re-ne-ge-the.

The creation of the alphabetical system of writing, in which symbols represented each single sound rather than syllables, probably occurred between 1800 B.C. and 1500 B.C. in the area of Palestine and Syria. The Egyptians had established trading posts in this area between Egypt and Mesopotamia, and the influences of many cultures were present. A knowledge of the various writing systems was necessary to invent the alphabetical system. The area where the cultures of the eastern Mediterranean, and in particular their writing systems, met is therefore the most logical geographical site for the most important, and final, step in the development of writing.

The most ancient system of writing known is cuneiform. It was invented by the Sumerians, *ca.* 3200–3000 B.C., and was later adopted and continued by the Assyrians and Babylonians. The Sumerians had emigrated to the southern part of Mesopotamia about 3500 B.C. and formed there, in an area between the Tigris and Euphrates rivers, the

Sumerian cuneiform clay tablets, third dynasty of Ur, *ca.* 2100–2000 B.C., concerning donkey and oxen skins.

Sumerian cuneiform clay cone, recording the building by Gudea of a temple in Girsu, second half of the twenty-second century B.C.

Sumerian cuneiform clay cone, recording that Sin-Kashid, king of Erech, rebuilt the Temple Eanna, 1865–1864 B.C.

Brick, bearing a cuneiform inscription of Nebuchadnezzar, king of Babylonia, *ca.* 605–562 B.C.

earliest known civilization. Culturally they are the most important and best known of the ancient peoples; they created an important literature as well as a complex system of law, religion, business, and administration.

Our knowledge of the existence and civilization of the Sumerians dates from the latter part of the nineteenth century, when a substantial group of clay tablets bearing cuneiform inscriptions was discovered. Excavations unearthed great quantities of their writings, principally on clay tablets, but also on bricks and clay cones.

The earliest examples of Sumerian writing are not actually cuneiform, that is, wedge shaped. They are pictographic and could serve only the most basic administrative functions. In a stratum of Erech (Uruk) approximately nine hundred different symbols were discovered, which may not represent all of the symbols that were in use. Their early writing system has the limitations that all pictographic systems share, and the Sumerians developed a new writing system combining ideographic and phonetic writing; a transitional ideographic script is not known.

This new script was true cuneiform writing: wedge-shaped characters impressed into wet clay tablets that were then fired; the durability of these clay tablets is attested to by the great numbers that have survived into the twentieth century. Scribes employed a straight length of reed with a broad head as a stylus to make the impressions in the clay.

As the ideographic influence decreased and phonetization became predominant, many ambiguities in meaning occurred. Determinative signs were introduced to place the text within a frame of reference. These determinatives were ideograms that were already in use and also new forms to clarify particular phonetic values.

The Semitic Akkadians (the Assyrians and Babylonians) took over the Sumerians' writing system about 2500 B.C. and continued to develop it, principally from a stylistic standpoint. It became more complex with the Babylonian influence; and in the late eighteenth century B.C., under Hammurabi, it became the instrument of the classical age of Babylonian science and literature. At this time the number of cuneiform symbols was approximately six hundred to seven hundred: six vowel sounds, ninety-seven simple syllables, approximately two hundred more complex syllables, and about three hundred ideograms.

The Assyrian kings, during the ninth to seventh centuries B.C., established libraries containing tens of thousands of clay tablets concerning religion, philosophy, astronomy, mathematics, mythology, law, history, medicine, science, and histories of the campaigns and activities of the kings. Many tablets were excavated at Nineveh, where very fine Assyrian dictionaries were also found. These were substantially larger and more

Egyptian hieroglyphic inscription painted on wood, from a Middle Kingdom sarcophagus. The inscription is part of a funerary text, an invocation to the god Re, 2133–1786 B.C.

comprehensive than their Babylonian counterparts. Artistically engraved tablets represented the final period of preeminence of cuneiform writing in Mesopotamia; the Aramaic nomads inundated the Tigris-Euphrates Valley commencing in the eighth century B.C., and gradually replaced cuneiform with their own alphabetical script and language.

Cuneiform was still used in specialized situations, such as astronomy texts, and was adopted by the Persians, who simplified it greatly under the influence of the Aramaic alphabet. This renaissance in Persia was short-lived, and the final cuneiform examples date from approximately A.D. 50.

The Egyptian system of writing is, together with cuneiform, one of the two most important scripts of the ancient Near East. Egyptian hieroglyphic writing is the most pictorial of analytic scripts and was used primarily for religious purposes. Hieroglyphs were carved in stone on temple walls, tombs, and sacred monuments; were painted on pottery and wood; and were written on papyrus and linen.

The earliest-known Egyptian hieroglyphic inscriptions are from about 3000 B.C., and it is generally believed that Egyptian writing developed in substantially the same manner as cuneiform: a pictographic

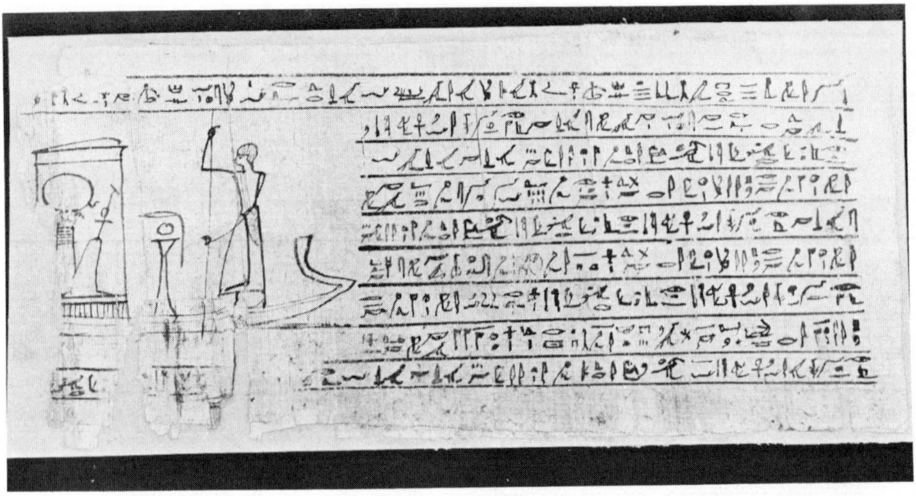

Papyrus fragment in hieroglyphic script from the Book of Gates, 663–525 B.C.

Egyptian hieroglyphic carving in stone.

Terra-cotta cone with a hieroglyphic inscription from the XVIII dynasty, 1567–1320 B.C.

A fragment from a Book of the Dead, written in hieratic script on linen, early Ptolemaic period, *ca.* 300 B.C.

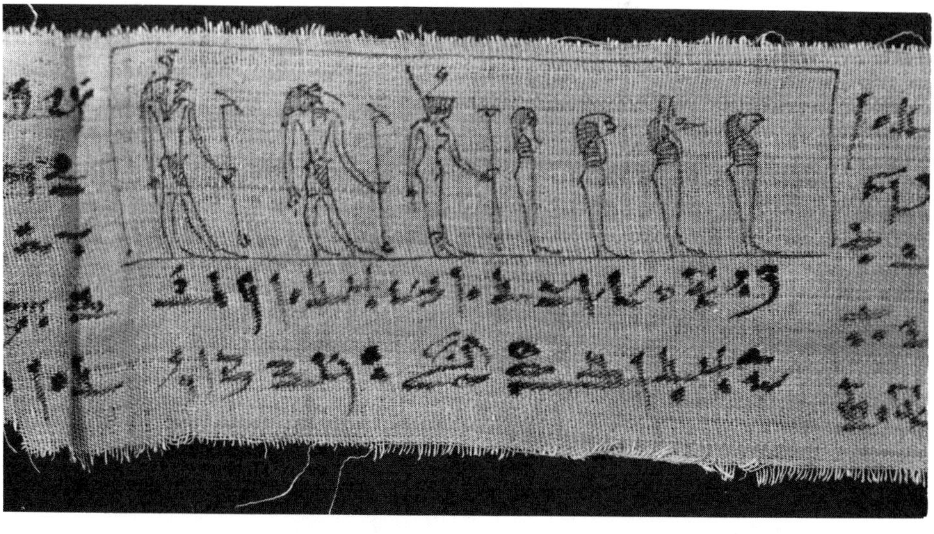

system evolving into a transitional one consisting of pictographs and ideographs, and finally a combination of pictographs, ideographs, and, most important, phonograms. The earliest extant hieroglyphics, on a group of slate plates found in Upper Egypt, are already a transitional script; it is believed that a phonetic system of writing was developed in the early years of the third millennium B.C. This system remained unchanged for the following thirty centuries.

Twenty-four single consonants (six homophones were later added) and seventy-five double consonants (approximately fifty of which were in common usage) represented the entire range of consonantal sounds.

The Rosetta stone, containing inscriptions in hieroglyphic, demotic, and Greek. Original in the British Library, London.

Vowel sounds were not represented, although they were, of course, pronounced in an oral reading of a hieroglyphic text. Determinatives were employed in the same manner as in cuneiform writing, to place the text within a particular frame of reference.

The unique sacredness of hieroglyphics in their employment in ritual, funerary, and royal texts ensured their continuation in their most elaborate, intricate, and monumental form. They required considerable time and space to carve and paint, and their narrow evenness was contrary to the type of writing that was most easily and quickly written on papyrus with a brush pen. Business documents, private correspondence, and literary manuscripts were executed in hieroglyphs with difficulty.

A script that would satisfy the requirements of these other forms of texts was developed about six hundred years after hieroglyphics and existed concurrently with it. This was a cursive form of hieroglyphics, without the pictorial quality, and is known as the hieratic script. Ligatured groups of characters were formed in the hieratic script; and in the period 2000–1790 B.C. the horizontal line, written from right to left, replaced the vertical line. Increasing cursiveness led the hieratic script to the point of serving only as a priestly shorthand, unreadable to most; and it was superseded by a new script, although it continued to be used for religious works until the second century of the Christian era.

The demotic script first appeared in the seventh century B.C. and was directly derivative from the hieratic and, therefore, the hieroglyphic. The new script showed an extraordinary degree of erosion from its predecessors. New and independent signs had resulted from the amalgamation of whole related groups of hieratic characters. Other hieratic signs were abbreviated; and while determinatives were still employed, they were used less, thus creating additional ambiguities. The extreme cursiveness of this script and its greater use of ligatures gave it an appearance unrelated to its predecessors. Its popularity in Egypt was such that it soon was the predominant script for all business and private writing, as well as for literary compositions. The Ptolemies considered demotic of greater importance than hieratic, and equal in importance to hieroglyphic and Greek writing.

After the entry of Alexander the Great into Egypt, the Greek language began to influence Egyptian writing, although the demotic continued until Christianity prevailed in Egypt. A new script emerged that employed twenty-five letters from Greek uncial writing and seven from Egyptian demotic writing to express Egyptian sounds that did not exist in the Greek language. This new writing was Coptic. The earliest known examples are from the third century of the Christian era. It continued in use until the ninth century, having begun to be superseded by the Arabic script after the seventh century.

The Greek group of scripts is the most important to the modern collector. Through its many offshoots the Greek script has provided the whole of modern Europe, the Americas, and parts of Asia with writing systems. The scripts considered here are the ones most frequently encountered by collectors; many others also developed and have had a prominent influence on writing systems in other parts of the world.

The origin of the Greek script is, like the origin of many other scripts, in considerable dispute; but the majority of scholarly opinion believes that the Greeks adapted their script from the Semites, probably in the tenth or ninth century B.C. The earliest Greek scripts, like those of the Semites, were written from right to left; they did not adopt a left-to-right method until approximately 500 B.C.

An example of a strong uncial script written in Coptic, giving an account of the martyrdom of Apachamoul, who was visited by Christ; Upper Egypt, A.D. 550–650.

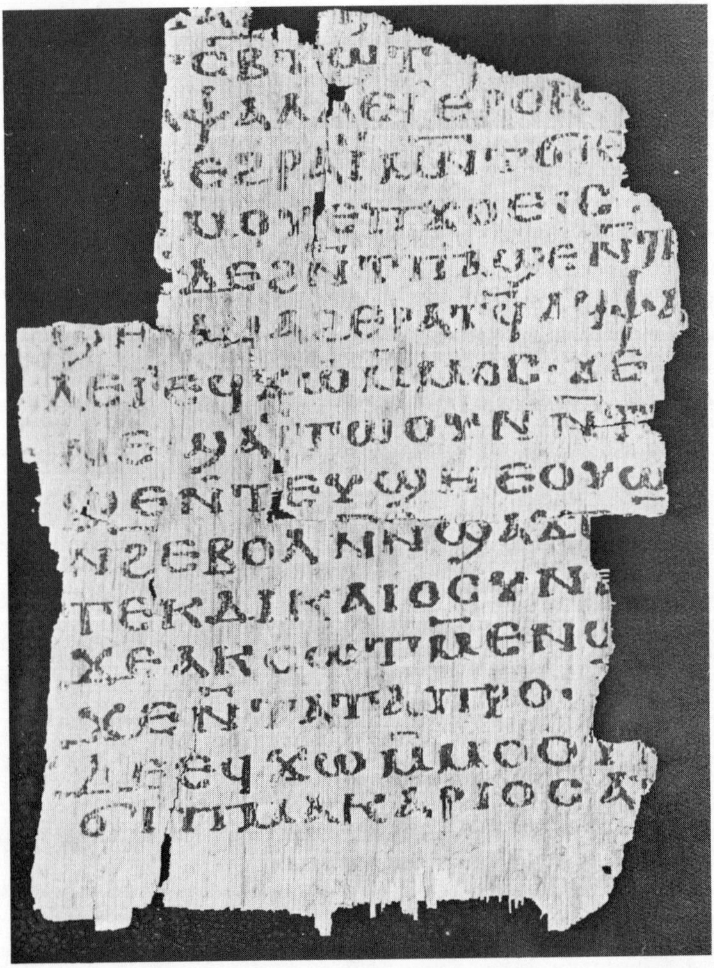

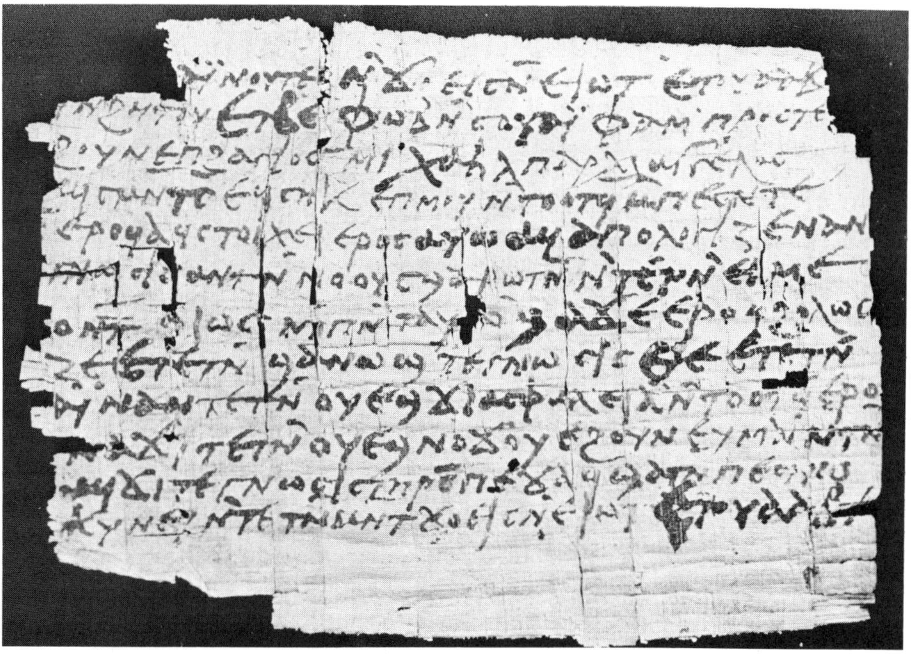

A letter to the bishop of Coptos from two priests discussing work on the Church of St. Michael the Archangel. Written in a semicursive Coptic script, Upper Egypt, A.D. 550–650.

A Coptic fragment of the eighth century of the Christian era, with contemporary notes at the conclusion in Arabic. Courtesy of The Rendells, Inc.

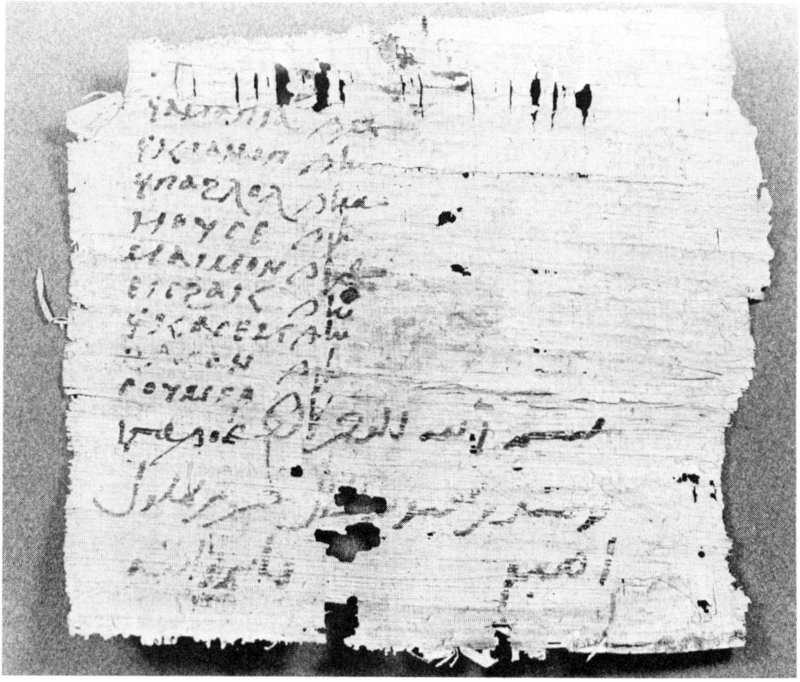

During the early centuries of Greek writing, many variations of the Greek alphabet developed; and many subdivisions were quite prominent. The two most important of these were the eastern (the Ionic alphabet) and the western (those of the Dorian islands of Thera, Melos, and Crete). Uniformity began to develop, and in 403 B.C. the Ionic alphabet of Miletus was established as the official Greek script. The occasion for its adoption was the restoration of the democratic constitution in Athens and the rewriting of the old laws. The Ionic alphabet consisted of twenty-four letters, and it did not undergo any further basic changes.

Greek writing did, however, undergo significant paleographical changes. Efforts to simplify the script signs continued after the adoption of the Ionian alphabet; at this time the script was known as the monumental script (or the lapidary script when effected in stone, or the capital script when employed in manuscripts). The simple straight lines of the monumental script were, of course, most appropriate for chiseling in stone; and the script required the development of rounded signs when writing with a reed pen or brush. The rounding of the signs began to emerge in the earliest Greek papyri documents (*ca.* 300 B.C.), and eventually this rounded script developed into the uncial script, which continued in use until about A.D. 900.

Contemporary with the uncial script, a cursive script developed for unofficial or everyday use. This is frequently encountered in papyri manuscripts and is characterized by the joining of the individual letters, in contrast with their isolation in the uncial script. Abbreviations also developed more with cursive writing as speed was emphasized in its execution.

Greek monumental script of the second century of the Christian era. From the Vatican Museum.

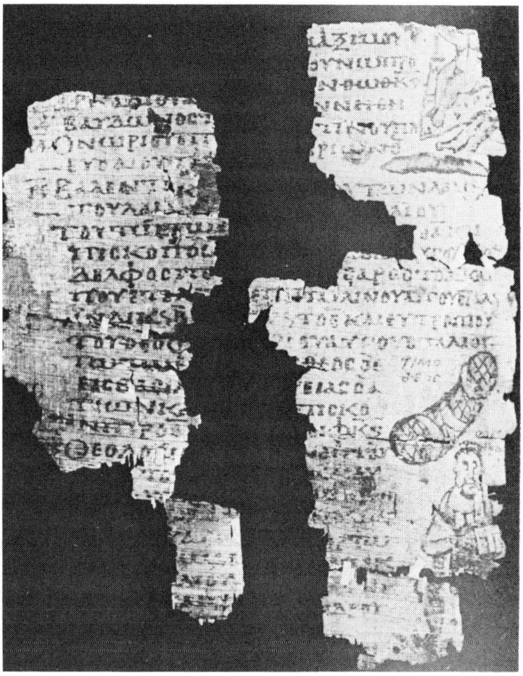

Greek uncial script, *ca.* A.D. 400. From the Museum of Fine Art, Moscow.

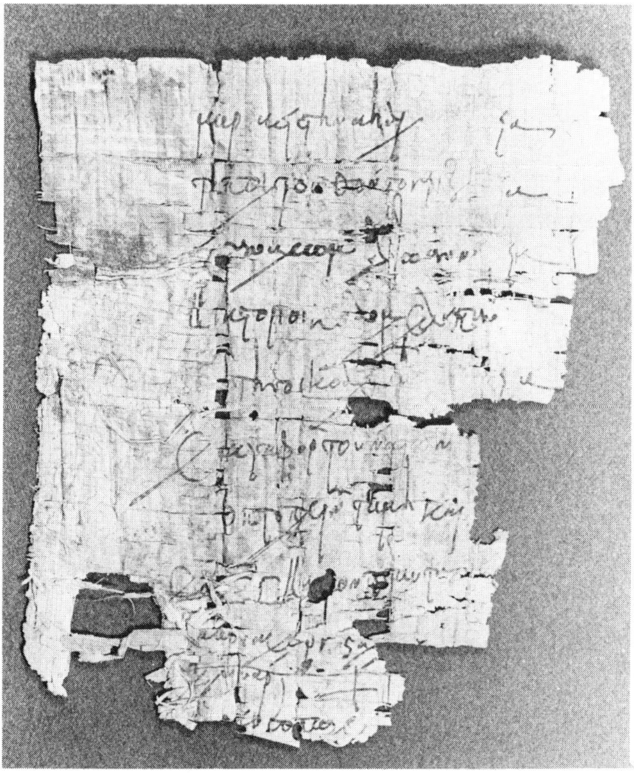

A papyrus fragment in Greek cursive script, concerning building expenses, sixth century of the Christian era. Courtesy of The Rendells, Inc.

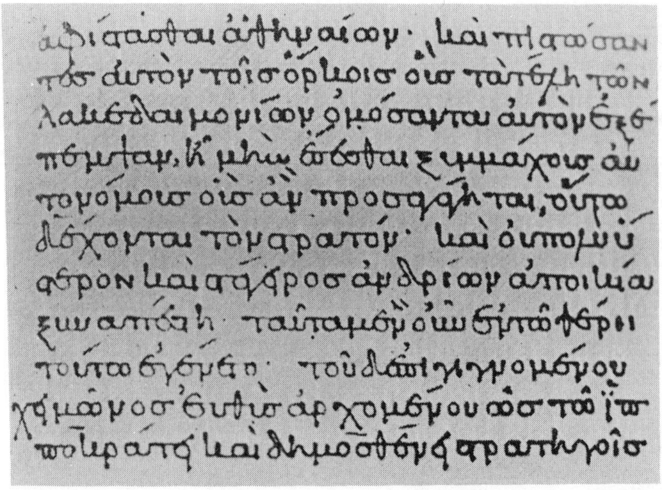

A carefully executed example of Greek documentary minuscule, early tenth century of the Christian era. (From Hans Jensen, *Die Schrift in Vergangenheit und Gegenwart* [1958], 439.)

A later example of Greek minuscule script, A.D. 1390. (From Jensen, *Die Schrift in Vergangenheit und Gegenwart,* p. 490.)

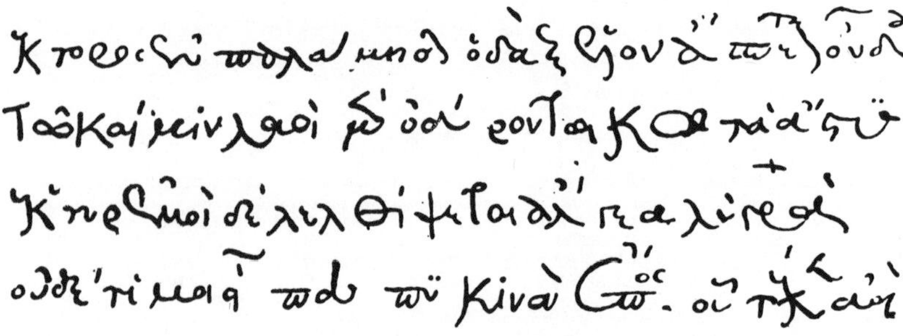

The gradual emergence of ascenders and descenders in the cursive script developed into a new script known as the documentary minuscule, which is characterized by a much greater emphasis of ascenders and descenders and the employment of lowercase letters. After the ninth century this new script gradually replaced both the cursive and the uncial, although the latter continued in use for headings and initials, with the new documentary minuscule being used for the text. This script remained in use through the Middle Ages and was the basis for the first Greek printing types developed in 1476. From this period to the present, the Greek style of script has remained relatively unchanged.

The Greek writing system gave birth to the early Italian scripts, the most important of these being that adapted to the language of the Etruscans, probably about the eighth century B.C. The Etruscans continued the development of their alphabet during the following three hundred years, when it reached its classical form of sixteen consonants (*g, v-digramma, z, h, th, l, m, n, p, san, r, s, t, ph, kh,* and *f*) and four vowels (*a, e, i, u*). Although this script remained in use until the early part of the first century of the Christian era, it was gradually supplanted by the Latin alphabet after the Etruscans' loss of political independence to the Romans.

The Latin alphabet developed from the Etruscan, probably during the seventh century B.C. In its earliest form it contained twenty-one letters from the Etruscans and, just prior to the Roman conquest of Greece, had developed into *A, B, C, D, E, F, G, H, I, K, L, M, N, O, P, Q, R, S, T, V, X.* After the Roman conquest of Greece, the Greek symbols *Y*

Roman monumental script of the first century of the Christian era. A dedication from Alexandria Troas to C. Antonius Rufus. From the British Library, London.

and *Z* were added in order to facilitate the transliteration of Greek words into Latin. From this period, the first century B.C., the Latin alphabet remained substantially unchanged until the additions of the letters *U, W,* and *J* in the Middle Ages. These added letters were actually differentiations from the existing letters *V* and *I*. While it remained unchanged in its characters, the Latin script did change significantly through the centuries in its writing styles.

In the first century B.C., the characteristics of Roman capital script began to develop. This script, also known as the monumental script, was employed in writing on both papyri and parchment, and was carved in stone. By the first or second century of the Christian era, the capital script had divided into three types: the lapidary capitals, principally employed in stone carving; book capitals, less formal in appearance than lapidary writing, being somewhat more rounded in shape; and rustic capitals, more quickly and easily written than lapidary letters but not as rounded as book capitals.

In the middle of the second century of the Christian era, a new script began to emerge for texts. This was the Latin uncial, which is less formal in appearance and more cursive in shape. The Latin uncial gradually replaced the capital script until it predominated in the fourth century, with the capital script being used for headings and initials. The Latin uncial maintained its prominent position until the ninth century.

A Latin cursive script had developed for ordinary writing; and while it initially employed many of the capital script forms, it eventually became quite distinctive. The earliest forms of this cursive script date from the first century of the Christian era, and it continued to develop until it became the cursive minuscule script.

Roman uncial script, *ca.* A.D. 700. A biblical passage. (From Jensen, *Die Schrift in Vergangenheit und Gegenwart,* p. 499.)

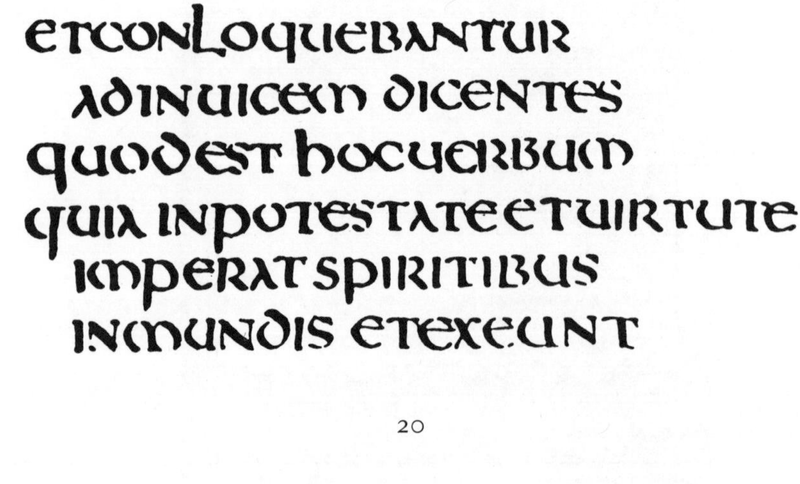

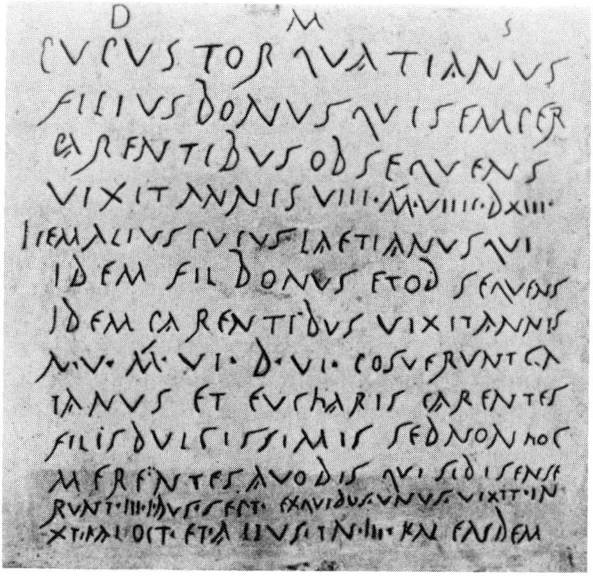

Roman cursive script, third century of the Christian era. An inscription of Pupus Torguatianus. From the Vatican Museum.

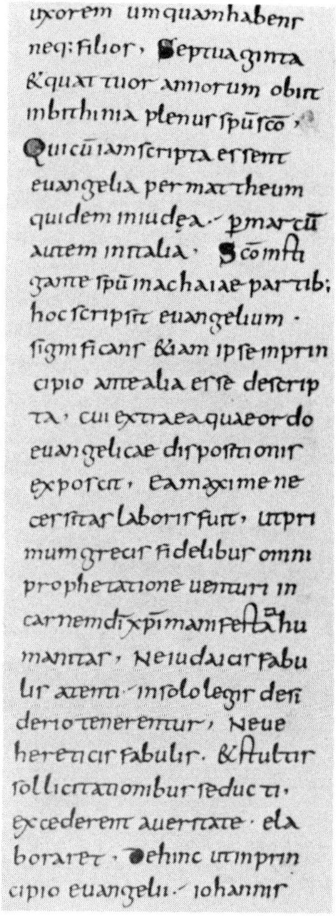

Carolingian script from an early ninth-century gospel.

The writing systems developed from the Greek system now began to emerge geographically, and forms that might be called national scripts emerged. In Italy several scripts evolved. The curial, the official script of the Papal Curia, is distinguished by a particularly careful style in some of the letter forms. The Beneventan script, cultivated in the writing schools of Benevento, Monte Cassino, and Salerno, as well as in other areas of southern Italy, and the Lombardic and Ravenna scripts were also prominent. The book hand found in northern Italy spread into France and Germany in the eighth and ninth centuries.

The Carolingian hand was introduced throughout the Frankish Empire during the time of Charlemagne, and in the ninth and tenth centuries it became the principal book hand of western Europe. This new script is distinguished by the clarity of its graphic image, the slight use

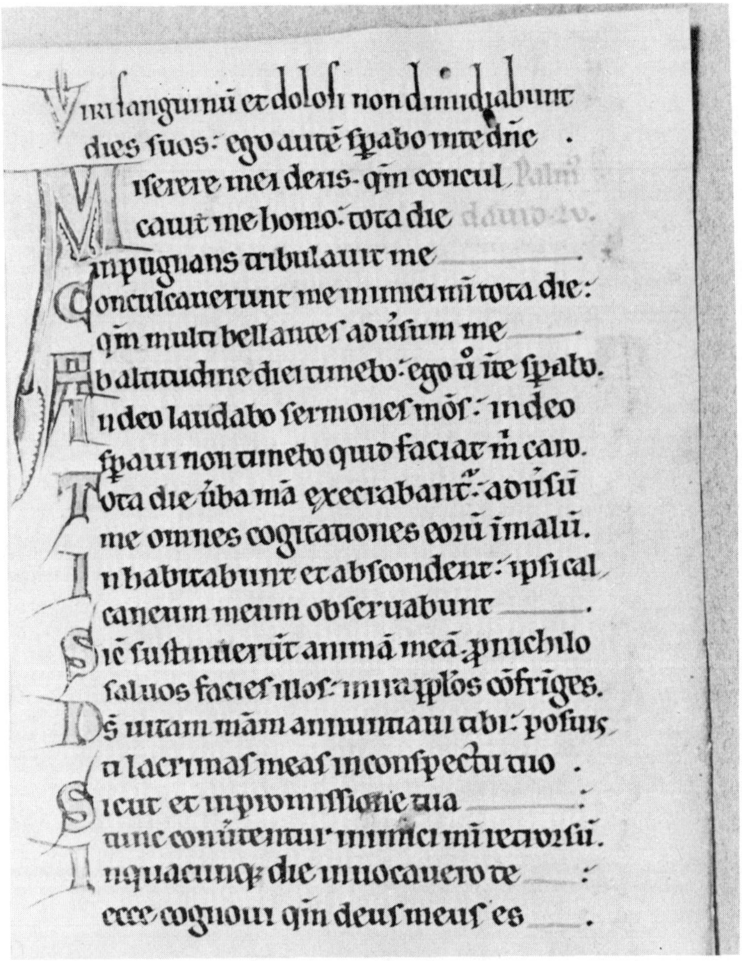

An early example of Gothic script from a thirteenth-century Spanish psalter. Courtesy of The Rendells, Inc.

of ligatures and abbreviations, and a regularity in the formation of the characters. Words are separated with some regularity, and the script blends both the majuscule and the minuscule scripts.

The Gothic script developed from the Carolingian and received wide acceptance in northwestern Europe until the sixteenth century, and in Germany until recent decades. The Gothic minuscule script originated in approximately the eleventh century as the curved elements of the Carolingian script were converted into angular combinations of strokes.

This transformation was not completed until the twelfth to the thirteenth centuries, by which time a more ornamental form of Gothic script had developed. The script employed fine lines to connect the individual characters, with decorative heads and feet. Gothic minuscule was widely used until approximately the thirteenth century. Contemporaneously with the other forms of Gothic scripts, a cursive form was occasionally used in manuscripts, with the minuscule continuing to predominate in most texts.

The Gothic text script was characterized by the joining of curves in adjacent characters, a closer pressing together of the characters, and the making of the final oblique strokes into curved feet and heads. Abbreviations became commonplace in this text, which was used very extensively, beginning in the fourteenth century, for books of hours and other religious works.

Efforts to develop a form of writing more easily read than the Gothic style led to the development of the humanistic antiqua, also referred to as Renaissance minuscule. This script emerged in the latter part of the fifteenth century, after its introduction in several printed works; and during the course of the following century, both the humanistic and the cursive types of antiqua pervaded Italy completely. It was introduced into England as a printer's type in 1509, and into France in 1530. Throughout Europe it replaced Gothic as the predominant script.

Antiqua script by Catherine de Medici's secretary, 1570.
Courtesy of The Rendells, Inc.

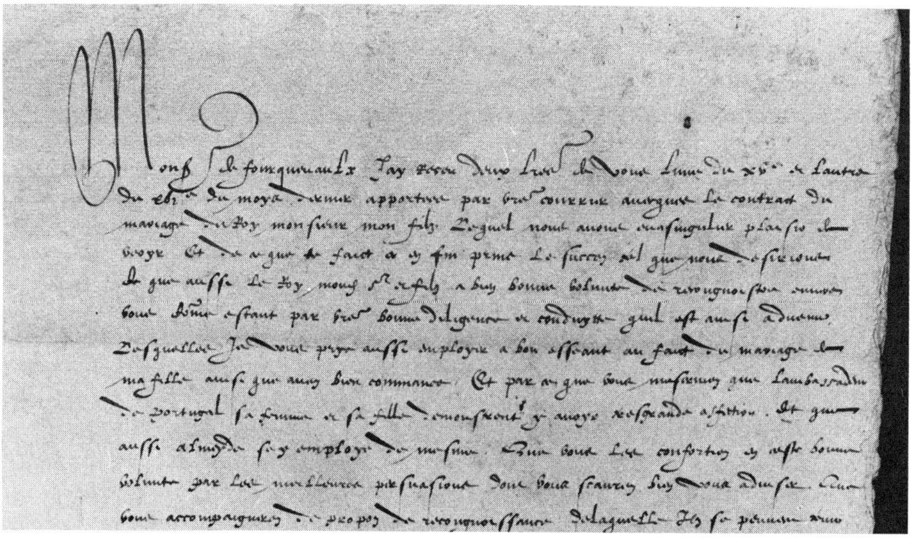

Dem durchleuchtigisten großmechtigen Fürsten vnd
herren/herrn Ferdinanden/ zu Hungern vnd Beh-
eym Konigen/Infanten in Hispanien/ Ertzhertzo-
gen zu Osterreich/zu Burgundi/Brabant/Grafen
zu Habspurg Flandernn vnnd Tyrol/Römischer
Kayserlicher Maiestat vnsers aller genedigstenn
herren statthalter im heyligen Reych meinem gene-
digsten herrenn.

Fraktur script. (From Jensen, *Die Schrift in Vergangenheit und Gegenwart,* p. 535.)

Germany, however, continued to use the Fraktur script that had emerged at the turn of the fifteenth century. This script was characterized by the distinction between the capitals and small letters, and continued in use in many localities until quite recently. A cursive form of antiqua appeared in Germany, and with many minor variations it continued until the development of the modern German script.

The Anglo-Saxon semiuncial script developed from the influence of the Irish and the Romans, who both brought Christianity to Britain. This style emerged in the seventh and eighth centuries and continued in use for the writing of Latin until about 940; it was used for Anglo-Saxon until after the Norman Conquest.

Carolingian minuscule, which succeeded Anglo-Saxon as the principal script used in Latin texts in the eleventh century, had the capitals and headings in rustic or square capitals and uncials. The Anglo-Saxon insular minuscule rapidly declined in usage and became increasingly confined to the vernacular. Gothic or text script developed in the early part of the thirteenth century, and replaced Carolingian minuscule as the principal script used in texts. At approximately the same time a contrast between the scripts used in texts and those used in business developed. The business hand was more cursive, written with fewer strokes of the pen and more rapidly.

The business hand continued to be written more and more rapidly, with a resulting loss in clarity. The widening gap between the text script and the business script led to the development of a hybrid commonly known as bastard. This new script became very popular about

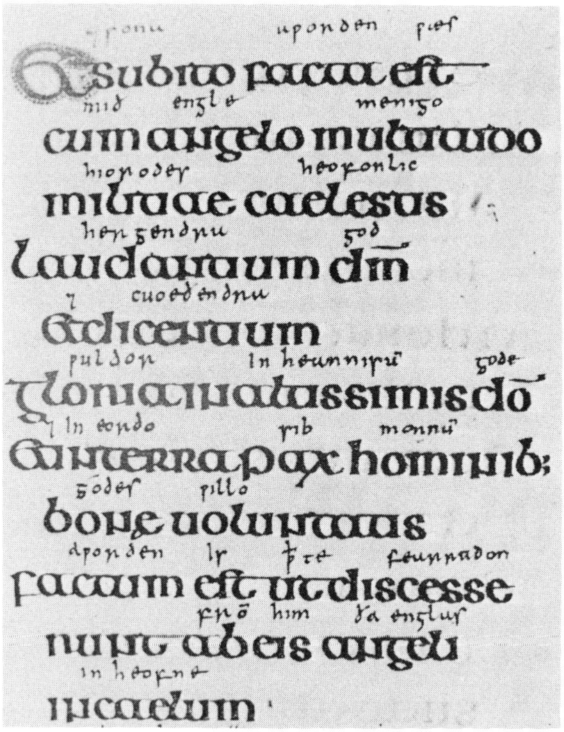

The Anglo-Saxon semiunicals in the Lindisfarne Gospels, *ca.* A.D. 700. From the British Library, London.

A royal charter illustrating the formal business hand, A.D. 1110. From the Public Records Office, London.

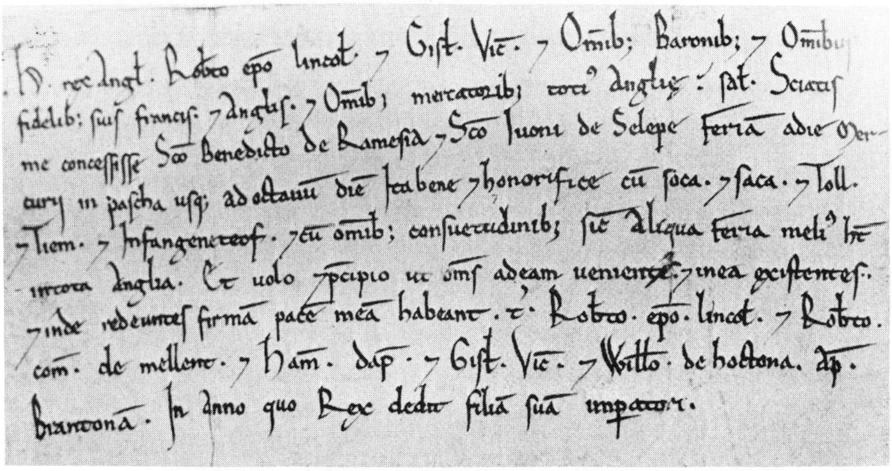

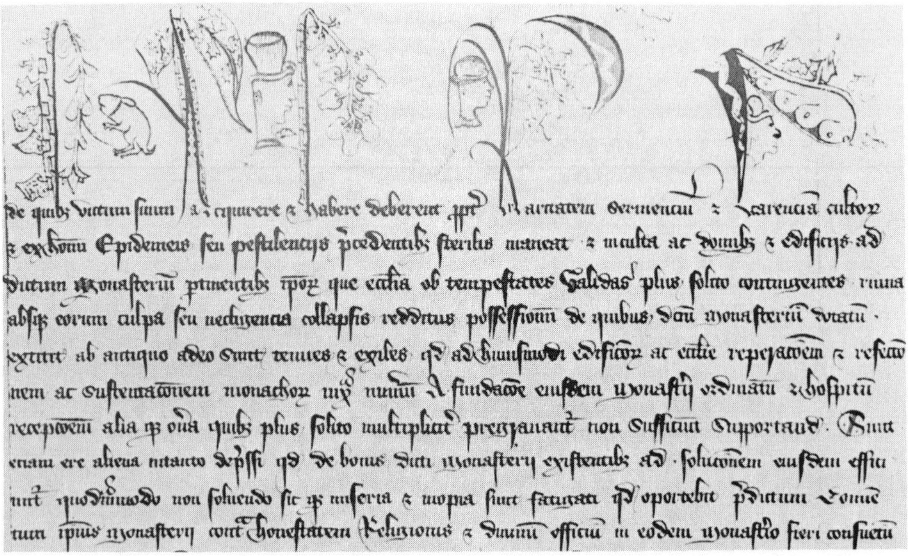

The bastard hand, fifteenth century. From the Public Records Office, London.

English secretary hand of the sixteenth century. From the Public Records Office, London.

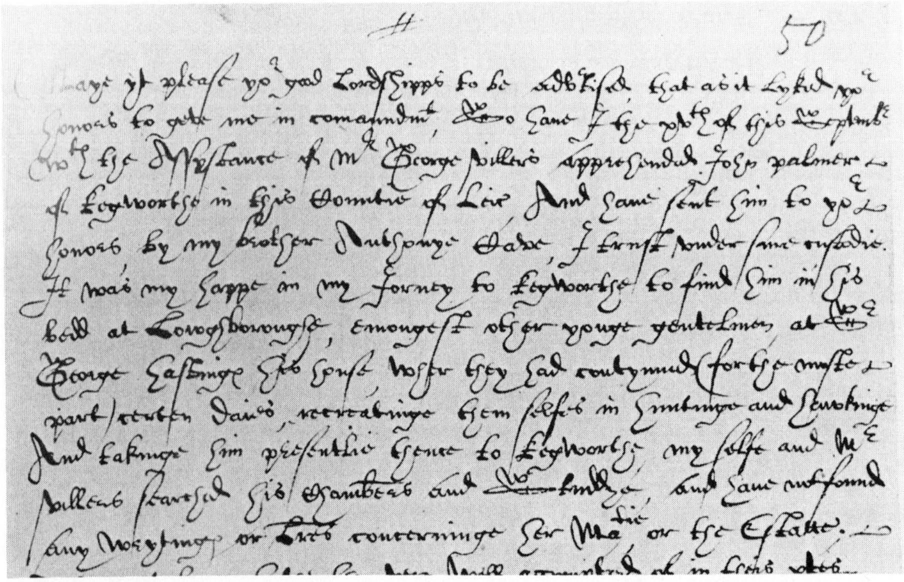

1350, and was used extensively for the vernacular literatures, business documents, and correspondence. One hundred years later, numerous free hands (various combinations of cursive and bastard styles) had developed in highly individual and personal ways.

The latter part of the fifteenth century witnessed significant changes in writing. Substantially increased literacy and new and varied business that required more correspondence and record keeping combined to put a new emphasis on writing skills. Writing masters taught on the Continent and, most probably, in England. The general new script that evolved, called the secretary hand, can be divided into various types. This script served the emerging group of new writers seeking ease of writing, clarity, and speed. The characteristic ligatures of the secretary hand are those that arise naturally from frequently writing common English letter combinations. The system of abbreviations also was altered, and many of the abbreviations employed in writing Latin were abandoned.

The humanistic antiqua style that had gained wide popularity in Italy was introduced into Britain in the early part of the sixteenth century. By 1550 it had achieved a substantial place in English writing as an alternative to the secretary style.

The simultaneous teaching of two structurally different writing systems and their general use, without specific purposes, will result in a hybrid style combining characteristics of both hands. The early years of the seventeenth century saw many examples of writing that were part secretary and part humanistic antiqua, or italic. This mélange continued through the seventeenth century until it was considered a new writing script, the English round hand. The superior speed of this new hand and its increased clarity commended it to writing masters and schools on the Continent as well; and it achieved the dominant position in France, Spain, and most of Italy. This hand has continued, relatively unchanged, to the present day.

WRITING INSTRUMENTS AND MATERIALS

EDMUND BERKELEY, JR.

THE FIRST WRITING INSTRUMENT undoubtedly was a finger, and the material, a piece of dusty ground. Writing, its instruments and materials, has progressed through many stages, and the modern collector should be familiar with those instruments and materials he may encounter.

INKS

Man experimented with many writing surfaces—from cave walls, stone and clay tablets, tree bark, and animal skins to wax-covered wood blocks, and cloth. Many of these required the use of a medium to mark the writing on the surface, and an instrument to carry the medium to it. Various fluids were tried: berry juice, dyes, blood, muddy water, and so forth. Some of them worked reasonably well on certain surfaces. The dyes used on cloth were the most satisfactory, and it probably was but a short step from a good dye to an ink. The search continued down the centuries for a writing fluid that would be ready for use on an instant's notice and that would dry quickly and be permanent. Man has striven to perfect his writing fluids, and that search continues today.

The early Hebrews used powdered charcoal or soot mixed with water, and also tried the ink of the cuttlefish, calling it *tekeleth,* or sepia. As a consequence of their experimentation, the Bible contains a number of references in the Old Testament to ink, including Jer. 36:18 and Ezek. 9:2, 3, 11.* The Arabs evolved a good ink. They invented lampblack, which is the soot resulting when oil, tar, or rosin is burned. They mixed this soot with gum and honey, and sometimes added a scent to it. The resulting mixture was dried and pressed into cakes onto which water

*David N. Carvalho, *Forty Centuries of Ink, or a Chronological Narrative Concerning Ink and Its Backgrounds* (New York: Banks Law Publishing Co., 1904), 5. Hereafter cited as Carvalho.

could be flowed to produce an ink. A similar process was developed in the Far East, and is still used there in some classical and artistic circles.

The best and most durable inks were produced when man discovered, about the eleventh century, that dried, powdered gall nuts could be mixed into a fluid containing certain iron salts to produce a very black, long-lasting ink. Gall nuts are formed on young buds of certain species of trees when they are punctured by the sting of female wasps. One can only wonder how someone came to add dried, powdered gall nuts to a solution containing iron salts, but it is likely that the mixture was prepared for some other purpose, and its use as an ink discovered quite by accident.

According to David N. Carvalho's *Forty Centuries of Ink* . . . , "The gall-nut contains gallic and gallotannic acid, and which acids, when combined with an iron salt, forms the sole base of the best inks."* This ink, though very black when first used, continues a slow chemical reaction after the water evaporates. Eventually, this ink changes color to the rich, rusty brown color so familiar to manuscript collectors. Because of the acid in the ink, it can damage paper. One often sees manuscripts where a flourish of the pen has deposited a large quantity of ink that has, over the years, entirely eaten away the paper.

Iron gall inks continued in use for many centuries after their discovery, and were in general use well into the twentieth century. However, experimentation with inks continued because of the danger that iron gall inks posed to paper. Various dyes were developed into usable inks and were popular because of the appeal of their colors. Few of them proved permanent, fading badly in daylight, or running when wet. Today, permanent colored inks are available for those persons not wedded to the ball-point pen or the fiber-tip pen.

PENS

Various writing instruments were tried in the early centuries of writing: twigs with their ends chewed to soften them; reeds with sharpened points; and sticks with sharpened points. The reed proved most usable and continued in use with primitive inks for many centuries. It was also used to impress marks in the wet clay of tablets. Metal pens were developed quite early, and examples were discovered among the ruins of Pompeii.

The goose quill pen displaced the reed pen in the seventh century, and remained the world's common writing instrument until the mid-nineteenth century, a remarkable record indeed. Goose quills have been the traditional favorite, and every school child had early to learn to cut

*Carvalho, 323.

and properly sharpen a quill into a pen. Most literate men carried a small penknife for this purpose. Various styles of handwritings required different cuts and shaping of the quill to achieve the distinctive characteristics of its script. The production of quills for writing instruments was a considerable business through the centuries, and a rather complex process of baking in hot sand and other procedures was evolved to produce a long-lasting, pliable pen quill. In 1809 Joseph Bramah of England patented a machine that cut many pen points out of one quill; these points were slipped into wooden pen holders for writing.

The steel pen point was produced in France as early as 1748, but was not popular because of its stiffness and cost. Metal nibs sold for two or three dollars each in London in 1803, but the price dropped within ten years to twelve cents as new manufacturing techniques provided a flexible, long-lasting point. Joseph Gillott, a Sheffield, England, cutler, developed the technique for large-scale manufacture, and various Americans apparently independently produced pen points of steel or other materials. According to Ray Nash, steel pens were advertised "as early as 1809 in Salem, Massachusetts."* The first pen company in the United States was formed in Camden, New Jersey, by Richard Esterbrook, and went into production as the Civil War began.

Because all these pens, quill or metal, held only enough ink for a few words of writing, they required the writer to have an open ink bottle at hand. Ink bottles were a nuisance, subject to embarrassing accidents. Inventors sought for years to produce a pen that would hold a quantity of ink within its own body. L. E. Waterman marketed the first fountain pen in 1884 in the United States. The pen was immediately successful, and hordes of new models poured onto the market, replacing the dip pen for most uses although the traditional pen was in use, particularly in accounting offices, for many years.

The ball-point pen is not a twentieth-century invention although its commercial success came after World War II. Models were on the market at the end of the nineteenth century after John Loud obtained a U.S. patent in 1888, but they did not catch the public's fancy. Laszlo József, a Hungarian living in Argentina, obtained a patent in 1937 for a ball point that was both workable and commercially successful. The United States Army adopted the pen in 1944, and its widespread use during the war made it popular and helped send sales soaring after the war. The ball point has virtually driven the fountain pen off the market, and the development of chemically treated papers, which, when written on with the heavy pressure possible with a ball-point pen, produce mul-

* Ray Nash, *American Penmanship 1800–1850: A History of Writing and a Bibliography of Copybooks From Jenkins to Spencer* (Worcester, Mass.: American Antiquarian Society, 1969), 58.

tiple copies, has made the use of a fountain pen a great inconvenience for most persons. Handsome scripts such as the Italic are not possible with a ball point, and there is a revival of interest in these scripts that has produced growing sales for fountain pens with the special points required.

Fiber-tip pens, in some ways similar to the primitive reed or twig with a chewed end, were placed on the market about 1951 strictly as markers for goods. The Japanese developed the pen as a popular writing instrument, and its success since it was introduced in 1964 has been remarkable. Because they require little pressure, the pens are easy to use. The ink colors available are legion, and specialty pens are available at modest prices. Many of the inks used in these pens are not permanent, and a few days' exposure to sunlight can fade their writing badly. One suspects that the ink will not last for many years even if protected from sunlight.

THE TYPEWRITER

Man worked for several centuries to invent a machine that would allow the average man to print at home. The result of this effort was the typewriter, without which the world would be quite a different place. The first patent for a home printing machine was issued in England in 1714 to a Henry Mill, but as the patent does not describe his machine, many persons are not willing to give him the credit for the original invention.

Inventors in many other countries obtained patents, notably one in France in 1784. The first patent in the United States was issued in 1829 to William Austin Burt of Detroit for a machine that worked much like the modern child's toy typewriter, or an embossing machine. One turned a wheel to bring the letter to be printed to the right place on the machine. This machine was quite slow to use and never became popular, as one of the hopes for the machine was that it would be able to produce printing much faster than a man could write.

Christopher Latham Sholes, collaborating with Carlos Glidden and Samuel W. Soulé, is credited with inventing the first practical typewriter. They obtained United States patents in 1868, and later filed a number of others. One of these was for the first machine that allowed "printing" to be done faster than handwriting. On March 1, 1873, Sholes signed a contract with E. Remington and Sons of Ilion, New York, an arms manufacturing company, for the production of the typewriter. The machine reached the market in 1874, and was called the Remington.

Though this first machine was not very efficient and did not sell well, it is notable for several features. One was the arrangement of the keyboard, the totally inefficient scheme that has disturbed efficiency experts ever since, and for which there is no good explanation. The model wrote only in capital letters, and it was not until the Remington Model 4, appearing in 1878, that today's shift key, which allows the same key to print a large or a small letter, was incorporated on the typewriter. Competitors placed on the market machines that had separate keys for the capital and lowercase letters. Competition between the two types of machines was strong, but the appearance of touch-typing—typing without looking at the keyboard—drove the double-keyed machines off the market in about ten years. By 1890 the touch system was the only method of instruction for the use of the typewriter.

Mark Twain acquired one of Remington's first typewriters, and he wrote in his autobiography that *The Adventures of Tom Sawyer,* published in 1876, was the first novel submitted to a publisher in typed form. Some argue that Twain's memory was not as good as it might have been and that his *Life on the Mississippi,* published in 1883, was the first submitted in typed form.

The typewriter caught on very rapidly with businesses, and women began to move into offices to take on the job of typing; they were called "typewriters" after the machine they operated because men were secretaries. In 1897 Grant Allen, using the pseudonym of Olive Pratt Rayner, published *The Typewriter Girl,* a novel that recorded some adventures in the life of one of these early typists.

Thomas A. Edison patented the first electric typing device in 1872, and in 1908 a German electric typewriter was on the market. It remained a novelty until James Smathers of the United States marketed a commercial machine in 1920, and in 1933 the International Business Machines Corporation entered the market with an electric machine. The real success of electric typewriters came after World War II, especially after the "Selectric" machine was introduced by IBM in 1961. It allowed the typist to change typefaces in seconds, and this feature appealed to many.

The collector may expect to find a few typed pieces dated as early as the late 1870's. The Centennial Exposition of 1876 featured typewriting demonstrations, and many persons paid twenty-five cents for samples of the new machine writing. By 1910 a "conservative estimate" is that there were over two million typewriters in use in the United States alone; there were eighty-nine companies in the United States, and many more companies manufactured machines abroad.*

*Bruce Bliven, Jr., *The Wonderful Writing Machine* (New York: Random House, 1954). This volume and encyclopedias provided the basic information for this section, together with the Carvalho book already cited.

HARTFORD CONN. FEB'Y 23D. 1882.

MY DEAR HOUSE:

COTO'S SHAWL WILL GO BY THIS AFTER-NOONS MAIL. MRS CLEMENS IS GETTING IT READY NOW. I GLANCED AT THE SCRIBNER CRITISISM AND INTERPRETED IT EXACTLY AS YOU DID. IT AMUSED ME A GOOD DEAL,TO OBSERVE THE STRUGGLE GOING ON IN THE WRITER'S MIND, TO FIND SOMETHING TO FIND FAULT WITH,AND I THOUGHT THAT IF I COULD HAVE BEEN AT HIS ELBOW,I COULD HAVE SAVED HIM THE HUMILIATION OF DISCOVERING SUCH INFINITEESIMAL DEFECTS,BY POINTING OUT COLOSSAL ONES, ALMOST WITHOUT NUMBER,WHICH HE WAS TOO BLIND TO SEE. I RECEIVED A LOT OF ENGLISH NOTICES YESTERDAY,AND TO MY ASTONISHMENT THEY ARE PROFOUNDLY COMPLIMENTARY; EVEN THE "LONDON TIMES" STOOPS TO FLATTER. THE ENGLISH SALE IS ONE THIRD AS GREAT AS THE AMERICAN,THE SAME PROPORTION ACHIEVED ON "THE TRAMP ABROAD",WHICH HAD AN EXCEPTIONATELY GREAT SALE FOR A HIGH PRICED BOOK. I COMFORT MYSELF THAT WHILE THE REST OF OUR

A portion of an early typed letter written by Samuel Langhorne Clemens (Mark Twain). Clemens bought one of the first typewriters that printed only in capital letters. Courtesy of the Clifton Waller Barrett Library, University of Virginia Library.

THE PENCIL

The pencil became popular after the discovery in A.D. 1564 of a mine in Borrowdale, Cumberland, England, which contained a heavy, almost greasy, substance that left dark gray-black marks when chips of it were rubbed on paper or cloth. Originally thought to be a form of lead, the substance was cut into strips and made writing instruments of high quality. By 1618, according to Carvalho, wooden cases for the "lead" strips were being made. In 1789 Abraham G. Werner coined the word "graphite" from the Greek *graphein,* meaning to write, and thus the substance has been properly known since, although most persons commonly refer to the pencil of today as a lead pencil.

Other graphite deposits were discovered, though few produced material as pure as that of Borrowdale, the supply of which was severely rationed, and finally was exhausted about 1845. Experimentation began early to devise methods of stretching the limited supply of graphite, and Kaspar Faber of Germany produced a composition pencil in 1662. N. J. Conté of France received a patent in 1795 for a process in which graphite and clay were ground, mixed, pressed into and dried in molds. This is the basic modern process, and was developed elsewhere about the same time. Pencil leads were square in the early days, and it was not until the Dixon Pencil Company (in business in the United States in 1827) developed the technique that they became round or octagonal. Pencils were first manufactured in the United States during the War of 1812, when the European supply was cut off.

PAPYRUS

One of the most important early writing materials was papyrus. The use of leaves, grasses, and so forth as writing surfaces in the early days of writing was rather common; but the only one to become widely popular and to remain in use for centuries was papyrus. By the fifth century B.C., according to Norman E. Binns, the Greeks had adopted papyrus for their major writing material, and the Romans, who frequently adopted things Greek, also made use of it.* Leo Deuel writes: "The oldest known papyrus appears to date back to the First Dynasty [of Egypt], at the end of the fourth millennium B.C. . . . Papyrus is a reed-like water plant (*Cyperus papyrus*) of the sedge family, native to Africa. . . .

*Norman E. Binns, *An Introduction to Historical Bibliography* (London: Association of Assistant Librarians, 1962), 9.

In ancient times . . . papyrus thickets grew all along the Nile and in the Delta." Deuel continues with an excellent description of the rather complicated process of producing a writing surface from the plant:

> The raw material taken from the tall plants, some as high as thirty-five feet, consisted of strips cut lengthwise from the pith of the three-sided stalks. Strips of equal length and quality were then arranged on a flat surface, in the manner of latticework, in a horizontal and vertical layer, the former representing the recto and the latter the verso side of the sheet. Through the application of pressure and water from the Nile—perhaps with the occasional addition of glue—the layers were merged into a fairly homogeneous mass, which was then exposed to the sun. After drying, the sheets were rubbed smooth with shells or ivory and perhaps whitened with chalk. Excess moisture was forced out by additional pounding. The papyrus was then ready to be written on with a reed pen. As a rule, only the recto sheet was inscribed.*

Sheets of papyrus were five to six inches wide and eight to nine inches high, and usually were glued together into a roll of perhaps twenty sheets. Such rolls, or scrolls, were widely used, but were a nuisance because one had to unroll a considerable amount of material to find particular information. Thus there were early attempts to fold the papyrus sheets in different ways to allow quicker access, and early forms of the codex evolved.

Papyrus as a writing surface lasted well into the first century, and only gradually was replaced with vellum and parchment as the standard writing surfaces; supplies of the papyrus reed diminished from over-cutting, and papyrus did not stand folding as well as it did rolling. By the third century, parchment had replaced papyrus except in Egypt itself.

PARCHMENT AND VELLUM

Man discovered very early that animal skins could be used for writing surfaces, and gradually he perfected a process for the production of a fine and durable writing material known as parchment or vellum.

There is a technical difference between parchment and vellum; the former is made from the split skins of sheep or goats, while the latter is made only from unsplit calfskins. However, the process of preparation is roughly the same. According to Norman E. Binns, the skins are washed, cleaned in lime, stretched, pared, dusted with chalk, and rubbed smooth with pumice.† The word "parchment" comes from the

---

*Leo Deuel, *Testaments of Time: The Search for Lost Manuscripts and Records* (New York: Knopf, 1965), 84–85.

†Norman E. Binns, *op. cit.,* 10.

city of Pergamum, where this process was developed by its king, Cleomenes II, in the second century B.C. Anthony G. Petti has written that "While it is true to say that vellum can sometimes be distinguished from parchment because of its relative smoothness, polish and thinness and the absence of the points caused by hair or wool, parchment was often so well prepared that it met these criteria."*

Parchment and vellum have proved useful writing surfaces over the centuries because they take ink very well, are durable, can be cleaned and used again, and may be folded and rolled with little damage. The term parchment is used today in the paper industry to refer to a fine grade of paper that resembles the genuine article, but real parchment is still produced, chiefly in Australia, and is used for diplomas and certificates of various types.

PAPER

Among the many contributions, and in many ways perhaps the most important, made by the Chinese to our civilization, is the invention of paper. Paper is a substance so common as not to be noticed, yet it is so basic and important that our modern civilization is entirely dependent upon it.

Ts'ai Lun is most often credited with the invention, about A.D. 105, of this most versatile and useful of materials, although Gordon A. Jahans has suggested that the Chinese acquired this art from another people. In any event, the process was so important that the Chinese guarded the secret jealously. It was not until A.D. 751, when the Arabs defeated the Chinese near Samarkand and took several papermakers captive, that the process escaped from China. The Arabs recognized the value of the process, and protected its secrets; although paper mills were established at Samarkand in 751, and at Baghdad in 793, the process did not reach Europe until 1150, when a mill commenced operations in Toledo, Spain. Paper mills spread rapidly over Europe after that, although they did not reach England until the end of the fifteenth century, and were not successful there until the end of the next century. All paper in the English colonies in North America was imported until the first paper mill opened in Germantown, Pennsylvania, in 1690. Others followed; there was one in 1726 in New Jersey, and a third in Massachusetts Bay in 1728.

"Paper is a material composed of vegetable fibres freely intertwisted with each other so as to form a sheet upon which to write," notes Binns.

*Anthony G. Petti, *English Literary Hands From Chaucer to Dryden* (London: Edward Arnold, 1976), 4.

The best source of the fibers for paper has been, and remains, rags. However, men have experimented with many other types of fibers. In South America the bark of fig trees was often used, and grasses and leaves also have been tried.

Collectors ought to know something of the process of manufacture and its changes because of their effect on the product. Jahans describes papermaking as follows:

> The pulp was produced by retting linen rags until they were soft enough to be broken by beating. This latter operation was carried out by means of heavy wooden beams shod with iron and actuated by manual or water power. . . . When sufficiently beaten the pulp was diluted by the addition of a large quantity of water and transferred to a vat. Here the vatman dipped his mould into the diluted pulp and raised upon its surface a thin layer of fibres. Some of the water was drained away from the fibres by the action of the suction box of the mould when it was lifted out of the vat. The wet pulp was next transferred to a piece of soft felt slightly larger than the sheet of paper. Upon the first layer of felt and paper was placed another . . . the process continuing until the pile was considered high enough to be placed in the press and squeezed. . . . The process continued until the paper-maker considered the paper firm enough to be separated from the felt; then it was finally dried by hanging the sheets over soft thick ropes in a current of air. Lastly, to prepare the dried paper for the reception of ink, the sheets were dipped into a solution of diluted gelatine, dried again, and polished by rubbing with a shell or hard stone.*

It is the mold that gives the paper many of its characteristics. Originally the mold was probably made of natural materials such as reeds or thin branches, but the Chinese used wire in their molds from a very early period, and gradually introduced progressively thinner wire. Wire in the molds was used in Europe from the early days. These wires leave marks in the paper when it is made, and the names of the wires give their names to the type of paper that is made using them.

In early premachine papermaking the chief and numerous wires that support the wet fibers in the mold were called "laid" wires, and the marks they left in paper were called chain lines. They were supported from below by wooden "bridges," and they were tied to a few strong wires running at right angles over them. After about A.D. 1285, the papermaker usually wired into his mold his emblem or trademark, which placed into his paper the designs known as watermarks.† Paper showing the marks of these laid wires is called laid paper, and it was the

---

*Gordon A. Jahans, "A Brief History of Paper," in *Book Collectors' Quarterly,* 15 (July–September 1934), 45–46.

†Petti, *op. cit.,* 5.

only kind of paper made until the process of weaving wire into a cloth was spread in Europe near the end of the eighteenth century.

When woven wire was adapted to the papermaker's mold, the resulting paper showed lines of uniform character running at right angles to each other and forming small squares in the paper. It is called wove paper.

Man worked to introduce machinery into the manufacture of paper to speed the slow and tedious process, and to produce more of this valuable and desirable product. The most important of the inventions applied to papermaking was that of Nicholas Louis Robert of France in 1798. The machine was not a success in France, and soon was moved across the Channel to England, where the brothers Henry and Sealy Fourdrinier engaged an engineer to perfect Robert's machine. Brian Donkin did so, and in 1803 production began in two mills using the new papermaking machine. So successful was it that it came to be called the Fourdrinier machine after its financial backers. Jahans notes that after 1810 "we may expect to find more and more printing being done upon machine-made paper," and that by 1851, there were 190 Fourdrinier machines working in England.*

Up to about 1800, almost all paper was made from rags except for occasional experimentation; but because rags became scarce about that year, men began searching for other sources of fibers. Wood was ground and used, as were various types of grasses. Later, Frederick Gottlieb's 1840 invention of a machine for grinding wood chips into fine powder, and the invention, eleven years later, of a process for disintegrating wood by means of chemicals, discovered by Englishmen Charles Watt and Hugh Burgess, were most important. These substitutes for rags, but chiefly wood fibers, made possible the widespread growth of newspapers and books as they proved both effective and inexpensive.

"Between the years 1803 and 1826 it was not possible to imitate either the watermarks or the laid lines of the older hand-made paper in the new machine-made papers," Jahans notes. But an 1826 invention called the dandy roll allowed marks to be pressed into the upper surface of the paper as it was being run through the machine. One can, with a magnifying glass and a strong light source, determine that the marks are pressed into the upper side while the wove wire marks are still visible on the lower side. The wove marks in machine-made paper are small diamonds rather than squares because the wire cloth must be stretched very tightly in a Fourdrinier machine, pulling the wires in the fabric out of their regular square alignment.

Mentioned above was the fact that handmade paper was dipped into a gelatin solution to give it a better writing surface. This practice con-

*Jahans, *op. cit.*, 51.

tinued with machine-made paper until 1807, when Moritz Illig discovered the process of adding processed rosin solution to the paper pulp. Later, when the paper was run over the heating drums at the end of the Fourdrinier machine's process, the heat melted the rosin and sized the paper. Unfortunately, alum had to be added to the pulp solution when the rosin was added, and it has since been found to be a prominent cause of paper deterioration. "Resin size can be easily distinguished from gelatine size, and we thus have another sharply defined dating point for our paper."*

Another factor contributing to the deterioration of the quality of machine-made paper as compared with handmade paper was that in the latter process, the vat man swirls the mold spreading the fibers in all directions. This is not possible in a Fourdrinier machine, and the fibers align in one direction only. As man attempted to speed and lessen the labor of making paper, he introduced processes and invented machines that produced more paper in shorter periods of time and that eliminated hand labor. But the effect of these "improvements" on the quality of paper was generally to reduce it. Paper has deteriorated in quality over the years until much of today's paper is very poor; books printed on most modern papers fall apart in a very few years.

The collector should investigate the history of paper in far more detail than it has been possible to include here. Most of the autographs and manuscripts that he will acquire will be written on paper, and it will be very helpful to him if he knows enough of the history of paper to be able to check it to be sure that it is of the period when the autograph purports to have been written. This knowledge will give the collector protection against the purchase of forgeries and will provide an extra measure of confidence in pursuing his avocation.

These, then, are the common writing instruments and materials that created the autographs that a collector of today may expect to acquire. Papyrus is rare, and parchment and vellum documents are not common, at least for United States collectors. Paper is the common material, and an iron gall ink applied with a quill pen was the most common method of producing the majority of the autographs moving in the market, although for those collecting autographs of the twentieth century, the fountain pen and the typewriter are the most common. The collector should know something of the other instruments and materials that man has invented and used for his writings over the centuries. Study of writing instruments and material can be a fascinating sideline to the collecting of autographs and manuscripts.

*Jahans, 56.

THE HISTORY OF AUTOGRAPH COLLECTING

JOSEPH E. FIELDS

MAN'S INTEREST in the preservation of his written word goes back into the mists of antiquity. He found it necessary to express his knowledge and ideas in a physical and visible form, first for his own enlightenment and soon thereafter for the benefit of his contemporaries. It then became imperative that he preserve his written records for the use of his successors, so that they might benefit from his experiences, regardless of the form his written thoughts might take.

As far as we are able to ascertain, man set forth his thoughts for the first time in the form of picture writing on the walls of caves. He had probably discovered that the elements had a deleterious effect upon his "writing" and that, in order to preserve his knowledge, he must record his thoughts away from molestation by the elements as well as from others of his own species. The picture writing of prehistoric man was likely the first attempt at collecting and preserving the written word.

There followed a long period of development from the picture writing of prehistory until the appearance of the cuneiform method of writing. Unfortunately, we know nothing of the evolutionary process nor of the period of time involved. We can be relatively certain that cuneiform writing was a modification of picture writing and that the process took thousands of years. Dr. Samuel Noah Kramer is of the opinion that the pictographic and ideographic script of the protoliterate era of the Sumerian period was modified over a period of many years into a phonetic system of writing and that it extended from about 3050 B.C. until 2300 B.C.*

By the middle of the third millennium B.C., the Sumerian cuneiform writing had become sufficiently developed to enable complicated histori-

*Samuel Noah Kramer, *From the Tablets of Sumer* (Indian Hills, Colo.: Falcon's Wing Press, [1956]); and "Sumerian Literature—Man's Oldest Manuscripts on Clay," in *Manuscripts,* 12, no. 2 (Spring 1960), 2–12.

cal and literary works to be written down instead of being preserved in an oral form. However, most of the inscriptions were of an economic and administrative nature. As Kramer has pointed out, Sumerian writings, preserved in the sands of time and still being discovered, deciphered, and studied, consist of myths, heroic tales, proverbs, fables, essays, laws, and narratives recorded a thousand years before Hammurabi. We are indebted to the early "collectors" of Sumer, for it was they, the teachers, priests, rulers, professional men, and civil administrators, who collected and preserved the written words that have been passed down to us. These cuneiform writings consisted of marks cut into flat pieces of clay by means of a stylus; the clay was then baked to preserve it.

The bulkiness of clay tablets naturally made preservation, either by a government or by a private individual, a major problem. It was to the ancient Sumerian as much of a storage problem as the megatons of paper archives are to us. Added to the bulk was the problem of weight, which made transportation of the written word difficult, and at times impossible.

Hieroglyphic writing of ancient Egypt developed approximately a hundred years after the cuneiform of Mesopotamia. Many of the rulers of Egypt are known to have had private libraries composed of written records of official events, business transactions, scientific knowledge, and religious beliefs and customs, as well as literary works. It would seem only logical that such writings would be preserved not only by the ruling monarch but also by his administration, priests, businessmen, scientists, professional men, and affluent citizens in all walks of life.

The Egyptians are credited with the invention of a writing material made from the papyrus reed that then grew in the Nile delta. Strips cut from the reed were laid close together, and another layer laid over the first at right angles to it. Whether a bonding agent of some gelatinous material or paste was used is not known. The resulting sheet was hammered, sundried, and then polished with a smooth, hard object. Successive sheets were pasted together into a long strip and then rolled from the bottom. Usually no more than twenty sheets constituted a roll. A fresh impetus was given to writing and its preservation by this discovery, and thus to its natural offspring—collecting.

The Egyptians recorded their public and private writings, laws, history, literature, and scientific data on papyrus. It is quite likely that the manufacture of papyrus was an Egyptian monopoly, and that its use spread from Egypt to Greece and the remainder of the ancient world. All of the classical Greek writers had their works recorded on papyrus. Strabo gives credit to Aristotle as the first Greek to collect a library, and says that he persuaded the Egyptian kings to form their collections, which ultimately became the most definitive in the ancient world. Ptolemy Philadelphus is supposed to have refused to supply wheat to the starving Athenians, caught in the ravages of a famine unless he was permitted to borrow the manuscripts of the Greek literary and philosophical giants so that he might have copies made. He is said to have retained the originals and sent the copies back to Athens. He is also reported to have persuaded the Hebrew scholars to come to Alexandria and translate the Hebrew biblical writings into the Greek language. The great library of Alexandria, one of the largest manuscript collections ever formed, was in reality the private collection of the Ptolemies.

It is known that Khufu, Khafre, and Ramses II had private libraries and, hence, were manuscript collectors. Undoubtedly there were many other pharaohs who had extensive collections. Gradually wars, natural disasters, climatic conditions, and conflagrations destroyed most of the papyracious libraries.

Cicero (106–43 B.C.) had a fine collection and speaks of it in his writings. One Pompeius Secundus had a collection of manuscripts, for Pliny the Younger states he had personally seen many fine examples. Pliny also had a collection, but placed his own as secondary to that of his friend Pompeius.

During the early Christian era the Egyptians shut off the supply of papyrus, and a new writing material had to be found. The skin of sheep, goats, and calves, called parchment, was used. A finer-textured parchment, called vellum, was also used; it was obtained from the skin of lambs, kids, calves, and the embryonic skin of these animals. It was apparently first developed by Eumenes II of Pergamum (ruled 197–160/159 B.C.). By the second century of the Christian era it was in wide use. Improvements in quality made it more universally accepted, although it never completely replaced papyrus. After the sixth century the product became inferior because increasing demand affected the supply.

Parchment had many inherent disadvantages: expense, bulk, short supply, easy prey to insects and vermin, attack by natural elements, lack of standard thickness, and poor absorbability of inks. All these made it an inferior writing material. The invention of printing in the middle of the fifteenth century, together with the introduction of paper into the Western world, sounded the death knell of vellum and parchment. Except for special occasions they have had no wide usage since early in the sixteenth century.

The invention of the camel's hair brush in 250 B.C. by the Chinese scholar Meng Tien greatly facilitated the writing of Chinese characters. For centuries the Chinese had written on woven cloth. The increased spread of writing naturally speeded the development of a more facile surface upon which to write. Paper made its appearance about A.D. 105. After some five hundred years the knowledge of papermaking spread to the Arabs of Samarkand, where in 751 a number of Chinese soldiers versed in the art were captured. By the tenth century the art had spread to Egypt and along the northern shore of Africa to Morocco. It reached Europe early in the twelfth century, when the Moors set up a paper manufactory at Játiva in Valencia, Spain. The art soon spread to Sicily and France. Paper was in use in England in the early part of the fourteenth century, but it was not until the late fifteenth century that John Tate set up the first English paper mill. A century later, in 1588, John Spilman was granted a patent by Elizabeth I to set up a paper mill at Dartford. Thus it took approximately fifteen hundred years for paper to reach the Western world. The first paper mill in the United States was erected at Roxborough Township, Pennsylvania, by William Rittenhouse in 1690.

The invention of printing further enhanced the replacement of vellum by paper. The art of calligraphy, a skill not difficult to acquire, also promoted education and the dissemination of ideas. Almost immediately documents and letters began to be collected, particularly by those associated with the court, the church, and the universities. Students and travelers often carried small notebooks called *alba amicorum*. In them were kept random jottings of interesting occurrences and quotations. Often professors, friends, and prominent people were prevailed upon to write some pearl of wisdom or a salutation upon their pages. A number of these books are in existence.

Gradually letters and documents, especially if of interesting or important content, came to be preserved, not just by the recipient but by others as well. The custom was particularly frequent in Germany. Not only were individual scholars collecting and preserving, but so were universities and libraries, to say nothing of the Vatican. The family archives of the nobility contained many literary and political treasures. Intellectuals preserved the letters of their contemporaries. A letter or a document was a precious possession, for paper was expensive and the delivery charge was dear.

The sixteenth-century collection of Antoine Loménie de Brienne, consisting of the 340 folio volumes now preserved in the Bibliothèque Nationale, was one of the most comprehensive of its day. Philippe de Béthune (1560–1641) also had an extensive collection. Roger de Gaignières, born in 1641, spent time and fortune acquiring and preserving historical letters and documents. In 1711 he presented them to Louis XIV. They are now housed in the Bibliothèque Nationale.

In Germany, Thomas Rehdiger (1540–1576) and Ludwig Camerorius (1573–1651) had notable collections.

In England, Sir Robert Bruce Cotton (1557–1631) amassed one of the largest private collections of his time. It consisted of charters, records, and manuscripts of a varied nature, some of which had been dispersed from the monastic and church libraries during the reign of Henry VIII. The collection was continued by his son and grandson, and was finally incorporated into the British Museum collection in 1752.

Sir Thomas Bodley (1545–1613) formed a large personal library and manuscript collection following his retirement from the diplomatic service in 1603. The collection, which made up the nucleus of the great Bodleian Library at Oxford, has been multiplied many times over since the original acquisition.

Sir Hans Sloane (1660–1753), president of the Royal Society, formed a great manuscript collection. He also purchased the collection of William Courten, a magnificent stroke that greatly augmented his growing collection. Sir Hans was an outstanding naturalist and scientist as well as personal physician to George II. His collection consisted of historical and scientific letters and treatises, scientific books and curiosities, as well as botanical and zoological specimens. He bequeathed his collection to the British government on condition that Parliament pay his family £20,000. Parliament agreed, and the collection became the nucleus of the present British Library. His manuscript collection consisted of 4,100 volumes.

Robert Harley, Earl of Oxford and Mortimer (1661–1724), was for many years Queen Anne's chancellor of the Exchequer and principal adviser. He formed a great library and manuscript collection. His son Edward, the second earl (1689–1741), enlarged the collection considerably. A portion of it was sold at auction in 1742. His widow sold the remainder to the British government in 1753 for £10,000. The Harleian manuscripts, forty thousand in number, are an integral part of the British Library collections. Other private collections of manuscripts, such as the Landsdowne, Hargrave, Burney, and Greville, have further augmented the British Library collections.

The nineteenth century saw an unprecedented growth in the number and quality of autograph collections. Queen Victoria and Prince Albert were avid collectors, their collection now being housed at Windsor Castle. Other large collections were formed by John L. Anderdon, Rev. Robert Bolton, Robert Cole, John Dillon, A. Donnadieu, Baron Heath, Alfred Morrison, Sir Thomas Phillipps, T. Stamford Raffles, Dawson Turner, William Upcott, and John Young.

Among the French collectors of the nineteenth century were M. Monmerqué, Lucas de Montigny, Benjamin Fillon, Étienne Pierre Louis Chambry, and Alfred Bovet. The Bonaparte family, including Joseph Cardinal Fesch, had outstanding and extensive manuscript holdings.

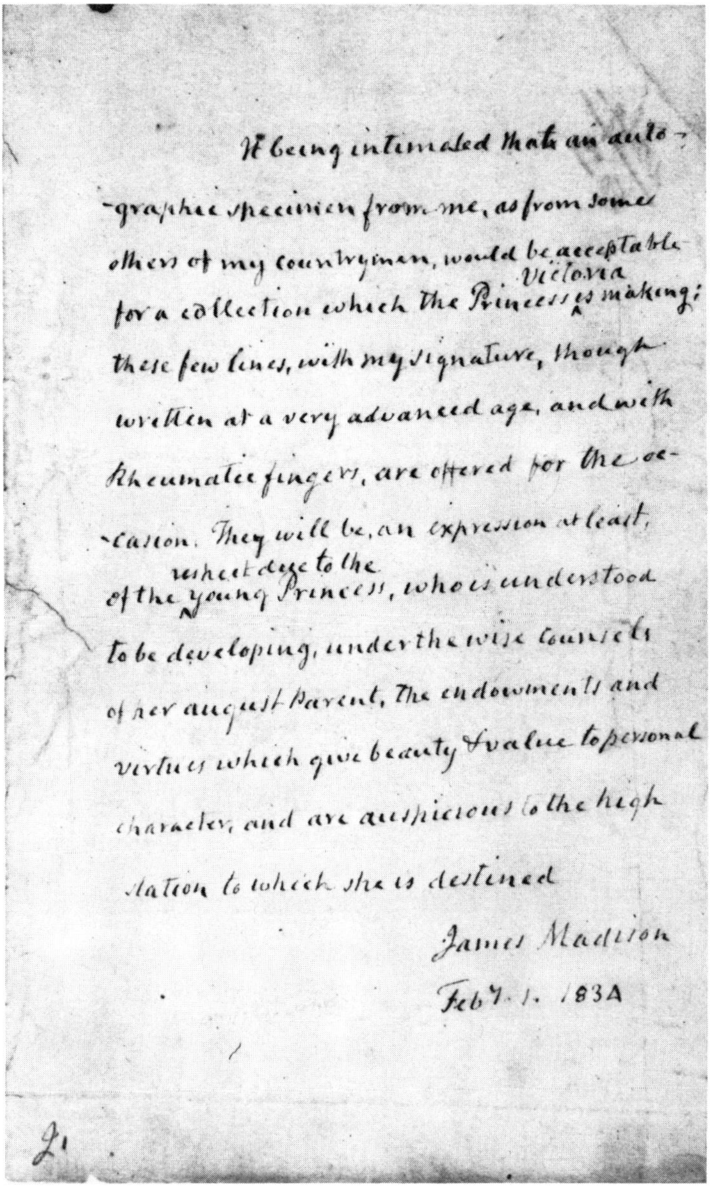

It being intimated that an auto-graphic specimen from me, as from some others of my countrymen, would be acceptable for a collection which the Princess Victoria is making; these few lines, with my signature, though written at a very advanced age, and with rheumatic fingers, are offered for the occasion. They will be, an expression at least, of the respect due to the young Princess, who is understood to be developing, under the wise counsels of her august Parent, the endowments and virtues which give beauty & value to personal character, and are auspicious to the high station to which she is destined

James Madison
Feby. 1. 1834

Queen Victoria began collecting autographs before she became queen. Here an aged James Madison complies with the request of the then princess for his autograph. Courtesy of the University of Virginia Library.

In Germany the collections of Count Ludwig Paar, Alexander Meyer Cohn, Dr. Carol Geibel, and Carl Herz von Hertenried of Vienna were notable. Probably the greatest continental collection was that formed by the Swiss collector Karl Geigy-Hagenbach.

Of the European collections, those of Alfred Morrison and Sir Thomas Phillipps are preeminent by virtue of the number, quality, and rarity of the items.

Apparently the first United States collector of autographs was Rev. William B. Sprague (1795–1876). He began his collection about 1814, when he became a tutor in the family of Maj. Lawrence Lewis in Virginia. Major and Mrs. Lewis were the nephew and adopted daughter of George Washington. While residing at Woodlawn, young Sprague was allowed by Judge Bushrod Washington to go to Mount Vernon and extract from General Washington's correspondence any letter he wished, provided he left a copy in its place. He thus came into possession of about fifteen hundred letters. It was probably Sprague who originated the idea of forming a set of signatures of Signers of the Declaration of Independence, a quest that was extremely contagious and that was to dominate the collecting pursuits of most of the nineteenth- and early twentieth-century collectors. At his death Sprague's collection numbered about forty thousand items.

Israel K. Tefft (1795–1862) started his collection about the same time as Sprague. Upon moving from Rhode Island to Savannah in 1810, he began collecting autographs. The collection grew extensively after 1830. He was on friendly terms with Sprague and other early collectors; an unusual rapport existed among them. They exchanged items freely, and thus strengthened their personal collections. Tefft, a bank clerk, was not a wealthy man, and probably never purchased an autograph for his collection. What he, as well as his fellow collectors, accomplished was by means of barter. After his death his widow auctioned off his thirty-thousand-item collection.

Other early collectors were Robert Gilmor, a wealthy merchant of Baltimore; Lewis J. Cist of Cincinnati; Eliza Allen of Providence; and Mellen Chamberlain, a judge and later librarian of the Boston Public Library.

Later in the nineteenth century, outstanding collections were formed by Dr. John S. H. Fogg, Dr. Thomas Addis Emmet, Ferdinand J. Dreer, Simon Gratz, Elliott Danforth, Frank Etting, Charles F. Gunther, James Lenox, John M. Hale, Zachary T. Hollingsworth, Charles Colcock Jones, Brantz Mayer, Bailey Myers, David McNeely Stauffer, John Boyd Thatcher, Joshua J. Cohen, and Charles Roberts. Some of these were disposed of at auction, others were sold privately, and still others gravitated to institutions.

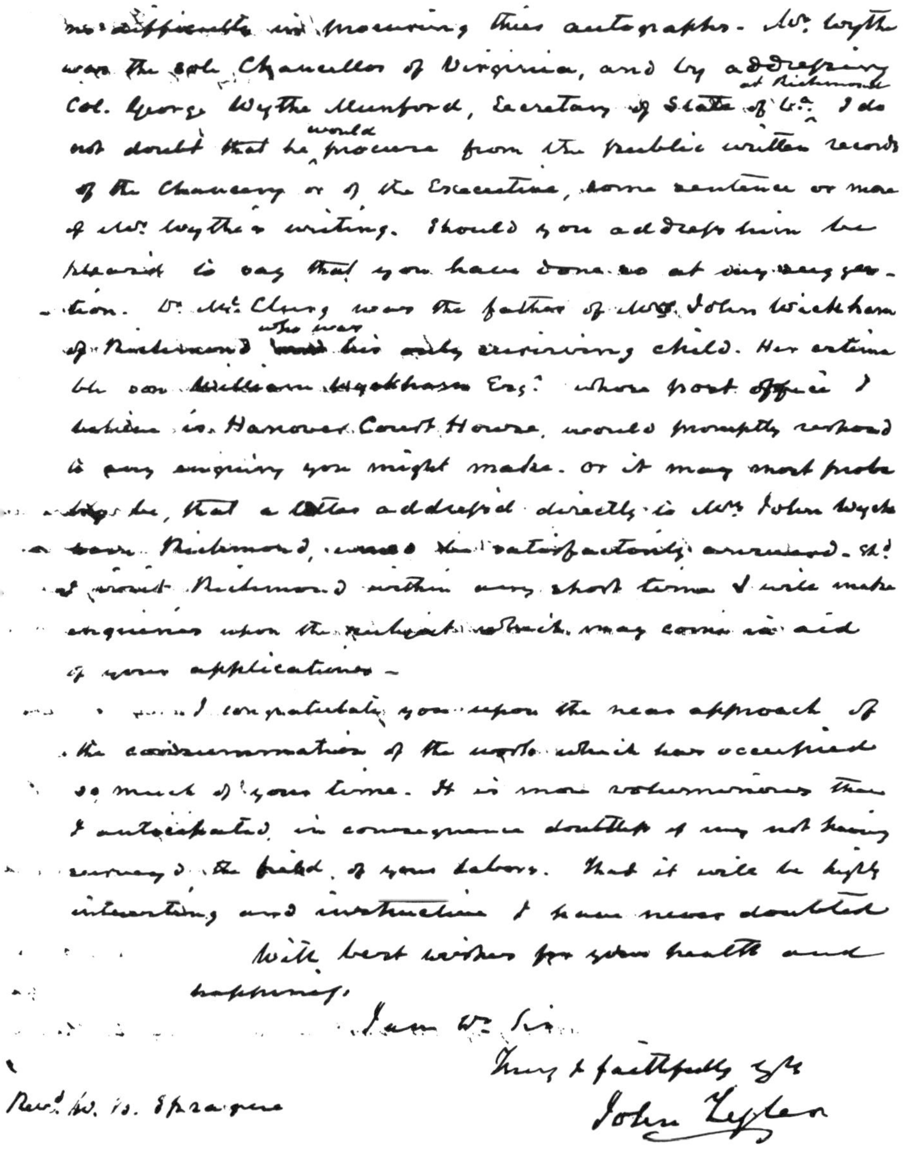
no difficulty in procuring these autographs. Mr Wythe was the sole Chancellor of Virginia, and by addressing Col. George Wythe Munford, Secretary of State of Va at Richmond I do not doubt that he would procure from the public written records of the Chancery or of the Executive, some sentence or more of Mr Wythe's writing. Should you address him be pleased to say that you have done so at my suggestion. Dr McClurg was the father of Mrs John Wickham of Richmond who was his only surviving child. Her eldest son William Wickham Esqr whose post office I believe is Hanover Court House, would promptly respond to any enquiry you might make. or it may most probably be, that a letter addressed directly to Mrs John Wickham Richmond, would be satisfactorily answered. Shd I visit Richmond within any short time I will make enquiries upon the subject which may come in aid of your applications—

I congratulate you upon the near approach of the consummation of the work which has occupied so much of your time. It is more voluminous than I anticipated in consequence doubtless of my not having surveyed the field of your labors. That it will be highly interesting and instructive I have never doubted

With best wishes for your health and happiness,

I am Dr Sir

Truly & faithfully yrs

John Tyler

Revd W. B. Sprague

Former president John Tyler wrote to Rev. William B. Sprague, the noted autograph collector, on July 20, 1853, concerning autographs that Sprague had solicited. Tyler also made suggestions in regard to individuals who might be able to assist Sprague in locating autographs he sought. Courtesy of the University of Virginia Library.

The early part of the twentieth century saw such collectors as Thomas Redfield Proctor, Augustin Daly, James H. Manning, Charles Francis Jenkins, Louis Bamberger, Herbert L. Pratt, Dr. George C. F. Williams, Frederick S. Peck, Roderick Terry, John Work Garrett, Robert C. Norton, Mrs. John Hubbard, George Cardinal Mundelein, Oliver R. Barrett, Josiah K. Lilly, William L. Clements, and Estelle Betzold Doheny forming outstanding collections of manuscripts, literary as well as historical.

No history of United States autograph collecting would be complete without the mention of the Morgan family. The founder of the financial dynasty, Junius S. Morgan, had a modest collection. His son, J. Pierpont Morgan, was busy gathering autographs at age sixteen. From then until his death in 1913 he was an avid collector of autographs, manuscripts, and books. His autograph collection was the cornerstone upon which his great collection of books and art was built. His son, J. Pierpont Morgan, also continued the collection, which is now housed in the Morgan Library, New York City, where scholars may use its fine source material. It is one of the finest and largest private libraries in the world.

Equally as great as the Morgan collection is that of Henry E. Huntington (1850–1927). Huntington began collecting about 1910 and was active until his death. In 1920 his collection of manuscripts, books, and art treasures was moved to the newly built Henry E. Huntington Library and Art Gallery at San Marino, California.

William Randolph Hearst, founder of the publishing dynasty, was also an avid collector of manuscripts, books, and art. He was no doubt stimulated to collect by his mother, Phoebe Apperson Hearst, an early collector of Washingtoniana.

Somewhat later, such collectors as Dr. Frederick M. Dearborn, Foreman M. Lebold, Richard M. Lederer, Allyn K. Ford, Dr. Otto Fisher, Dr. Frank L. Pleadwell, Dr. Arthur Elliott, and Philip D. Sang formed extensive collections of superb quality.

Mention of these great collections of the past brings to mind the dealers in manuscript material who have played such an important part in the formation of so many collections. Probably the first autograph dealer in the United States was Charles De F. Burns. He first set up business in New York in 1864. By 1871 he had become successful enough to publish a periodical, *The American Antiquarian,* in which he listed his items for sale.

Next on the scene in New York were the Benjamin brothers, William Evarts and Walter R. The former retired from the business, but Walter continued it until his death. Since then his daughter, Mary A. Benjamin Henderson, has continued it. This old and respected firm has been in business since 1887, and during that long period has been under the direction of only two individuals. The firm continues to publish *The Collector.*

In England a former Vermonter, Henry Stevens, became a noted bookseller. He was also the source of important manuscript material that was duly forwarded to his American customers.

Patrick F. Madigan and his son, Thomas F., were noted dealers in New York. The younger Madigan became an outstanding dealer and was imbued with a fine sense of showmanship. He was the source of much excellent material and had the ability to present it in an enticing fashion.

In Boston, C. E. Goodspeed, the well-known book dealer, also dealt in autographs. From 1927 Gordon Banks, the doyen of United States autograph dealers, was in charge of the autograph department until his recent retirement. The house publication, *The Month,* was published for forty years but ceased publication in 1969. It was, and remains, an excellent source of scholarly information.

The Rosenbach Company held sway in Philadelphia under the direction of A. S. W. and Philip Rosenbach. For many years they were the source of innumerable amounts of the finest literary and historical manuscripts. After the deaths of the Rosenbachs a portion of the stock became the Rosenbach Foundation, an educational foundation. The remainder was acquired by John F. Fleming of New York, who still deals in fine books and manuscripts.

Two of the most learned dealers were Forest G. ("Pop") Sweet and his son, Forest H. Sweet, who established their business in Battle Creek, Michigan. The father began dealing in autographs late in the nineteenth century, and was active until his death at the age of ninety. For many years he conducted his business in New York City. His shop was his bedroom, and his stock was kept in trunks and suitcases. Few dealers have had such a profound fund of knowledge at their fingertips as did "Pop" Sweet. His son carried on the business at Battle Creek. He is best remembered for his large, bold handwriting in India ink, his great store of knowledge, his stimulating advice to young collectors, and his indefatigable efforts on behalf of the Manuscript Society.

Other dealers, all having outstanding materials to offer, have played important roles in the trade. Ben Bloomfield, King V. Hostick, Emily Driscoll, Guido Bruno and his daughter Elenore, David Kirschenbaum of Carnegie Book Shop, Julia Sweet Newman, and Charles Hamilton are a few that come to mind.

Auction prices remained very low during the nineteenth and early twentieth centuries. There was a gradual upward climb until the 1920's. Spurred by an increased interest in collecting, intense dealer rivalry, and competition among a small group of collectors vying for high-quality items, auction room prices reached an all-time high in the late 1920's. After the financial collapse of the Great Depression, prices declined precipitously. They remained low until after World War II, when a gradual increase began. It has continued, and prices are now almost at the all-time high level.

Autograph auctions have been held in London for at least two centuries, Sotheby and Christie's being the most renowned houses. Auction sales in the United States were generally held in New York, Boston, and Philadelphia. One of the earliest auction houses was that of C. F. Libbie in Boston. In New York the leading auction house for autographs was Bangs and Company. Outstanding sales were conducted in Philadelphia by the firms of M. Thomas, Thomas Birch, and Stan V. Henkels. Freeman's has also conducted sales there for many years.

During the early part of the twentieth century, the American Art Association was formed in New York to conduct auctions of books and autographs. Its rival was the Anderson Galleries. The two firms eventually merged into a firm called the American Art Association–Anderson Galleries. It evolved into the Parke-Bernet Galleries under the direction of Arthur Swan; several years ago this firm was purchased by Sotheby. In 1977 Christie's, the well-known English auction house, made its appearance in the New York auction market.

In the 1920's and 1930's several abortive attempts were made to form a society composed of collectors and of dealers in autographs. Through the indefatigable efforts of a small group of collectors and dealers, an organization came into being that has thrived since 1948. The organization was originally incorporated as the National Society of Autograph Collectors. Its first publication was entitled *Autograph Collectors' Journal*. In 1953 the organization's name was changed to the Manuscript Society and its publication renamed *Manuscripts*. The society is composed of collectors, dealers, librarians, archivists, and all those throughout the world who have an interest in the written word.*

*There are today several other organizations for autograph collectors, such as the Universal Autograph Collectors' Club and the Check Collectors' Round Table.—*editor.*

SECTION II

RUDIMENTS OF AUTOGRAPH COLLECTING

THE LANGUAGE OF AUTOGRAPH COLLECTING

EDMUND BERKELEY, JR.

GROUPS OF PEOPLE who have considerable interaction with each other over a common interest or concern, such as their trades, hobbies, professions, or businesses, often develop specialized vocabularies either out of necessity or for convenience. A vocabulary sometimes develops because of new concepts and new programs that require new words, or new uses for old words. In other instances the vocabulary is a shorthand based on standard and accepted terms used in the trade, hobby, or other area.

The vocabulary of autograph collecting falls into the latter category, because most of its terms are abbreviations of longer phrases. Autograph dealers, probably to save space in their catalogs, began to use abbreviations for the standard phrases describing many of the common types of materials. Today these abbreviations are used universally in conversation and in writings by collectors, dealers, and professionals, although there is minor disagreement on the spellings.

The basic item sought by autograph collectors is the autograph. The concept evoked by this word in the minds of many collectors has evolved beyond the commonly held notion that an autograph is a signature. The latter is the traditional meaning of the word, and the one still used by the large number of collectors who specialize in signatures. Most dealers' catalogs list a few signatures, and there are some dealers who specialize in them; their offerings tend to include those of persons of current popularity in the cinema, sports, or public life.

To many collectors of today—and of yesterday as well—the word "autograph" implies much more than the mere signature of a person of interest. An autograph is considered to be a piece of writing in the hand of a person of consequence, or a piece of writing signed by the person. Unsigned writings by persons who appeal to the collector are desirable if the subject matter is significant.

The contents of autographs are important to these collectors because of the light they shed on their authors' thoughts or on some significant event in their lives. Many collectors are aware that the research value of an autograph collection focused on a person, area, or time period may be far greater than that of the single autographs; and in many instances they have developed collections eagerly sought by scholars.

Professionals working with autographs in libraries and in institutions use the word "manuscript" not only to mean what these collectors would term an "autograph," but also include typed pieces in their definition. Colton Storm and Howard Peckham have written a good definition of the word "manuscript" as employed by professionals, and much of their definition would be accepted by collectors as well.

> A "manuscript" means literally "handwriting," from the two Latin words that compose it. It has come to mean something written by hand, as opposed to printing. It may be used as a noun or an adjective. There is no limitation on subject matter; a manuscript may be official or personal, literary, reportorial, legal, or commercial. In America, there is no limit on the date or time of a manuscript. It may have been written in ancient Egypt or modern Detroit. So long as it is not printed, it is a manuscript. The typewriter has complicated things somewhat, but a typed page is still called a manuscript. A photocopy of a manuscript, however, is no longer a manuscript, but a reproduction of it. European usage confines the word manuscript to things written *before* the invention of printing. Pages written by hand since 1450 are called "documents," or sometimes "modern manuscripts."*

Professionals use the vocabulary of autograph collecting in describing the materials in their custody, and the collector must be familiar with this vocabulary in order to discuss readily materials of common interest.

The three types of handwritten material most commonly collected are the letter, the manuscript, and the document. Most persons know that a letter is a formal communication bearing both a salutation and a complimentary close. Particularly desirable, from a collector's point of view, is the letter entirely in the hand of and signed by its author. The word "holograph" is commonly used to describe such a letter or other writing. While the word "holograph" is a synonym for autograph, it is best used when one wishes to emphasize that the letter or writing was

---

*Colton Storm and Howard Peckham, *Invitation to Book Collecting* . . . (New York: Bowker, 1947), 127.

written and signed by the same person. A "holograph letter" is described as an "autograph letter signed," a phrase usually abbreviated to A.L.S.

Periods are often omitted from the abbreviations that will be mentioned in this article, but are included here. Some persons do not capitalize the letters in the abbreviations, a practice that occasionally can lead to confusion. Ms. is the abbreviation for manuscript; Mss. means manuscripts, while Ms.S. means a manuscript signed. If the capital letters were not used, one could not distinguish between the two.

Many busy people today do not have time to write letters by hand, and letters of such persons usually are typed by a secretary from dictation and signed by the author (though the collector must beware of the automatic signature-signing machines). This form of letter is called a "typed letter signed," abbreviated to T.L.S. Perhaps a typed letter will have a few handwritten words added by the author at the end; such a letter will be much more desirable for the collector than one that is merely signed. There is no special terminology for a letter of this type.

After the letter, a collector finds desirable a manuscript in the handwriting of the person in whom he is interested. It may be a poem, short story, draft of a novel, recipe, memorandum, or almost any writing in the hand of the author other than a letter, a note, or a document. The abbreviation for manuscript has been mentioned. A manuscript entirely in the hand of its author is abbreviated A.Ms., and one that is signed in addition is recorded as A.Ms.S.

"Document" is perhaps the most difficult term for the collector to define. A standard definition for the professional is that a document is a single writing, typing, or printed form completed by hand, used for the communication of information. The collector would narrow this definition considerably, because he ordinarily would be interested only in those that bear some writing as well as the signature of the subject (unless the document pertains to the subject, such as a military commission). A document, to a collector, usually had some official nature when originally prepared; thus the term is normally reserved for commissions, legal instruments, applications, ship's papers, and similar items. They may be autograph and signed, in which case the shortened term is A.D.S., or they may be written out by a secretary or consist of a printed form completed by hand and signed by the subject. The abbreviation is then D.S.

For centuries people have written notes to each other asking to borrow things, to make appointments, or for a multitude of other reasons. A handwritten note signed by its author is called an "autograph note signed," abbreviated as A.N.S.; a typed, signed note is T.N.S. Frequently it is difficult to decide whether a communication is a note or a letter, but the note rarely has the formal salutation or complimentary close, and usually is brief.

Postcards are collected and are a form of letter, but have their own abbreviation, P.C. This may be preceded by A., to indicate that the card is in the hand of the author; it also may be followed by S., to indicate the presence of the signature of the author.

Persons retaining communications for future reference frequently write comments on them. Such comments, acknowledgments, referrals to higher authority (chiefly on military documents), or notes are usually written on the back (or verso) of letters or documents, and are called endorsements, a term also used to describe the signature placed on the verso of a bank draft (check) by the person to whom it was made payable when it was cashed. Another form of notation placed on a letter or document by its recipient is the docket, always found on the verso in a blank area and often written after the item was folded for filing. The recipient notes the writer of the item, its date or the date received, and sometimes a brief summary of the contents. The docket was used extensively for filing purposes; in the late nineteenth century, government documents and business papers sometimes had a space on the verso reserved for the docket. A heading was printed, as were lines on which the information could be written.

It is helpful for the collector to know that the front, or first page, of a piece of writing is always called the recto, while the back is the verso. If a manuscript has many pages bound together, the right-hand pages are the rectos and the left are the versos.

Autograph collectors also have a shorthand for referring to the sizes of the materials they handle. These terms are derived from those originally used in book printing. The pages of a book were printed on large single sheets, or leaves, measuring about nineteen by twenty-five inches, which were then folded and cut to make the smaller book pages. Such a large sheet, when folded once, created two leaves, or four pages, and is known as a folio. If the sheet is not folded, but bears the printing on one side only, as a poster does, it is called a broadside. The number of pages obtained from the folding process determines the terms bookmen use to describe books. Autograph collectors have adopted these terms. An octavo book is one with sheets folded to give four leaves bearing eight pages. Today the term octavo (abbreviated 8vo) means a book or manuscript about eight by six inches. A quarto (4to) is approximately twelve by eight inches in size. The abbreviation 12mo is used to indicate a sheet about six by four inches, a size sometimes referred to as "small octavo." One should remember that the vertical dimension is always given first in autographic usage, and that today books are described by the heights of their bindings, not by their leaf foldings. Libraries measure books and manuscripts in centimeters, also giving the vertical dimension first, and rarely add the horizontal measurement unless it is unusual.

An author will, quite often, be asked to write out a well-known poem or story that he has composed. Such a manuscript, signed by the author, is called a fair copy because it was not involved in the original creative process. Sometimes an author, upon completing his composition, will prepare a clean copy, possibly to be used by a printer or just to have a clean copy on hand. Such a copy may be called a final draft or, if it can be determined from marks on the manuscript that a printer worked with it in setting type, it may be called a typesetting draft. Another type of copy made by the author of a writing is that designated as the retained copy. After completing a letter or other writing, the author may write out a copy to keep for his files. It may be difficult to distinguish such a copy from a draft, but the latter usually shows evidence of change and correction. Neither, however, will show evidence of having been sent through the mail if written before envelopes were first used (before the 1840's in the United States).

A transcript is a copy of a manuscript made by someone other than the original author, often for the purpose of providing a copy of the original that is easier to read. A dealer will sometimes prepare a transcript of a manuscript or a letter that he offers for sale if he feels that the obscurity of the handwriting may make the item difficult to sell.

In the centuries before the invention of the typewriter, carbon paper, and the electrostatic copier (those marvelous copying machines marketed by many companies but referred to by most of us by the trade name Xerox), people needed copies of manuscripts, letters, and documents. The only method of copying available was to have a scribe write one, or to do it yourself. Such copies are known today as contemporary copies if there is good reason to conclude that they were prepared not long after the original was composed. The collector must be cautious and not confuse a contemporary copy with an original. Reputable dealers' catalogs always state if an offered item is a contemporary copy.

A collector will see and hear frequent references to facsimiles. The word means "an exact reproduction," but facsimiles of autographs vary widely in quality. Dealers' catalogs often include facsimiles of autographs offered for sale, but rarely is an attempt made to reproduce the paper or the ink of the original. Only an expert may be able to detect the finest facsimiles when care has been taken in choosing the paper and matching the ink of the original autograph. Printing has developed so many sophisticated techniques in the past century that fine facsimiles of autographs can be reproduced with relative ease.

One of the most common facsimiles of an autograph is that of the letter of Thomas Jefferson dated November 27, 1803, at Washington; it is addressed to Craven Peyton and concerns Jefferson's debts and a loan. Some 30,000 copies of this facsimile were reproduced in a publicity campaign by a Richmond, Virginia, bank not long before World War II. The facsimile is excellent and does not bear any statement that it is a reproduction, thus deceiving many persons who discover copies in trunks or tucked into books. An envelope was reproduced with the letter and is a warning signal to the collector, for envelopes were not in use for almost forty years after the original letter was written. The University of Virginia Library receives so many inquiries from persons who have found one of these facsimiles that it has prepared a form letter to send in reply.

Careful examination of the ink of this reproduction, as with most facsimiles, reveals that the "writing" does not show the lighter and darker strokes so characteristic of ink applied with a pen. Uniform inking is a revealing sign of printing. With a magnifying glass one often can see that there are small flecks of the paper showing through the ink because the printing ink has not covered the type evenly.

Facsimiles of autographs have become rather common today. They are a favorite for the advertising fraternity, which may reproduce a letter of a company official appealing for business. The White House has used facsimiles of presidential signatures on White House cards and other items. An Autopen or Signa-Signer signature is a facsimile. When a skilled printer with a good knowledge of paper sets out to make a facsimile of an early document, he can do an excellent job that will cause considerable trouble for collectors unless they are cautious.

Copies made on electrostatic copying machines are a form of facsimile, because the machine will exactly reproduce the writing on the autograph. But normal copying paper is white and easily recognized. Old paper can be used in some electrostatic copiers, but close examination of the "ink" will reveal its slightly shiny surface and its thickness, as well as small specks of the toner around the lines of the "writing." As with a printed facsimile, the "ink" is uniform in density. A revealing characteristic of an electrostatic copy is that the "ink" can be rubbed off the page relatively easily, which is not true of writing or printing ink.

Photographic reproductions, often referred to by the generic term "photocopy," are easy to detect because of the slick surface of the thick, chemically treated paper. The texture of photographic papers is not the same on verso and recto. A photostat, the product of a photographic process in which the image is thrown directly on sensitized paper rather than first onto a film negative, may be slightly harder to detect, because the paper used is thin. But the surfaces of the recto and verso are different and, as with all photographic reproductions, there is no "life" or "feel" to the image.

Many official documents bear stamped signatures rather than

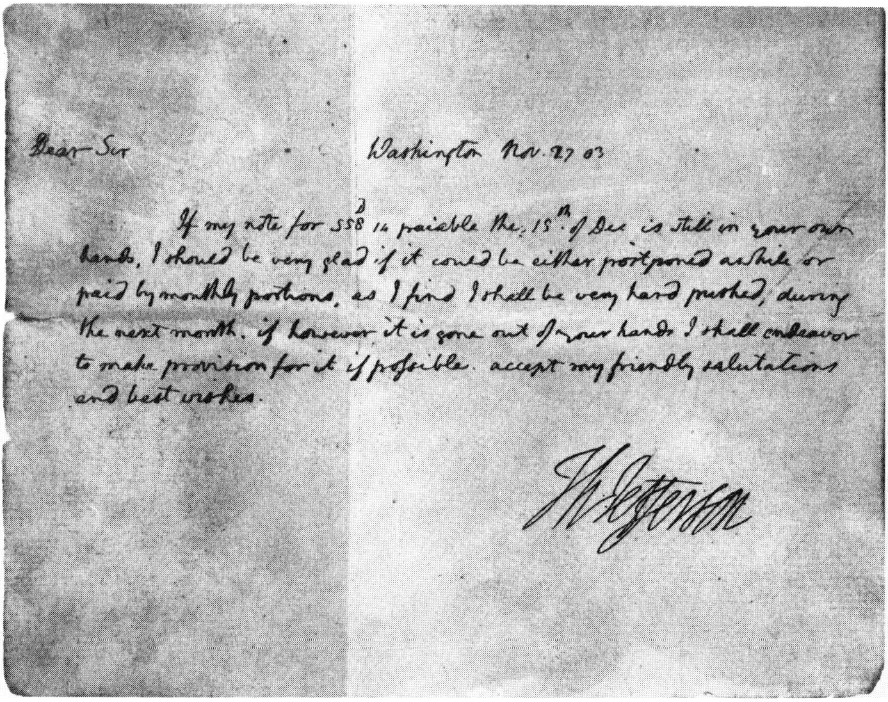

Dear Sir Washington Nov. 27. 03

If my note for 558 D. 14 paiable the 15th. of Dec. is still in your own hands, I should be very glad if it could be either postponed awhile or paid by monthly portions, as I find I shall be very hard pushed, during the next month. if however it is gone out of your hands I shall endeavor to make provision for it if possible. accept my friendly salutations and best wishes.

Th: Jefferson

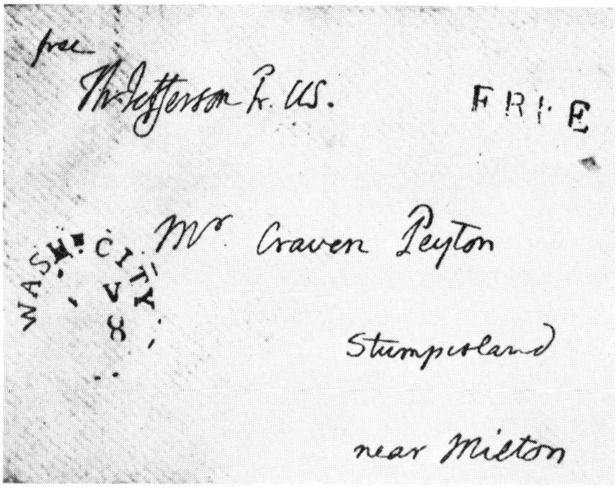

free
Th: Jefferson Pr. US.
FREE
WASH. CITY. V. 8
Mr. Craven Peyton
Stumpisland
near Milton

Thomas Jefferson's letter of November 27, 1803, was reproduced by the Morris Plan Bank, and some 30,000 copies were widely distributed. Note the envelope that was not used in Jefferson's time. Courtesy of the University of Virginia Library.

handwritten ones. The first metal signature stamps were succeeded by the rubber ones in wide use today. Stamped signatures show uniform inking, and frequently may bear signs of smearing if they were not applied carefully and allowed to dry. Caution is advised, because a stamped signature can be deceiving unless one is very careful.

A letterpress copy may occasionally appear in a dealer's catalog. This method of copying was in use fairly early in the nineteenth century; Thomas Jefferson made extensive use of it. The process involved dampening the surface of a letter or document, placing over it a thin sheet of paper, and pressing this sandwich in a special press. Enough ink would be absorbed by the thin paper for a copy of the letter to be made. Quite often too much liquid would be used, and the ink would blur badly as it transferred. In other instances, insufficient ink would be absorbed and the copy would begin to fade at once. Today many letterpress copies are almost illegible for one or the other of these reasons; but it was possible, with care, to make an excellent reference copy. Bound volumes of the thin sheets were often employed, and are known as letterpress-copy books. The process was in use until after World War II in a few offices.

Many items that are offered in the autograph market have been successively sold, auctioned, or otherwise transferred from collector to collector for generations. Most collectors are interested in the history of the materials in their collections. Such a line of ownership of a manuscript, letter, or document is called its provenance. Libraries are especially concerned with the provenances of the manuscript collections they acquire and keep careful records of them. It is interesting to note documents appearing in a dealer's or auction catalog and, later, to find the same item in another catalog—often at an increase in price.

The catalogers who prepare descriptions for dealers' and auction catalogs use other terms with which the collector must be familiar in order to understand the details given in the listings. In preparing a catalog entry for a document, letter, or manuscript, it is customary to give the author's name, date of writing, addressee of a letter, place of writing, and a note on the contents. If, however, the item bears no date but the cataloger can determine from its content that it was written on or about a certain date, he will supply that date enclosed in square brackets, which are used by those who work with manuscripts to indicate that the information within the brackets was not contained in the original but has been supplied by someone else. If the cataloger makes an educated guess about a date or place of writing, a question mark may be placed after the information inside the brackets. If the cataloger cannot find a date, and cannot determine a probable one from the internal evidence, the abbreviation n.d. will be used to indicate "no date." The abbreviation n.y. is used if the month and day are given but the year is not, and n.p. indicates that no place of writing was given.

A considerable number of terms are used in catalogs to indicate the physical condition of the items offered. "Worn along folds" means the document or letter has been folded so many times that there is definite deterioration at the folds and that the item must be handled with care lest it break. An item described as "foxed" bears the light brown spots (apparently thought to resemble fox paw prints) left by mold spores. An autograph listed as "spotted" has larger, heavier concentrations of stains, probably from having been splashed with a liquid. "Damp-stained" means that the item has acquired minor stains from dampness, while "water-stained" means that the item probably has been immersed in water, which has left serious stains on it. Both occurrences will leave the paper limp.

Various measures have been taken over the years to protect autographs and manuscripts that might suffer further damage if they were not stabilized. Often a limp or torn manuscript has been mounted on a stronger paper or on light cardboard. Unfortunately, these "stronger" papers often contain an excess of acid that causes further deterioration. Most mounting was done in the nineteenth century, and it is uncommon to find a modern document that has been mounted, because other methods of preservation are available.

Inlaying was also much more common in the nineteenth century. This practice involved cutting an opening a fraction of an inch smaller than the document in a sheet of paper or an album page. The document, being slightly larger than the opening, could be glued behind the opening, rather as a picture is placed behind a mat when framed.

Another protective method, and one still preferred by many collectors, is known as silking, in which very thin sheets of silk gauze are pasted, using a thin wheat or rice paste, to both sides of the document. Though the silk deteriorates and must be replaced periodically (every fifteen to twenty years), this is simple to do, because the paste can be dissolved easily in water. Silking, when applied by a skilled person, does not in any way damage most autographs; but it does make the text slightly harder to read.

A conservator occasionally will strengthen a document by pasting a thin piece of strong Japanese tissue to the blank side of a document worn along its folds; "strengthened along folds" may appear in the catalog. A document that is in extremely poor condition may be laminated, though this process finds little favor with collectors. It consists, in most conservators' shops, of washing the document to remove the acid in the paper and to introduce a mildly basic residue; the document is then placed between thin sheets of cellulose acetate, which are heated and pressed to bond them firmly to the document. The excess laminating material is trimmed away close to the edge of the document. This process obscures the writing about as much as silking, but the deacidification and the protection within the sandwich of laminating material ensures the survival of the document for hundreds of years. For this reason the process is used extensively by libraries and archives that must place long-term survival above the change in "feel" of the document, that being the chief argument against the process put forward by collectors and dealers.

A new process that may find favor with collectors for the protection of extremely fragile or deteriorating pieces is called encapsulation. The document (which may or may not be deacidified first) is placed within a sandwich made of thin sheets of Mylar, a strong, stable, acid-free plastic, that is held together by thin strips of double-faced tape placed just outside the edge of the document in the sandwich. Static electricity on the surface of the Mylar holds torn pieces of the document in place. The Mylar is absolutely transparent and may be removed at any time by peeling one sheet away from the other. Encapsulation is a simple process that may be learned readily by any collector; it offers great protection for any autograph, whether fragile or not.

This, then, is the basic language of autograph collecting. There are many other terms with which the collector will wish to become familiar as his knowledge of the avocation grows. These terms are included in the glossary of this book, or references are given to the articles where they are explained by other authors. But a knowledge of the terms in this section will enable collectors to read catalogs and discuss their collections with more experienced collectors, dealers, and professionals in the vocabulary those persons use.

WHO COLLECTS AUTOGRAPHS AND MANUSCRIPTS, AND WHY: THE PHILOSOPHY OF COLLECTING

KENNETH W. RENDELL

AUTOGRAPH AND MANUSCRIPT COLLECTORS are a very diverse group of individuals from widely varying social, financial, and professional backgrounds. Autograph collecting is not dominated by any one type of person, and the popular conception of manuscript collecting being limited to erudite scholars or wealthy collectors is far from accurate. Both of these groups are well represented, but they are only two of many elements. The common denominators among autograph collectors are an interest in history, literature, the arts, politics, music, or science, and a desire to obtain original handwritten records directly concerning the persons and events that are central to this interest.

Autograph collecting can, for analytical purposes, be divided into three categories: subject or special collections, those formed according to established guidelines or sets, and eclectic or general collections. Subject collections contain letters, manuscripts, documents, diaries, and journals relating to one subject or period of history, such as New York during the American Revolution, the Canadian fur trade, the English Civil War, French Impressionism, the Romantic period in music, the development of electricity, or the American Civil War. Alternatively, these collectors frequently concentrate on an individual, such as Napoleon I, Goethe, Beethoven, Abraham Lincoln, or Percy Bysshe Shelley, and usually obtain letters written by the person, letters by friends and acquaintances that relate to the person, and other material concerning the person's work and life.

Subject collections are almost exclusively the kind that institutions develop. The original source material in these collections is used extensively for research in the particular field and is, therefore, significant to the institutions. Subject collections are also formed by many private collectors, frequently in the areas of their own endeavors. Several modern composers have formed significant collections of musical manuscripts; the largest theatrical collection has been developed by a theatrical producer; physicians frequently collect letters of noted medical pioneers and experimenters; a number of psychiatrists collect the letters of Freud; and a major electrical manufacturer has gathered a comprehensive collection of material concerning developments in electricity. Many collectors, of course, do not collect in their own areas and have specialized in fields quite unrelated to their professions.

In both institutional and private subject collections, virtually all of the manuscripts and letters will have contents that significantly relate to the subject or person, and will have been written during an important period, from a particular place, or to an important correspondent. Letters or documents signed by persons central to the subject or person, but without significant content or other association, are usually included as representative examples if autographs with important content are not available.

After acquiring the available manuscript material directly concerning the central subject or person, the collection is usually expanded to encompass an ever-widening circle of material about events, associates, and works. It may eventually include various types of printed material, such as books, pamphlets, broadsides, and periodicals, as well as artifacts relating to the subject, photographs, and other memorabilia.

Many private subject collectors and, to a lesser extent, institutional collectors are interested primarily in the subject or person being collected, and are less concerned with the collecting of autographs. For this reason most of these collectors do not commence completely new areas when their principal collection has reached the reasonable and logical parameters of the subject or the individual's life and work.

Many private collectors concentrate on forming collections of letters and documents of persons who have accomplished a common goal, held the same official post, or signed an important document. Sets of the presidents of the United States, the kings and queens of various countries, the Signers of the Declaration of Independence, prime ministers of various countries, the signers of the United States Constitution, Nobel prize recipients, justices of the United States Supreme Court, the poets laureate of England, wives of American presidents, the New England poets and writers of the mid-nineteenth century, and Napoleon's marshals are extensively collected. Private collectors of sets of autographs may strive to obtain examples with fine contents, or may seek examples of a general nature, signatures on cards, portions of documents, or letters. When sufficient autograph material is available in an area—for example, the presidents of the United States—collectors can form collections of specific forms of autographs; of particular interest are signed bank checks, photographs, free franks, and books inscribed by the presidents.

To a substantially lesser degree, institutions also collect sets of letters and documents, principally for display purposes; these institutions usually do not gather autographs with significant content because the collection would not be sufficiently concentrated to be of research value. There are exceptions, of course; and a collection of presidential letters in which each president deals with the same or a similar subject would certainly be of considerable research value.

The majority of private collectors form eclectic or general collections of unrelated autograph material concerning subjects that interest them. Many institutions, in a sense, also follow an eclectic pattern by gathering unrelated subject collections. The eclectic collector may acquire a fine presidential letter, a poem in the hand of an admired author, a signed photograph that has a particular emotional or intellectual appeal, or an early deed for a plot of land that has special meaning. The possibilities are limited only by the collector's imagination and interests.

A very small percentage of the persons who acquire autograph material do so solely or principally for investment. They are, therefore, not collectors in the present context, nor are the persons who occasionally acquire a framed autograph principally for its decorative appeal.

Autograph collectors, therefore, are divided into private and institutional categories, each forming three basic types of collections: subject or special collections, sets of autographs, and eclectic collections. The two latter categories are further divided into collections containing material that is of interest principally because of its content or its association, and autographs that are collected as a representation of the person or period, with content of a more general nature.

ACQUIRING AUTOGRAPHS AND MANUSCRIPTS

HERBERT E. KLINGELHOFER

THE ACQUISITION of material for a manuscript collection should be undertaken with care if the collector is at all concerned about establishing a meaningful compilation. Clearly, the type of collection desired dictates a choice in the manner of its procurement. If the collector wishes to fill a scrapbook with the signatures of admired movie stars or baseball greats, he is likely to choose one avenue of approach. If, on the other hand, his aim is to establish a collection of original manuscript poems by Robert Burns, his method of doing so will be rather different. His budget also will have a bearing on the ways and means of putting together his collection.

A newcomer to the field of autograph collecting will be most fortunate if he can discuss his problems and interests with an experienced collector, particularly one whose specialty is similar to his own. Generally a veteran collector's advice on obtaining autographs and manuscripts is likely to be most useful; but manuscript curators and autograph dealers, under certain circumstances, can convey even more information. One good way to meet other collectors, curators, and dealers is through collectors' organizations. Many books dealing with the art and science of collecting are available. A novice to the field is likely to benefit from reading some of them. The best admonition for a fledgling manuscript collector is the same as that for a novice in any other field of collecting: Keep your ears and eyes open.

There are at least seven ways of acquiring autographs and manuscripts:

1. Letters received from correspondents
2. Directly requesting the autograph of a living celebrity
3. Receiving an autograph collection as a gift or an inheritance

4. Purchasing autographs from a dealer
5. Purchasing autographs at an auction sale
6. Buying autographs discovered in bookstores and antique shops
7. Obtaining autographs from other collectors by purchase or exchange

Since the first and third methods of acquisition usually do not require any effort on the part of the collector, nothing need be said about them. Requesting someone's autograph is inexpensive as well as easy; and such requests usually are not refused if a stamped, self-addressed envelope is enclosed with the request. For a person content with a signature or a few additional words in writing, this is a satisfactory way of building a collection. However, it is obvious that the collection is unlikely to contain autographs with significant contents unless the collector has the good fortune to receive a holograph of some consequence. One warning should be heeded: Requesting the signature of a political figure may result in receiving one written by Autopen or a secretary, or a facsimile.

Generally the best way for a novice to acquire autographs and manuscripts is to buy them from an established and reputable dealer. There is a set and fixed price for each item, and each is guaranteed genuine. The item may be returned if found unsatisfactory. In the case of a scarce and valuable piece, the dealer may furnish its provenance. Because of his experience and his knowledge of likely sources, he has a better chance of finding a piece that the collector particularly wants.

There are several ways of learning what manuscripts a dealer has in stock. The collector may ask him for information by letter or phone, read his catalogs, or visit his shop and inspect his merchandise. He may request that a dealer inform him if he should obtain an item that he thinks will appeal. The collector may provide the dealer with a list of desiderata, and the dealer will make an effort to find the items.

There are a number of advantages in being on several dealers' lists, buying at least one item from each occasionally. This will keep the dealers interested in the collector. It will assure him of receiving their catalogs, and it will be much more likely that one of them will turn up an obscure but much-desired item. There is the danger, if several dealers are aware of a collector's specialty and are anxious to supply him, that the price paid will be higher; but the chance of obtaining desired pieces will also be greater.

When a collector regularly receives a number of dealers' catalogs, he will begin to learn their specialties, if any. He will also be able to compare prices, which are often at great variance. Catalogs do differ. Some dealers barely give a hint as to the contents of the item and its condition, while others will give lengthy quotations or very detailed descriptions. Catalogs are arranged in various ways. Some list all items alphabetically, others subdivide according to subjects, and still others list items quite at random. Looking through the catalogs and inspecting dealers' stocks occasionally will turn up a "sleeper," an item that, because of a dealer's oversight or lack of knowledge, has been underpriced. This rarely happens, but it does provide exultation and excitement when it does.

The autographs and manuscripts found in a catalog constitute only a fraction of a dealer's stock, and he will gladly and readily tell the collector what other material he has. If possible, the collector should visit dealers' shops. Not only can he personally inspect all the manuscripts he wishes to see, but an interview will give him a much clearer impression of the dealer. The importance of dealing with a reputable and reliable firm cannot be stressed too strongly. It reduces to a minimum the hazard of buying forged, stolen, or greatly overpriced manuscripts.

When a collector has the inclination to turn to a specialized field of collecting, he had best ask dealers whether the specialty holds any promise of obtaining individual pieces readily, and whether collecting in this area is within his financial capacity.

Dealers' prices for similar items vary. Some will be egregiously high; some will be so low as to constitute a genuine bargain. There are reasons for discrepancies of this kind. A dealer's estimate of what an item is worth is a result of his calculations based on his existing stock, his personal interest, his specialized knowledge, the price he paid for the manuscript, his estimate of the demand, and his business location. How he arrives at his figure is discussed in the chapter "Values" in this book.

After scrutinizing dealers' lists for a period of time, a collector will be able to come to certain conclusions. There are no ubiquitously valid rules. If, for instance, a Charles Dickens autograph might be more expensive in Italy than in England because there are fewer specimens of Dickens on the market in Italy, it also could be less expensive there because the dealer might think that he would not sell it readily. Suffice it to say that the buyer must use his good judgment in each case.

When a dealer's catalog arrives, the collector knows precisely what each item will cost. He does not know, however, whether an appealing item is still available. He may be the first to receive the catalog and the first to send in an order. Therefore, he may be able to buy the item. He also may be too late. Whether the item listed be scarce or common, it behooves the collector to make up his mind quickly and to write or phone his order immediately. Foreign dealers almost invariably understand English, though they will be pleased to receive orders in their own language. The earlier the order reaches the dealer, the more likely the successful purchase. A French dealer once listed a very reasonably priced autograph of President William Henry Harrison, written during his brief term of office. Within a single hour he received several orders for it by telephone, and a number of orders by wire arrived the same day. Other orders arrived by air mail. The successful purchaser, a New York dealer, beat the next rival by two minutes.

When an autograph is ordered, it is implied that the collector will buy it. The dealer does not expect him to return it unless there are very good reasons. If the item is not as described, or the dealer has omitted to mention certain flaws, or if there is another cogent reason, the collector may return the item.

An autograph may be ordered "on approval," which tells the dealer that the collector believes he is likely to buy the item but feels that he cannot adequately judge the item from the catalog description alone. An item ordered on approval can be returned without stating a reason, but for the sake of continuing a cordial relationship, the collector ought to tell the dealer why he is not accepting the item. Whether an item has been ordered or requested on approval, the collector should return it promptly if he decides not to keep it. Twenty-four hours is a reasonable period to consider. When returning the item, one should wrap it securely and insure it. The collector must not make any sort of copy of the autograph while it is in his possession.

Acquiring autographs and manuscripts by bidding at auctions has several advantages, as well as dangers. It is possible to obtain desired items not available elsewhere, because some of the finest autograph collections eventually find their way to the auction block. At times some excellent pieces are auctioned off at amazingly low prices, for which one would hardly ever be able to buy such autographs from a dealer. If, on the other hand, an autograph is bid up to ridiculous heights, no one is forced to continue to bid. Someone else will be saddled with a vastly overpriced item.

Participating in an auction can be a thrilling experience. Generally, prices paid at manuscript auctions are a fair indication of how the market stands, and to some extent the price paid for a certain item serves as a guideline for collectors and dealers. This is why the annual volumes listing autograph prices at auctions are carefully studied. But, while the law of supply and demand seems to hold sway over the auction market, this is not invariably so. There are many exceptions to the rule that show why auction prices are not necessarily criteria of the true value of autographs and manuscripts. At a poorly attended auction from which the weather may have kept bidders away, prices may be much lower than normal. And if two or more bidders are absolutely determined to acquire an item, they may bid the price up to shocking heights. Often a very similar piece could have been bought from a dealer at a much lower price. The strange, almost feverish atmosphere—auction fever—prevailing among some participants at many auctions is also responsible for unexpected results.

Auction catalogs, on the whole, contain more mistakes than those of dealers. Items are often inadequately and sometimes wrongly described. It is always advisable personally to inspect the lots if the intention is to bid. This is particularly true when the auctioneer does not guarantee the genuineness of the autographs. Until fairly recently there was no such thing as an auction at which the items were guaranteed. Charles Hamilton in New York has always given a guarantee, and Sotheby Parke-Bernet is now following suit. At French auctions and some German auction houses the items are guaranteed to be as described, but everywhere else a collector is bidding at his own risk.

Auctions are not free of rackets, and the buyer must beware. The collector may protect himself at an auction by employing the services of an agent (usually a dealer) who will examine the item, give his opinion as to genuineness and value, and execute bids for the collector. The fee is commonly 10 percent of the price fetched. In England it is almost the rule that dealers represent clients. Dealers everywhere attend auctions in much larger proportions than do collectors; and while usually bidding for clients, they also bid on material for their own stock. Usually they are the ones bidding for large group lots that are rather useless to the individual collector.

Once the collector authorizes an agent to buy at auction, he cannot refuse the item if it is bought. A bill received from an auction house should be paid immediately, as should a bill from the agent whose bid has been successful.

It is the practice of some dealers to accept auction bids from several collectors on the same item at a sale. The dealer will start the bidding at, or one step above, his second highest bid. Other dealers will handle only one bid on an item, while others will inform an early bidder that a higher bid has been received. Quite definitely the client should ask his prospective agent to spell out his procedure clearly. The collector must ascertain the agent's course of action in order to protect himself. The chapter "Ethics" in this book deals with the agent-collector relationship, but only in the sense of what it ought to be.

It is possible to obtain from the auctioneer an estimate of what a certain item may bring. Both Charles Hamilton and Sotheby Parke-Bernet, as well as many European auction houses (but not the English, and usually not the French), add a list of estimates to their catalogs. These estimates are no more than the word implies, and may be far off the mark. The auctioneer may be quite ignorant of the true value of a given piece, and circumstances prevailing at the auction may be such as to nullify even an accurate estimate.

In the United States the price at which the item is knocked down will be the price the collector pays, plus shipping expenses and possibly sales taxes; but many European auction houses add an additional 5 to 20 percent surcharge.

A few other pointers concerning auctions may be appropriate. It is customary that of two identical mail bids, the one first received by the auction house wins. If during the auction the auctioneer receives two identical bids from the floor at the same time, he recognizes the bid of the bidder nearer the lectern.

As to the relative quality of the material presented at auctions, there are times when it is equal or superior to that offered by the dealers. During the past few years this has not been true, for the best material has not been coming up at auctions. Lately some dealers' lists have contained more important and exciting material than auction catalogs, with the exception of some prominent European auction houses. Therefore, it can be stated that there has been a general shift in recent years; the finest material now comes on the market through dealers rather than auction houses. This is certainly true in the United States. In Germany the finest autographs are still sold at auction; in England this pertains to the earlier items and less so to the rest. In France the dealers usually have the better material even though, in order to keep their taxes as low as possible, it does not always appear in their catalogs.

In selling autographs one should bear in mind that a dealer will offer a definite price based, above all, on his expectation of resale, whereas the price obtained at auction can be influenced not only by the circumstances mentioned above but also by the percentage of commission charged by the auction house.

Antique and secondhand book stores occasionally handle autographs. Here a collector must be especially wary, because the seller is rarely an expert. His knowledge of autographs is apt to be poor, and his ideas as to prices quite haphazard. It behooves the prospective buyer to use his judgment as to price and genuineness. It is true that some of the greatest autograph finds have been made in just such establishments, but the likelihood of finding a bargain is very small. However, the thrill of the "chance of a lifetime" can be quite comparable with that conveyed by auction fever.

Going through old trunks in attics may also yield real treasure troves; but here again, chance is against such happenings. Institutions often obtain vast amounts of material from attic cleanings. Local antique dealers often buy the right to remove the entire contents of an attic. Manuscript material discovered will then be sold to suitable institutions or to autograph dealers, who themselves give some of their time to going through letters found in attics and closets. Smaller dealers are more apt to ransack these dusty boxes, and they often sell more important items to bigger dealers able to place them quickly. For individual collectors possessing sufficient time and perseverance, searching for "buried treasure" will occasionally yield amazing results.

The occasions when a collector buys from a fellow collector can be very pleasurable. Often the older or more experienced collector will sell autographs to one who has collected for a shorter time. The latter can only benefit from the former's experiences and advice, which frequently can be obtained from no other source. Still, it is possible even for experts to make a mistake. Furthermore, there are dishonest collectors as well as dealers. If a collector sells an autograph to another collector, his guarantee, if any, means only that he believes the item to be what it purports to be. In the case of expensive items it is best to ask for a written statement that the seller will refund the purchase price should the item be found to be other than as claimed.

Swapping autographs is great fun. It is, of course, difficult to find items comparable in value; and since each autograph is sui generis, one can only approximate the likely absolute value. But as long as both parties are satisfied with the results of the exchange, no further words are necessary.

Every collection is begun by the acquisition of its parts. This is an important step. Without acquisition there can be no collection. But also implied is the accurate selection. The fewer mistakes made in choosing, the smoother will be the path in the building of a collection bringing satisfaction to the owner and to anyone able to appreciate the contents. While the old adage *caveat emptor* (Let the buyer beware) seems valid enough, it may be well to supplant it with the more comprehensive *sapiat emptor* (May the buyer be wise).

THE DETECTION OF FORGERIES

KENNETH W. RENDELL

THE POSSIBILITY of the acquisition of forged autographs creates understandable apprehension among collectors. Numerous forgeries do exist, and an even greater number of letters and documents exist that were not signed by the person to whom they are attributed.* It is, therefore, imperative for the collector to acquire a thorough knowledge of the methods of autograph authentication. Alternatively—and this is the only practical option for most collectors—they can rely upon dealers who are specialists in the field, give unconditional guarantees of genuineness, and most important, are experts in the authentication of autographs.†

The authentication of autograph material is a painstaking and meticulous procedure for the expert, requiring a thorough knowledge of the necessary equipment; characteristics of forged and genuine writing, paper, ink, and other materials; and the correct methods of comparing handwritings. Many of the factors considered in examining writing are not conclusive proof of authenticity by themselves, and must be evaluated in relation to other evidence. Obvious points, such as paper manufactured after the purported date of the letter or document, instantly indicate a forgery; however, it is a serious error to conclude from an examination of only a few factors that the writing is genuine or forged.

The microscope is the most important piece of equipment in the detection of both forgeries and facsimiles. From my experience the variable-power (10x to 100x) stereoscopic microscope equipped with

* See also the chapter "Confused Identities," which deals with the problem of confusion arising out of the existence of autographs of persons of the same name, one of them being famous and the others not.

† The collector may wish to inquire of the dealers with whom he does business what their methods of authentication are.—*editor.*

special mountings for examining documents is superior to other types. A substantial amount of time is spent in examining autographs with a microscope, and these special features lessen eye fatigue and allow the examiner to concentrate on the questioned writing without constantly changing eyepieces and adjustments.

In addition to this standard microscope, I also use a comparison microscope, which allows sections of two documents to be compared side by side. This microscope naturally has a much greater application in the comparison of handwritings than in initial detection of forgeries.

Both kinds of microscopes require good lighting. The ring type, which produces an even light, and the mounted high-intensity light are both very useful. Additionally, I have a high-intensity ultraviolet light mounted on the stereoscopic microscope. Ultraviolet light causes fluorescence in certain materials, including many types of ink and pencil writing; hence it is very useful in examining all types of questioned documents. Erased ink, for example, normally can be detected with the use of ultraviolet light. Infrared light has fewer applications but, in certain circumstances, can be very useful. A transmitted light table is necessary, and with proper adjustments it can be used in conjunction with the stereoscopic microscope.

The opaque projector, while not essential, is very useful in comparing several handwritings at one time. With this machine it is possible to project enlarged images of the handwritings on a screen, thus enabling substantial portions to be compared at one time, which is not possible with other equipment.

Test plates are measuring devices essential in comparing handwritings, and also have a number of applications in detecting forged writing. They are plates of glass, etched with lines, that can be placed over the writing in question while it is being examined through a microscope. Scales ranging from increments of one-tenth of an inch to one-thousandth of an inch are standard. Uniformly ruled squares in a number of sizes, and angle and slant plates, also have extensive applications. The wide variation in the sizes of handwritings necessitates having available several dozen of these plates.

Typewriting can be very accurately compared by the use of test plates designed to detect variations in the alignment or slant of the characters, and these devices are essential in such examinations. I maintain a complete selection of test plates that covers all the different European and American type sizes that have been manufactured.

The most prominent characteristics of the majority of forgeries relate to the manner in which they were written. Normal handwriting (with the exception of writing severely affected by age or illness) is produced with relative speed, consistency, uniform strength, and, normally, a degree of carelessness and a lack of attention to detail. The most immediate characteristic of forged writing is the care taken in the execution that results in slow, hesitating strokes giving the appearance of being drawn—as indeed they were. Strong, bold strokes are intermingled with weak strokes, and there is an unnatural attention to unimportant details that normally is not found in genuine writing. One of the most common and betraying habits of the forger is the lifting of the pen from the paper in sections of writing where this would not occur normally. The forger's attempt to connect the later stroke to the initial one is clearly indicated by the thickness of the ink where the continuing stroke has touched the initial stroke, causing the ink to flow back into the initial stroke.

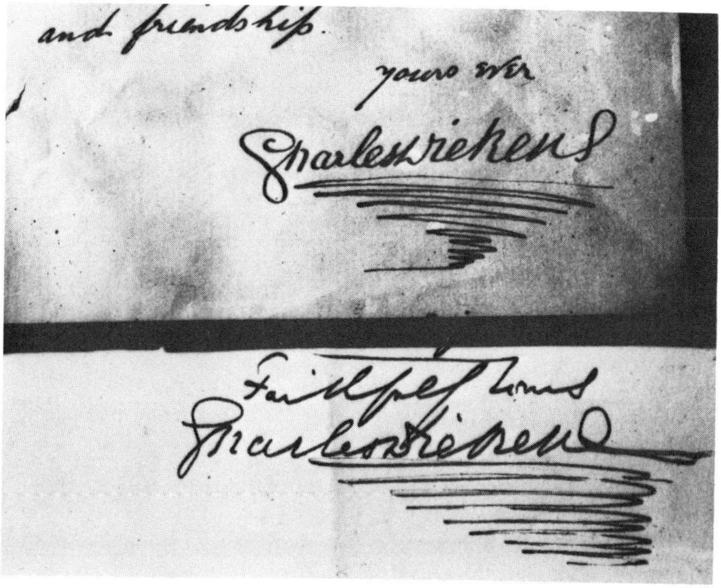

Note the unusual attention to detail and form in the forgery at the top, while the genuine example below is written in a much more carefree manner. The forger has also neglected to note Dickens' normal complimentary close.

Most genuine handwriting begins and ends with what can be described as flying starts and endings. The initial stroke commences as a very fine line, broadening as the line approaches the initial formation of the character. The writer also terminates the writing by rapidly moving the pen from the surface of the paper, causing the final stroke to decrease in width until it disappears. This characteristic of genuine writing is not true of all letter formations, nor is it a habit of all writers. However, few

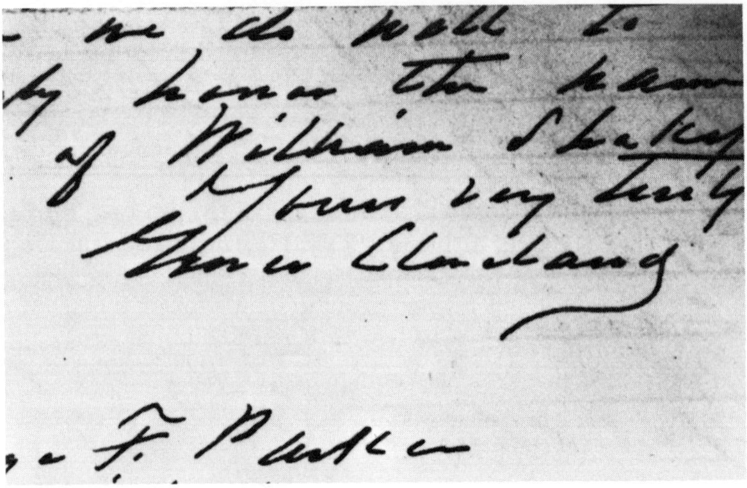

This is a portion of a forged Grover Cleveland signature, exhibiting the classical drawn appearance.

people begin writing by boldly putting the pen directly onto the paper and commencing the stroke. This is a common characteristic of forgers who are painstakingly attempting to copy or trace writing.

The relative smoothness of the upward and downward strokes should be examined. In general, forgeries exhibit less smoothness on the upward strokes, while the downward strokes are smoother and similar to genuine writing. The pressure that the writer puts on the pen can be determined from the depth the nib of the pen has cut into the paper and, more readily, by the flow of ink onto the paper. Significantly uneven pressure is a common occurrence in forgeries.

Retouching a stroke or a section of a word is a frequent habit of relatively unskilled forgers. Normal handwriting can give this appearance when the ink on a shaded stroke flows back onto an unshaded one. In genuine writing, this backward flow of ink can be distinguished from retouching by the smoothness of the edges of the pen stroke and the uniformity of distribution of the ink.

Another characteristic that I have found surprisingly common is the forger's habit of using the same form of writing when forging sections supposedly written by different persons. Dockets and endorsements or other notations purportedly written by the recipient will sometimes contain identical word formations or unusual consistencies in form when the forger has not changed the style of writing.

A natural tremor in writing due to age or physical infirmity can lead to the erroneous conclusion that the writing is forged. A tremor in genuine writing normally will show consistency; however, examinations of these types of writing frequently are inconclusive, and it is wise in such cases to ascertain whether the writer normally did have a tremor in his writing.

The final consideration in examining the writing alone is consistency of style and form with national characteristics of writing systems at that time. The system of forming letters, linking the characters, and spacing varies widely between countries and periods of time. A system of writing that was common in the United States during the early nineteenth century would be most suspect if it were employed in a letter supposedly written by a native German living in his country at that time.

Examination of the paper, as well as the examination of the other writing materials, can readily unmask many forgeries. A substantial

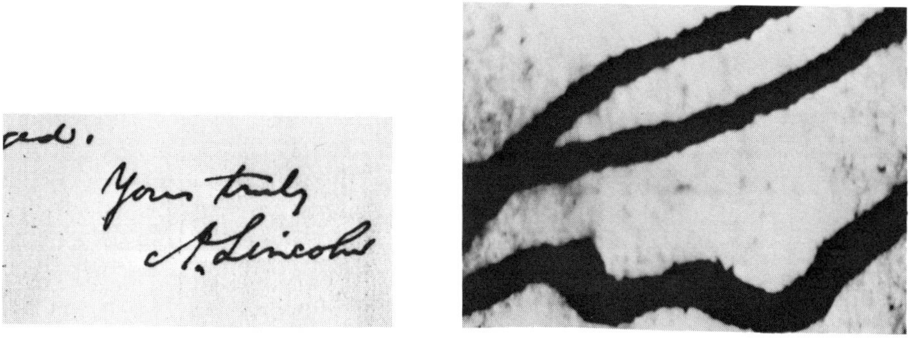

Although this is a well-executed forgery of an Abraham Lincoln letter, it betrays itself through the shaky downstroke on the letter *l*. Note the enlargement of this letter.

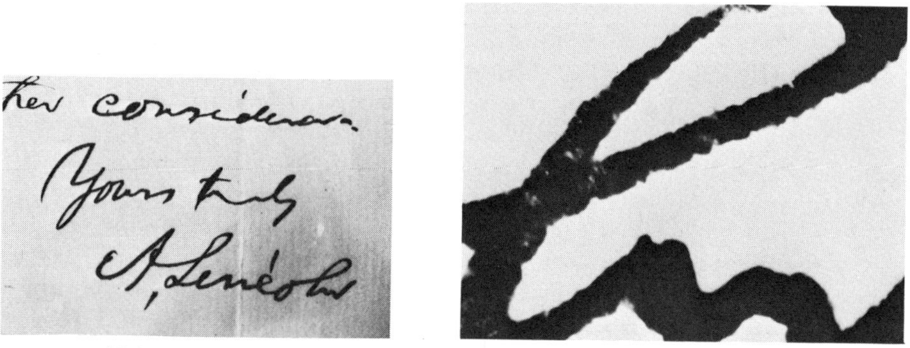

This is an example of a genuine Lincoln signature, together with an enlargement of its *l*, the strokes of which are firm and flowing.

number of forgers have neglected the importance of paper in dating letters and manuscripts, and have selected types of paper that either were no longer in general use at the time of the purported document or had not yet been invented.

Prior to 1300, parchment or vellum, made from animal skin, was used almost exclusively. Documents written on rag paper and dated before the fourteenth century are automatically suspect, and must be very thoroughly scrutinized. Laid paper—that is, rag paper made on a wire frame that creates a grid pattern as a watermark—was used concurrently with vellum and parchment after 1400, the former being used almost exclusively for letters and the latter for documents. Woven paper—that is, paper without the grid-pattern watermark—came into widespread use in Europe in the period 1750–1760, and in the United States in approximately 1800. The final substantial change in paper development, from an authentication standpoint, occurred in 1861 with the invention of wood-pulp paper.

Watermarks in paper are used principally in determining the year or period of manufacture, and a thorough knowledge of their patterns and periods of use is most helpful. This very extensive subject is discussed in detail in C. M. Briquet's *Les filigranes,* published in 1907 and reprinted at Amsterdam in 1968.

Particular sizes of paper were used during different periods of time, as were different colors of paper; and shape and color can provide the initial clue to a forgery. Oblong folio vellum was the most popular size for documents prior to 1600, as was legal folio for letters. In the seventeenth century, quarto became the most popular size for letters, and documents increasingly were written on larger folio-size parchment. Naturally there were overlaps in which varying sizes were used simultaneously.

An examination of the ink is necessary because the type of ink can determine the earliest date that the questioned document could have been written. To a lesser degree it is useful to know the probable time period after which a particular ink was no longer in general use. The oldest known ink was made of a finely ground carbon or a similar substance, and was extremely stable and permanent. It would not attack the medium on which it was written. Iron-gall ink, invented *ca.* A.D. 1020, was likely to be acid in content and to attack the paper or vellum. This ink also had a tendency to change color substantially with age, and the reddish tones acquired by many inks of this type over the years are impossible to reproduce. Equally impossible to imitate is the deterioration of the paper caused by highly acidic forms of this ink. Frequently a complete word will appear to have been burned through the paper, leaving only the outer traces of the pen stroke.

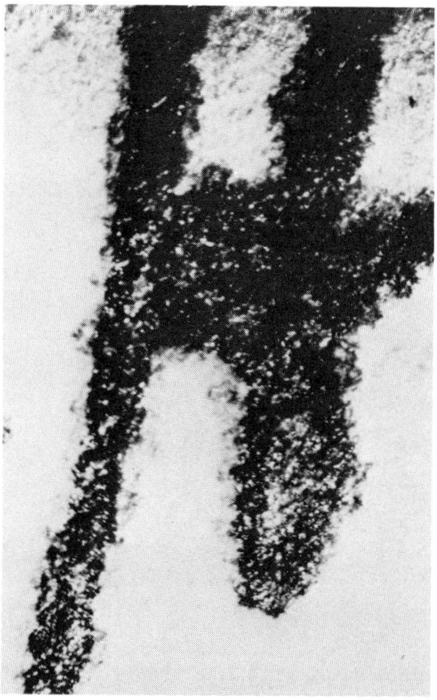

Fresh ink applied to old paper will cause a feathering of the lines of writing, as shown here in the *H* of a forged William Henry Harrison document.

Coloring matter was found in ink of this type as early as the American Revolution, although it was rare. It became increasingly popular, particularly in Europe after 1835. Logwood began to be added to ink in 1763, and in 1848 logwood ink of the potassium chromate type was invented. Indigo, with its characteristic bluish tint, was more commonly added to iron-gall ink after 1836 but was occasionally used prior to that date. Iron-nut gall ink, invented in 1836, differs from other inks, particularly iron-gall ink, in that a considerable part of the coloring matter is held in suspension and, as a result, penetrates the fibers of the paper rather than drying on the surface as other inks do.

The year 1860 was significant in the development of ink from the collector's standpoint; aniline inks were invented in that year. The chief characteristic of this ink was its solubility in water, with the result that it ran on contact with water; the primary advantage was that it did not attack the paper as iron-gall ink did.

Determination of the type of ink on a particular manuscript is done by chemical testing. A pinhead-size spot of ink is removed with a surgical scalpel and the effects of chemical reagents on the ink are observed under a microscope. The principal reagents used are hydrochloric acid (5 to 15 percent solution), oxalic acid (5 to 15 percent solution), stannous chloride (10 percent), potassium ferrocyanide (5 percent, containing 1 percent hydrochloric acid), and nascent hydrogen (obtained by adding zinc to 50 percent hydrochloric acid).

Visual observation frequently can reveal the type of ink. Oblique reflected light is used to observe the absorption of the ink by the paper (an unusual amount of absorption, with feathery strokes, indicates the ink was applied to aged paper), the amount and type of sediment in the ink (by examining thick or blotted strokes), and the gloss or sheen of the ink.

India ink has a uniformity of shading that is comparable with printer's ink, and it is frequently confused with printing. The sheen of India ink is the principal means of differentiating between this ink and printer's ink, which has a dull finish.

The traditional quill pen is the most ancient of the writing instruments normally encountered in autograph collecting. The steel pen began to be used shortly after its invention in 1780, a fact frequently overlooked by forgers who, mistakenly believing that quill pens were employed until recent times, have used them on letters written in the earlier part of the twentieth century. The writing of a quill pen differs notably from that of a steel pen, particularly in downstrokes and lateral strokes, which are broadly shaded largely due to the flexibility of the quill. Additionally, under microscopic examination the nib marks of steel pens (which create two "furrows" with the ink in between) are clearly visible. Many writers did continue to use the earlier form of instrument well into the nineteenth century, however. The expert should be aware of its decreasing popularity, and consequent comparative rarity during the middle and later part of the century.

The presence of nib marks rather than the absence of shaded lateral and downward strokes will instantly unmask many forgeries where a steel pen was used to write what purports to be a pre-1780 letter or document. Frequently these marks are so strong as to be clearly visible to the naked eye.

In some situations an examination of the person's writing where it crosses folds in the paper or crosses writing in another portion of the document may be revealing. Most paper, when folded, becomes more porous; and the rate of absorption of the ink in this porous area will differ from the rate of absorption in the unfolded areas. It is possible, therefore, to determine readily whether the paper was folded before or after the writing in question was executed. The feathering of the edges of lines written across folds, or the skipping of the pen across the fold line, is not in itself conclusive proof of forgery. However, these characteristics are clearly indicative of writing applied after folding.

When fresh ink crosses a line written at an earlier time, the more recent ink will sometimes, though not always, run out into the pen furrows of the original stroke. However, if the questioned portion of the document was written shortly after the main body of the document, especially if iron-gall ink was used, it may be impossible to determine the sequence, particularly if the strokes are shaded and well blotted. In these cases a microscopic examination of the distribution of the fibers is more useful, but still may be inconclusive.

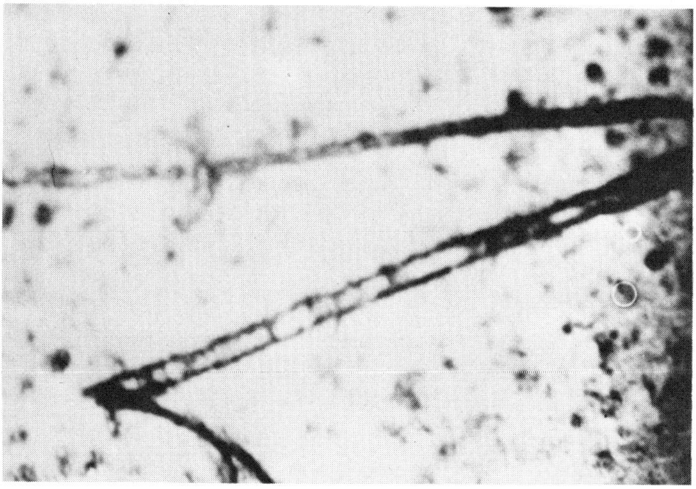

Above: A steel pen usually does not leave as readily visible nib marks as this one did. *Below:* The quill pen makes no furrows, and its writing appears as a smooth stroke.

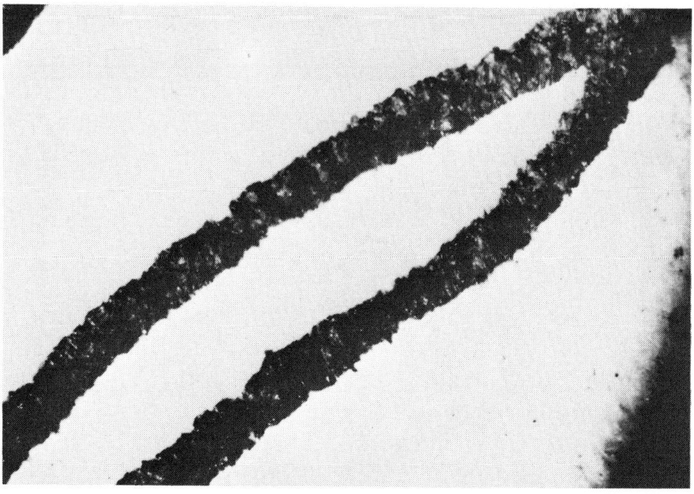

The use of a defective pen—for example, one with a broken nib that spattered ink or distributed the ink unevenly—usually indicates the document is genuine. Forgers generally have taken great care to use perfect materials and to avoid any variation from the normal.

Pencils came into general use *ca.* 1785; however, they were rarely used for letters or documents. Forged pencil writing is the most difficult of all writing to detect, because it can easily be retouched and it may not be possible to determine even the direction of the pencil stroke. A microscopic examination of the paper fibers may indicate the direction in which they were pushed by the pencil point, or to which side of the fibers the pencil particles have adhered. Definitive conclusions on pencil writing are, however, nearly impossible on the basis of the writing instrument alone.

Terminology, forms of address, salutations, closings, and the general layout and folding of letters have all changed significantly through the years; and a detailed knowledge of these characteristics is most important in document examination. A surprising number of forgers are unfamiliar with the significance of the internal content of a letter, and their creations are thus immediately apparent. Historical facts contained in a letter or document are also important; and if the authenticity is in doubt, such historical facts must be checked with other references to ascertain their accuracy.

Traced writing is one of the most common techniques of forgery, particularly of amateur forgers, and can be detected readily. The method of forging is quite simple: a facsimile or an original is placed on a light box or similar device, and a tracing is done in pencil or with a sharp instrument that will leave an indentation but no coloration. The pencil writing or indentation is then traced over in ink; and, in the case of pencil writing, the traces of the pencil are erased once the ink has dried. This type of forgery has all the characteristics of unnatural handwriting, with its appearance of having been drawn and with the lack of spontaneity and natural variations. The original indentations often can be revealed with the use of a microscope, and the abrasiveness of the erasing of pencil marks will also be visible in its effect on the ink.

Skillful forgers, notably Joseph Cosey, have acquired genuine letters or documents of the correct period, and added endorsements or other writing. The principal means of detecting these forgeries is by examination of the writing, ink, and content. The habits of the person whose writing is suspect should also be considered. Cosey imitated Lincoln's hand with remarkable accuracy, but failed to observe Lincoln's habit of invariably endorsing the reverse of letters written to him. Cosey consistently wrote his forged endorsements at the conclusion of the letter, an error that is an immediate indication of forgery.

A knowledge of postal history is necessary in authenticating documents. Fortunately such details were rarely considered by forgers. Postal handstamps came into use in England in 1661 and consisted of the month and day printed in a small circle; in 1695 a straight-line postmark bearing the name of the post town was introduced. Germany adopted this practice in 1720, Italy in 1740, and the United States in 1756. Adhesive postage stamps were first used in England in May 1840,

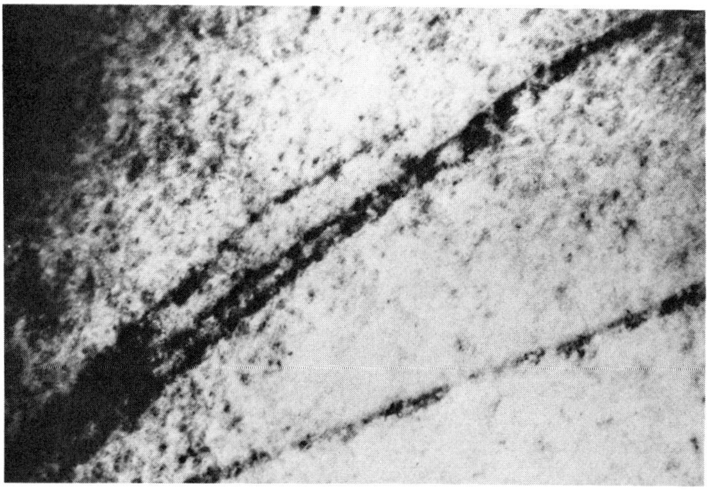

The rewriting of strokes or characters can result in the instant unmasking of many forgeries. The rewritten *h* (*above*) from a Washington document and the enlarged *2* (*below*) in a Lincoln document betray the work of Joseph Cosey.

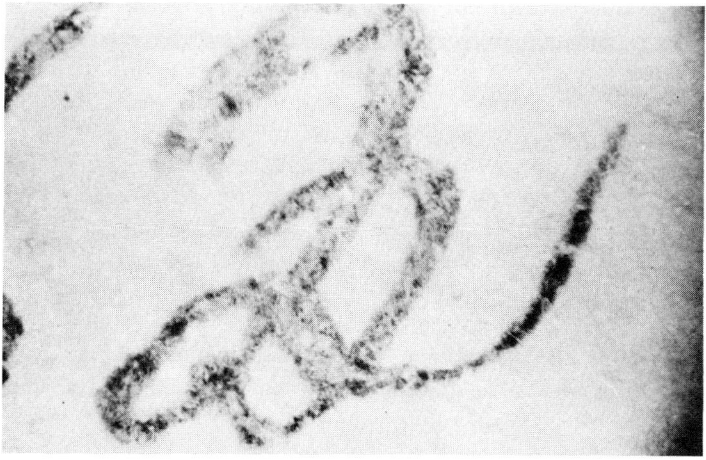

and in the United States seven years later (although private mailing companies employed their own adhesive stamps commencing in 1842, and the postmasters in New York, Providence, and St. Louis issued their own adhesive postage stamps from 1845).

Prior to 1845, letters were normally folded to employ the center of the final leaf as the address panel, and the folded letter was then sealed with wax for transmittal. Envelopes are rarely encountered prior to this date, although they became quite popular once they were introduced and rapidly replaced the older method. Before the introduction of the envelope, a separate piece of paper was sometimes folded around the letter to cover it for mailing; these pieces of paper are called letter covers, and the term "cover" is still used by stamp collectors to indicate an envelope with canceled stamp.

Erasures are most uncommon in forgeries, and the examination of the erased portions is more commonly undertaken in researching the contents of genuine letters. If it is suspected that the original signature, date, or any portion has been altered, an examination with ultraviolet light will frequently bring out traces of the original ink. The erasure will make the paper more porous, and therefore ink applied to the area will be absorbed in a manner different from that in the unerased areas. A marked difference in line quality appears under microscopic examination, as does the general disruption of the paper fibers. Reflected, transmitted, and direct light can, under some circumstances, illustrate erased portions. Ink eradicator removes only the coloring matter in the ink, leaving the basic solution in the paper; ammonium hydrosulfide in vapor form brings out the coloring in most forms of ink but does not otherwise affect the paper or other ink.

One of the most interesting techniques of forgery is false aging of the paper. The skillful forger obtains paper contemporary with the period; the amateur, however, attempts to duplicate aged paper by soaking it in tea, by burning small holes, by rubbing dirt into the fibers, or by other cosmetic means. When he writes on the paper, the amateur forger invariably avoids the holes and particles of dirt. A slightly less amateurish forger obtains paper that actually is old and follows some of the same "aging" processes to avoid having the paper look too fresh. These forgers seem to be unaware that most autograph material is in good condition, and that persons normally wrote letters and documents on paper that was in good condition, without holes or other defects. A significant exception to this general statement are the holes that frequently appear in parchment or vellum documents. These holes are caused by natural defects in the animal skin and are not the result of damage or deterioration. Parchment with these holes already present therefore was used by the scribes. They naturally avoided the holes when

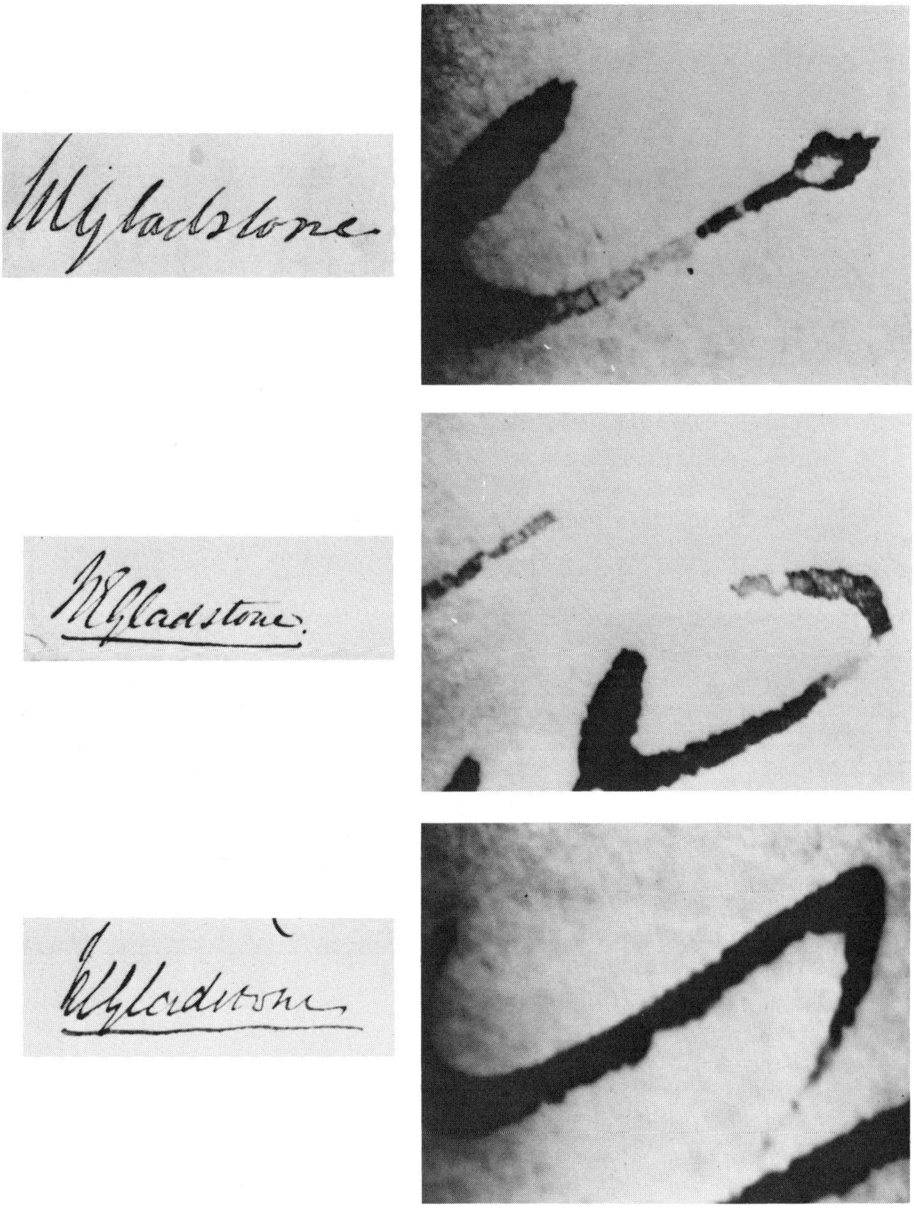

Two forged signatures of W. E. Gladstone (*top left*), with a genuine example (*bottom left*). Note the abrupt endings in the enlarged details of the endings from the two forged signatures as compared with the detail from the genuine example.

writing the text, and legal and business documents are frequently encountered with these characteristics.

Facsimiles of handwritten letters and manuscripts written by most of the major persons in the history of Western civilization are available in published volumes, and with a comprehensive library the expert can locate the majority of examples he will require. If the facsimile represents handwriting of the same period of time, comparison with a questioned autograph normally can yield definitive results. If it was written at a significantly different period of time, the basic characteristics normally are sufficiently similar or dissimilar to enable one to reach a determination. It is most important in comparing handwriting to observe the characteristics of examples known to be genuine before examining the questioned writing. Persons who were taught identical writing systems during the same period of time and in the same general geographic area frequently have very similar handwriting characteristics that can, therefore, be misleading.

There are a number of characteristics that are common to many writers and that should not be considered in making comparisons: dots of the *i* and crossing of the *t* made far to the right; the loop on the lowercase *e, a,* and *o* left open; dots of the *i* in the form of short strokes; pen raises after *v, w,* and *b;* and the habit of decreasing the size of characters toward the conclusion of a word.

The arrangement of a letter or document is important and should be studied, as should the content. The general layout of a letter—the location of the dateline, salutation, and closing; the indentations for paragraphs and the width of margins; the spacing between lines, words, characters, paragraphs, and between capitals and small letters in the same words—should all receive the attention of the examiner. Other aspects to consider are the relation of letters, words, and paragraphs to a theoretical baseline, the location of punctuation marks in relation to the theoretical baseline and in relation to the words they follow or precede, the general attention of the writer, the care in writing, and the care in following the outline of the letter. Are the terminology and writing style consistent with reference examples? Are the historical facts stated in the letter correct? Are the opinions and other subjective statements in the letter or document reasonable when compared with the known views and opinions of the writer?

The general characteristics of the questioned handwriting that should be compared with examples of the genuine handwriting include the connections between letters. There should be consistent variations before and after particular letters; the connections between all letters should be studied for angular or curved connections, pen lifts, and spaces; and the pattern of connections between particular letters should be noted. The fineness or bluntness of beginning and ending strokes should be considered, as should the length, slant, and shape of beginning and ending strokes and the distance that upward strokes are traced back at sharp angles in connections at tops of letters. A measurement of the length, width, and slant of the upper-loop letters *b, f, h, k,* and *l* should be compared with lower-loop letters *g, j, y,* and *z*. The form of certain letters should be examined, especially that of *a, r,* and *w* as final letters; *o, s,* and *t* as both initial and final letters; initial and intermediate *c;* the capital *E;* the words "of" and "the"; and any particular letter groups and forms the writer may have an unusual method of executing. One should note the slant of the letter *s* and its angularity, curvature, roundness, size, shading, and proportions.

Left: A forged signature of Thomas Carlyle (*top*) and a genuine example (*bottom*). *Right:* Note the blunt ending in the enlarged detail of the forgery as compared with the tapering ending of the genuine signature.

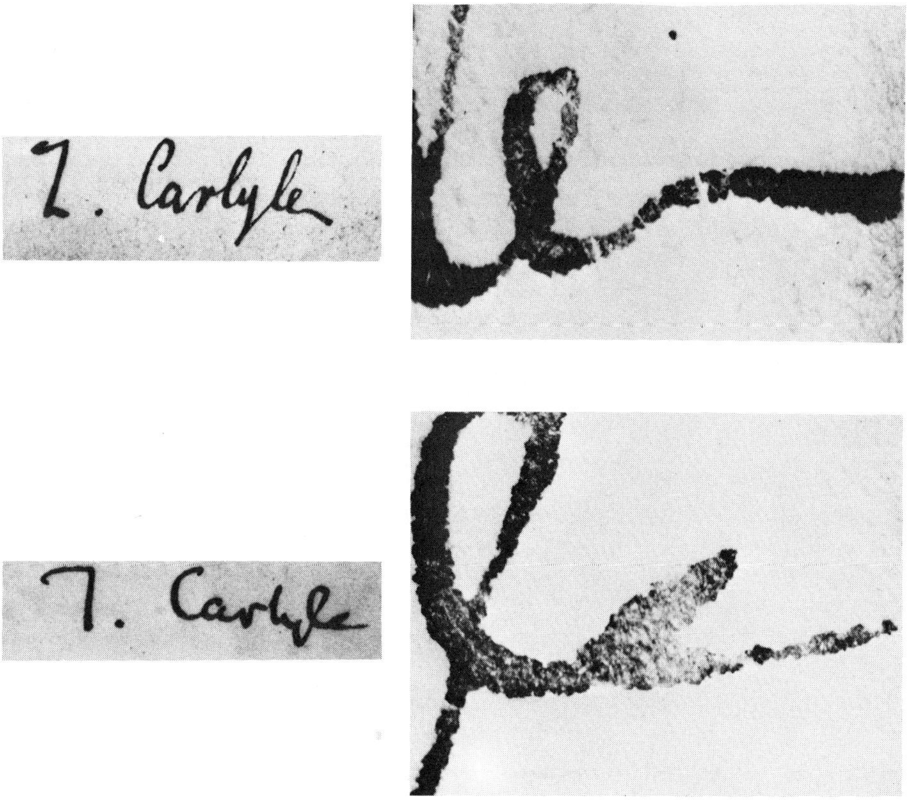

Next, one should examine the movement of the pen and the pressure applied by observing the smoothness or roughness of, and the apparent speed of, writing on upward and downward strokes. Pressure on the pen will be indicated by the width of the line and depth of indentation, and by variations in pen pressure in upward, downward, and horizontal strokes. Unevenness of pressure on the pen may be indicated by comparative smoothness or roughness of the right or left side of the pen stroke, but a writer's habit of applying more pressure to one side of the pen can be properly evaluated only when comparing characters written on similar paper with similar ink.

The shading of the pen strokes may provide valuable clues. The frequency of shading on each upward and downward stroke should be reviewed, as should the smoothness or roughness of shading and the vertical or horizontal shading (which depends on the position of the pen in the hand).

A page from a genuine account book, onto which the forged signature of Button Gwinnett has been inserted.

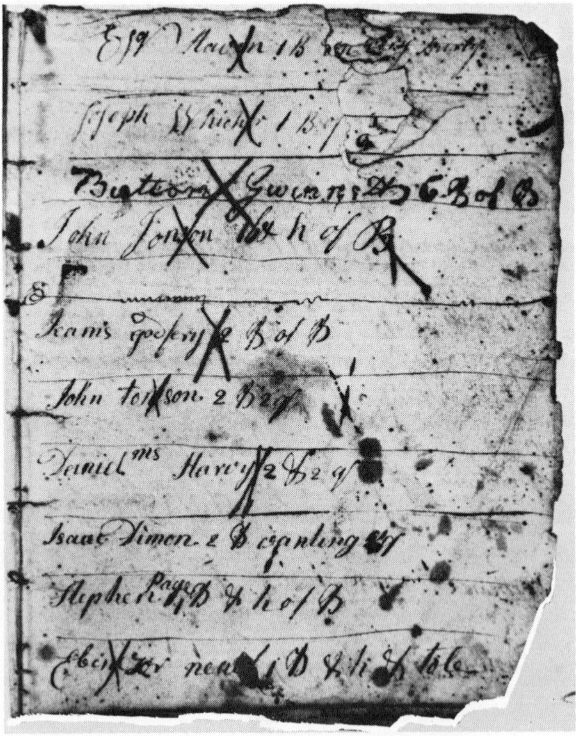

Still other characteristics to be considered are the slant of the writing, including the slant of the upward and downward strokes, the angle of slant of all vertical characters, and the angle of slant in the last part of the letters *h, m, n,* and *p.* The proportions of individual letters in relation to each other, and any characters that are consistently and significantly too large or too small in relation to other characters, must be studied.

Characters that are printed rather than written provide a special set of problems, and differing characteristics from script must be examined. These include incorrect formation of *a, g, r, m, n,* and *p;* the number of pen lifts to make each character; the direction of strokes; the general shading, slant, proportion, width, and height of characters; the alignment at the top and bottom of each character; any letters consistently written larger or smaller than the normal size; the spacing between lines, letters, words, and paragraphs; the angularity of the strokes in *A, K, M, N, V, W, X, Y,* and *Z;* the curvature in the left side of *C, G, O,* and *Q,* and in the right side of *B, D, P,* and *R;* the finishing strokes of *G, K,* and *R;* the proportions in *E, F,* and *L;* and, if all the letters are capitals, the relative size of each initial letter in each word, sentence, or paragraph relative to the following letters.

Comparisons between examples of typewriting frequently are made when it is suspected that typewritten letters or manuscripts supposedly written by different persons may have been prepared on the same typewriter, indicating the substantial probability of forgery. Fortunately, comparisons of typewriting normally are more readily definitive in their conclusions, and the criteria are fewer. Initial examination should reveal any unusual breaks in particular characters or defects in spacing. In the absence of such unique features, typewriting templates are used to compare the design, size, and proportion of the characters, and particularly the alignment of the characters in relation to each other and to the baseline. It is important to measure the vertical and horizontal slant of the characters and, if necessary, the pressure of the strike of the typewriter key—that is, the amount of pressure on each side of the character.

The lack of pen pressure, the evenness in the flow of ink, a dull finish, and the absence of nib marks will betray a facsimile, including those made on electrostatic copiers. To the novice the most immediately visible characteristic of a printed facsimile is the series of small breaks that appear as white dots in the pen stroke. These are apparent, without magnification, in all but the most sophisticated facsimiles. The detection of most facsimiles is a relatively easy task for the person experienced in examining handwritten examples.

Experience has taught me that the most difficult autographs to authenticate are those that bear the name of a person whose handwriting is

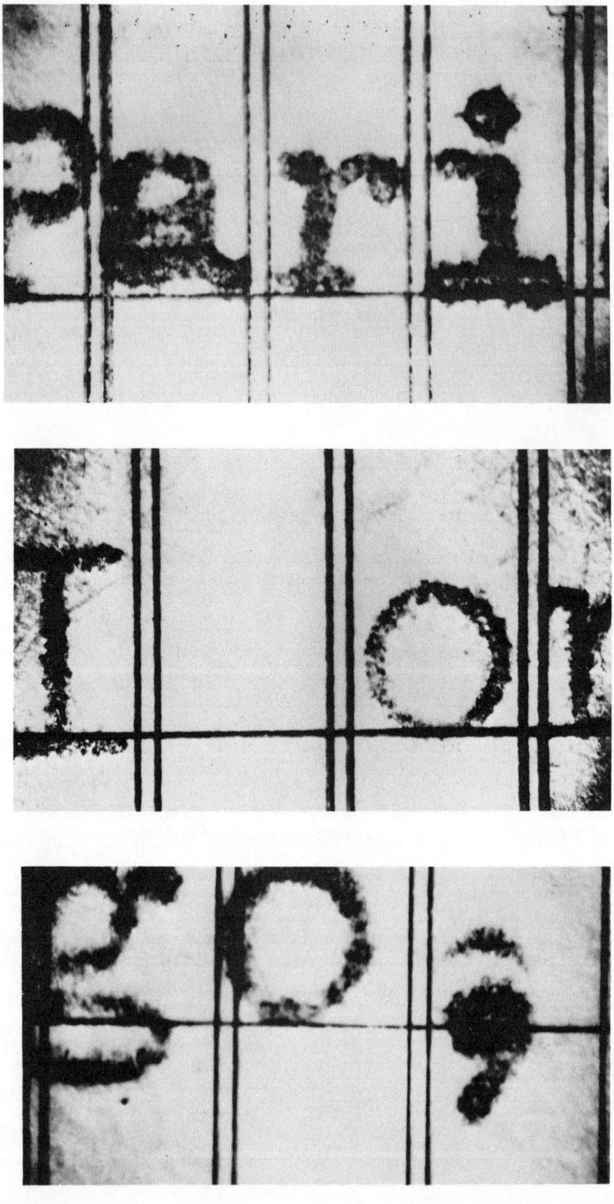

Typewriters have individual characteristics. Illustrated here (*from top to bottom*) are examples of the tilted *r* on Maurice Ravel's machine, the capital *I* below the baseline on Sir Ernest Henry Shackleton's typewriter, and a shadow over the comma on Woodrow Wilson's typewriter.

unfamiliar and were written during the period in question with the proper ink and paper. I maintain a very extensive reference library including files of facsimiles; and should I ever be without a sample, and unable to obtain one from a library, these autographs are kept aside until such time as definitive proof of the identity of the writer becomes available. Inconclusive examination occurs most frequently with letters purportedly signed by contemporary public personalities. Today the extensive use of the Autopen and Signa-Signer* makes modern autographs a treacherous area indeed; and without extensive research, as was done by Charles Hamilton on the signatures of John F. Kennedy, it is often impossible to make a definitive statement of authenticity.

Authenticating autographs is a painstaking and meticulous task; however, for the expert it is not an impossible one. With a thorough knowledge of the characteristics of forgeries and genuine writing, and the equipment and methods for examining writing, the expert can determine the authenticity of virtually all the autograph material he examines. There will always be a small percentage of autographs with characteristics of both genuine and forged writing. A reputable expert will candidly state the inconclusiveness of his examination in such a situation, and a reputable dealer will never offer such material for sale.

*See the chapter "The Autopen and the Signa-Signer" in this book.

FAMOUS FORGERS: THEIR SUCCESSES AND DOWNFALLS

KENNETH W. RENDELL

THE PTOLEMAIC RULERS of ancient Egypt were among the earliest patrons of literary forgers, offering substantial sums for manuscripts bearing the names of the leading writers of ancient Greece. J. A. Farrer states that forgers flourished in Greece long before the Christian era. In his classic work on this subject he discusses in detail the numerous literary hoaxes from ancient times to the nineteenth century and points out that prior to the nineteenth century, forgers, including the most noted, were chiefly concerned with the intellectual forging of literary works and paid scant attention to the details of handwriting and materials.*

Today, after examining one of these early forgeries, it seems inconceivable that such items could ever have been considered genuine; however, systematic and detailed document examinations were virtually unknown at that time, and forgers were therefore able to work almost without hindrance. These early forgeries occasionally appear in today's market, much to the delight of those collectors who specialize in forgeries. The stories of these early forgers are an interesting sidelight on autograph collecting.

Thomas Chatterton invented a fifteenth-century monk whom he named Rowley and attributed his own poetry to this fictitious character. The poems were written in an antique hand on parchment, and the young Chatterton intended to reveal his hoax once the poetry was acclaimed and accepted by the literary persons of his day. His deception died in its infancy when Horace Walpole, to whom he had appealed for aid in publishing the poems, consulted several experts, with the result that the manuscripts were quickly denounced as forgeries. Chatterton,

---

*James Anson Farrer, *Literary Forgeries* (London–New York: Longmans, Green and Co., 1907).

only seventeen years old, committed suicide—a great tragedy, for his poetic talent was considerable. Samuel Taylor Coleridge, John Keats, and Dante Gabriel Rossetti wrote poems lamenting his death,* and his forged manuscripts and others are today held by the British Library.

William Henry Ireland, on the other hand, was remarkably successful with his forgeries of Shakespearean documents. He was the son of Samuel Ireland, an engraver whose love of Shakespeare and ambition to own a Shakespearean letter inspired his son to begin his career as a forger. Ireland produced volumes from Shakespeare's library with annotations by the Bard of Avon, drawings by him, a love poem to Anne Hathaway, a correspondence between Shakespeare and his patron Southampton, and letters written to Shakespeare. The incredible acceptance of his literary creations encouraged Ireland to produce fragments of the manuscripts of *Hamlet* and *King Lear,* and finally to create a new drama attributed to Shakespeare, entitled *Vortigern and Rowena.* This work proved to be his undoing. Richard Brinsley Sheridan contracted to produce it at Drury Lane with John Philip Kemble in the lead, but Sheridan's disenchantment with the play increased as Ireland slowly produced each section of the manuscript. Sheridan finally refused to advertise the play as Shakespeare's, and rejected Ireland's offered compromise that it be advertised as a tragedy "discovered among the Shakespearean manuscripts in the possession of Mr. Ireland."

Kemble went considerably further, presenting on the same bill with *Vortigern and Rowena* a musical farce, *My Grandmother,* which concerned the gullibility of an art collector. He also expressed the intention of presenting the premiere of the play on April Fool's Day, but was frustrated in this; the first production occurred on April 2, 1796. Two days before, Edmund Malone had published his *Inquiry Into the Authenticity of Certain Miscellaneous Papers,* which combined an attack on Ireland's literary absurdities with a comparison of the handwriting of the forged documents. This excellent analytical work, coupled with the poor literary qualities of the fraudulent drama, led to Ireland's downfall. The interest in his forgeries gave rise to nineteenth-century forgers who specialized in forging Ireland's forgeries.

During the late nineteenth century the skillful forger Major George Gordon De Luna Byron (also known as "Monsieur Memoir" and "De Gibler") represented himself as the illegitimate son of Lord Byron, and his close physical resemblance lent credence to his claim. He resided in the United States but offered his forgeries in his native England, and was very accomplished in forging the writing of his "father" and his "father's" contemporaries, Keats and Shelley. His adeptness in forging

**Ibid.,* 145–146.

postmarks and seals, as well as the handwriting, paper, and ink, was unsurpassed at the time; and his forgeries are uncovered today only through very careful examination. His abilities were reflected in the fact that he was able to sell his forged Byron letters to Byron's own publisher—who, presumably, had a substantial number of genuine letters available for comparison. The detection of his fabrications occurred with a series of Shelley letters in which he plagiarized an obscure magazine article. Tennyson happened to show a copy of the letters to the son of the author of the original article, who was immediately able to reveal the source of the text of the letters, thus leading to the discovery of Byron as a major forger.

"Antique Smith," as Alexander H. Smith was known, was a highly skilled forger whose fabrications can cause problems for the collector of today. His career began in Edinburgh, Scotland, in the 1890's; and with great adroitness he forged letters and manuscripts attributed to Robert Burns, Sir Walter Scott, Mary Queen of Scots, Oliver Cromwell, Edmund Burke, William Pitt, William Makepeace Thackeray, James I of England, Charles I and II of England, and others. His calligraphy was excellent and was accomplished without tracing. His forgeries subsequently have acquired a genuine appearance of age, and they are frequently offered for sale in England and the United States.

The Frenchman Denis Vrain-Lucas perpetrated the most outlandish hoax of the major forgers. Beginning in 1861, he sold to Michel Chasles, a noted French mathematician, a collection of forgeries that over the years totaled 27,000 letters, manuscripts, and documents. No skill was involved in his forgeries, and his success was based upon his ability to gain the confidence of the gullible Chasles. Among the autographs sold by Vrain-Lucas (all of which were written in modern French) were love letters between Cleopatra and Caesar and letters by Judas Iscariot, Mary Magdalene, Pontius Pilate, Lazarus (before and after his resurrection), Joan of Arc, Attila the Hun, Alexander the Great, Herod, Cicero, Pompey, Sappho, and Dante. This fantastic undertaking was the subject of an interesting pamphlet written by the mid-nineteenth-century French dealer and autographs expert Étienne Charavay. Vrain-Lucas's revelatory error occurred when he forged a letter of Blaise Pascal to Robert Boyle in which the former claimed that he, rather than Newton, had discovered the law of universal gravitation. The date Vrain-Lucas supplied for the letter would have made Newton but ten years old at the time of its writing, and his fabrications were exposed.*

*Étienne Charavay, *Faux autographes: affaire Vrain-Lucas; étude critique sur la collection vendue à M. Michel Chasles et observations sur les moyens de reconnaître les faux autographes* (Paris: J. Charavay aîné, 1870).

Commencing *ca.* 1850, Baron Georg Heinrich von Gerstenbergk began to create excellently forged, and historically accurate, letters of the great German writer Johann C. F. von Schiller. This forger's knowledge of Schiller's life and writings, combined with his extraordinary ability to imitate his handwriting, necessitates a very careful examination of any purported Schiller material offered. During his lifetime Gerstenbergk's success was such that he was able to sell to Schiller's daughter letters purportedly written to her by her father. His acceptance eventually led to his undoing when, inspired by past success, he went on to write poetry that the literary experts of the day realized could not have been the work of Schiller. Gerstenbergk's career came to an end in 1856, when he was arrested by German authorities.

A contemporary of Gerstenbergk, Count Mariano Alberti in Italy, forged annotations in books supposedly from the library of Torquato Tasso. The books were genuine, and his imitation of Tasso's script and ink were excellent. Questions raised by the subjective opinions expressed in the annotations eventually led to doubt about the authenticity of the writing, and Alberti's efforts were discovered.

Robert Spring has the questionable distinction of being the first significant forger in the United States. His infamous career began in the 1870's. He is noted principally for his numerous forgeries of George Washington payment orders, initially written on genuine printed forms

A forgery by Robert Spring of a George Washington letter.

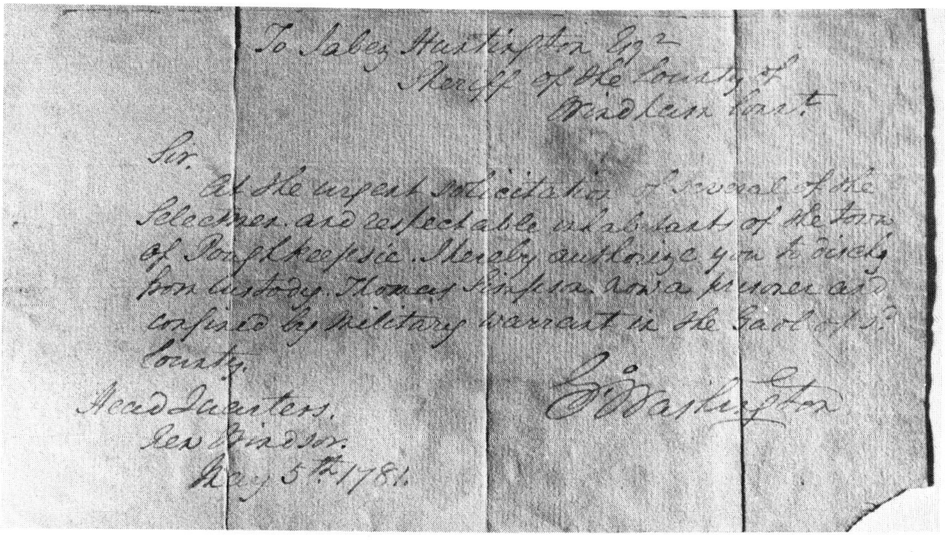

To Jabez Huntington Esq.
Sheriff of the County of
Windham Conn.t

Sir.
At the urgent solicitation of several of the Selectmen and respectable inhabitants of the town of Poughkeepsie. I hereby authorize you to discharge from custody Thomas Simpson now a prisoner and confined by military warrant in the Gaol of s.d County.

Head Quarters,
New Windsor.
May 5th 1781.

G Washington

of the Office of Discount and Deposit at Baltimore and later, when his supplies of these forms were exhausted, in completely holograph form. His forgeries of Benjamin Franklin payment orders are equally excellent, although not as numerous. All of Spring's work is characterized by a lack of hesitation, relative speed, and confidence. A careful study of his forgeries will reveal common characteristics, and the handwriting expert soon becomes adept at identifying his work.

While Spring was the first major forger in the United States, Joseph Cosey was undoubtedly the most prolific. Cosey devoted considerable time and care to the paper, ink, handwriting characteristics, and habits of particular periods. His forgeries can, therefore, cause considerable difficulty for modern collectors. Cosey's career began with his discovery of a batch of unused Monnier's 1851 watermarked paper of the same blue shade that Abraham Lincoln favored for his legal documents, and he undertook a series of legal briefs in the forged handwriting of Lincoln. These were followed by endorsements on genuine, contemporary letters of a type Lincoln frequently did endorse. Cosey studied the types and colors of paper favored by various persons, and dyed his own stock of antique papers to match that normally employed by the persons whose writing he was forging. Among the persons in whom he specialized are Francis Bacon, John Marshall, Patrick Henry, Richard Henry Lee, Thomas Lynch, Button Gwinnett, Aaron Burr, John Adams, Samuel Adams, Mary Baker Eddy, Samuel L. Clemens, Edgar Allan Poe, and Mary Todd Lincoln. Cosey's forgeries, like those of Spring, fortunately have their own characteristics that the expert learns to identify.

Charles Weisberg, also an American, was active principally in the 1930's. His work was neither as skillful nor as clever as Cosey's, and he was not as prolific; thus, examples of his forgeries are not as frequently encountered. Land surveys of George Washington were his specialty; but he also forged letters and manuscripts of Heinrich Heine, Walt Whitman, and Abraham Lincoln. Coincidentally, his Lincoln forgeries are similar to those of Cosey, and are principally endorsements written adjacent to the text of the letter to which Lincoln was replying, rather than on the reverse, which was Lincoln's custom. His nefarious activities led to his imprisonment during the 1940's, and he died in prison in 1945.

Contemporary forgers have been forced to be considerably less ambitious than their predecessors in the type of material they fabricate. They must contend with substantially more sophisticated collectors who are more cautious than their predecessors and who generally rely upon specialists to authenticate autograph material. These changes have been reflected in a decrease in the number of forged letters and manuscripts and a substantial increase in forged signatures on genuine photographs, sheets of postage stamps, first day covers, cards, and similar items.

These materials do not have to be fabricated, since they are easily obtained; the forger is therefore confronted only with the task of imitating the signature. Autographs on such material have increased substantially in value; and this rise, combined with the increased vigilance of collectors about letters and manuscripts, has focused the contemporary forger's attention on these other materials. The signatures of many contemporary persons, particularly that of John F. Kennedy, have been forged extensively in this manner.

A forgery by Joseph Cosey of a letter purportedly written by Edgar Allan Poe. Courtesy of the University of Virginia Library.

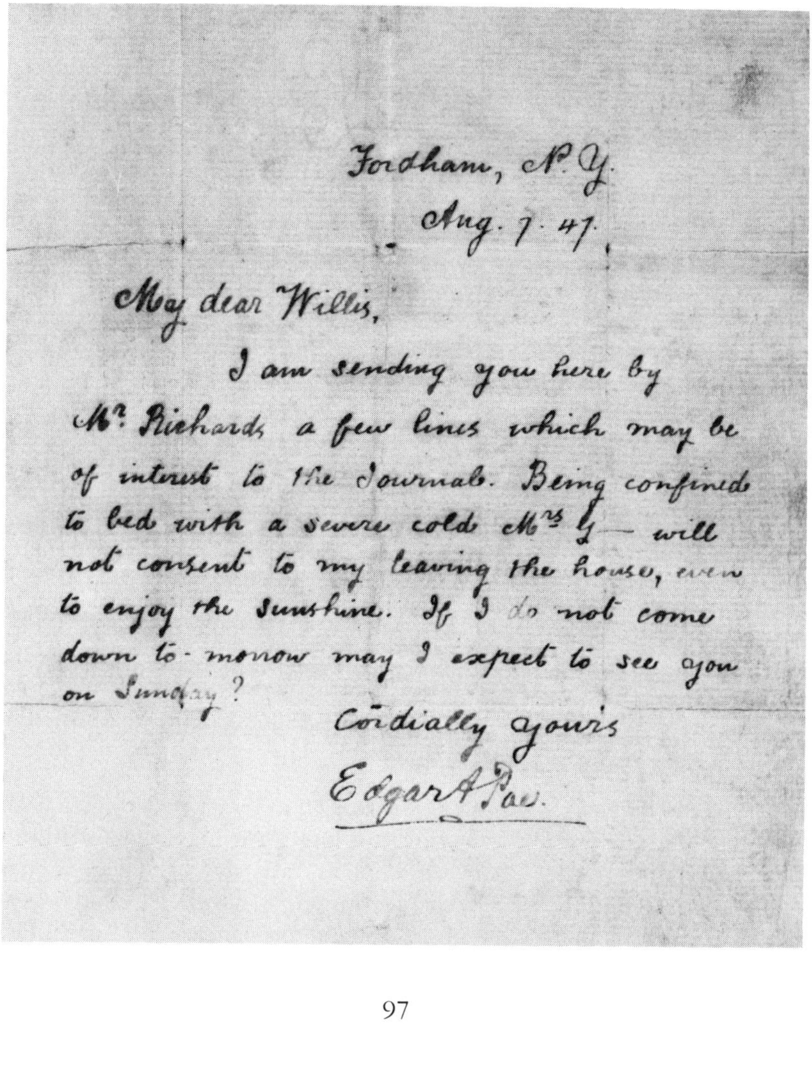

Fordham, N. Y.
Aug. 7. 47.

My dear Willis,

I am sending you here by Mr Richards a few lines which may be of interest to the Journal. Being confined to bed with a severe cold Mrs C— will not consent to my leaving the house, even to enjoy the sunshine. If I do not come down to-morrow may I expect to see you on Sunday?

Cordially yours

Edgar A Poe.

Two notable exceptions have occurred in recent years. In the late 1960's a skillful French forger fabricated a number of Hector Berlioz letters. These were offered to many specialist dealers, and the fraud was soon uncovered. Virtually all of the forgeries were recovered and destroyed; the forger was legally restrained from further activity.

The other exception has been forged manuscript poems of Robert Frost. At least two persons have been forging Frost manuscripts, and one has sold a sufficient number for them to be encountered with some frequency. To the uninformed these appear to be genuine; they are, however, readily detected through normal examination procedures. The second group of Frost manuscripts is less skillfully executed and has not been widely circulated. Early legal action was possible in this situation, and presumably will abort the forger's career.

The attractive prices of today's autograph market will undoubtedly continue to attract persons who possess reasonable handwriting and research skills, and who gain a sufficient knowledge of the autograph market to introduce their forgeries into it in a profitable way. The collector must be aware that forgeries are offered for sale, and be cautious when acquiring autographs from a source whose authentication procedures are unknown to him. The specialist autograph dealer who is accomplished and properly trained in the skills of authenticating autographs, and who unconditionally guarantees the authenticity and attribution of all material offered, will always exercise the greatest caution. His reputation depends entirely upon the accuracy of his judgment.

NOTE: In the catalog for his sale of February 24, 1977, dealer-auctioneer Charles Hamilton described the career of forger Arthur Sutton of Rumford, Maine, referring to Sutton's work as "abundant and varied and skillful. . . ." Sutton was apprehended through Hamilton's efforts, and pleaded guilty to one count of mail fraud on January 6, 1977. He received a suspended sentence of one year, and is making restitution to those he deceived. Hamilton commented:

> Certainly the most versatile forger of modern times, Sutton executed with considerable skill the signatures of W. C. Fields, Lyndon B. Johnson, Sitting Bull, Dwight D. Eisenhower, George A. Custer, Adolf Hitler, Picasso, Richard Nixon, Marilyn Monroe, Robert F. Kennedy, John F. Kennedy, N. C. Wyeth, Frederic March, Errol Flynn, Basil Rathbone, Lon Chaney, Jr., Walt Disney, Jacqueline Kennedy, Bela Lugosi, Hirohito, John Carradine, and Christopher Lee—and one example only of each of the following: Stan Laurel, Eleanor Roosevelt, Al Jolson, Judy Garland, Leonid Brezhnev, Betty Grable, Fay Wray, Otto Skorzeny, Charlie Chaplin, Boris Karloff, and Peter Lorre.

The catalog contains some facsimiles of Sutton's work. Other stories of forgers may be found in Hamilton's *Scribblers and Scoundrels* (New York: Paul S. Ericksson, 1968).

THE AUTOPEN AND THE SIGNA-SIGNER

H. KEITH THOMPSON

UNFORTUNATELY for autograph collectors and dealers alike, automation has brought a major curse to the hobby: the mechanical and electronic signature-signing devices. These faceless, mechanical robots are capable of reproducing thousands of "signatures" a day, and work for any master able to afford the cost of between $1,500 and $7,000.

The concept of creating a robot that could imitate the human skill of writing dates back to the ancient Arabs, but it was not until the eighteenth century that Friedrich von Knaus devised a successful mechanical writer. Thomas Jefferson invented and extensively used a polygraph (a precursor of the modern Autopen), and P. T. Barnum proudly exhibited his writing device. In 1916 a French inventor, P. M. Durand, invented a machine called the Signo, similar to the Autopen 50 currently used by many public officials.

"A fountain pen come to life" is the description of the Autopen by its manufacturer, the International Autopen Company of Arlington, Virginia. This machine can turn out as many as three thousand signatures in an eight-hour day from a "master" signature on a matrix, each an exact reproduction of the original. At its lowest speed the robot signs about as fast as the average man; at top speed, it signs twice as fast as any human.

The Autopen 50 is thirty-four inches high, thirty-four inches wide, and thirty-four inches deep. It weighs one hundred pounds and operates on standard house current. The machine is priced at about $1,500, with an additional charge for a signature recording on a plastic matrix shaped much like a boomerang. A foot pedal activates the Autopen, leaving the operator's hands free to feed in letters, checks, or other documents. The robot can be placed on "automatic" and will continue to sign as fast as the operator can insert material under the pen.

The plastic signature matrix is fitted into the machine on a large, flat wheel. When the machine is turned on, the signature is written as the wheel rotates, passing the matrix between two posts; there is a pause in each cycle until the matrix completes a full rotation and returns for another signature. Replacement of the matrix usually is required only when it becomes chipped.

Documents signed with a person's first name are created by the operator's halting the Autopen after the first name is written, thus dropping the last name. Even initials have been reproduced as patterns. Some collectors will claim that an item is genuinely signed because a ball-point pen was used; others will claim that felt-tip pen signatures are real. But any type of writing instrument can be used in the Autopen.

Although the pattern for each signature is basically identical, minor differences between signatures made from the same matrix can be produced because the operator moved the paper during the signing process, because a different pen was used or the pen failed to leave an ink deposit, or because the operator interrupted or jostled the matrix during

Thomas Jefferson's polygraph at Monticello. Courtesy of the University of Virginia Library.

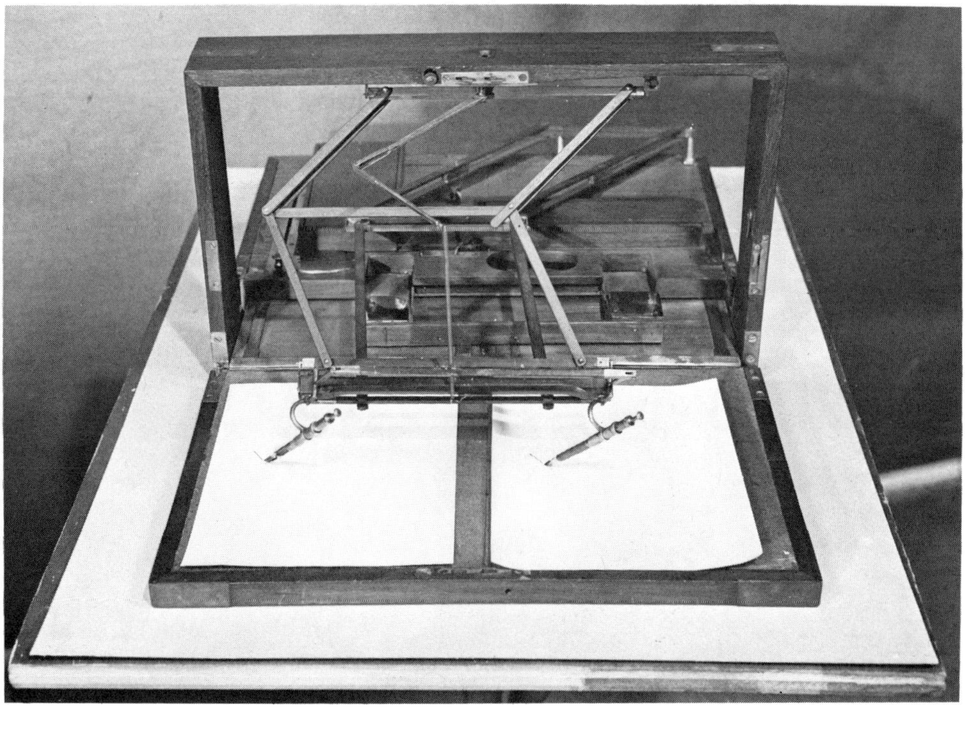

its operation. If the machine works at top speed, the *o*'s, *e*'s, and *a*'s tend to fill with ink. If the pen is fastened too low in the holder, an extra flourish may appear in the signature. Differences in spacing between the first and later units of the signature may appear, but portions of each signature will superimpose over comparable portions of other signatures of the same matrix pattern.

The Autopen 50 has been rendered relatively obsolescent by the Signa-Signer. This electromechanical device, invented by Harvey L. Huston, was designed to give the advantage over the Autopen of adding handwritten postscripts to letters, and to allow entire letters to be written. Another disadvantage of the Autopen 50, as cited in Huston's patent, is that only one signature is ordinarily recorded; thus the human element of error is not present in the handwriting reproduced, and each signature is exactly the same except for operator or machine inaccuracies. This is undesirable in obtaining the "personal touch" sought by utilizing a handwriting device in the first place.

The Signa-Signer in operation.

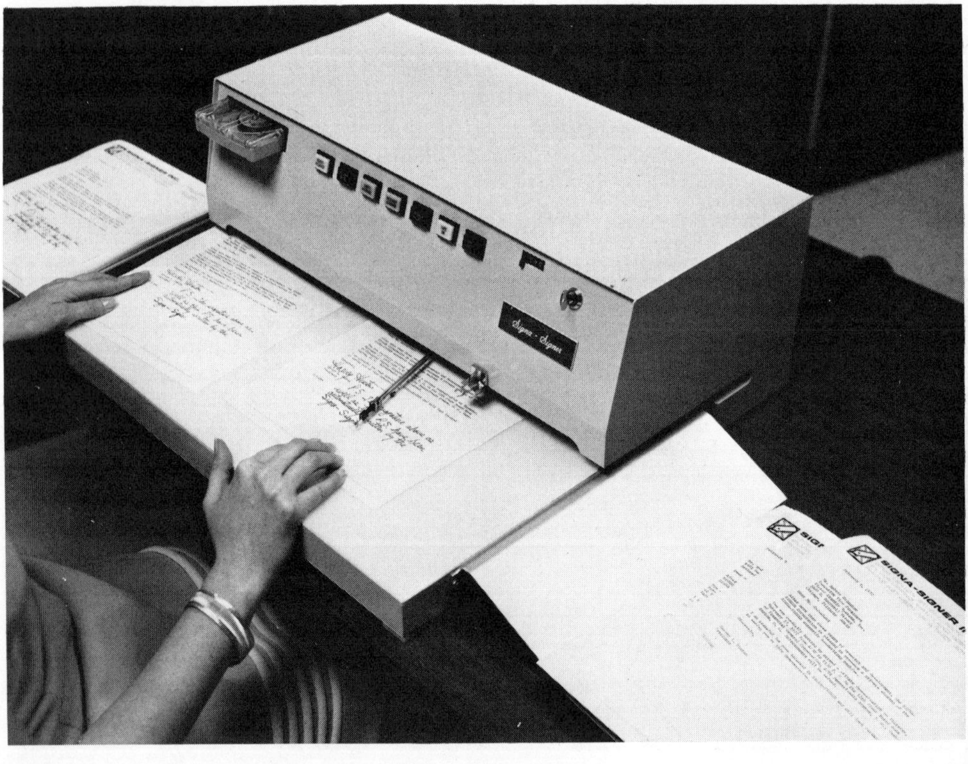

The Signa-Signer is capable of writing and signing entire letters and other memoranda, as well as of recording and reproducing an individual's handwriting, including the human element of error ordinarily involved therewith. Any direction of writing can be recorded and reproduced; thus a written insert along the side of the page or at an angle gives this invention greater versatility than the Autopen 50.

There are three models of the Signa-Signer. One automatically feeds continuous forms of any kind (stationery, stock certificates, envelopes, and so on) and permits anyone to record and instantly "play back" signatures, postscripts, or other messages. The second type has all the recording and playback features of the first, but is hand-fed. The last model automatically feeds single-sheet paper of various sizes.

The Signa-Signer is twenty-two inches wide, seven inches high, and seven inches deep. It can be mounted over an automatic-feed paper table and a paper enclosure resembling a two-drawer filing cabinet, twenty-three inches wide. It can also be mounted over a hand-feeding table. Depending on the model, it costs between $5,000 and $7,000. This price appears well justified because use of a Signa-Signer eliminates the need for an operator when utilizing the machine in the automatic-feed mode. There is no matrix cost, and the machine is simple to operate.

Serious collectors shun "Autopen signatures," for they are mechanically produced and tantamount to rubber-stamped or printed signatures. The evil of these machines—in addition to the fact that they could be dangerous if in the hands of unauthorized persons—is that one cannot identify a mechanically reproduced signature unless he has several examples to use for comparison. Even then, two different signatures could well be examples of two different Autopen patterns.

The deception is perpetuated by public officials and aides of the president who all but sign oaths in blood denying the use of automatic writing devices, and gleefully identify Autopen signatures as "authentic." According to the International Autopen Company, the robot signature is "as legal as though you had signed the paper yourself"; and this has been judicially confirmed in at least one state.* The writer has witnessed insurance company checks being ground out by Autopen, and the related opportunities for financial frauds seem limitless. The use of mechanical signing devices in business is entirely justified; the "autograph" of a business executive (with few exceptions) is hardly a collectible, and doubtless the presence of a personalized "signature" lends credence to the message conveyed in the letter to which it is affixed. But what about the use of the Autopen in government?

*See the editorial note at the end of this article.

When an official receives more than one hundred thousand letters in a year, obviously he would have to spend every minute of his office day signing replies if he signed any of his correspondence at all. Certainly his time is best spent working on the business of government rather than signing letters. It would be a much better practice for these officials to allow their secretaries to sign mail, but with their own names, not with the officials' alleged signatures, and to distribute only facsimile autographs so labeled.

The deception is quite provocative. Because a letter or document signed by the robot has been ruled "legal," could the robot continue to sign "legally" after its owner's death? And if a matrix made from a genuine signature of Abraham Lincoln was executed by the robot with an appropriate pen in reconstructed ink of the period on authentic paper, would it be considered genuine, or would it be a forgery?

The pioneer in the detection and exposure of mechanical signing devices is Charles Hamilton, and much of this article has been drawn from his three books: *The Robot That Helped to Make a President; Scribblers and Scoundrels;* and *Big Name Hunting.* Fred Casoni is making a valuable and serious study of the machine signatures of Lyndon B. Johnson, Richard M. Nixon, and Gerald R. Ford. He may as well add Jimmy Carter to his study, for most of Carter's mail bears machine or secretarial signatures. He is following the Kennedy pattern, attempting to lead the recipients to the conclusion that the signatures are genuine. Gerald Ford was honest, using mostly facsimiles; and his office, when asked, would reply that the president could not personally sign and therefore used machine and secretarial signatures.

The only way in which this problem can be contained is by seeking out, comparing, and classifying many hundreds—if not thousands—of examples. It is a costly, discouraging, and virtually endless labor, but it offers a partial solution to the revolution in the autograph market brought about by the mechanical and electrical signing devices.

NOTE: The author of this article was unable to furnish a citation to the case in which a mechanically reproduced signature was held to be valid. Officials of the International Autopen Company also were unable to provide a reference.

Thanks to Alan T. Gravitt, research librarian at the Arthur J. Morris Law Library of the University of Virginia, the editor has learned that the decision referred to probably is *State* v. *Watts,* 289 N.C. 445, 222 S.E. 2d 389 (1976), in which the Supreme Court of North Carolina held that the mechanically reproduced signature of a state official on a certification of a document was acceptable in place of a genuine signature. The court cited a case in the Utah Supreme Court in which a stamped signature of a police officer was held to be valid, and concluded, "We are of the opinion that the weight of authority and the better rule is that public documents may be authenticated by mechanical reproduction of the signature of the authorized officer when he intends to adopt the mechanical signature as his signature." The court did note that it agreed with the Utah court when it stated, "The general rule that a stamped, printed, or typewritten signature is a good signature appears to be subject to an exception where the signature is required by statute to be made under the hand of the person making it." In the North Carolina case the statute did not require a signature "under the hand," and the mechanically reproduced signature was accepted. In Gravitt's letter to the editor, dated February 21, 1977, he noted: "I am fairly confident that there is not another reported case where the issue is the validity of an authorized machine-produced signature."

There seems little question that a mechanically reproduced "signature" will be held valid if the person has authorized the use of such a "signature" as his own. However, the real question of legality, as far as collectors are concerned, will arise when a document required by statute to be signed "under the hand" of an official is, in fact, signed by an Autopen or a Signa-Signer, and this circumstance is discovered and challenged in court.

HIDDEN SIGNATURES

HERBERT E. KLINGELHOFER

A SIGNATURE is an individual's name written in his own hand. It is often written in a characteristic and distinctive fashion, and may be quite unlike his normal handwriting. Signatures exist in numerous forms, from that of the entire name (including first, middle, and last names plus titles and degrees) down to a single initial or part of it. The more complete the signature, the less doubt there is about the identity of the writer. Identifying the signer is, indeed, one of the two functions of a signature; the other is to serve as a means of providing authentication. The readiness and ease with which the reader will be able to establish this authentication depend on his familiarity with the handwriting. Establishing the identity of the writer, on the other hand, depends largely on how decipherable the signature is. Very often a person's signature varies from his normal handwriting because he writes his combination of letters more often than any other; this is especially true if the person's business or profession requires him to sign many letters and documents.

Signatures that, purposely or not, present a barrier to ready identification may be called hidden signatures. They can be divided into a number of categories: signatures indecipherable because of their illegibility; sign manuals; signums; monograms; paraphs; pictograms; titles; pseudonyms; total absence of a signature.

An execrable hand will hide the identity of the writer, whether intended to do so or not. Autograph collectors are frequently stumped by genuine but bad handwriting, and by scrawls. Horace Greeley, Giacomo Puccini, Leopold Stokowski, Walter Scott, and Reverdy Johnson come readily to mind, but the number of atrocious penmen is legion. It seems almost incumbent upon members of certain professions, such as bank clerks and government officials, to render their signatures indecipherable.

Other signatures may baffle the average reader because of his unfamiliarity with the type of writing. The court hand prevailing in England up to the eighteenth century, the Cyrillic alphabet, the Gothic hand, and every handwriting foreign to the reader provide a natural obstruction, though usually not to the initiate.

An example of a sign manual.

A sign manual, commonly used by monarchs of the fifteenth and sixteenth centuries, consisted of initials of their names, and often their titles, combined and connected by loops. It was always penned by the king himself. Fortunately, the scribe of the text spelled out the signer's name and title elsewhere in the document.

The same is true of a letter or document in which a signum occurs, for it would be impossible otherwise to identify the signer. A signum was a sign, usually in the shape of a cross but sometimes in the shape of a circle, a horizontal line, or some other simple design drawn by the signer. No matter how simple, it gave legal standing to the document. First used more than a thousand years ago, it is still employed as a signature by illiterates ("his mark").

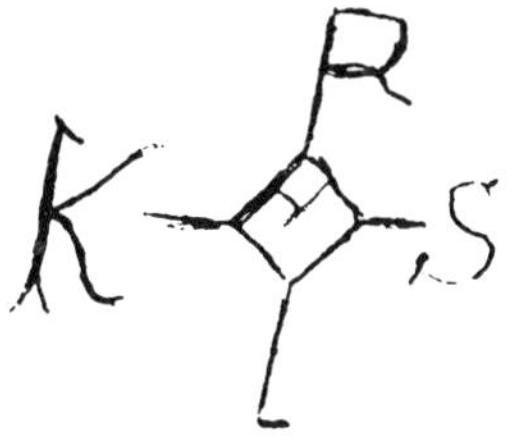

An example of a signum.

Somewhat related to the signum was the monogram, which was a cryptic design consisting of a number of letters arranged in a square, connected by vertical, diagonal, and horizontal lines, drawn by a scribe or secretary. A small portion, however, was personally added by the individual in whose name the document was written.

A paraph is not a true signature, but an addition to a signature—a flourish or swirl below or behind the signature proper. In certain cases—the Spanish conquistador Francisco Pizarro is a well-known example—the paraph was the only portion of the signature actually drawn by the author himself. In Mexico the paraph, or rubric, is legally more important than the rest of the signature. Paraphs were common in the eighteenth century, especially in France, where they often took the place of the signature proper and provided a certain incognito for the writer. At later times and in other countries, a paraph became a highly distinguishing mark of a signature, such as those of Charles Dickens, James Polk, and Franz Schubert.

This signature of Charles Dickens shows an excellent example of a modern writer's paraph.
Courtesy of the University of Virginia Library.

A pictogram is a pictorial design that a writer has adopted and is using in addition to or in lieu of a signature. Examples are James A. M. Whistler's butterfly, Carl E. Schultze's bunny, and Ernest Thompson Seton's paw print. American Indians often used pictograms as signatures on treaties with the white man.

Assumptions of and changes of titles are often a source of confusion for the reader, and England is the country where this occurs most commonly. While most collectors are familiar with such commonly known identities as Lord Beaconsfield (Benjamin Disraeli), the first Duke of Marlborough (John Churchill), and the Earl of Chatham (the elder William Pitt), they are less well acquainted with hundreds of others. The signatures on a letter from the Privy Council of Elizabeth I or James I have to be interpreted to the nonhistorian, and in general one must consult the *Encyclopaedia Britannica* to obtain information.

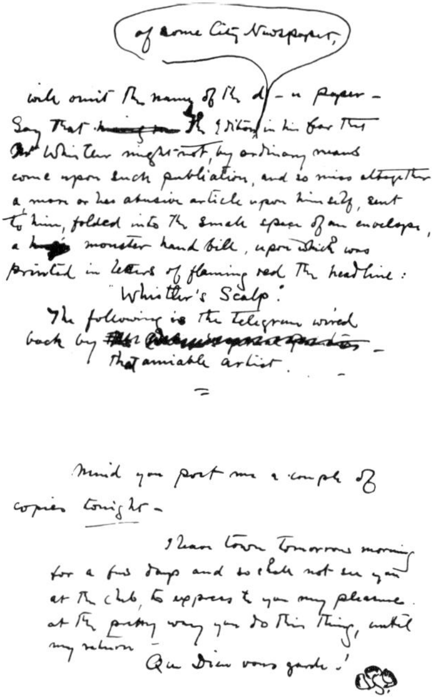

A portion of a letter by the artist James McNeill Whistler, illustrating his butterfly pictogram.

An original drawing by William Makepeace Thackeray for his *Book of Snobs,* illustrating both the artist's pictogram (the spectacles) and his monogram. Courtesy of the Clem D. Johnston Collection, University of Virginia Library.

Signatures of monarchs can be confusing, too. Queen Victoria signed "Victoria," "V.," "V.R.I.," and "The Queen." Napoleon signed in various fashions. All Castilian and Spanish kings hid in the same manner, signing *"Yo el rey";* it is necessary to identify the monarch by the date. The date is also important when trying to establish which North or Stanhope or Marlborough it was whose signature is encountered.

Among the dignitaries whose names changed are some American presidents who dropped their first names and used their middle ones before assuming the presidency. It was common for some of the electors of Brandenburg to sign by "manu propria" or even "mppria" ("by my own hand") instead of with their names. When Emperor Frederick III did not sign by his name "Fridericus," he used the words "praescripta recognoscimus" ("we acknowledge what was written before"); and his son, Maximilian I, usually wrote "per regem per se" or "p r p s." Some monarchs occasionally signed by initials only. So did the Renaissance popes, signing the *motus proprii* with the initial of the Latin version of their prepapal first name.

A list of pseudonyms and pen names could well run to book length were it intended to be exhaustive. Mark Twain (Samuel Langhorne Clemens) is perhaps the best-known example; but hundreds of authors used pen names for all their writings, and some habitually signed with both real and pen names. One good place to learn the real names of authors is the card catalog of a good library, for catalogers have for generations insisted on entering a writer's works under his real name; reference cards direct one from the pseudonyms to the real name. A great many pen names are better known than the authors' actual names. Included among pseudonyms are those used by individuals in past centuries who wished to preserve the anonymity of their observations of a political nature that they sent to newspapers for publication. During the American Revolution it was common to use a pseudonym.

Finally, some correspondents omitted signing altogether. This was usually done for reasons of safety. If the letter fell into hands other than those of the intended recipient, the reader would be at a loss to know who wrote the letter. On the other hand, the addressee would recognize the handwriting. Many collections contain an unsigned letter or two, and trying to establish the writer's identity by comparing various handwritings can be a difficult but fascinating pastime.

Knowledge of the types of signatures one may encounter is an interesting sidelight on the hobby of collecting autographs and manuscripts.

CONFUSED IDENTITIES

JOSEPH E. FIELDS

CONFUSED OR MISTAKEN IDENTITIES continue to be a vexation to the autograph collector. Perhaps the less frightening term "identical names" might be preferable. The problem is not a frequently occurring one, but it has been a pitfall since the very beginning of autograph collecting. Most collectors will eventually be faced with the problem in one way or another.

The inclusion of letters or documents written by the wrong person of the right name in an autograph collection should be of interest to the novice as well as experienced collectors, dealers, auctioneers, librarians, curators, genealogists, exhibit directors, historians, and biographers. Experienced collectors of a bygone era have made numerous errors of this type. Such collectors as L. J. Cist, Edward H. Leffingwell, that enthusiastic manuscriptophile Rev. William B. Sprague, and Charles Roberts were among the pioneer American collectors who had such inclusions in their collections. In more modern times Philip D. Sang and the present writer have had "wrong men" in their folders. There is probably no dealer who has not been a victim at one time or another. It is more likely that you will acquire an identical name than a forgery. You should not have an unreasonable fear of confused identities, but a healthy respect, alertness, knowledge, and curiosity about them. If nothing else, they are interesting.

The inclusion of a confused identity is usually an innocent error on the part of both the seller and the purchaser. The dealer is as unsuspecting as the buyer. He is genuinely sincere in his belief that he is selling an autograph of the desired individual. Perhaps, due to lack of specific knowledge or incomplete or unavailable facts, he is unwittingly selling an autograph of the right name but the wrong individual.

There is a much more frequent pathway whereby a mistaken identity may creep into a collection. The dealer, quite correct in the true identity of the writer of the autograph, has described, identified, and cataloged the item correctly. However, the prospective buyer, through lack of knowledge or just plain carelessness, purchases the item, blissfully ignorant that he has purchased the name he desired but not the writer he coveted. For instance, he may purchase an autograph of Benjamin West, the mathematician, astronomer, and almanac publisher, when he really desires a letter of Benjamin West, the artist. All this can be most distressing, for such occurrences detract from a collection and make for an unhappy collector. There may also be a considerable monetary loss. The discovery does have some redeeming features—it enhances the knowledge and skill of the collector. He is usually educated early in his collecting career.

An A.L.S. from Thomas Lynch, Jr., to Lt. Col. Huger, September 7, 1775. Courtesy of the Pierpont Morgan Library.

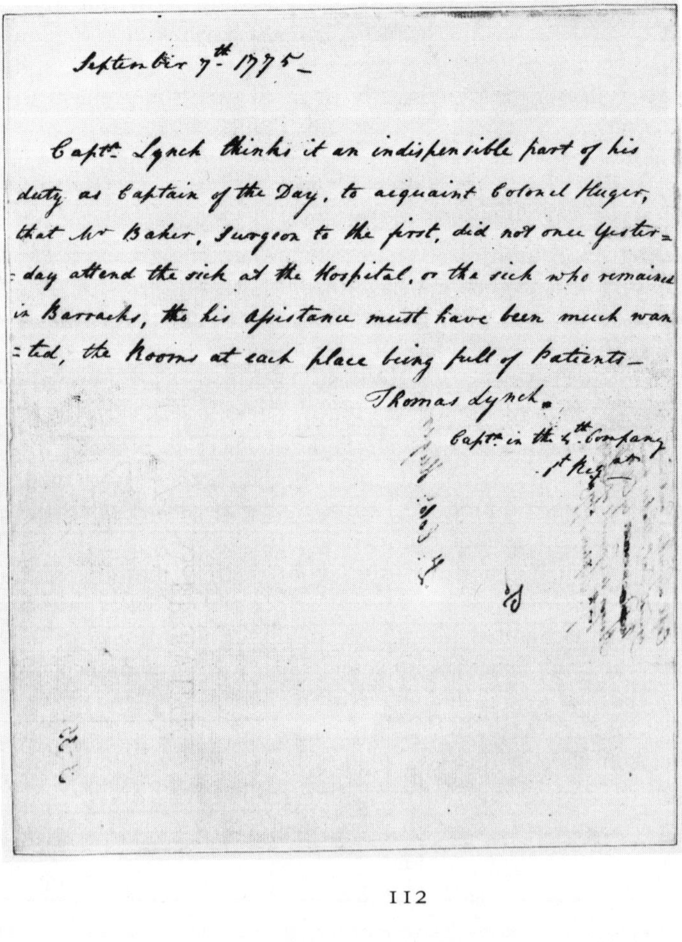

September 7th 1775—

Captn. Lynch thinks it an indispensible part of his duty as Captain of the Day, to acquaint Colonel Huger, that Mr Baker, Surgeon to the first, did not once Yester=day attend the sick at the Hospital, or the sick who remained in Barracks, tho his assistance must have been much wan=ted, the Rooms at each place being full of Patients—

Thomas Lynch.

Captn. in the 4th. Company
1st Regt.

Usually only one of a group of identical names is in great demand, more collectible, and therefore apt to bring a higher price. As an example let us consider the Thomas Lynches. We know of five men bearing this name who lived in the eighteenth century. The most collectible of them is the Signer of the Declaration of Independence. His autograph is extremely rare in any form, and brings prices into the thousands of dollars. Of much greater importance historically is the Signer's father, of the same name. His autographs are quite scarce; but since he was not capable of going to Independence Hall to place his name on the Declaration of Independence, his autographs bring relatively little compared with those of his son. Of much less importance and value are the autographs of Thomas Lynch, grandfather of the Signer; Sir Thomas Lynch, royal governor of Jamaica; and Thomas Lynch, New York merchant. A collector who is under the impression that he has purchased an autograph of the Signer would be considerably out of pocket should he later discover that he possessed an autograph of his father. A slightly less serious loss would be incurred by the inclusion of the wrong John Penn or Arthur Middleton in a collection of Signers. There are many other examples, but fortunately the financial losses would not be as pronounced as those mentioned above.

How may the collector avoid the inclusion of mistaken identities in his collection? First, buy from a known dealer who has an established reputation for reliability. He will not intentionally mislead a collector by selling him "the wrong man." Such an occurrence is as serious for the dealer as for the collector. In most instances the well-informed dealer is innocent of any wrongful act. Once the error has been called to his attention, he will make amends by a refund or by an exchange for the correct item if it should be available. The dealer's guarantee of authenticity covers you, and most dealers gladly rectify their errors.

Second, know the biographical details of the person whose autograph you desire. Special emphasis should be placed upon dates of birth and death, places of residence throughout his lifetime, nature and terms of public office, business ventures, and professional career. I recommend *Appleton's Cyclopedia of American Biography,* the *Dictionary of American Biography,* and, of course, their foreign counterparts. While *Appleton's* has inaccuracies, it does contain a wealth of material not found in the *Dictionary of American Biography* or elsewhere. In addition, many collectibles have been the subject of full-length biographies. Many of the historical and literary journals and newspapers can be most helpful in furnishing detailed information and identification.

Let me illustrate by citing the case of the three John Penns, all of whom are highly collectible. The eldest was the son of William Penn, founder of Pennsylvania. He was born in 1700, the only son of Penn to

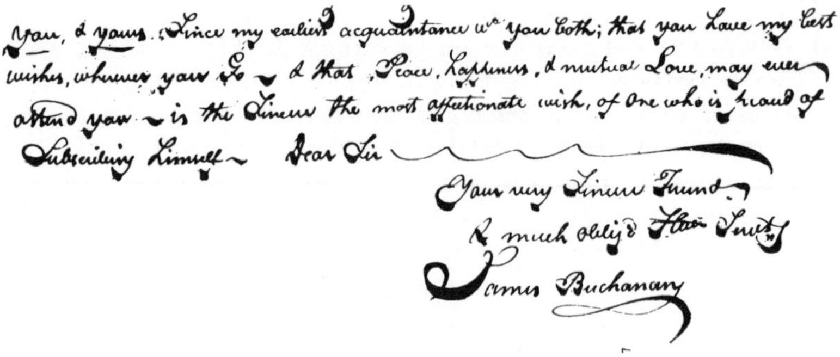

you, & yours: since my earliest acquaintance wt. you both; that you have my best wishes, wherever you Go — & that, Peace, Happiness, & mutual Love, may ever attend you — is the Sincere the most affectionate wish, of One who is proud of Subscribing Himself — Dear Sir

Your very Sincere Friend
& much oblig'd Hble Servt
James Buchanan

Illustrated are two signatures of men who might be confused with more famous namesakes. *Above:* The letter signed by James Buchanan was not written by the president; the clue is the date of the letter, which is September 29, 1789. President James Buchanan was born April 23, 1791. Courtesy of the Wilson Cary Nicholas Papers, University of Virginia Library. *Below:* The letter signed by "J Madison" was written by the president's cousin, Bishop James Madison. Familiarity with the handwriting of the two men would enable the knowledgeable collector to avoid confusion. Courtesy of the Edgehill-Randolph Papers, University of Virginia Library.

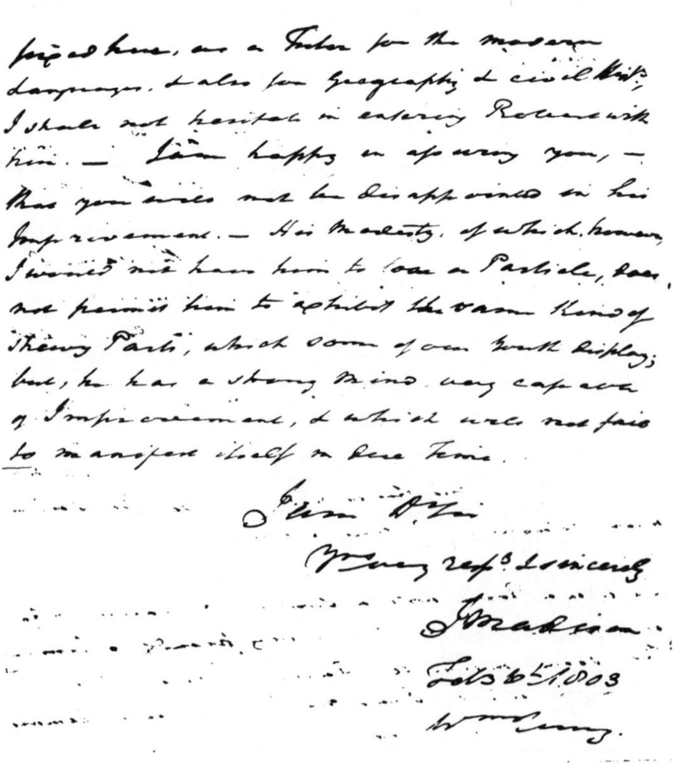

fix'd here, as a Tutor for the modern languages, & also for Geography & civil Hist.; I shall not hesitate in entering Robert with him. — I am happy in assuring you, — that you will not be disappointed in his Improvement. — His Modesty, of which, however, I wished not have him to lose a Particle, does not permit him to exhibit the same Kind of Shewy Parts, which some of our Youth display; but, he has a strong Mind, very capable of Improvement, & which will not fail to manifest itself in due Time.

I am D. Sir
Yrs very respy & sincerely
J Madison
Feb 6th 1803
Wm Cary.

be born in America, and has been known as "The American." From his mother he received half the proprietorship, but he spent little time in America. He died in 1746. Most of his autographs bear an English dateline. John Penn, nephew of "The American," was born in 1729 and died in 1795. He was a member of the provincial council, attended the Albany Congress in 1754, was lieutenant governor and later governor of Pennsylvania. He signed many official as well as personal documents during his long career in public life. Following the enactment of the constitution of Pennsylvania, he retired to private life. The Signer of the Declaration of Independence of the same name was not related. He lived from 1740 until 1788. Most of his life was spent in Virginia and North Carolina, where he practiced law. He was a member of the Provincial Congress of North Carolina, the North Carolina Board of War, and receiver of taxes under the Confederation. One can readily see that a familiarity with biographical details will materially aid in determining the identity of the John Penn under contemplation of purchase.

Third, pay close attention to catalog descriptions. They will usually give enough details to enable one to decide whether one is about to purchase an autograph by the correct name. If there is hesitancy or uncertainty, inquire of the dealer or order it on approval. A typescript or Xerox copy will often serve as well. If the item is the desired one, all that is necessary is to send a check to the dealer. If not, then the original or copy should be promptly returned. Do not belittle dealers' lists as being trite. Dealers will usually list in this fashion: "Hancock, John, Signer of the Declaration of Independence." Everyone knows that he was a Signer, but he is listed in that fashion to distinguish him from the three known John Hancocks who lived in eighteenth-century America.

Fourth, know the physical characteristics of the handwriting of the desired individual. This may be learned from photostats, facsimiles, reproductions from dealers' lists and auction catalogs, and comparison with known original examples. All dealers' lists and auction catalogs should be preserved for their reference value. Of course one must take into consideration the changes in handwriting that normally occur with the passage of time. Many authorities are able to date a document by an examination of the handwriting characteristics.

Fifth, if there is a question lingering in your mind, query the dealer, for he will gladly give you an opinion and will seriously attempt to verify the document. Consult the experts who may be authoritative concerning the individual in question. By all means consult your fellow collectors; there are many experts among them. Expertise is not confined to the professionals. No one would have ever considered consulting anyone other than the late Boyd B. Stutler should a doubt have arisen concerning the identification of an autograph of the abolitionist John

Brown. Stutler was a magazine editor and not a professional historian. Since there were many contemporary John Browns, Stutler was often called upon for an opinion.

An A.L.S. from Button Gwinnett to John Houston, May 5, 1773.
Courtesy of the Pierpont Morgan Library.

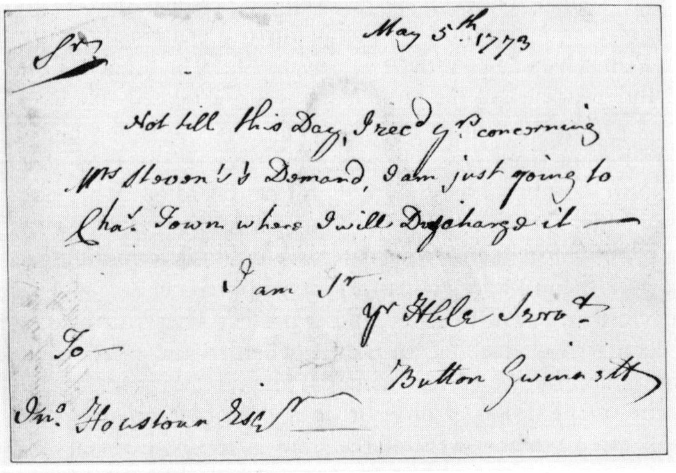

May 5th 1773

Sir

Not till this Day, I rec'd yrs concerning Mrs Moore's Demand, I am just going to Chas Town where I will Discharge it —

I am Sir

yr Hble Servt.

Button Gwinnett

To —

Jno. Houstoun Esqr

Confused identities are not something to be feared to the extent that one should be deterred from collecting. They should be studied assiduously. They may even be collected as such. Usually they are inexpensive, and will elicit much interest and admiration. At least one great collector of a former era, David McNeely Stauffer, collected men of the same name as the Signers of the Declaration of Independence. He succeeded in collecting thirty-five "wrong men" out of a possible fifty-six. Today one might even do better. And now, by a queer twist of fate, the elusive man of mystery, the nemesis of the collector, Button Gwinnett, rises to plague even those who may try to emulate Stauffer (as the writer has done). So far as we know, there has been only one Button Gwinnett in all of Christendom. If there was another, he might even be more rare than the "right one"!

CHANGING HANDWRITING

EDMUND BERKELEY, JR.

IT IS A COMMON AND ACCEPTED FACT of life that most people's appearances change as they age, but only a few are aware that many persons' handwriting also changes over the years. Most often these changes are a slow and natural process of evolution, one of which even the writer may not be aware. The changes are so subtle that it would be difficult to state that the handwriting changed after a particular date.

Sometimes, however, the change in a handwriting is sudden and dramatic, as when Lord Nelson lost his right arm in battle and had to write with his left hand thereafter. A changed handwriting may be only temporary, as when Thomas Jefferson, after tripping over a low fence while escorting Maria Cosway in Paris, so strained his right wrist that he wrote a number of letters with his left hand.

A collector must be aware of all the changes—evolutionary and dramatic—in the handwritings of the subjects of his collecting, and must study them with care. He must develop a comprehensive knowledge of these persons' writings. While he may not be able to purchase autographs from all the periods of his subjects' lives, he can acquire quite inexpensively from libraries, archives, and other sources copies of his subjects' letters and documents of different periods. These copies can be put into his reference files, and used both for study and for comparison purposes when he is offered an autograph. Knowledge of his subjects' lives is also mandatory, so that he will be familiar with their illnesses, accidents, and other events that may have affected their handwritings. If the collector does not acquire this thorough knowledge, he may pass up the opportunity to purchase an interesting autograph that does not immediately appear to be in the handwriting of his subject, or he may miss a sleeper in an auction sale, flea market, or antique shop.

Your sincere friend,
T. Woodrow Wilson

February 1, 1881

Your affectionate friend,
Woodrow Wilson

October 31, 1889

Very truly Yours,
Woodrow Wilson

December 5, 1897

Faithfully yours,
Woodrow Wilson

October 31, 1902

Faithfully Yours,
Woodrow Wilson

November 16, 1911

Affectionately yours,
Woodrow Wilson

January 30, 1913

Affectionately yours,
Woodrow Wilson

January 4, 1915

Affectionately yours,
Woodrow Wilson

April 13, 1917

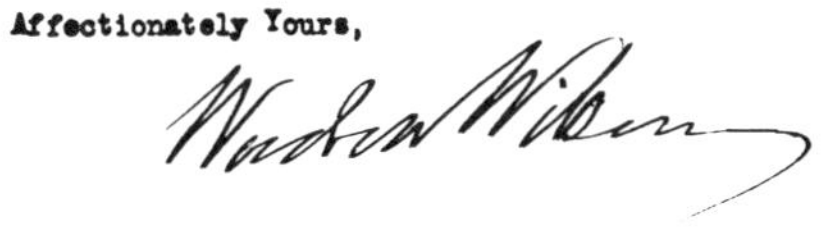

December 29, 1922

Autographs of President Woodrow Wilson over a forty-one-year period demonstrate a number of changes in his handwriting in this series taken from a collection of letters to his intimate friend, Richard Heath Dabney, of the faculty of the University of Virginia. Note that the paraph has been added by 1902 and that it then changes in length for the remainder of his life. Note also the effects of his stroke on the last signature in the group. Courtesy of the Wilson-Dabney Correspondence, University of Virginia Library.

It is not possible, within the scope of any book, to prepare essays on the handwriting of all the persons who might interest collectors. But to demonstrate the kind of subtleties to which collectors must be alert, we include an excellent article on the handwriting of President John Adams by Gordon Banks, long the doyen of American manuscript dealers. This article originally appeared in *Autograph Collectors' Journal* (3, no. 4 [Summer 1951], 37–40), and is reprinted with the permission of Mr. Banks and the Manuscript Society. A few minor editorial changes have been made to bring the article into conformity with the style of this book. References to a number of articles on handwriting that have appeared either in *Autograph Collectors' Journal* or in *Manuscripts* appear in the bibliography.

JOHN ADAMS—HIS HANDWRITING

GORDON T. BANKS

OUR SECOND PRESIDENT meets the scrutiny of time and emerges a solid, energetic, and well-trained political personality. There was no cradle-to-grave potential, followed slavishly and rising to a final zenith. His plans were altered twice; but when he made his decisions, set his course, and got under way, there were no side issues or diversions of consequence.

John Adams broke away from success at law to project himself into the leadership of the Revolution. His was neither a physical nor a social charm, but a sound melding of moral stamina and brilliant knowledge of history (what has been tried), economics (what can be done), and political philosophy (what will work). One can, almost with confidence, see such a man through a study of the orderly development and decline of his handwriting.

John Adams has not suffered serious neglect by autograph collectors. Yet, falling in the shadow of Washington, Franklin, Jefferson, and sometimes even of Hancock and Hamilton, he has been given less attention than he deserves. The study by Catherine Drinker Bowen (*John Adams and the American Revolution* [Boston: Little, Brown, 1950]) should spark the interest of many in the National Society of Autograph Collectors and lead to a more complete understanding of this early president.

I will not pretend to solve all the riddles of early, middle, and late handwriting styles of John Adams. In fact, there are none of the dramatic differences comparable with the vertical and sloping hands of William Makepeace Thackeray, or the youthful and mature hands of George Washington. Possibly it is of greater value to many of us if we study those men whose writing changes less markedly but has variations that lead to uncertainty and challenge.

My position is not that of a handwriting expert. This will save you some technical terminology and, I hope, leave the facts in your hands for preliminary use without special tools or equipment. Certain clear, confirmed results have come to my attention after the examination of close to five hundred original letters of John Adams. These results are offered as both warning and guide.

First the warning. I have identified at least fifty contemporaries of John Adams bearing the same name. Since the president was a well-traveled person, one cannot safely rule out letters written far from Quincy, Boston, Philadelphia, or any of his usual haunts. Nor can one too confidently rely on certain characteristics of the familiar Adams hand, for others affected the same *J* and the general size and shape of the last name. In fact, early in this investigation I wrote to one of our well-known institutions for a photograph of a John Adams letter of a period not represented in my own files. The photograph arrived and almost qualified. The appearance was not unlike his usual "small hand," but a scandal cropped up—John was making provision for several of his children in 1757, several years before his marriage (in 1764). The date, the place, the general appearance satisfied a former collector; but the text set the stage for a reappraisal of the writing and proof that President John Adams was not the writer. Moral: Always check the contents of your letters for sense.

THE WRONG ADAMS

Someone looking for a rewarding lifetime study can tackle all of the "wrong" John Adamses. I wager the box score will reach close to one hundred within the ninety years of the president's life. I must not even take time to tell about the easy fifty individuals I identified, except rapidly to indicate their locations and who they were.

There was a miller in Amherst, Massachusetts, of almost identical life span; a New Hampshire John Adams with a wife named Abigail; several from Barrington, Massachusetts; Captain John Adams of Boston, who became a prisoner of war at Dartmoor; a Revolutionary soldier from Brookfield, Massachusetts, who became an early settler in Vermont; an eccentric nicknamed "John Jeremy" while serving as a Revolutionary soldier; another who served at Bunker Hill and probably at Lexington; four or five from Chelmsford, Massachusetts; Deacon John Adams, who married widow Warren (incidentally, about twenty of these Johns married more than once); Reformation John Adams, a noted Methodist preacher from New Hampshire (he has a $3,000 tomb). You may find a John Adams in your locality, for these men were restless. Many left Massachusetts for Ohio-Wisconsin-New York-Vermont-Michigan-Pennsylvania-Virginia-Canada.

Enough of the wrong Johns; here briefly is John Adams the president as we look over his shoulder from 1756 to 1826 (seventy years of signing letters; there is also the early example owned by Dr. Joseph E. Fields, a schoolbook signed in 1748). Casually there appears to be a substantial variation in John's hand over the years and even within the period when he reached the full development of his handsome, angular, bold hand. The limitation of a lower margin often accounts for a small signature even on a boldly written letter. Frequently, with space to spare, he blew up his signature out of proportion to the text of the letter. This gives now and then the "L.S." appearance. The troubles of a poor quill or his state of mind will, in midlife, account for occasional untypical letters.

DEVELOPMENTS BY PERIODS

Adams' hand developed steadily until the bold "drawn" characters appeared about 1784. This bold hand is most common during the period of greatest responsibility—beginning in the winter of 1785 as minister to England and on through the presidency, nearly twenty years.

The decline set in and a tremulous shake appeared as early as 1803 (age sixty-seven), and became typical of the last decade.

Adams presents less trouble in authentication subsequent to 1770, and it is amazing how consistently he held to a few typical formations throughout his life. The final *s* is one of the best checkpoints, as are the *oh* connection in "John" and the top loop of the *J*.

Until 1780 the top of his small *a* was characteristically open, then for nearly twenty years it was closed; the backbone of the *a* was definitely raised above the loop by 1785. In late life (1810–1826) the *a* usually lacks both of these details.

The capital *A* evolved from a simple crossbar and curly-footed left stroke to a flourished cross stroke in the 1770's (occasionally up to 1785); then it reverted to the simple early style with little change, except a shift after 1805 to a narrow, more pointed *A*.

The *J* began with a full double loop, the lower attached to the *o*. The lower loop lost all but an end curl and became detached from the *o* about 1780. During the 1770's the *J* lengthened greatly and remained out of proportion until the mid-1780's.

The tie between the top of the *o* in "John" and the *h* held from early days until feebleness of the writer separated all letters.

The early small *n* had two well-balanced humps. By 1803 the *n* tended to break away from the *h* and the first hump was lost. This coincides with early years of the late hand in its pronounced separation of letters.

October 24, 1777

December 26, 1790

June 20, 1825

The small *s* was the most consistent and personal letter of Adams' alphabet. Early, middle, or late, it varied only slightly from the heavily top-looped, stand-out *s*.

Adams' written line started as a horizontal but soon (mid-1750's) developed a tendency to slope upward, although this was made more evident only in the 1790's.

Early and late there was an inclination to taper, starting a word in larger-size letters. This was very apparent in his signature, particularly the "Adams" from 1780 until his death.

One of the intriguing by-products of this analysis was the appearance of letters written under the stress of great events. Days could be swallowed up in a careful correlation of handwriting with the pressure of history in the making and being made by Adams.

EXAMPLES OF EXCITEMENT

Did you ever watch your own handwriting when you are angry, excited, exuberant? The effect on handwriting is of high interest as you read John Adams at critical periods.

In December 1773, the day after the Boston Tea Party: ". . . last night three cargoes of the tea were emptied into the harbour. This the grandest event which has ever yet happened!" (capital *A* nearly tipped over, *d* loop entirely gone).

Philadelphia, June [21], 1775, to [Joseph] Warren: ". . . impatient to be at Cambridge. We shall maintain a good army for you. How do you like your Gov't" (awkward shapes, irregular level).

June 23, 1776, to John Winthrop: "I am weary, thoroughly weary, and ought to have a little rest." "It is now universally acknowledged that we are and must be independent States but still objections are made to a Declaration of it" (cramped, irregular).

December 26, 1800, to Cotton Tufts: ". . . what shall I do with myself? I have forgotten all my law—lost my organs of Speech—given my books away" (jumpy, careless).

August 6, 1822: series of intimate reminiscences to Hancock, Tom Paine, Benjamin Rush (hardly able to control the quill).

One of the hottest periods of patriotic fervor brought almost a breakdown in writing style: "Gerry—a man of immense worth if every man here was a Gerry. The Liberties of America would be safe against the Gates of Earth and Hell.—New York—may Heaven grant us victory."

The leisure of the post-presidential period brought letters of phenomenal length, usually in the small, compact hand; he compressed a book into twenty-four pages to Benjamin Waterhouse in 1805. This was followed a few weeks later by eighteen pages on botany.

In summary, we can say the following:

1. Adams had a bold and a small hand (the bold hand was typical of 1790–1800).

2. His small *s* with the emphasized top loop was outstanding throughout his life.

3. There are three periods of the mature hand, roughly 1760–1785 (developing); 1785–1802 (bold); 1802–1826 (declining, wavering).

4. There is a distinct evolution and decline in the formation of individual letters, but numerous exterior influences account for stray formations. Almost never are these new; rather, they are throwbacks to earlier types of letters. In old age a period of physical well-being brought back much of the firm, bold hand of the presidency.

5. Haste in any period brought flashes of types of the previous decade.

In conclusion, let me suggest that less than 5 percent of the John Adams letters you see will present any problem beyond a reasonably careful check. Yet, were this study extended far beyond my preliminary work, it would still produce no magic by means of which some stray cut signature or fragment could be authenticated beyond doubt. However, I hope the results of this limited study will make it easier to arrive at a sound opinion whenever doubt arises.

FAIR COPIES AND WORKING COPIES

ROBERT L. VOLZ

COPIES are a class of manuscripts generally not so desirable as originals, yet they deserve both attention in a comprehensive discussion of manuscripts and consideration for their intrinsic or relative merit (or lack thereof), as well as for their textual significance, their saving graces, their charm (if any), and their market value. Copies present more variables than do originals. Qualification is the hallmark of discussing them, and "each on its own merit" becomes the guiding rule.

Essentially there are two types of copies: the work copy, intentionally created to preserve or transmit a text, and the fair copy, created primarily to please. The latter category is a chapter in taste and manners; but because fair copies are so prevalent, often so expensive, and too frequently naively acquired, they earn cautious consideration.

Fair copies are produced to provide a "manuscript" of an otherwise available text. The chief reason for their production is adulation of the writer, which creates a demand among collectors and admirers for a few lines from the author's pen transcribing a portion of a well-known work or bearing his autograph on a prepared transcription. Examples range widely, but include such actual items as stanzas of "Excelsior" carefully titled, written out, and signed by Henry Wadsworth Longfellow; eight lines of "Good Bye," in a secretarial hand, signed by an aged Ralph Waldo Emerson; and lines of "I'm Dreaming of a White Christmas," transcribed in neat calligraphy by a collector but genuinely signed by Irving Berlin. A variation in the production of fair copies is the goodwill of authors themselves, who, wishing to provide something more intimate for acquaintances, dear friends, or charity benefits, write out meaningful quotations that are added to personalized inscription. Recently seen examples include a quotation from *L'Enfer* written and inscribed by Henri Barbusse to Arthur Hartmann on stationery of the magazine *Clarté,* and a translation from the Greek of the Lord's Prayer written out for a dear lady friend by the cofounder of New York University, Rev. Samuel H. Cox. Many twentieth-century poets regularly inscribe a book with a stanza or two that is printed in the volume, a practice that gained vogue in the late nineteenth century, though instances can be found in several preceding centuries.

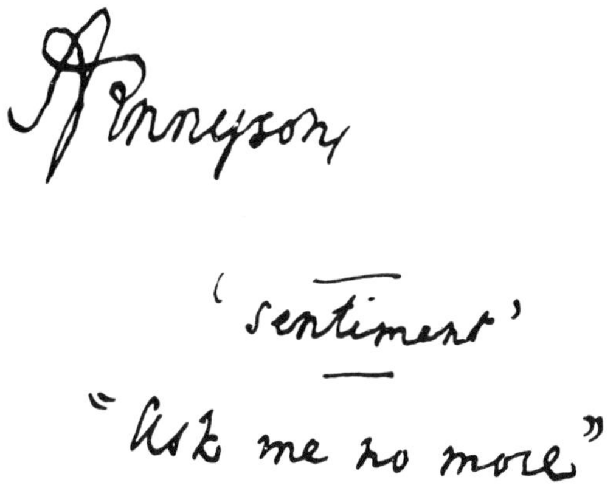
A Tennyson

'sentiment'

"Ask me no more"

Alfred Lord Tennyson's reaction to a request for
an autographed sentiment.
Courtesy of the Rush Rhees Library, University of Rochester.

Musical quotations of a few bars written on a postcard-size slip have gained great popularity. There is something very visual about musical notation that, when it is matted and framed with the composer's portrait, makes a handsome ensemble for the music lover's den. Thus, a recently offered Walter Piston fair copy of four bars of his Second Symphony is for $25 a charming bit of memorabilia, more meaningful than a note in which he refuses dinner, more displayable than a four-page letter to his music publisher, and therefore appropriately marketed and collected.

While most fair copies available today are single pages attractively written or typed and signed, the friendship and sentiment books of the eighteenth and nineteenth centuries are a little-collected source of fair copies equally or even more appealing in form. Kept most often by young persons, they were bound in leather and marbled papers, often with tinted pages and inserted engravings and drawings. The owner, family members, personal friends, and visitors wrote in them verses and thoughts of the famous and the unknown. Some of the compositions are original, but most are only transcripts of known printed pieces; though of these more than a few are known to be fair copies in their authors' handwriting. In 1976 a volume was sold that had been kept by R. P. Graves. It contained several poems of Arthur Henry Hallam and Felicia Hemans, on the surface authors' copies written out for their friend but very probably the only surviving contemporary manuscript versions of these poems.

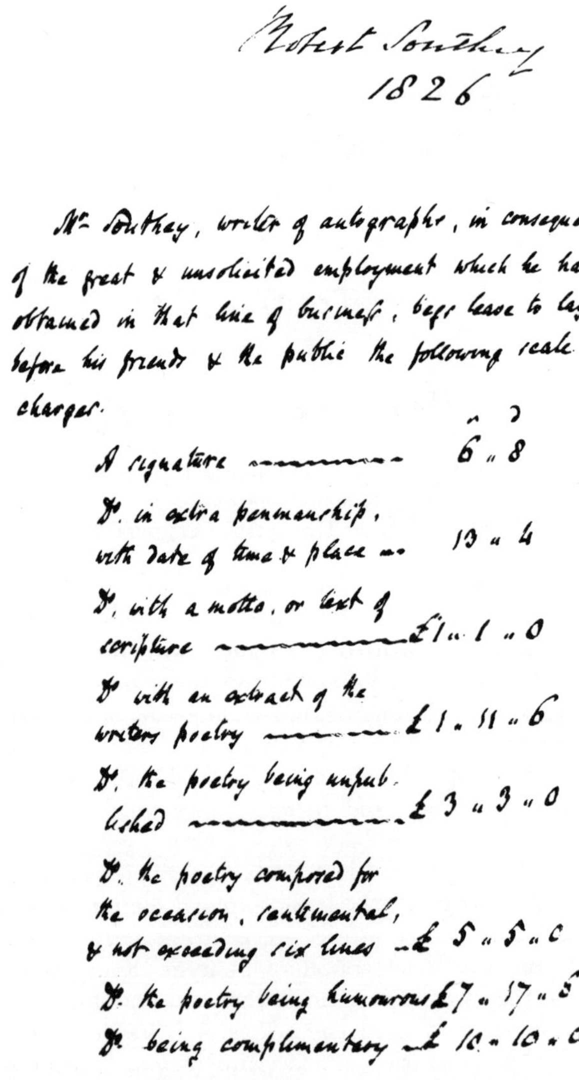

Robert Southey
1826

Mr Southey, writer of autographs, in consequence of the great & unsolicited employment which he has obtained in that line of business, begs leave to lay before his friends & the public the following scale of charges.

	s d
A signature	6 .. 8
Do. in extra penmanship, with date of time & place	13 .. 4
Do. with a motto, or text of scripture	£1 .. 1 .. 0
Do with an extract of the writers poetry	£1 .. 11 .. 6
Do. the poetry being unpublished	£3 .. 3 .. 0
Do. the poetry composed for the occasion, sentimental, & not exceeding six lines	£5 .. 5 .. 0
Do. the poetry being humorous	£7 .. 17 .. 6
Do being complimentary	£10 .. 10 .. 0

Robert Southey's "scale of charges" for the production of autographs.
Courtesy of the Rush Rhees Library, University of Rochester.

Though seldom so rare and of such research potential, for the inquisitive collector the sentiment books contain surprises among the verses copied in a variety of neat hands. Even when a daughter or sister of a popular author, statesman, or local poet has penned lines by her father or brother in a friend's album, the directness and authenticity of the piece recommends it to the collector. Unfortunately the pages of the famous are too often removed from sentiment books and scrap albums, thereby destroying their provenance. Probably among the bulkier discarded material there remain some equally interesting but unidentified collector's pieces.

Varying in form and importance, fair copies are not produced in a way that assures textual significance. Theirs is primarily a sentimental value. Yet a fair copy of "Dixie" written by an aged Dan Emmett forty years after its first appearance, or the Pledge of Allegiance to the Flag transcribed by Francis Bellamy for his son in 1924, is obviously more desirable than the commercially prepared typescripts of contemporary poets to which, to earn a few dollars, the authors have added their signatures. Verses written as fair copies, but into which the author has introduced a textual variant (not uncommon and usually unintentional), are of more interest than a fair copy that exactly follows the printed text. And the Emerson and Irving Berlin fair copies cited earlier are far less attractive than if the stanzas had also been in their authors' hands. But old age, the press of more important work, the desire for extra income, or just an attempt to maintain some sense of equilibrium among a sea of admirers has led many famous persons merely to approve and sign copies prepared by others. The market seems steady even for this type of fair copy, though at about one-quarter to one-half the full holograph copy price.

Because there are many reasons for collecting manuscripts, and because collectors come from all economic levels, it is inappropriate to discourage the collecting of fair copies. What must be realized, however, is that fair copies are a less-important kind of manuscript. They are not likely to appreciate so rapidly as drafts of manuscripts, they will have little value for scholarship, and they lack immediacy. Yet, for those who collect for sentiment, it is better to seek out fair copy verses of William Cullen Bryant's "Thanatopsis" for $150 than a fragment of a draft of a less-important Bryant poem offered at the same price. We write, though, not of the Bryant collector who would somehow acquire both, the first to have the author's most famous poem in his own handwriting, thus sharing the sentimental joy of the fair copy collector—the more because the original draft is no longer available—and the second to document the poet's life and work with whatever original sources can still be obtained.

A fair copy is potentially significant if the original manuscript drafts have been destroyed. The Hallam and Hemans poems described above are examples. Because they are the only known extant manuscript versions and some apparently never did reach publication, they become in fact original manuscripts because of their potential for study and their scholarly value. Yet technically they are fair copies, for there is no question that the poems had been worked out and drafted before their transcription into the Graves album. Having thus entered a gray area, how should one consider volumes of verse prepared and circulated only in manuscript form in the seventeenth and eighteenth centuries? These are not drafts. They are copies, but they are not fair copies. They are true work copies intended, in most instances, to suffice for publication. Only sometimes are they in the author's hand; but this matters primarily for attribution, authenticity, and, of course, price.

The variety of work copies is vast; and their importance depends upon the existence of originals, how far the copies are removed from the time of the original composition, the number of copies made, and similar considerations. In his foreword to the Parke-Bernet catalog of the Maurepas Papers (sale 2092, March 6, 1962), Robert F. Metzdorf gives a classic example of work copies:

> The papers offered in this sale were part of the Maurepas archives. They are, in many cases, secretary's copies, made for the Minister's use. The originals, for the most part, went into official government files and were destroyed in the disorders which later overwhelmed the country. These papers now offered, therefore, are important and unexploited sources for the rewriting and extension of the history of the times. They are unique.

On the other hand, the carbon copy or electrostatic copy of the final draft of the essay you are reading is a work copy, made and retained against loss of the original in the mails, as a point of discussion between the author and the editor should changes be required, and as an author's file copy of his unedited writing. After publication it will be of no value.

It is possible for a work copy to have a greater monetary or historical value than the original that is copied; but this is due to such special and extraneous circumstances as the fame of the copier, association, or added marginalia. In itself, the copy is less desirable. Also, drafts, however similar they are at times to a work copy, are not copies, though they sometimes serve the function of copies. As an example, William Henry Seward, because of his illegible handwriting, often had his son write out letters and memoranda intended for government officials. This is exactly what millions of secretaries and clerks do daily for their livelihood.

Seward sometimes had another secretary produce a copy for his personal file, and this parallels today's carbon or electrostatic copy or the letterpress book of the nineteenth and early twentieth centuries. These are the genuine work copies. But Seward also kept some of his scribbled drafts despite or in lieu of secretarial work copies. Thus, in the case of Lincoln's controversial proclamation suspending the writ of habeas corpus, the document Lincoln received for his consideration and signature is in the hand of Seward's son and one would tend to call it a copy when it is put in the presence of Seward's preserved original. But it is also an original, a final draft or version, and the only way the secretary of state communicated this important message to the president. Seward's draft, on the other hand, became the substitute for a work copy!

An understanding of how work copies are generated explains why so many are preserved and why they are frequently of significance. It is, however, futile and somewhat redundant to detail every possible manner and circumstance in which a work copy can be produced. What is essential is that the collector distinguish between a facsimile and a work copy, and between a fair copy and a work copy. Rather than just considering format, one must ask what is the likely process in the generation of the manuscript from conception to finish and what is the intended purpose of any draft or copy being considered. This will help the collector, whether institutional or private, to eliminate dross and intelligently get through the loosely used terminology found in both trade and library circles.

A work copy can be holograph, handwritten by another, typed by the author, or typed by another; it can also be a letterpress copy, an electrostatic copy, a photoreproduced copy, or a carbon copy. Some would venture that printers' galleys and page proofs are a stage of the manuscript (rather than of the printed book—advance proofs sent to reviewers excluded, of course) and that certain sets of these proofs would be work copies. Always it is the intended purpose that is dominant in determining a work copy. Copies "B" and "C" of Samuel Butler's *Notebooks* in the British Library and St. John's College, Cambridge, are pressed copies of the original manuscript (with additions) in the Chapin Library of Williams College. All, however, were for Butler's use. Likewise, many modern authors avail themselves of the quick and inexpensive electrostatic copying machine to produce one or more copies of their manuscripts for file purposes and working purposes such as corrections, revisions, and additions by themselves and their editors.

A recently offered thirteenth-century Ovid manuscript is a copy intended for a scholar's use, and for $18,000 one can study its place in the history of the transmission of the text of a first-century Latin poet. But what of the electrostatic copy a researcher makes of this manuscript for

Samuel Butler's letterpress. Courtesy of the Chapin Library, Williams College.

reference purposes or that the British Library requires to be deposited as part of the export license procedure? In many particulars such a modern copy is not unlike another copy of the same Ovid produced at the same scriptorium or recopied in the fifteenth century. Nor is it so very different from a seventeenth-century transcript of certain cartularies from one of the Cotton manuscripts in the British Library, nor from a near-contemporary secretarial copy of a 1495 Italian deed mentioning five times, as a frame of reference, Leonardo da Vinci's adjacent vineyard. Yet these copies were sold in 1976 and 1973 by two respected, experienced dealers for $925 and $900, respectively. And while our scholar's electrostatic copy of the Ovid manuscript would fetch next to nothing on the market and would generate even less interest in a non-Ovidian, an electrostatic copy of *The Reivers* found in William Faulkner's personal papers would fetch somewhat more than the cost of the paper on which it was reproduced.

The key to interest, desirability, and price lies, then, in the copy's uniqueness (the original is gone), its antiquity, its aesthetic and paleographic qualities (if any), its close association with the author or some famous person who copied it or formerly owned it, and so on. As we began with the cautions that the variety of copies is vast and that an assessment of them must be done carefully, so let us also admonish that the use of the word "copy" should be a careful, precise use. Then we no longer will find descriptions of Jefferson's "original" manuscript "copy" of the Declaration of Independence.

ORGANIZING AND DISPLAYING YOUR COLLECTION

DAVID HERR COBLENTZ

ANY SERIOUS AUTOGRAPH COLLECTOR, whether his holdings are large or small, will do well to give proper attention to the arrangement and housing of his manuscripts. A lackadaisical habit of keeping material boxed away on a closet shelf, tossed at random in some manila envelope, or carelessly mounted and placed on the wall of an overlighted room often results in serious damage to the material. Even excessive handling of an autograph may cause it to decrease in value if it becomes torn or stained or faded.

My advice to anyone who ventures into the green pastures of manuscript collecting is first of all to invest in a three- or four-drawer filing cabinet. (A number of collectors and some institutions prefer to file their manuscripts flat, and boxes are available that are designed for flat-filing. These persons argue that vertical filing may subject the edges of a fragile manuscript to unnecessary pressures.) The top drawers can hold the autographs, and the lower can be used to file folders on particular persons and events in which one has a special interest. Because of variations in the size of manuscripts, a legal-size cabinet is preferable. Though quite expensive, an insulated filing cabinet can protect a collection against most home fires.

Procure a legal-size manila folder with a cut tab to house each of your acquisitions, and on the tab indicate just what the folder contains; for instance, "James Madison to Dolley, 1 p., quarto, Oct. 11, 1812." Instead of merely writing the data on the tab, you may prefer to purchase a box of gummed labels, type the data on one of these, and affix it to the tab; this offers not only a neater effect but also a more apt way of filing.

The lower drawers of the filing cabinet can contain the special-interest folders in which you should place transcripts of the autograph material you have filed in the upper drawers; along with these may be kept Xerox copies of the manuscript in question plus clippings from magazines and newspapers relating to the person or event and any pictures, photographs, or engravings that also have a bearing on the individual or happening. Reference books on autographs, dealers' catalogs, and auction catalogs may also be deposited in the cabinet's lower drawers for handy retrieval.

When your filing cabinet reaches its capacity, retain it for the future filing of the type of material you have poured into the lower drawers, and then purchase a second filing cabinet, this one having a good locking system as well as being fireproof. Use the second cabinet solely for autographs. An alternative to buying a fireproof cabinet, of course, is to invest in a safe; another is to keep your autographs and manuscripts in a safety deposit box at your local bank. If you are doing research on a given manuscript in your collection, avoid overhandling it by working with the typescript and the Xerox of it instead of the original. For large folio items in your possession, such as vellum deeds, musical manuscripts, and commissions, you may wish to purchase a steel file of the type used by architects and building contractors to store drawings and blueprints. The drawers are large enough to allow the material to lie flat instead of having to be kept in an upright position and folded.

When placing an autograph item in a manila folder for filing, a collector may further protect it by placing the item within the folds of a sheet of acid-free paper, rolls of which may be secured from almost any large stationery company. The collector should be wary of clear plastic folders unless he can learn something about their chemical composition. Mylar folders, or encapsulation, are recommended and are in use in institutions. Acid-free file folders will also safeguard the autograph. In the case of plastic folders, I sometimes find it helpful to utilize a flexible or stiff-back leather loose-leaf book containing a dozen or so folio acetate or Mylar folders. On the recto page insert the manuscript, and on the verso facing it place a transcript or a picture of the personage who wrote it. Such procedure not only enhances the general appearance of the autographs, but also keeps together all the items that tend to form the set, whether it is presidents of Congress, presidents of the United States, monarchs of Great Britain, or manuscripts dealing with some particular poet, musician, general, playwright, politician, or other figure. It also permits easy viewing of the material without handling it. If the loose-leaf book system is used, I recommend to collectors who are working on a set of U.S. presidents or U.S. Constitution signers in particular that two such volumes house their collection, each volume containing not more than twenty acetate or Mylar folders. Such a method allows for more convenient, lighter handling.

One advantage in using the loose-leaf album is that you can thereby keep your material in chronological order, which you cannot do if the autographs are inlaid on paper and bound in. Another is that a specific item in the set can be replaced by another having greater significance or in superior condition, if occasion arises. A third advantage of the loose-leaf book over a bound book is that with the former you have room for needed expansion, which would certainly bear consideration if one were compiling a set of U.S. presidents or attempting to dramatize in sequence the life of some eminent individual.

Just as it is important for a library or similar institution to maintain a catalog of its holdings, so the manuscript collector should record and index his material as soon as it is acquired. Such registering may consist of a card index file or a loose-leaf binder, or a combination of the two. On the card that goes into your index file I would simply list the basic data: "D.S. of William Penn. 1 page, small folio,* with seal, on paper. Land grant to Jane Driver for a lot in Philadelphia. Dated April 17, 1684." However, in the loose-leaf binder I have always found it expedient not only to list the data given on the card, but also to add the purchase price of the item, the date of purchase, and from whom it was bought. As time goes on, you may wish to give access to your card index file to someone but sensibly withhold the private information you list in your loose-leaf record.

Another aspect of cataloging involves the collector's interest in a particular person or persons with respect to current market prices in dealers' lists and auction prices realized. By jotting down in a notebook from time to time the price, for example, of autograph letters signed by George Bernard Shaw, the British playwright, one gradually becomes familiar with the existing market prices for Shaw material. Naturally consideration must be given to condition and content; but, all in all, such listing can serve as a useful guide for the collector.

The private collector may be concerned about whether to use identifying marks on his manuscripts. In the mid-1950's the Library of Congress began stamping many of its millions of manuscript holdings with a small, light red institutional seal as a precaution against theft. The ink used is permanent and indelible, and the round seal is seven-eighths of an inch in diameter. Being very light in color, the mark is not too apparent to the casual viewer. However, while I sense the need for the Library of Congress to do this, I have my doubts as to the feasibility of the average collector's placing any sort of identification on his holdings.

*It is advisable to give the exact dimensions in centimeters (a library practice), placing the height first.

In years gone by I have seen autographs displayed on which the owner pasted a bright red label with his name, which certainly detracted from the overall appearance. Others thought they were doing the viewer a favor by underlining a signature on a manuscript with a blue pencil, or by drawing lines with red ink under significant words or sentences in a given letter. One collector used a small rubber stamp with indelible ink to initial his holdings, which, since his death, have been scattered to the four winds.

What to do for identification, then? Rather than resort to any of the above, I suggest keeping in one's files a receipt showing where and when the manuscript was purchased or otherwise acquired, and with it, if deemed valuable enough, a Xerox copy of the item and a typed transcript. When placing manuscripts on display, a small card with a simple statement such as "The items in this case are from the collection of John Doe" would be sufficient identification of ownership.

In the September 1948 issue of *The Collector,* the distinguished manuscript dealer Mary Benjamin wrote: "Autograph collecting, whether in the historical or the literary realm, is more than a hobby. It is a philosophy of quiet pleasure." And a continuing source of quiet pleasure it has been for many a white-collar worker, blue-collar worker, college student, housewife, or professional person. Sharing your collection of manuscripts with others by placing them on display can be an education in itself. Physicians, dentists, schoolteachers, professors, and other collectors often frame documents and letters from their collections and hang them on the walls of their offices or homes. They take great pride in explaining them to their beholders. Because improper framing can cause serious damage to a manuscript, the collector should consult the chapter "Preservation, Repairs, and Your Responsibility" in this book for advice about the proper method.

In considering temporary displays of his manuscripts, the private collector will benefit from visits to libraries and educational institutions where exhibits are set up, in order to study the arrangement, theme, lighting, and type of cases used. Over a period of time the collector can then devise ways of his own to set up an exhibit, whether it be in his office, a high school, a local library, a bank, or a university library. The general theme of the exhibit may be "A Collector's Showcase," or "A Collector's Choice," or "Autographs of Meaning and Significance," or "Manuscripts That Throw Light on the Past." Or, if you wish to incorporate your name in the topic, you may want to entitle it "A Display of Interesting and Unusual Manuscripts Selected From the Autograph Collection of John Doe."

A small printed leaflet or mimeographed brochure that can be made available to the viewer is a vital addition to a display of autographs. My experience along this line has been that the library or school where the display is to be set up will gladly cooperate in producing the leaflet if the collector will provide the copy for it. In so doing I usually preface the listing of the manuscript material on display by noting on one page just what manuscript collecting is and by giving other interesting information to the reader. Then I list the selected autograph material in numbered sequence. The latter should be logically laid out.

If dealing with a single personage, place your early letters or documents of the individual in the first showcase and follow through with various periods of the person's life, in systematic order, in the other cases. Thus, if you were displaying a collection of Dwight D. Eisenhower material, you would want the viewer to see letters and documents written by him at an early age, such as those of World War I vintage, when he was a captain at Camp Colt. Then would follow manuscripts signed as army general, as World War II commander of the Allied forces, as president of Columbia University, as commander of SHAPE, as president of the United States, and from the post-presidential period. In addition, manuscripts may be added that have a bearing on his sports activity (golf), his family, or his health. Books and pamphlets written by him, together with signed photographs of the general, his wife, their son, and the Eisenhower cabinet, would give added embellishment to the whole layout. In further arranging the above, the collector could also show variations of Eisenhower's signature—full, or "Ike," or "DE," or "Ike E," and so on—and add some signed by a secretary. The whole segment could be rounded out by a frank. Similar procedures could be followed if one were exhibiting the manuscripts of a writer, a poet, an artist, or a musician, utilizing in their cases perhaps not only letters but also corrected page proofs of their publications, music manuscripts, or manuscript poems signed by the author.

If your exhibit is a general one, your viewer will be happier if you coordinate it. In other words, if you have signed pen-and-ink drawings, keep them displayed in one case, Civil War material in another, musicians in another, writers and their manuscripts in another, French celebrities in another, and perhaps then have a case or two of unrelated material at the end. In describing the autographs in the leaflet, you may wish to note some particular feature about each exhibit piece. Perhaps the letter or document is important because of its date, or perchance something written in a letter shown can be given elucidation by an added sentence or two. If such information is not brought to the observer in the leaflet, it may be printed or typed on a small card placed below or beside the autograph.

Some attention needs to be paid to exhibit cases at this point. Institutions as a rule buy permanent, vertical wall cases or floor cases that are either sloping or horizontal in design. Custom-built cases or portable ones are preferred by others, depending on the area of use. The foyer of a building is often designed to accommodate, on either side, built-in vertical cases with glass shelving and doors that can be secured with a lock. If a special room for an autograph exhibit is set up, then chances are the exhibit cases will be horizontal ones placed around the four walls of the room, with perhaps an upright case or two in the center.

The collector or institution may use portable display cases. In such a situation the cases are made to order by a carpenter and set up in the exhibit room. They may be flat wooden cases that are placed side by side on long tables, or they may consist of two wooden cases supported by an arm that is bolted to an upright standard three and a half to four feet high. The latter cases are placed side by side in rows. At the end of each arm a case is attached at a viewing angle. The viewer goes down one line of cases and returns along the other. Such cases are constructed with a hinged front top and a small lock for security. The flat-top cases are generally considered more manageable and easier to store when not in use. A good size for this design is about thirty inches in length and eighteen inches in width. The framed glass top on the case should have a slope from five inches at the back down to three inches at the front. Like the other type of case this has hinges at the back; but instead of a hasp and lock, two long wood screws are inserted from the bottom front of the case and extend up into the glass frame, serving as security measures. The screws are inserted with little difficulty after the exhibit has been laid out in the case.

The collector may wish to add a green felt covering to the underside of each case to protect the surface of the table on which it will rest, and to make it more attractive to the eye by painting the case a neutral color and lining with black satin, ribbed corduroy, or velvet the interior base on which the manuscripts will rest. When preparing an exhibit, one may choose to draw attention to it by lining horizontal cases with such material, using light blue for royalty and U.S. presidents, bright red for the American Revolution, blue and gray for the American Civil War, and so on. Eye-catching displays at times implement as a backdrop a large map, framed portrait, national flag, or books by or about a person or event.

If the exhibition case is an upright one, then one may place the autograph in an acetate or Mylar folder and use pins to mount the folder on the back wall of the case, taking care in doing so not to perforate the manuscript itself. Or one can elect to place the manuscript in the folder on a small slanted metal or plastic stand that supports it without being in evidence. At printing companies one can often purchase sheets of fine-graded, soft-tinted paper that comes in pale pink, green, yellow, and brown. These sheets can be measured, cut, and placed under an exhibit piece with a half inch of the tinted paper showing all around the manuscript. This also serves to dress up a display. Still another suggestion that merits attention is not to crowd too many manuscripts into one case simply because you believe all of them are important enough to exhibit. If you determine that they are important, then use additional cases. Otherwise, be selective. A few carefully chosen items are better than a jumble.

If you are displaying a letter or document of more than one page in length, with writing on the verso, people will usually wish to see the signature of the individual featured. If the item contains a sentence or paragraph of major interest on the first page, then show the verso with the signature and lay beside it a Xerox copy of the other page. This will give clarification and added impressiveness to the whole.

Let us give some consideration now to lighting. We have noted that care should be taken in hanging a framed manuscript on a wall in home or office so that direct sunlight or artificial light does not continually shine upon it. In London's British Library the display cases of autographs are covered with very thick velvet weighted down with lead. One folds back the covering to view the contents, then replaces it when finished. For the most part, however, libraries and institutions of art and science today are equipped with showcases in which fluorescent lights* are installed. Such cases should have the small transformer affixed on the back of the case or, better still, placed underneath so that the heat is not given off inside the case. In the Lyndon B. Johnson Library in Austin, Texas, exhibition cases are being equipped with special filtered lights. This is a decided improvement, especially where manuscripts are shown.

Some table-type cases on the market today, though attractive in appearance and design, provide too small a space inside the cabinet. As a result, because of the close quarters, the fluorescent light or lights inside the case have a tendency to build up heat rapidly. What can be done to alleviate this problem? If the exhibit is to be on display for over two weeks, I have found it desirable to place a very small container of water in such cases. Set in an inconspicuous place, it not only helps the humidity of the closed case but also lets the manuscript "breathe," a point frequently underscored by autograph dealers and by the National Archives.

Attention should be given to the placement of fluorescent tubes or light bulbs inside exhibit cases. Often a poorly adjusted light results in reflections for the viewer as he bends over the case to inspect the mate-

*Fluorescent lights should be equipped with filters to screen out harmful rays, especially if displays are kept in the cases for great lengths of time.

rial. This is more likely to occur if the lighting illuminates the area from the back of the case than if the lighting is positioned inside, under the front lip of the case. Should the case be large, the illumination can come from the frontal top location. Some exhibitors prefer display cases with indirect lighting that does not focus down upon the manuscripts.

In rounding out this chapter, a word or two may be said regarding the advantages and disadvantages of publicizing an exhibit. If the display is set up in a place such as a local library, school, or hotel lobby, and is deemed large enough to merit more than average protection from vandalism or thievery, then insurance may be taken out to cover it. An added precaution might be to employ a security guard during the times when the exhibit is open to the public. Generally a library or gallery has a system of safeguarding its holdings as well as an exhibition, so that the displayer need have no qualms about leaving his layout up for an extended period of time. If the above procedures are followed, then any publicity given to the manuscript display or exhibition by newspapers, television, or radio will result in bringing it to the attention of the public in general and also will give good publicity to the collector and to the institution.

A few years ago the Manuscript Society set up a fine display of manuscripts owned by some of its members at one of its annual conventions. The exhibit was mounted attractively on large masonite boards and placed on easels around the lobby of the convention hotel. Wide publicity on it resulted in more than five thousand people from a wide area of the state descending on the hotel during the four-day showing, thereby advertising to advantage both the hotel and the Manuscript Society.

The display of original autograph material is an attraction that will appeal to a large segment of the public, provided it is tastefully done and effectively explained by a clearly visible commentary. This serves the purpose of enlightening and pleasing the public as well as possibly drawing a small number toward starting a collection of autographs. If one is on hand occasionally while the materials are on display, new friends may be made. While there is a good deal of work involved in preparing the display, the satisfaction it gives will prove well worthwhile.

NOTHING IS FOREVER: PRESERVATION, REPAIRS, AND YOUR RESPONSIBILITY

ROBERT C. WIEST

THE EXPLOSION ripped through the basement, shattering windows for two city blocks. There was no fire; but dozens of pipes ruptured, and tons of water rushed into the archival storage area in a new high-rise building. In fifteen minutes more than twenty thousand manuscripts and documents were submerged in two feet of filthy water. Countless business records shared a similar fate in an adjoining "safe" area. The trauma of discovery, the frantic call for help, the search for immediately available facilities large enough to handle the problem, and finally the safe return of the material seemed to be a bad dream. It was not. It happened.

Unfortunately, in many document and manuscript collections the manner of destruction is infinitely more subtle than that just described. No noise, no smoke, no streets jammed with fire and rescue equipment, and no heroics accompany most serious manuscript damage. Instead, the deterioration is spread out quietly over a period of years, not minutes. Much of it is far less obvious than two feet of water in a warehouse or basement. When these insidious problems are permitted to continue unchecked, they may result in total loss or severe and permanent damage.

The purpose of this article is to point out the principal causes of deterioration (excluding natural and unnatural disasters), what conservation problems can be handled by the collector, what problems are best left to professional conservators, types of conservation workshops and where you may find them, and what questions to ask conservators.

THE PRINCIPAL CAUSES OF PAPER DETERIORATION

Below we shall briefly consider the principal causes of paper deterioration: mankind, atmospheric pollution, insects, chemicals, humidity, heat, light, and self-destructive characteristics of paper and image materials.

MANKIND

Since the invention of paper, man has stored it in hot, dry attics, in damp basements, and in airless vaults. He has displayed it in direct sunlight and hung it over steam radiators and hot air vents. He has stored it in unheated warehouses; he has torn it, taped it, glued it, burned it, and spilled coffee, tea, and other chemicals on it. In short, he has folded, spindled, and mutilated it without mercy for nineteen centuries. This past carelessness need not continue; and you can demonstrate that what man creates, man need not rend asunder.

ATMOSPHERIC POLLUTION

While there may be little you can do about the environment without, it is well to be aware of its potential influence on your collection. Sulfur dioxide, ozone, and soot are the principal troublemakers known today, especially in urban areas. Airborne pollutants such as these can cause the development of sulfuric acid and other active reducing compounds that quietly and surely damage or destroy paper as well as other collectibles, such as leather and vellum. Fortunately, air conditioning and other forms of environmental control can be used to reduce the exposure of both people and paper to atmospheric pollution.

INSECTS

Insects have been around for at least 200 million years, and they will probably be around when we and our collections have disappeared. They cause more than $3 billion in damage to mankind each year. Their persistence and force of numbers make them a formidable enemy, an enemy that accomplishes most of its mischief in the dark, an enemy that moves so swiftly as often to remain undetected until irreparable damage is discovered. Paper and book collectors must be sensitive to the presence of silverfish, cockroaches, book lice, termites, and woodworms. Their destruction is total, and the disfigurement they cause is ugly and expensive to repair. Regular inspection of your collection and its immediate environs, moderate temperatures, light, and freely moving air are the simplest preventive measures.

If you are under insect attack, use local application of insecticides or hire professional help. Do not apply insecticides directly to any paper products except as an act of desperation and after discussion with conservators or museum personnel.

Chemicals and Chemical Migration

Material placed in intimate contact with paper—such as paper, cardboard, adhesives, pressure-sensitive tapes, inks, or plastics—can be the source of serious chemical migration damage. Acidic papers and cardboards, corrugated board, and similar materials will eventually discolor, spreading stains and causing serious acid damage to the paper mounted to, matted, or backed with these inferior products.

There are more than forty thousand proprietary adhesives on the market today, but only a few are suitable for use on valuable documents or artwork on paper. Most of these adhesives break the first rule of good conservation—never do anything that cannot be undone later—in that they become insoluble within a few years. They also can break down, spreading stains and destruction through the paper to which they are attached. This is especially true of pressure-sensitive tape.

Certain inks were ground in a medium that causes brown stains that will migrate to adjacent leaves. Acid-free slip sheets can be used to slow the spread of this damage.

Glazing in direct contact with a document or print can cause several problems. There is a chance of condensation forming between it and the paper, causing them to stick together or starting destructive mold growth. If the glazing is a plastic material, there is always the possibility of solvent attack upon the plastic from adhesives used in mounting, or from the image itself. Certain tinted plastics may transfer the tint dye directly to the paper.

Chemical migration can be controlled by the selection of correct materials and the knowledge of good mounting and framing procedures. Existing damage may or may not respond to treatment.

Heat and Humidity

The old adage "It's not the heat, but the humidity . . ." does not hold true in paper conservation. Heat is used in accelerated life tests for paper; and excessive heat can seriously dessicate paper, causing permanent damage. These tests are sometimes far less harmful than some attics I have seen. High humidity, in excess of 70 percent relative humidity, nearly guarantees mold growth. Some molds are colorless, making early detection improbable. In time these molds may react with materials in the paper, resulting in the familiar collection of reddish-brown spots called foxing. Paper people are generally happy with conditions approaching 70° F., with a relative humidity of 50 percent.

Even if you were able to sterilize your manuscripts and documents, such protection would last only as long as they were in a sterile environment. Once exposed to normal living conditions, mold spores would collect on the pieces, and would need only the correct conditions of heat and humidity to spring into life. Growing mold can be stopped, but frequently its scars remain.

The best way to handle mold is to prevent it. Do not let it get started. The spores are everywhere, and they require only a very short time in high humidity to bloom and flourish. Ethylene oxide kills growing mold; thymol does a similar job. Thymol is good to use during shipment, because it has a greater residual protection than ethylene oxide. Neither treatment is permanent. Keep your manuscripts dry, in air that is changed regularly, and check them frequently, especially in the summer.

Light

Although looking at a manuscript causes it no harm, illuminating it is a different matter. Fading and photochemical decomposition are directly proportional to the amount of light striking a paper object. Visible light is responsible for image fading, and the combination of visible and ultraviolet light causes papers to discolor or bleach and become brittle. In some cases the paper is so weak that it requires backing, mounting, or even lamination if it is to survive.

Direct sunlight and fluorescent lights are the prime source of ultraviolet radiation. This component of light can be controlled by employing various filtration materials. Framers can use Plexiglas UF-3 for glazing prints or documents, and shields made from the same material can be purchased as ultraviolet radiation protection for fluorescent lights.

While incandescent lights pose no threat in ultraviolet generation, they can be responsible for fading, and if mounted too close, they can generate excessive heat that will shorten the document's life. Some museums illuminate objects only when they are actually being viewed, by using proximity or demand switches. Obviously a piece must be lighted to be seen. Let that light be no greater than five footcandles, the equivalent of a one-hundred-watt light bulb three feet from the object. Anything you can do to remove light, and approach these recommendations, should be done.

Self-Destructive Characteristics of Paper and Images

The materials used in the manufacture of paper add to the problems of document life. While there are many additives and process materials used, the single most important problem being addressed today is acidity. Paper containing acid salts needs only a little moisture to activate the acid and destroy the paper, much as if you had played a lighted propane torch across it. The acid may take a little time to complete its mischief, but the results will be the same: lifeless, brittle, and discolored paper that breaks easily when handled.

Fortunately, many examples of this deterioration can be arrested by chemical means, using a technique called deacidification. Although this is done in one application in most cases, it is actually a two-step process. First, the acid content of the paper is neutralized, then an alkaline reserve is stored in the paper for additional automatic neutralizing in the future.

Currently there are several acid-free papers and boards available. These are used in the production of special books, the construction of archival envelopes, or simply as slip sheets to isolate art materials, documents, or manuscripts. They are referred to as "permanent" or buffered papers.

PROBLEMS THAT CAN BE HANDLED BY THE COLLECTOR

Environment

You are in a position to give your collection the best care it has ever had. The technology is available; all that remains are the determination of your specific problem and the money to carry out your plan.

You need a storage and display area free from sulfur dioxide, ozone, and soot. It should be kept at 70° F., with a relative humidity somewhere between 40 and 60 percent. The drier the air is, the less hydrolysis can take place. Because the strength of paper falls off rapidly under extremely dry conditions, however, some compromise is needed. These recommended figures may change, so the equipment you install must be capable of maintaining drier and cooler conditions. Air-washing devices, recording devices, and similar equipment require detailed knowledge unique to your situation. In some circumstances display and storage cabinets can be designed and built to house the collection, a sort of oasis in the wildly fluctuating climate of many homes, especially older ones.

A call to a nearby museum, historical society, or conservation studio should get you started in the right direction for the solution to specific environmental problems. A number of useful publications concerning collection management are available from the Library of Congress on request.

Display and Storage

The best approach for displaying a collection is to avoid extremes. A stable environment is most desirable. One should avoid hanging pieces over fireplaces, heat vents, or radiators, on outside walls, and similar locations. Do not put fine materials in the bathroom. Protect your material from ultraviolet radiation. In framing, wherever possible use Plexiglas UF-3 or other shielding material instead of glass. Always separate the glazing from the piece with a mat or strips of archival-quality material. Use ultraviolet shields over fluorescent tubes, or use incandescent lighting instead. Avoid high-intensity spotlights or any lighting that produces heat at the object in excess of 70° F. The recommended lighting limit is five candlepower. Do not display any work in direct sunlight.

Storage presents other problems. Do not use your attic, because the heat generated in summer will desiccate a piece and permanently damage it. Extremes of heat and cold experienced during a normal year can cause the paper to stretch or shrink, even tearing hinges or the document itself. Cellars are no better, for although high heat may not be a problem, high humidity is; and mold damage can be expected, especially during the summer months. There is the additional threat of flooding from plugged drains or water system failures.

The storage of manuscripts and documents can be handled in a variety of ways. Mylar envelopes can be made that allow the piece to be handled, yet protect it from greasy fingers and other physical hazards. In addition, the Mylar provides excellent support for weakened paper. The basic package consists of a sheet of Mylar, larger than the piece, with double-sided tape attached around the perimeter, perhaps one thirty-second of an inch from the very edge. The document should lie within this taped area, allowing at least one-quarter of an inch between the document edges and the tape. A second sheet of Mylar of the same size as the first acts as the top part of the sandwich. When the package is assembled, static electricity will keep the piece in place. There are numerous variations on this procedure, which is known as encapsulation.

Many archival board and paper suppliers have acid-free folders, boxes, envelopes, and other materials available for document storage purposes. It is far better to purchase these protective materials than to spend money on elaborate presentation boxes and cases that may not provide adequate protection. You can stretch your preservation dollar by using the proven materials.

Do not let anyone handle your material unless you are certain he knows what he is doing. Be sure hands are clean and free from oil or other easily transferred substances. Support the paper completely, not by one corner. Handle it firmly, and with authority. Do not smoke, eat, or drink while handling your material. Avoid moving the material quickly. Be especially careful of minute tears around its perimeter. They need little provocation to develop into long, expensive rips.

If you are trusting your material to a framer, ask to see his shop. Notice how material for framing is handled. Coffee cups and filled ashtrays—or any ashtrays—in the work area are sure signs of potential trouble. Some let their children play in the shop. If such is the case, you should find another framer.

Ask what materials the framer plans to use. His list should include neutral pH, or buffered, archival-quality matboard. Simply mentioning rag board is not enough, because it can contain harmful acid. Hinging or hanging material should be an acid-free tissue, preferably one of the Japanese varieties. It should be torn to shape, not cut. (This reduces the possibility of telltale straight lines showing through the front of the piece.) He should use an archival-quality paste, generally cooked wheat- or rice-starch paste. Under no circumstances should pressure-sensitive tapes be used directly on or next to your document. Be sure the framer understands the piece is not to be in direct contact with the glazing, which preferably should be an ultraviolet shielding material such as Plexiglas UF-3. This Plexiglas is not recommended for use in framing pastels, charcoal drawings, or very thin paper pieces, since static electricity may pull off pigment particles or draw the paper toward the glazing. Not all framers are aware of the damage they can cause, and some do not care. Be specific in your requests, and preferably obtain a signed statement as to how your work will be handled. A good framer is a welcome supporter of your collection.

PROBLEMS BEST HANDLED BY CONSERVATORS

Pressure-Sensitive Tape Removal

Unfortunately, many documents and books have been repaired with pressure-sensitive tapes. The adhesives in these tapes eventually discolor, spreading the stain to the paper. Their removal can be most difficult, and the elimination of the stain may be impossible. Solvents used to remove the residual adhesive and lessen the stain may also damage the image. Extreme caution is required to complete this kind of repair. The most tragic type of home repair starts when tape is discovered on the reverse of a piece, and a solvent such as trichlorethylene is applied to remove it. In all probability the tape will be removed, and perhaps the stain will lighten. But when you turn the piece over, you may discover, to your horror, that the stain has been forced through the paper to the front, possibly disfiguring it forever.

Repair of Tears and Voids

At this time there are no pressure-sensitive mending tapes that are acceptable for archival repairs. Heat-set materials may go through drastic chemical changes over time, discoloring and becoming difficult to dissolve should the need arise. Today the most responsible repairs are made with matching paper, pulp, or tissue.

These, being methods that use water-based adhesives or plain water, are best left to the specialist. Paper swells when wet, different amounts in different directions. If it is wetted or dried unevenly, a condition arises called cockling, that irregular waviness you can see from time to time in paper pieces. It takes special knowledge and care to make a local paper repair and not disturb the surrounding paper or image. If overall wetting is required, there is a further risk of image loss or other problems.

Deacidification

Today deacidification is recognized as one of the most important treatments for prolonging the life of paper. Two processes are most commonly used, one employing an aqueous solution of magnesium carbonate and the other, the same material in combination with methanol and freon. Since direct application of solvents is part of the process, it is best to leave it to professionals.

Image Replacement

Image replacement, sometimes known as image enhancement, is simply an overwriting process. It is a highly controversial operation, and the merits of whether to do it must be examined on a case-by-case basis. The decision to strengthen writing is a curatorial judgment. It has been stated that twentieth-century overwriting can be separated from older material. What will happen in the future, or what we do with fairly recent material, is a subject of great concern to all involved. While you may be tempted to have image enhancement done, you may get an argument or refusal by the conservator. The decision must resolve the question of how to deal with writing that is, or will shortly be, obliterated by natural fading. Be prepared for considerable discussion, and to accept the responsibility associated with your decision.

Stain Removal

The use of solvents or cleaning agents takes the sometimes controversial technique of stain removal out of the owner's hands. Considerable damage can occur during stain removal attempts, especially in inex-

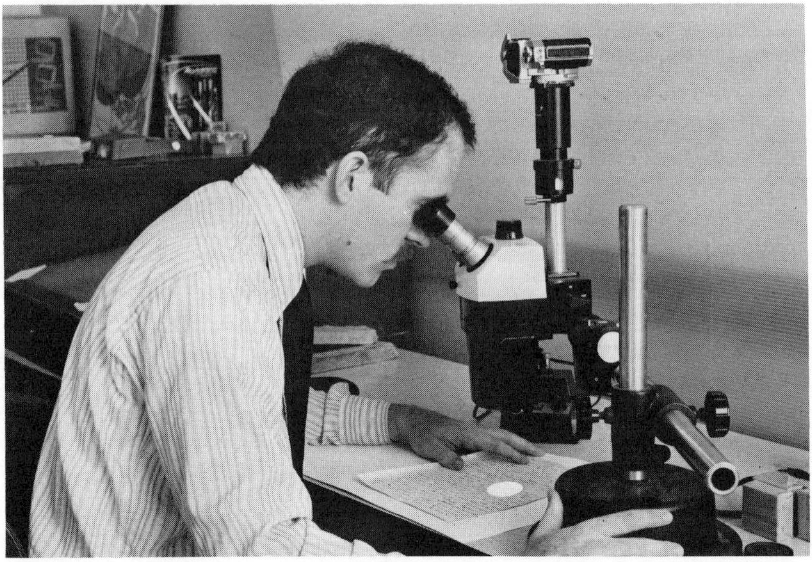

In the conservation laboratory a microscope is a useful tool for determining how to preserve paper and yet leave its images intact and sound. Courtesy of R. R. Donnelley & Sons.

A manuscript is being prepared for repair using a paper pulp-casting technique. Raw, dry pulp seen in the upper left corner will be made into a slurry, and cast into the void in the manuscript while it rests on the light box. The casting will be localized by surrounding the void with a dam of string. Courtesy of R. R. Donnelley & Sons.

Effective paper deacidification is assured by conducting regular quality tests of solutions prior to their use.
Courtesy of R. R. Donnelley & Sons.

perienced hands. If the conservator suggests you let the stain remain, take his advice. You may want to talk to another conservator, but be certain you are advised of the short- and long-term risks involved in the use of solvents or bleaches for stain removal. Do not try to remove stains yourself.

Seals, Grommets, Special Fasteners

Seals are often soluble in water; grommets and special fasteners may have to be replaced with some made of a benign material. Considerable harm can come to the documents involved if this is done by an inexperienced person.

Special Materials

Vellum or parchment is one of the more durable materials used in document work. It has a mind of its own, however, and will not tolerate inept handling. It is extremely hygroscopic, and will respond swiftly to sudden changes in humidity and temperature. If washed or heavily wetted, it can lose much of its opacity and tend to revert to the shape of the animal from which it was taken. In that state you would recognize it as rawhide. Definitely leave vellum to skilled conservators.

Fabrics

Do not do anything with fabrics until you talk with your local museum, historical society, or fabric conservator. The best a paper conservator could do is refer you somewhere else.

Demounting and Deframing

Demounting is a job for the professionals. Hinged items are not too bad, but perimeter-mounted or solidly mounted pieces present a challenge. It is generally time-consuming, expensive, and quite difficult to remove a fragile paper piece from an acid mount or other material. Even deframing can bring you an extra dose of trouble. In one case a vellum document had been deframed carelessly and then sent to me when the damage was discovered. It did not take the owner long to discover that he had left some of the document stuck to the glass. I was able to remove and replace the split-off material, but at a high cost to the owner. It could have been avoided if knowledgeable people had deframed the piece. If a decision is made to ship, very special attention should be given to protecting the document from damage if the glass is broken. Hand-carrying is still the safest and surest method of delivering extremely delicate pieces or pieces that are framed with glass.

Mounting

Paper in a badly weakened state may require mounting in one way or another. For a long period of time, silk chiffon was used for much of this work. Its main virtue was its transparency, for it could cover material and still meet minimum legibility requirements. Silk has a hard time resisting the environment today. It can be removed and replaced when necessary, which could be anywhere from five to twenty years later. Where possible, tissue mounting to various Japanese papers may give better service. Also, successful repairs can be accomplished by casting a new leaf of paper directly on the reverse of the piece. The least desirable form of mounting is lamination. Responsible lamination includes deacidifying before mounting between two sheets of cellulose acetate and thin tissue. This technique is often best for business archives and for documents so badly damaged that this is their last hope.

TYPES OF CONSERVATION WORKSHOPS, WHERE THEY CAN BE FOUND, AND WHAT YOU CAN EXPECT

There are four types of conservation workshops available today: full-time commercial conservators, part-time commercial conservators (sometimes in conjunction with a framer or sales outlet), institutional conservators with outside commission privileges, and institutional conservators without outside commission privileges. There is a fifth category just becoming established, the regional conservation center. The New England Document Conservation Center is the first example of this type.

The commercial, full-time paper conservators are frequently small shops. A few have the size and facilities to handle complicated and difficult jobs. You can best locate these by talking to print curators, museum conservators, or manuscript and book dealers.

Sometimes conservation services are offered in conjunction with frame shops and galleries. Be certain they have the facilities and skills to accomplish what you wish. A good conservator will discuss all aspects of the job, no matter where he or she works.

Some institutional conservators can take on private commissions, and they may be able to handle your problem. They generally have excellent facilities. Others cannot accept private commissions, but they can generally refer you to several responsible studios.

When looking for a conservator, check with public and private museums, reputable dealers, and galleries. When you find a conservator, feel free to discuss the problem over the telephone; but do not expect price quotes if an examination of the document has not been made. Be wary of those willing to quote without going through this formality. Be sure you specify the time limitations you may have, and do not be afraid to mention money. This may save you and your prospective conservator valuable time. Keep in mind that shipping considerations are becoming more and more important in conservation. Be sure you have these details before you make your decision.

QUESTIONS YOU SHOULD ASK CONSERVATORS

Keep in mind that you are the custodian of a particular document or collection of documents. Generally this is a temporary situation, but you do have the responsibility to see that the best is done to keep the items in good condition for future generations. In that light, do not let yourself be bullied by conservators. You have a right to know exactly what is to be done to your property. Bearing this in mind, the following guidelines might be helpful:

1. Will you be supplied with an examination report?
2. Is the proposed treatment described clearly? If there are areas of risk, are they detailed?
3. Does the conservator require written approval before commencing treatment? Do not expect a conservator to start work without such approval.
4. Will a report of treatment be available upon completion of the work? If so, will there be an additional charge for it?
5. Are the stated costs firm? If not, how are cost increases handled?
6. How does the conservation studio handle insurance? Many insist that the owner be responsible for coverage while it is out of his hands. When you ship, be sure you are conforming to your policy. Sometimes the types of crates or other limitations are spelled out in detail in the policy.
7. Be sure to get a delivery schedule. Expect to pay a premium for special handling.
8. Does the studio maintain photographic records? There is no telling when this might be handy.
9. Is the conservator willing to discuss details of his treatment with you? Does he use archival-quality materials? Is he specific in his descriptions of these materials? If you are not satisfied, find another studio and try again. You are the custodian, and you have the final word as to what is done.

CONCLUSION

Paper is a marvelous material, much of it tougher than is generally imagined. It was, and is being, manufactured in a variety of ways. Some materials used in its manufacture are helpful to its life; some are harmful. Unless understood and checked, sizing procedures, inks, environmental conditions, and a host of other detractors hasten the premature loss of unique and valuable historic items. The known threats to paper and the myriad images found on it must be controlled in a manner providing that delicate and sometimes controversial balance between preservation and utility. The ideas contained in manuscripts and documents may be immortal, but paper and ink are not.

YOUR MANUSCRIPTS AND THE SCHOLARLY WORLD

CAROLYN HOOVER SUNG

UNLIKE MANY COLLECTIBLES, manuscripts are not merely artifacts, art objects, or curiosities; they are the most abundant evidence on which our beliefs about the past rest. The substance of a manuscript is usually the communication, not its artistic or decorative value. Thus, the way in which the communication is used is crucial to all owners of manuscripts. This article attempts to give examples of the results of scholarly use of manuscripts, criteria for determining the use that collectors wish to permit, guidelines for supervising use, and ways in which collectors may learn more about their own manuscripts.

In recent article in the *Quarterly Journal of the Library of Congress,* Paul H. Smith, editor of *Letters of Delegates to Congress, 1774–1789,* a letterpress publication sponsored by the Library of Congress, reported a discovery concerning the time of the vote on the Declaration of Independence on July 4, 1776.* A letter written on that date, by the committee appointed to confer on the defense of New Jersey and Pennsylvania, led Smith and his associates to inquire more deeply into the sequence of events on that historic day. After considering the evidence, they concluded that the Declaration of Independence was adopted sometime before 11:00 A.M., and not in the evening, as historians and popular dramas have commonly asserted. The traditional assumption about an evening vote was based on the language of Thomas Jefferson's notes describing the events:

> The debates having taken up the greater parts of the 2d. 3d. & 4th. days of July were, in the evening of the last closed. The declaration was reported by the commee., agreed to by the house, and signed by every member present except Mr. Dickinson.

---

*Paul H. Smith, "Time and Temperature: Philadelphia, July 4, 1776," in *Quarterly Journal of the Library of Congress,* 33, no. 4 (October 1976), 294–299.

According to the official journal of the Continental Congress, the appointment of the committee to confer on the defense of New Jersey and Pennsylvania was the third item of business for the day and immediately followed the approval of the Declaration of Independence. The new evidence found in the committee letter supports the morning vote in the first lines: "Gentlemen, The Congress this morning directed us to confer. . . ." The official journal records that that body convened about 9:00 A.M., disposed of one minor matter, and then "resolved itself into a committee of the whole to take into their farther consideration the declaration." Thus, Smith concludes that the committee was actually appointed on the morning of July 4, following the adoption of the Declaration of Independence.

The significance of this discovery may seem inconsequential at first. It may call for minor revision in future dramatizations such as *1776*. But it is of much greater importance to scholarship because it has raised significant questions concerning heretofore accepted information about the adoption of the Declaration of Independence and, more important, questions Jefferson's notes, on which many historians have relied heavily for their understanding of the steps leading to the Declaration of Independence. In addition to Smith's evidence regarding the time of the vote on the Declaration of Independence, it has been recognized for some time that Jefferson erred in recording that the signing took place on July 4; the actual signing did not take place until August 2. These errors of fact in Jefferson's notes on the independence debates in Congress indicate that the notes are not literally accurate in all significant detail, and cannot be used uncritically in reconstructing precisely the actions of the delegates to the Continental Congress in the summer of 1776.

The evidence or documentation on which Smith based his conclusions came from manuscripts in the hands of a private collector, from another private collection now owned by a historical society, and from collections in the Library of Congress and the National Archives. The printed broadside containing the defense committee's letter that sparked Smith's initial interest has long been in the collections of the Library of Congress. The original draft of the letter, written by committee member Robert R. Livingston of New York, provides independent confirmation of the authenticity of the document and its date. Collector Sol Feinstone made this draft available to the *Letters* project through a microfilm copy of his collection in the Library of Congress Manuscript Division. Another important document substantiating Smith's hypothesis is a letter written early on the morning of July 4 by Delegate Abraham Clark of New Jersey to Elias Dayton, in which Clark discussed the recent work of the Continental Congress on the Declaration of Independence as follows:

> . . . Our Congress Resolved [i.e., on July 2] to Declare the United Colonies *Free and independent States*. A Declaration for this Purpose, I expect, will this day pass Congress. It is nearly gone through, after which, it will be Proclaimed with all the State and Solemnity circumstances will admit. It is gone so far that we must now be a free independent State, or a Conquered Country.

The passage "It is nearly gone through" is, of course, Clark's statement that supports the morning vote. Ferdinand Julius Dreer, a nineteenth-century Philadelphia capitalist and collector, acquired Clark's letter for his collection of letters written in the hands of distinguished persons from different countries and from almost every field of intellectual activity. Although Dreer acquired the Clark letter primarily for its signature, it contains an important account of the consideration of the Declaration of Independence. Dreer gave his beautifully bound and lavishly illustrated collection, including Clark's letter, to the Historical Society of Pennsylvania. The letter was published in *Letters of Members of the Continental Congress*.*

Thus, in the bicentennial year, through the use of manuscripts and a printed broadside held in both public and private repositories and in private hands, a scholar-editor, upon close examination of only a few documents, reopened discussion, research, and interpretation of the setting and of the events surrounding the vote on the Declaration of Independence. For the present, the discovery may reach only a small portion of the public who are particularly concerned with this historic event. Perhaps by the time of the tercentenary, if not long before, this discovery will become more generally known. The information will become a part of the historical record when scholars incorporate this discovery, along with others obtained through a new examination of the evidence discovered by other collectors, archivists, scholars, and editors. The *Letters* project has made, and no doubt will continue to make, an important contribution to a deeper understanding of the Continental Congress that governed the United Colonies in revolt, handling the momentous decisions along with the mundane but often crucial affairs of state throughout the American Revolution. The *Letters* will put into perspective the Declaration of Independence and the events of one of the most important days in American history. The vote was not taken amid pomp and ceremony. The fireworks did not come until later. The Continental Congress approved the Declaration of Independence and immedi-

*Edmund S. Burnett, ed., *Letters of Members of the Continental Congress, 1774–1789*, 8 vols. (Washington, D.C.: Carnegie Institution of Washington, 1921–1936), I:534–535.

ately went to the next issue, the preparation of the defense against the great military force that the British were bringing to bear against the United Colonies.

Recording the minute details of history is essential in order to base generalizations on fact and not on fiction. Indeed, facts destroy myths and qualify generalizations. When the past is examined in detail and perspective, great people are seen in their proper dimensions and great events in the total context of the times. Frequently manuscripts provide the essential detail necessary for an accurate reconstruction of the past. Thus it behooves all of those who hold manuscripts to recognize that their holdings are frequently unique and part of the legacy of the past. As such, they must be used, researched, and preserved with the utmost care.

Both public and private collectors should remember that they own only the physical object—the paper on which the words are written—and not the words or sentiments expressed. A manuscript has its own life. It will pass from one collector to another, and will be used by scholars of numerous generations, nationalities, and points of view. Thus collectors should view themselves as keepers whose duty it is to preserve and use the manuscript in such a way that it can pass unharmed to the next generation.

In considering the collections that they hold, private collectors should realize that they will be confronted by requests from scholars to use their manuscripts. The new collector or owner of manuscripts may wonder how a scholar knows a particular manuscript exists. Most scholars aim at completeness. One of their greatest fears is that their studies will be outdated by the discovery of evidence that might have been available with a little extra effort. Thus scholars become adept detectives. Their curiosity can be aroused by the mere mention that a document of possible significance to their study exists. They will spend hours searching for clues to the identity of the current owner and will show great perseverance in seeking access. Scholars read manuscript auction catalogs regularly, and many are bitten by the collecting bug. On seeing an item of interest, they will almost automatically send a stamped, self-addressed envelope and a letter of appeal to the dealer, asking that it be forwarded to the buyer of the manuscript, in the hope that the collector will permit access. Thus you may be confronted with a request to consult your manuscript at the same time you make a purchase. A clever scholar may even have already consulted your new item before you, by visiting the dealer on the pretext of purchasing the manuscript.

Collectors should recognize that a manuscript, even if new to them, may be well known to scholars. In deciding how to meet scholars' requests, you must consider many issues; but the first decision must be your own plans for its use. Why are you collecting manuscripts? The answer to this question will color many of your subsequent choices.

The effect of scholarly use and publication on monetary value is often the first consideration. Collectors find themselves in the middle on this issue. Some dealers encourage collectors to disregard requests for use and not to permit access, and certainly not publication, because they feel that publication automatically reduces the resale value. On the other hand, the scholar and the editor, anxious to see the manuscript or print it, may suggest that its value would be enhanced by publication in an important and prestigious edition.

Who is correct? Because price is dependent on a number of variables—supply and demand, rarity, content, length, condition, date, and association—the fact that an item has been published in a recognized scholarly edition is but one of many factors in determining its price. The effect of publication on price cannot be measured with certainty. According to Mary Benjamin, a well-known authority on autographs, in the revised edition of her *Autographs: A Key to Collecting* (1946; revised edition, 1963), "librarians and those who specialize, because they wish their material to be used for research purposes definitely prefer the unpublished manuscripts. . . . A few collectors and institutions even refuse to buy items which have appeared in print despite the fact that they are offered at nominal figures." Undoubtedly Miss Benjamin's discussion of preferences has validity. Certainly items by lesser-known persons or such manuscripts as journals, diaries, and orderly books are less attractive to autograph collectors. Frequently the main attraction of such material is its research potential and the possibility of making an attractive publication. Undoubtedly, in such cases, the price would be affected if the manuscript had been previously published in its entirety. If the manuscript has merely been used as background or mentioned in part in a monograph of recognized historical importance, it may well be easier for an institutional purchaser to justify the expenditure. Certainly it is extremely unlikely that an attractive manuscript would fail to sell merely because it had been published.

There is no evidence that the price of manuscripts written by such leading figures in American history as George Washington, Abraham Lincoln, and Thomas Jefferson has been adversely affected by publication. The demand for autograph manuscripts written by important historical personages is too great to be destroyed by the fact that the content is well known. For example, according to the *New York Times* of May 17, 1967, the Carnegie Book Shop paid the record price of $20,000 at the Parke-Bernet Galleries in New York for a George Washington letter dated July 4, 1776, written in New York and addressed to

Gen. Artemas Ward in Boston. The letter, printed in volume VI of *The Writings of George Washington,** was owned at the time of printing by Thomas F. Madigan of New York, a dealer in American manuscripts and a noted collector. George Washington signed, but did not write, the short note, the text of which follows:

> The Distress we are in for want of Arms induces me again to urge your sending on all such as can possibly be spared with the greatest expedition,—The enemy have landed under cover of their Ships and taken possession of Staten Island from which in all probability they will soon make a descent upon Us,—The Arms would have [to be] sent to Norwich and from there by Water to this place provided there is no Risque—otherwise by Land.

Publication does not appear to have depressed the price of this letter because its $20,000 price tag was well above the $2,800–3,500 average auction price of a George Washington military letter at that time, and $3,000 above the previous record price for a Washington item, set at a Parke-Bernet Galleries sale in April 1963. The latter item was a long, revealing letter written entirely in Washington's hand from the Falls of the Delaware in December 1776 to his cousin Lund Washington, telling of the capture by the British of an important officer, Gen. Charles Lee. The text of this letter also was published in the 1932 edition of *The Writings of George Washington,* and was taken from an 1890 edition of his writings edited by Worthington Chauncey Ford,† who had printed it from the copy of the original made in 1862 by C. F. Lee, Jr., of Alexandria, Virginia; the 1932 edition noted that the whereabouts of the original were unknown. These two examples of the highest prices brought at auction by George Washington letters support the contention that substantial prices can be had for manuscripts even though they have been previously printed and the content is well known.

Of course the resale value should not be, and is not, the only consideration of private collectors, many of whom have responded to the needs of historians and scholarly editors, making their manuscripts available for editing and publication. Scholarly use of one's collection is not without benefits to the owner. In addition to the new friends one may make, and the pleasure of knowing that one has contributed to the advancement of knowledge, collectors who share their manuscripts reap the benefits of any discoveries that scholars might make concerning the

*John C. Fitzpatrick, ed., *The Writings of George Washington,* 39 vols. (Washington, D.C.: U.S. Government Printing Office, 1931–1944), 6:345–347.

†Worthington Chauncey Ford, *The Writings of George Washington,* 14 vols. (New York: G. P. Putnam's Sons, 1890), 5:77–80.

manuscript. When a manuscript is included in a recognized edition of published papers, its authenticity is assured and can be cited in establishing provenance and ownership.

Although twentieth-century collectors find it more difficult and more costly to build collections of significant manuscripts and research materials than did their nineteenth-century predecessors, they can still make a significant contribution to scholarship by astute collecting based on specialized knowledge. Some collectors become authorities on their subjects and make substantial contributions through their own publications, by assisting others, and by sharing their specialized knowledge and their collections. Since the possibilities for collecting are practically infinite, even the greatest library or research institution must limit its acquisitions. Thus there will always be room for the astute collector. Within the last few decades, members of the Manuscript Society have assembled important and useful collections around such diverse subjects as the presidents of the Continental Congress, the French spoliation claims, Roscoe Conkling, and Algernon Charles Swinburne.

In addition to their specific contribution of creating and shaping collections, collectors make a more general contribution. The demand created by collectors establishes a market for manuscripts. Since manuscripts have monetary value, many are preserved that might otherwise have been destroyed. The occasional newspaper account of a high sale price for a manuscript is an asset in the preservation of manuscripts because it is a reminder of the potential value of old documents. Therefore, when people discover old papers in their attics or in their grandmother's trunk, they are more cautious and generally will check with a book dealer or a library before disposing of them. The hope that their old papers will provide them with extra income is an added inducement to preservation.

Valuable and legitimate scholarly use of private collections can be made to the mutual advantage of collectors and scholars. When collectors decide to permit scholars to consult their collections, specific conditions of access and use should be agreed upon before scholars see them. The rules of the road must be established; and it may even be advisable to spell out the terms in writing, in order to avoid later misunderstandings. However, in the end these agreements rest on the integrity of the persons involved. As discussed in the chapter on law and manuscripts, ownership of a manuscript is not tantamount to the right to publish. By the common-law tradition and now by statute (effective January 1, 1978), the owner of a manuscript owns the physical object but not the intellectual content or the right to reproduce the manuscript for gain without the permission of the creator, unless the creator's copyright is in the public domain. However, it is possible, as a condition of access, to restrict publication of the content without your permission and/or without the copyright holder's permission.

Here are some practical points about the security of the collection. First, the person who seeks access should be able and willing to provide identification and state the purpose for which access is sought. It is advisable to verify this information, since the potential for theft or harm is always present. Collectors should decide and specify whether the scholar may see the original, photographic copies, or handwritten or typewritten transcripts. In cases where only one or two documents are sought, it may facilitate matters to mail a typed or handwritten copy, or in some cases, for reasons of security or preservation, a photographic or Xerox copy. Never send a manuscript through the mail unless it is registered. If you send anyone a copy, especially a photocopy, your control over the manuscript is lessened. To maintain the maximum control while permitting access, allow a scholar to read the item for substance, but without note-taking or quotation.

Even if you have the highest regard for the person consulting your collection, do not leave him alone with your collection, for manuscripts may tempt persons who are otherwise quite reliable. Naturally a precise inventory of your collection is a must. It is wise to have photocopies of your entire collection stored in a building separate from the originals. These admonitions may appear harsh or exacting, but owners of manuscripts must be mindful of the problems of physical security as well as of preservation, value, and a host of others. Perhaps collectors will find it more convenient to deposit their collections or photocopies of them in a library or institution that will administer the collection under mutually acceptable terms.

If you decide to provide a scholar with a photocopy of a manuscript, most unbound manuscripts of legal size or smaller can be reproduced satisfactorily on a Xerox or electrostatic copying machine of the type that is generally available in libraries and in some post offices. Avoid machines that draw the document to be copied inside, and use a machine that has a glass plate on which to place the manuscript for copying. If the manuscript is to be used as an illustration, a professional photographer should photograph it under careful supervision. More and more scholars are photographers capable of making an acceptable copy with high-speed film and hand-held camera without lights. Remember to supervise copying, for an enthusiastic scholar-photographer may be so eager to get the correct angle that he may temporarily forget to use proper precautions in handling the manuscript. The face of the photocopy, whatever its form, should have a statement of ownership such as "Reproduced from the collection of Andrew Jason Hoover, Statesville, N.C., December 24, 1976." If the scholar wishes to copy the document with his own camera, ask him to photograph a three-by-five-inch card bearing the ownership statement as he photographs each page of the document; the card can be laid over the edge of the document so that it does not obscure any of the writing, but so that it cannot be cut out of the print made from the negative. Scholars collect large numbers of photocopies in their work. If you wish to eliminate confusion over the source of the document, be sure it is clearly marked with all information necessary to identify it. The ideal statement is one that can be used as the citation in a published work. For reasons of security, some collectors choose to omit a specific address and provide only the state and the city.

For many collectors and manuscript curators, and for most scholars, one of the greatest pleasures is exploring the research avenues opened by a single manuscript to see how much can be uncovered about the people, the setting, and the incidents mentioned. The number of research possibilities opened by the investigation of a single letter can be extensive. An example of a historically inconsequential yet very human letter is one that Abraham Lincoln wrote, signed, and sent to Gideon Welles. The Library of Congress purchased it as the first acquisition of the Mearns Fund, established in honor of the retirement of David C. Mearns, a past president of the Manuscript Society and chief of the Manuscripts Division. John McDonough, manuscript historian in the division, explored and reported some of the aspects of this letter in his "Lincoln, Welles and the Public Service," in the *Quarterly Journal of the Library of Congress.** The letter reads as follows:

Executive Mansion
Washington, Aug. 2, 1862

Hon. Sec. of Navy
My dear Sir
Lieutenant Commanding [sic] James W. A. Nicholson, now commanding the Isaac Smith, wishes to be married, and from evidence now before me, I believe there is a young lady who sympathizes with him in that wish. Under these circumstances, please allow him the requisite leave of absence, if the public service can safely endure it.

Yours truly
A. Lincoln

Even a letter as short and straightforward as this brings with it a force and vitality that compels involvement. Who was this naval officer, James W. A. Nicholson? What was the history of his ship, the *Isaac Smith?* How did the president know that a young lady sympathized with

*John McDonough, "Lincoln, Welles, and the Public Service," in *Quarterly Journal of the Library of Congress,* 26, no. 4 (October 1969), 213–215.

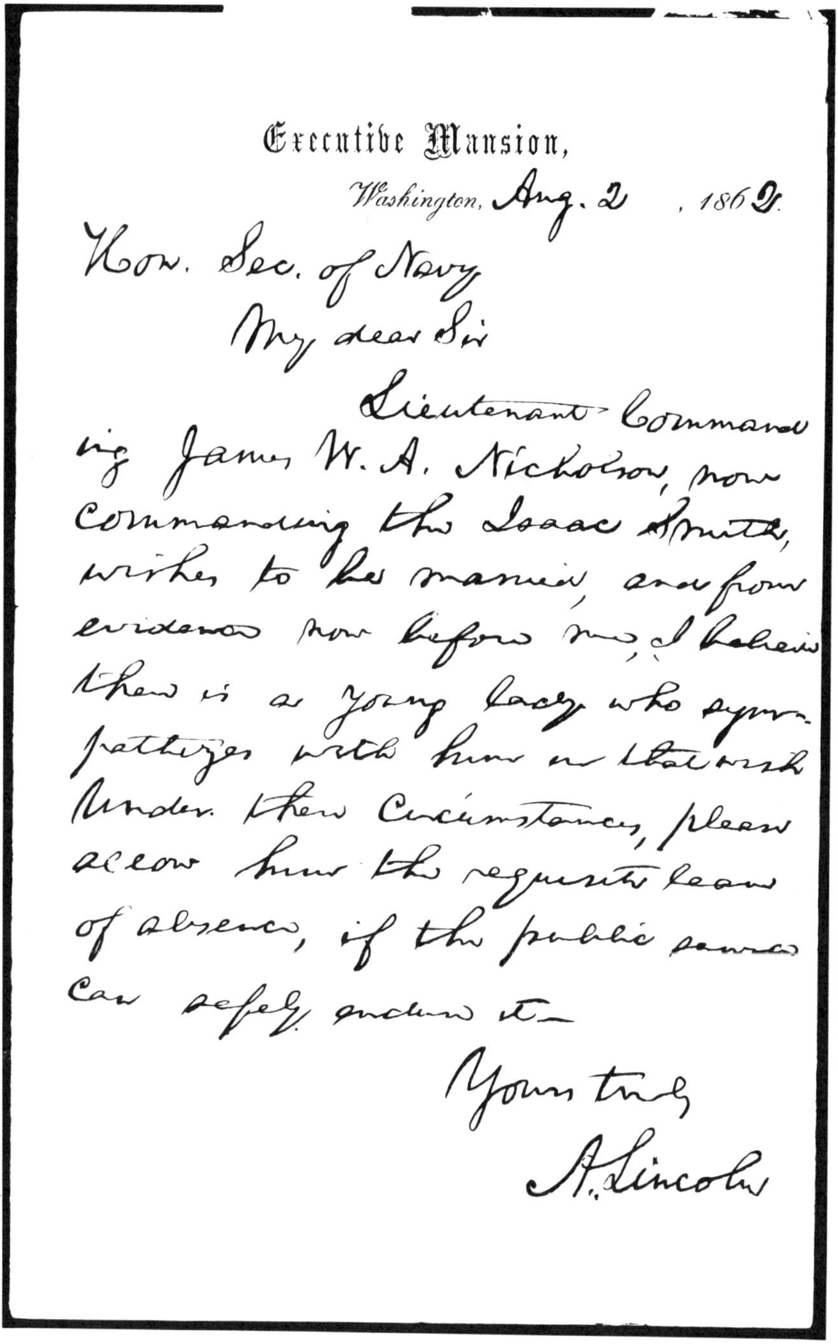

Executive Mansion,

Washington, Aug. 2, 1862.

Hon. Sec. of Navy

My dear Sir

Lieutenant Commanding James W. A. Nicholson, now commanding the Isaac Smith, wishes to be married, and from evidence now before me, I believe there is a young lady who sympathizes with him in that wish. Under these circumstances, please allow him the requisite leave of absence, if the public service can safely endure it—

Yours truly

A. Lincoln

The A.L.S. of Abraham Lincoln to Gideon Welles discussed in this article. Courtesy of the Library of Congress.

Nicholson's wish to be married? Did the young lady herself make a personal plea to the president? In addition to the problems of recruitment and emancipation, what were some of Lincoln's specific preoccupations on August 2? What was Secretary Gideon Welles concerned with on that day?

One question leads to others. Some can be answered and others cannot. From the brief entry in the *Dictionary of American Biography,* Nicholson can be identified as James William Augustus Nicholson (1821–1887), born in Dedham, Massachusetts, the son and grandson of American naval officers. He served as a young man with Matthew C. Perry, was in the African Squadron, and had been aboard the *Pocahontas* in the expedition for the relief of Fort Sumter. From the thirty-volume publication of the U.S. Navy Department, *Official Records of the Union and Confederate Navies,** we can determine that the *Isaac Smith,* Nicholson's first command, was in the New York Navy Yard for repair on August 2, having recently been at Port Royal, South Carolina. Nicholson's subsequent Civil War career included service in both the North Atlantic and South Atlantic blockading squadrons. He remained in naval service after the war, retiring as a rear admiral in 1883.

That Secretary Welles acceded to Lincoln's good-humored intercession is seen from his endorsement of the letter: "Leave granted the first opportunity G.W." A newspaper clipping pasted onto the letter relates: "Nicholson–Martin.—At Washington, D.C., on Wednesday, August 20, in St. John's church, by Rev. Dr. Pyne, Commander J. W. Nicholson, United States Navy, and Mary H. Martin, of St. Louis, Mos." The provenance of the letter is not known, but the small remains of glue along its top edge is evidence that it was once mounted in a scrapbook or volume. It was not previously recorded in the standard works, including *The Collected Works of Abraham Lincoln,* edited by Roy P. Basler,† and the consigner who forwarded it for sale was not identified.

These questions and many more could be answered through ingenious and diligent research. All of the information McDonough used in his article was found in published sources, the logical place to begin. For a novice at research, it is best to start at the local public library. Most towns, regardless of size, have a public library that is linked to a county, regional, or state library system. Through this network of cooperation, many resources will be available in the community. Before visiting the local library, make an appointment with the reference librarian to

** United States Navy Department, Official Records of the Union and Confederate Navies,* 30 vols. (Washington, D.C.: U.S. Government Printing Office, 1894–1922), 1st ser., vols. 12, 13, 21.

† Roy P. Basler, ed., *The Collected Works of Abraham Lincoln,* 9 vols. (New Brunswick, N.J.: Rutgers University Press, 1953–1955).

discuss the research. It is important to find a time when he can speak without constant interruption and can give full attention to your request. Ask the librarian to point out various reference works and their location in the building, and to recommend other possible resources in your area, such as a university library, a local historical society, a historical park, or a museum. *Directory of Historical Societies and Agencies in the United States and Canada* is published regularly by the American Association for State and Local History, and lists nearly five thousand historical organizations with the address, telephone number, names of officials, and information on membership, programs, publications, and staff. The *American Library Directory* provides information on holdings, services, and personnel in libraries in the United States and Canada. Both can be very useful tools in evaluating resources in your region.

Because most American collectors acquire American manuscripts with some historical connections, this brief discussion of bibliographies will be limited to American resources. Similar resources are available in almost any field of collecting. Three bibliographies that are widely available and cover a broad range of historical sources are *The Harvard Guide to American History, A Guide to the Study of the United States of America* and its *Supplement,* and *Writings on American History.** *The Harvard Guide* is a basic tool that includes valuable essays on research methods (of special interest are those on dating and transcribing manuscripts) and research materials, as well as extensive listings of books by period and subject. Its list of published biographies and local histories is especially useful. *A Guide to the Study of the United States of America,* prepared by staff members of the Library of Congress, is a selected, annotated bibliography describing nearly 6,500 works from various academic disciplines published before 1955 (the *Supplement* brings the coverage to 1965). The *Guide* is especially strong in American literature. *Writings on American History,* sponsored by the American Historical Association, is a comprehensive bibliography of works for study and research on United States history. Volumes were published for 1902–1903, 1906–1940, and 1948–1960. For the period 1962–1973, the American Historical Association published a four-volume bibliography, *Writings on American History: A Subject Bibliography* (1976), which includes chronological, geographical, subject, and author access. Beginning in 1974 the association published *Writings on American History 1973–74: A Subject Bibliography of*

*Frank B. Freidel and Richard K. Snowman, *The Harvard Guide to American History,* 2 vols. (Cambridge, Mass.: Belknap Press of Harvard University Press, 1974); Donald H. Mugridge and Blanche P. McCrum, *A Guide to the Study of the United States of America* (Washington, D.C.: U.S. Government Printing Office, 1960), and *Supplement, 1956–65,* Oliver H. Orr, Jr., ed. (Washington, D.C.: U.S. Government Printing Office, 1976); *Writings on American History,* 1902/1960 (Washington, D.C.: U.S. Government Printing Office, 1904/1972–).

Articles; subsequent annual volumes include completed dissertations in history. This bibliography lists about 3,800 articles drawn from the "Recently Published Articles" section of the *American Historical Review,* which, as of 1976, is a separately published list. The subject bibliography is organized in broad chronological periods and/or broad subjects with only an author index; however, each article can be listed under several subjects.

As illustrated by the Lincoln letter, research should begin with published works such as biographies, editions of an individual's writings, published government records, general histories, and local histories. In exploring the Lincoln letter, other questions might arise. Did Lincoln attend the wedding? If he did, it is not listed in *Lincoln Day by Day: A Chronology,* edited by Earl Schenck Miers.* The local newspaper could be examined for a list of guests. Was the wedding in St. John's Church on Lafayette Square or St. John's Church in Georgetown? This could be checked by verifying the names of the ministers in local church histories or in church records.

After exploring the printed sources, one could turn to unpublished manuscripts by identifying the locations of personal papers of the principals. The standard reference works do not list a collection of Nicholson's papers. There is no mention of papers in the article in the *Dictionary of American Biography* (*DAB*), Philip M. Hamer's *Guide to Manuscripts and Archives in the United States,*† or *The National Union Catalogue of Manuscript Collections* (volumes from 1959 to 1976). An examination of the repository guide to Nicholson's native state's historical society, the Massachusetts Historical Society, revealed no papers; and the *Naval Historical Foundation Manuscript Collection: A Catalog*‡ lists no papers. The *Index to the Abraham Lincoln Papers* in the Library of Congress indicates there is a letter from a James Nicholson on May 18, 1861; but from the content the writer can be identified as another person. The Gideon Welles diary and the papers in the Library of Congress could be examined for mention of Nicholson.

In addition to printed and manuscript sources, naval records at the National Archives could be examined, especially the file on naval officers and the pension file (for Nicholson's wife). The pension file would include information on the marriage and other family matters. The clipping indicated that the bride's name was Martin, but the *DAB* indicates

* Earl Schenck Miers, *Lincoln Day by Day: A Chronology,* 3 vols. (Washington, D.C.: U.S. Lincoln Sesquicentennial Commission, 1960).

† Philip M. Hamer, *Guide to Manuscripts and Archives in the United States* (New Haven, Conn.: Yale University Press, 1961).

‡ *Naval Historical Foundation Manuscript Collection: A Catalog* (Washington, D.C.: U.S. Government Printing Office, 1974).

her maiden name was Heap. Perhaps the pension file or a marriage record in a local government office or archive, or on file in the church, could clear up this point. Was she a Civil War widow who knew Lincoln? The records already mentioned might address this question.

In examining a manuscript, the physical object should not be overlooked. The torn places, traces of glue, fold marks, color, texture, and watermarks on the paper all provide clues to its past. The traces of glue on Lincoln's letter compel one to speculate on the provenance. We know only that it was purchased in February 1969 from Swann Galleries. Did Welles give the letter to Nicholson as a wedding gift? Did it then become a family treasure, glued in an album? Was it pilfered by a government clerk or saved from a dump by a trash man? Where was the letter from its writing at the White House on August 2, 1862, until it returned to Washington, to the Library of Congress, in February 1969?

Manuscripts can indeed be fascinating and offer intellectual challenge and intrigue. Fully identifying one's manuscripts can be among the most challenging and creative aspects of collecting. The search can lead the collector to various libraries and archives and acquaint one with a wide range of research materials. Using one's manuscript to learn more about the past will widen one's vistas and understanding, and can be one of the greatest joys and pleasures of collecting.

LEGAL RAMIFICATIONS OF MANUSCRIPT COLLECTING

LESLIE J. SCHREYER

As every collector knows, an autograph letter or manuscript, like a work of art, is simultaneously a piece of tangible property and an embodiment of its author's creative process, a reflection of his intellectual interests and concerns. This dual nature of the autograph, which forms the basis of its appeal to the collector, is acknowledged also by the law, which has formulated one set of rules to deal with the manuscript or letter as physical property, and another to deal with it as intellectual property.

As a general rule the private collector is likely to encounter practical problems only in the first area, which includes income and estate taxes and the rights of a purchaser of stolen, forged, or improperly described items. The scholar and the institutional collector are also faced with complex problems in the second area—namely, possible limitations on their right to publish, exhibit, or give access to the content of letters and manuscripts. This chapter first considers in very general terms some of the laws dealing with the physical property aspects of autographs, including in particular some tax planning considerations that may affect collectors, and then turns briefly to the restrictions applicable to use of the intellectual content of an autograph. Since this discussion is generalized and abbreviated, and speaks only as of the date of writing (January, 1977), readers should consult their own legal and tax advisers when confronted with specific questions.

FEDERAL INCOME TAX

The recent sharp rise in the value of autographs has made income and estate taxation an area of increasingly important concern to the collector, and proper tax planning can often produce substantial tax savings. With certain exceptions, the general federal income tax rule for private collectors who hold autographs for investment is that a sale of a letter or manuscript produces capital gain or capital loss, which will be short-term or long-term depending on how long the collector held the autograph. The Tax Reform Act of 1976 replaced the six-month holding period that had been the dividing line between short-term and long-term capital gain or loss with a longer period: nine months for sales during 1977 and one year for sales after 1977. Capital gain treatment is not available (and ordinary income is the general rule), however, if the seller of the letter or manuscript is its creator, the person for whom it was prepared, a person who acquired the letter or manuscript from either of the foregoing by gift or in various similar transactions, or certain other similar persons.

In recent years, as many collectors undoubtedly know, the advantageous tax treatment of capital gains has been substantially eroded. The federal income tax system has introduced the maximum tax on personal service income and the minimum tax on tax preference items, both of which are adversely affected by the presence of capital gains; and some states impose a higher tax rate on investment-type income than on so-called earned income. Accordingly, collectors wishing to dispose of autographs that have increased substantially in value might consider two possible alternatives to taxable sales: tax-free (or partly tax-free) exchanges and charitable contributions.

For the collector who plans to invest some or all of his sale proceeds in other autographs, a wholly or partly tax-free exchange may provide a particularly advantageous alternative to a taxable sale. Although most exchanges of property (for example, an exchange of a Lincoln letter for a Buick or for IBM stock) are taxed as if they were sales, special tax-deferral treatment is accorded to a collector's exchange of property held by him for investment solely for other property "of a like kind" that is also to be held for investment. While there is no precise definition of "like-kind" property, it would appear that all autographs and manuscripts are probably of like kind to each other. An exchange of a letter for a rare book, or even perhaps for a drawing, might also qualify, depending on the exact nature of the items involved. Instead of selling an autograph, paying capital gains tax, and having only the after-tax proceeds available for reinvestment, therefore, a collector who has already selected another autograph to purchase with the proceeds might instead consider an exchange. If the like-kind exchange is not an even one and the collector "trades up," paying some money in addition to his letter in order to receive a more valuable letter, he will still have tax-free treatment. If the collector "trades down," receiving not only like-kind property but also money or property other than like-kind property, he will have partially nontaxable treatment.

It is worth noting that with proper tax planning, a tax-free exchange can be accomplished by a collector even if the person who wishes to acquire his manuscript is not the owner of the autograph the collector wishes to acquire. For example, assume collector Lee owns a group of Confederate officials' letters that he bought several years ago for $3,000 and that is now worth $10,000. He now wishes to obtain from dealer Grant a group of Civil War letters worth $10,000, and plans to obtain the purchase money by selling the Confederate letters for that amount. Since dealer Grant wants only cash and is not interested in buying the Confederate letters, Lee plans to sell them to dealer Davis. If he follows this plan, Lee's $7,000 gain will be taxable. To defer the tax, however, Lee could arrange a tax-free exchange by asking dealer Davis to buy the Civil War letters from dealer Grant for $10,000, and then exchange those letters with Lee for the Confederate letters. All of the parties end up with the property they want (Lee gets the Civil War letters, Grant the cash, Davis the Confederate letters), but there is no taxable event for collector Lee until he disposes of the Civil War letters.

Because there are technical requirements to qualify for a tax-free exchange (especially a three-party exchange, as in the above example), and because in some circumstances tax-free treatment is not desirable as a tax goal, collectors should consult their tax advisers before entering into such an exchange. It should also be noted that dealers cannot obtain tax-free treatment in an exchange involving property they hold for sale in their business, but collectors can qualify regardless of whether the other exchanging party is a collector or a dealer.

As mentioned above, charitable contributions can, in some circumstances, provide a good tax alternative to a sale of letters or manuscripts. Although the Tax Reform Act of 1969 placed restrictions on the deductibility of charitable gifts of property that has appreciated in value, a gift of autographs by a collector to a tax-exempt charity (other than certain private foundations) still generates a deduction equal to the current value of the autographs, as long as the charity uses the donated property for one of the purposes giving rise to its tax exemption. A gift of autographs to a university or other tax-exempt rare book and manuscript library, therefore, will generally satisfy this requirement, unless there is an understanding or plan for the library to sell the donated item. This full deduction rule does not apply, however, to letters or manuscripts donated by their creator, by the person for whom they were prepared, by a person who acquired the letters or manuscripts from either of the foregoing by gift or similar transaction, or by certain other similar persons. A charitable gift by any of these classes of donors only generates a deduction equal to the tax cost of the letter in the donor's hands.

FEDERAL ESTATE TAX

The sweeping and much-publicized 1976 changes in the federal estate and gift tax structure have added greater complexity to an already difficult area. As in the past, the federal estate tax is imposed on the value of property owned by a decedent at the time of his death (and certain other property); and deductions continue to be available for bequests to charities. The most significant change in the estate tax law as it affects collectors, however, involves not the estate tax itself but the income tax payable when a person who receives an autograph by inheritance sells it. In the past a person who inherited property was treated, for income tax purposes, as if he had purchased the property for its value at the time of the decedent's death. This rule no longer applies to property inherited from persons dying after 1976, which will be considered to have a tax cost determined by reference to the cost of the property to the decedent, subject to certain exceptions and adjustments.

The principal adjustment is a partial "grandfather clause" applicable to appreciated property owned by a decedent both on December 31, 1976, and at the time of his death. Such property will be considered to have a tax cost in the hands of the heir equal to its supposed value on December 31, 1976, which must be computed, in the case of autographs, manuscripts, and other collector property, on the mandatory assumption that the property appreciated in value at an even rate during the period of the decedent's ownership. If collector Adams purchased a Jefferson letter in 1960 for $500 and it is worth $2,000 when Mr. Adams dies in 1980, for example, the December 31,1976, value of the letter is considered to be $1,700 (the $500 original cost plus 16/20 of the $1,500 appreciation). The letter will, therefore, as in the past, be included in Mr. Adams' estate for federal estate tax purposes at its full $2,000 date-of-death value; but the person who inherits the letter from Mr. Adams will be treated for income tax purposes as if he had purchased it for $1,700, subject to certain other adjustments. If he sells the letter at its value of $2,000, therefore, he will have a gain that will be subject to income tax.

In order to reap the benefits of this grandfather clause (which in the above example reduced the taxable gain to the heir from $1,500 to $300, in both cases subject to certain adjustments), it will be necessary for Mr. Adams' beneficiary to prove not only what Mr. Adams paid for the Jefferson letter but also the date Mr. Adams acquired it. It is important, therefore, that collectors maintain or reconstruct records of their pre-1977 purchases, and many attorneys are recommending that collectors prepare a December 31, 1976, inventory of their holdings.

The preceding discussion is an extremely generalized summary of an estate planning factor that collectors should consider. A more detailed discussion of estate planning for the collector is beyond the scope of this chapter; and collectors are advised to consult their attorneys in this regard, especially if they have not reexamined their estate plans in light of the 1976 changes in law.

STOLEN, FORGED, AND IMPROPERLY DESCRIBED AUTOGRAPHS

An informed collector purchasing property from a reputable dealer or auction house generally can have confidence that the material he buys is as described. Of course, the volume and prices of autograph material being offered on the market today make it inevitable that some stolen or forged letters, manuscripts, and documents find their way into the hands of even the knowledgeable and reputable dealer—and eventually the collector. The collector who later learns that an item he purchased is stolen, forged, or otherwise not as described by the seller is not without legal remedies. While state law is controlling as to the rights of a buyer—and, therefore, there are variations in the law in different jurisdictions—it is a legal maxim that a thief cannot pass title to a piece of property. In other words, if a stolen autograph subsequently turns up, the victim of the theft is entitled to recover the stolen autograph from the present owner, whoever that may be. This is so even though the present owner may have purchased it in total innocence, not from the thief but from, say, a dealer who acquired it from another dealer who in turn purchased it unknowingly from the thief. The innocent owner, although obliged to surrender the autograph, would generally be entitled to recover damages from the seller; and the same would be true down the line until the original purchaser from the thief, who would have to catch a solvent thief in order to obtain restitution.

With forged or improperly described items, the victim's rights are more circumscribed; and as a general rule the greatest protection for a collector is to purchase from a reputable and reliable seller. The rights of a buyer of an improperly described item (including a forged manuscript) depend on the law of the jurisdiction in question, usually the place of sale; and because laws vary from state to state and from country to country, only generalities can be discussed here. In most jurisdictions in the United States, a seller who describes a letter to his prospective purchaser as, for example, a "Washington letter" warrants that it is in fact just that; and if he is wrong, he is liable to the buyer for damages. Statutes of limitation restrict the period of time during which a buyer can institute a lawsuit to recover his damages (usually a few years), and the buyer generally has the burden of proof to establish that the item he purchased was not what it purported to be.

In general, the faster a purchaser discovers the problem, the more likely he is to have a legal remedy. Many dealers who sell by catalog or by mail, for example, permit a customer to return an item within a specified number of days without having to state a reason; and some of the principal autograph auction houses expressly guarantee the authenticity of items they auction for a set period of time. It is also important that a collector read and understand the "terms of sale" that appear in many catalogs, especially auction catalogs, and in invoices, for they sometimes restrict the purchaser's rights by disclaiming a warranty of authenticity or of proper description. Such disclaimers are not always effective under the applicable law, and a collector confronted with a recalcitrant seller should consult competent legal counsel.

Often of greater importance than the technicalities of the law in this area is the reputable dealer's pride in his good name, and an aggrieved collector would generally be well advised to talk to his seller before considering legal action. The dealer is often willing to return the buyer's money even if he is not required as a matter of law to do so.

THE CONTENT OF A LETTER OR MANUSCRIPT

When a collector—whether a person or an institution—acquires a letter or manuscript, he becomes the owner of a piece of physical property; but he does not thereby acquire the right to "publish" the content of the letter or manuscript. "Publication" for this purpose is a technical term of copyright law that is much broader than the ordinary nonlegal usage of that term.

Prior to legislation enacted in 1976, statutory copyright law did not apply to "unpublished" letters and manuscripts; and the right to control their "publication" remained, under the common law, in the author and his estate or heirs (or in transferees of this specific right). This "common-law copyright" did not lapse with a defined period of time, as does a statutory copyright; and questions arose as to whether a letter or manuscript was "published," which depended, among other things, on the author's intent. If a work was not "published" by the author (or his estate, heirs, or transferees), the issue became whether an intended use of a letter or manuscript—for example, exhibition of the item or reproduction in a catalog—constituted a prohibited "publication" of the letter or manuscript or was permissible under various legal doctrines.

After many years of consideration by Congress, the Copyright Revision Act was passed late in 1976; it transforms the former common-law copyright into a statutory right. In attempting to provide greater certainty as to the rights of the author, the legislation expands some aspects of the author's protection while contracting and limiting others. When the Copyright Revision Act becomes effective (generally on January 1, 1978), statutory copyright protection will apply to letters and manuscripts, whether "published" or "unpublished"; and the author (and his estate, heirs, or transferees of the copyright) will have the exclusive right to control reproduction of the work as well as certain types of "public display" of the work, subject to the doctrine of "fair use," which permits other persons to make "fair use" of the copyrighted work.

"Fair use" is a legal term appearing in copyright law that has received a vast amount of attention and definition by the courts. Some of the many factors determining whether the use made of a work is "fair use" (and hence permissible) include the purpose and character of the use (for instance, is it for commercial purposes or for nonprofit educational purposes?); the nature of the copyrighted work; the amount and substantiality of the portion used in relation to the copyrighted work as a whole; and the effect of the use on the potential market for or value of the copyrighted work. Libraries, archives, and educational institutions are given certain limited rights not available to other users, provided they comply with various statutory requirements.

The Copyright Revision Act preserves the distinction between "published" and "unpublished" works for some purposes, although much more limited ones than formerly. The provisions of the act are applicable, for example, beginning January 1, 1978, to all works whether or not then published; but the term of the copyright protection varies somewhat depending on whether or not a work was "published" on that date. Works created on or after January 1, 1978, are given statutory copyright protection for the author's life plus fifty years, while works created before 1978 but not yet published receive statutory copyright protection beginning January 1, 1978, and until the later of (a) the author's life plus fifty years or (b) December 31, 2002 (extendable to December 31, 2027). Works in the public domain before January 1, 1978, are not protected by the act. The concept of "publication" remains significant for various other purposes, among which are the marking of the work with a notice of copyright, the deposit of copies with the Copyright Office, and the types of remedies available to the copyright owner.

As can be seen from even this brief and very generalized description of the Copyright Revision Act, the general principle is continued that ownership of a letter or manuscript as a material object is distinct from ownership of the copyright in the work, the right to use its content. A rather entangled area of the law has actually become even more complex as a result of the legislation; and, as in the past, scholars and institutions will need the advice of copyright counsel when specific questions arise. Authors will continue to require permission to quote their letters and manuscripts, and scholars and institutions would be wise to consider the admonition of Robert Penn Warren: "As for my own letters or manuscripts, if anyone quotes anything whatsoever without my permission, I promise to sue him from hell to breakfast and back by slow freight if I can get a lawyer to take the case."

VALUES

MARY A. BENJAMIN

SOME YEARS AGO the famous collection of Lincolniana owned by Oliver Barrett came up for sale at public auction. Those attending the sale wondered why what seemed an uninteresting item sold for $350. It was a marriage certificate signed by Mordecai Lincoln, an uncle of the president, issued to A. Johson [*sic*] and Eliza McCardle. Shortly thereafter the same item was featured in a dealer's catalog at $850. The profit at first glance appeared somewhat excessive; but it soon became apparent that, if anything, the document was modestly priced. The obscure piece of Lincolniana was none other than the marriage license for the future seventeenth president of the United States and a seventeen-year-old schoolteacher. Andrew Johnson, a runaway tailor's apprentice, had never found time to learn his ABC's and could not even spell his name at the time of his marriage. His misspelled signature had not been identified by the cataloger nor by anyone else but the dealer and one private collector.

What, then, determines the price of an item in the autograph field? First and foremost, knowledge and experience—knowledge of authenticity, of supply and demand, of the significance of contents and date, of rarity, and of association value. The dealer must be experienced in all these areas. The private collector develops such knowledge over the years.

When one speaks of autographs, simple signatures unattached to a letter or document are not necessarily implied. The word "autograph" in the professional sense may be a fully handwritten letter, a dictated letter signed, an endorsement, a page of manuscript, or a document—in other words, anything that has writing on it, with or without a signature. Unlike stamps or books, every autograph is unique; and each one must be individually evaluated. Much depends on the knowledge of the appraiser in a variety of fields. Since it is impossible to be knowledgeable in all areas, dealers and collectors tend to specialize in the field that attracts them most. This very specialization often explains the difference in valuations placed on a given item by two individuals. The one who knows more about the subject will, in all probability, price the item higher than one who is not as familiar with background details.

Genuineness is of paramount importance, though even forgeries of autographs are collected, especially if they are by well-known forgers such as Robert Spring or Joseph Cosey. Forgeries have sold at public auction for surprisingly high prices. They are sought for purposes of comparison with authentic items and are occasionally placed on display by librarians as a warning to collectors. Forgeries are unfortunately plentiful, and many a collector has accidentally acquired one or more.

Despite the pessimists who gloomily forecast the end of the supply of autographs due to their gradual absorption by institutions or destruction by time and the elements, there is no reason to fear a shortage. Fine accumulations of important material are constantly coming on the market. Special anniversaries such as the bicentennial of the American Revolution or the centennial of the Civil War tend to flush out family collections long overlooked in attics and cellars. A new biography of some well-known individual will call forth a spate of his letters. True, the supply of material of the Elizabethan period, or of early American colonial times, is shrinking; but no one can deny that items of the American Revolution and later periods are still plentiful. Literary material regularly comes on the market, though letters of Edgar Allan Poe, Herman Melville, and Henry David Thoreau are admittedly scarce. In past years the contents of customhouses, storage warehouses, courthouses, and other government buildings were not infrequently discarded. In recent years institutions hard-pressed for funds have occasionally been known to dispose of portions of their holdings that have no bearing on their particular locality or region. By so doing, they earn money for the purchase of material more relevant to their particular interests.

However, family collections, often acquired directly by librarians, dealers, and auction houses, are, for the most part, the chief source of supply for the collector. Most librarians, when consulted, if not interested for their own institutions, will refer parties to dealers who are members of the Antiquarian Booksellers Association of America. In recent years, with rare books becoming more difficult to secure, rare book dealers have entered the autograph field. At times antique stores and stamp dealers will offer items but, understandably, their ability to guarantee the authenticity or correctly evaluate what they handle is not as reliable as that of the specialist dealer. *Caveat emptor* must be considered when purchasing items from such sources.

On the whole, values are fairly standard; and it may come as a surprise to see how closely letters of equal merit, say of a Ralph Waldo Emerson or a Daniel Webster, are priced by different dealers. Dealers do not pick prices out of the sky, as some would seem to think. A somewhat general rule of thumb may be said to exist. Supposing that the items in question average about the same in content, the rule is as follows: If an A.L.S. is valued at $100, an A.D.S. would be priced at $75, an L.S. at $50, a D.S. at $25, and a signature at $10. But here the rule stops, and various factors enter the picture. One specific point must be remembered: the age of an item has little bearing on its value. Many a land deed or legal document dated in the 1700's is not worth more than $10 to $20. What is considered old varies between the United States and abroad. In the United States items are not considered old unless they date back to the early seventeenth century, while in Europe one hardly considers anything old that is dated after the fourteenth century.

There is no doubt that material of good content commands the highest prices. It must, however, be realized that there is a difference between historic value and monetary value. An item that has interest for scholars may have no monetary value, and vice versa. A simple signature of Thomas Lynch, Jr., the South Carolina Signer of the Declaration of Independence, is so rare that it carries a high price tag; yet it provides no biographical information. Few librarians would consider using their limited funds to acquire one, but a private collector must have it to complete his set of the Signers. On the other hand, a letter of a little-known person may fetch a high price because of the contents. Such a case some years ago was that of a letter of Elizabeth Dixon, wife of the United States senator from Connecticut, James Dixon. Mrs. Dixon's letters normally are totally unsalable, and at public auction would be lumped together with other material or added to a dealer's grab-bag lots. This particular letter, however, gave a play-by-play description of President Lincoln's last hours in the Peterson House on the night of April 14, 1865, and of Mrs. Lincoln's agonized behavior. Mrs. Dixon had chosen not to attend the performance of *Our American Cousin* that fateful night and had remained at home. A frenzied call for help from the theater caused her to rush to the side of the president's wife, to stand by and give comfort. The letter sold many years ago for $500. Today it would be worth many times that sum.

Again, the correspondence of a governor may have historic interest as a whole but little monetary value. This is because his retained papers consist of carbons of his own correspondence and a multitude of invitations, newspaper clippings, and letters of minor politicians, senators, congressmen, bankers, and others. The contents of such a correspondence may afford an excellent picture of the times, possibly of a man's campaigns for higher office; but individual items of this type are not collected. If offered at all, they appear in large lots sold at auction and fetch minimal amounts. The correspondence undoubtedly has interest for the student, but no monetary value for the collector. A reputable dealer will hesitate to undertake the appraisal of such a correspondence, for he cannot back his valuations with any known records.

Autograph collecting has attracted persons of culture the world over. Collectors are of two kinds: those with small budgets and those with some means. The former are, for the most part, forced to limit themselves to simple, inexpensive examples. What they collect nevertheless enriches them, for each name added to their collections and researched will increase their knowledge of history, literature, and the arts.

The more affluent collector, whatever his financial bracket, is able to be more selective. Above all he wants his purchases to be meaty and informative. The holdings of such a person often form the basis of new biographies and other scholarly works. He collects the records of the past, records without which much valuable information would never come to light. All the items collected by him are not necessarily high-priced. Some years ago a fascinating article appeared in a Harvard publication based on a letter listed by a dealer at $1. No one had ordered it, since the writer had no great standing. But the collector who acquired it appreciated the significance of the contents and had no trouble placing an article based on it in a scholarly magazine.

DATES, SUBJECT MATTER, AND SIGNATURES

The specialist collector or librarian does not place too much stress on dates, providing the contents of an item are good. On the other hand, the nonspecialist collector, seeking to own a single item of a given president, for example, strives to secure one of the presidential period. A Civil War buff prefers a letter of a general written during the war rather than one written before or after. The letter of a Signer of the Declaration of Independence written in 1776 will command a far higher price than his letter written in 1768 or 1794, or even in 1777 or 1779. In the field of the American Revolution, 1776 is the "magic" date.

The collector of musical items is equally discriminating. He prefers a letter of a composer mentioning one of his compositions to a letter of a social nature. Signed bars of music strongly appeal to him and command good prices. For him, too, there is another requirement—an appreciation and understanding of the merits of a specific composition in contrast with other works of the same composer. Some years ago an original composition for the piano by Richard Wagner came on the market. Collectors refused to consider it. Those seeking an example of the noted composer stated that Wagner was known chiefly for his operas, not for his piano compositions, of which he had written only four. They preferred having an unsigned page of one of his operas to the fully handwritten and signed piano composition. The item, on which the price was necessarily held low, was finally sold in Europe. The significance of a composer's work therefore enters the picture for a proper evaluation.

Collectors generally want the letters of the individuals they collect to discuss their own subjects. Benjamin Rush sells more readily if he speaks of medical matters or writes about the progress of the American cause during the Revolution. A letter of Sir Arthur Conan Doyle discussing one of his Sherlock Holmes stories will command a far higher price than one mentioning his psychic experiences.

Undoubtedly the most valuable material one can find is original manuscripts of authors, scientists, composers, and poets. Such originals or working copies, as they are called, fetch very high prices. Though copies of stanzas of well-known poets, signed by them, are in considerable demand and sell readily, the original manuscript, which may carry corrections and deletions, even though unsigned, will bring a much higher price than the "fair" copy signed. Collectors tend to prefer the signed copies to the unsigned originals, but the librarian who seeks unpublished material will unhesitatingly express a preference for the unsigned original.

The manner in which letters are signed affects valuations. Most collectors want their acquisitions signed in full, preferably not with initials or first names only. In recent years, however, the custom of signing first names only has become quite common. In other days such familiarity was anathema. As recently as the Civil War period, husbands writing to their wives invariably signed their names in full; and it would have been the exceptional wife who would have addressed or written to her husband by his first name. Attitudes are changing, however, and collectors are becoming reconciled to the new informality. Letters by President Eisenhower signed "D.E." or "Ike" have fetched good prices at auction, as have letters of presidents Lyndon B. Johnson and Harry S. Truman signed with their first names.

Other practices existed in earlier centuries. Louis XVI, Mme de Maintenon, and Mme de Staël, to name three, quite regularly wrote letters that they either did not sign at all or to which they simply appended their paraph, a flourish used instead of a signature. The paraph, according to Webster, may have been intended as a safeguard against forgery. Each writer had his own paraph that never varied.

It was also customary to write in the third person. Such letters read: "Th. Jefferson requests the pleasure . . ." or "Mr. Smith begs to be excused. . . ." Queen Victoria as often as not signed her letters "V.R.I." (Victoria Regina Imperatrix) or wrote third person letters: "The Queen wd. merely observe that she does not wish her two Nephews to be upon the same Ship. . . ." All such variations from the normal way of signing letters are apt to cause a lower estimate unless the contents are particularly good.

Still another factor affecting valuations is the medium used. A letter written in ink will often command a higher price than an equally good letter written in pencil, despite the fact that ink will fade if not properly protected and pencil, though it may get smudged if carelessly handled, will not fade.

RARITY

The rarity of letters may or may not affect valuations. There may be a very few autographs of a given person available; but if there is no demand for them, prices will remain low. On the other hand, if the supply is plentiful but the demand strong, prices will be high. Supply and demand go hand in hand, and cannot be separated. Letters of Mozart, Mary Queen of Scots, and Martin Luther are in great demand but small supply. Their many admirers fight eagerly to acquire them, and high prices result. Similarly, prices for signatures of the presidents tend to be quite out of proportion to letters of these same men. Being far less expensive than letters, there is a greater demand among collectors for them; but the supply is far from commensurate. Some collectors making up a set limit themselves to signatures of presidential date and, where possible, on Executive Mansion or White House cards. The result is that a White House card signature may fetch as much as or more than a nonpresidential letter. Complete sets of the presidents, consisting of letters and documents, may be formed at any time; but to complete a set of signatures only may take years, since some of them are quite scarce. Recipients of letters treasured them and wisely refrained from cutting off the signatures.

A depressed economy will, of course, affect valuations adversely even in times of great rarity. In the boom times of the 1920's a Roger Williams A.L.S. sold for $7,350 and an A.D.S. for $950. In 1934, during the Great Depression, an equally good A.L.S. fetched only $3,000; and in 1940 another A.L.S. went for $400. The original 1920's prices will unquestionably be topped in the present inflationary market. In the early 1930's a Mozart letter could be secured for a few hundred dollars. In December 1975 a letter sold at auction in Germany for $17,500. And because of rarity, prices on such items may be expected to reach new heights in the years to come.

There is another type of scarcity that must be considered with caution. This is the scarcity on the market of letters of living persons who are in the limelight, in part due to the introduction of machine and secretarial signatures. Prominent statesmen have little time to attend to their immense correspondence, and turn with relief to the use of the Autopen or to clerical help in signing their letters. The resulting shortage of authentically signed letters pushes prices upward. In addition, most owners of letters of prominent persons hesitate to place them on the market even though the demand for them is strong. They are, perhaps, ashamed to have the writer know that they have sold his letters. Or there may be a touch of reflected glory in retaining them and boasting of them. Yet, the demand being strong, prices at the time will be high. However, when the writer of these same letters dies, owners have no hesitation in offering the material for sale. Other owners may think along the same lines, with the result that what was once rare becomes common and, if the demand has weakened, prices plummet.

Fads in collecting will also run prices up. There may be a run on autographs of popular baseball players or a movie star. In the same way a major event may cause prices of available material bearing on the event to skyrocket. Such was the case with letters of those connected with the Watergate scandal. The letters of any man who becomes president are immediately in demand. The many collectors of presidential sets require an example. This was true of President Kennedy. Shortly after his death his letters climbed to new highs, as did those of Mrs. Kennedy, whose letters until then had had only nominal value. Mrs. Kennedy's conduct at the time of the tragedy aroused much admiration; and when, shortly after the assassination, a letter of hers dated when her husband was a senator appeared at auction, it fetched the extraordinary price of $3,000. The contents of the letter in no way warranted the price, but sentiment entered the picture and the buyer felt that no price was too high. Few of Mrs. Kennedy's letters had, up to that time, been offered. With the passing of the years, and perhaps due to her remarriage, some of the glamour attached to her name has worn off. Those of her letters that have appeared on the market have tumbled in price. A recent six-page A.L.S. sold in June 1976 for $150. It is not unlikely that her letters, aside from those written during the White House years, will go even lower, for she is still young and may have a long life ahead in which to correspond. Her letters written prior to the presidential years and during those brief two years at the White House will always command higher prices than those written after November 22, 1963.

Letters of the wives of many of our presidents are, with a few exceptions, very common and fetch nominal sums unless written from the White House. They have a slightly higher value if of the presidential period.

In recent years the market has been flooded with letters of both the Roosevelts—Franklin D. and Theodore—with a resultant lowering of prices. These prices will, however, start climbing once the material has been absorbed. A collector who paid a stiff price for a letter when it was scarce, and suddenly discovers values slumping, may feel that the dealer has treated him unfairly. He may even suspect fraud. He forgets that the dealer, who may have a number of Roosevelt items in his stock, will himself be suffering an even greater loss. The dealer is forced to lower his prices to reflect current market values, and forfeits profit on his holdings.

Handwritten letters of prominent persons of today are far scarcer than the typewritten or dictated ones. Such persons rarely have time to write longhand, and prices for A.Ls.S. are very much higher than for dictated ones. Yet a good dictated L.S. may at times far exceed in value a handwritten letter of minor content.

The early letters of well-known men are always rarer than those written during the period of their fame. Letters of young people are seldom kept, but those of the famous are treasured. Yet, despite the rarity of the earlier letters, they will not necessarily be priced higher than the later ones of more significant date.

LENGTH

In the early days of collecting, the length of a letter was of no consequence; but as interest in autographs became more widespread, it became popular to display or frame them. This development caused single-page letters, or letters written on the first and third sides of a double lettersheet, which can be separated without damage to the letter, to be in considerable demand. A two-page letter, written on both sides of one sheet, must be framed in double glass. Or, if it is displayed, only one side can be shown. Since most letters with good contents run over one page in length, good single-page letters are accordingly priced perhaps 25 percent to 50 percent higher than the longer ones of equal merit.

CONDITION

Condition is an important factor for many collectors. A letter in poor condition is less salable, and must be priced accordingly. Collectors often fail to realize, however, that some aging must be expected. Letters are repeatedly handled, folded, and unfolded over the years. A letter that is old may well have minor defects, such as light stains, fraying, or occasional breaks at folds. Also, depending on where the letters have been stored, they may suffer from having been exposed to excessive moisture or dryness. Fortunately there are excellent repairers of old letters, and most minor defects may be corrected at no great cost; however, all such defects should be noted in cataloging. Librarians do not worry too much about condition, providing the writing is legible, since content is of greatest importance to them. Regrettably, there is no known method of permanently restoring ink that has faded. But it is a fatal error for a collector to attempt to darken the writing of a faded letter by retracing it. By doing so he perpetrates a forgery, and the item becomes unsalable. There are, for the librarian, scientific methods by which faded writing may be deciphered; but this does not interest the collector, who usually shuns a badly faded item.

ASSOCIATION VALUE

The prominence of the addressee will raise the value of a letter to a considerable extent. The letter of a famous scientist, for example, written to another scientist of note on scientific matters, will be far more valuable than a letter written to his tailor about a suit of clothes or one to his brother on family matters. The records show that letters of one president to another, or even referring to another, or of an author or composer to his publisher, or of an artist to his dealer, will enhance the value. Absence of the addressee's name, on the other hand, will detract somewhat from the value of the letter.

AUCTIONS

As mentioned above, dealers and auctions are the main sources of autographs for collectors. Auction houses differ from dealers in their approach to evaluation and guarantee. Many auction houses attach lists of tentative appraisals of value to their offerings. These, if accurate, are very helpful; but often they are not so, being either far too high or too low. True, no one can really predict what an item will bring, but there are printed records that may be consulted as to previous prices realized. The most important one is *American Book Prices Current,* published yearly, which contains a section on autograph auctions. Many a private collector, attending a sale or sending in his bid directly to the auctioneer, on whose estimate he has based it, ends up sadly disappointed. The valuation suggested was far too low. One auctioneer claims that if a high appraisal is printed, collectors are frightened away and do not bid. Others have been known to overappraise items in the hope of inducing higher bids. While this may be good business for the auction house, the collector who has trusted the appraisal may find himself acquiring an item on which he is unlikely to recoup what he paid.

Auctions are affected by a variety of circumstances that cause prices to fluctuate widely: weather conditions, the attendance, and the overall quality of the material offered for sale. The current economic situation of the country or of the individual will temper the bidding. Actually, prices realized at auctions depend entirely on the presence and the whim of those attending the sales. Under no circumstances can they be considered an accurate record of market value. It has frequently happened that a certain letter will sell at one price on one occasion and, when resold a year or two later, will go for either half that amount or double it. The dealer is aware of these facts. In appraising letters he must consider not only the rarity of what comes on the market in his own country, but also what supply of similar items exists abroad. He can hardly charge a high price for an item that sells reasonably in Europe.

APPRAISALS

The appraising of autograph material is by no means an easy matter. Estate appraisals are required, as are appraisals for insurance purposes. Collectors often donate their collections to institutions during their lifetimes for tax deductions. The government is interested in knowing that the appraisal is a correct one and that material is not overestimated. No dealer wishes to be challenged on this score. Insurance companies also have a great interest in proper valuations, especially if they must make good on a loss. Normally, material owned by a collector is appraised for insurance purposes at its replacement value. If the insurance is solicited at the time of purchase, the bill of sale is proof of value. It should be noted, especially in an inflationary period, that a collection should be reappraised for insurance purposes at intervals of five to ten years.

For estate purposes, auction records are often used. However, approximately 40 percent of the sale prices should be discounted; current auction charges run 10 to 30 percent. To these charges must be added insurance and incidental costs, and possibly charges for reproductions in the catalog.

AUTOGRAPHS AS INVESTMENTS

Perhaps a word is in order on the subject of investment in autographs. "Investment" is a dangerous word. Though the records show that prices have zigzagged up and down over the years, with the high always higher than the last high and the low always higher than the last low, the fact remains that though a collector may profit on what he sells, he may also suffer a considerable loss. He who buys primarily to invest and who is not familiar with price fluctuations may find himself obliged to sell unexpectedly, sooner than he had planned. Family problems, an operation or illness, or some other catastrophe may force him to raise money at short notice. His outlet is one of two—the dealer or the auction house—and the chances are that he will secure less than what he originally paid. The average dealer, as has been said, pays only about 50 percent of what he hopes to get at retail. However, on items for which he has a ready market he will consider a lower margin of profit. Should the owner sell at auction, the results are uncertain. Collectors who hold on to what they buy for ten or more years almost invariably see their acquisitions increase in value, in addition to having the pleasure of ownership that their purchases have afforded them.

CONCLUSION

It is obvious that there is much more than is generally realized to the fair evaluation of autographs. What has been written here could be called the basics, but there are many more points of which the collector must have knowledge. In the long run, it is not dealers who set prices, but collectors themselves. The infinite variety of their tastes and interests brings pressure on the market and determines valuations. Understandably, each country will, in all likelihood, value its own greats more than those of other countries. Germany, for example, holds in high esteem the works of Beethoven, Goethe, Johann C. F. von Schiller, Heinrich Heine, Arthur Schopenhauer, and Immanuel Kant. France treasures the writings of Jean Baptiste Molière, Jean Racine, Blaise Pascal, François M. A. de Voltaire, and, especially, Napoleon I. Similarly, England, Italy, and Spain hold precious examples of their outstanding men and women.

Certain areas of collecting are more popular than others and command higher prices. Music, for example, is the international language; letters of the great composers, violinists, and opera singers are competed for the world over, and are on an ever-increasing spiral of demand. Letters of the great painters and artists of all countries are on a rising market. Those of Paul Gauguin, Paul Cézanne, Pierre Auguste Renoir, Pablo Picasso, Sir Joshua Reynolds, Gilbert Stuart, and others command very high prices. In recent years Nazi material has increased tremendously in value. All items bearing on the history of slavery in the United States and the emancipation and gradual assimilation of blacks have found many collectors seeking letters of Frederick Douglass, George Washington Carver, and Booker T. Washington. Other specialties include whaling, Alaska, medicine, and photography. The horizons are limitless. Catalogs will feature material along all these lines and, as he progresses in building his collection, the collector will gradually develop an awareness of values that will guide and safeguard his pursuit.

THE MARKET FOR AUTOGRAPHS: THE EUROPEAN SCENE

MICHEL CASTAING*

VERY OFTEN, people who are not familiar with the collecting of autographs ask me, "How do you determine the value of an autograph? After all, isn't the decision yours in the end?"

This is true to a certain extent, because it is impossible to establish a price list, as is done for stamps or books, for which the physical aspects are the sole factor influencing their worth.

However, a certain classification is established through auctions taking place all over the world, and according to catalog prices of French and foreign dealers as well. The standards of scarcity are indicated by this mean classification, which also gives the dealers an indication of the average price, for instance, of a letter from Alphonse de Lamartine (quite common), Honoré de Balzac (slightly less common), Arthur Rimbaud (rare), or Isidore Ducasse de Lautréamont (very scarce), to cite only relatively recent French authors.

Thus, the dealer's free choice in determining the value of an autograph plays a limited part and depends chiefly upon his intelligent evaluation with respect to the interest of the text. An easy illustration of this fact would be that the few lines Napoleon I wrote in the margin of an administrative report can be bought for less than $200, whereas a love letter to Josephine (the last one was sold in Vienna in 1975) was sold for more than $4,000 (a reasonable price).

Another recent example is that of the numerous and uninteresting letters of Charles de Gaulle, which are appearing on the market everywhere and are hardly worth more than $50, whereas the few pages that form the first draft of the appeal of June 18, 1940 (in which de Gaulle urged the French people to resist the Germans, even though the Pétain

*Translated from the author's French by Christine Guyonneau Crowley.

government had surrendered), considered a unique historical document, reached more than $200,000 in 1977.

Those two striking examples aside, the range of evaluation is affected by a certain perspicacity as well as a good knowledge of the life and works of both prominent and lesser figures in literature, the sciences, the arts, and other areas.

Thus, the degree of scarcity and the interest of the text are two essential considerations in determining the commercial value of an autograph.

Besides these factors, intermittent and unexpected influences, such as fashion or a specific event, play an important role. This was the case on the hundredth anniversary of Charles Baudelaire's death—or, even more recently, on the 150th anniversary of Louis Pasteur's birth. The last few years have witnessed a great demand for musical works, especially outside France. The law of supply and demand also regulates the transactions involving such collectors' items.

The European autograph market now revolves about three main centers of public auctions that are regarded as dependable sources of information on prices: Paris, with its eight to ten auctions a year at the Hôtel Drouot; Marburg, Germany, with the two important auctions organized by the excellent Mecklenburg; and London, where in 1975 Sotheby offered more than ten auctions including documents and autographs. Some auctions for autographs and for books also take place in Switzerland and in Belgium, but irregularly.

The general trend is identical in those three places. Whatever the area—be it music, the sciences, the arts, or history—documents of universal interest are most in demand. Certain items, such as autographs of famous musicians, have maintained a constant value, taking the depreciation of currency into consideration.

It is also obvious that national documents have a better commercial value in their country of origin, although the market for autographs has shown a tendency to become international. Today most clients place their bids directly at the centers mentioned above or through agents.

The international character of the autograph market is indicative of an increased interest in this type of collecting. In the last few years prominent French figures have become fascinated with autographs and manuscripts, thus influencing the purchase of documents by public organizations.

I will add a minor bit of history: when Valéry Giscard d'Estaing visited the Soviet Union, his gift to Leonid Brezhnev was a marvelous letter signed by Leo Tolstoy.

ETHICS

JOHN F. REED

ETHICS are moral standards by which human endeavors should be governed for the best interest of those endeavors. There are certain basic rules, such as honesty, that apply to all aspects of this governance, while other particular rules apply to specific subjects, such as dealing in and collecting manuscripts—which is the subject of this essay. Although certain discretions (such as refraining from exposing specific modern unethical occurrences and names connected with them, which is not the purpose of this essay) must be exercised in writing of dealing in and collecting autographs and manuscripts, no adverse issues in general should be evaded or softened. The basic rules should be strictly adhered to; slighting or breaking them may result in threatened or actual loss of reputation by the guilty. Although parts of this chapter will be accepted without cavil or argument, parts may be controversial. Anyone writing on the subject of ethics can be open to criticism, since different ideas can be maintained about identical things.

This chapter is based on positive rather than on negative ideas, but negative exceptions to accepted rules occasionally must be noted. Manuscripts have been stolen, destroyed, illegally copied, illegally (even wittingly) purchased and sold, and subjected to less scandalous acts. However, the aim of this chapter is to accentuate and explain the positive rather than the negative. The negative can be taken for granted as inadmissible, as the opposite of ethical. In all fields of human endeavor, knowledge of acceptable practices and a respect for veracity, if learned early, should become habitual; faulty knowledge, erroneous practices, and aversion to truth can become dangerous and destructive.

The manuscript trade is an interaction of various interested persons: collectors, auctioneers, archivists, librarians, researchers, dealers and other vendors, and appraisers. This interaction must be based throughout on mutual trust, since all these persons have mutual obligations to each other, whether direct or indirect. The same ethical behavior governs all, whether collector vis-à-vis collector, collector and dealer, collector and auction house, or some other relationship.

Basic to the trade is ownership of the manuscript. All rights to ownership of manuscripts are vested in the legal owner with the exception of the right of first publication, which remains with the writer and his legal heirs in many cases.* A legal owner can be defined as a person or institution—whether dealer, collector, investor, archives, or library—that purchases manuscript material at an honest sale, obtaining clear title to the material, or who receives such material by gift or inheritance, again with satisfactory title. In the instance of sale/purchase, a doubtful title should be investigated by the vendor, not by the purchaser, unless doubt is discovered by the purchaser subsequent to the transaction. When a purchaser learns some fact that clouds his title to a manuscript, he should inform the vendor at once. Within a time limit honorably set at the vendor's discretion, the vendor should accept return of the material. A prospective purchaser should not attempt to acquire material when any doubt of flawless title is entertained, and a vendor is morally obligated to inform a prospective customer of any such doubt.

In purchasing, although the age-old theory of *caveat emptor* may possibly hold true under certain remote circumstances (such as carelessness by the purchaser rather than his ignorance), the vendor should nevertheless exhibit at all times the honesty expected of him. If he does not, and a trespass on honesty is publicly exposed, the vendor risks perpetual ostracism by the trade; once a reputation is lost, it cannot easily, if ever, be recovered. Honesty, however, is a two-way proposition: the purchaser is also obligated to establish and sustain his credibility. Payment for purchased material should be made promptly unless otherwise arranged with the vendor. Material received on approval and rejected should be returned speedily to the vendor in the exact condition in which it was received, carefully wrapped and protected from injury in the mails.

Although the owner of manuscripts has the legal right to destroy or alter them at his discretion, if the manuscripts are historically important, he has a moral obligation not to do so. The occasional practice of some dealers and collectors of detaching from a letter a franked address leaf in order to sell it separately is most reprehensible. Often this address leaf is the sole indication of the recipient of the letter; and once the leaves are separated, the recipient may never be known thereafter. It

* The complicated problem of who controls the right to publish the words on a letter or document, or excerpts from them, is dealt with in the chapter "Legal Ramifications of Manuscript Collecting" in this book.

is neither ethical nor unethical, being a matter of judgment (though in many cases perhaps to be censured), to separate any groups of manuscripts that belong or seem to belong together. Archivists consider such separation unprofessional.

If certain manuscripts may prove of an embarrassing nature to living persons, whether the writer or the recipient or the family, descendants, or friends of either, the fate of those manuscripts, especially when they are historically important, should not be destruction, excision, or alteration, but impoundment for a defined period. This holds true especially for material donated to a public archives.

A public archives, whether federal, state, or other, cannot seize or confiscate a private manuscript unless theft from its custody is proven to the satisfaction of a court when the private owner legally resists such seizure. Two such attempts by government agencies have been defeated in the courts in recent years because the public origin of the material could not be proved. Of course, if theft can be proven, then the material obviously must be returned to the archives.*

A purchaser should be particularly cautious about buying any letter or document that may have been held in a public archives unless the manuscript is accompanied by a release from that archives. When a dealer is involved in a transaction that results in a buyer's having to return unwittingly purchased stolen property to an archives, the dealer should, within a reasonable time after the sale, make some mutually satisfactory arrangement with the buyer to assume some or all of the monetary loss to the buyer. However, an extended period of time between the date of purchase from the dealer and the discovery by the purchaser that the material was stolen may well absolve the dealer from any responsibility. Proof of theft from a public archives, as with any legitimate owner, is the burden of the archives and not that of the present apparent owner.

Public archives should, and often do, indelibly mark (sometimes in code) their manuscripts for easy recognition of their legal ownership. If properly done, such marking does not damage the contents and appearance of the material. Since no future sale of the material is contemplated at the time of acquisition, this marking system is quite ethical. Material released by an archives as superfluous or duplicate property should be equally prominently, though not obtrusively, marked as such, to avoid

*In 1977 the state of North Carolina established a very important and controversial precedent when its supreme court upheld the right of the state to seize at any time public documents that have strayed from official custody. It held that the state did not have to prove continuous custody of the documents but only that they were created on the public business and that they had never officially been discarded. North Carolina dealer B. C. West was forced to turn over to the state two American revolutionary period documents that had not been in official custody in many years.

any taint of theft. Unfortunately, some private collectors also place identifying marks on their manuscripts as protective devices. In so doing they have often been careless of the manner in which the identification is executed, thereby damaging the appearance of the manuscripts. Such private marking, when carelessly done, surely may border on the unethical, since it may in measure lessen the value of the manuscripts for future vendors and purchasers even though it assists in partially establishing the provenance of these manuscripts.

Theft of manuscripts, as any theft, is certainly not to be condoned; and he who may harbor knowledge of a theft and does not demand surrender of the material by the thief to the legitimate owner, threatening public exposure of the thief if the material is not instantly returned, is morally as guilty as the thief, and also in violation of the law. If private threat of exposure is not effective, public exposure should be implemented immediately, including notification of the proper authorities.

There have been instances in which dealers have unwittingly purchased stolen manuscripts. Extreme care must be exercised by dealers to ascertain an untainted provenance of their purchases, especially when material is offered by strangers or when a suspicion of illegitimate provenance is present. Collectors, librarians, and archivists, when buying privately from other than reputable dealers, should exercise even more caution, since most of them have less practice than dealers in negotiating with people they do not know. The natural acquisitive enthusiasm of collectors should always be tempered with reason. Both dealers and collectors are liable to prosecution as purchasers of stolen property, an accusation that can present considerable trouble to the accused.

Experienced dealers need not be cautioned concerning the accepted practices of the trade, but novice dealers should be warned of some of the ramifications and possible pitfalls. A dealer certainly should endeavor, to the best of his ability, to guarantee the authenticity of his sales material. No dealer, whatever his experience, is infallible; and, if proved in error, he should readily admit it and endeavor to rectify that error to the satisfaction of the customer. If there is some doubt concerning authenticity, but absolute proof is lacking, the prospective purchaser should be informed. Once a sale has been consummated and the authenticity subsequently questioned, the dealer will expect the buyer to submit proof of his allegations before he will cancel the sale.

One complaint voiced by some dealers concerns the practice of some manuscript owners who "shop around" among dealers in an effort to gain a larger sale price from one dealer at the expense of others. This "system" consists of offering material to an initial dealer in the expectation of acquiring a free appraisal; then, upon receiving that appraisal, the offer of sale is withdrawn, ostensibly through indecision whether or not to sell. Thereafter, the same material is offered to a second dealer. The second offer is often accompanied by a statement that the vendor has already been offered a certain price, or if a price is first offered by the second dealer, the vendor states that a better price has already been offered. He hopes that the second dealer will offer more in either case, and perhaps subsequently contacted dealers even more. Some of these vendors even have the temerity to name previous dealers to whom the material has been offered, in an effort to impress a subsequent dealer. However, some dealers encourage "shopping around" as advantageously apprising them of available material (rarer material not being as obtainable as formerly), and because they feel they offer the highest prices possible, given their necessary markup and the possible market price.

Fortunately, the practice of "shopping around" is usually confined to novice vendors who are unacquainted not only with current values of material but also with the ethics of the trade. These tyros can usually be spotted by wary dealers and collectors who, apprised of the intent of this type of vendor, refuse to make an appraisal-purchase offer without some definite assurance that a sale will be consummated. Perhaps the best solution to this problem is that of some dealers who charge for all appraisal-purchase offers, the charge being remitted if the vendor sells the material to the appraiser. Also, a manifestly honest approach by a dealer or collector to an obviously novice vendor may well so gain the latter's confidence as to obviate any attempt by the latter to practice the trickery discussed in the previous paragraph. Novice vendors are naturally fearful of being taken advantage of by even the most amiable dealer or collector unless the latter's reliability has been established previously by a mutually familiar third party.

Conversely, should not a dealer or collector be at least morally required to tender a reasonably decent price, based on resale value, for any material offered to him? This suggestion has purposely been presented in the form of a question, since some dealers and collectors may reason that since their knowledge is valuable to them, it is therefore proper, both morally and legally, to take advantage of the lack of knowledge of the novice vendor—a sort of reverse of the "let the buyer beware" theory. Such semiethical dealings undoubtedly do occur, but eventually may result in repercussions to the dealer's or collector's ultimate disadvantage. Indeed, this policy could well disadvantage other, more ethical dealers and collectors if publicized. Reputable dealers and collectors, aware of the dangers, endeavor to be scrupulously fair in all aspects of their dealings. Also, when a dealer catalogs a price for a manuscript and the manuscript is not immediately sold, that price should remain in effect for a reasonable time, at the dealer's discretion, before he raises it.

When material is submitted on approval by a dealer to a prospective customer, the latter has no legal or moral right to copy that material for any purpose whatever, least of all for publication. If a prospective purchaser does copy material without purchasing it, the dealer, if made aware of this action, may not only refuse to deal further with that customer but also has every legal right to bring suit to recover damages. The prospective customer has no right prior to, or without, purchase to permit any other person to read or use the material for any purpose, or to quote the contents from memory to any other person either orally or in writing. Until purchase is consummated, all rights to the material belong exclusively to the owner-dealer. Conversely, the sale of manuscript material is the relinquishing by the vendor of all copying and publishing rights, and no copies should be knowingly retained by the vendor without the buyer's explicit permission.

Forgeries, more extensively discussed in another chapter, also fall within the domain of unethical practices. No person has the right to forge manuscripts, or even to deal in forgeries executed by others without apprising a prospective customer that the material is, or is suspected of being, a forgery. Some forgeries maintain a market value, but only as forgeries. Forgeries should either be indelibly marked as such, or destroyed. A prospective customer should also be advised of the fact when a manuscript is amanuensis-written or -signed. Reproductions should be labeled distinctly and traded as such, and marked in such a way that the information cannot be deleted without irreparably damaging or destroying the reproduction.

Appraisals also fall within the ethics of the trade. These, at all times, should be honestly computed by dealers and other appraisers. Knowledge of current values is a prerequisite. No increased monetary gain should be sought by the appraiser through any deliberately false increment of values. Since a few appraisers still charge a percentage of the appraised value of the property (unless the appraiser is purchasing the material), there is sometimes room for suspicion of an unusually high appraisal. For this reason most appraisers now charge a flat fee, by the hour or day, which protects them from any accusation of high appraisal figures.

Appraisers should not allow themselves to be improperly influenced by customers seeking a tax deduction through gift of manuscripts to public archives, or for any other purposes, such as inheritance taxes. The Internal Revenue Service keenly watches for such malpractices, which, if engaged in, may result in prosecution, imprisonment, fines, or all three. The taxpayer is held responsible for a false appraisal value, and the Internal Revenue Service reviews appraisals and sometimes challenges them.

Auctions of manuscripts, like any auctions, should be a public display of trust on the part of all parties concerned, for here again, if trust is lost, it is not easily, if ever, regained. The auction house has an obligation to a vendor to derive the best possible price for his material, and an obligation to a purchaser to handle his interests in a manifestly candid manner. It exceeds the intent of this chapter, however, to attempt to establish any binding rules for auction houses. Most, if not all, such houses devise their own conditions of sale based on accepted practices; and their regulations are prominently displayed in their catalogs. These regulations state a guarantee of authenticity of material, the terms of sale, methods of resolution of disputes between bidders and disputes with the auction house, the method of return of unsatisfactory material within an established time limit, and so on.

Although the regulations of the various auction houses are basically identical, some divergences do occur. Occasionally these divergences may cause complaints among customers, but all auction houses of repute endeavor to present an honest set of rules. These regulations should be understood prior to bidding, so that no misrepresentation can be claimed. If there is any question in the prospective bidder's mind, he should at the earliest possible time consult with the auctioneers to clarify the matter. All material cataloged by an auction house, as by any dealer, should be clearly and fully described within the limits of printing costs, including a full description of damaged material. Unfortunately, some auction houses are careless or unknowledgeable in their descriptions, occasionally to their embarrassment at the hands of irate customers. The most reprehensible practice of any auction house is the employment of mock bidders in an attempt to increase the bidding. No reputable house would engage in such an unethical practice.

Bidding at auctions by persons representing other parties is a delicate subject, since each representative may abide by a different self-devised system. The system used by a representative should be fully clarified to a prospective customer if the latter is not already conversant with it. All representatives guarantee the authenticity of the purchased material, usually as the result of personal inspection (though a reliable third party may be employed) prior to the sale; acquire the lot at the lowest possible price; and charge only a reasonable fee for their services. If the material is spurious, questionable, damaged, or inaccurately described in the catalog, the customer should be so informed by his representative prior to the sale, in order that he may decide whether or not to bid.

It is perfectly ethical, if he chooses, for the same representative to accept more than one bid for the same lot. Probably the most efficacious method to be employed by a representative when more than one customer for the same lot is involved is that the first bid received is that first honored. If this bid is lower than that offered by a second or other customers, the lower bid is honored only until the bidding exceeds it. The second offer should then be attended to in like manner, and subsequent offers in turn, if the bidding rises that high. A representative should inform a second and any subsequent bidders, prior to the sale, that a previous bid has been accepted and takes precedence over their bids if the purchase price falls within the initial customer's limit. Otherwise a representative should refuse other representations; and he of course will refuse to handle a lower bid when a higher bid already has been accepted. Under no circumstances should a representative divulge, or be expected to divulge, the amounts of the bids given to him or the names of his customers.

A collector may require a researcher using his collection to abide by any rules he may establish. This governs both access to material and research and publishing rights. Some collectors refuse access entirely; even if moral obligation might point to permitting the use of privately owned material, legal obligation does not. Many collectors sequester their material to protect its market value, since publication or other use of it may reduce that value, though this presumption does not always hold true. Some collectors, however, regard their holdings with paternalism, discovering great pleasure in owning unknown or unpublished material.

Under no circumstances should a dealer reveal a collector's interests, especially coupled with his name, without the collector's permission; nor should a dealer reveal the purchaser of material without like permission.

All dealers can rightfully be expected to refuse to allow a researcher access to their manuscripts, for they have not only an obligation to themselves to withhold material lest they risk financial loss through reduced value, but also an even stronger obligation to a prospective buyer who may desire to purchase only unresearched, unpublished material or who may expect a reduced price if he discovers that the material has been researched or published. Librarians and archivists in particular will often refuse to purchase previously published material even though that material definitely complements their collecting interest. Dealers therefore have no obligation to researchers, inhumane as this rule may sometimes prove; their obligation is to the purchaser of the manuscript. Not infrequently a researcher's work is obstructed by lack of access to dealer-owned or privately owned material. The researcher then must either purchase the material from the dealer or, if he cannot afford it, locate some philanthropic agency that might buy it and make it available to him.

A discussion of the preservation of manuscripts belongs to another chapter of this book, and no further comment will be made here except to assert that all owners of manuscripts have a moral, if not a legal, duty to preserve such material to the best of their knowledge, ability, and finances. If such knowledge is lacking, the owner should seek the best advice available. This is true of both public and private ownership. Such preservation applies not only to manuscripts of historical importance but also to a great quantity of lesser material that is worth preserving if it fits into the whole historical sequence.

In conclusion, the present exceedingly expanded interest in, and hence the greatly increasing value of, manuscripts is perhaps a threat to the ethics of the trade, since riches breed temptation. Ethics are one of the principal social mores of mankind without which decent civilization cannot exist. The manuscript trade might well be threatened with moral, and perhaps actual, ruin if the ethical practices of today are not followed in the future.

SECTION III

SOME AREAS IN WHICH TO COLLECT

SPECIALIZED COLLECTING

RICHARD MAASS

ALTHOUGH the earliest form of autograph collecting may well have been the assemblage of writings of a particular person or a group of individuals in a certain occupation or profession, the importance of specialized collections as tools for research into the development of political, scientific, and philosophic thought has been recognized only in recent times if measured over the three hundred or more years during which there has been such collecting.

Beginning in the seventeenth century, it was not uncommon for religious leaders in England to amass collections of important figures in the Church of England, not only archbishops and bishops but divines, writers, local curates, and heretics as well. Some of these collections have survived intact and others were dispersed, but they have provided a major resource for the study of church history in the English-speaking world. Similar collections of Roman Catholic church history were assembled, not by individuals as such but, rather, by church leaders who deposited their work in the Vatican Library or in the vaults of cathedrals or monasteries where they, too, remain intact.

This emphasis on religion and its spokesmen became the dominant influence on autograph and manuscript collecting in the United States when the practice began early in the nineteenth century. For example, William Buell Sprague, a Congregational and Presbyterian minister who is remembered for his vast collection of autographs of American Revolution heroes and participants, begun in 1820, prized his collection of American church leaders above all else. He was perfectly willing to trade an autograph of an important Signer of the Declaration of Independence for one of an obscure pastor of a New England church who had written an unimpressive commentary on a biblical passage. Voluminous correspondence between Sprague and contemporary collectors reveals that he was not alone in this predilection.

Aside from these "religious" collectors, the majority of the collectors of autographs through the nineteenth century seem to have been interested in obtaining examples of the writing of anyone whom they deemed to be "important," in any age, in any sphere of endeavor. Sir Thomas Phillipps (1792–1872), England's great antiquary and bibliophile, bought hundreds of manuscripts at a time. He owned four or five hundred volumes of oriental manuscripts; a splendid collection of Italian writing covering many centuries; historical and literary items illustrating the history of Wales and Ireland. In fact, there was no nation, no language, no arena of the world in which he was not interested. Sales from his holdings are still being held.

Few collectors during Phillipps' life and even fewer today could aspire to the breadth and depth of his purchases. What is more evident, however, is the fact that current collecting interests no longer are devoted to single representations of the writings of so diverse an aggregation. Rather, contemporary collectors who have progressed beyond the rudimentary stage tend to concentrate their interest in specific fields. These fields themselves may be broad or narrow, chronological, occupational, national, or regional; but what they have in common is a sense of purpose, of integrity or wholeness, and they undoubtedly return to the collector a richer reward in knowledge and satisfaction than the most catholic collection of larger numbers assembled haphazardly by someone of greater means.

The origin and development of a specialized collection may be illustrated by my own experience. The collecting groups may not be typical, but the manner in which they evolved and the extent to which they have been developed may provide both insights and cautions to some who have not yet set their collecting patterns.

Upon returning from naval service in 1945, I was shown by my father-in-law a small collection of bank checks that were signed by presidents of the United States. A former banker, he had been given a check signed by James Garfield and had decided to try to obtain all of the presidents in similar form. At that time he lacked only two or three and wished to complete the group, then move on to Signers of the Declaration of Independence. He asked me to help. I was fascinated with the idea, and for the next seven years helped to obtain most of the Signers in either check or negotiable instrument form. Several were impossible on financial documents and were bought in other styles.

By 1952 the collection was as complete as it could be made. What now? We displayed, gave talks at financial gatherings, and enjoyed the ownership; but the sense of history, the personality of the check signers, the continuing interest were all absent. I decided to expand my interest into historical fields that were less restricted and certainly more exciting than that of financial instruments. The entire collection was sold at auction and the proceeds were used to buy autographs in the areas of interest I had newly developed.

To me the most exciting period in American history is that of the Revolution and the ten years immediately prior to the war. Accordingly, I decided to collect in that period. But since the war and all of its participants are too broad an area of collecting, I decided to limit my collecting to New York and, even more specifically, to Westchester County, my adopted residence. Having chosen one topic for collecting, it was natural to expand into other, related ones. The Dutch and English colonial administrations in New York were then neglected areas of collecting, and prices for rare and interesting selections were not too high. A third, and obviously more restricted, choice was an attempt to gather autographs pertaining to the actions at Lexington and Bunker Hill and the British occupation of Boston up to January 1776. The fourth and final specialty, which grew out of the surrender of New Amsterdam to the British by the Dutch in 1664, is a group of autographs that cover the English Restoration years of 1660–1667, and are political and naval in nature.

Each of these four categories of collecting could be carried as far as time, attention, and the purse would allow. In each there was an abundant supply of material on the market; at the time I started collecting there was not too much competition for the less-important items and, consequently, prices were not beyond my reach.

My Westchester collection consists of letters and documents written in the county, ones dated outside the county but pertaining to events or military operations there, and others by or related to prominent residents of the area. Since Westchester was a continuous arena for military action from 1776 to 1783, literally hundreds, if not thousands, of autographs were written from and about the county during those years. Some that I acquired are from little-known officers or enlisted men, but the contents might be of more interest than more expensive letters from George Washington or Nathanael Greene. I prize a description of the Battle of White Plains, written by a Connecticut foot soldier three days after the engagement, even more than a letter from Washington that calls a court-martial to sit at the same place. There are military documents signed by Baron Friedrich von Steuben, Johann Kalb, James McHenry, and Charles Lee, to mention a few of the top generals, and a host of then-junior officers and enlisted men. There are seven Washington letters, written from White Plains and Dobbs Ferry, including a long and detailed order completely in his hand for an attack on New

York in 1781, shortly before removal of the army to the Yorktown Peninsula in Virginia.

Of a political nature there is a letter of John Jay in 1777, describing his work in composing the New York State Constitution and a tender letter written by him from Bedford to his wife Sally in New Jersey, with an account of military action in Westchester. Nathaniel Woodhull, first president of the New York Committee of Representatives, successor to the Provincial Congress, is represented by a document signed only a week after the Declaration of Independence. There is an account of the execution of a Peekskill man charged with recruiting for the British and a journal describing the arrest, captivity, trial, and death of Maj. John André, in the hand of Col. Benjamin Tallmadge, in whose charge André was placed after his capture.

Of an earlier period, there is an Indian deed to one John Dibble, from three Indian sachems, for the town of Bedford, dated in 1703; also a partition agreement for a large number of acres in the same area, signed by eleven of the most prominent New Yorkers in 1702. Autographs of the "lords of the manors" such as Van Cortlandt, Pell, Philipse, and Heathcote render a view of a local society that had a patrician and wealthy landed class. There are documents about boundary disputes in the early 1700's between the towns of Eastchester and Westchester, and between Mamaroneck and Scarsdale, as well as a coroner's inquisition about the murder of a deputy sheriff that is signed by a Roosevelt and a Livingston. Of great interest is a letter of Thomas Paine that, though dated in New York City, fits into the collection because he complains about having been disenfranchised in New Rochelle when he was living on his farm in that community. It can be seen from these autographs that the selection of a geographic area for a subject collection can provide a wide variety of topical autographs.

Events such as the actions in April and June 1775 provide a more limited opportunity for collecting. In order to present a full picture of the times, events preceding and following "the shot heard 'round the world" and Bunker Hill might be included. In my group there are some muster rolls of minutemen dated just prior to April 19 and a letter from John Hancock to Elbridge Gerry, thanking Gerry for the information that "the British are out Concord Road." The latter is dated "Lexington, 9 P.M. April 18, 1775." For Bunker Hill there are two descriptions of the action, one by Gen. John Burgoyne written to his father-in-law, and another by a Massachusetts soldier, barely literate, to his father. Surrounding these prime autographs are more routine ones that nevertheless furnish an exciting picture of those dangerous times.

Enough of personal accounts. What about a collector who has not yet chosen a specialty? Are there any rewarding fields that one could enter without having to depend upon a fat pocketbook? I think there are a number worthy of consideration. A neglected subject from the standpoint of collecting is abolition and abolitionists. The field would encompass both England and America, and would cover a period of more than one hundred years. Extensive research could be done and letters of relatively unknown supporters of the cause uncovered. Prices for William Wilberforce, William Lloyd Garrison, and even Francis Scott Key are modest today.

Those who are musically inclined cannot expect to begin with musical scores or even letters by Mozart or Bach unless they are prepared to spend twenty-five to fifty thousand dollars, but a fine collection of twentieth-century composers and musicians could be assembled at modest cost.* Aaron Copland, Ned Rorem, Antonin Dvořák, George Gershwin, Darius Milhaud, Igor Stravinsky, Gian-Carlo Menotti, Kurt Weill, Béla Bartók, Jean Sibelius, and Benjamin Britten, to mention a few, are available in letter form at prices that, by today's general level of autograph prices, are not excessive.

A very interesting subject for a specialized collection would be the world of travel and exploration. One could develop this topic in as broad or as limited fashion as time and research would allow, for autograph material is available in all of the centuries in which discoveries were made and in all of the languages of the explorers themselves. A collector could decide to restrict his interest to the western hemisphere or even to the twentieth century. The latter would include Arctic and Antarctic expeditions as well as space exploration and certainly would have a future value, both academic and monetary, beyond its current worth.

Autograph collectors are frequently asked if they limit themselves to holographic material. The answer will vary, of course, with the outlook of the individual, but the specialized collector for whom the acquisition of autographs is as much for reasons of study and scholarship as it is for mere ownership will inevitably expand his horizon from solely handwritten items to printed works, etchings, lithographs, maps, newspapers, and other material. Take my Bunker Hill collection, for example. I think it is greatly enhanced by the printed materials that accompany it: firsthand accounts of the battle, in books published both in England and America; maps of the action published by both sides; newspaper accounts of the battle published in papers printed in various of the colonies, with calls for support of the New Englanders; broadsides put out by Gen. Thomas Gage to justify his action; and broadsides printed on behalf of the Continental Army, in which farmers and merchants are requested to supply food and equipment for the fledgling troops. All of

*Average letters of no special content, at 1976 prices, range from Bartók at $750, Dvořák at $500, and Gershwin at $350, to Britten at $50.

these printed works add knowledge and color to the collection and, in this collector's judgment, should not be neglected simply because they are not handwritten.

There are certain advantages for the specialized collector in making his particular desiderata known to as wide an audience as possible. This view flies in the face of earlier custom, when collectors not only kept their valuables hidden from sight but told their interests to only a few dealers. This reclusive attitude was based (falsely) on the assumption that if the trade knew what the collector was interested in buying, prices would be marked up especially for him. My experience does not justify this suspicion. By letting all the book and autograph dealers from whom I receive catalogs know my areas of interest, I am certain that I receive more offerings of relevant material than I would if I kept my specialties to myself. Further, it is not uncommon for a dealer to send me page proofs of particular items that will soon appear in his catalog, in the belief that they will be of interest and which, because of the vagaries of the postal system, I might not be the first to order from the catalog. It is possible that a dealer might advance the price of a particular autograph beyond its "market value" because of the knowledge that one collector is buying in that field, but the collector can always refuse to buy. One or two such experiences for a dealer would be enough to give him the picture, and I am sure the overpricing would stop.

Individuals with autographs to sell have been referred to me by librarians, universities, historical societies, and even the local newspaper, because they knew of my collecting interests. If I am not willing or interested enough to buy, I refer the vendor to a dealer who, in my opinion, would be. As a matter of policy it is best not to estimate a value on such items. A collector is not a professional, and he can be—usually is—wrong in monetary judgments of autographs other than those he collects.

Some collectors attend autograph auctions and bid in their own items. This is a decision more personal than one of business. Certainly bid yourself if you are thoroughly familiar with autographs of the persons on which you are bidding; if you have the time to inspect carefully the lots in the sale; if you enjoy attending sales and know enough about the manner in which they are conducted so that you do not unwittingly bid against yourself; then, by all means, be your own bidder. I prefer, however, to give my bids to a reputable dealer to execute in my behalf. Taking all a dealer's services into account, I long ago decided to give a dealer all my bids at auction. I have never regretted the decision.

In concluding this article on specialized collecting, I should say something about the ultimate disposition of the collection itself, although this is a most delicate, even distressing, subject to approach. A specialized autograph collection, which may have required many years to assemble, and which perhaps could not be replicated at any cost were the individual items that compose the collection dispersed through sale, presents a challenge to the imaginative collector. If the collector is wealthy and is in a position to bequeath the collection to an institution, there is no problem. Dozens of college and university libraries, historical societies, and other public and private institutions would be interested; and the collector would have to be guided only by instinct as to which of the many possible recipients would best maintain, conserve, display, and use the collection. The real problems arise when the collection represents a major portion of the assets of one's estate. A bequest may be out of the realm of financial reason. Here the collector or his executors have a number of options.

If the collector has definite thoughts on disposition, then he must include them in his will as directions to his executors. If he wishes the collection to remain intact (sold to one buyer), he must so state; otherwise the executors, who have the responsibility to obtain the highest possible price, may find that they will have to break up the collection. If the latter is the case, there are still various methods of sale. Some collectors, having bought largely through auction, may desire others to have the same opportunity and specify that the sale should be at auction. The old Anderson Galleries of New York used to print a quotation from the will of Edmond de Goncourt on its manuscript folders that expresses very well this feeling about disposition at auction:

> My wish is that my Drawings, my Prints, my Curiosities, my Books—in a word, these things of art which have been the joy of my life—shall not be consigned to the cold tomb of a museum, and subjected to the stupid glance of the careless passer-by; but I require that they shall all be dispersed under the hammer of the Auctioneer, so that the pleasure which the acquiring of each one of them has given me shall be given again, in each case, to some inheritor of my own tastes.

One thing is quite clear: if no instructions are given in the will and no provisions made in advance of death, the collection may not be handled in a manner of which the collector, were he alive, would approve. Fortunate, but rare, is the collector with descendants who are interested in preserving the group intact and who have the means to make such a provision after the payment of inheritance taxes.

Someone embarking on a specialized collection would be well-served by establishing the boundaries of his collection in advance. If his object is to assemble a collection that is representative in its field, then he should resist the temptation to acquire less-important and peripheral items. If, on the other hand, his goal is a definitive collection, then he can justify to himself the purchase of every item that relates to the subject matter. In either event, his decision to acquire should not be influenced by the character of the material available: for his purposes an autograph letter signed, a letter signed or unsigned, a document or a note may have equal value to the collection although the prices will, of course, vary. The acquisition of printed materials and related graphics such as prints, drawings, and engravings is a matter of personal taste. After initially purchasing related graphic material, I soon reached the conclusion that the limits of storage and display facilities were such that it simply was not feasible to continue to collect these items; not so with books, for somehow one always seems able to squeeze in additional volumes. Depending upon the degree of scholarship and research that the specialized collector is willing to devote, he can become the authoritative source for historians and writers in his particular field and if his collection is to serve any useful purpose other than personal gratification, it as well as his accumulated knowledge should be made available to serious students and authors. A fine collection locked in a vault serves no one well, least of all the owner.

AUTOGRAPHS OF AMERICAN PRESIDENTS

CHRISTOPHER C. JAECKEL

IT SHOULD COME as no surprise that the fledgling American collector, bitten by the autograph bug but uncertain where or how to start, most often turns to his own presidents. Such a collection, no matter how modest, can be both inexpensive and readily acquired but, more important, it also provides the collector with a tangible link to the course of American history through the men who lived and shaped that history. The variety of examples is almost limitless, depending on pocketbook and availability; and there is the added advantage that a collection of American presidents can be relatively easily disposed of should the collector's interest wane or veer in another direction. Finally, should it be necessary to dispose of a collection, the collector, over the long term, can be assured that he will at least recoup his expenses and, very often, realize a handsome profit. This possibility must, however, be qualified on two counts: the collection must be held for a number of years—in other words, considered as a long-term investment—and it must not include poor or damaged examples.

One of the commonly asked questions about autographs, and certainly pertinent here due to the number of collectors of presidents, is whether material will continue to be available or whether supplies are drying up. It is certainly true that much of the material acquired by institutions disappears permanently from the marketplace. Yet museums and libraries will sometimes sell a part of their holdings either to raise money or to make room for different material. Material purchased by private collectors may remain out of circulation for years and may be given or willed to institutions, but ultimately much of it reappears. And new material is constantly being discovered, thereby adding to the supply. It is quite common for material of one man, scarce in one generation, to flood the market in another. Thus there is no reason to believe that presidential autographs will be permanently unavailable.

The possibilities of what to collect are almost endless. The first consideration, of course, must be one of finances. Where these present no barrier, the collector may choose to limit himself to handwritten letters of presidential date. Such a collection may take a lifetime to complete and, indeed, may never be completed due to the difficulty of obtaining presidential material of men like William Henry Harrison, who served only thirty days in the White House before his death, or Herbert Hoover, who rarely wrote his own letters at any time.

Much more specialized sets have also been made where a common theme, such as references to religion, health, or even shoes, provides a link between the men who filled the nation's highest office. Other sets are often made of checks, signatures, or documents. The possibilities are limited only by the imagination and interests of the collector; the location and acquisition of material for these specialized sets—the thrill of the hunt—are often as important to the collector as completion of the set itself.

The neophyte may wonder just what is available. The most obvious are the handwritten and dictated letters, the signatures, signed photographs, and checks. But there are also endorsements and dockets, and the great variety of documents that, over the presidential signature, keep the governmental machinery running. A brief summary of some of the more commonly seen documents may be of some use.

Land grants are quite common, having been issued into the twentieth century. It is important to remember, however, that they were signed by the president only until the beginning of Andrew Jackson's second term. So many were being issued by that time that they were subsequently, with very rare exceptions, signed for the president by a secretary, and were so designated.

Commissions are, most commonly, military appointments, with those for the army most prevalent. The naval appointments are more decorative and scarcer, the navy being the smaller service.

Sea letters were paper documents given to all American vessels traveling in foreign waters (except the Mediterranean); they gave particulars of the voyage and requested safe passage for ship and crew. Printed in four languages (English, French, Spanish, and Dutch), they were signed by the president and the secretary of state.

Ships' passports resulted from the treaty of September 5, 1795, with the dey of Algiers. Printed in English, on parchment, these passports are distinguished by an engraving at the top and by a peculiar scalloped or indented top edge. A master "counterpart" was furnished to the Algerian cruisers. The cruisers, manned by the pirates of Tripoli, harassed American ships. When boarded, the American captain would produce his passport; and if it matched the upper portion held by the pirate, his ship was allowed to pass. The United States paid tribute to the Barbary pirates for this protection.

The Executive Mansion card is a small card, approximately two and three-quarters inches by four and one-quarter inches, bearing the Executive Mansion imprint at the upper right-hand corner. They were introduced by President Grant, although very few signed by him have come on the market.

White House cards are the same size as the Executive Mansion cards and bear the White House imprint. They were introduced by Theodore Roosevelt shortly after he assumed the presidency in 1901, apparently because he felt the Executive Mansion cards were too ostentatious. Signed White House cards are in great demand, but the collector should be especially wary of those signed by the more recent presidents. From Harry S. Truman on, the cards are often, if not always, signed by secretaries or the Autopen. Many bear facsimile signatures that are sometimes, but not always, identified as such on the verso.

Executive Mansion vignette of the style used by President Truman.
Courtesy of Walter R. Benjamin Autographs, Inc.

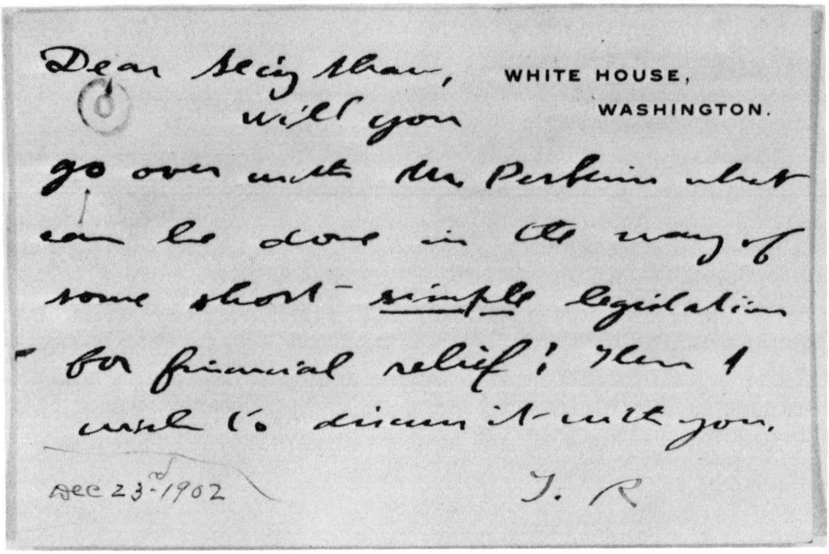
WHITE HOUSE,
WASHINGTON.

Dear Sec'y Shaw,
will you
go over with Mr. Perkins what
can be done in the way of
some short-simple legislation
for financial relief? Then I
wish to discuss it with you.
T. R
Dec 23-1902

White House card.
Courtesy of the George Perkins Papers,
Rare Book and Manuscript Library, Columbia University.

A warning with regard to the use of the Autopen is particularly appropriate at this time. Material of the recent presidents is more difficult to come by than that of the earlier presidents. Either the president is still alive and people are holding their letters in the hope that they will appreciate in value after the president's death, or they are embarrassed at the prospect of being discovered selling a personal letter, or quite simply not enough time has elapsed for material to have come on the market. In any event, the difficulty in acquiring material of the recent presidents, and the extensive use of the Autopen by all presidents from Kennedy on, make the eager collector vulnerable to adding an Autopen signature to his collection, thinking or hoping that it is the real thing. Even the experienced dealer is often in doubt about such signatures; but the ethical dealer will sell a presidential signature, as such, only if he is absolutely sure that it is the real thing.

With such a wealth of possibilities, where should the tyro start and how should he plan his collection? That, of course, must be his own decision, based on his own interests. But two possibilities may help inspire the beginning collector. The first, and perhaps finest, collection would include handwritten letters of all the presidents, regardless of date, with the finest contents available. Such a collection would establish the strongest possible link between collector and president, with the latter's most profound thoughts and observations on the events of his day, written in his own hand, in the possession of the collector. Although assuredly the most expensive way to form a set of presidents, such a set is easily started on a more modest level and can be upgraded as finances improve and finer material becomes available.

The second collection, perhaps for the collector with a more limited budget, would not only establish a link with the presidents but would also be a representation of the fascinating variety of personal and administrative records. Such a collection would encompass as great a variety of material as possible, with perhaps an emphasis on representing each president by an item particularly appropriate to him. For example, John Adams or Grover Cleveland, known for the quality of their writing, might be represented by particularly fine handwritten letters. For George Washington one might have a membership in the Society of the Cincinnati or a Revolutionary War discharge. For Chester Arthur one might have a White House vignette card (he introduced them); for Lincoln, perhaps an endorsement approving the pardon or release of a prisoner of war; for Grant, a military commission. The possibilities are enormous and would depend to a great extent on the individual collector's interests and how he himself views the different presidents. Part of the fun of such a collection would be in determining what to include for each president.

What then of the men themselves, the thirty-eight men who have held the highest office in the land? What characteristics of personality and penmanship should the new collector be aware of as he begins his quest? The following sections are but a brief introduction to what, one hopes, will bring lifelong pleasure.

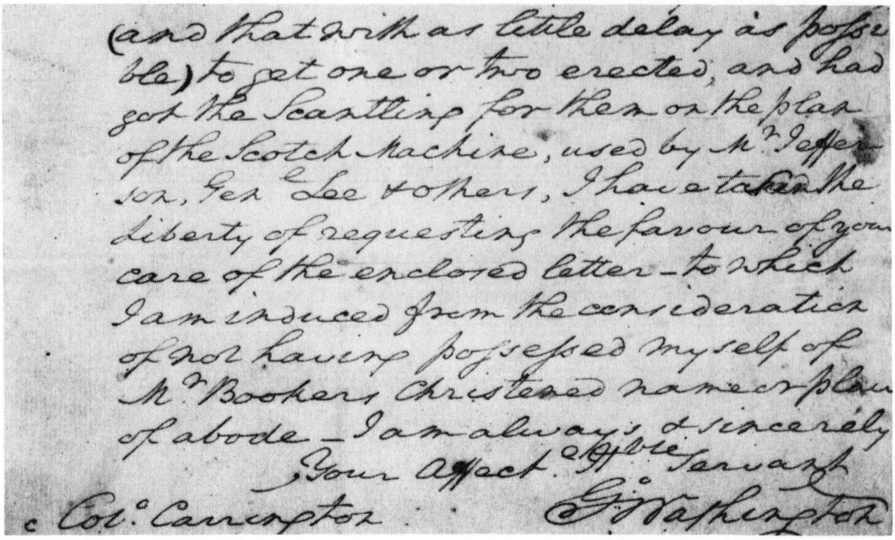

(and that with as little delay as possible) to get one or two erected; and had
got the Scantling for them on the plan
of the Scotch Machine, used by Mr Jefferson, Genl Lee & others, I have taken the
liberty of requesting the favour of your
care of the enclosed letter—to which
I am induced from the consideration
of not having possessed myself of
Mr Bookers Christened name or place
of abode—I am always & sincerely
Your Affect.e Hble Servant
Col.o Carrington
Go: Washington

Courtesy of the Cabell Memorial Foundation, Charlottesville, Virginia.

GEORGE WASHINGTON

It is somehow surprising that our most prolific penman had, at the same time, the most beautiful calligraphy. Washington's early script was somewhat sharp and pointed but gradually developed into the near copperplate of his later years. Pedantic in style, Washington nevertheless displayed a grace and logic seldom matched by his successors. Many of his letters are on routine matters but others are magnificent, dealing with the Revolution, matters of state, or the like. This diversity helps to explain the wide range of prices, with some letters selling for ten times the price of others dealing, perhaps, with maintenance at Mount Vernon. Pre-Revolution material of any kind is scarce, and surveys are particularly desirable. Documents signed, once fairly plentiful, are now less so, although Revolutionary discharges do still come on the market. Washington signed the discharge of every soldier released from service at the conclusion of hostilities with England. Memberships in the Society of the Cincinnati and ships' papers are very scarce. Most in demand are Revolutionary and presidential letters, with handwritten letters of these periods bringing the highest prices.

It is worth noting that, other than in legal documents, Washington rarely signed his full name, preferring the abbreviated "G.o Washington." Forgeries of our first president are not uncommon, with Revolutionary passes and checks done by Robert Spring, in the mid-1800's, and the wide variety of Joseph Cosey forgeries in the twentieth century, most prevalent.

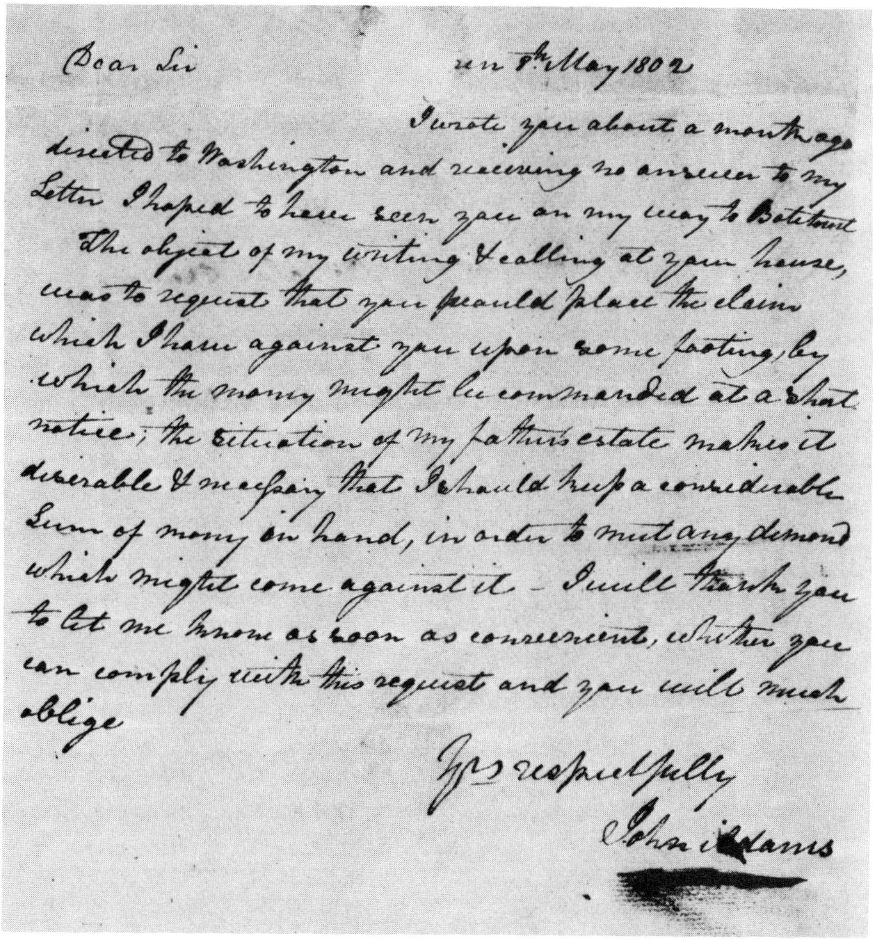

Dear Sir [illegible] 8th May 1802

I wrote you about a month ago directed to Washington and receiving no answer to my Letter I hoped to have seen you on my way to Botetourt

The object of my writing & calling at your house, was to request that you would place the claim which I have against you upon some footing, by which the money might be commanded at a short notice; the situation of my fathers estate makes it desirable & necessary that I should keep a considerable Sum of money on hand, in order to meet any demand which might come against it — I will thank you to let me know as soon as convenient, whether you can comply with this request and you will much oblige

Yrs respectfully

John Adams

JOHN ADAMS

Our second president's hand underwent dramatic changes during the course of his lifetime. Always unpretentious and legible, his early handwriting was small and irregular, almost cramped. With his election to the presidency his script grew larger and his signature, during that period, was the boldest of all the presidents. Following his years in the White House, Adams' handwriting shrank to the palsied efforts of his later years, when his signature became almost illegible.

Highly educated, Adams wrote letters of consistently fine quality: dramatic, forceful, and generally interesting. He is the rarest of the early presidents, with signed documents of particular scarcity owing to his single term in office. Letters are rare in all forms, those of Revolutionary and presidential date being particularly hard to come by.

The collector should be aware that the name John Adams was not an unusual one, and it quite often happens that the wrong Adams is included in a set.

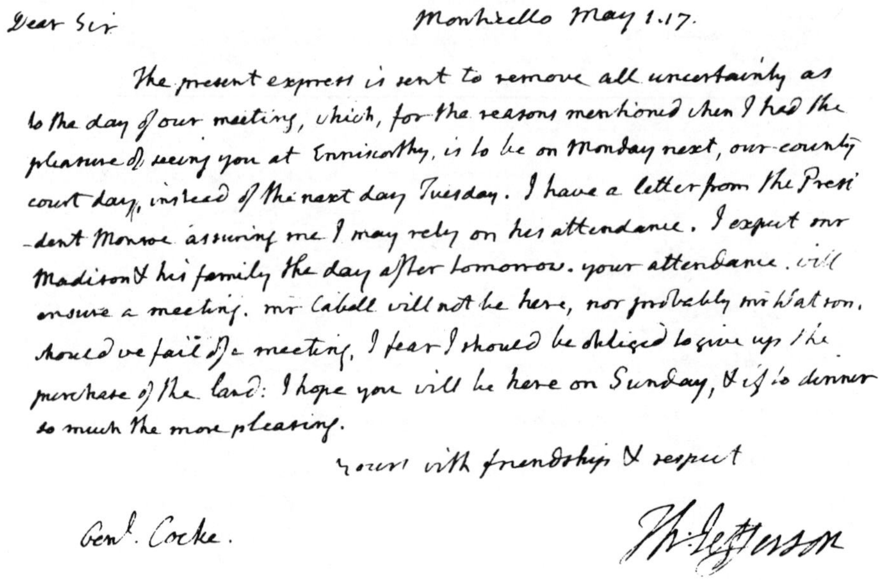

Dear Sir Monticello May 1. 17.

The present express is sent to remove all uncertainty as to the day of our meeting, which, for the reasons mentioned when I had the pleasure of seeing you at Enniscorthy, is to be on Monday next, our county court day, instead of the next day Tuesday. I have a letter from the President Monroe assuring me I may rely on his attendance. I expect mr Madison & his family the day after tomorrow. your attendance will ensure a meeting. mr Cabell will not be here, nor probably mr Watson. should we fail of a meeting, I fear I should be obliged to give up the purchase of the land: I hope you will be here on Sunday, & if to dinner so much the more pleasing.

Yours with friendship & respect

Genl. Cocke. Th: Jefferson

THOMAS JEFFERSON

Jefferson's small, neat, irregular script varied little during his lifetime. It often lacked punctuation and capital letters, especially at the beginning of sentences. His handwritten letters are frequently mistaken for dictated letters, since his signature is invariably written in larger characters than the body of the letters.

Although lacking the fire of his predecessor, Jefferson nevertheless wrote letters that were good; and some were superb. The demand for them is increasing and, although handwritten letters are becoming scarce, third-person letters are available, as are dictated letters and documents. The latter usually appear as land grants and ships' papers.

Although forgeries do not show up often, there is one facsimile of which collectors should be aware. It is of a handwritten letter signed, Washington, November 27, 1803, addressed to Craven Peyton with accompanying envelope (not used at this time) bearing reproduced postal markings and frank. The facsimile was issued shortly before World War II by the Morris Plan Bank of Richmond, Virginia, as an advertisement.

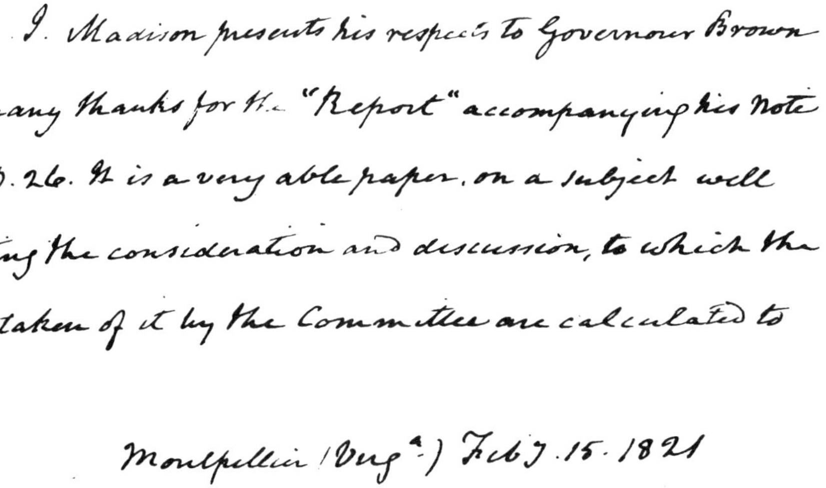

J. Madison presents his respects to Governour Brown with many thanks for the "Report" accompanying his Note of Jany. 26. It is a very able paper, on a subject well meriting the consideration and discussion, to which the views taken of it by the Committee are calculated to lead.

Montpellier (Virga.) Feby. 15. 1821

JAMES MADISON

Small, angular, and easily read, Madison's hand was devoid of flourish and, as he neared the end of his life, it diminished further in size, becoming increasingly difficult to read. Known as the "Father of the Constitution," Madison is increasingly in demand and the trend undoubtedly will continue as we approach the bicentennial of the Constitutional period. Most prized are his early letters, then those written as president. Subsequent letters were, for the most part, routine and indifferent. Madison is common in document form, particularly ships' papers signed jointly with James Monroe. Collectors are sometimes confused by, and have bypassed, Madison's early letters, which he signed "James Madison, Jr." Later in life his wife, Dolley, wrote many of his letters for him and he signed in a labored, printlike hand.

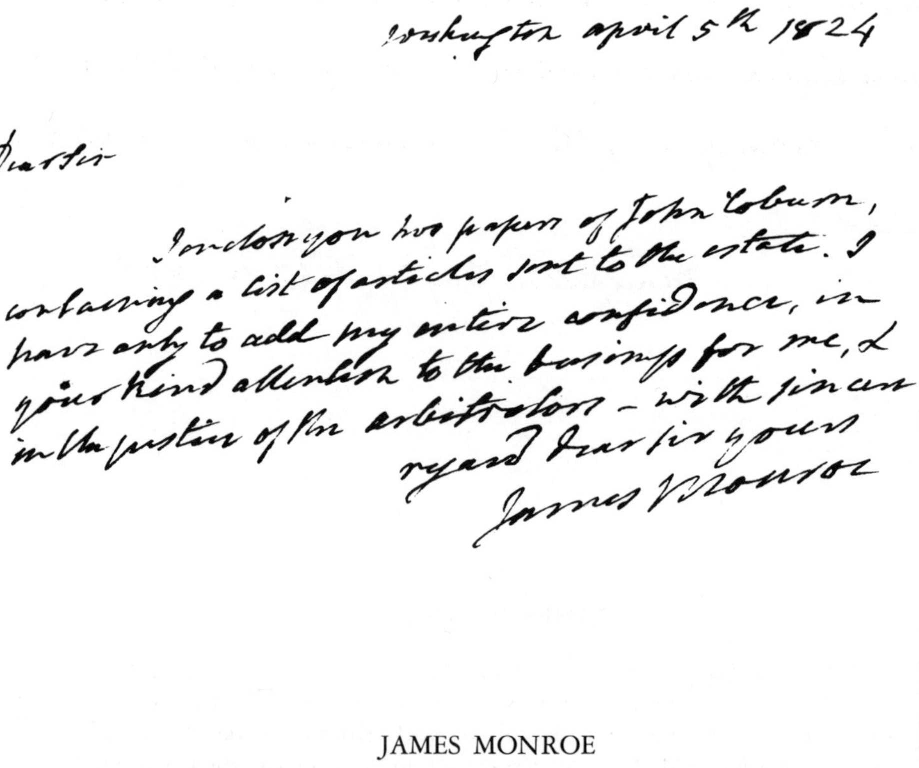

Washington April 5th 1824

Dear Sir

I enclose you two papers of John Coburn,
containing a list of articles sent to the estate. I
have only to add my entire confidence, in
your kind attention to the business for me, &
in the justice of the arbitrators – with sincere
regard dear sir yours
James Monroe

JAMES MONROE

In contrast with that of his predecessor, Monroe's handwriting underwent marked changes. His early letters are in a roundish, irregular script, considerably more legible than the scrawl of his later years. Monroe is in good supply but the demand is small, in part because of the uninspired length of his letters. Those of Revolutionary date are scarce but later, during his political career, he is common in all forms except dictated letters. Most common are land grants, issued to veterans in lieu of cash, which was in short supply.

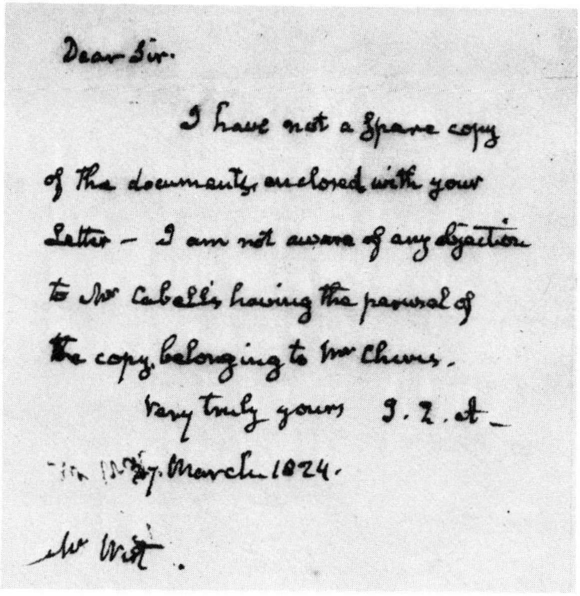
Dear Sir.

I have not a spare copy of the documents enclosed with your Letter — I am not aware of any objection to Mr Cabell's having the perusal of the copy belonging to Mr Chaves.

Very truly yours J. Q. A —

Wn 17. March 1824.

Mr Wirt.

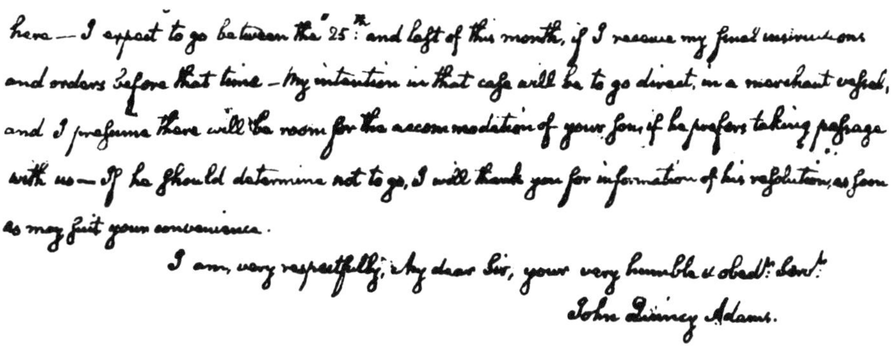
here — I expect to go between the 25th and last of this month, if I receive my final instructions and orders before that time — My intention in that case will be to go direct, in a merchant vessel, and I presume there will be room for the accommodation of your son, if he prefers taking passage with us — If he should determine not to go, I will thank you for information of his resolution, as soon as may suit your convenience.

I am, very respectfully, My dear Sir, your very humble & obedt. Servt.

John Quincy Adams.

JOHN QUINCY ADAMS

Like his father, John Quincy Adams suffered from a palsy that made his hand shaky and nearly illegible at times. His early letters, however, display a small, neat hand. Never quite measuring up to his father, Adams nevertheless wrote a fine letter, although he tended toward a flowery turn of phrase. His best letters are perhaps those in which he engaged in long, bitter tirades against Masonry. He was also the only president to publish a volume of verse, and occasionally a manuscript poem turns up. Since he was a one-term president, letters written then naturally are rarer than those of other periods. Most common are land grants. Adams' secretary, Daniel Brent, had a very similar hand; and collectors occasionally mistake letters dictated to Brent for handwritten ones.

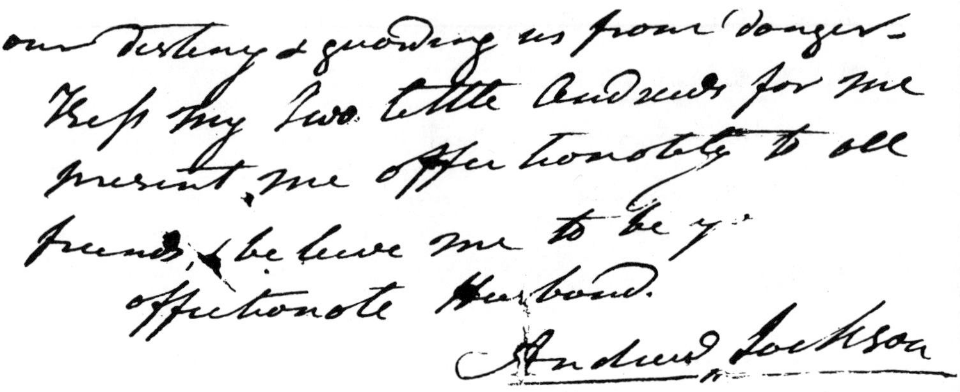
our destiny & guarding us from danger—
Keep my two little Andrews for me
present me affectionately to all
friends, & believe me to be yr
affectionate Husband.
Andrew Jackson

ANDREW JACKSON

Jackson was the first "common" man to gain the White House, and his background is reflected both in his handwriting and in the language of his letters. Crude and boldly penned, characterized by atrocious spelling, his letters lacked the formal, courtly tone of his predecessors and occasionally contained quite strong language. A truly colorful figure in American history, Jackson is in good demand. His letters are becoming scarcer, although military A.Ds.S. and land grants are still readily available.

The first of the presidents to delegate his signatory power, Jackson stopped signing land grants at the beginning of his second term. The printed form specifically states "By ______ Sec." but this is often overlooked. The hand of Jackson's nephew and occasional secretary, Andrew Jackson Donelson, also causes confusion. Similar to that of the president, it frequently leads dictated letters to be confused with handwritten ones. Adding to the confusion is the fact that Donelson often wrote and signed Jackson's checks for him.

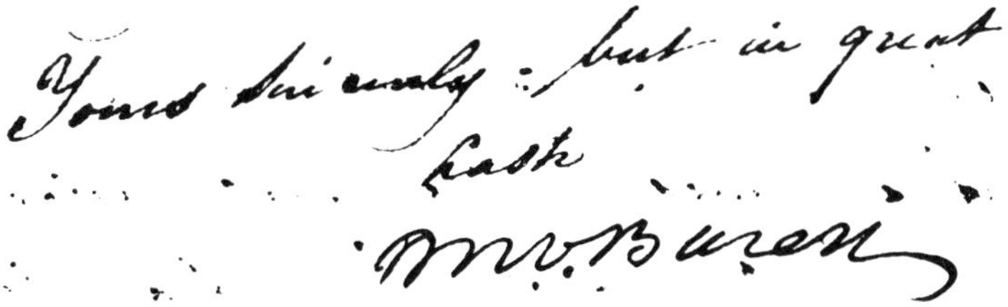
Yours sincerely: but in great haste
M. V. Buren

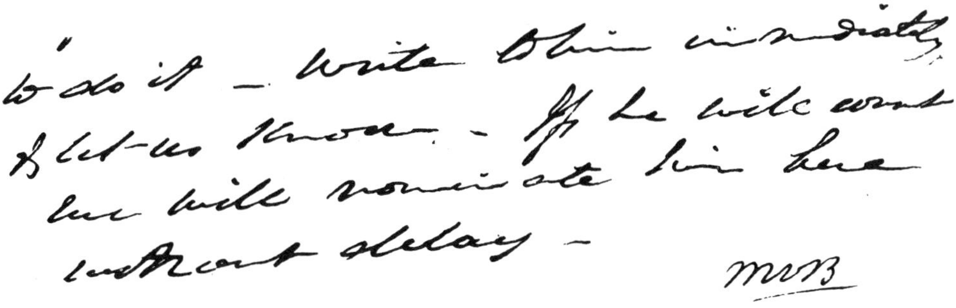
to do it — write to him immediately & let us know — If he will come we will nominate him here without delay —
MVB

MARTIN VAN BUREN

Van Buren was the first professional politician to sit in the White House and, perhaps appropriately, his hand, although originally small and quite legible, grew larger and almost unintelligible. His was normally an uninteresting scrawl that matched the usual quality of his letters. However, he could, on very rare occasions, write interestingly. His material is not common during any period, and presidential material is scarcer still.

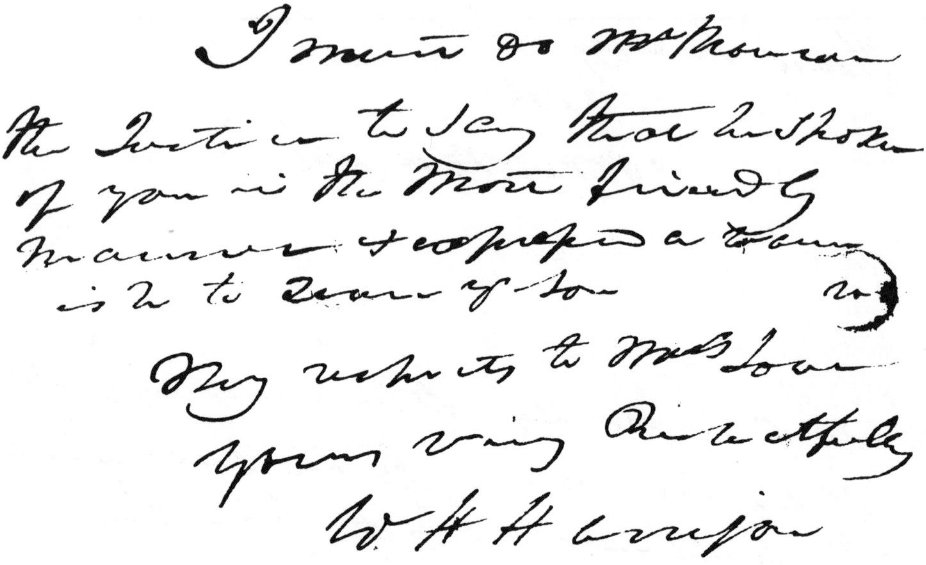
I must do Mr [illegible] the Justice to say that he spoke of you in the most friendly manner [illegible]

My respects to Mrs [illegible]

Yours very Respectfully

W H Harrison

Courtesy of Turner McDowell.

WILLIAM HENRY HARRISON

Harrison's early handwriting was large and irregular but, during his brief time in politics, and presumably due to the press of his duties, his hand became small and cramped. His early letters were generally routine, but during his political career they were often quite good—clearly expressed and finely worded.

Harrison caught cold at his inauguration and never recovered, dying one month later. As a result, he is the main stumbling block to the completion of a presidential set of material written while in office. Only three handwritten letters, one or two dictated letters, and perhaps a dozen documents are known. Needless to say, those that do come on the market bring very high prices. Luckily, material of prepresidential date has recently been fairly common, with dictated and handwritten documents signed, from Greenville, most in evidence. Some six hundred of these were unearthed in the early 1930's by the dealer E. V. Heise.

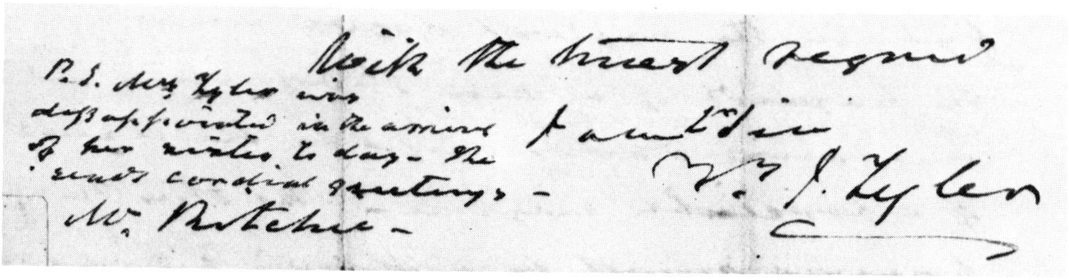
P.S. Mrs Tyler was disappointed in the arrival of her sisters to day - She sends cordial greetings - Mr Ritchie -

With the truest regard I am D Sir, Yrs J. Tyler

JOHN TYLER

The first vice-president to assume office upon the death of the president, Tyler showed marked variations in his handwriting. At first small and cramped, it developed into the strong, forceful script of his presidency. Yet it also varied depending on what, or how much, he had to say and the size of the paper he was using. Usually brief and to the point, Tyler's best letters are normally those written to his son. With little demand, his handwritten letters are fairly common, although dictated letters and documents are more difficult to come by.

JAMES KNOX POLK

Small and precise, Polk's script is overshadowed by his signature, which he usually embellished with an elaborate paraph. Although generally routine in nature, his letters did, on occasion, achieve some distinction. The best were usually campaign letters discussing politics. Little in demand, handwritten letters, documents, and signatures are relatively scarce and dictated letters are practically nonexistent.

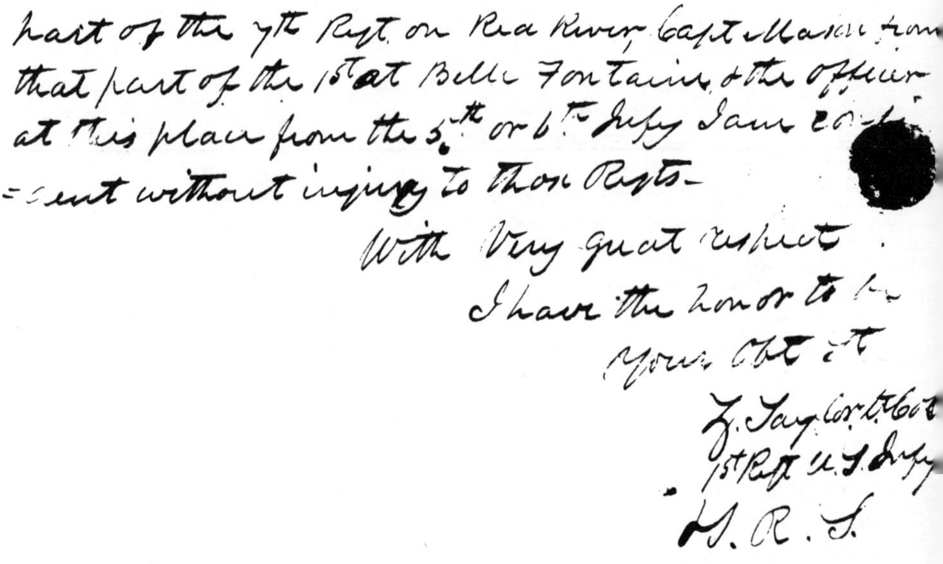

part of the 7th Regt. on Red River, Capt. Mason from that part of the 1st at Belle Fontaine, & the officer at this place from the 5th or 6th Infy I am co[illegible]-ent without injury to those Regts.—

With very great respect
I have the honor to be
Your Obt. st
Z. Taylor Lt. Col.
1st Regt. U.S. Infy.
H.R.S.

Z. Taylor Col.
1st Regt. U.S. Infy.
Comdg.

ZACHARY TAYLOR

Letters of Taylor are distinctive, since they were often written with such a broad quill point that the ink has eaten right through the paper. Never a facile penman, Taylor wrote letters that are generally long and rambling yet quite interesting; the best are those written to his family while campaigning for the presidency. Also good are those letters dictated during his Indian-fighting days. Presidential material of Taylor is scarce—he served only fifteen months in office before his death—and those that do come up generally are dictated. Prepresidential handwritten letters are common but usually of a routine military nature.

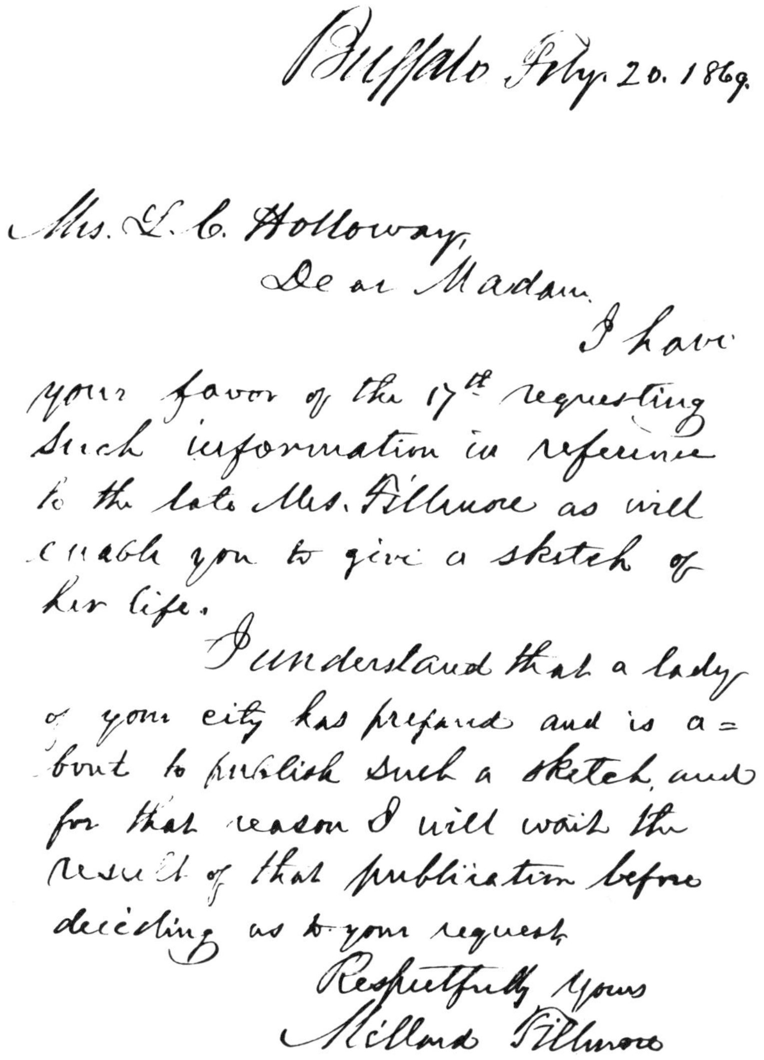
Buffalo Feby. 20. 1869.

Mrs. L. C. Holloway,

Dear Madam,

I have your favor of the 17th requesting such information in reference to the late Mrs. Fillmore as will enable you to give a sketch of her life.

I understand that a lady of your city has prepared and is about to publish such a sketch, and for that reason I will wait the result of that publication before deciding as to your request.

Respectfully Yours

Millard Fillmore

MILLARD FILLMORE

Never one to excite the imagination, Fillmore penned letters that were generally routine and dull, with strong opinions rarely expressed. His hand was clear, straightforward, and legible, without the flourishes and mannerisms of some of his predecessors. Although presidential material is scarce, handwritten letters of other periods are quite common, since Fillmore wrote a great deal during the twenty-one years following his presidency. Although photographs of earlier presidents (as far back as John Quincy Adams) do exist, Fillmore is the first known to have signed one—in the familiar carte de visite style.

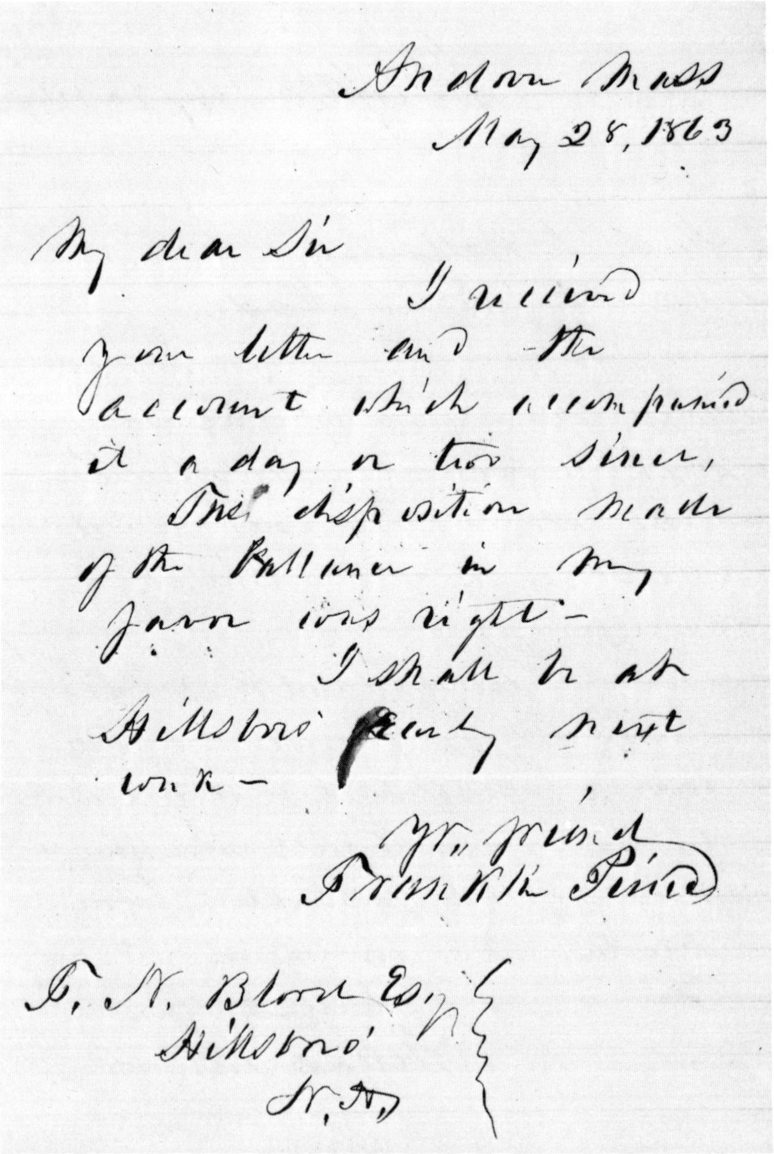
Andover Mass
May 28, 1863

My dear Sir
I received your letter and the account which accompanied it a day or two since,
The disposition made of the balance in my favor was right —
I shall be at Hillsboro' early next week —
Yr friend
Franklin Pierce

P. N. Blood Esq
Hillsboro'
N. H.

FRANKLIN PIERCE

What he lacked in literary quality Pierce made up for with flourishes and ostentation. His handwriting is marked by up-and-down strokes in a large angular hand, yet he was an indifferent writer and even letters to his family were dull. Handwritten letters and documents (usually commissions) are common, but dictated letters are quite scarce. Also scarce are signatures and signed photographs.

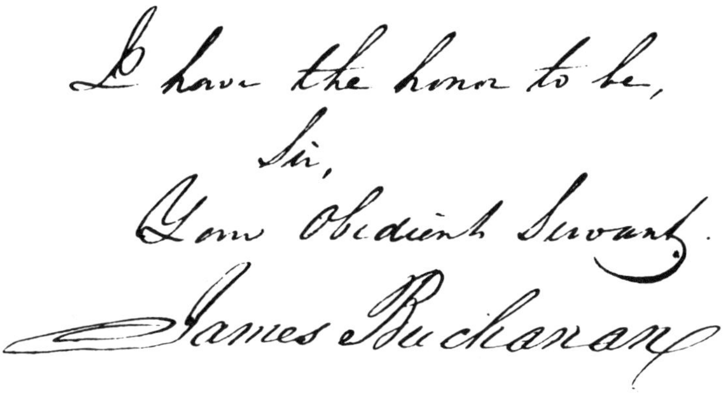

I have the honor to be,
Sir,
Your Obedient Servant.
James Buchanan

JAMES BUCHANAN

Buchanan rivaled Washington for the most attractive handwriting of all the presidents. Legible and graceful, almost artistic, his script complemented the content of his letters, which were often excellent. Demand for Buchanan material is slight, and limited chiefly to those wishing to complete a presidential set. He is quite common in all forms, although handwritten letters of presidential date are somewhat less so.

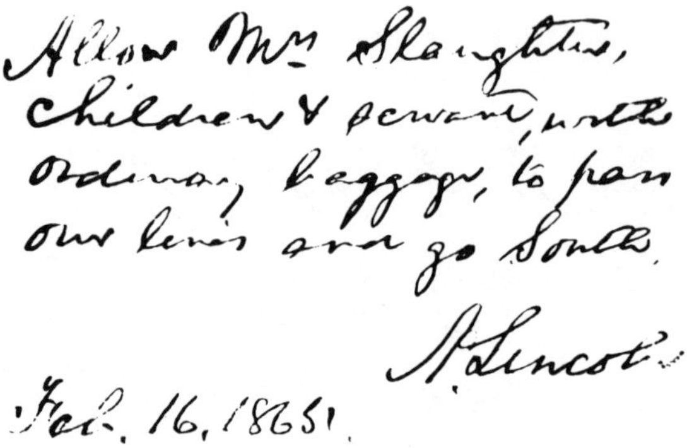
Allow Mrs Slaughter, children & servant, with ordinary baggage, to pass our lines and go South.

A. Lincoln

Feb. 16, 1865.

ABRAHAM LINCOLN

Much like the man himself, Lincoln's hand was rugged and virile, with no pretensions. A prolific writer, he did not mince words. His letters were short and to the point, yet displayed humor, graciousness, and firmness. The main impression gained from Lincoln's handwriting is that this was a man in a hurry. Dictating relatively few letters, he wrote so quickly that it is not at all unusual to find a grammatical error, a misspelling, or even an omitted word. He is an interesting contrast with Washington, who, although more prolific, rarely made an error in his correspondence. Far and away the most popular president with collectors, Lincoln's material is in great demand and its prices are high. Early letters are scarce but later, more routine letters are still readily available. On his letters Lincoln almost invariably signed "A. Lincoln," whereas his full signature just as invariably appears only on official documents and formal papers signed as president. Very fine handwritten letters are becoming quite scarce, with most of them having been absorbed by institutions. Signed photographs, although in great demand, are extremely scarce. Because of his great popularity, and because his hand varied so little, Lincoln is an inspiration to forgers more than any other president.

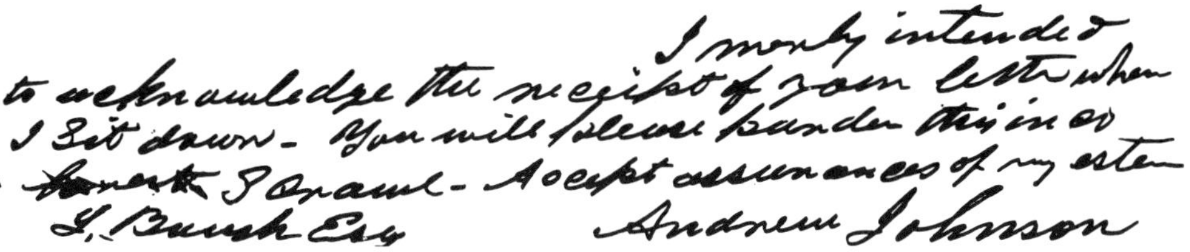
I merely intended to acknowledge the receipt of your letter when I sit down - You will please render this in so ~~honest~~ I could - Accept assurances of my esteem
G. Bush Esq Andrew Johnson

ANDREW JOHNSON

An uneducated man, Johnson did not learn to write until he was an adult; and his hand was a reflection of that lack of schooling. Labored and angular, with frightful spelling, Johnson's letters are nevertheless often long and strongly worded, forcefully expressing his views. Handwritten letters of Johnson are not common, a result, in large part, of a game right arm. For this reason also, he was the first to use a hand stamp on many of his presidential documents. However, signed documents are obtainable, usually in the form of commissions and pardons. Signed photographs are not common, with those that do appear often signed in a cramped hand on the front and more boldly on the blank verso.

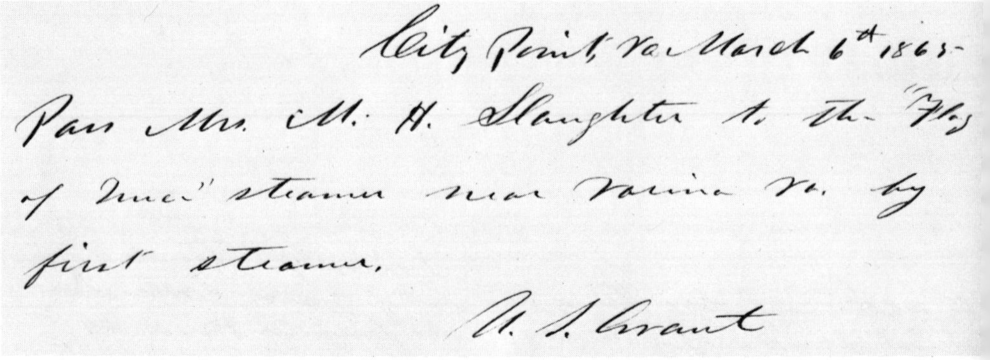
City Point, Va. March 6th 1865
Pass Mrs. M. H. Slaughter to the "Flag of Truce" steamer near Varina Va. by first steamer.
U. S. Grant

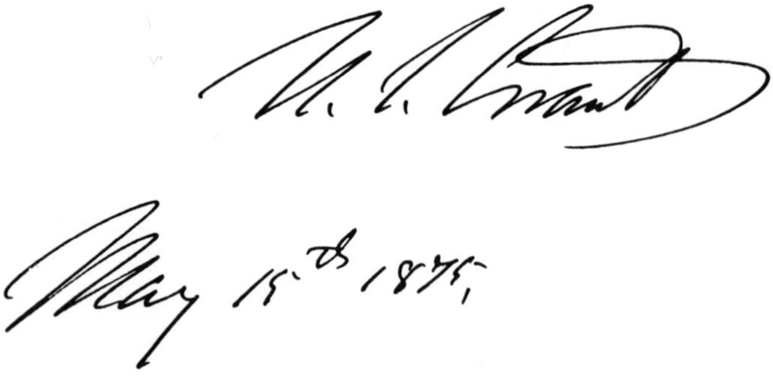

ULYSSES SIMPSON GRANT

Those few early letters of Grant that turn up display a small, pointed script. In his later, more successful years he changed to a thicker pen and his hand was larger, free-flowing, easily read, and devoid of flourishes. His finest letters were those written during the Civil War, being both authoritative and forceful; material of this period is in steady demand. Grant is common in all forms, although dictated letters are somewhat more difficult to come by. He also introduced the formal Executive Mansion card, probably for short notes, but very few have come on the market signed by him.

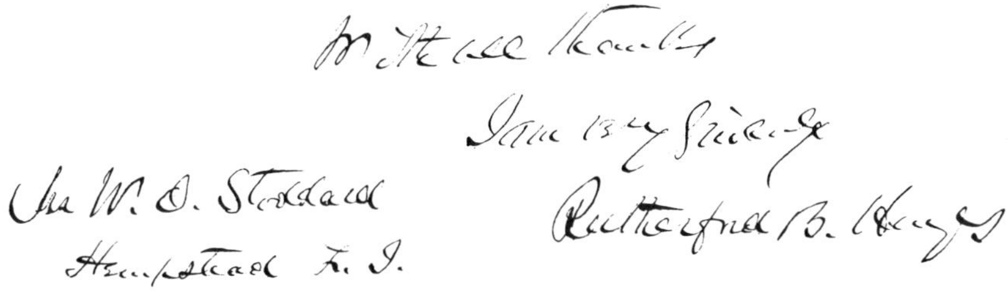

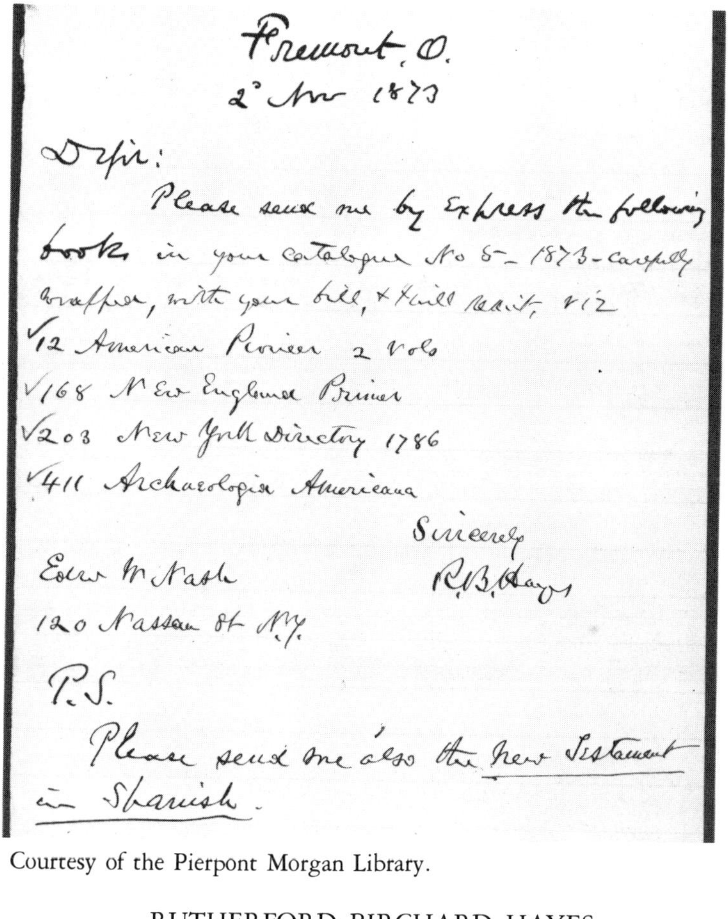

Fremont, O.
2° Nov 1873

Dr Sir:

Please send me by Express the following books in your catalogue No 5 – 1873 – carefully wrapped, with your bill, & I will remit, viz

√12 American Pioneer 2 vols
√168 New England Primer
√203 New York Directory 1786
√411 Archaeologia Americana

Sincerely
R. B. Hayes

Edw W. Nash
120 Nassau St N.Y.

P.S.
Please send me also the New Testament in Spanish.

Courtesy of the Pierpont Morgan Library.

RUTHERFORD BIRCHARD HAYES

Hayes had a small, almost feminine, hand that varied little. He is not in demand except to round out sets, and much of his material has been absorbed by institutions. Dictated letters are quite scarce, documents somewhat less so.

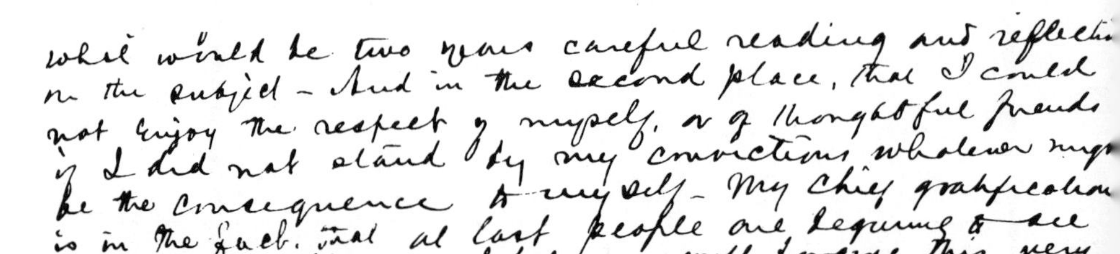
which would be two years careful reading and reflection
on the subject – And in the second place, that I could
not enjoy the respect of myself, or of thoughtful friends
if I did not stand by my convictions whatever might
be the consequence to myself – My chief gratification
is in the fact that at last people are beginning to see
& appreciate this – I hope you will forgive this very
long letter. All the family send love – As ever Yours
Harmon Austin. Warren O. J A Garfield

JAMES ABRAM GARFIELD

Garfield wrote a fluent, graceful, and legible hand but was an indifferent writer; good letters are rare. Since he was assassinated just four months after taking office, presidential material is very scarce in all forms. Prepresidential handwritten letters are quite common, although in little demand. Collectors should be aware that, during the year prior to this election, Garfield's secretary, J. Stanley Brown, deliberately imitated his handwriting; letters dictated to Brown are often mistaken for handwritten ones.

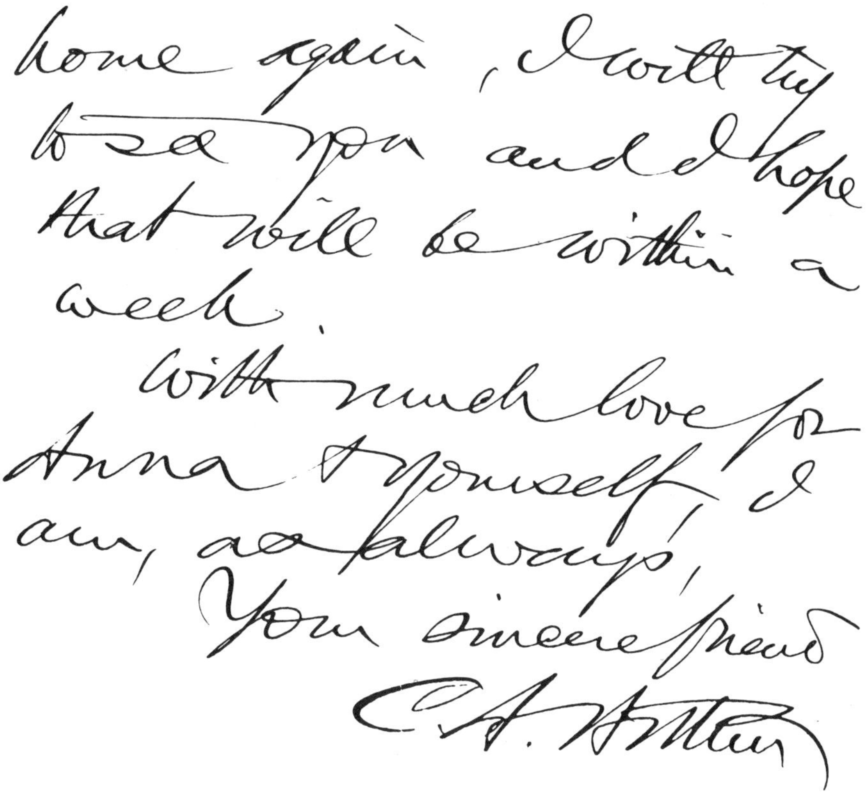

home again, I will try
to see you and I hope
that will be within a
week.
With much love for
Anna & yourself I
am, as always,
Your sincere friend
C. A. Arthur

CHESTER ALAN ARTHUR

Arthur wrote a large, striking hand, but his letters did not live up to the promise of his pen. They are poor in quality, and there is little demand for them. Although handwritten letters in office are scarce, those written as quartermaster general of New York are relatively common. He did initiate an elaborate card bearing an engraving of the White House, which he signed and distributed; but these did not replace the Executive Mansion cards introduced by Grant.

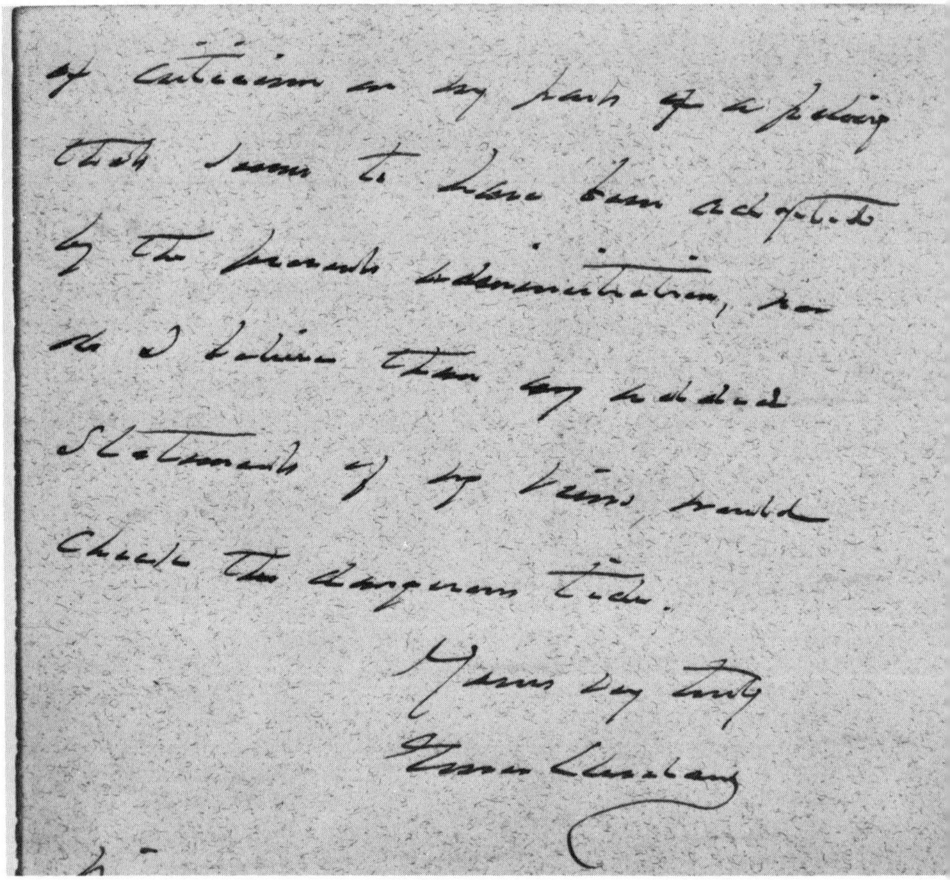

of criticism on my part of a policy
that seems to have been adopted
by the present administration, nor
do I believe that any added
statements of my views would
check the dangerous tide.

Yours very truly
Grover Cleveland

GROVER CLEVELAND

Cleveland's hand was in stark contrast with his personality and physical presence. A virile "man's man," he had a small and dainty hand quite difficult to read. Yet his letters were consistently good, and he can certainly be considered one of the better writers to serve in the presidency. There is not a great deal of demand for Cleveland and his letters are quite common, although material of presidential date is somewhat less so. He is the only president to have served two nonconsecutive terms.

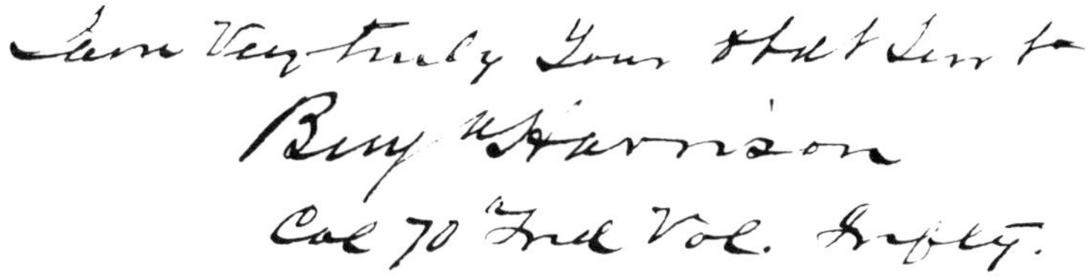

BENJAMIN HARRISON

Another president whose hand varied greatly, Harrison had an early script that was rounded and fairly legible. In later years it became pointed and nearly illegible, having some similarity to that of Cleveland. Demand is not great for letters of Harrison, and he generally had little of interest to say. It is notable that his dictated letters seem to have better content than his handwritten ones. He apparently was better able to marshal his thoughts and speak his mind when he did not have to be concerned with guiding his pen across a page. Handwritten letters of Harrison are fairly scarce, while other forms are readily available.

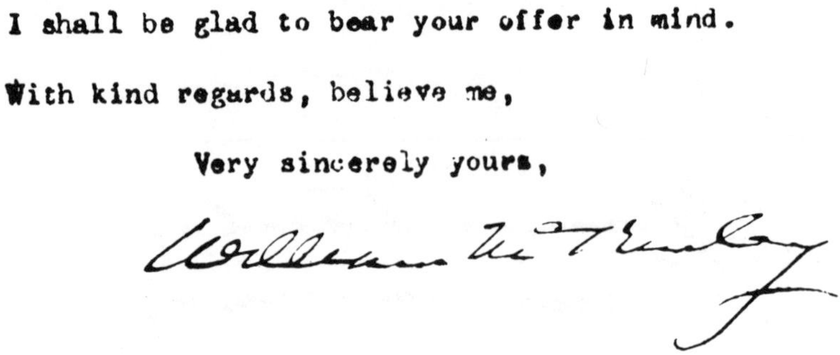
I shall be glad to bear your offer in mind.

With kind regards, believe me,

Very sincerely yours,

William McKinley Jr

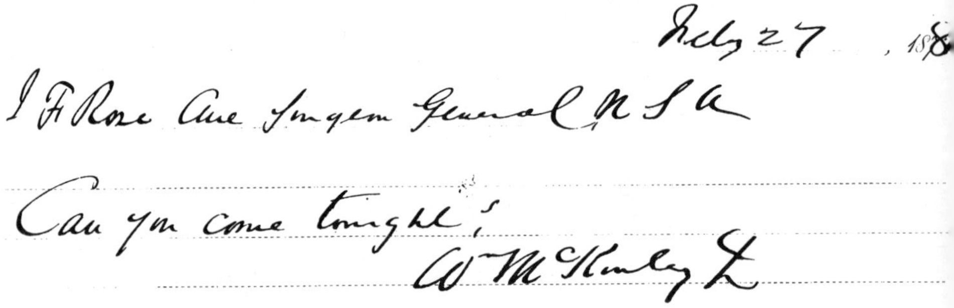
July 27, 188

J F Rose Asst Surgeon General U S A

Can you come tonight?

W McKinley Jr

WILLIAM McKINLEY

The restrained and precise hand of his early years gave way to a vigorous, forceful script late in McKinley's career. He was a colorless writer, and there is little demand for his letters. Prepresidential handwritten letters are available; but letters as president, whether handwritten or dictated, are scarce. Although Cleveland and Benjamin Harrison had made use of the typewriter, McKinley was the first to do so regularly; typewritten letters of prepresidential date are fairly plentiful. The presidential document most often encountered is the commission, and these are in good supply. One does come across handwritten drafts of telegrams written during his term in office.

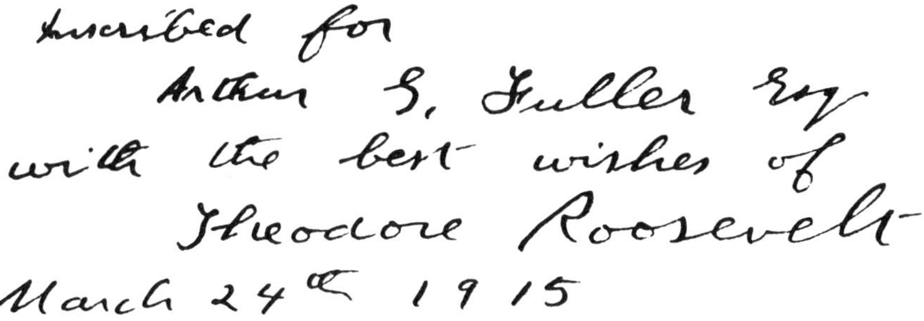
Inscribed for
Arthur G. Fuller Esq
with the best wishes of
Theodore Roosevelt
March 24th 1915

THEODORE ROOSEVELT

One of our most popular presidents, Roosevelt wrote with a sprawling, immature hand that varied little. He was an excellent writer despite the immense volume of his correspondence during his literary and political careers. Always a fighter, he wrote fiery but fluent letters when angry or upset. Roosevelt is most common in typewritten letters, which often bear extensive handwritten corrections and postscripts. Also common are typewritten manuscripts bearing handwritten corrections and interlineations. The demand for Theodore Roosevelt is quite strong, much more so than for his cousin Franklin.

Shortly after assuming the presidency in late 1901, Roosevelt changed the Executive Mansion cards to White House cards, apparently feeling the former were too ostentatious. The collector should be wary of dictated letters written while governor of New York and vice-president. Roosevelt was the first president to permit his secretary to sign his name for him.

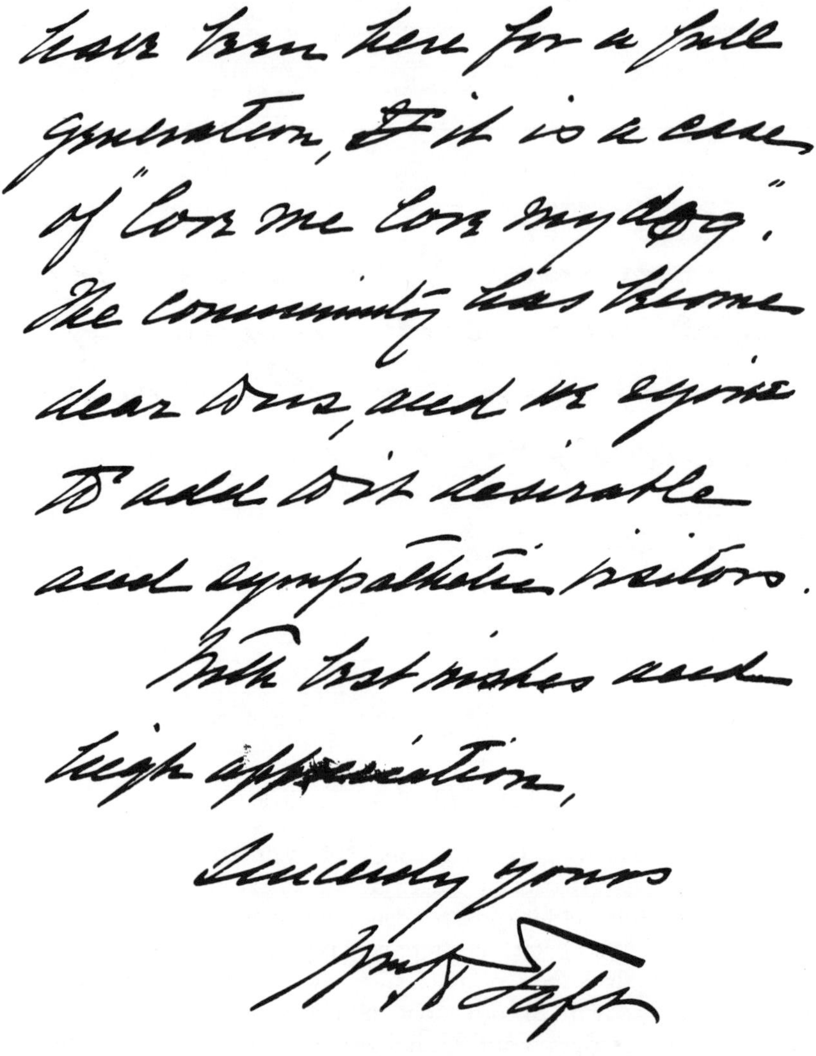
have been here for a full generation, & it is a case of "Love me love my dog". The community has become dear to us, and we rejoice to add to it desirable and sympathetic visitors.

With best wishes and high appreciation,

Sincerely yours

Wm H Taft

WILLIAM HOWARD TAFT

Taft wrote an attractive and pleasing hand and, although capable of writing a fine letter, seldom did so. It can be said that his letters were always gracious but seldom interesting. Taft is as much in demand writing as chief justice of the Supreme Court as he is as president, and the supply is limited.

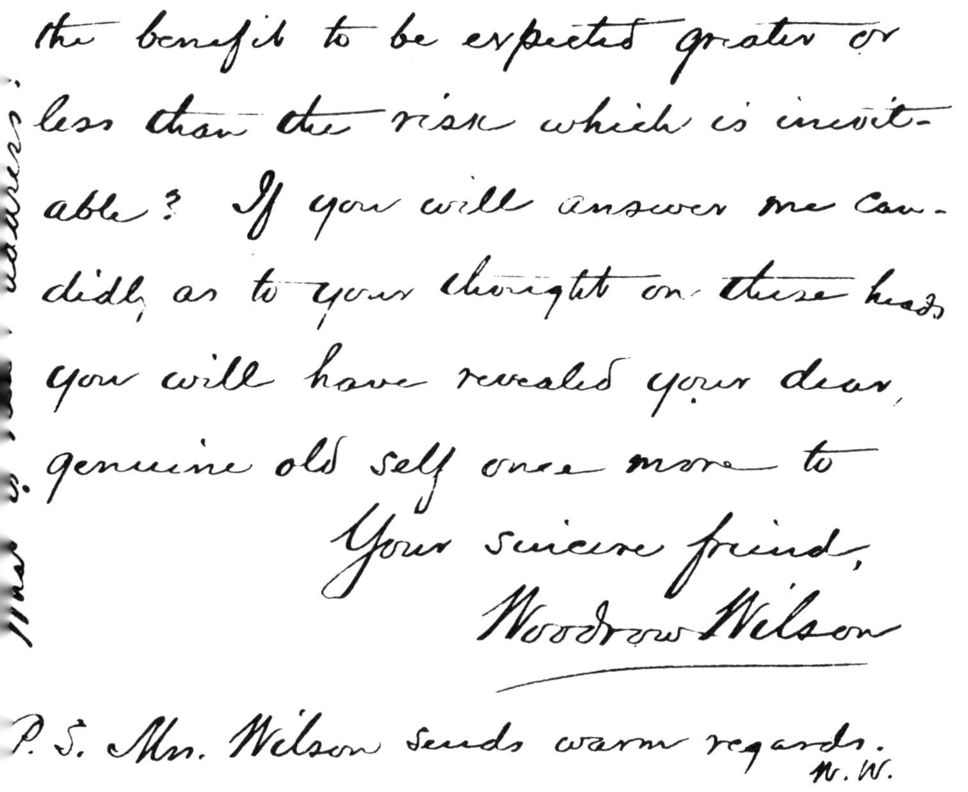

the benefit to be expected greater or less than the risk which is inevitable? If you will answer me candidly as to your thought on these heads you will have revealed your dear, genuine old self once more to

Your sincere friend,
Woodrow Wilson

P.S. Mrs. Wilson sends warm regards.
W.W.

WOODROW WILSON

Wilson had an extremely legible hand, certainly one of the finest of all the presidents, and, during his early years, wrote splendid letters. Later, as his responsibilities and political activities increased, he tended to limit himself to short notes. While preceding presidents had used the typewriter, Wilson was the first to make extensive use of one; and the distinctive, small type of his personal machine turns up regularly. Handwritten letters are quite unusual, and his typewritten letters are often very good. Wilson was apparently able easily to impress his thoughts on his typewriter keys. Documents are not common, and those that do appear are generally commissions. The collector should be wary of material signed while governor of New Jersey and while running for the presidency. Wilson used rubber stamps during those periods.

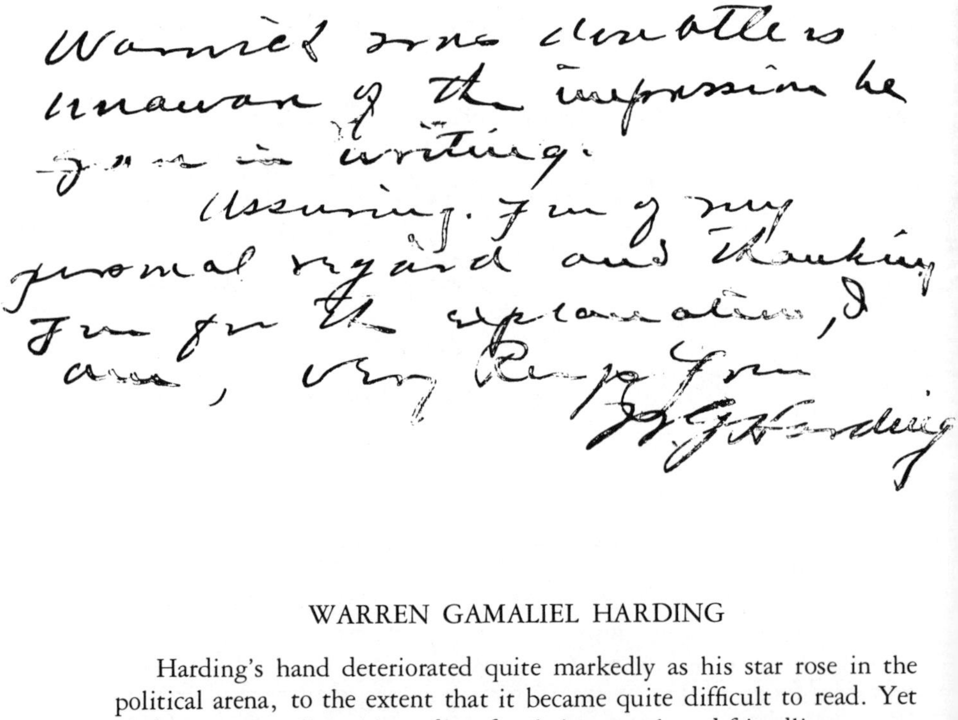

WARREN GAMALIEL HARDING

Harding's hand deteriorated quite markedly as his star rose in the political arena, to the extent that it became quite difficult to read. Yet his letters are well worth reading for their warmth and friendliness, even the routine ones. To his intimates he displayed a marvelous wit and humor. Surprisingly, there is little demand for his letters. Very few handwritten ones as president have ever appeared, nor is he common of prepresidential date. Dictated letters are available, while documents are uncommon. Handwritten documents, while editor of the *Marion Star,* are frequently encountered. Watch for the authorized forgeries of his secretary, George B. Christian, Jr. He deliberately imitated Harding's signature, and it was nearly identical to the real thing.

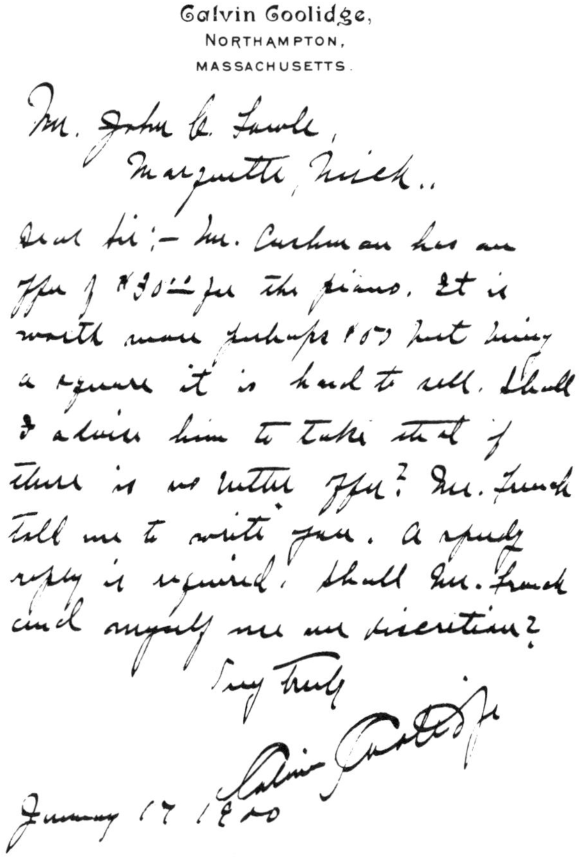

Calvin Coolidge,
NORTHAMPTON,
MASSACHUSETTS.

Mr. John C. Fowle,
Marquette, Mich..

Dear Sir:— Mr. Cushman has an offer of $30.00 for the piano. It is worth more perhaps $100 but being a square it is hard to sell. Shall I advise him to take that if there is no better offer? Mr. French tells me to write you. A speedy reply is required. Shall Mr. French send anyway or use our discretion?

Very Truly
Calvin Coolidge

January 17 1900

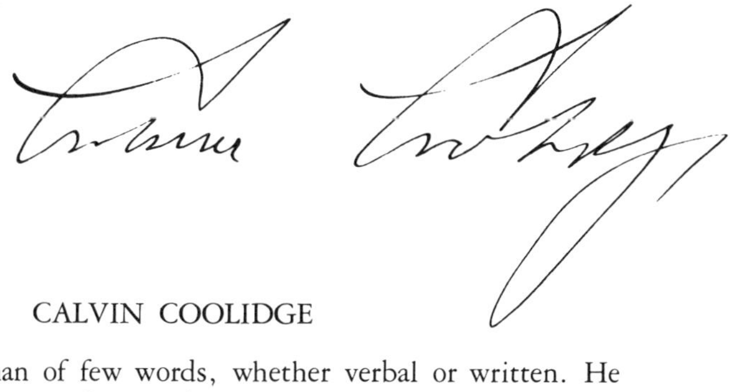

CALVIN COOLIDGE

Coolidge was a man of few words, whether verbal or written. He would fill a page with just a few words or lines of his large, scratchy, indecipherable scrawl. One of the dullest of the presidential letter writers, Coolidge is in little demand. His handwritten letters are very rare, while dictated letters are common. As with most of the modern presidents, documents, especially those of presidential date, are scarce. Collectors should be wary of dictated letters, particularly as governor. Coolidge authorized his secretaries to sign his name for him, and these signatures sometimes bear a resemblance to his own.

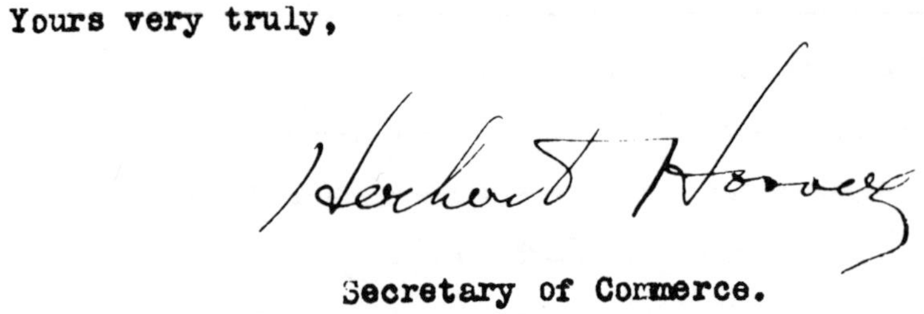

Yours very truly,

Herbert Hoover

Secretary of Commerce.

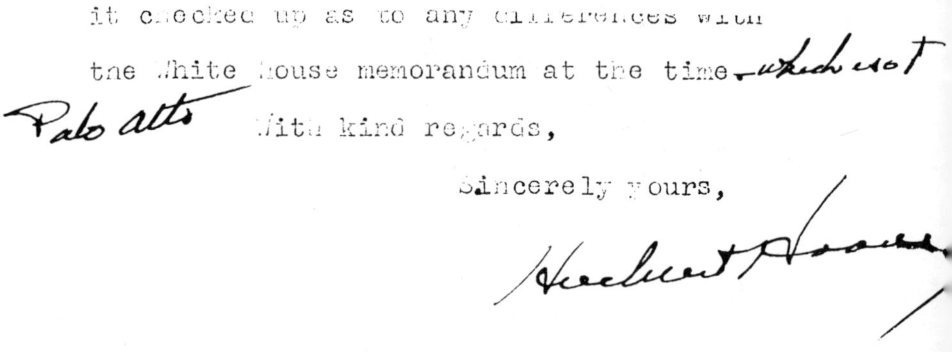

it checked up as to any differences with
the White House memorandum at the time — which is not Palo Alto

With kind regards,

Sincerely yours,

Herbert Hoover

HERBERT CLARK HOOVER

Although Hoover wrote with a graceful and legible hand, his handwritten letters, particularly as president, are extremely scarce. Dictated letters are fairly common, although less so as president. Demand for Hoover appears to be picking up, although the contents of his letters are generally indifferent. Hoover's secretary's hand greatly resembled his own, and dictated letters are often mistaken for handwritten ones. He also permitted others to sign his letters for him, and these items must be guarded against. A final caution: Hoover used facsimile Christmas greetings and thank you notes for birthday greetings. These are so well done that they are often mistaken for the real thing.

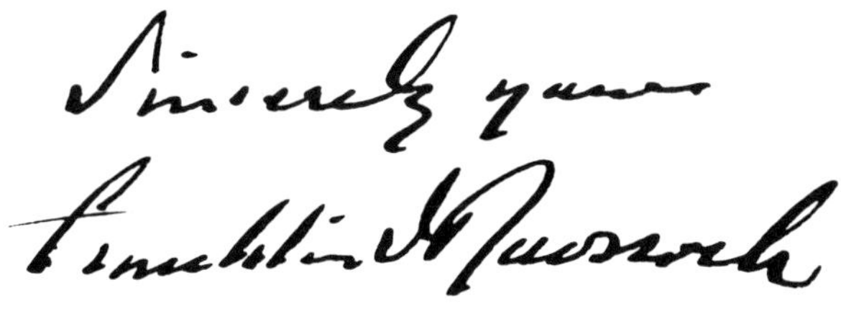

FRANKLIN DELANO ROOSEVELT

Although many of Roosevelt's letters were warm and friendly, few were interesting; those to his intimates generally are the best. Demand is waning but the supply is plentiful, with dictated letters and documents quite common. Handwritten letters, particularly as president, are scarce, as are signatures. Roosevelt often signed his letters with his initials and, like Harding, used a professional forger; thus, many of his letters were not actually signed by him. Adding to the confusion is the variety of signatures he himself used. The only president to serve more than two terms, Roosevelt died shortly after his fourth inauguration. Some months prior to his death, in the fall of 1944, his signature began to show the unmistakable downward slant of an ill man who can no longer control his pen.

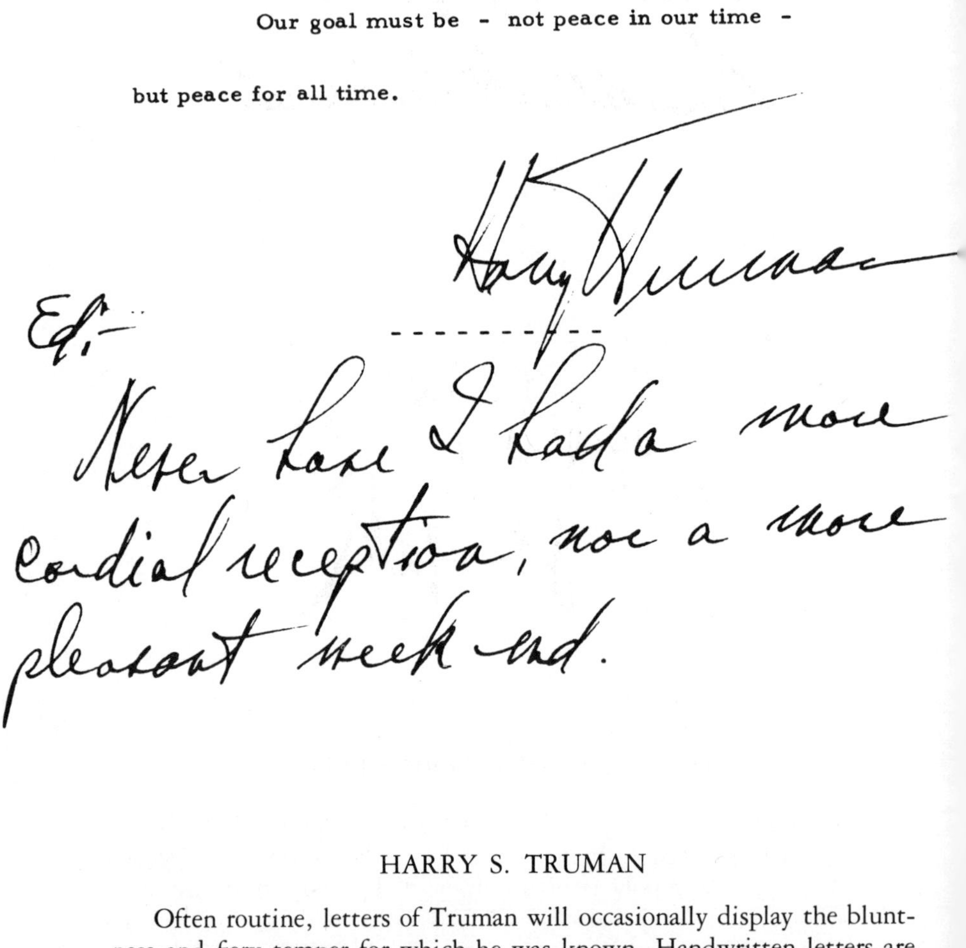

Our goal must be - not peace in our time -

but peace for all time.

Harry Truman

Ed.—

Never have I had a more cordial reception, nor a more pleasant week-end.

HARRY S. TRUMAN

Often routine, letters of Truman will occasionally display the bluntness and fiery temper for which he was known. Handwritten letters are very scarce, with dictated presidential letters less so and those of other periods quite common, particularly those following his presidency. Respect and admiration for Truman have increased dramatically in recent years, and demand for his letters is on the rise. The collector should watch for letters written while in the Senate, since many of these were signed by secretaries. He also, on occasion, distributed White House cards bearing secretarial signatures.

Will you please convey to His Excellency
the Archbishop of Brooklyn and accept
for yourself my appreciation for your
good wishes, which I fully reciprocate.

Sincerely,

DWIGHT DAVID EISENHOWER

Letters of Eisenhower, who was much admired as a general, are in good demand and his dictated letters are generally available. Handwritten letters and documents are scarce. Signed photographs of him in uniform are also popular. Demand for Eisenhower's signature was so great that he had prepared facsimile inscriptions and signatures on White House cards. A printed statement, identifying the facsimile as such, appeared on the verso of the card. Collectors should watch for such cards that have been pasted down, thereby obscuring the disclaimer.

With every good wish, I am

Sincerely,

John F. Kennedy

I hope to see you some time soon to thank you personally – Best regards Jack Kennedy

JOHN FITZGERALD KENNEDY

Second in popularity only to that of Lincoln, the demand for Kennedy material remains high, although the wild prices following his assassination have abated somewhat. Few handwritten letters have come on the market, but those few are generally well written and friendly. Dictated letters as president are scarce, but prepresidential dictated letters are increasingly available. Many of his dictated letters carry handwritten postscripts.

Identifying Kennedy's handwriting, or his signature, can be a frustrating adventure, since both varied almost daily. In addition, Kennedy made greater use of secretarial signatures than did any of his predecessors. They would often write inscriptions, as well as signatures, particularly on photographs. Kennedy was also the first president to use the Autopen, and great care is needed to avoid such signatures.* Recently a number of scratch sheets bearing doodles of sailboats and signatures of Kennedy have appeared on the market. The inclusion of the sailboat makes these believable and desirable items, yet they have so far proved to be spurious.

---

*See Charles Hamilton, *The Robot That Helped to Make a President* (New York: [Charles Hamilton?], 1965), for more about Kennedy's use of the Autopen.

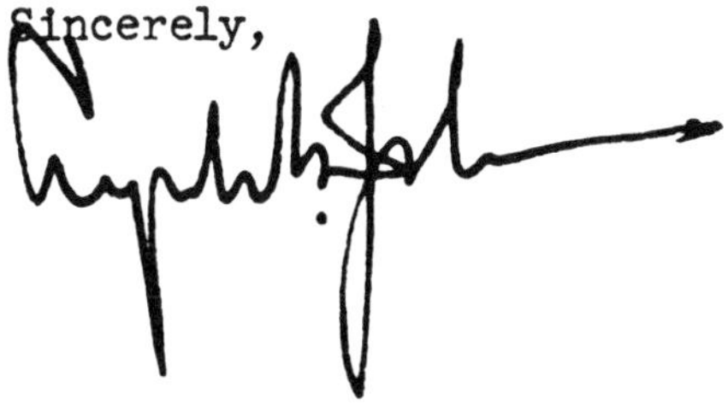
Sincerely,

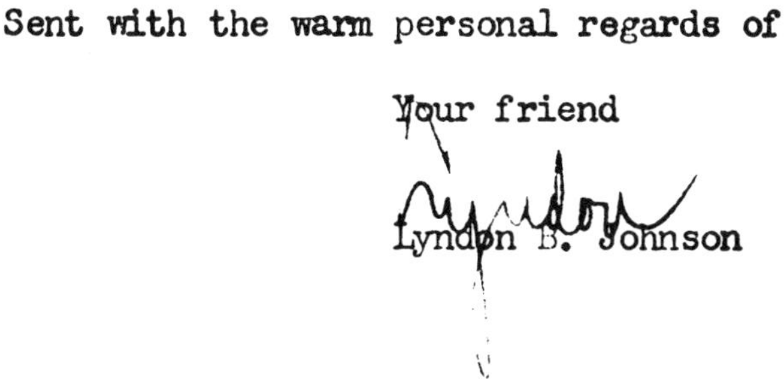
Sent with the warm personal regards of

Your friend

Lyndon B. Johnson

LYNDON BAINES JOHNSON

Demand for Johnson is good, primarily to complete sets. Yet material signed by him is scarce because of his extensive use of secretarial and Autopen signatures. Most common are dictated letters written after his presidency, many of which he signed with initials. Johnson also distributed White House cards bearing facsimile inscriptions and signatures. As with Eisenhower, the cards bore a statement on the verso identifying the signature as a facsimile.

RICHARD MILHOUS NIXON

In demand primarily in order to complete a set, or for his being the central figure in the Watergate scandal, authentic Nixon letters are difficult to identify and secure, with handwritten letters virtually unobtainable. Countless letters bearing secretarial and Autopen signatures have flooded the market. White House cards with Autopen signatures are also in great abundance, and have fooled many an unwary or trusting collector. There is no disclaimer on the verso of these cards, in contrast with the facsimiles of his predecessors.

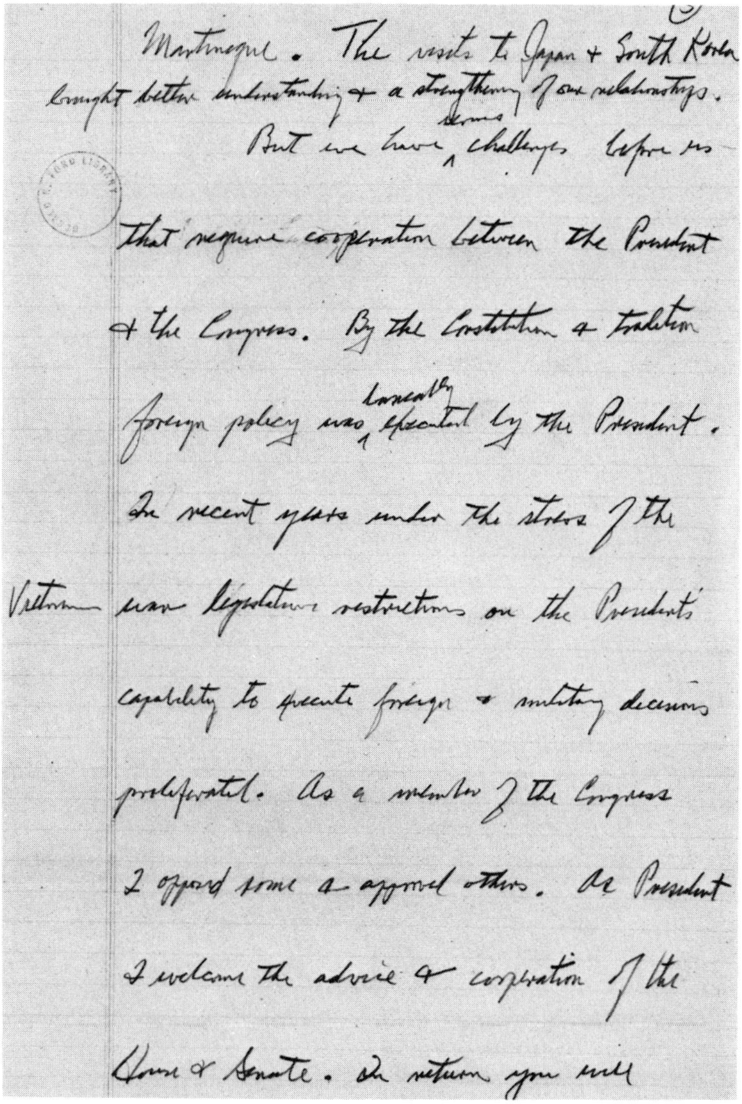
Martinique. The visits to Japan & South Korea
brought better understanding & a strengthening of our relationships.
But we have serious challenges before us
that require cooperation between the President
& the Congress. By the Constitution & tradition
foreign policy was basically executed by the President.
In recent years under the stress of the
Vietnam war legislative restrictions on the President's
capability to execute foreign & military decisions
proliferated. As a member of the Congress
I opposed some & approved others. As President
I welcome the advice & cooperation of the
House & Senate. In return you will

Courtesy of the Gerald R. Ford Presidential Materials Project.

GERALD RUDOLPH FORD

A number of dictated letters have come on the market but, as with the three presidents preceding him, care must be taken to avoid the Autopen signature. It is interesting to note that President Ford reportedly stopped writing his own checks because he had been bedeviled by persons who refused to cash them, preferring to keep them as souvenirs.

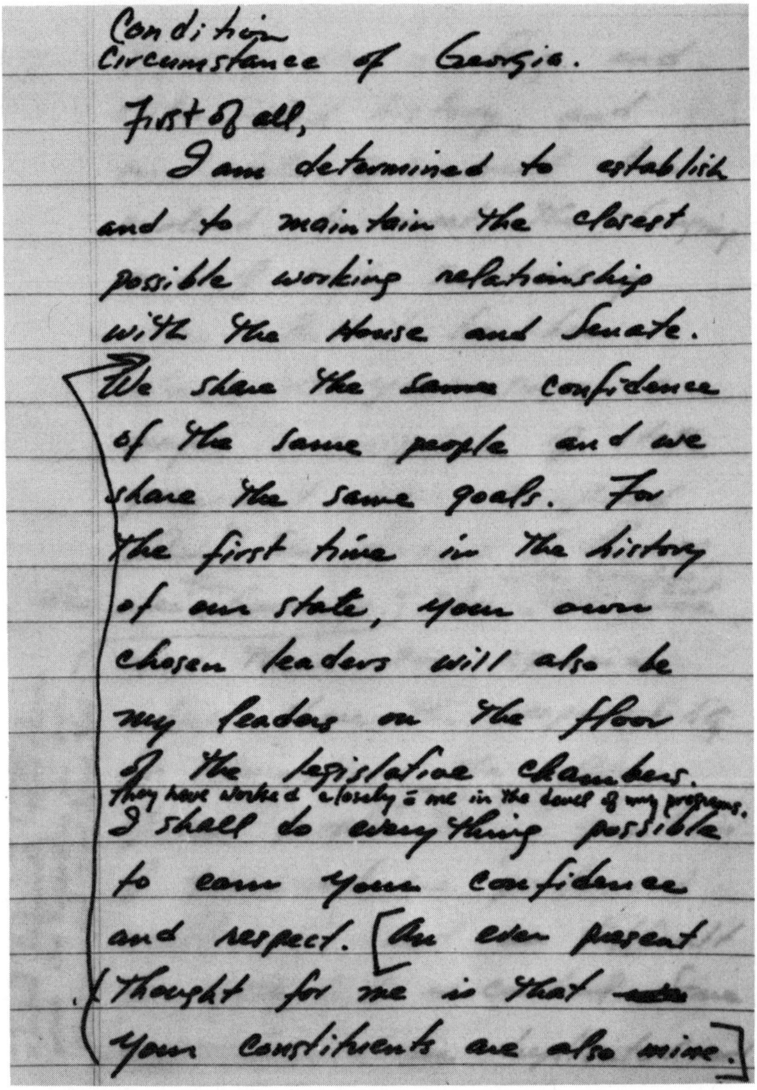

Condition
Circumstance of Georgia.

First of all,

I am determined to establish and to maintain the closest possible working relationship with the House and Senate. We share the same confidence of the same people and we share the same goals. For the first time in the history of our state, your own chosen leaders will also be my leaders on the floor of the legislative chambers. They have worked closely c̄ me in the devel of my programs. I shall do everything possible to earn your confidence and respect. [An ever present thought for me is that your constituents are also mine.]

JAMES EARL CARTER

As with other presidents of the Autopen era, letters of Carter are, as yet, scarce. During his campaign for the presidency he did send out a number of postcards bearing facsimile handwritten notes. Then, upon assuming office, he apparently added a new refinement—a machine, similar to the Autopen, which can reproduce entire handwritten letters. Using stock paragraphs, completely "original, handwritten" notes and letters can be sent out over the "presidential," or Autopen, signature. Where it will all end, or how collectors will be able to deal with this new problem, remains to be seen.

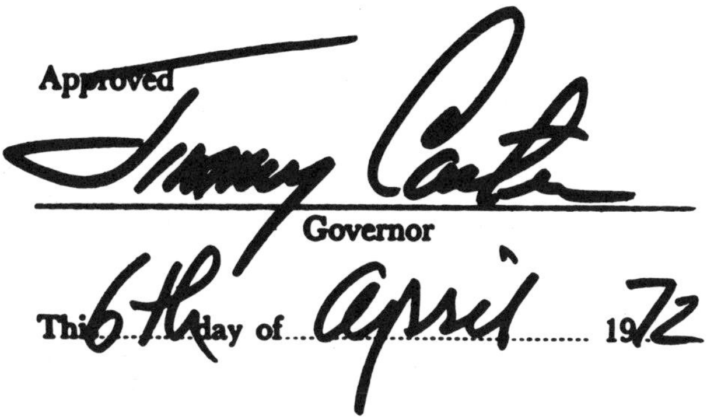

Left and above: Courtesy of the Georgia Department of Archives and History.

CONCLUSION

Collecting a "presidential" set can be a relatively simple endeavor, as well as an intensely personal one. Yet the road to completion can be full of pitfalls, all waiting to trap the unwary novice. The determined collector can learn much about secretarial signatures, the Autopen, forgeries, facsimiles, investment prospects, and other factors pertaining to his hobby. But the best friend a collector can have, in terms of knowledge, guidance, and as a source of the right material for his collection, is a reputable dealer in whom he can place his complete trust. With such a friend, building a collection of autographs of the presidents of the United States can be a marvelously stimulating and profitable venture.

PRESIDENTS OF THE UNITED STATES

President	*Date of Birth*	*Date of Death*	*Period of Service*
GEORGE WASHINGTON (Fed.)	Feb. 11/22, 1732	Dec. 14, 1799	Apr. 30, 1789 – Mar. 3, 1793 Mar. 4, 1793 – Mar. 3, 1797
JOHN ADAMS (Fed.)	Oct. 19/30, 1735	July 4, 1826	Mar. 4, 1797 – Mar. 3, 1801
THOMAS JEFFERSON (Dem.-Rep.)	Apr. 2/13, 1743	July 4, 1826	Mar. 4, 1801 – Mar. 3, 1805 Mar. 4, 1805 – Mar. 3, 1809
JAMES MADISON (Dem.-Rep.)	Mar. 5/16, 1751	June 28, 1836	Mar. 4, 1809 – Mar. 3, 1813 Mar. 4, 1813 – Mar. 3, 1817
JAMES MONROE (Dem.-Rep.)	Apr. 28, 1758	July 4, 1831	Mar. 4, 1817 – Mar. 3, 1821 Mar. 4, 1821 – Mar. 3, 1825
JOHN QUINCY ADAMS (Dem.-Rep.)	July 11, 1767	Feb. 23, 1848	Mar. 4, 1825 – Mar. 3, 1829
ANDREW JACKSON (Dem.)	Mar. 15, 1767	June 8, 1845	Mar. 4, 1829 – Mar. 3, 1833 Mar. 4, 1833 – Mar. 3, 1837
MARTIN VAN BUREN (Dem.)	Dec. 5, 1782	July 24, 1862	Mar. 4, 1837 – Mar. 3, 1841
*WILLIAM HENRY HARRISON (Whig)	Feb. 9, 1773	Apr. 4, 1841 (12:30 A.M.)	Mar. 4, 1841 – Apr. 4, 1841
JOHN TYLER (Whig)	Mar. 29, 1790	Jan. 18, 1862	Apr. 6, 1841 – Mar. 3, 1845
JAMES KNOX POLK (Dem.)	Nov. 2, 1795	June 15, 1849	Mar. 4, 1845 – Mar. 3, 1849
*ZACHARY TAYLOR (Whig)	Nov. 24, 1784	July 9, 1850 (10:35 P.M.)	Mar. 5, 1849 – July 9, 1850
MILLARD FILLMORE (Whig)	Jan. 7, 1800	Mar. 8, 1874	July 10, 1850 – Mar. 3, 1853
FRANKLIN PIERCE (Dem.)	Nov. 23, 1804	Oct. 8, 1869	Mar. 4, 1853 – Mar. 3, 1857
JAMES BUCHANAN (Dem.)	Apr. 23, 1791	June 1, 1868	Mar. 4, 1857 – Mar. 3, 1861
†ABRAHAM LINCOLN (Rep.)	Feb. 12, 1809	Apr. 15, 1865 (7:22 A.M.)	Mar. 4, 1861 – Mar. 3, 1865 Mar. 4, 1865 – Apr. 15, 1865
ANDREW JOHNSON (Union)	Dec. 29, 1808	July 31, 1875	Apr. 15, 1865 – Mar. 3, 1869
ULYSSES SIMPSON GRANT (Rep.)	Apr. 27, 1822	July 23, 1885	Mar. 4, 1869 – Mar. 3, 1873 Mar. 4, 1873 – Mar. 3, 1877
RUTHERFORD BIRCHARD HAYES (Rep.)	Oct. 4, 1822	Jan. 17, 1893	Mar. 5, 1877 – Mar. 3, 1881
†JAMES ABRAM GARFIELD (Rep.)	Nov. 19, 1831	Sept. 19, 1881 (10:35 P.M.)	Mar. 4, 1881 – Sept. 19, 1881

CHESTER ALAN ARTHUR (Rep.)	Oct. 5, 1830	Nov. 18, 1886	Sept. 19, 1881 – Mar. 3, 1885
GROVER CLEVELAND (Dem.)	Mar. 18, 1837	June 24, 1908	Mar. 4, 1885 – Mar. 3, 1889
BENJAMIN HARRISON (Rep.)	Aug. 20, 1833	Mar. 13, 1901	Mar. 4, 1889 – Mar. 3, 1893
GROVER CLEVELAND (Dem.)	Mar. 18, 1837	June 24, 1908	Mar. 4, 1893 – Mar. 3, 1897
†WILLIAM McKINLEY (Rep.)	Jan. 29, 1843	Sept. 14, 1901 (2:15 A.M.)	Mar. 4, 1897 – Mar. 3, 1901
			Mar. 4, 1901 – Sept. 14, 1901
THEODORE ROOSEVELT (Rep.)	Oct. 27, 1858	Jan. 6, 1919	Sept. 14, 1901 – Mar. 3, 1905
			Mar. 4, 1905 – Mar. 3, 1909
WILLIAM HOWARD TAFT (Rep.)	Sept. 15, 1857	Mar. 8, 1930	Mar. 4, 1909 – Mar. 3, 1913
WOODROW WILSON (Dem.)	Dec. 28, 1856	Feb. 3, 1924	Mar. 4, 1913 – Mar. 3, 1917
			Mar. 4, 1917 – Mar. 3, 1921
*WARREN GAMALIEL HARDING (Rep.)	Nov. 2, 1865	Aug. 2, 1923 (7:30 P.M.)	Mar. 4, 1921 – Aug. 2, 1923
CALVIN COOLIDGE (Rep.)	July 4, 1872	Jan. 5, 1933	Aug. 3, 1923 – Mar. 3, 1925
			Mar. 4, 1925 – Mar. 3, 1929
HERBERT CLARK HOOVER (Rep.)	Aug. 10, 1874	Oct. 20, 1964	Mar. 4, 1929 – Mar. 3, 1933
*FRANKLIN DELANO ROOSEVELT (Dem.)	Jan. 30, 1882	Apr. 12, 1945 (3:35 PM.)	Mar. 4, 1933 – Jan. 20, 1937
			Jan. 20, 1937 – Jan. 20, 1941
			Jan. 20, 1941 – Jan. 20, 1945
			Jan. 20, 1945 – Apr. 12, 1945
HARRY S. TRUMAN (Dem.)	May 8, 1884	Dec. 26, 1972	Apr. 12, 1945 – Jan. 20, 1949
			Jan. 20, 1949 – Jan. 20, 1953
DWIGHT DAVID EISENHOWER (Rep.)	Oct. 14, 1890	Mar. 28, 1969	Jan. 20, 1953 – Jan. 20, 1957
			Jan. 20, 1957 – Jan. 20, 1961
†JOHN FITZGERALD KENNEDY (Dem.)	May 29, 1917	Nov. 22, 1963 (2:00 P.M. EST)	Jan. 20, 1961 – Nov. 22, 1963
LYNDON BAINES JOHNSON (Dem.)	Aug. 27, 1908	Jan. 22, 1973	Nov. 22, 1963 – Jan. 20, 1965
			Jan. 20, 1965 – Jan. 20, 1969
‡RICHARD MILHOUS NIXON (Rep.)	Jan. 9, 1913		Jan. 20, 1969 – Jan. 20, 1973
			Jan. 20, 1973 – Aug. 9, 1974 (12:00 Noon EST)
GERALD RUDOLPH FORD (Rep.)	July 14, 1913		Aug. 9, 1974 – Jan. 20, 1977
JAMES EARL CARTER (Dem.)	Oct. 1, 1924		Jan. 20, 1977 –

*Died in office.
†Assassinated.
‡Resigned.

WIVES OF THE PRESIDENTS

Name	*Born*	*Married*	*Died*	*Years as First Lady or in White House*
Martha Custis WASHINGTON	June 2, 1731	Jan. 6, 1759	May 22, 1802	Apr. 30, 1789 – Mar. 3, 1793* Mar. 4, 1793 – Mar. 3, 1797
Abigail Smith ADAMS	Nov. 11, 1744	Oct. 25, 1764	Oct. 28, 1818	Mar. 4, 1797 – Mar. 3, 1801
Martha Skelton JEFFERSON	Oct. 19, 1748	Jan. 1, 1772	Sept. 6, 1782	Died before Election
Dorothea Todd MADISON	May 20, 1768	Sept. 15, 1794	July 12, 1849	Mar. 4, 1809 – Mar. 3, 1813 Mar. 4, 1813 – Mar. 3, 1817
Elizabeth Kortright MONROE	*ca.* 1763	Feb. 16, 1786	Sept. 23, 1830	Mar. 4, 1817 – Mar. 3, 1821 Mar. 4, 1821 – Mar. 3, 1825
Louisa Johnson ADAMS	Feb. 12, 1775	July 26, 1797	May 15, 1852	Mar. 4, 1825 – Mar. 3, 1829
Rachel Robards JACKSON	June 15, 1767	Aug. 1791†	Dec. 22, 1828	Died before Inauguration
Hannah Hoes VAN BUREN	Mar. 8, 1783	Feb. 21, 1807	Feb. 5, 1819	Died before Election
Anna Symmes HARRISON	July 25, 1775	Nov. 25, 1795	Feb. 25, 1864	Mar. 4, 1841 – Apr. 4, 1841‡
Letitia Christian TYLER	Nov. 12, 1790	Mar. 29, 1813	Sept. 10, 1842	Apr. 6, 1841 – Sept. 10, 1842
Julia Gardiner TYLER	May 4, 1820	June 26, 1844	July 10, 1889	June 26, 1844 – Mar. 3, 1845
Sarah Childress POLK	Sept. 4, 1803	Jan. 1, 1824	Aug. 14, 1891	Mar. 4, 1845 – Mar. 3, 1849
Margaret Smith TAYLOR	Sept. 21, 1788	June 21, 1810	Aug. 14, 1852	Mar. 4, 1849 – July 9, 1850
Abigail Powers FILLMORE	Mar. 17, 1798	Feb. 5, 1826	Mar. 30, 1853	July 10, 1850 – Mar. 3, 1853
Caroline McIntosh FILLMORE	Oct. 21, 1813	Feb. 10, 1858	Aug. 11, 1881	Married after Presidency
Jane Appleton PIERCE	Mar. 12, 1806	Nov. 19, 1834	Dec. 2, 1863	Mar. 4, 1853 – Mar. 3, 1857
Mary Todd LINCOLN	Dec. 13, 1818	Nov. 4, 1842	July 16, 1882	Mar. 4, 1861 – Mar. 3, 1865 Mar. 4, 1865 – Apr. 15, 1865
Eliza McCardle JOHNSON	Oct. 4, 1810	May 17, 1827	Jan. 15, 1876	Apr. 15, 1865 – Mar. 3, 1869
Julia Dent GRANT	Jan. 26, 1826	Aug. 22, 1848	Dec. 14, 1902	Mar. 4, 1869 – Mar. 3, 1873 Mar. 4, 1873 – Mar. 3, 1877
Lucy Webb HAYES	Aug. 28, 1831	Dec. 30, 1852	June 25, 1889	Mar. 5, 1877 – Mar. 3, 1881
Lucretia Rudolph GARFIELD	Apr. 19, 1832	Nov. 11, 1858	Mar. 13, 1918	Mar. 4, 1881 – Sept. 19, 1881
Ellen Herndon ARTHUR	Aug. 30, 1837	Oct. 25, 1859	Jan. 12, 1880	Died before Election
Frances Folsom CLEVELAND	July 21, 1864	June 2, 1886	Oct. 29, 1947	June 2, 1886 – Mar. 3, 1889 Mar. 4, 1893 – Mar. 3, 1897

Caroline Scott HARRISON	Oct. 1, 1832	Oct. 20, 1853	Oct. 25, 1892	Died before Election
Mary Dimmock HARRISON	Apr. 30, 1858	Apr. 6, 1896	Jan. 5, 1948	Married after Presidency
Ida Saxton McKINLEY	June 8, 1847	Jan. 25, 1871	May 26, 1907	Mar. 4, 1897 – Mar. 3, 1901 Mar. 4, 1901 – Sept. 14, 1901
Alice Lee ROOSEVELT	July 29, 1861	Oct. 27, 1880	Feb. 14, 1884	Died before Election
Edith Carow ROOSEVELT	Aug. 6, 1861	Dec. 2, 1886	Sept. 30, 1948	Sept. 14, 1901 – Mar. 3, 1905 Mar. 4, 1905 – Mar. 3, 1909
Helen Herron TAFT	June 2, 1861	June 19, 1886	May 22, 1943	Mar. 4, 1909 – Mar. 3, 1913
Ellen Axson WILSON	May 15, 1860	June 24, 1885	Aug. 6, 1914	Mar. 4, 1913 – Aug. 6, 1914
Edith Galt WILSON	Oct. 15, 1872	Dec. 18, 1915	Dec. 28, 1961	Dec. 18, 1915 – Mar. 3, 1917 Mar. 4, 1917 – Mar. 3, 1921
Florence Kling HARDING	Aug. 15, 1860	July 8, 1891	Nov. 21, 1924	Mar. 4, 1921 – Aug. 2, 1923
Grace Goodhue COOLIDGE	Jan. 3, 1879	Oct. 4, 1905	July 8, 1957	Aug. 3, 1923 – Mar. 3, 1925 Mar. 4, 1925 – Mar. 3, 1929
Lou Henry HOOVER	Mar. 29, 1874	Feb. 10, 1899	Jan. 7, 1944	Mar. 4, 1929 – Mar. 3, 1933
Anna Eleanor ROOSEVELT	Oct. 11, 1884	Mar. 17, 1905	Nov. 7, 1962	Mar. 4, 1933 – Jan. 20, 1937 Jan. 20, 1937 – Jan. 20, 1941 Jan. 20, 1941 – Jan. 20, 1945 Jan. 20, 1945 – Apr. 12, 1945
Bess Wallace TRUMAN	Feb. 13, 1885	June 28, 1919		Apr. 12, 1945 – Jan. 20, 1949 Jan. 20, 1949 – Jan. 20, 1953
Mamie Doud EISENHOWER	Nov. 14, 1896	July 1, 1916		Jan. 20, 1953 – Jan. 20, 1957 Jan. 20, 1957 – Jan. 20, 1961
Jacqueline Bouvier KENNEDY	July 28, 1929	Sept. 12, 1953		Jan. 20, 1961 – Nov. 22, 1963
Claudia Taylor JOHNSON	Dec. 22, 1912	Nov. 17, 1934		Nov. 22, 1963 – Jan. 20, 1965 Jan. 20, 1965 – Jan. 20, 1969
Thelma Ryan NIXON	Mar. 17, 1913	June 21, 1940		Jan. 20, 1969 – Jan. 20, 1973 Jan. 20, 1973 – Aug. 9, 1974
Elizabeth Bloomer FORD	Apr. 8, 1918	Oct. 15, 1948		Aug. 9, 1974 – Jan. 20, 1977
Rosalynn Smith CARTER	Aug. 18, 1927	July 7, 1946		Jan. 20, 1977 –

* Did not occupy the White House.
† Second marriage ceremony performed Jan. 17, 1794.
‡ Mrs. Harrison was taken ill one month before her husband's inauguration and did not accompany him to Washington. She intended to follow later, but was not able to do so during her husband's brief term in office.

AMERICAN LITERARY AUTOGRAPHS

MICHAEL PAPANTONIO

AMERICAN literary autographs, letters, and manuscripts have been collected for well over a century. By the 1880's there were serious collectors of this material, but the great majority (as in present times) were primarily book collectors; letters and manuscripts were considered an adjunct to their primary interest.

Book collectors early realized the importance of autograph material. An author's letter regarding one of his writings frequently contains bibliographical information or an interesting observation on the background, source, or inspiration of the work. Such letters were often tipped or laid into a copy of the work to which they referred or, if a manuscript, put into the volume where it was first published. The Jacob Chester Chamberlain collection of American authors, sold in 1909, had many examples, as well as numerous individual letters cataloged separately. Stephen H. Wakeman, who obtained a number of items from the Chamberlain sale, continued this practice. He had scores of letters or short manuscripts inserted in his books.

Carroll A. Wilson also was fond of collecting for this purpose. Letters or manuscripts were inserted in many books by the major New England writers. Wilson's account of the search for and discovery of two customhouse documents signed by Nathaniel Hawthorne and used as source material for *The Scarlet Letter* is a fascinating story recorded in his *Thirteen Author Collections*. . . .

By the turn of the twentieth century, at least one noted collection was already well along and rapidly expanding. The Stephen H. Wakeman collection, rich in manuscript material of New England authors, was sold in 1924 through George S. Hellman to J. P. Morgan. More than 250 manuscripts, now in the Morgan Library* and valued at $165,000, were involved, including Hawthorne's *The Blithedale Romance, Dr. Grimshawe's Secret, The Dolliver Romance, Septimius Felton,* and all the surviving notebooks and a journal; Ralph Waldo Emerson's manuscripts of seven essays and poems; six Henry Wadsworth Longfellow poems; Oliver Wendell Holmes's *The Autocrat of the Breakfast-Table,* incomplete but the only surviving portion; Edgar Allan Poe's *Tamerlane* and *Politics;* and Henry David Thoreau's manuscript *Journals* in thirty-nine volumes. Wakeman continued collecting until his death; his library was then sold at the American Art Association on April 28–29, 1924. This is not the place to describe the books, which were superb and included many association copies, in numerous instances with autograph letters relating to them laid in, as well as individually cataloged letters. A considerable buyer was William T. H. Howe through Walter H. Hill. The Howe collection eventually was purchased en bloc and now forms a part of the noted Berg Collection at the New York Public Library.

Other notable early collectors with significant manuscript material included Charles B. Foote, William Harris Arnold, and Jacob Chester Chamberlain.

The period between the world wars saw the start of a new group of collectors: William T. H. Howe; Carroll Atwood Wilson, who primarily collected nineteenth-century New England authors; and H. Bradley Martin, whose collection includes superb and extensive holdings of Edgar Allan Poe, Herman Melville, and Lafcadio Hearn. Another collection is that of Charles Feinberg, now dispersed except for the Walt Whitman manuscripts and letters. Shortly before World War II, Clifton Waller Barrett began to assemble what became a spectacular collection of American autograph letters and manuscripts, the largest accumulation of American literary material ever brought together by a single individual. The collection is destined for the University of Virginia, and a large portion has already been presented. William H. Koester's collection of Poe includes scores of letters and some manuscripts, and was purchased shortly after his death by the University of Texas.

After World War II a gradual but significant change became apparent. Prior to the war institutional libraries had been relatively inactive, but by the early 1950's librarians and scholars became more aware of the research value of American autograph letters and manuscript material. An astute and early mover in this field was Charles D. Abbott of the University of Buffalo, now part of the State University of New York. He

* Wakeman's collection is described in detail in Herbert Cahoon *et al., American Literary Autographs From Washington Irving to Henry James* (New York: Dover Publications, Inc., in association with the Pierpont Morgan Library, 1977).

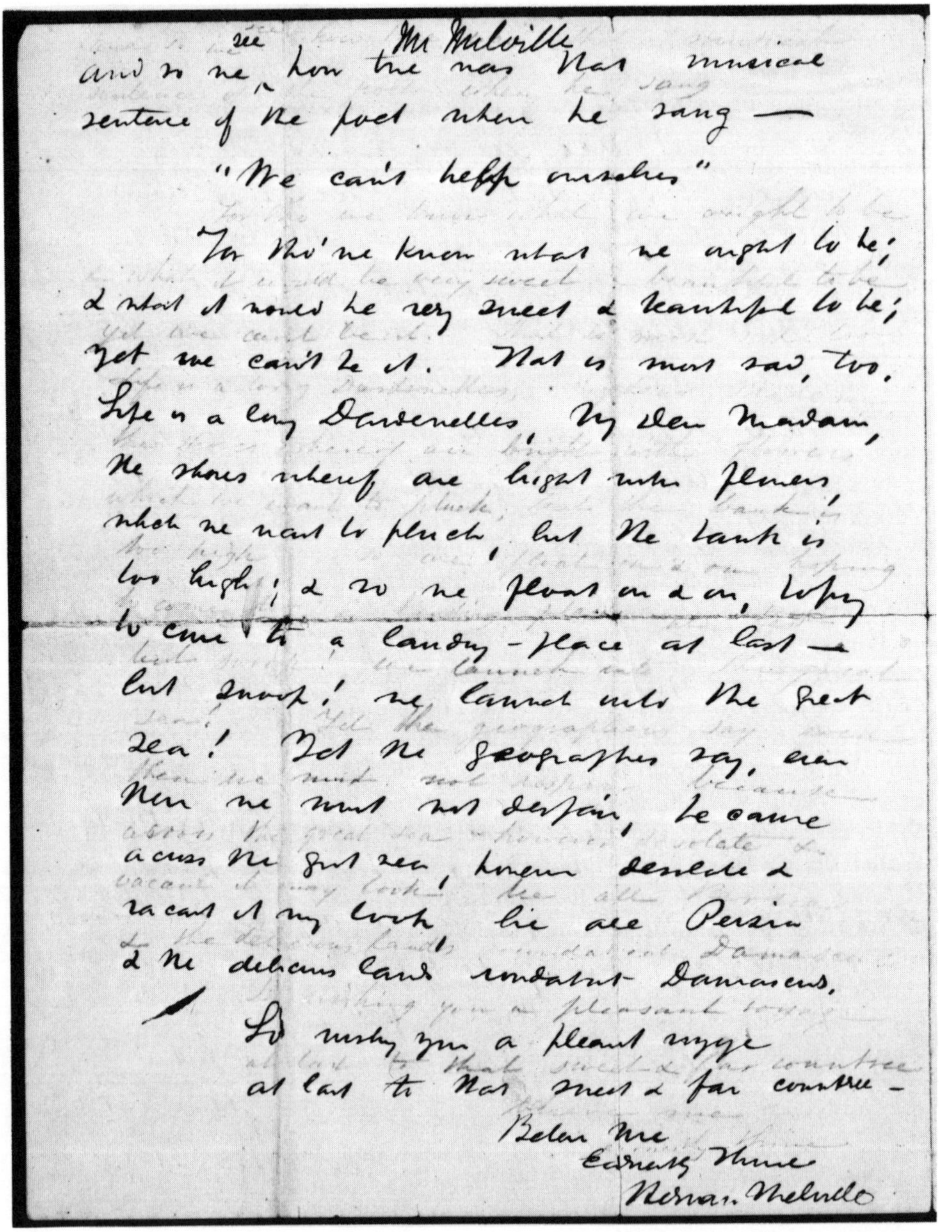

Mr Melville

and so we see, how true was that musical sentence of the poet when he sang —

"We can't help ourselves"

For tho' we know what we ought to be; & what it would be very sweet & beautiful to be; yet we can't be it. That is most sad, too. Life is a long Dardenelles, My dear Madam, the shores whereof are bright with flowers, which we want to pluck, but the bank is too high; & so we float on & on, hoping to come to a landing-place at last — but swoop! we launch into the great sea! Yet the geographers say, even then we must not despair, because across the great sea, however desolate & vacant it may look, lie all Persia & the delicious lands roundabout Damascus.

So wishing you a pleasant voyage at last to that sweet & far countree —

Believe me
Earnestly Thine
Herman Melville

Above: Portion of a letter from Herman Melville to Mrs. Hawthorne. Courtesy of H. B. Martin.

Right: Portion of a letter of Emily Dickinson. Courtesy of Robert H. Taylor.

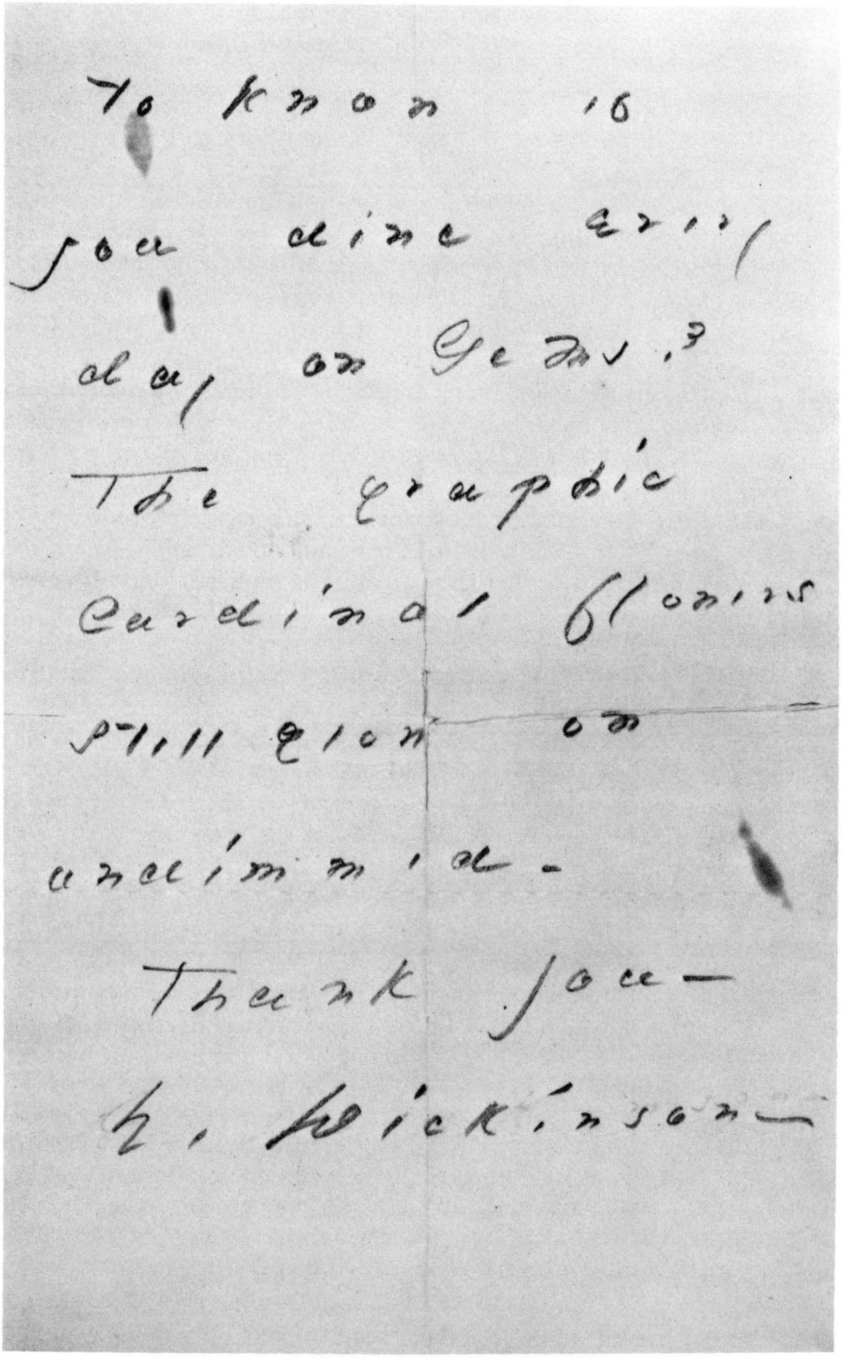
To know it
you came every
day on Genius?
The Graphic
Cardinal blooms
still glow on
undimmed.
Thank you —
E. Dickinson —

was able to persuade some authors to present their manuscripts; others were acquired by purchase. The William Carlos Williams archive is now at Buffalo.

The Huntington Library has been acquiring vast quantities of American literary material over the years. Eighteenth-century materials include the manuscripts of Benjamin Franklin's *Autobiography* and William Byrd's *Journal.* The nineteenth century is well represented, with extensive holdings of Thoreau, Emerson, Hawthorne, Longfellow, John Greenleaf Whittier, Holmes, Samuel Clemens, and Henry James. Holdings of twentieth-century writers include a vast collection of Jack London and the recent acquisition of the complete archive of Wallace Stevens.

Yale University has important collections of twentieth-century material acquired both by gift and by purchase. Major collections include Eugene O'Neill, Edith Wharton, Gertrude Stein, and the recently acquired archive of Ezra Pound.

Harvard is noted for its New England authors, a vast collection of Henry James letters, Emily Dickinson manuscripts (roughly half of the surviving portions; the other large group is at Amherst), and the extensive Thomas Wolfe collection presented by William B. Wisdom.

Princeton has extensive holdings of F. Scott Fitzgerald, Booth Tarkington, and Allen Tate, as well as much Woodrow Wilson material, both literary and historical.

The New York Public Library has acquired fine collections of Washington Irving and Herman Melville and the entire W. T. H. Howe collection mentioned above, now a part of the Berg Collection and especially rich in manuscripts and letters of the major nineteenth-century authors. The Owen D. Young collection, also in the Berg, includes the manuscript of Mark Twain's *Following the Equator.*

The Clifton Waller Barrett Library of American Literature at the University of Virginia numbers thousands of items, including manuscript letters of Washington Irving, Henry James, James Fenimore Cooper, Poe, Melville, and Twain; all the major nineteenth-century writers; and vast holdings of autograph material of twentieth-century writers. Major single items include manuscripts of Irving's *Sketch Book* and *Bracebridge Hall;* Cooper's *The Pathfinder;* a large segment of the manuscript of the earliest surviving portion of Whitman's *Leaves of Grass;* Ambrose Bierce's *Tales of Soldiers and Civilians;* and Stephen Crane's *The*

Right: The first page of "Rip Van Winkle," from Washington Irving's *Sketch Book of Geoffrey Crayon, Gent.* Courtesy of the Clifton Waller Barrett Library, University of Virginia Library.

Rip Van Winkle.

a posthumous writing of Diedrich Knickerbocker

By Woden, God of Saxons,
From whence comes Wensday, that is Wodensday,
Truth is a thing that ever I will keep
Unto thylke day in which I creep into
my sepulchre —

Cartwright.

Whoever has made a voyage up the Hudson [redacted] must remember the ~~Kat~~ Kaatskill mountains. They are a dis-membered branch of the great appala-chian family, and are seen away to the west of the river swelling up to a noble height and lording it over the surroun-ding country. Every change of season, every change of weather, indeed every hour of the day, produces some change in the magical hues and shapes of these moun-tains, and they are regarded by all the

The Red Badge of Courage.
An Episode of the American Civil War.
By Stephen Crane.

[illegible]

The cold passed reluctantly from the earth and the retiring fogs revealed an army stretched out on the hills, resting. As the landscape changed from brown to green the army awakened and began to tremble with eagerness at the noise of rumors. It cast its eyes upon the roads which were growing from long ~~[illegible]~~ troughs of liquid mud to proper thoroughfares. A river, amber-tinted in the shadow of its banks, purled at the army's feet and at night when the stream had become of a sorrowful blackness one could see, across, the red eye-like gleam of hostile camp-fires set in the low brows of distant hills.

Once, ~~Jim Conklin~~ a certain tall soldier developed virtues and went resolutely to wash a shirt. He came flying back from a brook waving his garment banner-like. He was swelled with a tale he had heard from a reliable friend who had heard it from a ~~reliable~~ truthful cavalryman who had heard it from his trust-worthy brother, one of the orderlies at division head-quarters. ~~Conklin~~ He adopted the important air of a herald in red and gold.

"We're goin' t' move t'morrah - sure," he said

Red Badge of Courage. Twentieth-century holdings include the Vachel Lindsay archive, two versions of James Branch Cabell's *Jurgen* (the possession of which was instrumental in bringing most of the other Cabell manuscripts to the university), and vast collections of Robert Frost, Richard Harding Davis, and Thomas Nelson Page.

Virginia also has a superb collection of William Faulkner presented by Linton R. Massey, as well as Faulkner's own archive of his manuscripts and working papers. The most recent acquisition is one of the six manuscript copies of *The Marionettes* (the university recently published the first edition of this work), acquired through the efforts of numerous of Massey's friends and added to the collection in his memory. Other Virginia holdings include John Dos Passos' archive of more than sixty linear feet of material, and Ellen Glasgow's papers.

The Morgan Library holdings include manuscripts of Cooper's *Deerslayer,* Clemens' *Life on the Mississippi* and *The Tragedy of Pudd'nhead Wilson,* and material by New England writers as mentioned.

Indiana University is rich in Poe and James Whitcomb Riley materials; Newberry Library holdings include Sherwood Anderson; and the University of Pennsylvania has important collections of Theodore Dreiser and Edgar Lee Masters.

With all of this material in institutions, what is left for the collector? A great deal. Trends in collecting American literary autographs follow a pattern set many years ago; the greatest demand is for material by contemporary writers. T. S. Eliot, Faulkner, Frost, Ernest Hemingway, Fitzgerald, Eugene O'Neill, Thomas Wolfe, Wallace Stevens, William Carlos Williams, and Ezra Pound are eagerly sought. Fewer manuscripts by contemporary authors will be donated to institutional libraries because the Tax Reform Act of 1969 ended tax credits for the material created by an author; thus more will come on the market.

Demand for the nineteenth-century New England writers is more selective. Hawthorne and Thoreau command high prices; Emerson, a shade less; Holmes, Longfellow, Whittier, and Lowell may still be obtained at comparatively moderate prices. Other nineteenth-century American authors have had spectacular rises. In the late 1940's a collection of nine autograph letters from Herman Melville to James Billson, an English writer, brought $900 at auction. In recent years single letters of comparable importance averaged $2,000 each. Prices of Poe letters and manuscripts have been high throughout the century. A letter of Poe's brought $19,550 (perhaps an all-time high for a single letter), and another brought $12,000 in 1970.

Left: First manuscript page of Stephen Crane's *Red Badge of Courage.* From the Clifton Waller Barrett Library, University of Virginia Library.

In the late 1950's, manuscripts and letters of Washington Irving and James Fenimore Cooper could be had for comparatively reasonable prices. The rise has been steady rather than spectacular; but an outstanding exception was the sale at auction in 1973 of the manuscript of *The Pathfinder,* which brought $35,000.

Walt Whitman and Mark Twain letters and manuscripts are steadily increasing in price. The latter author in particular has enjoyed widespread popularity for many years, perhaps more so than any other American writer since the 1920's.

The importance and use of autograph material is steadily growing. Editors for the ambitious series authorized by the Modern Language Association through its Center for Editions of American Authors are generally collating printed texts with their manuscripts, when available. A recent example is the new edition of *The Pathfinder.* Richard Rust had progressed with his collation of the printed forms of the text. The manuscript was thought to be extant but had not been located. By coincidence it "surfaced" just at the right moment at a sale in Chicago in September 1973. It was purchased by Clifton Waller Barrett for the University of Virginia and immediately was made available to Rust, who has found hundreds of errors between the first edition and the manuscript that he will be able to correct in his text.

A recent trend is the publication of facsimile reproductions of manuscripts; some examples are *The Waste Land, The Red Badge of Courage,* and *The Great Gatsby.* Another recent publication has been Richard M. Bucke's *Walt Whitman,* which contained thirty-five pages of facsimile reproductions of the manuscript, showing Whitman's collaboration in the work.

An unpublished letter or manuscript will generally, but not always, have more prospective buyers and bring a higher price than published material. Even though published, however, an important American manuscript or autograph letter can still command a high price.

Though much purchasing emphasis is given to the research use of original autograph manuscripts, the autograph collector (perhaps a vague and rather broad term) is still a considerable factor in the field. The whole of the *Spoon River Anthology* is said to have been dashed off more than once by Edgar Lee Masters and to have found a ready market. T. S. Eliot copied out *The Waste Land,* the proceeds from the sale of which went to the London Library. Robert Frost liked nothing better than to be asked by an admirer to write a favorite poem into a volume of his own verse. Institutional libraries also are glad to have fair copies of well-known literary manuscripts as exhibition pieces.

Possibly too much emphasis has been placed on the research value of autograph material through the vast flow of this material to libraries.

This trend is inevitable. When an important private collection appears in the auction room, frequently a large or even a major portion is purchased for or by institutions. Private collectors have always been active, and will continue to accumulate material. Many are not unaware of the importance of unpublished material; others are less interested in this aspect but are content with specimens they are proud to possess, often to frame with a portrait of the author. A letter or a stanza from a well-known poem will find eager purchasers.

Institutional activity should not necessarily discourage the private collector. Enough material comes onto the market to satisfy the average collector. Several prominent collectors of means have complained about the lack of material in their fields, but in the next breath they will say that they never seem to be caught up; they are able to spend all of their available funds and must pass up an occasional expensive item.

Letters and manuscripts of some writers are scarce in the present market. Much may be extant but is locked up permanently in institutions. Of the major nineteenth-century authors, materials of Poe and Melville are prime examples. Little is likely to come on the market. Few Hawthorne letters appear. Something like a thousand or so of his letters are recorded; but of the thousand, two series of correspondence—one to his wife and the other to his publisher, William D. Ticknor—account for a considerable number of the surviving letters. Thoreau letters are very scarce. Pages of manuscript keep turning up, but only because wads of manuscript pages were widely distributed around the turn of the century. Stephen Crane and Ambrose Bierce letters and manuscripts seldom come up. Among the older writers, William Gilmore Simms is scarce. Some minor nineteenth-century writers are difficult to find, but the competition for them is far less. One exception would be Thomas Holley Chivers, who, because of his controversy with Poe, would bring far more than his literary standing warrants.

Most of the major authors are expensive; and a few are really rare, if we may use that overworked term. Collectors of modest means cannot hope to assemble significant collections of the major writers, but moderately priced material by scores of American authors can be obtained. Some examples are Louisa May Alcott, Mary E. Wilkins Freeman, Sarah Orne Jewett, Eugene Field, Joel Chandler Harris, and William Dean Howells. Some later significant writers are Edna Ferber, Ellen Glasgow, Katherine Anne Porter, and Edith Wharton. Also available are James Branch Cabell, Theodore Dreiser, Sinclair Lewis, and Thornton Wilder. These random selections are not meant to be recommendations. There are numerous other worthwhile writers. Collectors can make their own selections; and if they concentrate on writers that they like, they will derive much satisfaction in assembling such a collection. Letters and

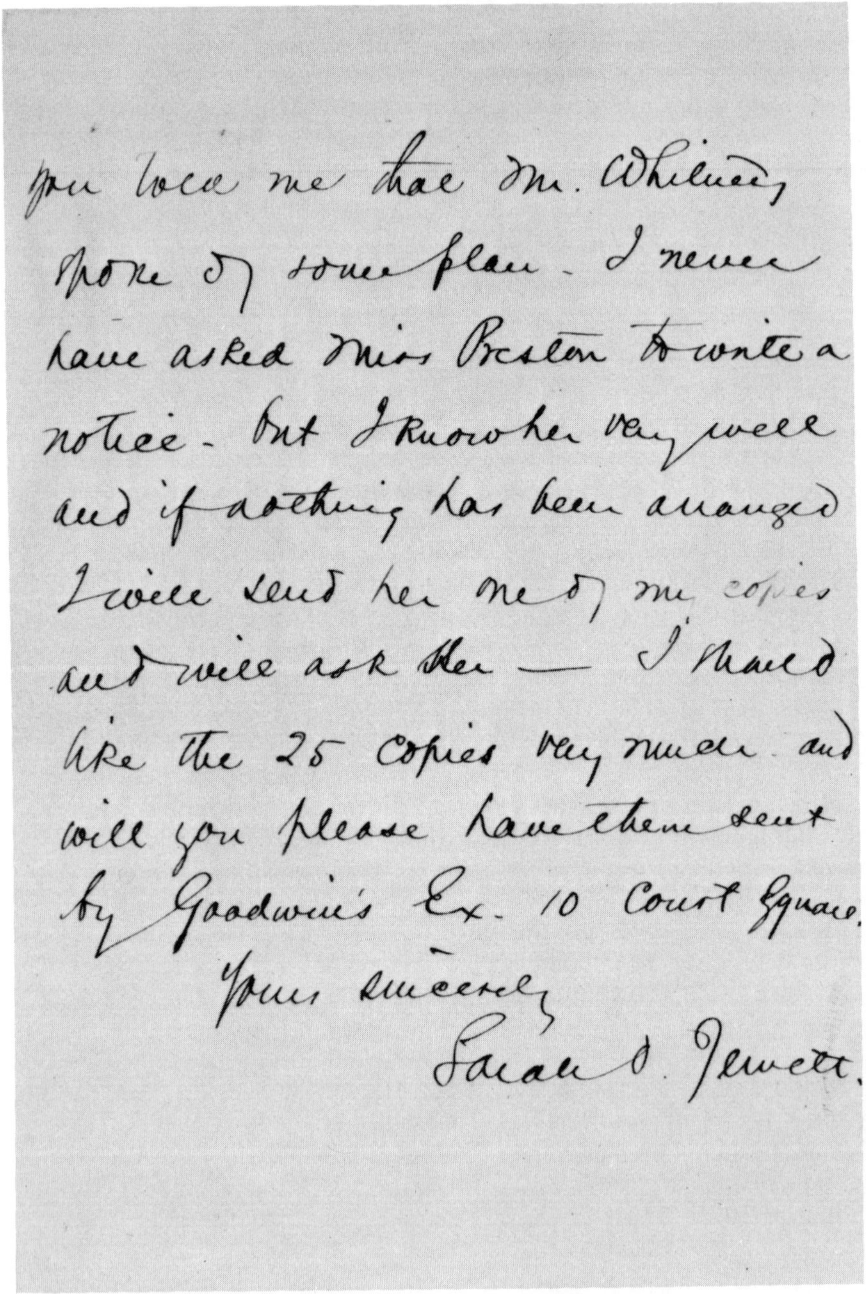
you told me that Mr. Whitney
spoke of some plan - I never
have asked Miss Preston to write a
notice - but I know her very well
and if nothing has been arranged
I will send her one of my copies
and will ask her — I should
like the 25 copies very much - and
will you please have them sent
by Goodwin's Ex. 10 Court Square.
Yours sincerely
Sarah O. Jewett.

Portion of a letter of Sarah Orne Jewett to Mr. Osgood.
Courtesy of Robert H. Taylor.

manuscripts of earlier American authors will be more difficult, but not impossible, to find.

Some of the major post–World War II authors currently in favor with collectors and institutions include Robert Frost and Ernest Hemingway, both fairly plentiful but likely to be expensive. Hart Crane is scarce and expensive; Tennessee Williams is easier to obtain. William Faulkner and F. Scott Fitzgerald appear less frequently, particularly the former, and material by both is likely to be very costly. Eugene O'Neill and Ezra Pound material is more plentiful, the former bringing substantial prices. John Steinbeck material is scarce and costly. Edna St. Vincent Millay and E. A. Robinson are less sought after, and can be obtained at reasonable prices. Scores of other writers of the period are collected. Some will live, and your judgment will be vindicated. Others will not, but what matter?

Though few worthwhile writers are neglected by the collector, there are instances of a gradual or a sudden revival of interest in authors who had been fashionable in earlier periods or had been entirely neglected by collectors during the authors' lifetimes. This revival is often shared by the general reader and collector alike. The classic example is Herman Melville, who was almost totally forgotten during the last twenty-five years of his life, and thirty years after his death emerged as one of the giants of the nineteenth century. Ezra Pound was dropped, along with a score of others, from the fourth edition of Merle Johnson's *American First Editions* in 1942 because of the lack of collector interest; and F. Scott Fitzgerald does not appear in any of the four editions.

A glance at the names of the winners of the Pulitzer Prize for fiction since the 1920's shows that at least a dozen winners are not now seriously collected. The same can be said for the dramatists. Winners of the poetry award do include a larger number of writers who are actively collected.

Your greatest joy in collecting American literary autographs and manuscripts will be in assembling the material piece by piece. Once you have it, you will enjoy it; but the average collector is always thinking of the next item to be acquired.

ENGLISH LITERARY AUTOGRAPHS

ROY L. DAVIDS

"CHARLES LAMB was a man, not a book." This striking perception by Arnold Bennett in *Literary Taste* hints at an essential difference between the collector of literary manuscripts and the collector of printed books, although, of course, the two species are not necessarily mutually exclusive and their interest in literature springs from the same sensibilities and emotional responses. The sense of contact experienced by collectors of manuscripts perhaps found its most exuberant and misplaced expression in 1795, when Boswell fell on his knees and kissed the then undetected forgeries of Shakespeare's papers manufactured by William Henry Ireland. Among manuscript collectors in the English-speaking world, literature has had the most constant appeal; and until recently, when historical manuscripts have really come more into their own, literary ones attracted most of the highest prices for postmedieval manuscripts. This appeal is due to the universal interest in literature itself; to the demands of doctoral dissertations; to the desire among some individuals, librarians, and editors for definitive collections; and no doubt also to the relative ease, in comparison with historical manuscripts, of selecting an area for collection.

Most collectors in this field begin by acquiring a letter or manuscript of their favorite author. This first impulse, usually accompanied by a delightful bewilderment that it is at all possible to obtain anything in the autograph of a writer whose genius has touched them, is prompted by the purest desire, sadly often later abandoned, to collect pieces directly related to personal interests. Acting on this impulse makes overpriced purchases easier to accommodate; gives the beginner real advantages over rivals and dealers; and, depending on the nature of the interest and its degrees of novelty and specialization, may put the novice ahead of the market.

Even experienced collectors sometimes buy pieces of indifferent quality, through enthusiasm or the desire to make their collections exhaustive. Comfort, if not from a bottle or Shakespeare, can be found in the reflection that the purchase of items of minor interest, or those not at the time fashionable, does at least tend to ensure their preservation—surely one of the justifications of the collector's passion. Many manuscripts in the celebrated collection of Sir Thomas Phillipps would not have survived at all had that self-styled "vellomaniac" collected on

A copy of a part of *Dreams, Waking Thoughts, and Incidents,* annotated by William Beckford. Courtesy of Blackwell's of Oxford.

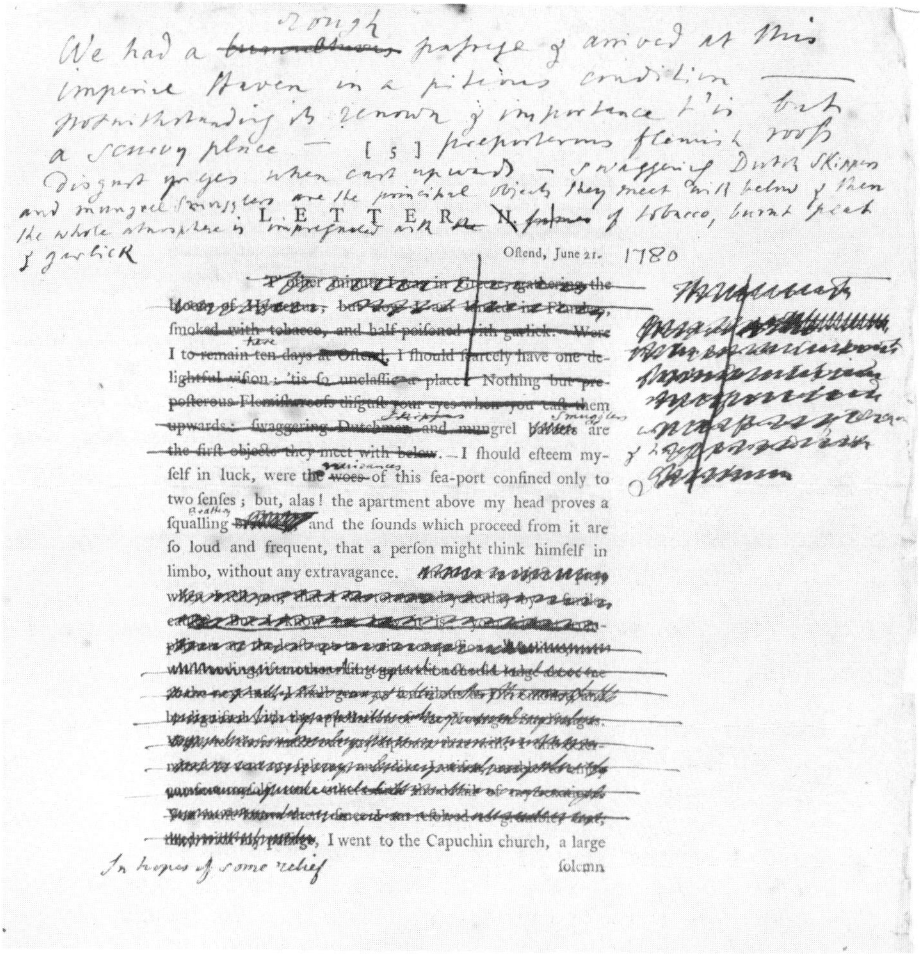
We had a rough [illegible] passage & arrived at this imperial Haven in a pitious condition — notwithstanding its renown & importance t'is but a scurvy place — [5] preposterous flemish roofs disgust yr eyes when cast upward — swaggering Dutch Skippers and mungrel Smugglers are the principal objects they meet with below & then the whole atmosphere is impregnated with the fumes of tobacco, burnt peat & garlick

LETTER V.

Ostend, June 21. 1780

[illegible] ... smoked with tobacco, and half poisoned with garlick. Were I to remain ten days at Ostend, I should scarcely have one delightful vision; 'tis so unclassic a place! Nothing but preposterous Flemish roofs disgust your eyes when you cast them upwards; swaggering Dutchmen and mungrel sailors are the first objects they meet with below. — I should esteem myself in luck, were the nuisances of this sea-port confined only to two senses; but, alas! the apartment above my head proves a squalling [illegible] and the sounds which proceed from it are so loud and frequent, that a person might think himself in limbo, without any extravagance. [illegible] I went to the Capuchin church, a large solemn

In hopes of some relief

any basis according to reason. The avoidance of the inferior specimen is a particular problem to the collector who ranges across the whole field of literature or who collects within a medium, such as poetry, rather than the papers of a specific author.

Signatures cut from letters or complete letters of a formal nature cannot, unless immense rarities, afford much lasting pleasure to the lover of literature, and are really no more than examples of handwriting. Just as the polar explorer is of greater interest to posterity on the ice than in the boudoir, so in the field of literature a writer's manuscripts in his characteristic medium—the novels of Dickens, the essays of Hazlitt, the poems of Keats—will be the collector's highest aspiration. Fortunately, it is possible, as it is often necessary, to compromise.

At present, complete literary compositions, particularly of unpublished books or long works, only rarely find private collectors, a circumstance largely determined by price and the worthy resolution of librarians to harvest such original manuscripts for scholarly use. The collector may find, however, that he has a stronger appreciation of manuscripts as relics than do many librarians—as objects, not just vehicles for the transmission of texts—and he may be able to secure those prizes whose texts have been published. To be fair to librarians, their choices have often to be taken, in these days when budgets are greatly restricted, for financial rather than sentimental reasons so that they feel obliged to abandon the published for the unpublished.

Such a decision has its dangers, for there are innumerable instances of texts being seriously mistranscribed or bowdlerized, of editors being blind or indifferent to significant details, of alterations and revisions going unrecorded, of changes of hand unnoticed, and other nuances of originals passing unobserved. An extreme and notorious case is Edmund Gosse's edition of *The Works of Thomas Gray,* which he claimed to "have scrupulously printed as though they had never been published before, direct from the originals . . . [They] have hitherto been so carelessly transcribed," he prided himself, "that I regard this portion of my labour . . . with great satisfaction." In fact, he had employed a scribe who, "wearying of the script [of the originals], and finding that the letters had been published by Mitford, soon began to copy from the printed word in preference to the manuscripts. Mitford's edition of the letters differed from the originals, and these differences reappeared in the work of the copyist."

The catalogues of auction houses and dealers are littered with corrections to standard editions and, regrettably, it is too easy to find examples of editors whose sensibilities are dull to the finer points of manuscripts. The editor of Jane Austen's *Volume the Third* thought that the manuscript might have been completed in a hand other than the au-

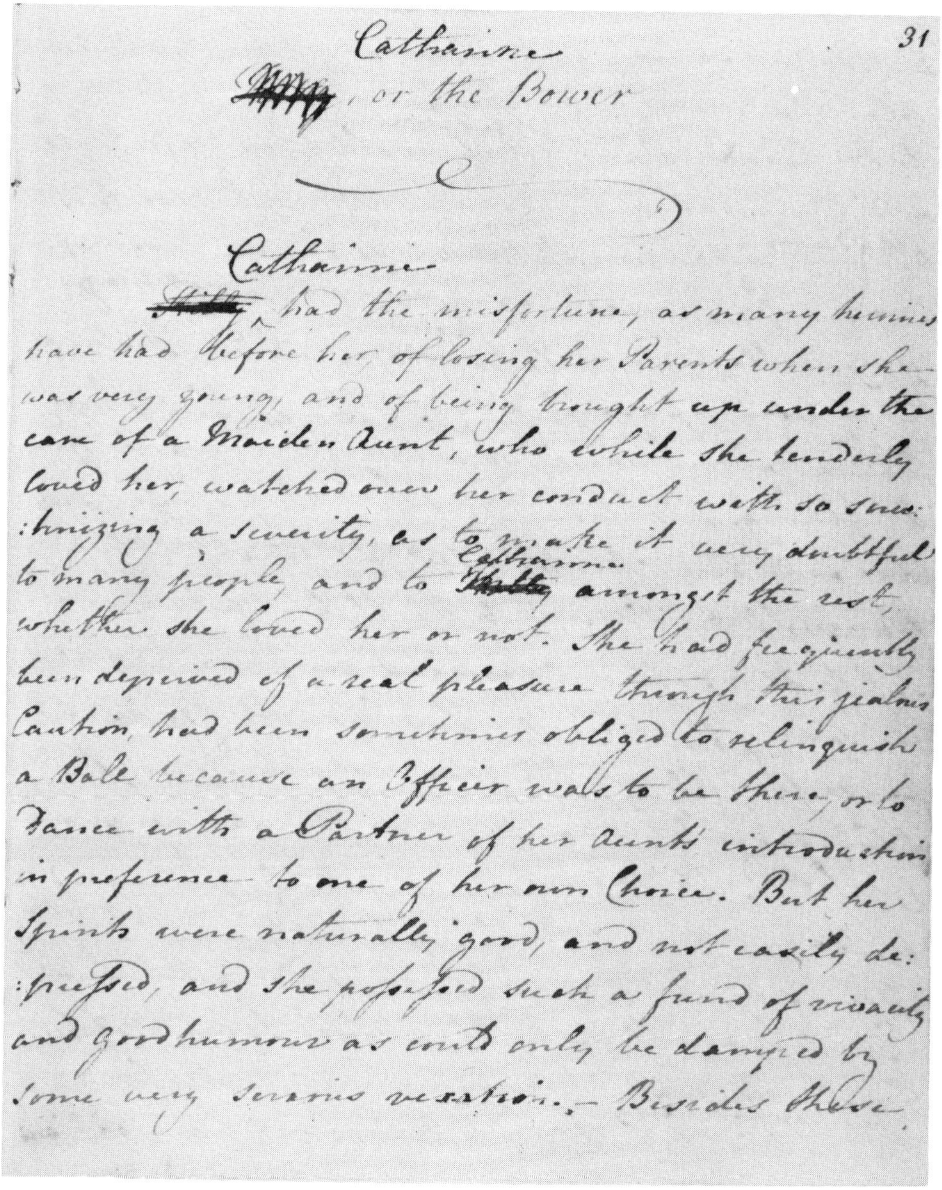

31

Catharine

~~Kitty~~, or the Bower

Catharine

~~Kitty~~ had the misfortune, as many heroines have had before her, of losing her Parents when she was very young, and of being brought up under the care of a Maiden Aunt, who while she tenderly loved her, watched over her conduct with so scru:tinizing a severity, as to make it very doubtful to many people, and to Catharine ~~Kitty~~ amongst the rest, whether she loved her or not. She had frequently been deprived of a real pleasure through this jealous Caution, had been sometimes obliged to relinquish a Ball because an Officer was to be there, or to Dance with a Partner of her Aunts introduction in preference to one of her own Choice. But her Spirits were naturally good, and not easily de:pressed, and she possessed such a fund of vivacity and Goodhumour as could only be damped by some very serious vexation. — Besides these

The first page of "Catherine, or the Bower," from Jane Austen's *Volume the Third.*

170

Mary

Mary

This woman had the good luck of being advanced to the throne of England, inspite of the superior pretensions, Merit, & Beauty of her Cousins Mary Queen of Scotland & Jane Grey. Nor can I pity the Kingdom for the misfortunes they experienced during her Reign, since they fully deserved them, for having allowed her to succeed her Brother— which was a double peice of folly, since they might have foreseen that as she died without Children, she would be succeeded by that

Above and right: Two pages from Jane Austen's *Volume the Second.*
Courtesy of the British Library.

disgrace to humanity, that pest of society, Elizabeth. Many were the people who fell Martyrs to the protestant Religion during her reign; I suppose not fewer than a dozen. She married Philip King of Spain who in her Sister's reign was famous for building Armadas. She died without issue, & then the dreadful moment came in which the destroyer of all comfort, the deceitful Betrayer of trust reposed in her, & the Murderess of her Cousin succeeded to the Throne. —

Elizabeth —

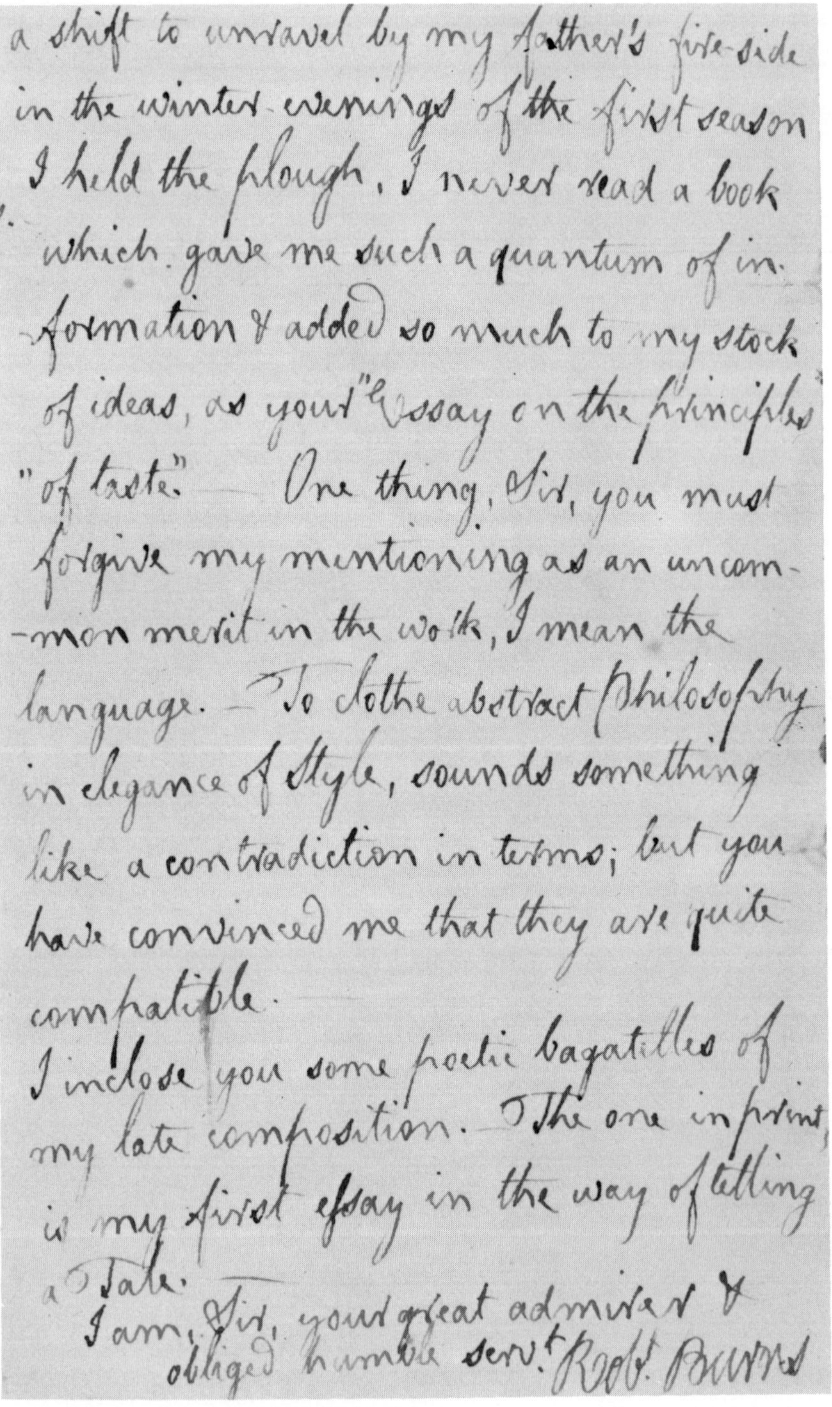
a shift to unravel by my father's fire-side
in the winter-evenings of the first season
I held the plough, I never read a book
which gave me such a quantum of information & added so much to my stock
of ideas, as your "Essay on the principles
"of taste." — One thing, Sir, you must
forgive my mentioning as an uncom-
-mon merit in the work, I mean the
language. — To clothe abstract Philosophy
in elegance of Style, sounds something
like a contradiction in terms; but you
have convinced me that they are quite
compatible.
I inclose you some poetic bagatelles of
my late composition. — The one in print,
is my first essay in the way of telling
a Tale. —
I am, Sir, your great admirer &
obliged humble servt. Robt. Burns

The final page of a letter by Robert Burns.

thor's, a suggestion subsequently confirmed by another scholar. Recent reexamination of the manuscript has revealed that it was completed not in one, but in two, other hands. The manuscript of the first part of *The Confessions of an English Opium-Eater,* sold in 1975, showed a great deal about the composition of the work; the stages of its dispatch to John Taylor, the editor of the *London Magazine,* in which it was first published; about Taylor's functions as editor; and about the anonymous appearance of the work under the initials "XYZ"—all previously unknown to De Quincey scholars.

The autograph manuscript of a verse-letter by Robert Burns was recognized at Sotheby's among a pile of papers brought in for inspection, the text of which had been previously dismissed from the canon of the poet's work by his latest editor on stylistic grounds. The survival of the autograph is vital, whether published or not, and the collector can play an invaluable role that impecuniosity may deny to the institutional buyer.

The manuscripts of poets, more than those of long works in prose, afford opportunities for collecting the working papers of authors, since they frequently survive in drafts, final versions, and fair copies on single

An autograph of Alexander Pope. Courtesy of the Clem D. Johnston Collection, University of Virginia Library.

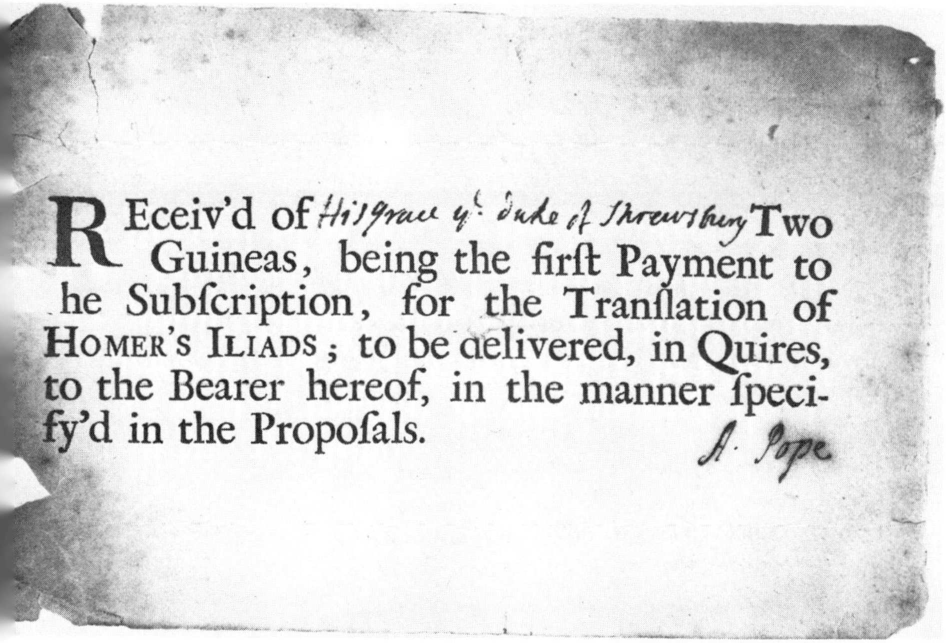

Receiv'd of His grace ye Duke of Shrewsbury Two Guineas, being the firſt Payment to he Subſcription, for the Tranſlation of HOMER'S ILIADS; to be delivered, in Quires, to the Bearer hereof, in the manner ſpeci-fy'd in the Propoſals.

A. Pope

Madame,
Here, where by all all Saints invoked are
T'were too much Scisme to bee singulere
And gainst a practise generall to war;
yett, turninge to Saints, should my Humilitee
To other Saint, then yo^w directed bee,
That were to make my Scisme Heresee.
nor would I bee a Convertite so cold
As not to tell yet; If thys bee to bold,
Pardons are in thys markett cheaply sold;
where because Fayth ys in too lowe degree,
I thought yt some Apostleship in mee
To speak things wch by Fayth alone I see:
That ys, of yo^w, who are a firmament
Of vertues, where no one ys growen, nor spent,
Thay'are yor Materialls, not yor Ornament.
Others, whom wee call vertuous, are not so
In theyr whole Substance, but theyr vertues grow
But in theyr Humors, and at Seasons show.
For when through tastles flatt Humilitee,
In Doe-bak'd men, some Harmelesnes wee see
Tis but hys flegme that's vertuous, and not hee.
So ys the Blood sometymes; who ever ran
To danger vnimportun'd, hee was than
no better then a Sanguine vertuous man.
So Cloystrall Men who in pretence of fear,
All Contributions to thys Lyfe forbear
Haue vertu in Melancholy, and onely there.
Spirituall Cholerique Critiqs, wch in all
Religions find faults, and forgiue no fall
Haue, through thys Zeale, vertu, but in theyr Gall.
wee'are thus but parcell-gilt; To Gold wee'are growen,
when vertu ys our Soules Complexione;
who knowes hys vertues Name, or Place, hath none.
Vertu ys but Aguishe when tis Severall;
By'Occasion wak'd, and Circumstantiall;
True vertu ys Soule, allways in all deeds all.
Thys vertu, thinkinge to giue Dignitee
To yor Soule found there no infirmitee;
for yor Soule was as good vertu as shee.
Shee therfore wrought vpon that part of yo^w
wch ys scarse ~~[illegible]~~ lesse then Soule as shee could doe,
And soe hath made yor Beauty vertue two;

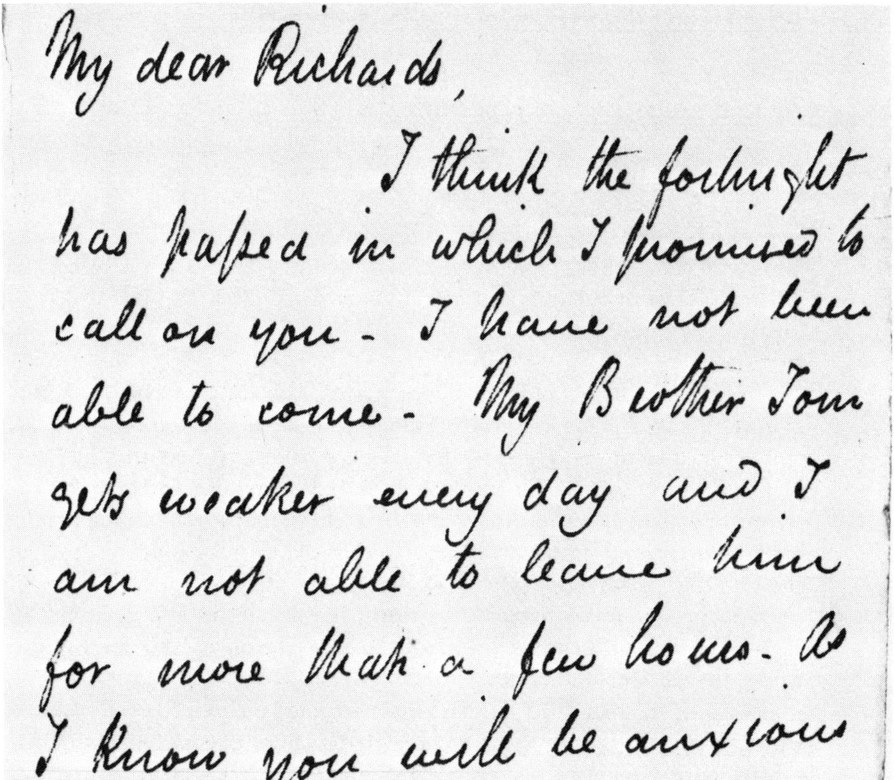

My dear Richards,

I think the fortnight has passed in which I promised to call on you - I have not been able to come - My Brother Tom gets weaker every day and I am not able to leave him for more than a few hours - As I know you will be anxious about us, if I cannot come I will send you now and then a note of this nature that you may see how we are - Remember me to Mrs R - and Mr Vincent.

Yours most sincerely
John Keats

Above: A letter by poet John Keats. Courtesy of the Tracy W. McGregor Library, University of Virginia Library.

Left: The first page of John Donne's verse letter "to the Lady Carey, and Mrs. Essex Rich from Amyens." Courtesy of the Bodleian Library, Oxford.

or a few sheets of paper. Moreover, poems create patterns on paper pleasing to the connoisseur of handwriting. There is an understandable prejudice against fair copies and quotations in albums, although, as with Wordsworth, they sometimes contain otherwise unrecorded, though not necessarily superior, variant readings. The current preference is for drafts and rough notes that reveal the creative processes, although there is a lobby for the author's final version commanding as much interest as his jottings. Unattributed autograph manuscripts offer the possibility of great discoveries to the collector with a strong visual memory for handwriting.

Poems can turn up in unlikely places: the only known autograph manuscript of a poem by Philip Sidney was found written on the flyleaf of a book, and the only one by John Donne among papers that had been in a public repository for about a hundred years. Recently, poems by Byron and Shelley were discovered in a chest in the vault of a London bank. Coventry Patmore was once able to claim possession of "perhaps the greatest literary treasure in England—the manuscript of Tennyson's next poem." It was written "in a thing like a butcher's account book." Tennyson had no other copy of it, and no memory even for his own work. It was "In Memoriam."

Serendipity may lead the fortunate to one of the scraps of paper on which John Keats was wont to scrawl his short poems, and which he subsequently sometimes used as bookmarks. Charles Armitage Brown discovered his friend Keats thrusting four or five such scraps behind books on his shelves, and was subsequently instrumental in piecing together the original of "Ode to a Nightingale."

The autograph letters of writers are by no means merely substitutes for imaginative compositions or only sources for biographical information—on the contrary, fine examples rank as literary works couched in epistolary form. "Nothing," said Horace Walpole, "gives us so just an idea of an age as genuine letters, nay history waits for its last seal from them." Samuel Johnson gave it as his opinion to Mrs. Thrale that "In a man's letters . . . his soul lies naked—his letters are only the mirror of his heart." Especially desirable are those referring to the author's literary work or circle and including, as do many of the letters of Gray or Dickens, for instance, vivid descriptions and reflections. Letters have both the advantages and the disadvantages of showing a writer in less formal or considered mood, playing to a private audience. Writers seldom abandon their art in their letters, and sometimes, perhaps because of the economy imposed by the medium, produce in them some of their noblest effects. A letter of consolation by George Eliot sold at Sotheby's in 1975 springs to mind in this respect:

> We women are always in danger of living too exclusively in the affections, & though our affections are perhaps the best gifts we have, we ought also to have our share of the more independent life, some joy in things for their own sake . . . surely women need this sort of defence against passionate affliction even more than men. . . . I do not believe there is any consolation. The word seems to me to be the drapery for falsities. Sorrow must be sorrow, ill must be ill, till duty & love towards all who remain recover their rightful predominance. . . .

Robert Browning began his fine "Essay on Shelley" thus:

> An opportunity having presented itself for the acquisition of a series of unedited letters by Shelley, all more or less directly supplementary to and illustrative of the collection already published by Mr. Moxon, that gentleman was decided on securing them. They will prove an acceptable addition to a body of correspondence, the value of which towards a right understanding of its author's purpose and work, may be said to exceed that of any similar contribution exhibiting the worldly relations of a poet whose genius has operated by a different law. . . .

Regrettably, all the letters proved to be forgeries, the skillful productions of Maj. George Gordon de Luna Byron. It has been claimed in Browning's defense that he did not see the "originals."

The careers of the arch literary forgers—William Ireland (Shakespeare), Alexander Howland Smith, known as "Antique" Smith (Burns), and Major Byron (Shelley, Keats, and Byron), and the less culpable hoaxers James Macpherson (Ossian) and—the saddest case—Thomas Chatterton (Rowley) have been too often told for further disquisition here. "Some forge for love, some for money, and some for the glory of having done it."* Some dupe experts, some could scarcely deceive their spouses. Everyone dealing in manuscripts or collecting them has perforce been confronted with the problem of forgeries—the clever and informed should not be, but occasionally are, deceived; the fortunate have the opportunity to learn from their mistakes. Of course, forgeries can be detected by vigilance and observation, and the invocation of science and all her mysteries; but these are only the handmaids of perception—one must first realize that a test is necessary and then know what is to be looked for to determine the result. Provenance can be important, but it can never be unimpeachable—externals must always be inferior to a thorough examination of the manuscript itself.

Among the personalities of English literature whose handwriting has

*Lola L. Szladits, *Documents Famous and Infamous, Selected From the Henry W. and Albert A. Berg Collection of English and American Literature* (New York: New York Public Library, 1972).

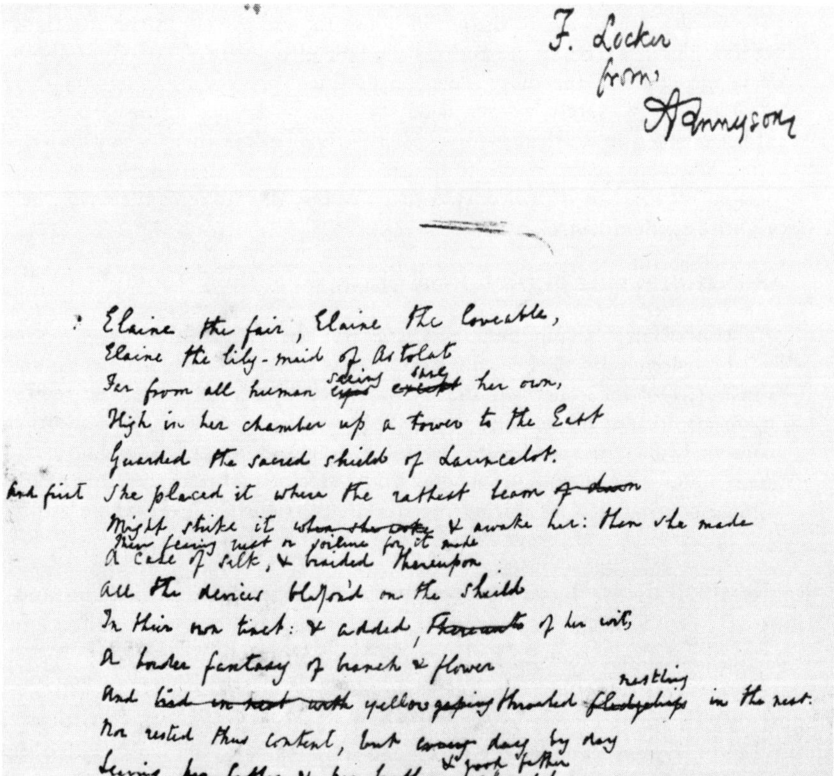

F. Locker
from
A Tennyson

Elaine the fair, Elaine the loveable,
Elaine the lily-maid of Astolat
Far from all human ~~eyes~~ seeing ~~except~~ save her own,
High in her chamber up a tower to the East
Guarded the sacred shield of Lancelot.
And first She placed it where the earliest beam ~~of dawn~~
Might strike it ~~when she woke~~ & awake her: then she made
Then fearing rust or soilure for it made
A case of silk, & braided thereupon
All the devices blazon'd on the shield
In their own tinct: & added, ~~...~~ of her wit,
A border fantasy of branch & flower
And ~~bird in nest~~ with yellow ~~gaping~~ throated ~~fledgelings~~ nestling in the nest.
Nor rested thus content, but ~~every~~ day by day
Leaving ~~her father &~~ her brethren & good father climb'd
The eastern tower, & entering, barr'd her door,
And stripping off the case, read the naked shield
Now guess'd a hidden meaning in his arms
And made a pretty history to herself,
Now

~~And~~ Of every dint a sword had beaten in it
And every scratch a lance had made upon it
Conjecturing when & where: this cut is fresh
That ten years back - this ~~given~~ dealt at him at Caerlyle
This at Caerleon, ~~that at~~ this at Camelot:
And Ah God's mercy, what a stroke was there ~~...~~
~~God~~ But bless the goodly shield that warded it
And here a thrust that might have ~~reached his heart~~ kill'd, but God
God broke the strong lance & roll'd his enemy down

Page from Alfred Lord Tennyson's "Elaine." From the Crocker-Tennyson Collection, University of Virginia Library.

been forged, other than those already cited, are Charles Dickens, Sir Walter Scott, Edward Lear, Charlotte Brontë, Oliver Goldsmith, Tennyson, Ben Jonson, Samuel Johnson, Thackeray, Oscar Wilde, Shaw, Rudyard Kipling, Mrs. Gaskell, William Blake, Elizabeth Barrett Browning, Coleridge, and Maria Edgeworth. Dickens was well aware of the problem, as is shown in a letter to his sister-in-law, Georgina Hogarth, written in 1868: "Forgery of my name is becoming popular. You sent me this morning a letter from Russell Sturgis, answering a supposed letter of mine (presented by 'Miss Jefferies') and assuring me of his readiness to give, not only the Ten Pounds I asked for, but any contribution I wanted, towards sending that lady and her family back to Boston." Dickens, however, apparently did not know of the truly uncanny resemblance that the handwriting of Charles Thomas Clement James, of Woodlands, Shorne, by Gravesend, Kent, had to his own. So similar are their handwritings that one suspects some consanguinity, perhaps well outside the prohibited degrees. The letter to Frederick George Kitton in which James comments on the similarity is worthy of quotation in full:

> Friday, eighteen September 1896
>
> Dear Sir
>
> With reference to your letter of yesterday's date, the similarity of my handwriting to that of the great Charles Dickens was first brought under my notice in this way: The printers to the Publishers who accepted my second or third novel, five or six years ago, were the now extinct firm of Dickens & Evans. On my story being sent to them for setting-up, the first-named partner, (the but recently deceased eldest son of the novelist) waited personally upon my publisher and pointed out the remarkable similarity of "hand"—his expression being, as repeated to me, that mine was "like a ghost" of the great original. This appeared to me to be so curious a coincidence, that I (who had, up to that moment, never seen Dicken's [*sic*] writing in my life) went purposely to South Kensington Museum where, I feel sure, the shock was as great to me as to the discoverer of the likeness.
>
> So much for *that*. But, here comes the really curious point in connexion with the resemblance.—Whenever a reviewer gets to work on one of my books, nine times out of ten there is a reference to Dickens in his critique—sometimes complimentary to me, sometimes v[er]y much the reverse. In short, a reviewer can no more keep a mention of Dickens out of a notice of one of my books, than Mr Dick could keep King Charles's head out of his own; and it is with rather a grim smile, I fancy, that I at such times remember the so-seldom quoted line with reference to there being "more in heaven and earth, Horatio"—et cetera et cetera!
>
> It has certainly often occurred to me that a graphologist might be interested in the resemblance; but, until your letter, I have never given any details to anyone on the subject.

I feel ashamed, even now, of writing such an extremely egotistical letter; but yours was a natural to provoke a personal explanation, and I know you will overlook it.

In conclusion, may I say: Will you come and spend a day down here in the sacred neighbourhood? I am almost as great a Dickens enthusiast as yourself, and though you know this locality so well, I think we might possibly even yet turn up something new and interesting on the inexhaustible subject.

Believe me, Dear Sir,
Faithfully Yours
Charles James *

Generic—one might almost say genetic—similarities in the handwritings of members of the same family or circle can be misleading, as in the cases of John Donne and John Evelyn with their sons and namesakes; the Wordsworths (William and Dorothy; Dorothy and Mary; Mary and Sara; Mary and Dora); the circle of Robert Louis Stevenson; and, outside literature, of Spencer Perceval and his son Spencer. A slightly different problem arises from an inability to distinguish the essential characteristics of a hand and the differences between hands. Similarities fly first to the eye of the uninitiated. An example of this failing is the much-vaunted "Donne discovery," when the poems and papers proved to be in the hand of Nathaniel Rich and not, as was claimed, of John Donne. A habitual exposure to the handwriting of an admired master can lead to the adoption, by design or accident, of characteristics of it, as was true of Conan Doyle's secretary.

Facsimiles, some immediately very convincing, are (or should be) easily uncovered by the discerning eye, human or instrumental. More deceptive is the contemporary copy, not necessarily done to deceive, where one does not know the genuine handwriting or cannot (perhaps one does not bother to) check against a verified example of an author's hand. Worse, however, are those forgeries that gain such wide acceptance as "genuine" examples that all exemplars used for authentication are merely other forgeries from the same stock. Fortunately, this problem is not likely to arise with post-Renaissance figures. Manuscripts should be considered on at least three levels: as texts, as examples of a particular person's handwriting, and as objects.

In his letter of August 3, 1650, to the General Assembly of the Church of Scotland, Oliver Cromwell delivered a characteristically violent homily, to which we might do well to incline an ear: "I beseech you, in the bowels of Christ, think it possible you may be mistaken."

The supply of any writer's papers is, of course, variously influenced

* *Ibid.*

by their survival, their sale and dispersal, and (given these factors) by the demand for them. Working for an auction house leads one to believe that anything is possible, be it only once; but it is generally true that there is a direct correlation between age and availability, and consequently there tend to be fewer opportunities to purchase sixteenth- and early seventeenth-century literary manuscripts than those of the eighteenth century, and so on. Except for those engaged in government or administration, like James I, Fulke Greville, and Thomas Sackville, it seems true to say now that the papers of no authors before the end of the eighteenth century are really common on the market.

Only six signatures, and perhaps three pages of Anthony Munday's manuscript "The Booke of Sir Thomas More," survive in the hand of Shakespeare. There are no known literary manuscripts in the hand of Edmund Spenser and only one autograph poem respectively by John Donne, Philip Sidney, and John Dryden. Nothing but one signature remains of the handwriting of Christopher Marlowe. Opportunities have occurred, however, in recent years to buy manuscripts of many of even the rarest writers. The poem by Donne was sold at Sotheby's in 1972, and a Latin poem by John Milton in 1967. Also sold since the late 1960's were a receipt by Robert Herrick; a letter by Sir Walter Ralegh; books from Ben Jonson's library, signed by him (of which, incidentally, there are a number of forgeries); and a book annotated by Dryden. Manuscripts by Oliver Goldsmith and William Collins are particularly rare and those of Keats, Shelley, and Jane Austen are uncommon; but in the years 1975–1977 one letter each by Keats and Shelley (also two promissory notes by the latter) and three literary manuscripts and a letter by Jane Austen have been on the market in London. The appearance of three literary manuscripts by Jane Austen (one an unknown play) cannot be thought to make her manuscripts common; on the contrary, it makes them rarer on the market because, according to B. C. Southam's census of them, nearly all the others are already in public collections.

Letters and manuscripts by Byron cannot be described as rare, although they may be expensive (the autograph manuscript of *Beppo* realized £50,000 at Sotheby's in June 1976) and fewer seem to be coming onto the market each year, despite such widely publicized finds as the Scrope Davies hoard. The facsimile of the "Vampire" letter is, of course, in good supply. Large-scale discoveries or caches released by descendants can for a time affect prices, as was true when papers of Thomas De Quincey came in profusion into the salesrooms in the early 1970's; but recent sales of large collections of manuscripts by William Cowper, Robert Louis Stevenson, and the Wordsworths have been quickly absorbed. At present there are opportunities to purchase manuscripts by almost all the leading literary luminaries of the nineteenth century. Letters by

Lord Byron's dog's collar.

Below: A page from the autograph manuscript of Lord Byron's *Beppo*.

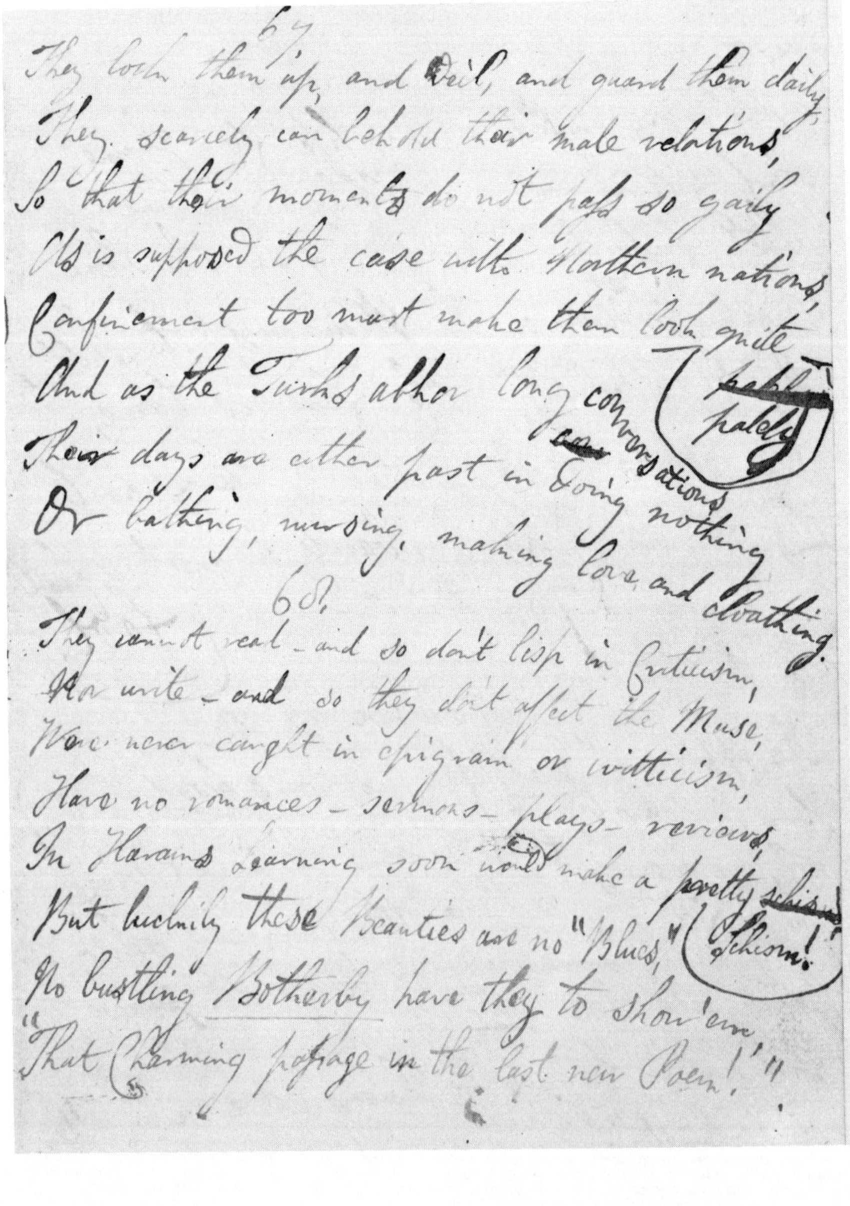
67

They lock them up, and veil, and guard them daily,
They scarcely can behold their male relations,
So that their moments do not pass so gaily
As is supposed the case with Northern nations;
Confinement too must make them look quite ~~pale~~ palely
And as the Turks abhor long ~~con~~ conversations
Their days are either past in doing nothing
Or bathing, nursing, making love, and cloathing.

68.

They cannot read - and so don't lisp in Criticism,
Nor write - and so they don't affect the Muse,
Were never caught in epigram or witticism,
Have no romances - sermons - plays - reviews,
In Harams learning soon would make a pretty ~~schis~~ Schism!
But luckily these Beauties are no "Blues,"
No bustling Botherby have they to show 'em
"That Charming passage in the last new Poem!"

"Verses by W[illia]m Cowper In memory of
the late John Thornton Esq[uir]e."

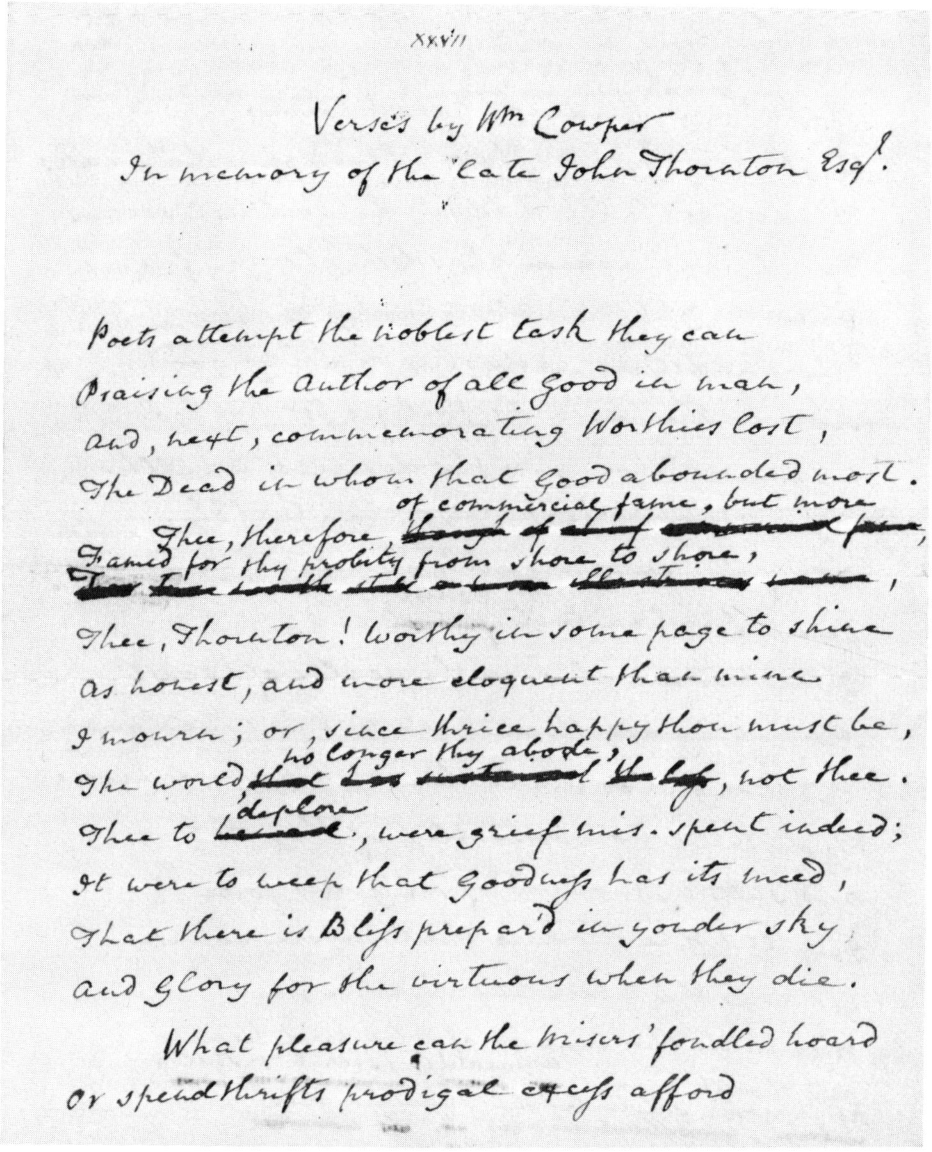
XXVII

Verses by Wm Cowper
In memory of the late John Thornton Esqr.

Poets attempt the noblest task they can
Praising the Author of all Good in man,
And, next, commemorating Worthies lost,
The Dead in whom that Good abounded most.
Thee, therefore, ~~[illegible]~~ of commercial fame, but more ~~[illegible]~~,
Famed for thy probity from shore to shore,
~~[illegible]~~,
Thee, Thornton! worthy in some page to shine
As honest, and more eloquent than mine
I mourn; or, since thrice happy thou must be,
The world, ~~[illegible]~~ no longer thy abode, not thee.
Thee to ~~[illegible]~~ deplore, were grief mis-spent indeed;
It were to weep that Goodness has its meed,
That there is Bliss prepar'd in yonder sky,
And Glory for the virtuous when they die.
What pleasure can the Misers' fondled hoard
Or spendthrifts prodigal excess afford

Dickens survive in great quantity, but are rightly becoming increasingly expensive. Letters to him are rare, because he burned his correspondence in the year before his death. Lesser lights can be distinctly hard to find—I number among the treasures of my own collection autograph poetical manuscripts by Ernest Dowson and Henry Kirke White. Particularly rare among twentieth-century writers are the manuscripts of Gerard Manley Hopkins, Edward Thomas, and Wilfred Owen. Autograph manuscripts by Ezra Pound, who habitually used the typewriter, are not often to be seen.

It is perhaps worthy of note that examples of the handwriting of the great poets of the sixteenth and seventeenth centuries may be available by indirect means to the vigilant collector. Many poets served as secretaries at certain times in their lives: Donne was secretary for a time to Sir Thomas Egerton, Spenser to Arthur Gray, Carew to Sir Dudley Carleton, Marvell to John Thurloe, Milton to Oliver Cromwell,* Cowley to Henry Jermyn and thus also to Henrietta Maria, Gay to the Duchess of Monmouth, Swift to Sir William Temple, and Addison to Thomas Wharton. Thus the texts of documents and letters signed by their masters or mistresses may well be in the hands of these poets. Literary figures often had patrons, and may have turned their penmanship to humble tasks when necessity demanded—Philip Ayres, for instance, kept the household accounts of the Drake family at Agmondesham (Amersham).

The making of a great or interesting collection does not depend exclusively on opportunity and money. The choice between the wise and the foolish virgins has never seemed a very real one: nothing of lasting artistic importance was ever done by prudence or prodigality alone. Moreover, knowledge, while vital, can in the last analysis only inform a judgment. The concept of taste is often shunned because it is so imperial, and the consequences of its definition are too rigorous and unpleasing. It shares with "style" a necessary preservation of simplicity and innocence, and a simultaneous recognition and rejection of the overly sophisticated, the incestuous, and the bizarre. Reflected glory, or the goal of definitiveness, or pecuniary advantage—each is a poor barter for impassioned interest: desire is purer than necessity and is a better basis for collecting.

*Marvell is also to be found acting as secretary to Cromwell, particularly during compassionate and other absences of Milton.

FRENCH LITERARY AUTOGRAPHS

WALTER G. LANGLOIS

FEW NATIONS in the world can boast of a literary tradition that is as long, as rich, and as varied as that of France. For nearly a thousand years French writers and intellectuals have been major contributors to Western culture, and there is a legion of names—both famous and less well-known—to stimulate the interest of collectors of autograph materials. Many foreigners who have little or no knowledge of the French language have collected extensively in this domain, as have the French themselves. (Fortunately, most major American dealers routinely provide translations or summaries of their foreign-language items.) The present essay is intended to provide a brief general outline of French literary history as it relates to autographs and to suggest what kinds of items today's collector might reasonably expect to find on the market.

As in any other collecting area, in gathering a meaningful ensemble of French literary materials the collector ought to be governed above all by his personal interest and tastes. If he has long been fond of William Wordsworth or Walt Whitman, for example, he will probably find it more rewarding to acquire an A.L.S. or a manuscript fragment by the Romantic poet Alphonse de Lamartine rather than something signed by the surrealist André Breton. Likewise, someone with an interest in the novels of Sir Walter Scott would probably be more satisfied by an item of Victor Hugo or Honoré de Balzac than by a manuscript page of André Gide or of the existentialist Jean-Paul Sartre. In addition to his personal interests, today's collector of French literary items will find himself limited by two other factors: the availability of materials (often closely related to their age) and their price (usually a reflection of rarity or of quality of content).

It should be noted at the outset that, as a general rule, the collector of average means cannot hope to acquire examples of French literary materials dating from before the seventeenth century, even if he is passionately interested in them. Indeed, it would probably require the resources of a Ford or a Rockefeller to purchase so much as a late copy of the medieval *Chanson de Roland,* while authentic signatures of great Renaissance authors like François Rabelais, Pierre de Ronsard, and Michel de Montaigne have always been as rare as Shakespeare's in English.

However, this does not mean that pre-seventeenth-century periods of French literary history need remain totally unrepresented in a collection. The French have always been very concerned with property rights, and there is a wealth of legal documents—wills, marriage contracts, property transfers, rental agreements, lawsuits over inheritances—that have survived from as early as the high Middle Ages. If such items relate to routine matters and do not involve important historical figures, they are usually available at very reasonable prices; in them the imaginative collector who wishes to have the early literary periods represented in his collection will find a rich source of potential materials. For example, by careful search it would be perfectly possible to acquire an Anglo-Norman legal document from the early twelfth century (the date and area of the principal manuscript of the *Chanson de Roland*), or a rental contract of the early 1530's from Lyons (where Rabelais was living and writing *Gargantua* and *Pantagruel*), or a legal writ from Bordeaux, dated in the 1580's (when Montaigne was mayor of the community).

To a certain extent the same situation prevails for materials dating from the classical age of the seventeenth century, one of the high points of French—and European—culture. The names of great authors like Pierre Corneille, Jean Baptiste Molière, and Jean Racine are of course known to educated men everywhere; but autographs of these writers are virtually nonexistent on today's market. Gone is the time when the dispersal of a great collection like that of Benjamin Fillon in the late nineteenth century would make available a certain number of items by these and other major figures of the classical period. Today's collector will have to be content with a letter signed by the son of the great Racine, or perhaps the receipt for a pension paid to one of the theatrical troupes playing in Paris when Molière was active there. He might also be able to obtain copies in a seventeenth-century hand of verses by Corneille, or a collection of epigrams in the style of François de La Rochefoucauld, written by a provincial gentleman with literary pretensions.

However, he will find that original materials—even when signed by classical authors slightly less well-known to Anglo-Saxons (Madame de Sévigné, Jacques Bossuet, Nicolas Boileau-Despréaux, and others)—are so rare as to be prohibitively expensive. (It should be noted in passing that since a number of historical personages of the seventeenth century—including even Louis XIV—were interested in literature and were closely associated with literary endeavors, materials signed by them would be entirely appropriate in a literary collection.)

For those with a great interest in the seventeenth century, as well as for those who like to collect series or sets of autographs, there is fortunately one area that is still collectible by individuals of average means. In 1635 the prime minister of France, Armand Cardinal Richelieu, founded the Académie Française to encourage belles lettres and to protect the purity of the French language; this prestigious institution has survived until the present. Although the character of the membership has changed somewhat, it has always been predominantly literary in character. However, the deep conservatism of the academicians has in many cases led them to elect colleagues whom subsequent generations have judged to be secondary literary talents. Autograph items by many of these individuals—even as early as the seventeenth century—are often available, at fairly reasonable prices.*

In French intellectual history the eighteenth century is known as the Age of Enlightenment. An eminently "rationalist" period on the whole, it saw an explosion of interest in all kinds of philosophical and scientific areas. Although most of the major authors of the period were not involved primarily in belles lettres, they deserve a major place in French literary history because of the importance of their ideas, the polish of their writing style, and the quasi-literary forms they often used to convey their philosophical or scientific messages.

Unquestionably the four figures who dominate the eighteenth century are Charles de Montesquieu, Denis Diderot (together with his associates on the *Encyclopédie*), François Marie Arouet de Voltaire, and Jean Jacques Rousseau. Although autograph materials by Montesquieu are rare and expensive, items by the other individuals are usually available at prices within the range of many collectors. Diderot letters and fragments of texts are seen in dealers' catalogs from time to time, as are autographs of most of those who worked with him on the *Encyclopédie* (notably Jean Le Rond d'Alembert, Jean Marmontel, and François Tronchin) or who were otherwise associated with the scientific and philosophical movements of the period (Georges Buffon, Marie Jean de Condorcet, and Jacques Henri Bernardin de Saint-Pierre).

Voltaire lived to a ripe old age, and he remained active to the very end of his life. His personal correspondence was enormous, particularly during the years following his retirement to his estate at Ferney, Swit-

*For a full list of those who have occupied the forty chairs of the academy, consult *Le Grand Larousse encyclopédique du XXe siècle* under the heading "Académie Française." A list of contemporary academicians may also be found in the *Encyclopedia Americana,* under the heading "Institute of France: I. The Académie Française."

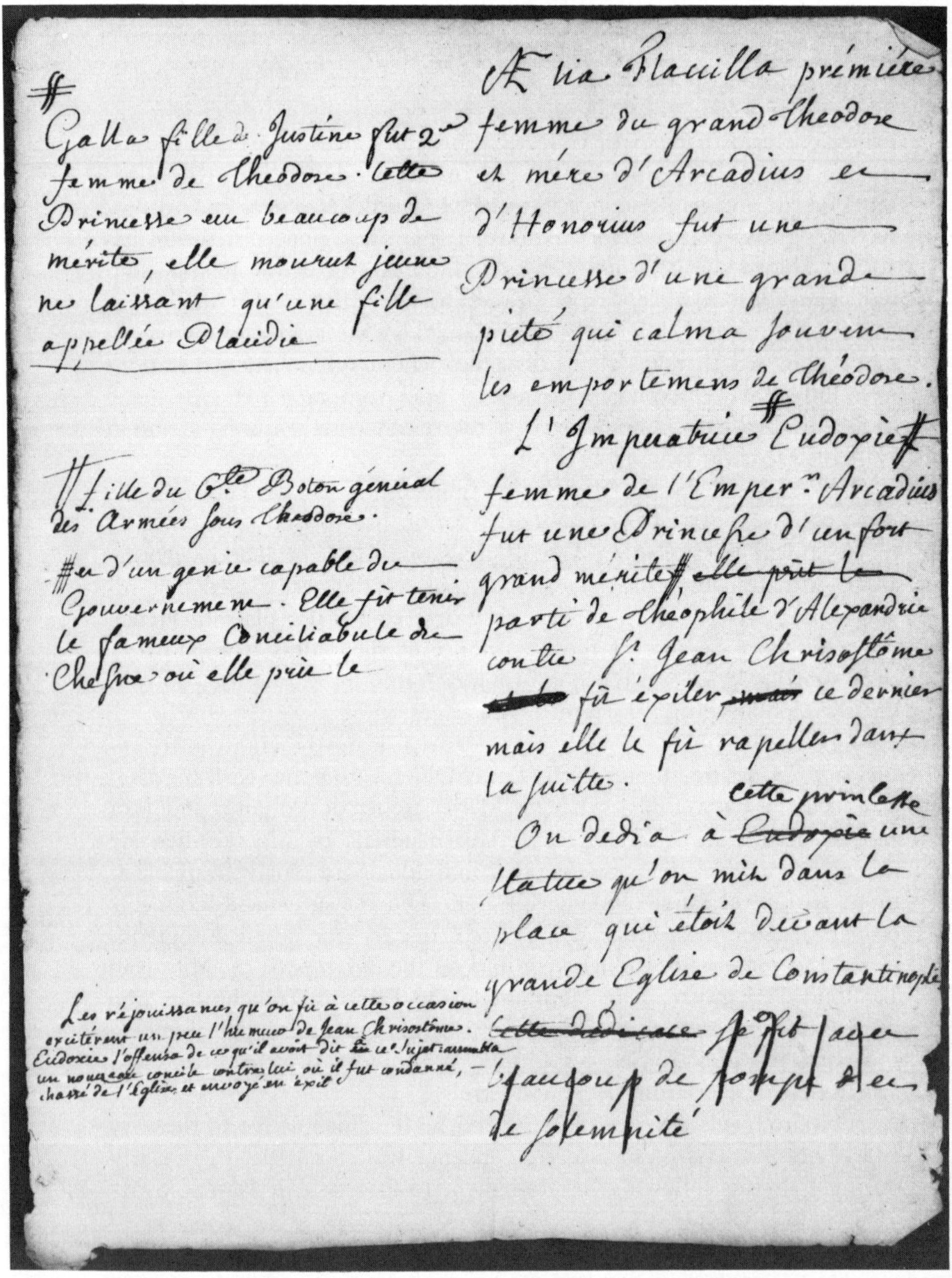

Galla fille de Justine fut 2.e femme de Théodore. Cette Princesse eut beaucoup de mérite, elle mourut jeune ne laissant qu'une fille appellée Placidie

Ælia Flacilla prémiére femme du grand Théodore et mére d'Arcadius et d'Honorius fut une Princesse d'une grande pieté qui calma souvent les emportemens de Théodore.

L'Impératrice # Eudoxie # femme de l'Emper.r Arcadius fut une Princesse d'un fort grand mérite # ~~elle prit le~~ parti de Théophile d'Alexandrie contre S.t Jean Chrisostôme ~~[illegible]~~ fit exiler, ~~mais~~ ce dernier mais elle le fit rapeller dans la suitte.

On dédia à ~~Eudoxie~~ cette princesse une statue qu'on mit dans la place qui étoit devant la grande Eglise de Constantinople ~~cette dédicace~~ se fit avec beaucoup de pompe et de solemnité

fille du C.te Boton général des armées sous Théodore.

et d'un genie capable du Gouvernement. Elle fit tenir le fameux Conciliabule du Chesne où elle prit le

Les réjouissances qu'on fit à cette occasion excitérent un peu l'humeur de Jean Chrisostôme. Eudoxie offensée de ce qu'il avoit dit sur ce sujet assembla un nouveau concile contre lui où il fut condanné, chassé de l'Eglise et envoyé en exil

A manuscript in the hand of Jean Jacques Rousseau, a leading figure of the French Enlightenment.

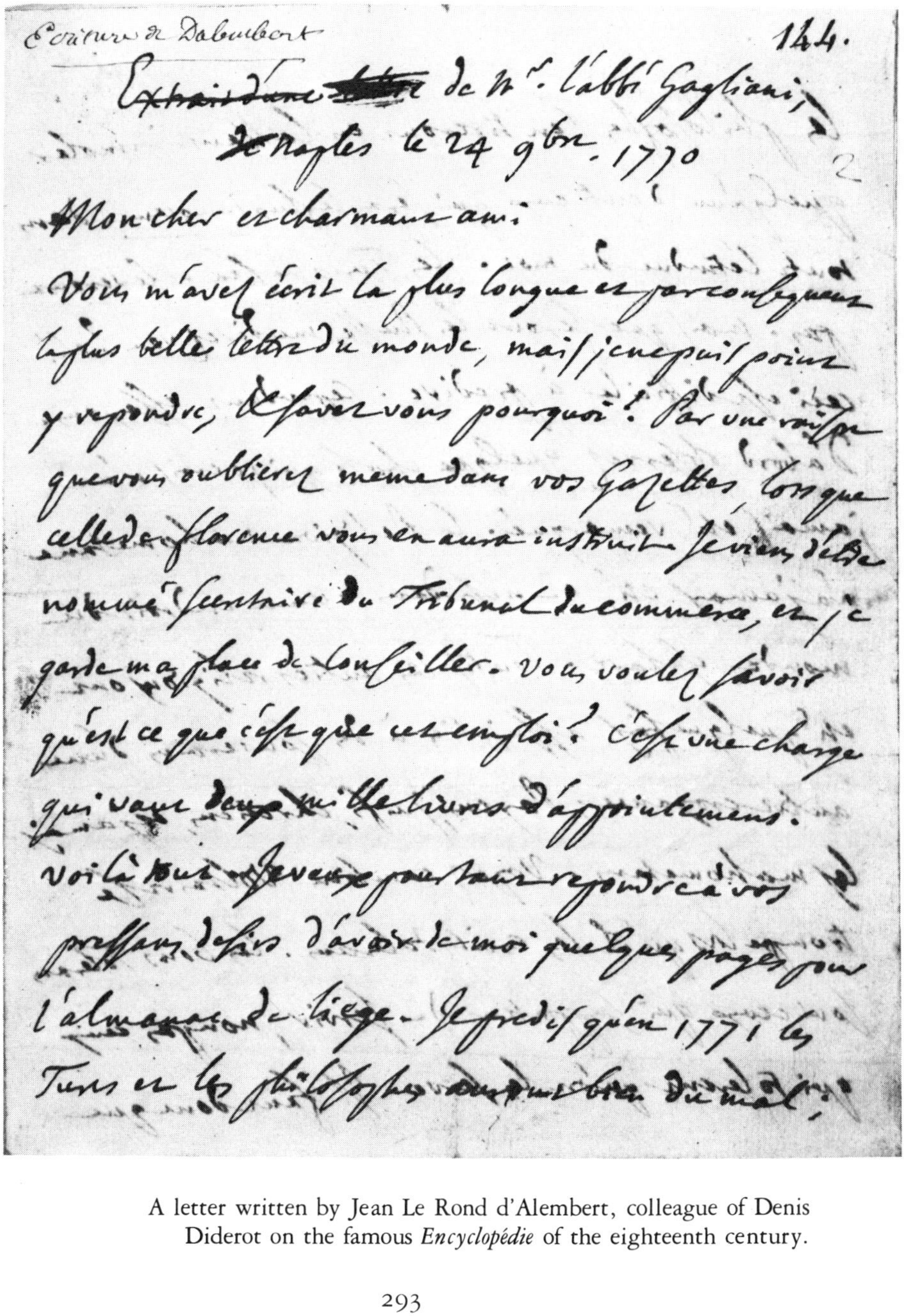

Ecriture de Dalembert 144.

~~Extrait d'une lettre~~ de Mr. l'abbé Galiani,
~~de~~ Naples le 24 9bre. 1770

Mon cher et charmant ami

Vous m'avez écrit la plus longue et par conséquent
la plus belle lettre du monde, mais je ne puis point
y répondre, et savez vous pourquoi? Par une raison
que vous oublierez même dans vos Gazettes, lorsque
celle de Florence vous en aura instruit. Je viens d'être
nommé secrétaire du Tribunal du commerce, et je
garde ma place de conseiller. vous voulez savoir
qu'est ce que c'est que cet emploi? C'est une charge
qui vaut ~~deux~~ mille livres d'appointemens.
voilà tout ~~Je veux~~ pour tout répondre à vos
pressans desirs d'avoir de moi quelques pages pour
l'almanach de liège. Je predis qu'en 1771 les
Turcs et les philosophes ~~auront~~ bien du mal;

A letter written by Jean Le Rond d'Alembert, colleague of Denis Diderot on the famous *Encyclopédie* of the eighteenth century.

zerland. Over the years much of this material—as well as other, more directly literary items—has disappeared into the huge Theodore Besterman archives in Geneva, Switzerland, but Voltaire letters still come onto the market fairly regularly. (They are usually written in a secretary's hand, signed with a simple "V.") As for Rousseau, A.Ls.S. or Ls.S. by him are very rare, although a few years ago a number of manuscript notes in his hand (relating to the history of the Byzantine empire) came onto the market, thus permitting alert collectors to acquire a text of one of the most unusual figures of the eighteenth century. Rousseau is now (1976) rare in all forms.

There are other individuals from this period whose autographs are available from time to time and who deserve to be included in a French literary collection. Among prose writers are Sébastien Chamfort, the Marquis de Sade, Abbé Prévost, and Honoré de Mirabeau, as well as

Letter written by Jacques Henri Bernardin de Saint-Pierre in 1807.

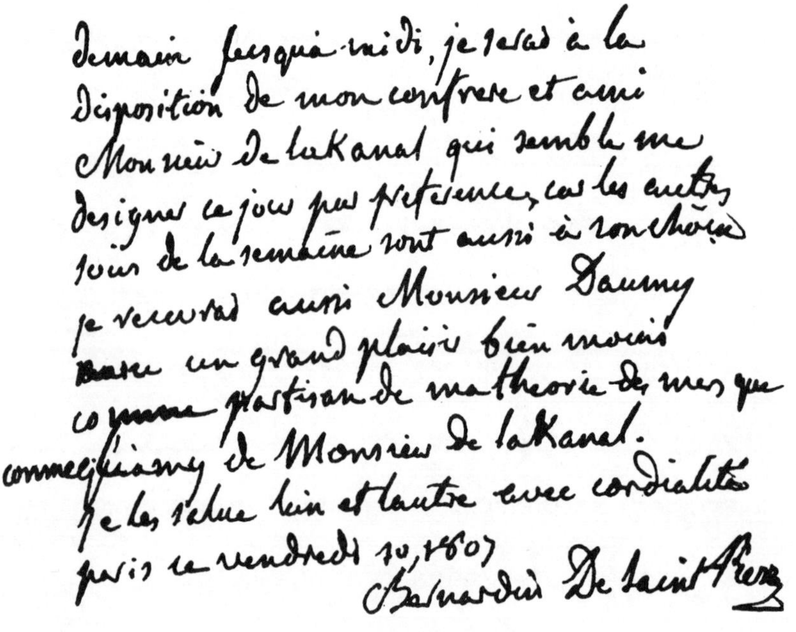
Demain jusqu'à midi, je serai à la
disposition de mon confrère et ami
Monsieur de Lakanal qui semble me
designer ce jour par préférence, car les autres
jours de la semaine sont aussi à son choix
je recevrai aussi Monsieur Dauny
[illegible] un grand plaisir bien moins
comme partisan de ma theorie des mers que
comme [illegible] de Monsieur de Lakanal.
Je les salue l'un et l'autre avec cordialité
paris ce vendredi 10, 1807
Bernardin De saint Pierre

lesser authors who were members of the French Academy. Although drama was an important literary form in the period, today virtually the only eighteenth-century playwrights who are considered significant are Pierre de Marivaux and Pierre Beaumarchais. Both are rare in autograph form, as is virtually the only lyric poet of any stature, André Chénier.

From a literary point of view, the nineteenth century in France is a complex period. The early decades saw the development of the great Romantic impulse, followed by the gradual emergence of the movements known as realism and naturalism in prose, and by symbolism in poetry and in much of the theater. The end of the century witnessed a confused search for new literary directions, most of which did not really emerge until after World War I. Because it is fairly close to us in time—and because many of the literary figures of the period were unusually active men—there is a great deal of nineteenth-century autograph material on the market. However, here we shall be concerned primarily with two dozen authors who are generally recognized as the outstanding representatives of various aspects of that era.

The early years of the Romantic movement are dominated by two major writers: François de Chateaubriand and Alphonse de Lamartine. Strictly literary materials by these two individuals are fairly rare. However, both were involved in politics at various times in their lives (Chateaubriand as ambassador and minister under the Restoration, Lamartine as a member of the Chamber of Deputies from 1833 to 1851), and documents and letters related to these activities are usually available. As a whole, Romanticism is probably best represented by one of France's greatest and most prolific authors: Victor Hugo. As a young man the energetic and prolific Hugo was very active in Romantic literary circles, but unfortunately relatively little material from this period is still available. Later, in 1851, his outspoken opposition to the regime of Napoleon III forced him to flee France and take refuge on the Channel Islands. Between 1855 and 1870, from his Guernsey retreat at Hauteville-House, Hugo carried on an extensive correspondence with various literary personalities in England and on the Continent before returning to France in glory for the last decade and a half of his life. Examples of autographs from these periods of his life are continually coming onto the market, and at fairly reasonable cost. Likewise, autograph materials of various kinds by the other major figures of the Romantic period also are usually available, price depending on content. These would include the poets Alfred de Musset, Alfred de Vigny, Théophile Gautier, and Charles Leconte de Lisle; the novelists Benjamin Constant, Étienne Pivert de Senancour, and Mme de Staël; the historian Jules Michelet; and Alexandre Dumas, father and son.

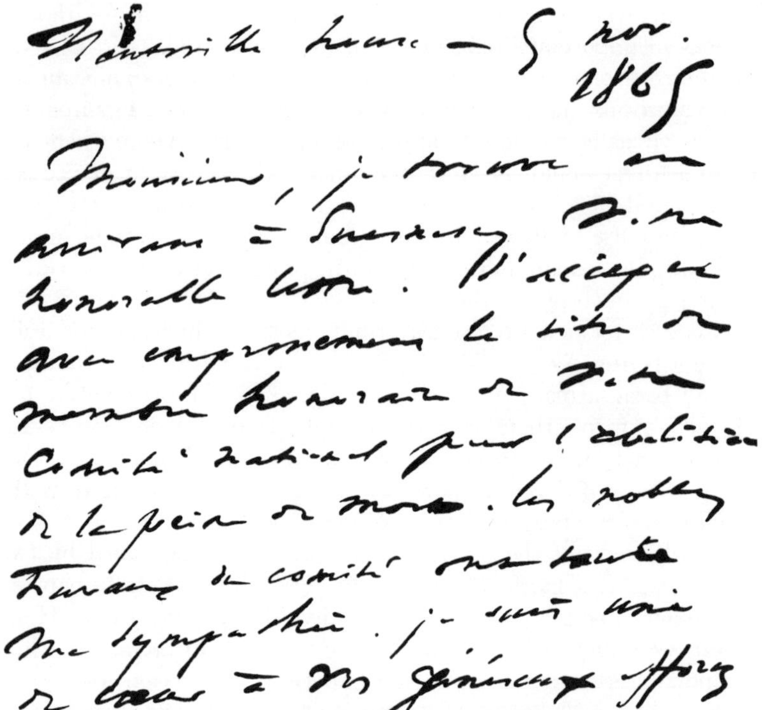
Hauteville House — 9 nov.
1869
Monsieur, je trouve en
arrivant à Guernesey votre
honorable lettre. J'accepte
avec empressement le titre de
membre honoraire de votre
Comité national pour l'abolition
de la peine de mort. Les nobles
travaux du comité ont toute
ma sympathie. Je suis uni
de cœur à vos généreux efforts.
Veuillez transmettre mes
remercîments à M. Ch. Gilpin
et à M. Beggs, qui m'ont fait
l'honneur de plaider mon
nom aux suffrages du comité,
et recevez, Monsieur, l'assurance
de ma considération distinguée.
Victor Hugo

A letter written by the novelist Victor Hugo, from his Guernsey Island retreat, November 9, 1869.

In prose the middle decades of the nineteenth century saw the emergence of three major authors: Stendhal (Henri Beyle), Honoré de Balzac, and Prosper Mérimée. Autograph material of Stendhal is very rare, and Balzac items tend to be quite expensive, so the average collector may have to content himself with a less costly Mérimée letter or manuscript fragment. Fortunately, these are still fairly plentiful. The same may be said of the letters of the novelist George Sand (Aurore Lucie Dupin-Dudevant), who—in later years—carried on a voluminous correspondence from her home at Nohant. Among important prose writers (not all *littérateurs*) associated with this middle period are Eugène Fromentin, the critic Charles Augustin Sainte-Beuve, Alexis de Tocqueville, Ernest Renan, and Hippolyte Taine. Since these latter all had official or semiofficial posts of some kind at various times in their lives, they generated a certain amount of bureaucratic paper that is still available. It is often highly interesting, even if only indirectly literary in content.

In poetry, the middle period of the nineteenth century was dominated by Charles Baudelaire, followed a few years later by Arthur Rimbaud and Paul Verlaine. Rimbaud, a precocious genius, gave up his literary career and left France when he was only twenty-one years of age; thus material by him is exceedingly rare. Baudelaire is expensive but available, usually in the form of notes rather than letters, and signed (often in pencil) with his initials. In his declining years Verlaine was little more than a destitute alcoholic, and he wrote a large number of letters regarding money problems to publishers and friends. From time

A document signed by the poet Charles Baudelaire, December 27, 1861.

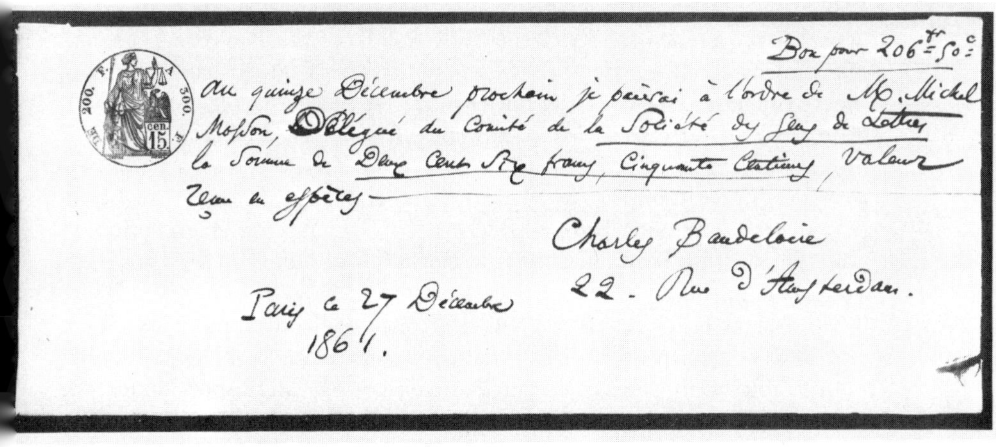
Bon pour 206f 50c

Au quinze Décembre prochain je paierai à l'ordre de Mr. Michel Mosson, Délégué du Comité de la Société des Gens de Lettres la somme de Deux Cent Six francs, Cinquante Centimes, Valeur reçue en effets —

Charles Baudelaire
22. Rue d'Amsterdam.

Paris le 27 Décembre
1861.

to time these are listed in dealers' catalogs. As for the lesser poets active during this period—Henri de Regnier, José María de Heredia, Jules Laforgue, and Émile Verhaeren—routine autograph material is usually available and not too expensive. The two major poets of the declining symbolist movement are Stéphane Mallarmé and, somewhat later, Paul Valéry. Letters in their hands are fairly common; since both knew English, it is occasionally possible to obtain a text written in that language.

Generally speaking, there were two dominant literary personalities in prose writing during the last half of the nineteenth century. One is Gustave Flaubert, and the other is the founder of the naturalist school, Émile Zola. Flaubert material is still readily available, and until fairly recently it was also possible to acquire Zola letters at a very modest cost. There are a number of other literary (or related) figures from this late period who have a certain importance and whose letters—or in some cases manuscripts—are generally in dealers' files. These include writers such as Guy de Maupassant, Pierre Louÿs, Pierre Loti, Camille Huysmans, Alphonse Daudet, the Catholic novelist Léon Bloy, the Goncourt brothers Edmond and Jules, and the dramatists Henri Becque and Maurice Maeterlinck. A host of less well-known individuals is also available—sometimes in fairly large quantities—for those collectors willing to leave the highroads of literary history for the more challenging and less popular bypaths of collecting.

To anyone interested in French literature, the twentieth century offers a particularly wide choice of collecting areas. Indeed, the very abundance of materials contributes to the difficulty of formulating a coherent acquisitions program. For those who wish to complete a series, for example, several possibilities present themselves (in addition to the members of the French Academy). The Nobel prize for literature is, of course, international; but when the very first award was made in 1901, it went to a French writer, René Sully-Prudhomme. Between 1901 and the present about a dozen other Frenchmen have won this coveted prize. These include Frédéric Mistral (1904), Maurice Maeterlinck (1911), Romain Rolland (1915), Anatole France (1921), Henri Bergson (1927), Roger Martin du Gard (1937), André Gide (1947), François Mauriac (1952), Albert Camus (1957), St.-John Perse (1960), Jean-Paul Sartre (1964, refused), and Samuel Beckett (1969). With the exception of Camus, St. John Perse, and perhaps Beckett, autograph material of these authors is generally available.

As far as other autograph sets are concerned, one should not forget the Prix Goncourt, the most notable literary prize in France, roughly comparable with the American Pulitzer prize. Established under the wills of Edmond and Jules Goncourt, this award has been made annually since 1903. However, with relatively few exceptions the list of more than seventy laureates includes fewer than a dozen individuals who could be called truly outstanding writers. Indeed, many are such minor figures that one rarely sees them mentioned, even in the catalogs of French dealers. In general, the same may also be said of the recipients of the half-dozen or so other literary prizes awarded each year in France, including the Prix Fémina (1904–), the Prix Théophraste-Renaudot (1925–), and the Prix Interallié (1930–).*

To help organize the profusion of material in twentieth-century French literature, serious collectors may find it convenient to divide the period into about five broad general divisions. Chronologically, the first group is composed of those writers who began their literary careers about 1890. Of these, two—André Gide and Marcel Proust—are literary giants by any standard, while three others are of major stature: Paul Claudel, Romain Rolland, and Charles Péguy. Although much of Gide's material is now in institutional hands (notably in the Jacques Doucet collection at the Ste. Geneviève library in Paris), he lived a long life and was a prolific letter writer; his autographs are generally available on the market at fairly modest prices. Marcel Proust died in 1922, and his materials are much less common than those of Gide. They also tend to be quite expensive if they have any content at all. Of the remaining figures from this early period, Péguy is extremely rare in any form, while Rolland and Claudel are fairly readily available.

Another easily discernible group in twentieth-century French literary history includes those writers who were associated, however loosely, with the movement known as surrealism. Although there were some important predecessors, it was not until the early 1920's that this school began to take shape around the person of André Breton. As a unified movement it exerted a major influence on the literary and artistic scene for only about a decade, but its influence continues to be felt today, primarily in poetry and in art. Of the authors associated in one way or another with surrealism, the following are the most important (except for those marked with a dagger, all are fairly readily available): Guillaume Apollinaire, Louis Aragon, Blaise Cendrars, René Char, Jean Cocteau, †René Crevel, †Robert Desnos, Paul Éluard, Pierre Emmanuel, Max Jacob, †Francis Ponge, †Pierre Reverdy, and Jules Supervielle. With the exceptions of Aragon and Cendrars, all are known primarily as poets.

Of the various periods of twentieth-century French literary activity, most critics, scholars, and collectors would probably agree that the two

* For lists of these laureates, see *Le Grand Larousse encyclopédique du XXe siècle,* under "Prix littéraires"; and Jane Clapp, *International Dictionary of Literary Awards* (New York: Scarecrow Press, 1963).

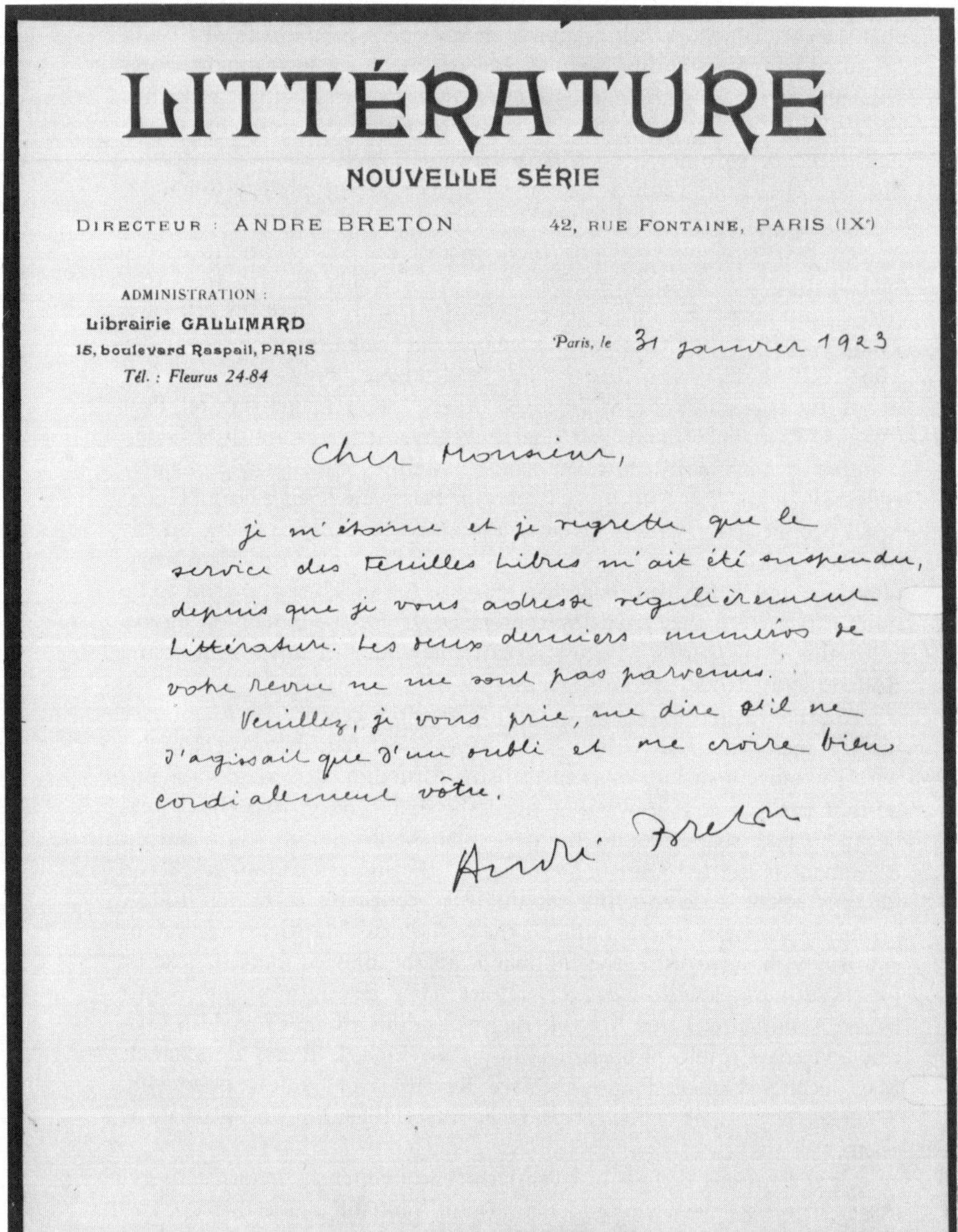

LITTÉRATURE

NOUVELLE SÉRIE

DIRECTEUR : ANDRE BRETON 42, RUE FONTAINE, PARIS (IXe)

ADMINISTRATION :
Librairie GALLIMARD
15, boulevard Raspail, PARIS
Tél. : Fleurus 24-84

Paris, le 31 janvier 1923

Cher Monsieur,

Je m'étonne et je regrette que le service des Feuilles libres m'ait été suspendu, depuis que je vous adresse régulièrement Littérature. Les deux derniers numéros de votre revue ne me sont pas parvenus.

Veuillez, je vous prie, me dire s'il ne s'agissait que d'un oubli et me croire bien cordialement vôtre.

André Breton

Letter, January 31, 1923, by surrealist André Breton.

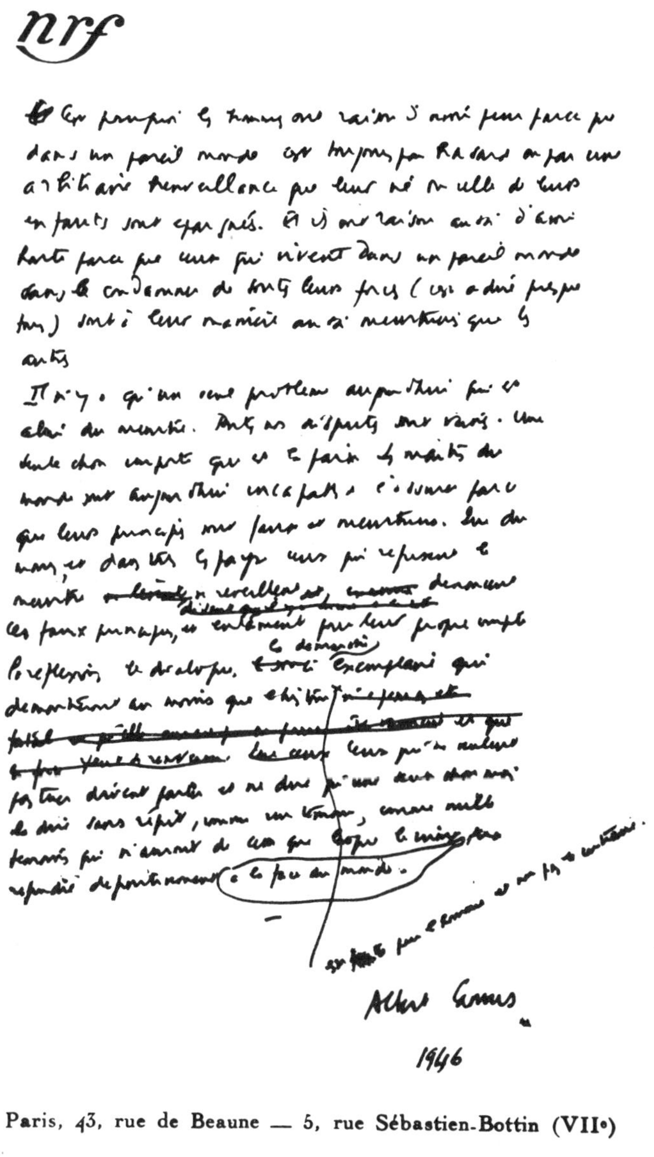

Page of a manuscript written in 1946 by the existentialist Albert Camus.

decades between the wars are the most rich. Of the four or five dozen authors of merit whom one could mention from this 1919–1939 period, about fifteen stand out clearly as being in a class by themselves. By far the largest proportion of these are the novelists and dramatists whom one might call "gifted traditionalists," those who in subject matter or technique remain essentially within the broad mainstream of French literary history. Such authors include Jean Anouilh, Colette, Georges Duhamel, Jean Giono, Jean Giraudoux, Roger Martin du Gard, Jules Romains, and Antoine de Saint-Exupéry. Except for Giraudoux, Saint-Exupéry, and perhaps Martin du Gard, materials by these individuals are fairly regularly available. A second group, generally characterized as "Catholic" writers, includes François Mauriac, Georges Bernanos, Julien Green, and Henri de Montherlant. Except for Green, all are listed from time to time in the catalogs of many French dealers. Finally there is a third group that includes a number of socially conscious authors like Eugène Dabit, Jean Richard Bloch, Henri Barbusse, and two novelists of particularly remarkable talent: Ferdinand Céline (Louis Ferdinand Destouches) and André Malraux. Céline remains a controversial figure because of his rabid anti-Semitism and his pro-Fascist sympathies, but most critics now tend to agree that his literary importance is very great. In recent years letters and occasional manuscript fragments by him have begun to come onto the market. Malraux led a long and very active life in several fields in addition to literature, and routine letters by him are often available, but at prices that tend to be high. Really significant materials of his are very expensive.

The French literary movement that attracted worldwide attention in the immediate post–World War II period is known as existentialism. Led by Jean-Paul Sartre, this school dominated the French literary scene for nearly two decades. Although existentialist ideas influenced many writers during this time, there are only three authors of major stature who were directly associated with the movement: Sartre, Simone de Beauvoir, and Albert Camus. Sartre material—including extensive manuscript fragments—is quite available at present, and in recent years one has usually been able to find items by Beauvoir as well. On the other hand, Camus items are rare and likely to remain so, since the bulk of his personal papers is destined for a literary repository.

Although Sartre and Beauvoir are still alive and active, in recent years they have increasingly led their movement into involvement with political rather than literary matters. Thus the period since the death of Camus in 1960 has been characterized by the decline of literary existentialism and the emergence of a cluster of younger writers, generally grouped as "New Novelists" (principally Michel Butor, Marguerite Duras, Alain Robbe-Grillet, Nathalie Sarraute, and Claude Simon), or dramatists of the "Theater of the Absurd" (the precursor Antonin Artaud, Beckett, Eugène Ionesco, Jean Genet, and Fernando Arrabal). This literature is often difficult for the average reader or collector to appreciate, and it is not surprising that items by these authors do not yet often appear in dealers' catalogs in either the United States or France.

This brief survey of the sweep of French literary history of the last four centuries has made it clear that, as is the case with comparable materials in English, it is the periods closest to our own that offer the greatest collecting opportunities to those of modest means. Yet it is precisely this period that also presents the greatest challenge, for here the collector has little to guide him in his acquisitions except his own taste and judgment. But whether a collector seeks autographs by the time-honored authors of the past or by those contemporaries whose gifts have yet to be fully appreciated, he will find French literary history a fascinating and stimulating collecting field.

EUROPEAN AND WORLD LITERATURES

HENRY STRUTZ

At last count there were 138 countries in the United Nations and 160-some countries in the world. It's a big, variety-filled world. Yet, autographically speaking, it's a small world. The literature of countries such as China and India is ancient and venerable. Autograph activity, however, is largely confined to the industrialized nations of the West. In many areas of the world, political autographs are more collected than literary ones. Balkan royalty, usually from German princely houses, appears on the autograph market with its Graustarkian trappings; but few writers do. A song popular in World War II proclaimed that "They're Either Too Young or Too Old." This could be applied to the literature of many countries of the world. They're either too young or too old or, in cases like Finland, Israel, and many others, both. My task of reporting on European (France and Britain excepted) and world literature is therefore made easier.

GERMAN LITERATURE

By far the greatest number of autographs I am to discuss is German. Although German literature is qualitatively and quantitatively very important, there are many reasons for this abundance of German autographs, some of them extraliterary.

The German literary tradition is very old. In contrast with Russia and many East European and African countries, literature flourished in Germany during the Middle Ages (the *Minnesingers* and many epic poets like Gottfried von Strassburg) and has continued to do so. There are literary survivals from the Old High German period and the era of tribal migrations. Much material from this and earlier "pagan" periods was destroyed in the wake of Christianization although, paradoxically, some fragments survive because of copies made by monks.

German dealers and collectors were active in the nineteenth century, and still are. The firm of J. A. Stargardt, for instance, was founded at Berlin in 1830. This house, now located in Marburg and owned by Klaus Mecklenburg, continues to be very active.

Many German-speaking individuals are active in other European and American autograph centers. Rudolf Kallir (International Autographs), an Austrian, has long issued catalogs in New York. The American autograph dealer Kenneth Rendell includes French and German translations of the "terms of sale" in his catalogs. The role of German immigrants and émigrés in the United States has also been significant. German narrowly missed being declared the second official language of Pennsylvania in American Revolutionary days; and in the nineteenth century the historian Frederick J. Turner and others spoke of the probable necessity of making German the second official language of many Midwestern states. As of this writing, Lawrence Welk's North Dakota German accent can still be heard on television. The émigrés of 1848 and the refugees from Hitler were usually middle-class and more literarily oriented than the farmers, workers, and brewers who constituted the bulk of immigrants. Many prominent émigré writers took up residence in the United States in the 1930's and 1940's, either permanently (Franz Werfel and Lion Feuchtwanger) or for a time (Bertolt Brecht and Thomas Mann, both of whom returned to Europe after the war with a few parting shots at America and Americans).

German at one time was the most widely studied foreign language in the United States. During World War I, however, many state legislatures passed laws forbidding its teaching. The political importance of Germany and the many attendant controversies have both helped and hindered all things German. Frankfurters are no longer styled "liberty sausages," but the German language has never returned in its old vigor. Many German-language publications and legitimate theaters in New York and other cities have disappeared. Nevertheless, traces of the German influence remain.

German public and private archives were looted on a massive scale after World War II, thus making more German autographs available on international markets. Some dealers, with questionable ethics, feel no compunction about handling these "liberated" autographs. Some, however, were of such antiquity and value that they couldn't be easily "fenced." Fragments of priceless eighth-century manuscripts turned up in a garbage can in Kansas after the war. The Russians also took a great deal. Although many manuscripts are still missing, they have returned most of the art and archives.

The same factors—supply, demand, and literary fashion—operate in all autograph markets. In European and world literature the situation is further complicated by accessibility, translation, and general popularity in the English-speaking world. Political and propaganda considerations also have affected German autographs. Woodrow Wilson delighted in quoting William Wordsworth and other English authors to the English ambassador during World War I. If he had taken equal or greater delight in dropping gems from Goethe to the German ambassador, the course of the twentieth century might well have been different.

Authors such as Christoph Martin Wieland, Gotthold Ephraim Lessing, Friedrich Hölderlin, Novalis, Heinrich von Kleist, Joseph von Eichendorff, Adalbert Stifter, Gottfried Keller, Theodor Storm, Conrad Ferdinand Meyer, and many others are considered literary giants in German-speaking countries and their autographs command great prices. In the United States, when they do appear, purchasers are often Europeans or institutions with special archival collections. A few authors like Arthur Schnitzler are in good supply and not excessively expensive. A routine example would sell for about $20, a content letter for more.* Schnitzler's famous correspondence with Sigmund Freud, and movie and stage presentations of his work, have made him well known to Americans. The BBC television series "Vienna 1900," based on his works and shown in the United States in 1975, may affect his autograph in the same way the BBC's "Forsyte Saga" series affected John Galsworthy's. Schnitzler's contemporary and fellow Austrian, novelist Leopold von Sacher-Masoch, is available and sells for considerably less than the more important Marquis de Sade, despite the fact that Leopold von Sacher-Masoch is occasionally spicy, whereas de Sade's letters rarely concern anything other than his financial difficulties.

Samuel Taylor Coleridge thought Schiller the greatest of writers. John Quincy Adams translated Wieland's fairy-tale epic *Oberon.* Ralph Waldo Emerson and the transcendentalists held many German authors in high esteem. Henry Wadsworth Longfellow translated many of them. Lord Byron once declared that Franz Grillparzer's name was impossible to pronounce but that all would have to learn it because of the Austrian dramatist's great literary merit. Lessing said that everybody was prepared to praise Friedrich Klopstock but few were willing to read him. Lessing declared that he wished to be less uplifting and more widely read. Neither is much read by most Americans, although both are "classics" in Germany; both are expensive autographs, and Lessing is still widely read. Many have heard of Goethe and Schiller, yet, as T. S. Eliot

*The prices mentioned in this article are current as of the time of publication (1978), and may bear no relation to those of the market at the time of reading.

points out, few have read them. Despite Byron's dictum, most English-speaking people are not familiar with Grillparzer's name, let alone his works; and Schiller is less widely known than he was in the days when Richard Mansfield and Maude Adams appeared in English translations of his plays in the United States. Eduard Mörike is considered a literary figure of classic stature in German-speaking countries. Like the others mentioned earlier, his autograph is expensive and most likely to be found in German, Austrian, and Swiss catalogs. In 1975 the West German government issued a commemorative stamp bearing his signature and complimentary close "Ihr ganz ergebener, E. Mörike." In the United States, however, he is perhaps best known through the Hugo Wolf settings of many of his poems.

The fact that an author's works have been set to music by composers does not necessarily help the author's autograph. Jean Paul (Richter) is still revered as a classic writer, though less read than formerly, and brings high prices in Europe. His works furnished programmatic material for Gustav Mahler's first symphony (*The Titan*) and Robert Schumann's *Papillons.* Yet despite the Mahler vogue there is not much demand for Jean-Paul's autograph in the United States. In France, Henri Meilhac and Jacques Halévy fashioned many excellent librettos for Georges Bizet (*Carmen*) and Jacques Offenbach, Jules Barbier and Michel Carré for Gounod, Augustin Eugène Scribe and Victorien Sardou for many composers, yet all are cheap autographs. Even the famed romantic E. T. A. Hoffmann, himself a musician of note, is best known in the United States through Offenbach's opera and Peter Tchaikovsky's *Nutcracker.* He is still read in Germany and is an expensive, moderately scarce autograph there.

Some of the reasons why so many authors are considered giants in the German-speaking countries and fetch high prices there have already been mentioned. Another reason for the fact that they are less well-known abroad is that the philosophical has long loomed large in German literature. The *Bildungsroman,* or developmental novel, is a favored genre. In these works the hero's philosophical, aesthetic, and religious transformations are often more important than the recounting of experience or action. Notable examples are Jakob von Grimmelshausen's *Simplicissimus* in the baroque period, Goethe's *Wilhelm Meister* (especially the *Wanderjahre*), Hölderlin's *Hyperion,* Eichendorff's *Ahnung und Gegenwart,* Keller's *Der grüne Heinrich,* and Mann's *Der Zauberberg.*

German poetry, too, is often "philosophical." There are of course scores of notable German works that cannot be so described, such as Christian Morgenstern's nonsense verse and Wilhem Busch's *Max und Moritz* (Busch is sometimes called the father of the comic strip). Yet there is no German Molière despite some famous, classic comedies by

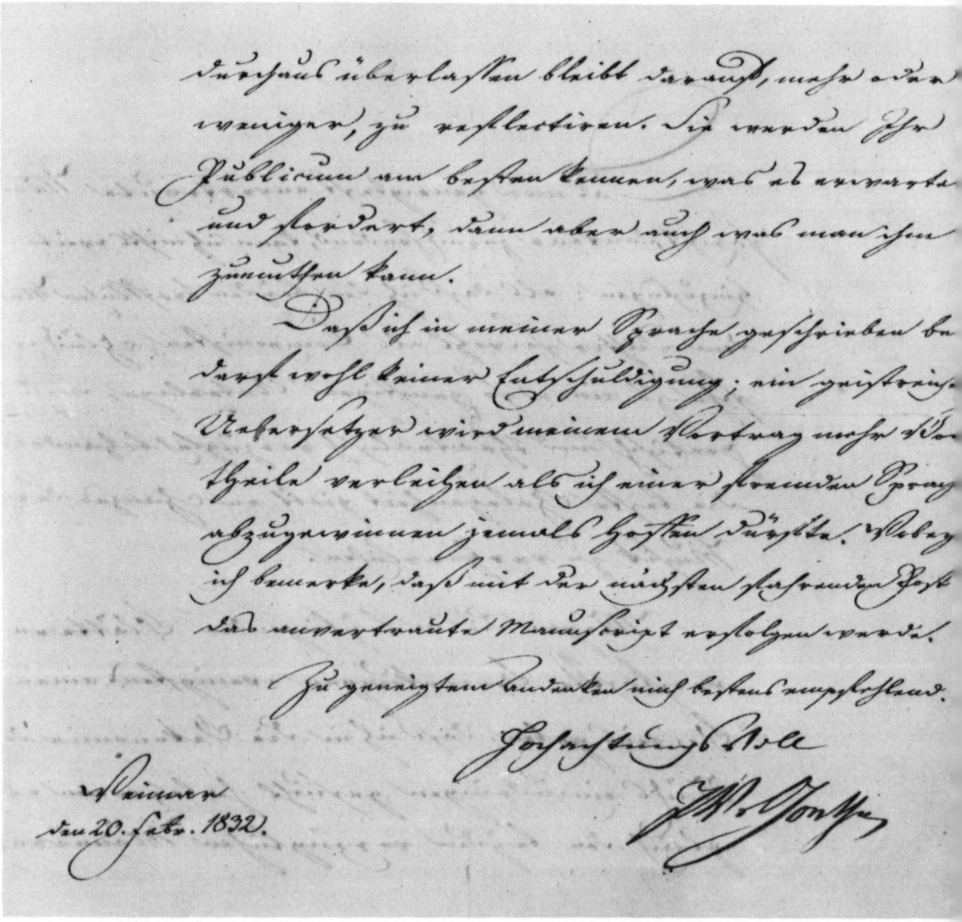

Johann Wolfgang von Goethe's signature in Old German script, dated February 20, 1832, with the body of the letter written by a secretary. From the John Batchelder Autograph Collection, Library of Congress.

Lessing, Kleist, Gerhart Hauptmann, and Brecht. Even in Brecht's comedies, however, there is usually a mighty propaganda axe grinding away, not for the "true, good, and beautiful," as in Schiller, but for some parodistic, proletarian version of them. It is natural that philosophically minded poets, such as Coleridge and Emerson, were fond of Schiller, whose poetry is sometimes more philosophy than poetry. Coleridge felt that "no man was ever yet a great poet, without being at the same time a profound philosopher." Goethe qualifies, although he wrote some dithyrambic verse (such as *Wanderers Sturmlied*) that he later, in a more Olympian mood, dismissed as "half-nonsense." On the other hand, the

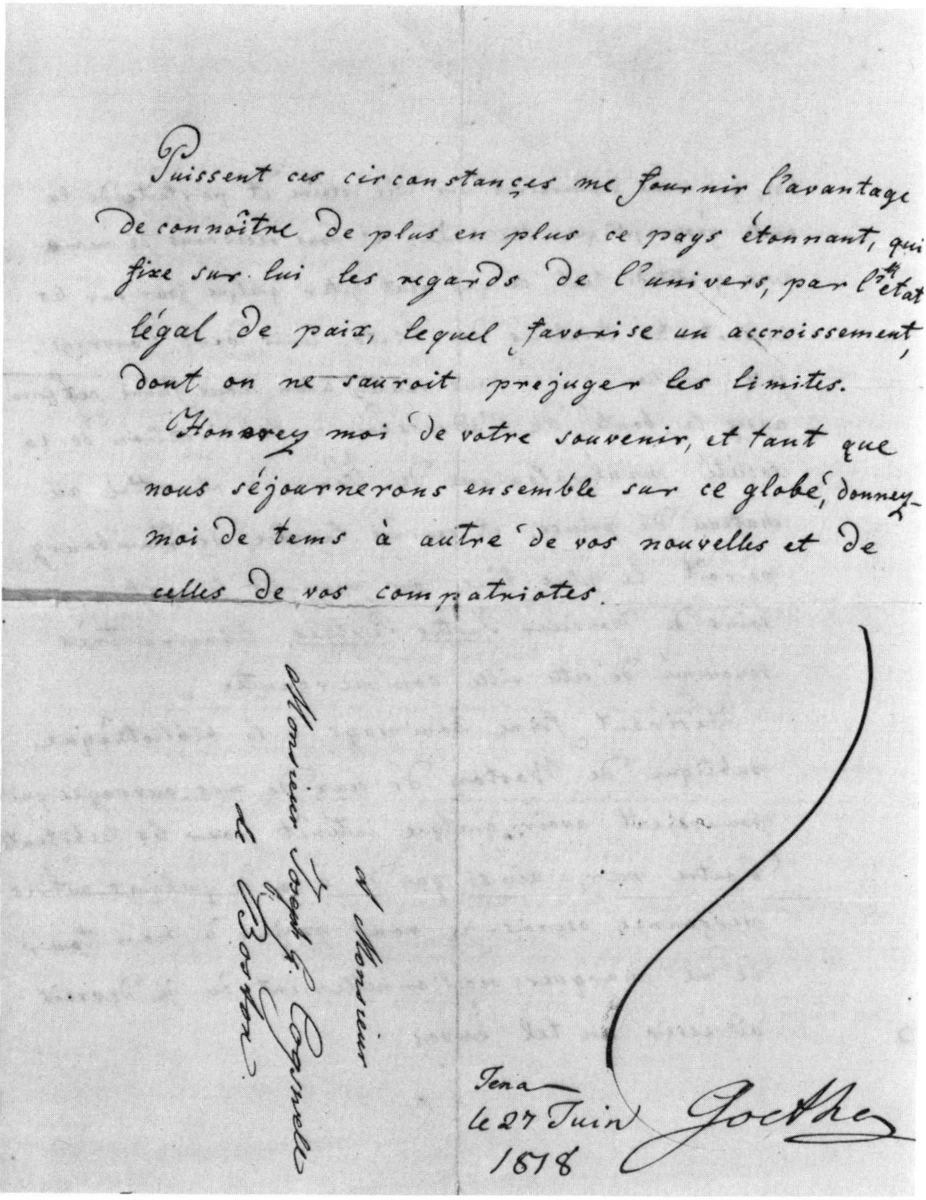
Puissent ces circonstances me fournir l'avantage de connoître de plus en plus ce pays étonnant, qui fixe sur lui les regards de l'univers, par l'état légal de paix, lequel favorise un accroissement, dont on ne sauroit prejuger les limites.

Honorez moi de votre souvenir, et tant que nous séjournerons ensemble sur ce globe, donnez-moi de tems à autre de vos nouvelles et de celles de vos compatriotes.

Jena
le 27 Juin
1818

Goethe

A Monsieur
Joseph G. Cogswell
à Boston

A letter in French, written by a secretary,
but signed and addressed by Goethe.
Courtesy of the Chapin Library, Williams College.

twentieth-century poet Stefan George said of Nietzsche that he should have sung instead of spoken; that is, written more poetry and less philosophy. Although Nietzsche's style is often rhapsodic and difficult to translate, there is much interest in him, perhaps in part because of nonliterary considerations such as the controversial "superman" concept. He is infrequently seen on the autograph market and is expensive.

Goethe has been described as the "last Renaissance man." His is a very special case. What does appear outside of Germany is usually receipts and Ds.S. of little content. Even these sell for more than $500. In Germany his stature has reached almost mythic proportions. He is a "patron saint" of the Anthroposophical Society, of which the center in Dornach, near Basel, Switzerland, is appropriately called the Goetheanum. A compendium of thoughts for each day called *Mit Goethe durch das Jahr* is widely sold in almost all German bookstores. Goethe lived so long and wrote so much in so many styles that he has been compared to the Bible as a font from which anyone can draw whatever he wants. His greatest works, the towering masterpiece *Faust* and the poetry, are difficult to translate adequately. Perhaps this is why he is only a name to many outside of German-speaking countries. Nevertheless, most collectors have heard of him and want his autograph. His autographs are about as common as Washington's or Lincoln's, say; but, as in their cases, prices are high because of demand.

Hans Sachs, the Renaissance cobbler-poet, is not of great stature. However, because of Wagner's *Die Meistersinger,* and because, in an age before the widening gulf between bourgeois and artist, he symbolized the fusion of craft and literature admired by Goethe and Thomas Mann, he is sought after, rare, and expensive.

There are great numbers of collected literary autographs of regional and dialect authors, such as Klaus Groth, Fritz Reuter, Johann Peter Hebel, Ludwig Thoma, Peter Rosegger, and Johann Nepomuk Nestroy (whose *Einen Jux will er sich machen* Thornton Wilder adopted for *The Matchmaker*). Some are of considerable literary merit and are revered beyond their dialect or regional boundaries—in German-speaking countries, that is. Here again German literature reflects political conditions. The regional is more important in German literature than in many others partly because of the lack of political unity. Many of these regional literary autographs are expensive in Germany but rarely seen elsewhere. The local is usually best marketed locally. Just as certain wines do not travel well, dialect poets may enjoy great stature in their native habitat but do not "make it" on the international market. The local is more exportable musically than literarily—as witness Manuel de Falla, Edvard Grieg, and Modest Moussorgsky—although even in music the local is a factor. For instance, the Viennese are said to prefer Franz

Schmidt to Mahler among symphonists. One also finds in European, and sometimes in American, catalogs huge lots of once-fashionable literary figures, such as Ludwig Fulda, Jakob Wassermann, Christian Grabbe, Heinrich Laube, Ernst von Wildenbruch, Richard Dehmel, and Emanuel von Geibel. As is the case with English or American authors, large and interesting collections of lesser lights can be compiled economically.

Great numbers of non-Frenchmen from many countries have written works in French. The Americans are a notable exception, since most of them (Hemingway, Fitzgerald, Henry Miller, Richard Wright, James Baldwin, James Jones) seem to write only English-language works when living in France. Oscar Wilde, Algernon Swinburne, Strindberg, the Cuban José María Heredia, the Greek Jean Moréas (Iannis Papadiamantopoulos), the Irishman Samuel Beckett, and several Rumanians have written some or all of their works in French. Many refugees from Metternich's political system, authors of the literary school known as "Young Germany," lived and worked in France. Outstanding among them is Heinrich Heine. His autograph is perhaps more common in French than in German. The examples are usually of little content, however. Rainer Maria Rilke, for a time the sculptor Rodin's secretary,

German poet Richard Dehmel is among those "once-fashionable literary figures" whose letters are often seen in the catalogs of European dealers. Courtesy of Herbert E. Klingelhofer.

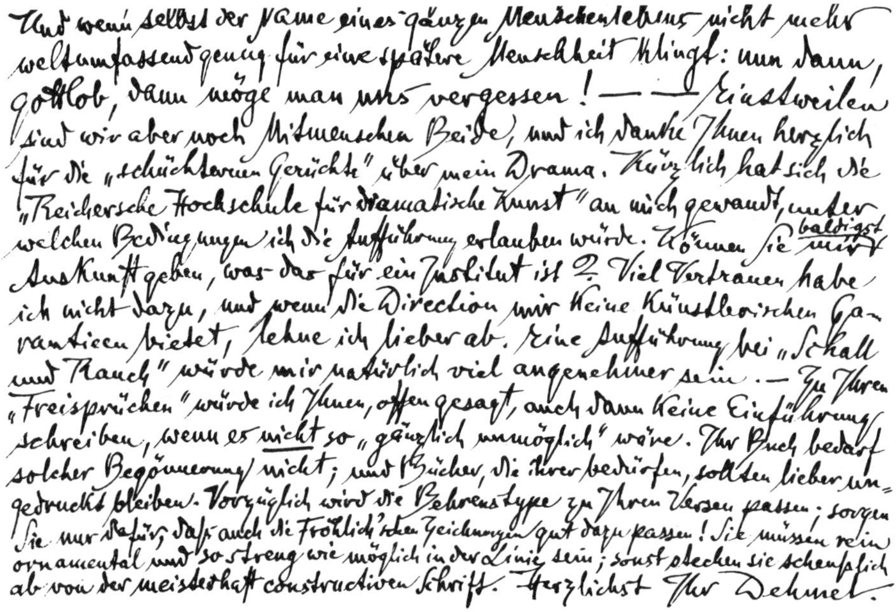

Und wenn selbst der Name eines ganzen Menschenlebens nicht mehr weltumfassend genug für eine spätere Menschheit klingt: nun dann, gottlob, dann möge man uns vergessen! — — Einstweilen sind wir aber noch Mitmenschen Beide, und ich danke Ihnen herzlich für die „schüchternen Gerüchte" über mein Drama. Kürzlich hat sich die „Reichersche Hochschule für dramatische Kunst" an mich gewandt, unter welchen Bedingungen ich die Aufführung erlauben würde. Können Sie mir baldigst Auskunft geben, was das für ein Institut ist? Viel Vertrauen habe ich nicht dazu, und wenn die Direction mir keine künstlerischen Garantieen bietet, lehne ich lieber ab. Eine Aufführung bei „Schall und Rauch" würde mir natürlich viel angenehmer sein. — Zu Ihren „Freisprüchen" würde ich Ihnen, offen gesagt, auch dann keine Einführung schreiben, wenn es nicht so „gänzlich unmöglich" wäre. Ihr Buch bedarf solcher Begönnerung nicht; und Bücher, die ihrer bedürfen, sollten lieber ungedruckt bleiben. Vorzüglich wird die Behrenstype zu Ihren Versen passen; sorgen Sie nur dafür, daß auch die Fröhlich'schen Zeichnungen gut dazu passen! Sie müssen rein ornamental und so streng wie möglich in der Linie sein; sonst stechen sie schändlich ab von der meisterhaft constructiven Schrift. Herzlichst Ihr Dehmel.

wrote many famous poems in the Jardin des Plantes in Paris. He also wrote a few poems, much admired and anthologized, in French. Rilke and Heinrich Heine are expensive in French but more expensive in German, since their best-known work is in German.

Adelbert von Chamisso, a notable German romantic author (Schumann's song cycle *Frauenliebe und -leben,* and the famous *Peter Schlemihl* story), reverses the trend. He and his family were political refugees from the French Revolution. His autograph is expensive (about $200 for a content letter), but less so than the other great German Romantics. Theodor Fontane and Friedrich de La Motte-Fouqué are other German authors whose background was French. Many German émigré writers, the most famous of them Thomas Mann, are also available in English. Mann, who considered himself simultaneously *praeceptor Germaniae* and a Goethean *Weltbürger,* is a common autograph because he scrupulously answered all correspondence, often in holograph. This was part of the ethical code he felt it necessary to impose upon himself to offset the tumultuous inner life of the artist. Demand is great, and increasing. Prices are still high for content letters. Other examples can be obtained for $30–$75.

Hermann Hesse, although an intellectual and aesthetic elitist in the German Romantic tradition, is popular with young people, perhaps because of his interest in Oriental religions, neuroses, and, in *Steppenwolf,* drugs. This popularity is reflected on the autograph market. As with William Makepeace Thackeray, Jean Cocteau, and Adolf Hitler, Hesse's drawings and watercolors occasionally appear on the market. Franz Kafka and Brecht, widely known internationally, are rare and expensive autographs. Günter Grass and Heinrich Böll, contemporary writers also active in politics, are internationally known but available and inexpensive.

Although the Third Reich lasted but twelve years, it continues to cast a shadow. The Nazis denigrated what they styled "asphalt-literature"—for them, rootless, cosmopolite, folk-corroding literature—and exalted *Blut und Boden,* earthbound, "folk-conscious" literature. In contrast with Italy, where statues of Mussolini are sold openly and the neo-Fascist party is a political force, many Germans, including writers, have, in a sense, had to "pass muster," first by the Nazis, then by the de-Nazification courts, then by the constant scrutiny of an overzealous domestic and foreign press. Germany's turbulent history is reflected in autographs, too. German literature, at home and abroad, has been affected, perhaps more than any other, by the intensity and violence of political controversy. In the late 1960's the West German consul in New York declared that Lessing and Schiller would most certainly have left Germany during the Third Reich.

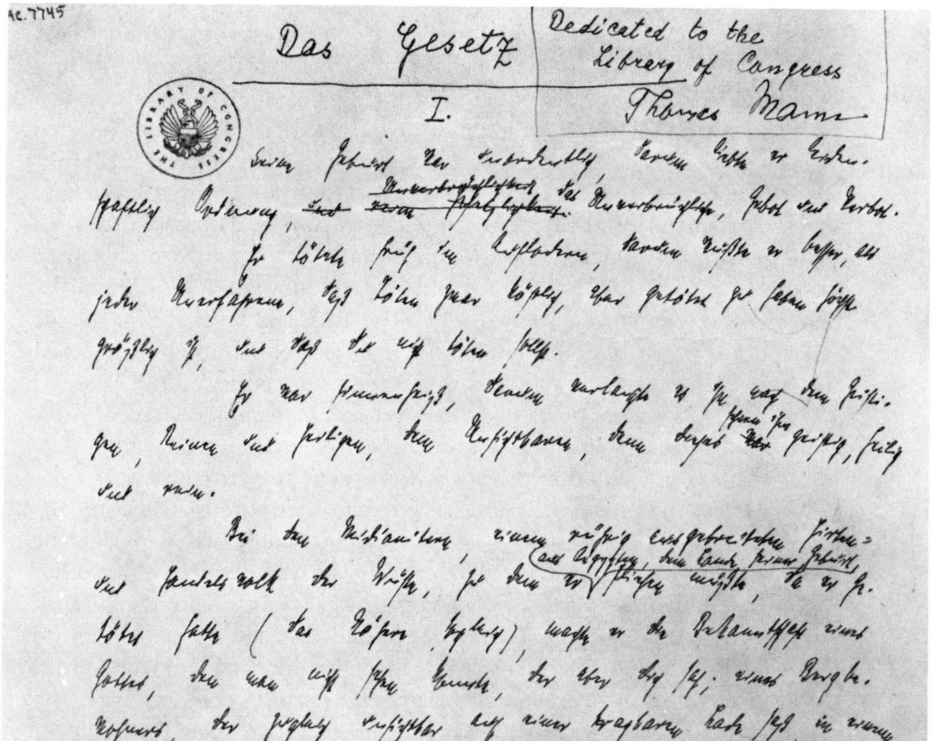

First page of Thomas Mann's *Das Gesetz,*
dedicated to the Library of Congress, and published in 1944.
From the Thomas Mann Papers, Library of Congress.

Some collect only anti-Nazi or refugee authors; others, only folk-oriented or Nazi authors. The former are more in favor. Some authors allege they went into "innere Emigration" in the Nazi era, which period is often referred to as "die unbewältigte Vergangenheit" ("the unsettled past"). Joseph Goebbels, although a novelist (*Michael*), is not collected as such. Other Nazi or allegedly Nazi authors—Hans Friedrich Blunk, Josef Weinheber, Erwin Kolbenheyer, Ernst Bertram, Hanns Johst, and the most famous of them, Gerhart Hauptmann—are surrounded with much controversy. Goethe and Mann moved from German nationalism in youth to cosmopolitanism in old age. Hauptmann moved in the opposite direction, from left to right. The Russians revered him for his early anticapitalist play (*The Weavers*) but nevertheless moved him out of his native Silesia, with most of the population, after World War II. Hauptmann's autograph has declined in price, perhaps more out of literary fashion than any political considerations. Nevertheless, a content letter or manuscript would still fetch a high price (in Germany).

There are thus many divisions in German literature that bear on autograph values. One additional, contemporary, and obvious one is the division between East and West Germany. In the former, as in other "socialist" countries, writers are expected to hew to a line of socialist realism. As in the Soviet Union and the satellites, they do not always do so. Among such East German writers are Uwe Johnson and Wolf Biermann, who have either gone to or maintain strong contacts with the West. I have seen inexpensive autographs of them offered for sale in Germany.

To compare the present condition of Vienna and Berlin, two former power centers, with their literary image and tradition is to realize what has happened to German as a literary and linguistic influence in Europe. Schiller wrote once to Goethe, "Unsere Sprache wird die Welt beherrschen" ("Our language will rule the world"). What he meant was the language of humanity and harmony. Some Germans understood it differently. Nevertheless, literarily and autographically, German is still an important presence in both the East and the West. As Nikita Khrushchev put it to President John F. Kennedy, "You have your Germans, and we have ours." There is often a correlation between literary and political importance. In the case of England (the Elizabethan and Victorian eras) and France (the age of Louis XIV), this has been particularly apparent. German literature, however, flourished in the politically unimportant duchy of Saxony-Weimar and, despite enormous political and territorial losses, continues to do so today.

ITALIAN LITERATURE

Although Italian literature and culture were a seminal influence on many European countries in the Renaissance and baroque ages, the great medieval and Renaissance names rarely appear on the market. When they do, they are extremely expensive. Michelangelo, for instance, was also a major Italian poet and, like Dante, Petrarch, Torquato Tasso, and Boccaccio, is of the utmost rarity.

Political (foreign domination and lack of unity) and economic considerations also bear on Italian autographs. There is less autograph activity in Italy than in Britain, France, and Germany. Occasionally Italian bookstores, such as the Libreria L. Gonelli & Figli in Florence, issue autograph catalogs. Most of the literati offered are not well-known internationally; but they are usually described in glowing superlatives like "illustrissimo" and "celeberrimo," and given prices that reflect their particular Italian interest. Renato Saggiori in Apt, France, issues lists with much Italian material but described with more French restraint. Ugo Foscolo, Giovanni Berchet, Giacomo Leopardi, Giuseppe Giusti, Giosuè Carducci (Nobel prize, 1906), Giovanni Pascoli, and Dino Campana are authors much esteemed by students of Italian literature but not frequently encountered on the autograph market outside of Italy. Many prominent Italian poets were much involved with the Risorgimento and are thus of more specific Italian interest. In the case of the composer Giuseppe Verdi, whose very name was used to stand for "Vittorio Emmanuele Re d'Italia," the association with politics has not diminished interest or value; rather, it perhaps has added some romantic panache. Alessandro Manzoni's novel *I promessi sposi* is a revered classic, but its author is best known internationally by the requiem that Verdi wrote on the occasion of his death.

Since Italian has long been held in lower academic esteem than its Romance language sisters French and Spanish, many important Italian writers are not well-known. Italian scholarship after the trial of Galileo was eclipsed by northern Europe. Universities, even Catholic ones, in American cities with large Italian-American populations have only minimal offerings in Italian, despite the generous endowments of Italian-American millionaires for *case italiane.* Although Italian-American groups have become outspoken in protesting the Mafia stereotype, it is also striking that some of the best-known chroniclers and portrayers of Italian-American life are non-Italians: Arthur Miller (*A View From the Bridge*), Tennessee Williams (*The Rose Tattoo*), Frank Loesser (*Most Happy Fella*), and Barry Newman ("Petrocelli" in the television series of that name).

The decadent poet and freebooter Gabriele D'Annunzio is the most collected (and most frequently seen) of the nineteenth- and twentieth-century Italian autographs. No doubt his colorful life is in part responsible—lover of Eleonora Duse and many others (despite his reputed lack of good looks), his aerial exploits in World War I, freebooter (the Fiume seizure), and his association with Mussolini, who said of him, "D'Annunzio is like a rotten tooth. Either you yank it out or fill it with gold." Mussolini made him prince of Monte Nevoso and published his works (1927). Although many literary critics prefer Giuseppe Ungaretti, Eugenio Montale, and Mario Luzi, and dismiss his writings as proto-Fascist bombast, D'Annunzio is sought after and available at moderate cost, in French as well as in Italian (he wrote *Le martyre de St.-Sébastien* for Debussy).

International interest is also lively in the case of Luigi Pirandello. His works continue to be performed, and there is some demand for his autograph. It is moderate to expensive in cost. Because he studied in Germany, he is sometimes found in German. A collection of letters to a German girl friend was sold recently. Though in German, the compli-

This postcard was written by the Italian "decadent poet and freebooter" Gabriele D'Annunzio to A. Garro, on August 16, 1908. From the John Batchelder Autograph Collection, Library of Congress.

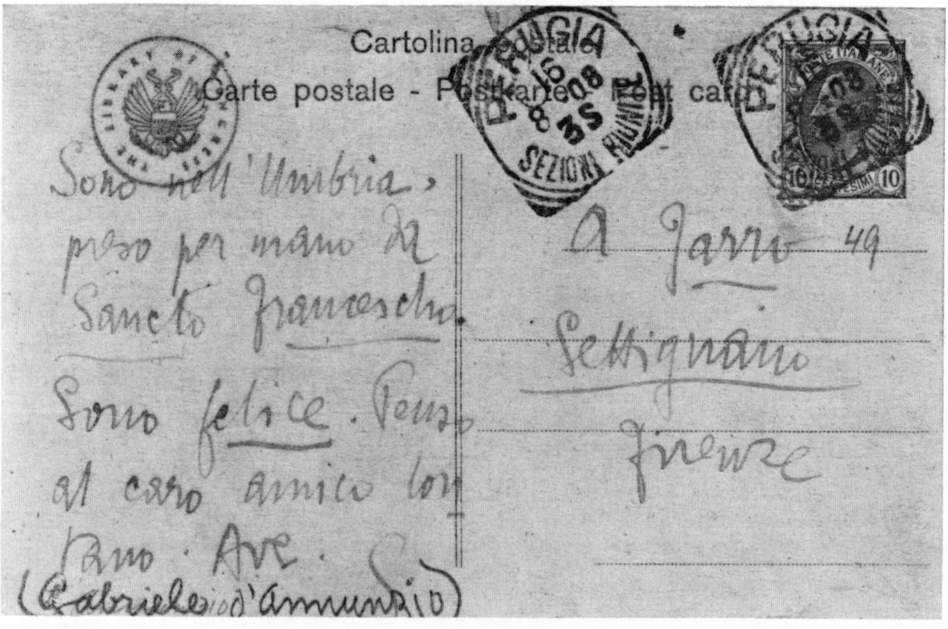

mentary close that he favored was "Con un baccio siciliano" ("with a Sicilian kiss"). Other collected Italian names occasionally seen are Giovanni Verga (inexpensive) and Count Carlo Gozzi (expensive). Mascagni's *Cavalleria rusticana* (Verga) and Puccini's *Turandot* (Gozzi) are among the very few major Italian operas drawn from an Italian source. It is striking that with few exceptions, they are taken from foreign authors, such as Schiller, Dumas fils, Sir Walter Scott, Augustin Scribe, Shakespeare, Antonio Garcia Gutiérrez, Ángel de Rivas, and Goethe.

Despite the Nobel prize (1959), Salvatore Quasimodo is neither widely read nor widely collected, and is available inexpensively. Well-known modern authors like Alberto Moravia, Cesare Pavese, Italo Svevo, and Carlo Levi are available and usually appear in inexpensive lots.

SPANISH, PORTUGUESE, AND LATIN AMERICAN LITERATURE

As with Italians, few Iberian classical authors of the Renaissance and baroque appear on the autograph market. *Siglo de oro* (Golden Age) authors such as Félix Lope de Vega Carpio, Pedro Calderón de la Barca, and Tirso de Molina turn up on rare occasions, usually at major European auctions, and are very expensive. I have never seen Cervantes or Vaz de Camoẽs. As in Italy, there was a decline in literary activity until the nineteenth and twentieth centuries.

The most commonly seen Spanish autographs are the early twentieth-century authors Jacinto Benavente y Martínez (Nobel prize) and Vicente Blasco Ibáñez. They are available at modest cost. There is much interest in Federico García Lorca; his autograph is not common, and when he does occur, prices are high. Miguel de Unamuno and José Ortega y Gasset can be obtained at modest cost. Hemingway once called himself a disciple of Pío Baroja y Nessi. Many important and interesting Spanish and Portuguese authors are not widely known internationally, however. There are a number of reasons for this.

The Iberian Peninsula, isolated from the rest of Europe by the Pyrenees, has lagged behind economically. Until recently the middle classes in Spain, Portugal, and Latin America have been relatively small. The lack of a large book-buying public does not provide a good base for autograph collecting. Until recently these areas have been considered somewhat out of the mainstream and "exotic." "Spanish music is always written by Frenchmen or Russians" is an unfair and untrue quip that reflects this attitude.

Anglo-Saxon attitudes toward Spain may be colored by traditional enmities and rivalries. The United States may have inherited some prejudices from Britain and in the days of "manifest destiny" developed some of its own. As was the case with the Indians of the New World, the conquerors rarely respect the language and culture of those they've conquered.

Spanish poetry (Gutiérrez, Duke Rivas, José de Espronceda, Gustavo Bécquer) is often too rhetorical, florid, and emotional for Anglo-Saxon tastes.

The many significant writers of the "Generation of '98" addressed themselves to specifically Spanish problems in the wake of the loss of the last vestiges of colonial empire.

The autograph market in Iberian and Latin American authors is behind the times. The great international literary interest in authors such as Juan Ramón Jiménez, Gabriela Mistral, Pablo Neruda (all Nobel laureates), Joaquim Machado de Assís, Fernando Pessoa, Jorge Amado (contemporary Brazilian novelist, eight of whose nineteen novels have been published in the United States), Mario Vargas Llosa, Miguel Covarrubias, Camilo Cela, and Antonio Machado has not yet been reflected on the autograph market. Since Spanish has suffered less than other languages from the culture-destructive cutbacks in foreign-language programs in American schools, perhaps the picture will change.

Much of the indigenous culture of the Indians in the western hemisphere was destroyed as part of Christianization, as had happened much earlier in Europe. The Incas of South America had an oral, not a written, tradition; and the writings of Central American Indians that survived Christianization rarely come on the market, in contrast with the massive amounts of plundered pre-Columbian art and artifacts encountered. These literary remains pose many problems for anthropologists and ethnologists. There is more respect, at least superficially, for Indian culture in Latin America than in North America. Only Paraguay, however, has an Indian language, *guaraní,* as a second official language.

In many circles in Latin America there is little respect for American culture. The Uruguayan José Enrique Rodó in *Ariel* characterized the United States as a materialist, machine-mad Caliban in contrast with spiritual and idealist Latin America as Ariel. Teddy Roosevelt's action in Panama in 1903 inspired similar sentiments in the great Nicaraguan poet Rubén Darío. Because of the spectacular failure of the massive American commitment of machines and money in Vietnam, some Americans have become more sensitive to the many international critics of the United States as a money- and machine-mad society.

Many feel that Latin America has a great future. Perhaps this will be true autographically also, unless there is a rise of communism, since that system's prescriptive obsession with "socialist realism," enforced mass togetherness, and hostility to the "personality cult" are inimical to au-

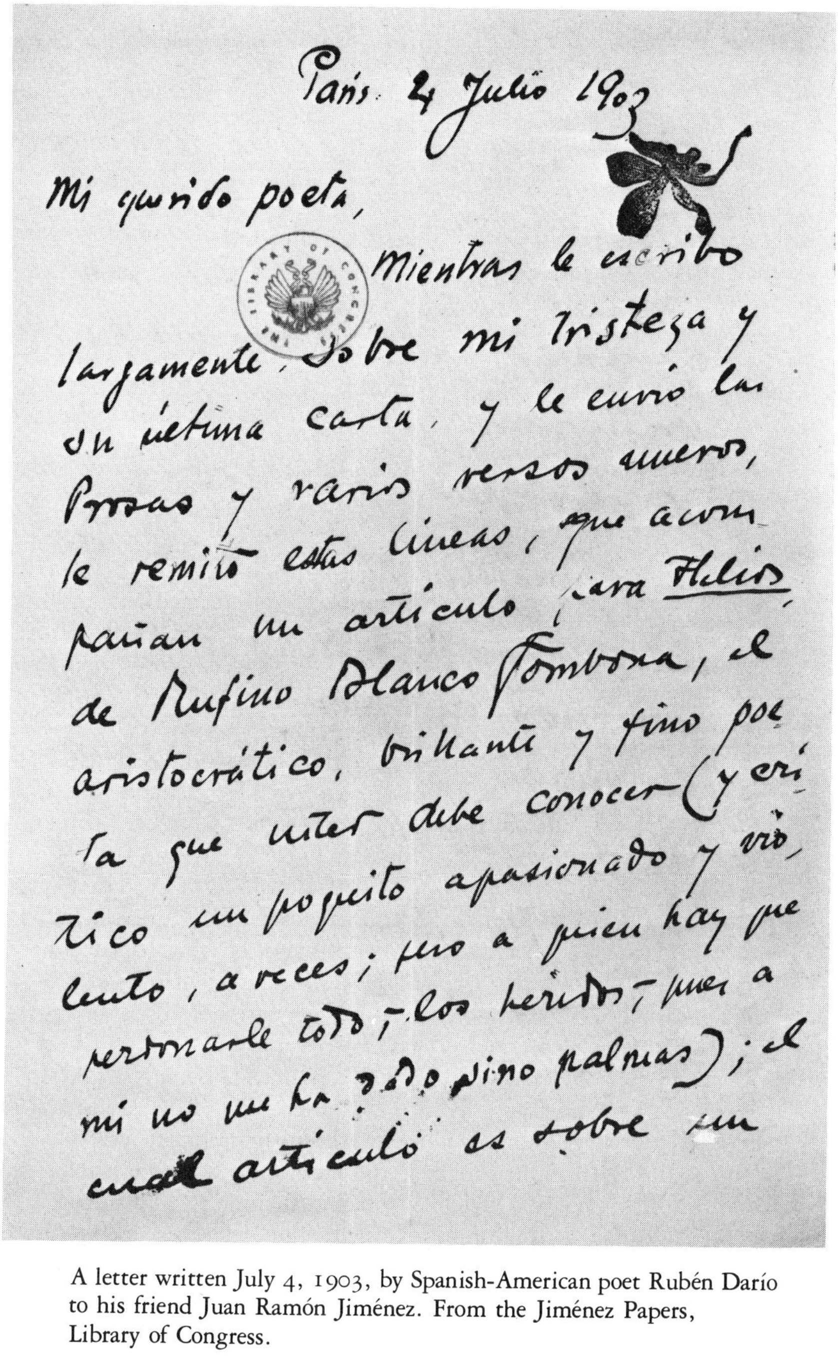

París. 4 Julio 1903

Mi querido poeta,

Mientras le escribo
largamente, sobre mi tristeza y
su última carta, y le envío las
Prosas y varios versos nuevos,
le remito estas líneas, que acom-
pañan un artículo para Helios,
de Rufino Blanco Fombona, el
aristocrático, brillante y fino poeta que usted debe conocer (y crí-
tico un poquito apasionado y vio-
lento, a veces; pero a quien hay que
perdonarle todo, — los heridos, — pues a
mí no me ha dado sino palmas); el
cual artículo es sobre un

A letter written July 4, 1903, by Spanish-American poet Rubén Darío to his friend Juan Ramón Jiménez. From the Jiménez Papers, Library of Congress.

tograph collecting. To judge by the amount of literary activity, there may well be more interest in Latin American literary autographs. Now, however, political (especially Mexican) autographs constitute the bulk of material from that area. Bogotá styles itself "the Athens of America," yet I know of no autograph dealers there. Some bookstores in Buenos Aires and other cities do occasionally offer autographs.

SCANDINAVIAN LITERATURE

Inexpensive examples of Nobel laureates Sigrid Undset, Pär Lagerkvist, Selma Lagerlöf, Bjørnstjerne Bjørnson, and Knut Hamsun are frequently seen. Interest in Hamsun has risen markedly in recent years since he has emerged from under the cloud of alleged pro-German activities in World War II. The same is true of his countryman Vidkun Quisling, who, according to some revisionist historians, was not at all what propaganda has made him out to be. A very high percentage, in fact the highest (19 percent), of Nobel laureates in literature have been Scandinavian. This is not reflected on the autograph market. Earlier observations on the local are pertinent here, too. Adam Oehlenschläger, Denmark's greatest poet, does better in Europe. The Norwegian-Danish Baron Ludvig Holberg, styled the "Molière of the North," is held in great esteem in Scandinavia, but is best known internationally as the literary source for Arnold Schoenberg's *Gurrelieder* and Frederick Delius' *Fennimore and Gerda.* Hans Christian Andersen is available and expensive. Like Henrik Ibsen and Strindberg, he often wrote in German, although he is sometimes erroneously cataloged as "in Danish," as in the case of some of his German poetry offered for sale in 1975. There is little international interest in many Scandinavian Nobel laureates like Erik Karlfeldt and Halldór Laxness (Iceland), and interest has declined in Bjørnson and some of those cited earlier. Interest continues strong (and prices high) in Andersen and the great playwrights Ibsen and Strindberg. Strindberg is the rarer of the two.

Finland, strictly speaking not in Scandinavia, is represented on autograph markets primarily by the composer Jean Sibelius and the soldier-statesman Carl von Mannerheim. Finnish literature is a good example of the "either too young or too old, or both" pattern referred to at the beginning of this article. The Finnish literary tradition was oral and not collected in the famous *Kalevala* and *Kanteletar* until the nineteenth century. The development of Finnish literature was further inhibited by the presence of a large and, until recently, more articulate Swedish minority and by czarist (later Soviet) oppression.

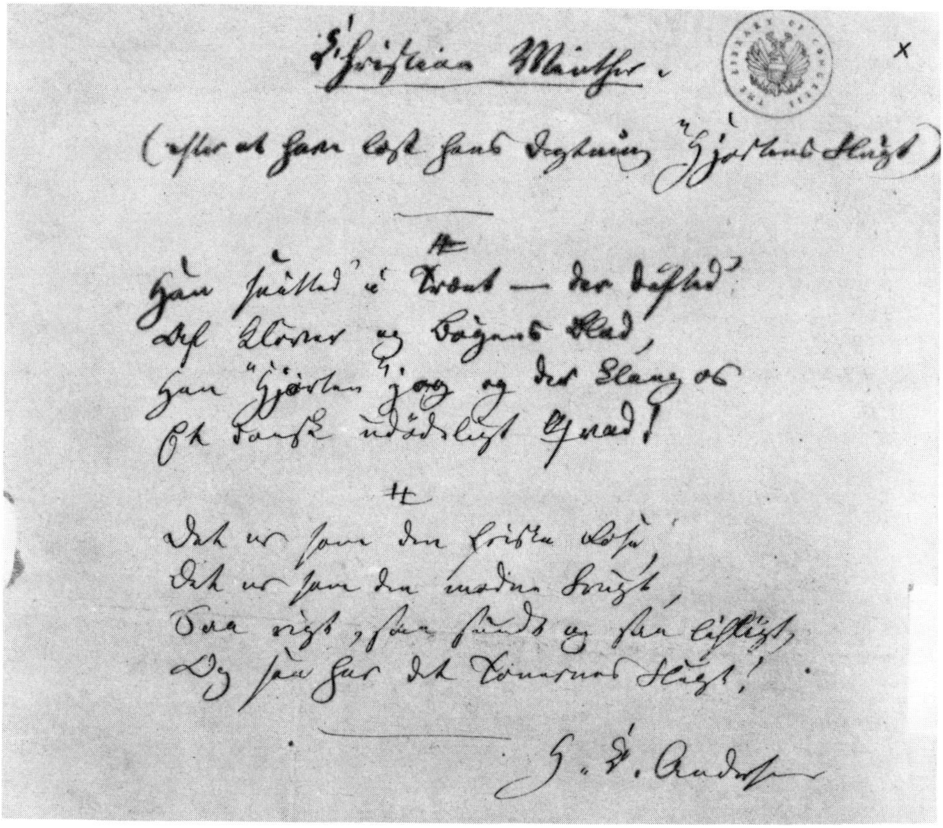

Christian Winther.

(efter at have læst hans Digtning "Hjortens Flugt")

H. C. Andersen

A brief poem entitled "Christian Winther (After Having Read His 'The Flight of the Hart')," by the Dane, Hans Christian Andersen. From the John Batchelder Autograph Collection, Library of Congress.

Norwegian dramatist and poet Henrik Ibsen wrote out this quotation on August 6, 1892, for Miss Jarrett, "the inspiration of Ibsen's old age." From the John Batchelder Autograph Collection, Library of Congress.

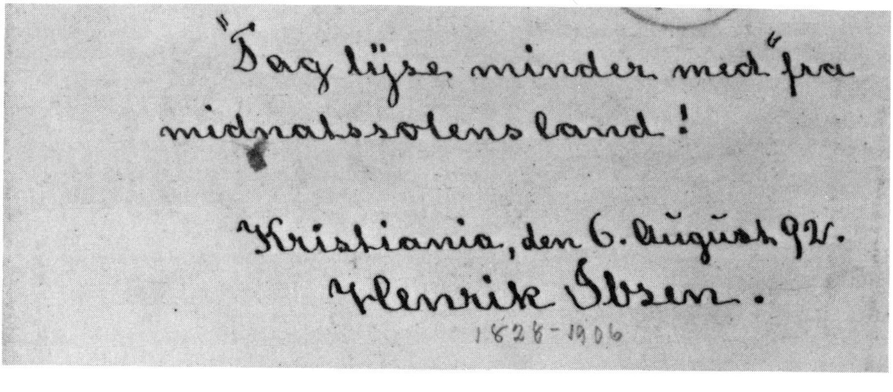

"Dagslyse minder med" fra midnatssolens land!

Kristiania, den 6. August 92.
Henrik Ibsen.

1828-1906

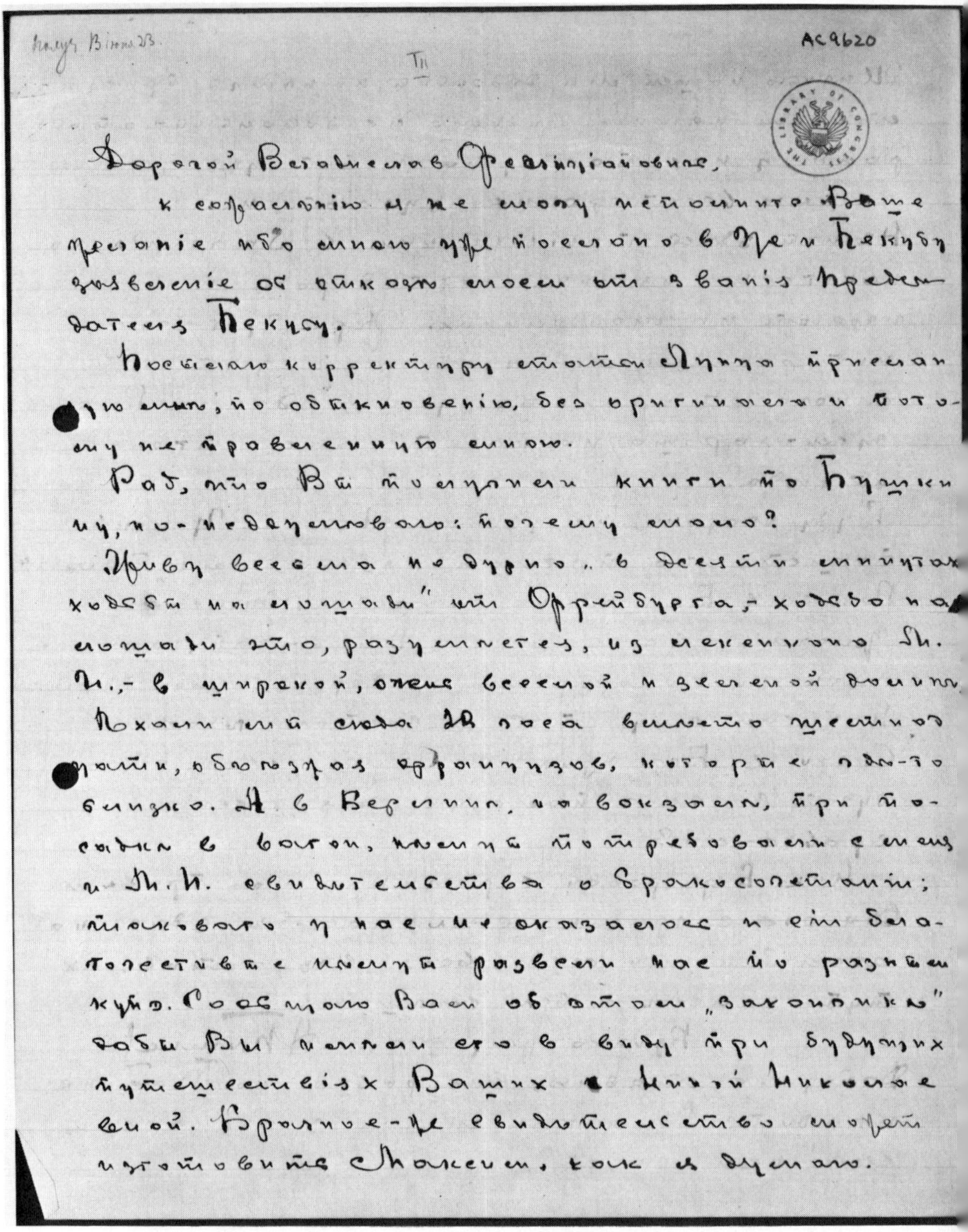

Page of an undated letter written by Russian novelist Maxim Gorki to the poet and literary critic Vladislav Khodasevich.
From the Gorki Papers, Library of Congress.

RUSSIAN LITERATURE

Russian literary autographs occur but are in short supply. Demand for them is active, and prices are consequently high. Russian literature, in comparison with other European literatures, was a late bloomer. Nevertheless, it is greatly esteemed. Madness, self-laceration, terror and ecstasy, metaphysical and psychological malaise, are often portrayed more intensely and vividly than in other literatures. Thomas Mann referred to it as "venerable"—not, however, on account of its age—and Freud called *The Brothers Karamazov* the "eighth wonder of the world." All the great names are rare and expensive, especially Aleksandr Pushkin, Mikhail Lermontov, Feodor Tyutchev, Anton Chekhov, Nikolai Gogol, and Feodor Dostoyevsky. Leo Tolstoy is common, but moderate to expensive. Of the better-known Russian authors, Ivan Turgenev is in best supply, and is most frequently found in French or German. Maxim

A letter of Russian author Ivan Turgenev written in French. Courtesy of the Clifton Waller Barrett Library, University of Virginia Library.

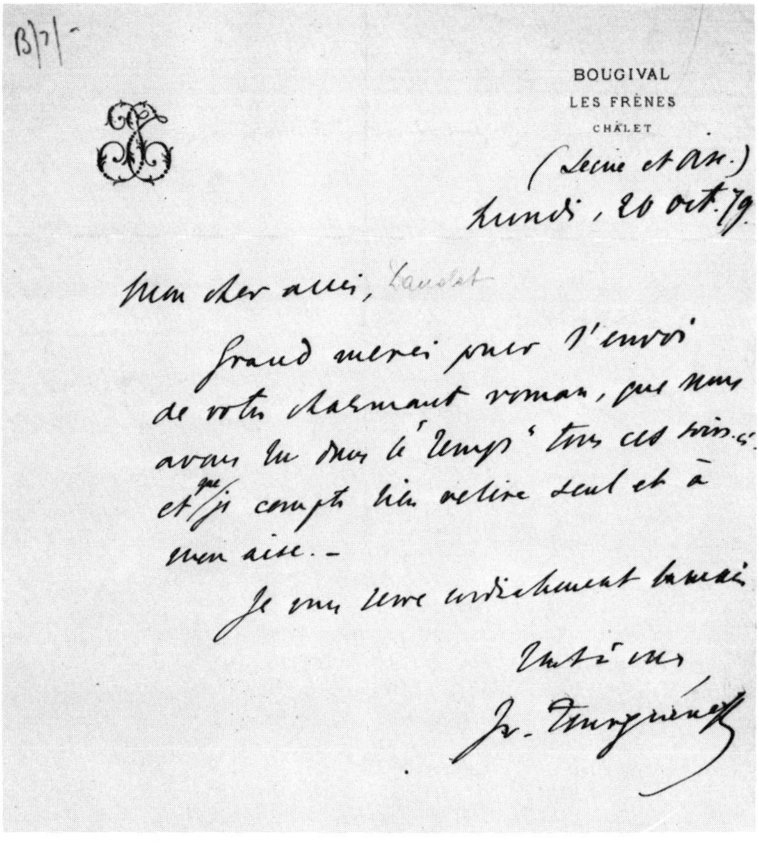

BOUGIVAL
LES FRÊNES
CHALET

(Seine et Oise)
Lundi, 20 oct. 79.

Mon cher ami,

Grand merci pour l'envoi de votre charmant roman, que nous avons lu dans le 'Temps' tous ces mois-ci et que je compte bien relire seul et à mon aise.—

Je vous serre cordialement la main

Votre
Iv. Tourguéneff

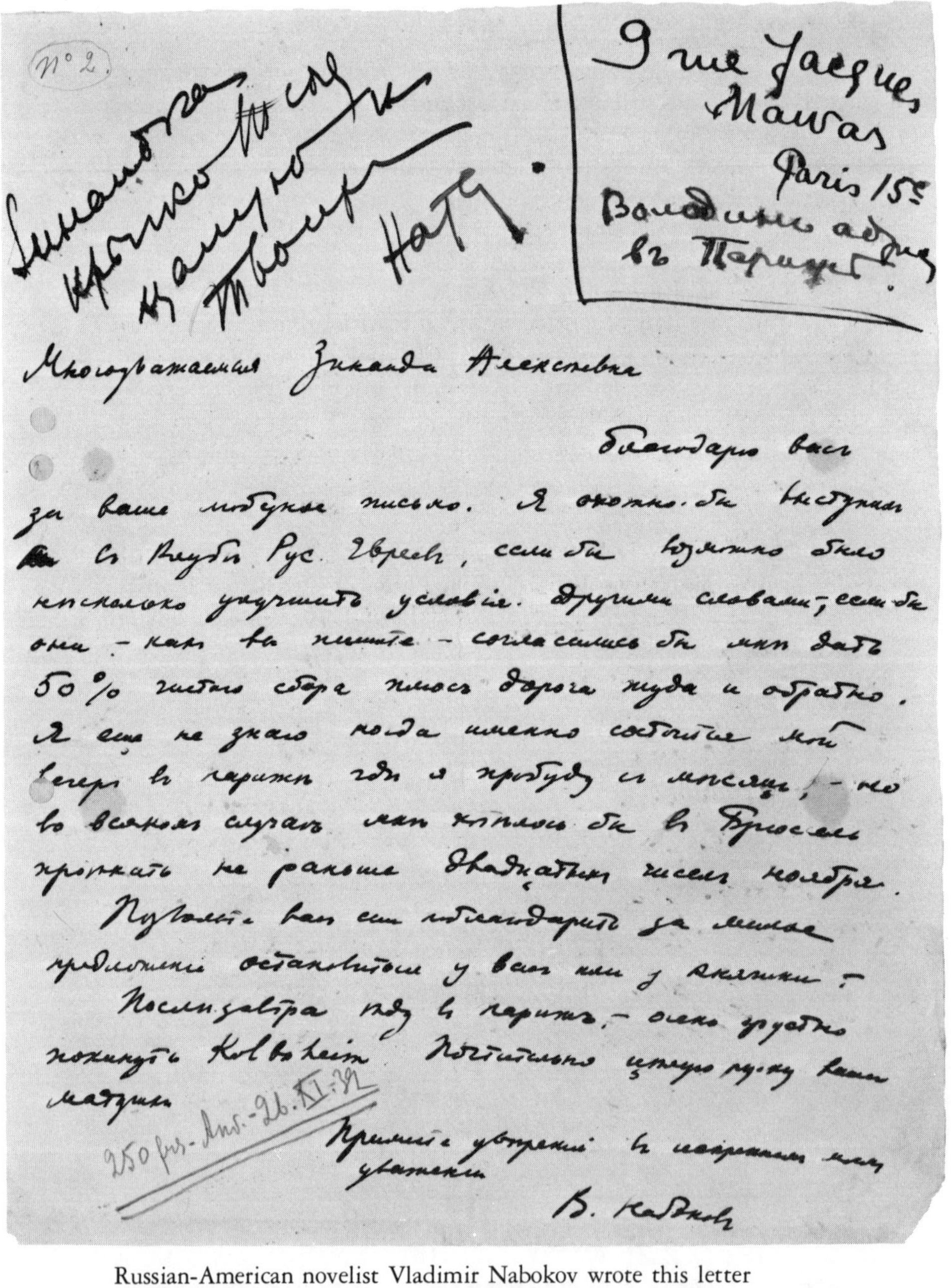

№ 2

9 rue Jacques Mawas
Paris 15e
Володин адрес в Париже.

Многоуважаемая Зинаида Алексеевна,

благодарю вас за ваше любезное письмо. Я охотно бы выступил в Клубе Рус. Евреев, если бы возможно было несколько улучшить условие. Другими словами, если бы они — как вы пишете — согласились бы мне дать 50% чистого сбора плюс дорога туда и обратно. Я еще не знаю когда именно состоится мой вечер в Париже, где я пробуду с месяц, — но во всяком случае мне хотелось бы в Брюссель приехать не раньше двадцатых чисел ноября.

Позвольте вас еще поблагодарить за милое предложение остановиться у вас или у княгини.

Послезавтра еду в Париж, — очень трудно покинуть Kolbsheim. Почтительно целую руку вашей матушки.

Примите уверения в искреннем моем уважении

В. Набоков

250 frs. - Anv. - 26. XI. 32

Russian-American novelist Vladimir Nabokov wrote this letter to Princess Zinaida Schakovskoy, on September 26, 1932. From the Nabokov Papers, Library of Congress.

Gorki is more available than his protégé Leonid Andreyev, but both are now expensive. Vladimir Nabokov's early works were in Russian; and since his great successes in English, he has translated many of them into English. His autograph is not common and is expensive.

Josef Stalin, when a young man, was a Georgian nationalist and contributed poems to a Georgian literary magazine. Autographs of Stalin are rare and I have seen none in Georgian, though it was his first language. Many Soviet authors have had well-publicized difficulties with the government. Interest in them is great, but few appear on the market. Some, like Osip Mandelstam, disappeared into the prison system. Boris Pasternak is rare and expensive, occasionally found in German and in English. Vladimir Mayakovsky was an early suicide, and Aleksandr Blok died at the age of forty-one. Yevgeny Yevtushenko, an anti-Stalinist poet, traveled widely in the United States on reading tours. Signed copies of poems and signed photos are encountered at modest cost. I have never, as yet, seen Aleksandr Solzhenitsyn on the market. Since he is now in the West, his autographs will soon be available. There is only moderate interest in authors who have not run afoul of the regime, like Ilya Ehrenburg (one-time apologist for Stalin) and Mikhail Sholokhov (accused of plagiarism by Solzhenitsyn). A long Ehrenburg typescript with extensive holograph corrections sold in 1974 for less than $50.

EAST EUROPEAN AND OTHER LITERATURES

Although Greece is the fountainhead of Western literature, few Greek autographs are seen. Some members of the U.S. Congress at the end of the Revolutionary War proposed that Greek be adopted as the language of the new state. Once again, the "too young, too old, or both" pattern applies. Time, Christianization, and Turkish domination are responsible for the fact that only a few examples of noted modern Greek authors appear on the market. C. P. Cavafy, George Seferis, and Nikos Kazantzakis occasionally occur and are inexpensive.

Henryk Sienkiewicz (Nobel prize, 1905) is one of the few Polish literary names seen on the market. He is inexpensive. The most famous Polish literary name is, of course, Joseph Conrad (né Korzeniowski). All autographs of him I've seen have been in English. Polish history (the partitions) is reflected in the fact that the most famous literary, scientific, and musical Poles often worked elsewhere and in other languages, or, as in the case of Copernicus, probably were not Polish at all. Poland has, in a sense, been "in transit" for centuries. A quip attributed to Bertrand Russell in 1946 has it that "If Poland keeps moving westward at this rate, she'll soon be in Brazil." Things have probably stabilized now, although, as in all the satellite countries, there is the ever-present demand to adhere to "socialist realism."

Similarly, in the case of Rumania, the best-known authors did not write in Rumanian. French influence is great. Emil M. Cioran, widely discussed philosopher of the negative, and Eugène Ionesco, famed playwright of the absurd, live in France and write in French, as did symbolist poet Tristan Tzara. Queen Elizabeth of Rumania, who wrote under the pseudonym Carmen Sylva, is also found in French but mostly in German. Cost is inexpensive to moderate.

The greatest Ukrainian poet, Taras Shevchenko, is a collected and expensive autograph. I have never seen any Belorussian (the language was long banned in czarist Russia) or other Soviet minority-language writers on the market.

The Greek influence in Bulgaria (the clergy), and the German in many other East European countries, retarded the development of national literatures there. Johann von Herder's famous collection of folk songs, *Stimmen der Völker in Liedern,* added to the collection and study of many East European literatures. In the nineteenth century, nationalism lent impetus to the development of these literatures. The region now called Czechoslovakia had a very old and important German tradition until 1945. The Karlsbad and Marienbad spas are better known by those names than by their contemporary Czech designations. Similarly, Pilsen and Budweis live on in beer brands. Bedřich Smetana, called "the father of Czech music," wrote a symphony for Emperor Franz Joseph's birthday in which the imperial anthem (later the same Haydn melody was used for *Deutschland über alles*) figures prominently. Authors such as Rilke, Kafka, Franz Werfel, and many others wrote in German. Like Freud and Mahler, they are included in the German-Austrian sphere.

With the advent of nineteenth-century nationalism, many Czechs became sensitive to the German-Austrian influence. The famous Königinhof manuscript forgery attempted to show that Czech culture antedated the German in Bohemia. There are two official languages today in the state created out of former Austrian territories. One is Czech and the other is Slovak, despite frequent erroneous references to "Czechoslovakian." With the exception of Pavol Országh, the Slovakian epic and lyric poet who wrote under the pseudonym Hviezdoslav, whom I once saw in an inexpensive lot in Vienna, I have seen no autographs of Slovakian literati. Slovakia achieved statehood briefly in the 1940's. There are many Czech authors active today (in the 1960's there was something of a vogue in things Czech), but few are seen on the autograph market. Jaroslav Hašek (*The Good Soldier Schweik*) is available and inexpensive. The best known is Karel Čapek, author of the play

R.U.R. (*Rossum's Universal Robots*), which made the word "robot" (from the Czech word for compulsory service or work) current in the West. He is uncommon, but in 1975 the California autograph dealer Doris Harris offered an autograph manuscript of the conclusion of this play (one page) at $275.

Although most Belgians speak Flemish (a Germanic language), almost all the internationally known Belgian poets wrote in French. Maeterlinck is available and inexpensive; Georges Rodenbach is rarer and more expensive, as is Verhaeren. Similarly, the most famous Dutch autographs encountered are in French. Among these are Vincent Van Gogh (whose name, to the displeasure of Dutchmen, is usually pronounced as in French and whose autograph French poetry sold for a high price at auction in 1975). Pieter Hooft, Joost van den Vondel, and the other great writers (and painters) of the seventeenth century (Holland's golden age) rarely appear. As with many Italian and Spanish authors of the Renaissance and baroque, they occasionally appear in Europe at high prices. Most Dutch autographs on the American market are on old New York (New Amsterdam) documents or commercial ships' papers.

Breton and various other Gaelic cultural communities have become literarily and politically more active of late, but they are almost never seen on the autograph market. Gaelic, the "sweet wee maternal tongue," was proscribed in the Education Act of 1872 but, along with Scottish nationalism, is experiencing a minor revival now. Some Irish authors write in Gaelic as well as English, although I have seen only examples in English. Sean O'Casey is available and expensive, as is J. M. Synge.

Because of World War II and the creation of the state of Israel, Yiddish literature has flourished less vigorously, although chairs of Yiddish literature exist at Israeli universities. Despite the many collectors of Judaica and the fact that Yiddish theater still flourishes in New York (unlike many ethnic theaters, which have disappeared) and is a considerable factor even in the commercial Broadway theater, most collectors seem more interested in political autographs. Israeli novelists like S. Y. Agnon (Nobel prize, 1966) and David Shahar are inexpensive and far less sought after than David Ben-Gurion, Theodor Herzl, or even signers of the Israeli Declaration of Independence. This is perhaps influenced by the fact that Signers, like U.S. presidents, are old standbys on the American autograph market. Another consideration is that Hebrew is still not a widely known language. Yiddish, a linguistic amalgam, is felt by many Jews to be a symbol of the Diaspora; and they feel that it will eventually be replaced by Hebrew. Yiddish-language authors like Isaac Bashevis Singer (still productive and widely read in English translation), Isaac Peretz, and Sholom Aleichem (Solomon Rabinowitz) are available and inexpensive.

Arabic and Persian authors are almost unknown on the international market. Material from these areas is often collected for calligraphic or artistic reasons. Despite the enormous popularity of the Syrian Khalil Gibran, his autograph is available at moderate cost. He also wrote in Arabic, but I have seen only examples in English. Although many Arabic countries have a rich literature, it is not widely known in the West. Major ancient literary finds such as the Dead Sea Scrolls of a Jewish Essene community, rediscovered in 1947, or the remarkable library of Gnostic scriptures known as the Nag Hammadi Codices, rediscovered in 1946, wind up in museums or national libraries almost immediately.

AFRICAN LITERATURE

Although Africa has long fascinated the imagination of Western writers such as André Gide, Joseph Conrad, Isak Dinesen, Ernest Hemingway, Rider Haggard, Edgar Rice Burroughs, and others, no black African writer is widely popular or widely collected in the West. Some of the newly emerged African nations are still seeking their identities, attempting to blend their precolonial traditions with their recent colonial past and the modern world. *Elima,* the official journal of Mobuto Sese Seko's Zaïre (new name for the Congo yet, strangely, of probable Portuguese derivation), decreed in 1975 that a national literature emerge and that official literary salons be established. French and English are the major languages of black African writers. French is also the language of many black Indian Ocean and Caribbean writers—for instance, Aimé Césaire, who first spoke of negritude in 1944. Léopold Sédar Senghor, poet and president of Senegal, appears more frequently in lots of statesmen than of authors, although he is very active literarily. Unlike Ignace Paderewski, who is sought primarily by musical collectors, not because he was briefly president of re-created Poland, Senghor is considered an able statesman despite the assertion that poets (like Robert Southey) draw up "Great Models" for government that in practice turn out to be "Great Muddles." One would expect more interest in him literarily, since the idea of the poet as statesman has intrigued many since the days of Plato.

Julius Nyerere of Kenya and Wole Soyinka of Nigeria have been active literarily but are always included in political lots. Swahili is a Bantu language much influenced by other African languages, as well as by many corruptions of Arabic and English words, and has now (1975) been chosen as the language of Africa by the Union of African Writers. The Kenyan poet Ahman Hassir bin Juma Bhalo's Swahili verses have been published in the United States. Many African novelists, perhaps because they write in English, are becoming increasingly known internationally.

Among these are the Nigerians Chinua Achebe and Buchi Emecheta. Most African countries, until recently, had only an oral literary tradition. The only South African writers I have seen on the market (both inexpensive) are Alan Paton and Nadine Gordimer. Two black South African plays, *Sizwe Bansi Is Dead* and *The Island* by John Kani, Winston Ntshona, and Athol Fugard, appeared on Broadway in 1975. Most South African literature is white Afrikaans or English. Nevertheless, there may be "mute, inglorious Miltons" in the underdeveloped countries who are simply unknown, unheralded, unchronicled, and uncataloged in the autograph markets of New York, London, Paris, Vienna, Milan, Marburg, Hamburg, and Munich. The activity of writers like Cedric Makepeace Phatudi, a South African novelist who translated *Julius Caesar* into Sepede as *Julease Sisare,* and others may, in time, be reflected on autograph markets.

Africans have begun to write about Africa, its past, its present, and its future. This has, until recently, not been the case. In 1975, *Longing for Darkness* by Kamante, Isak Dinesen's majordomo, was published in the United States with a foreword by Jacqueline Bouvier Onassis. Attitudes toward Africa and other nonoccidental areas have changed drastically. Gone are the days when the art, artifacts, and literature of "primitive" peoples were destroyed as part of Christianizing the "heathen." Since the late nineteenth century such artifacts have been collected and transported to anthropological museums or are much sought for private collections. In the old days the white man sold trinkets and beads to the natives. Today it is the natives who sell trinkets, beads, and carvings to the tourists.

INDIAN LITERATURE

Perhaps East is East and West is West, yet the twain did meet in Rabindranath Tagore (seen in Bengali and more often in English, sometimes in both together). He is available at moderate cost. Many other contemporary authors, like Santha Rama Rau, R. K. Narayan, Raja Rao, Mulk Raj Anand, and Khushwant Singh are widely read, if not collected, in the West. They, and others, often write in English, which is still something of a *lingua franca* in India. Yoga, an Indian discipline widely practiced in the West, means joining, uniting. Recent biographies of Kipling allege that it was he who felt out of place both in English and Anglo-Indian society.

The literatures of the Far East do not fall into the "either too young or too old, or sometimes both" pattern that applies to many African and other countries. As far as the West is concerned, however, this is the case. An anthology of Urdu poetry, *The Golden Tradition,* published in the United States in 1973, is a case in point. Although it spans eight centuries, few in the West are familiar with any of the authors. The *Dhammapada,* published in a new translation in 1976, is a collection of twenty-six poems attributed to Buddha himself. The great Indian epics (the *Ramayana* and *Mahabharata*) are of such antiquity that no autograph material is available.

CHINESE LITERATURE

As in the case of India, interest in Oriental religions has stimulated interest in the literatures. Although Americans are "into" the *I Ching* and Lao-tzu's *Tao Te Ching,* one sees few Chinese autographs on the market. The religious, erotic, political, and philosophical writings of China (from many centuries) are enjoying a great vogue, yet the only authors appearing on the autograph market with any frequency are those who were active in the West and wrote in English as well as Chinese. Most notable among these are Lin Yutang and Chiang Yee, both of whom are inexpensive. A copy of the latter's book *Silent Traveller in London,* bearing an inscription to Pearl Buck and Chiang Yee's signature in English and Chinese, was sold inexpensively at auction in 1975. China's Chairman Mao Tse-tung and Vietnam's Ho Chi Minh have both written poetry and "philosophy." The latter's verses have even been set to music by the German composer Hans Werner Henze. I have never seen Mao's autograph, and only two of Ho's. They have not obliged collectors. The official aversion to elitism and the "cult of the personality" is not a climate that encourages autograph collecting. The emphasis is on the collective in everything, but not on collecting as such.

The Western individualistic tradition notably exemplified by Thomas Carlyle, Henry David Thoreau ("enlightened self-cultivation is everything"), Voltaire's "cultivating our garden," Emily Dickinson, and many others is not deeply rooted in China. The committee mentality, and the sterile, stultifying rituals that accompany it, are becoming rife elsewhere, notably in American academia. I have even seen a form printed up by Chou En-lai in ungrammatical English, stating that it is not a Chinese custom to give autographs. A musical case in point is the *Yellow River Concerto,* now enjoying some popularity in the West. It is based on the work of a Western-trained composer, but in accordance with Chairman Mao's dictates it was rearranged and its authorship ascribed to a committee. Many Chinese (and Japanese, Persian, and Arabic) manuscripts are sold on the market merely as examples of ornate calligraphy and are collected for their aesthetic value. Since relatively few in the West can read them, it is possible that some literary luminaries lurk there.

JAPANESE LITERATURE

Western interest in all things Japanese has grown steadily since the days of Matthew Perry, Lafcadio Hearn, and Gilbert and Sullivan's *The Mikado.* In part because of the economic importance of Japan and the vogue of Zen Buddhism in the United States, new translations of Japanese works from all periods appear with increasing frequency. In the wake of Japan's great industrial prosperity, there were a number of dramatic purchases by Japanese in the art market in the early 1970's. Although less spectacular, there were also direct outlays of Japanese capital in the autograph market. Although Japan has no tradition of autograph collectors or dealers, this condition may well change, since the nation has so wholeheartedly adopted so much from the West. Even the Kabuki Theater, once the popular theater of Japan, has now become elitist and exotic to the Japanese. Western music is the most popular music in Japan. As yet, however, one sees few Japanese autographs other than political and military ones. The latter have usually been happy to oblige Western collectors. Lt. Hiroo Onoda appeared personally in New York to autograph his book *No Surrender: My Thirty-Year War.* The Japanese are thus conscious of autographs and obviously aware that an autograph in a book is a selling point. Other than Yukio Mishima and Yasunari Kawabata (Nobel prize, 1968), few Japanese literary autographs are encountered. They are uncommon but inexpensive.

TIBETAN LITERATURE

The 1959 annexation of Tibet by China caused the departure of many literary and religious leaders. Many Tibetan Buddhists have formed art and meditation centers in several American cities. Naropa Institute, founded by Tibetan Buddhists in Boulder, Colorado, is extremely active in sponsoring poetry courses and workshops with the participation of noted American poets like Allen Ginsberg, Gregory Corso, Ed Sanders (of "Fug" fame), and William Burroughs.

CONCLUSION

Although a revival of American isolationism and the existence of American linguistic arrogance is pointed out by some, culturally and literarily American interest in the literature of the world, in all its exciting diversity, is growing markedly. This should, in time, be reflected on the autograph market.

AMERICAN COLONIAL AND REVOLUTIONARY AUTOGRAPHS

JOHN C. DANN

OPPORTUNITIES FOR COLLECTING

Although two centuries have passed since the American colonies declared themselves independent from Britain and waged a war to give their lofty rhetoric substance, colonial and Revolutionary manuscripts remain a thoroughly viable field of collecting. The relatively plentiful supply of autograph items can be explained largely by the breadth of the colonial period. Well over half of America's recorded history occurred before Washington's inauguration. There were almost three centuries between Columbus' discovery and 1789, and 172 years between the first permanent settlement at Jamestown and the implementation of the federal constitution. Many of the nation's citizens were, by that time, fifth-, sixth-, even seventh-generation Americans. Their ancestors had been writing letters and diaries, creating a growing body of institutional and governmental records since earliest settlement.

The colonial period culminated in the American Revolution, a war the preliminaries of which had encompassed a decade of incidents from the Stamp Act to the march on Lexington. The armed conflict lasted eight years and involved every one of America's 2.5 million citizens in some manner. In terms of a tangible legacy, the Revolution, because of its democratic character, left a great quantity of manuscript records, from orderly books and correspondence to pay receipts, promissory notes, and signed currency.

The nation's first heroes were its Revolutionary statesmen and military leaders. Letters and documents of George Washington, the Marquis de Lafayette, Thomas Jefferson, and Benjamin Franklin were eagerly sought when autographs captured the imagination in the nineteenth century. Washington's generals, the Signers of the Declaration of Independence and the Constitution, members of the Continental Congress, and British military and political leaders of 1765–1783 held preeminence in the collections of William B. Sprague, Robert Gilmor, Israel K. Tefft, Lewis J. Cist, Thomas A. Emmet, Frederick J. Dreer, and Mellen Chamberlain. In keeping with the Romantic age in which they lived, these pioneering collectors characteristically combined one or two letters of each historical figure with a fine steel engraving. The sumptuously bound volumes that they created, still found on the shelves of major historical libraries, were as much memorials to their aesthetic and patriotic attitudes as records of the past; but they set an example that continues to shape autograph collecting. Prints and manuscripts remain frequent companions in auction lots and dealers' catalogs.

In relative terms, important letters of Revolutionary leaders have always been highly desirable and quite expensive. As investments they

Richly bound manuscripts and engraved portraits assembled by nineteenth-century collectors.

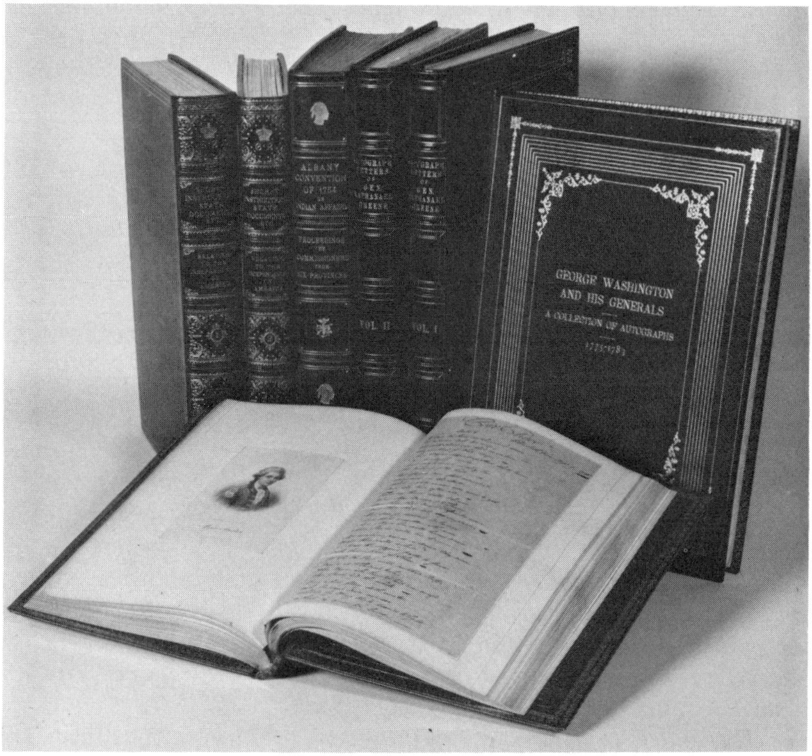

have traditionally been the "blue chips" of the market, subject to the general fluctuations but steady and substantive gainers under normal economic conditions. Dealers' catalogs and auctions since the late 1960's would suggest that there probably will be an adequate supply of colonial and Revolutionary War autograph material, ranging from historically important and expensive wartime letters to relatively inexpensive non-wartime autographs, for years to come.

In contrast with the War for Independence, the earlier and far longer colonial period, because of its breadth and complexity, has aroused collecting interest only in piecemeal fashion. Historical events are less well known and their importance less directly obvious than are those of Revolutionary and post-Revolutionary America. The collector is far less able to acquire particular items on demand than is true of the Revolutionary era. But the unpredictability of the market, the greater historical knowledge required to comprehend the significance of manuscript items, the limited competition, and consequently the enhanced possibilities of obtaining "sleepers" at bargain prices make colonial manuscripts an especially exciting field for those who dare to enter it.

Considering their antiquity, the colonial manuscripts that appeared on the market in 1965–1975 are remarkable both quantitatively and qualitatively. Land grants and documents signed by the governors of each of the colonies, letters of all but the most famous political and military figures, and business and retained copies of court records from seventeenth-century New England and New York were available in dealers' catalogs at well under $200. Documents signed by Ferdinand and Isabella appeared regularly at prices ranging between $400 and $1,200. Substantive letters of early figures such as Count Louis Frontenac, Lord Baltimore, and William Penn continue to change hands through dealers and at auction with surprising regularity.

An orderly book for James Wolfe's expedition to Quebec, the papers of General John Forbes, a series of unique manuscript American maps from the archive of Jeffrey Amherst, the Nathaniel Rich papers with outstanding contemporary material on the settlement at Jamestown, and even a journal and maps of an engineer who accompanied Robert de La Salle on his Canadian and Mississippi explorations appeared on the market in 1965–1975. They sold at prices that, in the light of their importance, future generations of collectors will undoubtedly think eminently reasonable. Supplies of better items, eighteenth-century personal and business letters, and documents of all sorts, written and signed by persons without historical reputation but illustrating everyday life in the period, were bountiful at prices well within the average collector's financial reach.

The sources of the colonial and Revolutionary manuscripts that come up for sale are varied. A surprising number of the proverbial "trunks in grandmother's attic" continue to turn up; and manuscript curators at the state historical societies, who are in a position to know, agree almost unanimously that many descendants still possess family papers with significant colonial and Revolutionary content.* While the era when owners of eighteenth-century autograph materials were oblivious to potential monetary value is gone, the enhanced profit motive on the part of initial sellers will undoubtedly bring an increasingly higher percentage onto the open market, particularly if estate taxes are raised or deductions for charitable gifts are abolished. The rising "per item" value of colonial and Revolutionary manuscripts has already driven the price of many large lots beyond the reach of most historical libraries. As much as it is to be regretted from the scholarly viewpoint, there is a noticeable and logical trend on the part of auctioneers and dealers, desiring to maximize profits, to subdivide large collections of family papers. The practice works to the advantage of private collectors by making available small lots and single letters that formerly would have gone in bulk to institutions.

Many of the very finest manuscripts have come from Europe, especially from British descendants of early American political and military leaders. Tightened export legislation and restrictive estate taxes for the wealthy have diminished the chances of large collections migrating across the Atlantic, but the effect is felt almost exclusively by libraries. Individual letters of American interest, which private collectors can afford and for which they are generally willing to pay far more than institutions, continue to be readily available in European auction and dealers' catalogs. There is no obvious reason to think the annual injection into the American collecting market of some first-rate colonial and Revolutionary autograph items from European sources will not continue, at gradually slackening pace, for years to come.

Occasionally, although often with guarded silence, institutions sell manuscripts. As escalating values raise economic incentives, as historical libraries tighten territories of collecting interest and struggle with the vast bulk of modern records, institutional selling of odd, geographically "misplaced" colonial and Revolutionary autograph items may become increasingly common.

More than half of the manuscripts listed in almost any catalog, however, come from private collections. The longevity of prime autograph material on the open market is often greater than one might realize. Items from the stock of dealer Forrest G. Sweet, auctioned between 1957 and 1963, and even of the American Autograph Shop, sold in

* See author's note at end of article.

1944–1945, turn up regularly. James McHenry letters that continue to surface in the mid-1970's are the residue of a 1944 Parke-Bernet sale; Lewis Morris letters, common in today's catalogs, come from sales in 1938 and 1971. Once a large collection is broken into small lots, reuniting by collectors and libraries will often take decades, if it can be accomplished at all.

THE MARKET FOR COLONIAL AND REVOLUTIONARY MANUSCRIPTS

The market in colonial and Revolutionary autograph manuscripts is dominated by individual collectors. The leading dealers and auctioneers polled by the author estimate that three-fourths of the manuscripts passing through their hands go to private collectors.* Charles Hamilton, Inc., reported that only 5 percent of its auction lots go to institutions; 45 percent go directly to collectors; 50 percent to dealers. The dealers, in turn, sell an average of 65 to 85 percent of their stock to private individuals, 5 to 10 percent to fellow dealers, and only 15 to 25 percent to libraries.

To autograph dealers, private collectors are, for good reason, their most valued customers. They are more flexible than the librarian can be; they can be "educated" and introduced to new avenues of collecting. Once committed to a particular subject area, they will pay more for desired items and generally can pay more promptly. Of particular importance, private collectors are not only purchasers but, as their tastes shift, or when they or their heirs decide to sell, are suppliers of manuscripts as well. Several dealers estimate that as much as 50 to 75 percent of the better manuscripts sold to private collectors are likely to reappear on the market—which is, of course, to their business advantage. Manuscripts sold to libraries, except in rare cases, are permanently removed from circulation.

There are some twenty libraries actively searching for and collecting American colonial and Revolutionary manuscripts. The state historical societies in the areas inhabited before America's independence, although acquiring most of their holdings by donation from descendants, frequently will bid on substantive letters of local significance. State libraries, state archives, and local historical societies occasionally go after items or collections of particular interest. The Southern Historical Collection at the University of North Carolina specializes in regional material; the American Antiquarian Society of Worcester, Massachusetts, in anything relating to early American printing and bookselling. The Li-

*See author's note at end of article.

brary of Congress, the Huntington Library, and the special collections departments or rare book libraries at several leading universities, although spreading their fields of collecting interest widely, occasionally purchase colonial or Revolutionary items. The Clements Library at the University of Michigan places primary emphasis on colonial and Revolutionary materials.

In almost every case, libraries are interested in a manuscript or a collection on the basis of content. They will pick up the large body of personal papers that few private collectors would handle because of sheer bulk. They occasionally will buy odd letters of unique importance in the areas of interest, thereby supplementing existing collection strengths. Most libraries have a few historical figures whose correspondence they will acquire whenever they can afford to. But, overall, institutions are very selective buyers, offering relatively infrequent competition to private collectors for any manuscripts on the open market.

Colonial manuscripts are a field of particular complexity, and a collector often needs assistance in order to transform the faded ink and yellowed paper into living historical documents. A wise collector will join and generously support historical societies and "friends of the library" organizations appropriate to his collecting interest. In return, curators are generally more than happy to help solve problems of identification and to verify signatures. Librarians are well aware that collectors are potential donors; and, while they resent being "used" selfishly by either collector or dealer, they will extend themselves graciously to someone sincerely interested in a subject and in their library's holdings.

BUILDING A COLLECTION

The greatest personal collections of early American manuscripts—Lyman C. Draper's materials on the Ohio Valley frontier and William L. Clements' British manuscripts on the Revolution—were assembled far more by ingenuity and perseverance than with money. It is a lesson that, even on a far smaller scale, is worth remembering.

The individual who can afford to invest several thousand dollars a year has great opportunities to obtain outstanding autograph letters. The least expensive Washington Ls.S. and A.Ls.S. climbed from $500 to $600 to over $1,000 between 1965 and 1975, but supplies of these and others of greater content and expense seem almost limitless. Fine letters of Nathanael Greene or Benjamin Franklin have been relatively common, though Greene's would sell in the $2,000 range by 1975, and Franklin's much higher. Correspondence of Baron Friedrich von Steuben, Thaddeus Kosciusko, Francis Marion, and Benedict Arnold, al-

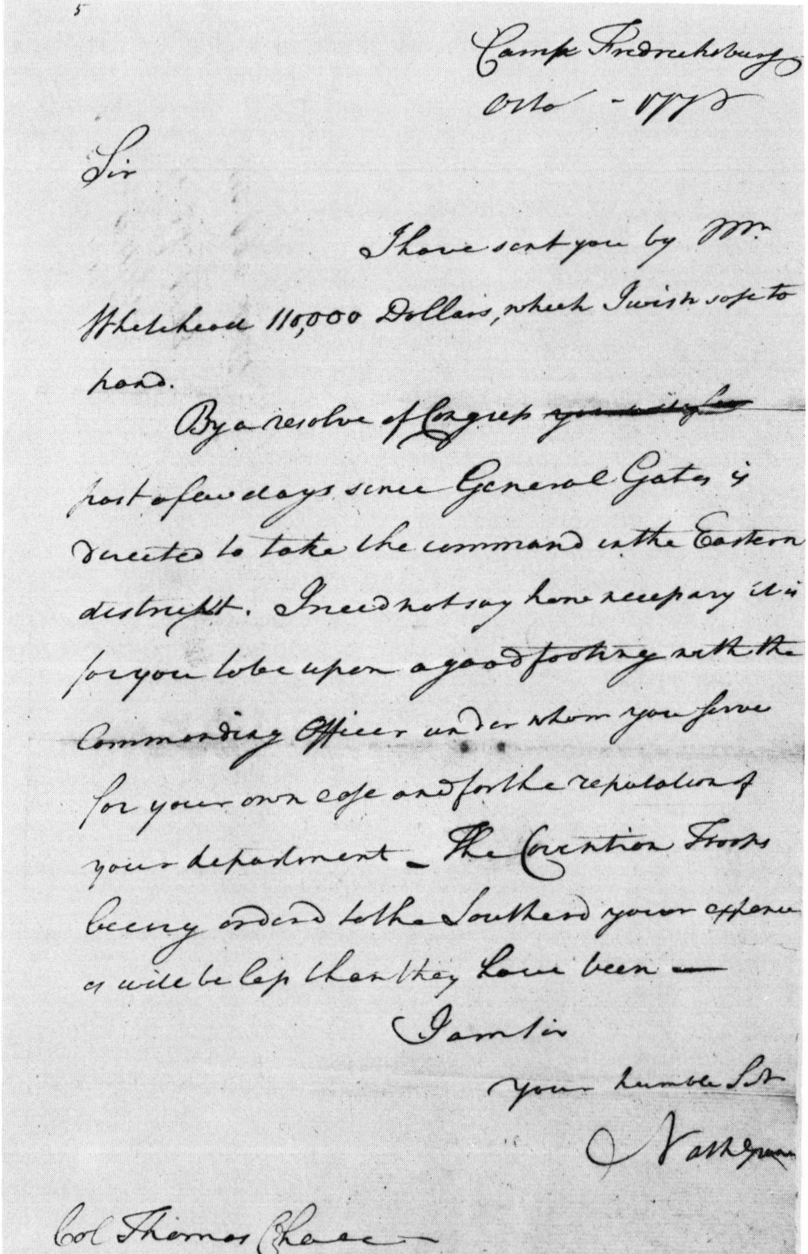
Camp Fredericksburg
Octo – 1778

Sir

I have sent you by Mr. Whitehead 110,000 Dollars, which I wish safe to hand.

By a resolve of Congress ~~you will see~~ past a few days since General Gates is directed to take the command in the Eastern district. I need not say how necessary it is for you to be upon a good footing with the Commanding Officer under whom you serve for your own ease and for the reputation of your department – The Convention Troops being ordered to the Southward your expences will be less than they have been –

I am Sir

your humble Servt

N Greene

Col Thomas Chase –

Autograph letters of Nathanael Greene. The letter above sold at auction for $35 in 1952; the letter on the right, for $880 in 1974.

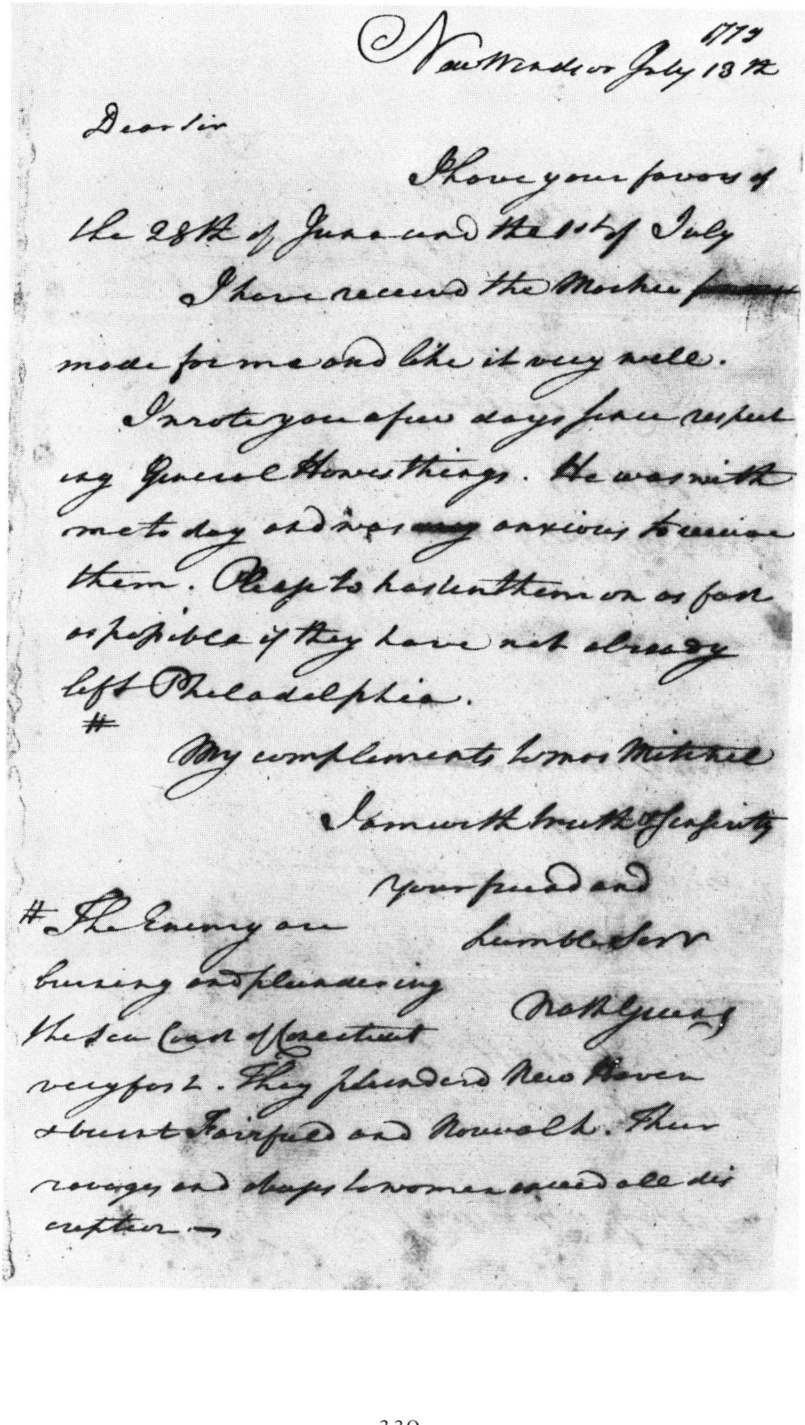
New Windsor July 13th 1779

Dear Sir

I have your favors of the 28th of June and the 1st of July

I have received the Markee made for me and like it very well.

I wrote you a few days since respecting General Howes things. He was with me to day and was very anxious to receive them. Please to hasten them on as fast as possible if they have not already left Philadelphia.
#

My compliments to Mrs Mitchell

I am with truth & sincerity

Your friend and

humble Serv

Nath Greene

The Enemy are burning and plundering the Sea Coast of Connecticut very fast. They plundered New Haven & burnt Fairfield and Norwalk. Their ravages and abuses to women exceed all description. —

though far less plentiful, costs somewhat less and is generally to be found in the course of a year's catalogs. Letters or important signed documents of key historical figures who were greater letter writers or who enjoy less popular reputation—for example, Alexander Scammell, Alexander McDougall, the Marquis de Lafayette, and William Heath—all changed hands in the mid-1970's at less—often considerably less—than $500. Letters of late colonial and Revolutionary political figures, unless they were rarely met Signers, and Revolutionary era British political and military leaders, were even less expensive. Actual copies of letters sent, or retained drafts written and signed by the author, having significant content and previously unpublished, traditionally have been the most desirable and valuable type of autograph material.

The unpredictability of supplies and of general economic conditions makes any discussion of manuscripts as investments problematic. For certain early American manuscripts, prices realized in 1927–1929 have never been equaled, even with inflation. The chances are, though, that in spite of today's seemingly high prices, anyone who can buy first-rate autograph letters of the period and hold them for two decades or more will reap a handsome return on a delightful hobby.

But a very important point to emphasize is that great wealth is not essential for building an exciting and valuable collection. Enthusiasm, shrewdness, and tireless persistence are greater assets. Anyone willing to invest perhaps $500 or so per year (1978 buying power) consistently for a decade can build a noteworthy collection of colonial and Revolutionary manuscripts.

Periodically, great bargains surface in the market. Every year or two, perhaps because of timing, or weather, or postal mixup, an auction fails to draw major bidders, and the finest items sell well under estimates. Or dispersal of a large body of manuscripts may glut the market in a certain type of material. In the early 1970's manuscript legislative acts of colonial New Jersey and legislative payrolls of Connecticut in the 1760's with autograph signatures of prominent political leaders, highly desirable autograph items in their normal scarcity, sold as low as $50 each. Because of temporary abundance, substantive letters of Charles Lee and Robert Morris sold at less than $100, a quarter or a third of what they will command when supplies dwindle. And once in a while, more often with colonial manuscripts than those of any other period because of general unfamiliarity with the era's history, an inadequate or inaccurate catalog description will bring the purchaser a prize item at a fraction of its value.

For colonial manuscripts, dating from an era when territorial divisions carried great political and social significance, geographical collecting limits (a single colony or city) make particularly good sense. Or there is subject collecting, building around an event of political, social, or military importance: one or more of the colonial wars, a particular campaign or battle of the Revolution, the Great Awakening, the Stamp Act dispute, and the like.

Letters and even signatures of Washington and Franklin have climbed beyond the average collector's budget; but items about these men (letters to or mentioning them, family correspondence, printed items), known as "association items," are plentiful and priced within reason. With several of the lesser American generals and many of the British officers, significant biographical collections could be assembled at moderate "per item" cost.

For the colonial period in particular, where dominant individuals with historical impact beyond a particular colony were few, there are numerous possibilities in group biography: collecting graduates of Yale or Harvard; the clergy of a particular denomination; the proprietors of South Carolina, or New Jersey, or Georgia; members of a colony's governor's council; or the great landholders of the Hudson Valley, for in-

Low in price, deeds, receipts, and business letters can be rewardingly collected around a theme.

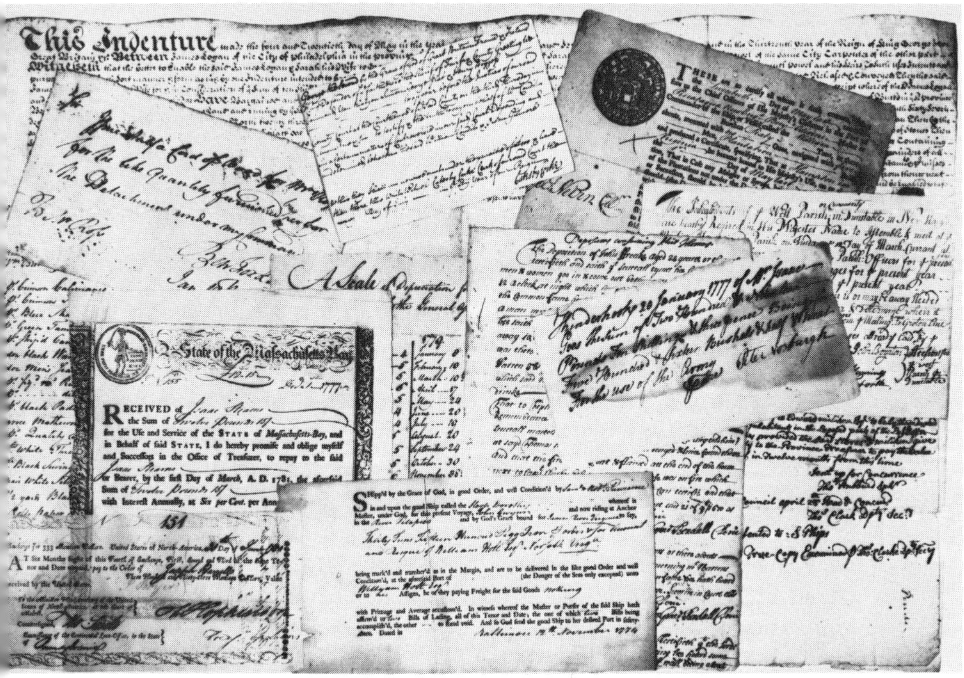

stance. Occupational groups are a relatively unexplored area of concentration. One could build collections relating to medicine, law, domestic industry, milling, iron production, privateering, travel, or intercolonial trade. For the Revolution a collector could specialize in items relating to recruiting, to arms and equipment, or to prisoners of war.

In the field of business, one could assemble at minimal expense a "type collection" that includes samples of the various records and documents involved in commercial transactions: daybook, ledger, promissory note, bill of lading, customs manifest, bill of exchange, and so on. Attractively arranged and described, such an assemblage of individually unimportant manuscript items would tell the story of colonial trade in a way that the printed word alone could never match.

By adopting a thematic approach, the collector can pursue purposeful accumulation on a limited budget, can learn a great deal about early American history in the process, and can create a collection that is unified, valuable, and appropriate for eventual sale or gift to a historical library. For a person deeply interested in colonial America and sensitive to the romance of direct contact with the written records of the nation's founders, collecting colonial and Revolutionary manuscripts is a uniquely exciting activity.

AUTHOR'S NOTE

In order to acquire a firm sense of the market in early American manuscripts, I sent questionnaires to dealers and manuscript curators at major libraries. Although the opinions expressed here are my own, the general statements and statistics could not have been presented without the generous assistance of Gordon T. Banks, Goodspeed's Book Shop, Inc.; Mary A. Benjamin, Walter R. Benjamin Autographs, Inc.; Irving Halpern, Carnegie Book Shop; Doris Harris, Los Angeles, California; Julia Sweet Newman, Battle Creek, Michigan; Kenneth W. Rendell, Newton, Massachusetts; Joseph Rubinfine, Pleasantville, New Jersey; H. K. Thompson, Jr., Charles Hamilton Galleries, Inc.; Edmund Berkeley, Jr., University of Virginia; John C. Broderick, Library of Congress; Howson C. Cole, Virginia Historical Society; Richard J. Cox, Maryland Historical Society; William L. Joyce, American Antiquarian Society; Peter J. Parker, Pennsylvania Historical Society; Jean F. Preston, Huntington Library; Mattie Russell, Duke University; Allen H. Stokes, South Caroliniana Library; and the manuscript curators of the New Jersey Historical Society, New-York Historical Society, Rhode Island Historical Society, and the Southern Historical Collection at the University of North Carolina.

AUTOGRAPHS OF THE AMERICAN CIVIL WAR

CHARLES F. COONEY

ON JANUARY 13, 1863, a young Alabamian sent a small package home to his father. In an accompanying letter he noted, "I send you just for a curiosity some Yankee letters picked up by one of my men on the battlefield." Thus, the collecting of Civil War manuscripts began even before the dust and smoke had settled on the battlefields. And ever since, interest in the Civil War as a collector's field has continued unabated.

Many historians have called the American Civil War the first "modern war." They of course are referring to the advanced technology turned to the arts of war and to the evolution of new strategies to cope with the changes in warfare wrought by technology. Yet the term also applies to the mountain of paperwork generated during the four years of fratricidal strife. The published official records of the Union and Confederate armies occupy 130 volumes of closely printed type, and that is but a portion of the entire mass of records accumulated. In addition the level of literacy in both the Union and Confederate armies was surprisingly high, and countless soldier letters, diaries, and reminiscences flowed from the war. The Civil War collector is consequently faced with a wide latitude for his collecting interests.

Manuscripts of virtually every figure who achieved prominence during the Civil War are available to the collector. A 1976 dealer's catalog offered for sale the famous letter Abraham Lincoln wrote to Grace Bedell, the schoolgirl who urged him to grow a beard, for $48,000. At the same time, catalogs were offering letters from Union soldiers for between $10 and $50. Confederate letters were somewhat higher. Between these two extremes are the manuscripts of the statesmen, generals, senators, and soldiers who shaped the Civil War years.

Because of the vast number of orders, reports, endorsements, passes, and other documents that military figures were required to sign, manuscripts of only a few of the generals or other prominent Union Army officers are hard to obtain or prohibitively expensive. The names of

George McClellan, Irvin McDowell, Don Carlos Buell, Ambrose Burnside, Joseph Hooker, Henry W. Halleck, George G. Meade, William T. Sherman, and others appear frequently in the pages of autograph and manuscript dealers' catalogs. Prices rarely exceed $200 for any but the most exceptional items, and fall as low as $10 to $15 for some items.

The Confederate military hierarchy is generally a little more difficult to obtain, and prices are concomitantly higher. The destruction of Richmond and many other places in the Confederacy resulted in the loss of countless war-related documents. Despite the generally greater rarity of Confederate items, the majority of Confederate commanders are still well within the reach of most collectors.

There are, of course, military figures on both sides whose autographs and manuscripts are difficult to obtain. One category of rarities is the men who fell in battle. Among those in this category are Thomas J. ("Stonewall") Jackson, J. E. B. Stuart, Albert Sidney Johnston, and A. P. Hill on the Confederate side; on the Union side there are Philip Kearney, James B. McPherson, and Nathaniel Lyon. Another category, which exists almost exclusively on the Confederate side, is the records of guerrillas or partisan rangers. Perhaps the most famous among the partisan rangers was the renowned John Singleton Mosby; his letters of war date are rare, though postwar materials are common. John Hunt Morgan and Nathan Bedford Forrest are also difficult to obtain.

Many of the prominent figures who opposed each other between 1861 and 1865 had served during the Mexican War; many achieved fame in other fields after the Civil War. Thus, for any particular person, material may originate either before the Civil War or long afterward. Postwar items often contain lengthy comments on wartime activities or recollections of other personalities, and thus can be more desirable than war-dated items of a routine nature. Prewar items are occasionally of interest. Mexican War service produced some association items that bring together future foes. A personal favorite in this category (although not, strictly speaking, a manuscript) is the broadside for Zachary Taylor's inaugural ball bearing the names of the ball managers. Listed together are the names of Abraham Lincoln, Jefferson Davis, and Robert E. Lee. War-dated items of good content are the most desirable, however.

Autographs may be as diverse as a simple clipped signature, a signed carte de visite or cabinet photograph, a personal letter, a routine business letter or bank check, and a lengthy military report. Date and content play a significant role in determining the value of the item. War-dated items of good content are rapidly increasing in value, while clipped signatures and signed photographs merely keep pace with inflation. Prices for prewar and postwar items depend largely on content. As in any collecting field, the better the content, the higher the value.

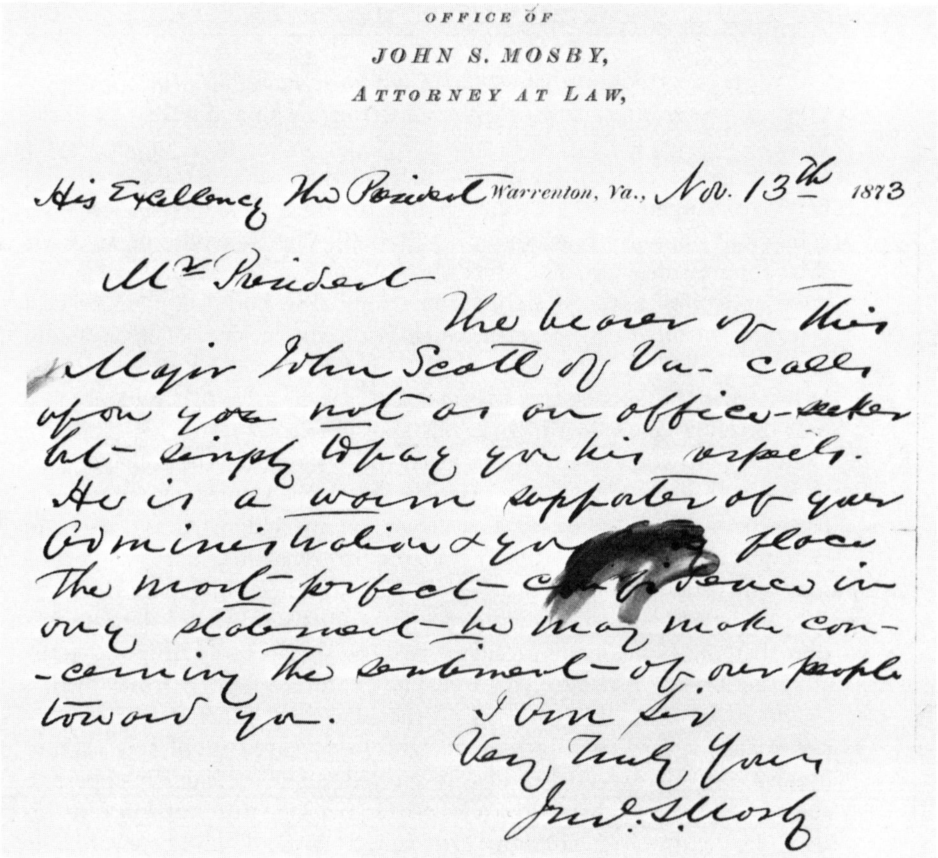

OFFICE OF
JOHN S. MOSBY,
ATTORNEY AT LAW,

His Excellency The President Warrenton, Va., Nov. 13th 1873

Mr President —

The bearer of this Major John Scott of Va. calls upon you not as an office-seeker but simply to pay you his respects. He is a warm supporter of your Administration & you [illegible] place the most perfect confidence in any statement he may make concerning the sentiment of our people toward you.

I am Sir
Very Truly Yours
Jno. S. Mosby

This letter, written a few years after the end of the Civil War by the noted Southern guerrilla leader John S. Mosby and directed to then president U. S. Grant, draws together two of the most noted leaders of the great American conflict. From the Jeffress Collection, University of Virginia Library.

In nonmilitary Civil War collecting, there remains the general rule of thumb that Confederate material is more difficult to obtain; but most figures are not impossible to acquire. Abraham Lincoln is available to collectors most often in dockets on the verso of letters received by him and forwarded to an executive department and also in signed official documents. There is a danger, however, that Lincoln may completely vanish from catalog pages in the future. Institutional collecting (most notably by the Library of Congress and the Illinois State Historical Library) may some day account for virtually every Lincoln item. On the other hand, Jefferson Davis, Lincoln's Confederate counterpart, is fairly common, although postwar items predominate. Most of Lincoln's cabinet are readily available for moderate sums; and with a few exceptions congressmen of the period are scandalously inexpensive.

With the ready availability of Civil War materials, the most perplexing question for the Civil War collector is who and what to collect. Most collections of Civil War manuscripts are well defined in one way or another. Some collectors look for material that pertains to a particular battle or campaign; others focus on an individual. A few try to assemble collections containing examples of all Civil War generals, or all Civil War congressmen, or some other "comprehensive" collection. Some creative collectors have developed collections that both supplement and complement other collecting interests. For example, one collector of cavalry equipment and accoutrements has also developed a manuscript collection that contains only items related to the cavalry. It is undoubtedly best to follow one's own inclinations and interests.

There are a few cautions that need to be stated for the collector new to the field of the Civil War. Jefferson Davis, the Confederate president, had a namesake who served as a general in the Union Army, Jefferson Columbus Davis. In a letter, memorandum, or similar document, content will usually make it clear whose signature it is; but more than one clipped Jefferson Davis signature has been purchased under the assumption that the Confederate president was the signatory when it was actually the Union general. The well-known forger Joseph Cosey had a weakness for Lincoln documents on the blue-lined paper that characterizes many of the legal documents Lincoln prepared in Illinois. While usually clumsily executed and easily spotted, a few occasionally appear at antique auctions and flea markets. Secretarial signatures of Lincoln can also fool the unwary. Jefferson Davis collectors should also be aware that in the postwar period, Varina Davis wrote and signed many of her husband's letters. Her handwriting very closely approached that of her husband, but she always added a period at the end of the signature.

Many collectors are tempted, when starting, to purchase the clipped signatures and signed photographs that are so readily available and inexpensive. Curb the temptation, for these items add little, if anything, to a collection. Except for the rarest autographs they do not, and never will, have any intrinsic value; and of course they are devoid of historical value or interest. A good letter from a private soldier describing the battle of Antietam seems to me worth far more than a clipped signature of Ambrose Burnside.

All in all, the Civil War is one of the richest and most satisfying fields available to the manuscript collector. There is an abundance of material available, a great deal of drama in the era, and even the opportunity to visit most of the places described in the letters and documents one collects.

BRITISH HISTORICAL AUTOGRAPHS

JOHN WILSON

THE COLLECTOR of British historical autographs is faced with what appears at first to be a bewildering choice. A glance at most dealers' and auctioneers' catalogs will show that there is no great difficulty, even with modest financial resources, in assembling some sort of collection including documents that go back almost nine hundred years. But where to start? Typical offerings include an early thirteenth-century document, perhaps written soon after Magna Carta, still clear and legible; a document signed by Queen Elizabeth I, its price reflecting the great demand as well as the rarity; a letter written by Lord Nelson not long before the battle of Trafalgar; a rather illegible letter of the great Duke of Wellington, surprisingly modest in price; and documents signed by any King George. Perhaps we should begin with the great statesmen of all periods and ignore the more valuable kings and queens: a letter signed by Lord Burghley, or by Essex, Queen Elizabeth's one-time favorite; one of the countless statesmen of the seventeenth century; or such worthy Victorians as Gladstone, Palmerston, and Peel. Perhaps we could expand a little? If we acquire letters of Burghley and Essex, can we later add something by Sir Walter Ralegh or Sir Francis Bacon? Probably not, for autographs of these two are particularly rare.

The questions are many, and the answers cannot always be precise. We are dealing with an ever-changing body of documents, and time usually brings a diminishing supply of older material as more and more is absorbed into private and institutional collections. A short time ago one could have said that the chances of buying anything signed by King Edward VI, the young son of Henry VIII who reigned for six and a half years, were quite remote; but a good document appeared in an auction, brought a predictably high price, and vanished. It is not likely to be offered again in the near future, and may never come back on the market.

Recently one could have said with conviction that any collector wanting a document or letter signed by Mary Queen of Scots would have to act quickly when and if his chance came. But again, such a letter came onto the market from a private source, and was followed shortly afterwards by two more at auction, one of them signed also by the ill-fated Darnley as king of Scotland. May one say that Mary is not rare? One might think so now, but the picture will soon be different. All these letters will quickly be absorbed and virtually forgotten by all but their fortunate owners. The new collector will find his chances of such an acquisition slimmer than ever.

It is this constantly changing pattern, caused by the sudden arrival on the market of a rare autograph, and its equally sudden departure, that can cause confusion for the collector and at the same time give a delightfully kaleidoscopic—and certainly distorted—view of history. It can also lead to frustration. Disappointed collectors, although wealthy enough to build a fine collection, will give up in despair if they always seem to be seeking the unattainable.

It would not be wise to advocate a completely random approach to collecting historical documents; but it is certainly better to start tentatively, perhaps a little haphazardly, and develop and strengthen the collection in one area at a later date when it has become possible to resolve the conflict between one's personal preferences and what can be found. A sympathetic dealer is sure to give the help and advice that is essential from the outset, and will perhaps agree to accept documents in exchange for part of the purchase price of other items.

It is possible to obtain routine legal documents, and sometimes more important items like royal charters, dating from the early thirteenth century and occasionally from the previous century; but one cannot expect to find autographs or signed pieces from much before 1500. It would obviously be impossible to assemble a complete set of documents signed by the kings and queens of England, for many of the earlier sovereigns could not sign or write. Even if we start with, say, a document signed by Edward IV (reigned 1461–1483), there will be many gaps: no Edward V or Richard III unless we are extremely fortunate; not much chance of Edward VI; and Mary Tudor is quite rare. A collector would have to spend as much on either Henry VIII or Elizabeth I as on all the rest from James I (reigned 1603–1625) to the present day. The later monarchs are a more practical proposition, for not only are examples of all kinds of documents more plentiful as one moves forward through history but they are also less expensive. There are a few problems, of course; documents signed by Mary II during her joint reign with William III, for instance, are rather scarce. It is difficult to avoid buying tedious military commissions, by far the most common sort of royal autographs; and it would be more rewarding in the long run to try to obtain an autograph letter. Autograph letters signed in full by Queen Victoria are not easy to find, but run-of-the-mill documents are common. Consider that almost every day throughout sixty-four years on the throne she signed at least ten documents, often many more; that makes between 250,000 and 500,000, without a rubber-stamped or secretarial signature among them!

In the long and checkered history of Great Britain there have been a sizable number of revolts, revolutions, and wars, both civil and international. This field for the collector of documents is a large one, and most will by inclination or choice decide to limit themselves. Bearing in mind that autograph material before 1600 is rather scarce, we must for practical purposes begin in the seventeenth century, though an occasional item relating to the Spanish Armada (1588) would enrich any collection.

Rulers of England and Great Britain, 1413–1978
(including dates of reign)

Henry V, 1413–1422

Henry VI, 1422–1461, 1470–1471

Edward IV, 1461–1470, 1471–1483

Edward V, 1483

Richard III, 1483–1485

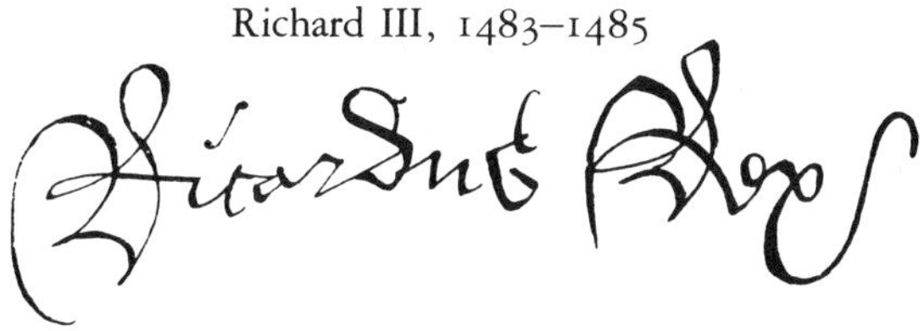

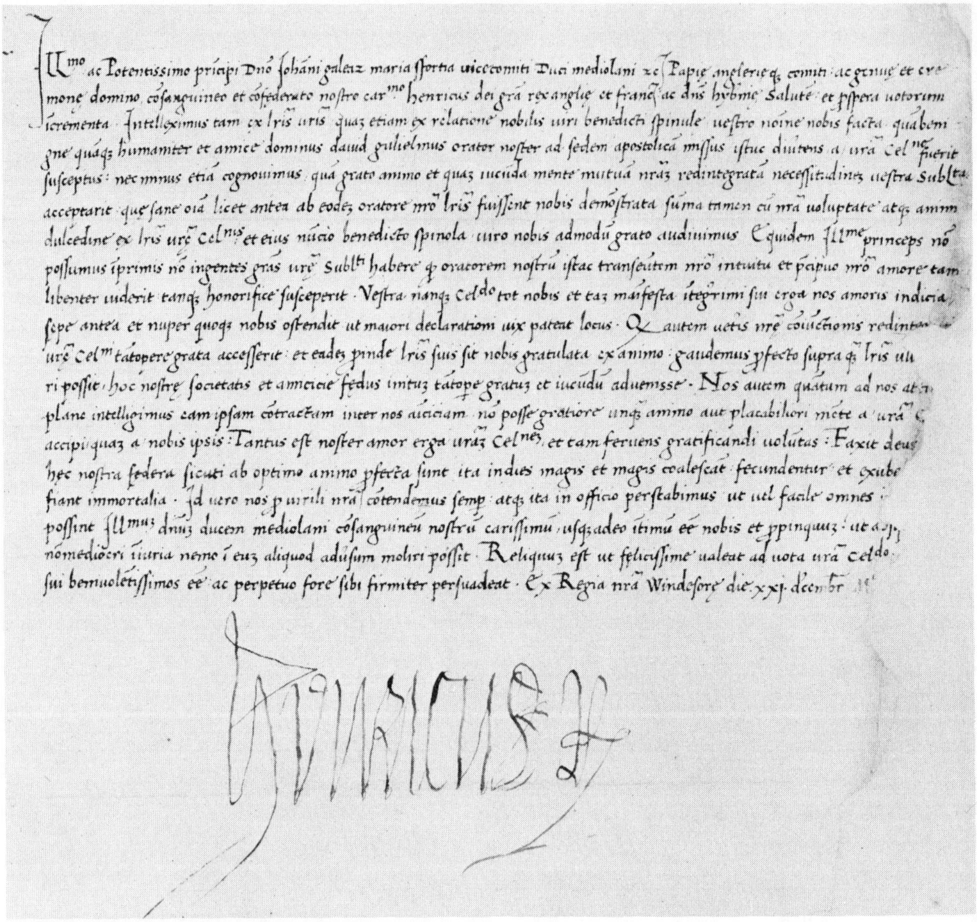

Illmo ac Potentissimo principi Dnō Johāni galeaz maria sfortia uicecomiti Duci mediolani &c Papie angerieqz comiti ac genue et cre-
mone domino cōsanguineo et cōfederato nostro carmo henricus dei grā rex anglie et franc ac dns hybnie salutē et pspera uotorum
icrementa · Intelleximus tam ex lris urīs quaz etiam ex relatione nobilis uiri benedicti spinule uestro noīe nobis facta quā beni-
gne quāqz humaniter et amice dominus dauid gulielmus orator noster ad sedem apostolicā missus istuc diuertens a urā Celne fuerit
susceptus: nec minus etiā cognouimus quā grato animo et quāz iucūda mente mutuā nrāz redintegratā necessitudinē uestra Sublta
acceptarit que sane oīa licet antea ab eodē oratore nrō lris fuissent nobis demōstrata sūma tamen cū nrā uoluptate atqz animi
dulcedine ex lris urē Celnis et eius nūcio benedicto spinola uiro nobis admodū grato audiuimus · Equidem Illme princeps nō
possumus iprimis nō ingentes grās urē Sublti habere q oratorem nostrū istac transeuntem nrō intuitu et pcipuo nrō amore tam
libenter uiderit tamqz honorifice susceperit · Vestra namqz Celdo tot nobis et taz manifesta itegrrimi sui erga nos amoris indicia
sepe antea et nuper quoqz nobis ostendit ut maiori declarationi uix pateat locus · Q autem uetis nrē coniunctionis redinte[illegible]
urē Celm tātopere grata accesserit et eadē pinde lris suis sit nobis gratulata ex animo · gaudemus pfecto supra q lris [illegible]
ri possit hoc nostre societatis et amicicie fedus intuz tātope gratuz et iucūdū aduenisse · Nos autem quātum ad nos at[illegible]
plane intelligimus eam ipsam cōtractam inter nos aiciciam nō posse gratiore unqz animo aut placabiliori mēte a urā C[illegible]
accipi quaz a nobis ipsis: Tantus est noster amor erga urāz Celnes et tam feruens gratificandi uoluntas: Faxit deus
hec nostra federa sicuti ab optimo animo pfecta sunt ita indies magis et magis coalescat fecundentur et exube[illegible]
fiant immortalia · Id uero nos p uirili nrā cōtendemus semp atqz ita in officio perstabimus ut uel facile omnes [illegible]
possint Illmus dnūz ducem mediolani cōsanguineū nostrū carissimū usqz adeo itimū eē nobis et ppinquū: ut a[illegible]
nō mediocri iiuria nemo ī euz aliquod adusum moliri possit · Reliquū est ut felicissime ualeat ad uota urā Celdo [illegible]
sui beniuolētissimos eē ac perpetuo fore sibi firmiter persuadeat · Ex Regia nrā Windesore die xxj decembr M[illegible]

Henry VII L.S. (in the hand of Petrus Carmelianus) to the Duke of Milan, December 21, 1490. Courtesy of the Pierpont Morgan Library.

Henry VII, 1485–1509

Henry VIII, 1509–1547

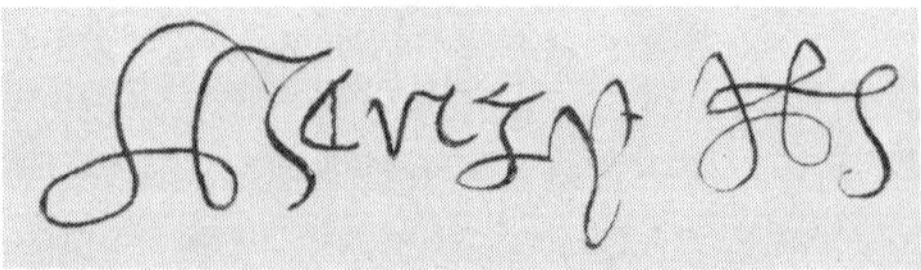

Edward VI, 1547–1553

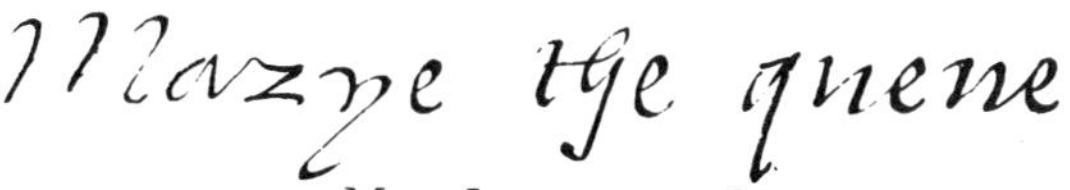

Mary I, 1553–1558

Elizabeth I, 1558–1603

James I, 1603–1625

Charles I, 1625–1649

Oliver Cromwell,
lord protector, 1653–1658.
Courtesy of The Rendells, Inc.

Richard Cromwell,
lord protector, 1658–1659
Courtesy of the Pierpont Morgan Library.

Charles II, 1660–1685

James II, 1685–1688

William III; ruled jointly with Mary II, 1689–1694; ruled alone, 1694–1702

Mary II; ruled jointly with William III, 1689–1694

Anne, 1702–1714

George I, 1714–1727

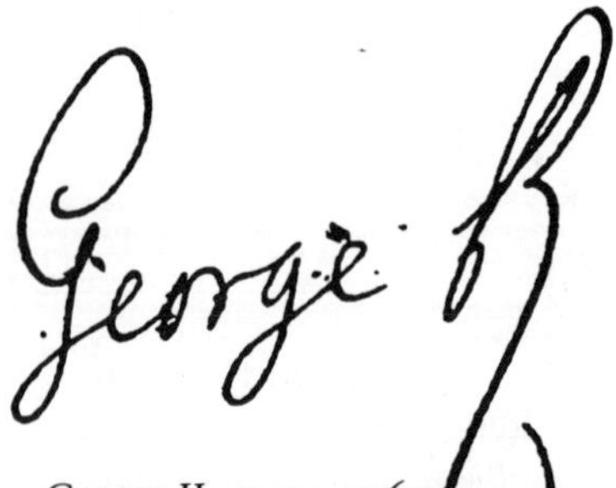

George II, 1727–1760

George III, 1760–1820

George IV, 1820–1830

George III.
From the Clem D. Johnston Collection, University of Virginia Library.

William IV, 1830–1837

Victoria, 1837–1901

Edward VII, 1901–1910

George V, 1910–1936

Edward VIII, 1936

George VI, 1936–1952

Elizabeth II, 1952–

The English Civil War, beginning in 1642, is a rich field for the military historian and collector, who will find a surprising amount of documentary material on the market, both from the years leading up to Charles I's execution in 1649 and particularly throughout the Commonwealth until the Restoration in 1660. There is a good deal more to be found of the Parliamentarian than of the Royalist faction because they were for the greater part of the time the winning side. It was hard enough to be detained on suspicion without being found in possession of incriminating commissions or letters.

A curious sidelight on the intrigues of the period is given by the commissions signed by the future King Charles II during his continental exile. These are remarkably small, usually about three and one-half by seven and one-half inches; and although they convey wide powers to raise soldiers "For the opposing and destroying those who are in Rebellion against Us . . . and to fight, kill and destroy all who are in armes against Our Authority," there are spaces for inserting the name of the officer and the date and place of writing. These documents, small enough to be smuggled safely, contained only the essential king's signature during their hazardous journey.

The early part of the eighteenth century is of interest for the military campaigns of the first Duke of Marlborough, especially the victory at Blenheim in 1704. Documents signed by Marlborough are regularly offered for sale, and autograph letters are occasionally found. There are also letters of Marlborough's wife, Sarah Churchill, the friend and confidante of Queen Anne. The Scottish rebellions of 1715 and 1745 also provide an interesting field for study, although direct documentary evidence, perhaps again because of its incriminating possibilities, is not so easy to find. On the home front, the years 1711–1720 give us the bizarre case of the South Sea Bubble, a massive speculation involving—and ultimately ruining—thousands of the country's richest families. Many documents, especially receipts for dividends, can be found to illuminate the story.

The major figures in Britain's military and naval history are, of course, Horatio Nelson and the first Duke of Wellington; but it is unwise to forget the many admirals, generals, and leaders of lower rank contemporary with these national heroes whose exploits were often as courageous and whose letters are not only more common but also a great deal less expensive. It has often been remarked that letters of Lord Nelson are much more valuable than those of Wellington, but the reasons are fairly obvious. Nelson died in battle at the height of his fame, and many of his surviving letters were written on active service and on board ship; the Duke of Wellington, reaching the peak of his military prowess at Waterloo in 1815, survived to serve his country in political and functionary capacities until his death in 1852 at the age of eighty-three. He was, moreover, a prolific though rather illegible letter writer.

The wars in the Crimea (1853–1856) and South Africa (the Boer War of 1899–1902) are good sources of autograph material, since letters and documents signed not only by the commanding officers but also by ordinary soldiers writing to their families are available. There is a particularly keen demand from South Africa for autograph material relating to that country; this naturally has an effect on the value, especially of the better pieces.

It has always been popular to collect autographs of the British prime ministers, and not least because they can be assembled as a set, so that the excitement of the pursuit itself can make up for the sometimes dreary nature of the material. Collecting sets often causes problems. Kings and queens do not always rule for an equally long time, Signers of the Declaration of Independence are inconveniently killed in duels, and prime ministers have equally contrived to put snares in the collector's path.

There is some argument over how many prime ministers there have been. In the early days the title was never used, and the principal minister of the government was nearly always the first lord of the treasury. Sidney Godolphin (1645–1712) is sometimes regarded as the first prime minister; and if we accept his claim, we shall have to admit Robert Harley, Earl of Oxford; Charles Talbot, Duke of Shrewsbury; Charles Montagu, Earl of Halifax, and Charles Howard, Earl of Carlisle, before we come to Sir Robert Walpole (1676–1745), who is generally accepted as the first prime minister in the modern sense. There are still two more, James Stanhope, Earl of Stanhope, and Robert Spencer, Earl of Sunderland, who are not always accepted on the list; but from 1742 to the present day the succession is undisputed except for the case of the second Earl of Waldegrave (1715–1763), who was premier from June 8 to June 12, 1757, and for that reason is sometimes neglected.

Many of Britain's prime ministers are household names, the holders in their days of the greatest political power in the world. William Pitt, Benjamin Disraeli, Gladstone, Lloyd George, and Sir Winston Churchill are known to all; and the first Duke of Wellington was also at one time head of the administration, though he is far better known for his military exploits. But many have been forgotten, perhaps rightly so. The collector will, however, find most prime ministers easy to obtain in any form, and relatively inexpensive. The rarest are the fourth Duke of Devonshire (1720–1764), a reluctant prime minister from November 1756 to July 1757, who signed himself "Hartington" until he succeeded to the dukedom in 1755; and John Stuart, third Earl of Bute (1713–1792).

There are two particular problems that face the collector of British documents. These are the question of dating and the confusing use of titles by many eminent historical figures. Until about 1280 legal documents, which are all that the collector will find from medieval times, are not dated; and it is necessary to use the evidence of the names in a document, especially where the list of witnesses is long, as well as the handwriting, to arrive at an approximate date. Throughout the fourteenth and fifteenth centuries, where dates are given, they may be found expressed in the form "the day before the feast of Saint Luke in the fifth year of the reign of King Richard the second"; this can be translated as October 17, 1381. Although the day of the month is usually given, the use of the regnal year, which always happens to span two calendar years, is common. Even when documents are dated in full and in the modern form, one still has to remember that until the end of 1751 the civil and legal New Year's Day was March 25, which means that a document plainly dated February 15, 1662, was, in fact, written in what we now

Right: This letter of British Prime Minister Gladstone, written on stationery printed with one of the most important and well-known ministerial addresses in the world, is typical of the attractive items that may be acquired in building a set of the autographs of the prime ministers of Great Britain. Courtesy of the Jeffress Collection, University of Virginia Library.

Autograph of Benjamin Disraeli. From the Clem D. Johnston Collection, University of Virginia Library.

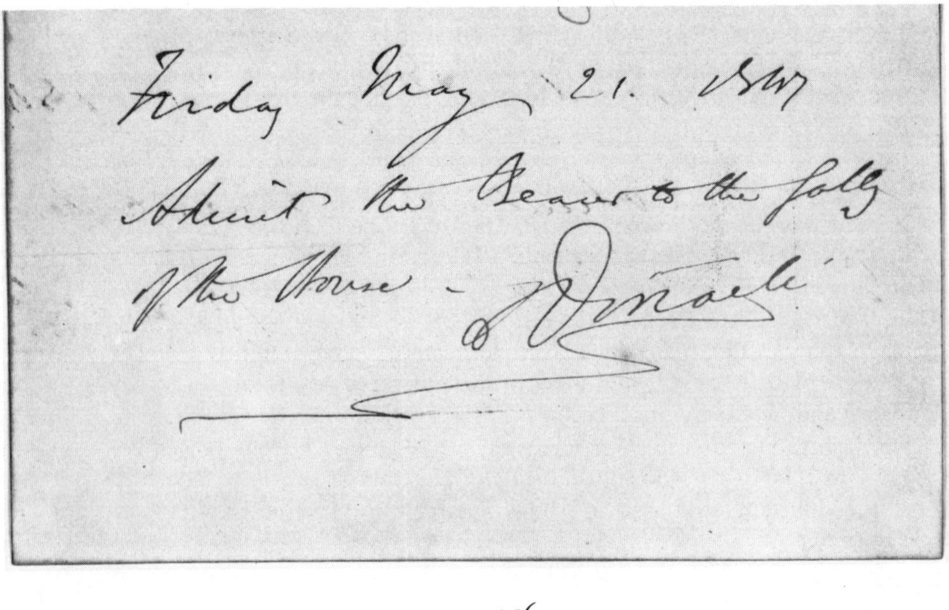
Friday May 21. 1847
Admit the Bearer to the Gally
of the House – B Disraeli

Send this to Forman.

Write to Mr G. & say I am better — but tho' able to work well in bed suffer a good deal when I get up — signature

Aug 19th 80

10, Downing Street,
Whitehall.

My dear Sir,

I will see that the case of Madame Llanos is thoroughly considered; for Keats' sake as well as her own. We were all extremely sorry to hear that you were ill, & I trust that the good account which I heard yesterday holds good to-day.

Believe me my dear Sir
Yrs sincerely

Sir C. Dilke Bart. M.P. Herbert Gladstone

know as 1663. The change had already been made in Scotland after December 1599, which was followed by January 1600. Descriptions now often give the date as 1662/3, for instance, to prevent confusion.

In the year of the adoption of the "new style" or Gregorian calendar, Great Britain and Ireland shed the eleven days by which they had fallen behind the European countries that had already adopted the form. One must bear in mind that in earlier correspondence from outside Britain, the continental dating is likely to be used without any warning. If James II could leave England before Christmas in 1688 and land in France to find the festival already over (although one must assume that he was aware of the different calendars), the student of history certainly can make false assumptions from the date of any letter or document before 1752. Even later, when dating is fairly simple, there are peculiarities. The logbook entry for the battle of Trafalgar made on board H.M.S. *Victory* shows October 22, 1805, whereas the battle took place on October 21. This is explained by a formality used only in naval logbooks, later abolished by admiralty decree.

The most important basic reference work for the student of British history is the *Dictionary of National Biography* and its convenient epitome volumes; it contains the biographies of every important figure. Do not waste time, however, looking for Burghley, Marlborough, Clarendon, Wellington, Palmerston, Castlereagh, or Derby, since none of them are there except as cross-references. All these men were members of the nobility and are entered under their family names of Cecil, Churchill, Hyde, Wellesley, Temple, Stewart, and Stanley. The problem extends to the style in which many important historical figures signed their names. Lord Nelson does not cause much confusion, but his signature varied a good deal during his lifetime. Until 1797 he signed "Horatio Nelson" with his right hand, and continued the same signature with his left hand until 1798, when he became Baron Nelson of the Nile and began using the signature "Nelson." A year later, when created Duke of Brontë, he added the second title to his signature and signed "Nelson and Brontë." Similarly, Wellington began his life as Arthur Wesley, changing the spelling of his name to Wellesley in 1798. He became Viscount Wellington in 1809, and thus did not need to change his style of signature when created a duke.

Not all changes of name or title are as easy to follow, however. Lord Fitzroy Somerset, Wellington's aide-de-camp and the commander of the British troops in the Crimea, became Baron Raglan; his letters may be found signed in either form. Benjamin Disraeli was elevated to the peerage with the title Earl of Beaconsfield; and since he was particularly given to signing notes with his initial in later life, these may often end with "B." Bishops sign with the names of their sees preceded by their

Christian names or initials. The bishop of Manchester might sign "James Manchester," whereas the Duke of Manchester would sign "Manchester," and his wife would sign "Susan (or "S") Manchester." The bishop's wife would use the family name. This complicated use of different styles and titles is a particular problem for the collector of British historical papers, since so many great men in the British historical field were either born with titles or acquired them later in life by inheritance or in recognition of their achievements. A further complication is that some forms of a person's signature are more desirable to the autograph collector, either because they are less common or because a person is better known by one style than by another. For instance, Cromwell's earlier signature, "O. Cromwell," is rarer than "Oliver P" (the "P" stands for "Protector") and is more desirable; this is certainly true of Disraeli, whose "Beaconsfield" signature is less valuable.

The export of manuscripts from the United Kingdom is controlled by the statutory export licensing regulations, but collectors should not form the impression that there is any insuperable problem. The exact requirements of the law have varied over the years, and in 1977 are as follows: Any manuscript, letter, or document more than seventy years old will need an export license from the Department of Trade. Leading dealers and auction houses, however, are granted open general licenses that enable them to export, without reference to the department, any piece or group of related pieces up to a value of £100 at a time; they need only render a simple quarterly return of exportations in brief detail (the names of the purchasers need not be given). In the case of items over £100 in value (and seventy years of age) a special license is called for and, in the great majority of cases, is quickly granted. It is extremely uncommon for an export license to be refused altogether for an autograph letter.

The opportunities are so varied, and the amount of material available from the last 450 years of British history is so great, that it is sensible for a collector to follow his own inclinations wherever possible and to study with care the catalogs of the major dealers both in England and in the United States. Few collectors buy purely for investment, and those that do so will tend to buy the rarest and most valuable items and prize them more for commercial reasons than for their historical or literary merit. Most collectors rightly regard the intrinsic interest of their documents as a matter of first importance and, therefore, will buy what appeals to them within the price bracket to which they may be limited. One collector might wish to have a document relating to the plague of 1665 or the great fire of London in 1666, while another would prefer an item that would illuminate the long history of Britain's conquest of India or give a new insight into one of the celebrated trials of the nineteenth century—the impeachments of Warren Hastings and Lord Melville and the divorce action brought against Queen Caroline. The invention and development of the railways is another example of a field in which the collector with a natural interest in such matters will find letters and documents to add to his knowledge, or at least to illustrate and embellish his collection. Indeed, it is not possible in a short article to suggest many of the byways of history into which a collector might find himself drawn, nor to mention more than a very few of the names of those men and women around whose lives and through whose influence the course of British history has been shaped.

EUROPEAN HISTORICAL AUTOGRAPHS

MEMBERS OF THE EDITORIAL BOARD

THE REALM of European historical autographs is so vast that several volumes devoted to the subject would not suffice to cover it adequately. This chapter can provide only a cursory survey. Those genuinely interested must resort to studying its specific bibliography or at least to reading a score of dealers' catalogs. Since for several reasons it is impossible to build a general collection of historical autographs that would approach completeness, a collector must restrict himself either to what he considers highlights of history or to manuscripts of a particular period or those illuminating a particular event.

The first method is of greater popular appeal and, on the whole, easier to accomplish. The second, after the first flush of success, becomes more difficult and frustrating. Both are rewarding, each in its own way. Examining the special-epoch or special-event collection first, it is easy to see that a compilation covering the French Revolution, or Queen Victoria's reign, is easier to put together than one of the Hundred Years War or of the Reformation. As is true of all autographs, it is easier to collect those readily available in sufficient quantity and those lying outside any intensive collecting interest.

Much depends also on whether the collector insists on full autograph specimens or not. Any period or event of the twentieth century is only sparsely represented in holograph material. Indeed, almost all historical personages are much easier to obtain in the form of signed pieces, although it is, of course, possible to find autograph letters and notes of, say, Napoleon, Frederick the Great, even Gustavus Adolphus, at a price—let alone Metternich, François Guizot, Lord Nelson, Bismarck, Charles de Gaulle, Marlborough, Alexander I, and Konrad Adenauer. The list is practically without end. Dealers' and auction catalogs present them month after month.

Competition for autographs of the last hundred years is not great, except for those of certain towering personages. It should be relatively easy, for instance, to build a significant collection of the rise and fall of Italian fascism. Likewise, it would not be difficult to trace, autographically, England's resistance to the French Revolution or the German rebellion against the Napoleonic regime. An attempt to collect material illustrating peace negotiations from the two world wars, the Franco-Prussian and the Napoleonic Wars back to the Peace of Paris, the Peace of Utrecht, and the Peace of Westphalia would be most rewarding.

Since the completing of any event or period collection is a matter of relativity, there are no limits—a collector can stop whenever he wants to consider his collection as brought to a conclusion.

Turning now to a collection of highlights of history, a time-sanctioned method has been to build one of autographs of those rulers who have a special appeal, or who have brought about important historical changes. The danger of this method is that it entices the collector into trying to obtain the autographs of other rulers as well. If you collect several French kings, it seems that the thing to do is to try to collect them all, back to Jean II (ruled 1350–1364), even if it is practically impossible to obtain a D.S. of this ruler. But it is possible to acquire autographs of kings and queens, as well as ministers of state, back through several centuries without much trouble or too much expense, always excepting those individuals in great demand.

The available autographs of French kings for all intents and purposes start with Louis XI, the "Spider King," although very, very rarely documents signed by one of his predecessors come on the market. In addition to the existence of a fierce competition for any such piece, it would also be very expensive. The later Valois kings are moderately rare, with Charles IX more so and Francis II quite rare. The Bourbons are all obtainable without difficulty, though they vary in price. The few genuine examples of the handwriting of Louis XVII, the unfortunate dauphin, are exceedingly scarce. Of the Bonapartes, Napoleon II is not very easy to find, though obtainable. Although there are probably more autographs available of Napoleon I than of his nephew Napoleon III, the demand for the former greatly exceeds that for the latter. Again, autograph letters are much more difficult to procure and much more expensive (Napoleon I A.L.S., $5,000 and up), but they do exist; occasionally one can find some with extraordinarily interesting contents, such as Francis I in captivity writing to Emperor Charles V, or Napoleon I scribbling a note expressing very intense feeling.

Everything written above pertains to genuine autographs, of course; letters signed for the king by a secretary would be considerably cheaper.

Rulers of France, 1380–1870
(*including dates of reign*)

Charles VI, 1380–1422

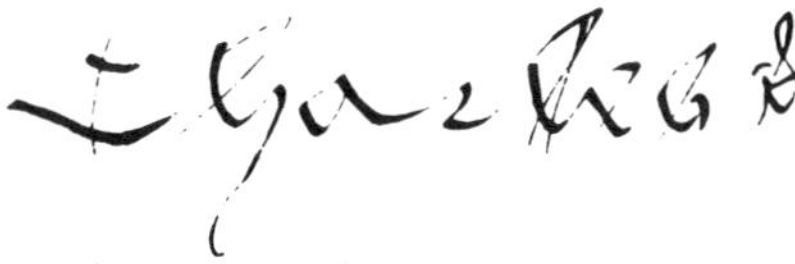

Charles VII, 1422–1461

Louis XI, 1461–1483

Charles VIII, 1483–1498

Louis XII, 1498–1515

Francis I, 1515–1547

Henry II, 1547–1559

Francis II, 1559–1560

Charles IX, 1560–1574

Henry III, 1574–1589

Henry IV, 1589–1610

Louis XIII, 1610–1643

Louis XIV, 1643–1715

Louis XV, 1715–1774

Louis XVI, 1774–1792

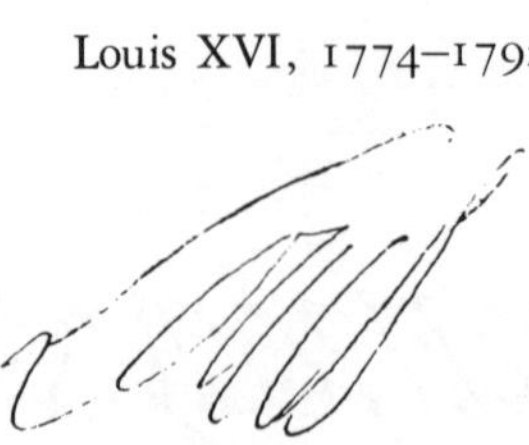

Louis XVII

Napoleon Bonaparte, first consul, 1802–1804
From the Clem D. Johnston Collection,
University of Virginia Library.

Napoleon I (Napoleon Bonaparte),
emperor, 1804–1815.

Napoleon II,
Duke of Reichstadt.

Louis XVIII, 1814–1824

Charles X, 1824–1830

Louis Philippe, 1830–1848

Louis Napoleon Bonaparte, 1848–1852
Courtesy of the Pierpont Morgan Library.

Napoleon III
(Louis Napoleon Bonaparte), 1852–1870

The French kings from Charles VIII to Louis XVIII had the deplorable habit of having most documents and letters, including nonroutine pieces, signed by their secretaries, who sometimes attempted to imitate the sovereign's signature but usually penned the name in their own handwriting. During the reign of Louis XVI the treasurers were so suspicious of the signature on orders to pay that the king often had to certify his secretary's "Louis" with his own "Bon Louis" written underneath.

An interesting collection could be built around the subject of female influence on matters of state in France, which would comprise the kings' mistresses as well as wives and other powers behind men of influence. The French cabinet ministers are an entertaining lot and readily available. Costs vary according to desirability, with Richelieu, Mazarin, Colbert, Turgot, Vergennes, and Talleyrand commanding a higher price.

The entourage of Napoleon I is being avidly collected, and so are the men connected with the French Revolution. The most expensive are not necessarily the most famous (or infamous), but of the latter Maximilien Robespierre and Georges Jacques Danton are among the most highly priced. Then there are the republican statesmen, beginning with Louis Adolphe Thiers and ending with de Gaulle and the present-day leaders, who are increasingly hard to find in holograph pieces as time advances. In regard to special periods of French history, there are the innumerable wars in which the monarchs engaged, from the Crusades and the Hundred Years War on, during which Joan of Arc (unobtainable) and Jean de Dunois (very rare) brought about the decisive turn-around in favor of France; there is the time of Protestantism and the Huguenots (still largely available); the spellbinding reigns of Louis XIV and Louis XV, the four French revolutions (1789–1793, 1830, 1848, and 1871), and so on up to modern times.

The rulers of the Holy Roman Empire go back in full signatures to Frederick III, who is difficult to acquire. His successors can be found very easily and are not expensive, except in A.L.S. form. Earlier documents either in the name of the monarch or signed by him in the form of signum, sign manual, or monogram are expensive and increasingly rare as you approach the eleventh century, at which point the supply ceases altogether. None of the emperors after 1520 are rare in autograph form, though because of their short reigns Joseph I, Charles VII, and Leopold II are a little hard to find.

The various German states, the more or less sovereign kings, dukes, margraves, and prince electors and their courts, as well as the governments of the free cities, produced a profusion of autographs. These princely houses provided dynasties for most of the European thrones, and a detailed study of their lineage is required before one can collect in

Holy Roman Emperors, 1438–1806
and German Emperors, 1871–1918
(*including dates of reign*)

Albert II, 1438–1439

Frederick III, 1440–1493

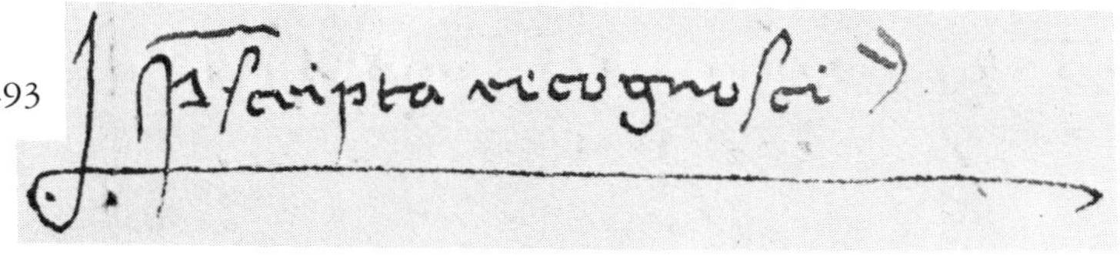

Maximilian I, 1493–1519

Charles V, 1519–1558

Ferdinand I, 1558–1564

Maximilian II, 1564–1576

Rudolf II, 1576–1612

Matthias, 1612–1619

Ferdinand II, 1619–1637

Ferdinand III, 1637–1657

Leopold I, 1658–1705

Joseph I, 1705–1711

Charles VI, 1711–1740

Charles VII, 1742–1745

Francis I, 1745–1765

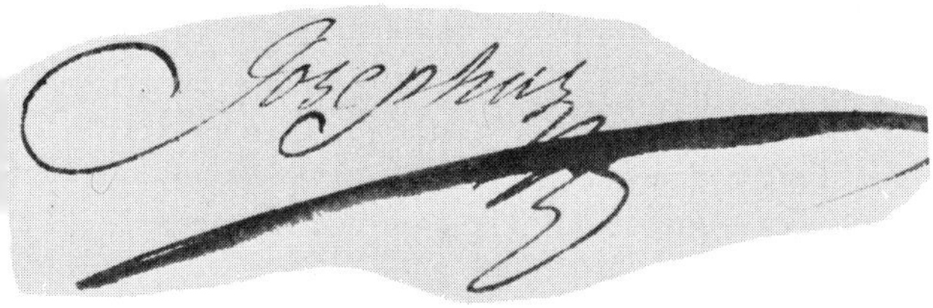

Joseph II, 1765–1790

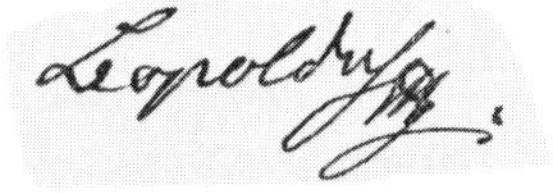

Leopold II, 1790–1792

Francis II, 1792–1806

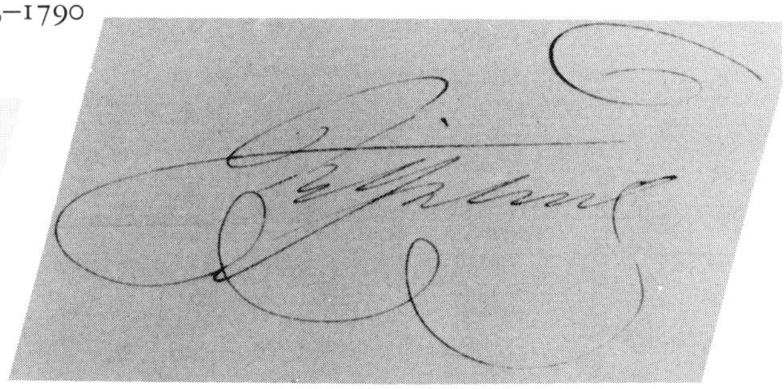

William I emperor of Germany, 1871–1888

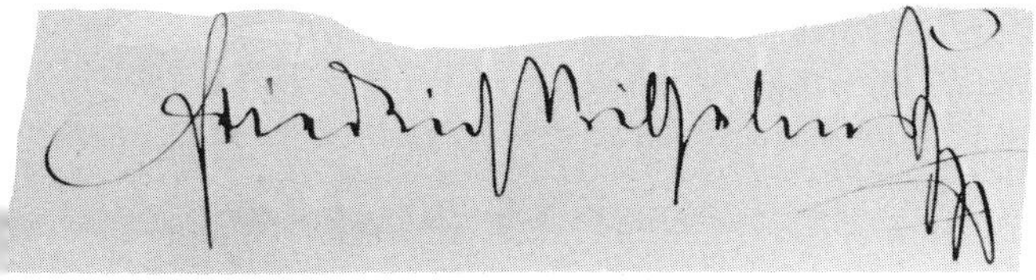

Frederick III, 1888

William II, 1888–1918

depth. Such study, of course, is advisable for any collection of monarchs.

The interplay of history and such other collecting fields as philosophy, theology, art, and science is ever present in Germany, as it is in other nations; but for the sake of accuracy a historical collection excludes these other fields except in cases where they are inseparable—as when rulers also happen to be authors, musicians, artists, or inventors.

Even though signed letters and documents of rulers are easy to come by, A.Ls.S. are much rarer, if only because monarchs had scribes at their command. One interesting form of royal autograph is that of marginal annotations on a letter or document received, which can be very enlightening as well as amusing.

The Protestant Reformation in Germany, because it produced a country of divided loyalties and three Christian faiths, is a fascinating period for collectors. Items are still readily available, except for the founders themselves. The Thirty Years War (1618–1648), to some degree a war of religion, provides a large field. The eighteenth century and the first part of the nineteenth are attractive for many collectors, partly because of the variety of events taking place and partly because of the large number of interesting historical personages. Autographs from the reunification of Germany in the latter half of the nineteenth century (with the exclusion of Austria), Bismarck's diplomacy, the events leading up to the two world wars, the Hitler period, and the postwar decades are relatively easy to procure and not too expensive.

As the Allied armies swept over Germany to victory at the end of World War II, it was relatively easy for troops to sweep up documents and correspondence in the government offices of towns and cities that they overran. These documents were carried out of Germany as the troops were sent home, and today many of these former soldiers are cashing in on their military days by selling Nazi documents on the manuscript market. A Jewish soldier in the American army managed to obtain a large number of particularly fine Nazi autographs during the war that he now sells, donating the proceeds to orphanages in Israel. Nazi material is quite popular with collectors at present (1978), and sells readily at good prices.

Not unexpectedly, autographs of Adolf Hitler are eagerly sought and not difficult to find if the collector is willing to settle for a routine document signature. However, Hitler is very rare in A.L.S. form, and often used a lithographic signature on routine letters and some documents. Of other Nazi leaders, Hermann Goering, Joseph Goebbels, Heinrich Himmler, Alfred Jodl, Wilhelm Keitel, and Martin Bormann are available, like Hitler, on routine documents and are rarer in A.L.S.; Rudolf Hess is somewhat scarcer. As one would expect, those leaders that survived the war and the war crimes trials are much more common and easy to acquire. Albert Kesselring, Karl Doenitz, and Albert Speer are in this category, while Reinhard Heydrich and others who were killed early in the war are much more difficult for the collector to locate. Since men have always been interested in evil, it is likely that the popularity of Nazi material will continue.

The history of Italy, particularly the time between 1200 and 1600, is so fascinating in its multiplicity of politicians of all shades, including those of the Roman Catholic Church, that there are innumerable possibilities for the collector. European autograph catalogs abound with samples. There are many specializations: the popes; the religious councils; the members of the many noble houses of Italy, many of them benefactors of art or literature, such as the Medici, Gonzaga, Borgia, Este, Sforza, Farnese, and Rovere families; the doges of Venice. The list is almost without end. The Italians, more literate than most nations, wrote voluminously; the autographs of practically every man or woman of note are available. And because most of them wrote in a "fine Italian hand," their letters are also a pleasure to the eye—there were few scrawlers among them.

It is an odd phenomenon that scoundrels and people to whom scandal is attached exert so great a fascination on autograph collectors. Thus also in Italian history, where the names of Cesare and Lucrezia Borgia have a great attraction. Which Italian autographs are particularly hard to obtain? Because the popes between 1198 and 1484 very rarely signed documents or letters, they are the ones quite difficult to find. Most of the more illustrious princes of the Renaissance are also quite rare—for example, Lorenzo the Magnificent. It is a fortunate circumstance that many men noted as poets, writers, and artists were in the employ of princes or popes and, as such, acted as secretaries. Thus we are able to obtain autographs of some who would otherwise be nonexistent on the market. Pietro Bembo comes to mind as just one example.

Collectors of royal autographs will do especially well in Spain. The autographs of the kings of Aragon and Castile extend to the beginning of the fourteenth century and thus form the longest continuous line anywhere. While those of earlier kings are somewhat expensive and rather rare, they are at least obtainable. Some of the royal charters are exceptionally handsome. Documents bearing the signatures of both Ferdinand II and Isabella are particularly high in demand, for obvious reasons.

All documents pertaining to the early Spanish and Portuguese explorations and the settlements of the colonies are nearly impossible to procure, but after 1600 they become more obtainable. The hero of the battle of Lepanto in 1571, John of Austria, half brother of Philip II, is much in demand. So is Margaret of Parma, a daughter of Charles V. All the other Spanish regents of the Netherlands in the sixteenth century

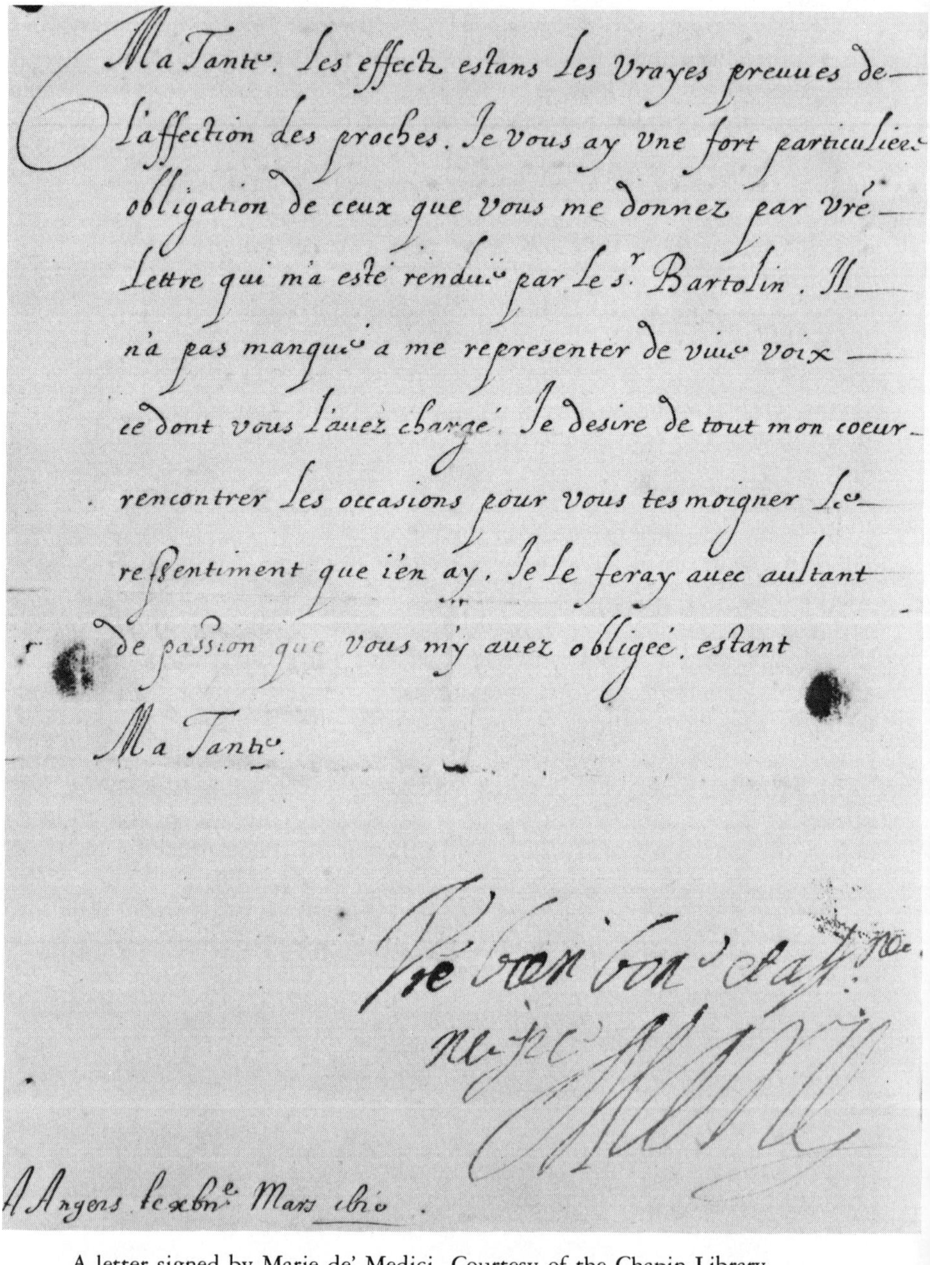

Ma Tante. Les effectz estans les vrayes preuues de
l'affection des proches. Je vous ay vne fort particuliere
obligation de ceux que vous me donnez par vre
lettre qui m'a esté rendue par le sr Bartolin. Il
n'a pas manqué a me representer de viue voix
ce dont vous l'auez chargé. Je desire de tout mon coeur
rencontrer les occasions pour vous tesmoigner le
ressentiment que i'en ay. Je le feray auec aultant
de passion que vous m'y auez obligée. estant

Ma Tante.

A Angers le xxbre Mars 1620

A letter signed by Marie de' Medici. Courtesy of the Chapin Library, Williams College.

were interesting individuals, well worth collecting. So are the heroes of the Dutch war of independence, such as William the Silent and Count Lamoral d'Egmont.

Russian historical autographs start rather late, with the czars Ivan the Terrible and Peter the Great. As to their successors, there is a steady market for Catherine the Great, Alexander I, and Nicholas II and his czarina. Again, fascination with evil in human form shows itself in the high demand for autographs of Lenin, Trotsky, and Stalin, of whom the first and last are very difficult to obtain and expensive, as are those of Karl Marx and Friedrich Engels.

The fact that a European naturally emphasizes collecting the history of his own country—because he is familiar with it—need not deter anyone from building a collection without regard to his background or schooling. Dig in wherever your fancy will lead you! The life of Charles XII of Sweden is a case in point. His adventures led him all over Eastern Europe; and while it would be difficult to document his exploits, it would not be too hard to obtain collateral material and create a most interesting assortment. Other figures include Admiral Maarten Tromp of Holland, Ferenc Kossuth of Hungary, Ignace Paderewski of Poland, Maria Theresa of Austria, Francisco Franco of Spain, Count Hans Fersen of Sweden, Camillo di Cavour and Garibaldi of Italy, Carl von Mannerheim of Finland, Joannes Capodistrias (Giovanni Capo d'Istria) of Greece—history is teeming with totally engrossing figures in smaller countries. You do not have to collect Napoleon.

The market for European historical autographs is large, probably the largest in the world. Because the supply is so vast, the prices even for fairly good material are surprisingly low. In comparison, in the field of music the supply is limited and the demand very great, with the prices correspondingly high. Furthermore, available historical material goes back into the past many centuries further than do musical, scientific, and even literary items.

Naturally European autograph dealers carry the largest stock, catering first to their compatriots and second to collectors in other countries. While French dealers congregate mostly in Paris and the English in and around London, and those in small countries conduct their business in the capitals, such as Vienna, dealers in Germany, Italy, and Switzerland are more widely distributed. Dealers' supplies vary greatly, and so does the composition of their stock. A few tend to specialize. Some are dealers in books as well. It is best to obtain catalogs or, preferably, to visit their shops and inspect the material. A goodly portion of the autograph trade is handled by auction houses.

A number of the larger dealers in the United States also have a fine stock of European historical material, though it generally is more selec-

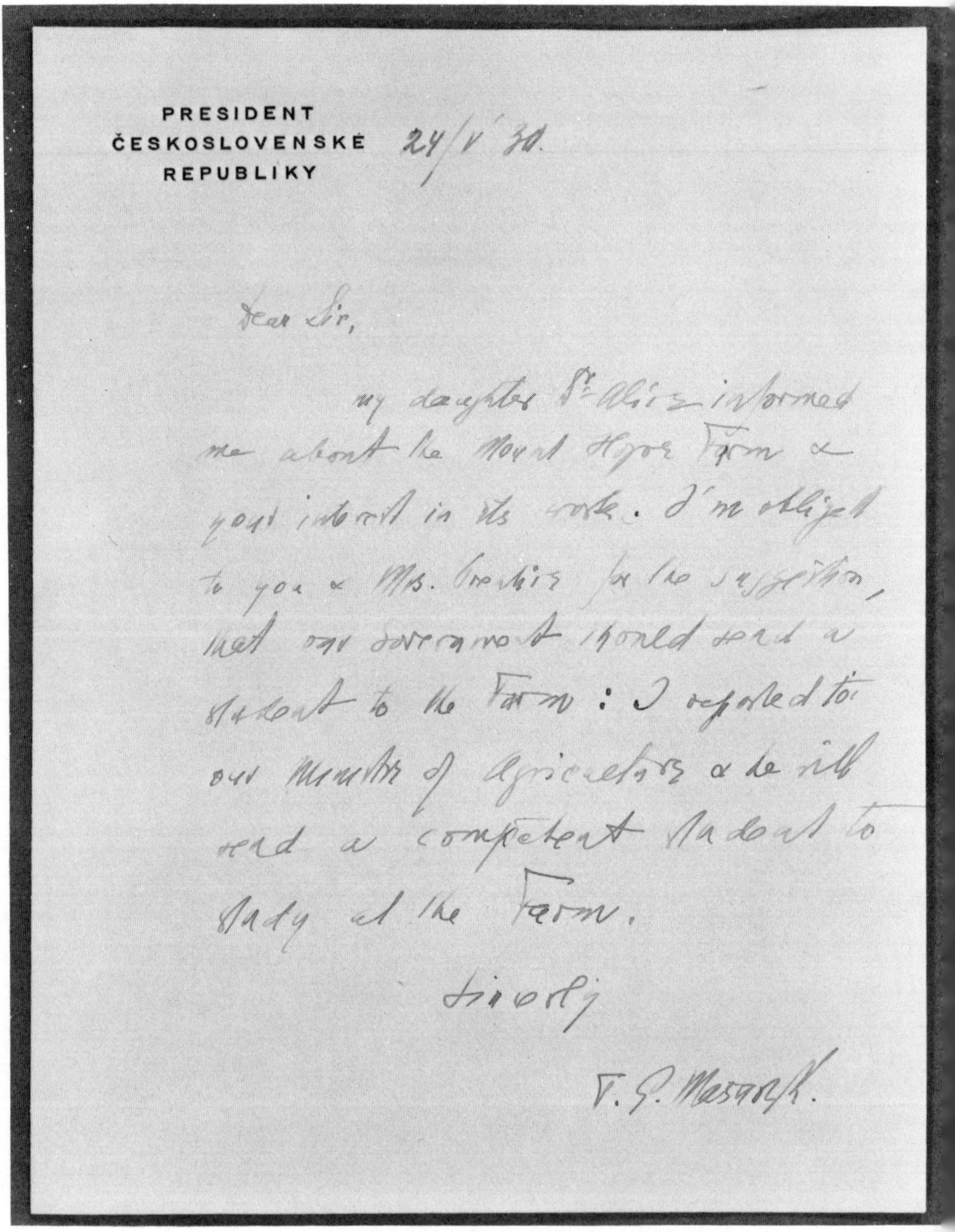

PRESIDENT
ČESKOSLOVENSKÉ
REPUBLIKY

24/V 30.

Dear Sir,

my daughter Dr. Alice informed me about the Mount Hope Farm & your interest in its work. I'm obliged to you & Mrs. Prentice for the suggestion, that our government should send a student to the Farm: I reported to our Minister of Agriculture & he will send a competent student to study at the Farm.

Sincerely

T. G. Masaryk.

A letter by Tomáš G. Masaryk, the first president of Czechoslovakia. Courtesy of the Chapin Library, Williams College.

tive; naturally they prefer to acquire mainly those pieces for which there is a ready market in America. Two or three dealers, who happen to be the largest in the United States, handle a considerable number of European autographs and have a ready market for them in Europe as well. The old pattern of American dealers buying in Europe but selling only to American collectors has changed noticeably. They now buy from and sell to European dealers and collectors. The smaller American dealers only occasionally have European autographs of any significance. American auction houses can also be expected to present a fair share of European items. Often autographs are considerably underpriced when there is no demand or interest, even though there may be eager competition for them in Europe.

One interesting feature found in a few European catalogs is the grouping of autographs into historical, literary, and other categories, or according to periods or personalities. For instance, a French catalog may feature only material pertaining to the Duke of Reichstadt (Napoleon II), or Lamartine and other statesmen around 1850, or the court of Louis XIV. The catalogs of J. A. Stargardt of Germany often are arranged chronologically, one running from 1100 to 1600, the next from 1600 to 1700, and so on. The reading of these specialized lists provides an engrossing lesson in history. Many auction catalogs are divided into sections, according to whether the pieces are of historical, literary, musical, or art contents. This enables the specialist collector to locate his field quickly. The Rosenbach Company of Philadelphia issued the *History of America in Documents* in three parts (1949, 1950, 1951). They make good reading. It would be good to see other dealers with a large enough stock occasionally do likewise in presenting the history of other countries or of a more limited area or period in documents.

Collecting European historical autographs presents a particular challenge to the collector, since he may have to learn a foreign language in order to understand the autographs that he has acquired. Paleography, the study of ancient documents, is another field in which he will have to acquire special knowledge, for the handwriting used in Europe over the centuries has varied and changed enormously. Paleography and languages are useful skills to acquire, and the collector will be increasingly proud of his knowledge as his collection and skills grow.

For an individual genuinely interested in history, there can be no greater thrill than to be able to bring back to life his favorite period with the aid of pertinent autographs. He will aim for intimate letters of salient personalities, preferably written by themselves and not dictated. If these deal with important events, express innermost thoughts, or are of a philosophical nature, they will form the finest jewels in his collection.

That it is possible to acquire such letters of some individuals, but not of others, does not alter the fact that many true building blocks of history are still obtainable. For instance, an order written by the Polish king Jan Sobieski (John III) pertaining to the movement of his army toward Vienna in order to raise the siege imposed by the Turks; or the oath to obey the constitutional charter signed by Louis Philippe on August 9, 1830, after he had been chosen French king; or an A.L.S. of Benito Mussolini, written two hours after he had become prime minister of Italy, beginning with "Finalmente siamo giunti!" These autographs not only record history, they *are* history!

MUSICAL AUTOGRAPHS AND MANUSCRIPTS

IRVING LOWENS

"THE FOLLOWING HIGH PRICES were obtained recently in Berlin for some musical autographs," according to the *Etude* for January 1894: "Three Bach manuscripts brought 1,600, 1,400 and 1,300 marks each. A collection of numbers of his autographs brought 5,566 marks. An autograph letter of Mozart's brought 325 marks, and a letter of Beethoven's brought 148 marks."

According to the *Washington Post* for May 11, 1977, "a touching letter from Mozart to his wife, Constanze, written in 1789 was sold yesterday for $25,500 at Christie's auction house. Put up for sale anonymously, it was bought by an unnamed English private buyer in a sale of musical instruments and manuscripts."

Things have changed; at one time the autograph manuscripts of musicians were worth next to nothing. The March 1894 issue of the *Etude* reports:

> At an auction sale of manuscripts lately in Vienna, the well preserved original song Op. 39, bearing Franz Schubert's name and dated April 24, 1824, sold for the small sum of $41.20. An autograph letter of Ludwig van Beethoven to the master's own copyist, H. Rampel, written in 1824, sold for $17.

Not so today, when music manuscripts of the great composers are among the most expensive and most eagerly sought of all autograph materials. A single instance can serve to document this point. In 1971 the holograph of a Beethoven piano work (not a sonata) was purchased by a German industrialist from a well-known German antiquarian bookseller for the mind-boggling sum of one million Deutsche marks (DM). And today Beethoven letters—when they appear in the open market—normally would fetch from $5,000 to $10,000.

Why the precipitous rise in prices? One of the reasons is surely the fact that musical notation is universally comprehensible regardless of the language spoken by those who use it. Except in most unusual cases, the demand for an autograph letter written in Cyrillic or Greek is likely to be limited to those who read the language. But the demand for a musical manuscript penned by a Russian or Greek composer is likely to be global rather than national in scope. Thus the market potential for the holographs of the major composers is greater than the market potential for the holographs of famous writers, and the increased competition tends to boost prices higher and higher.

The potential collector of musical autographs will find that the materials available to him can be conveniently broken down into the following categories:

1. Autograph musical compositions. These come in several different forms—the initial sketch, the reduced score, the full score, the first finished version, the final version that goes to the engraver, a clean copy (*Reinschrift*) in the composer's hand intended as a gift. Normally this category contains the items that are likely to be most expensive.
2. Autograph musical quotations written out and signed by the composer. These were usually intended to serve as mementos, and frequently were included in autograph albums. Although their value to the historian is slight, they make very attractive display pieces and good examples fetch good prices.
3. Autograph letters signed by the composer. As with all letters, there are many factors that affect the price: content, length, condition, and scarcity are some of the most obvious ones. Letters—with some exceptions—generally are more reasonably priced than items in musical notation.
4. Memorabilia, such as printed scores or programs signed by the composer, signatures, photographs, tickets, checks, menus, calling cards, and other ephemera.
5. All categories except the first pertaining to musicians who are not composers—singers, instrumentalists, conductors, critics, musicologists, and so on. Letters with musical content written by nonmusicians are also collectible.

Like all fields of endeavor, music embraces an elite whose autographs are of the highest interest to collectors. There is usually some rough correlation between a composer's popularity and the price of his autograph; but for purposes of the collector, the elite (the "great composers") may be defined pragmatically as those whose musical manuscripts fetched $1,000 or more on the open market between 1951 and 1975. The list, not overly long, includes Johann Sebastian Bach, Béla Bartók, Ludwig

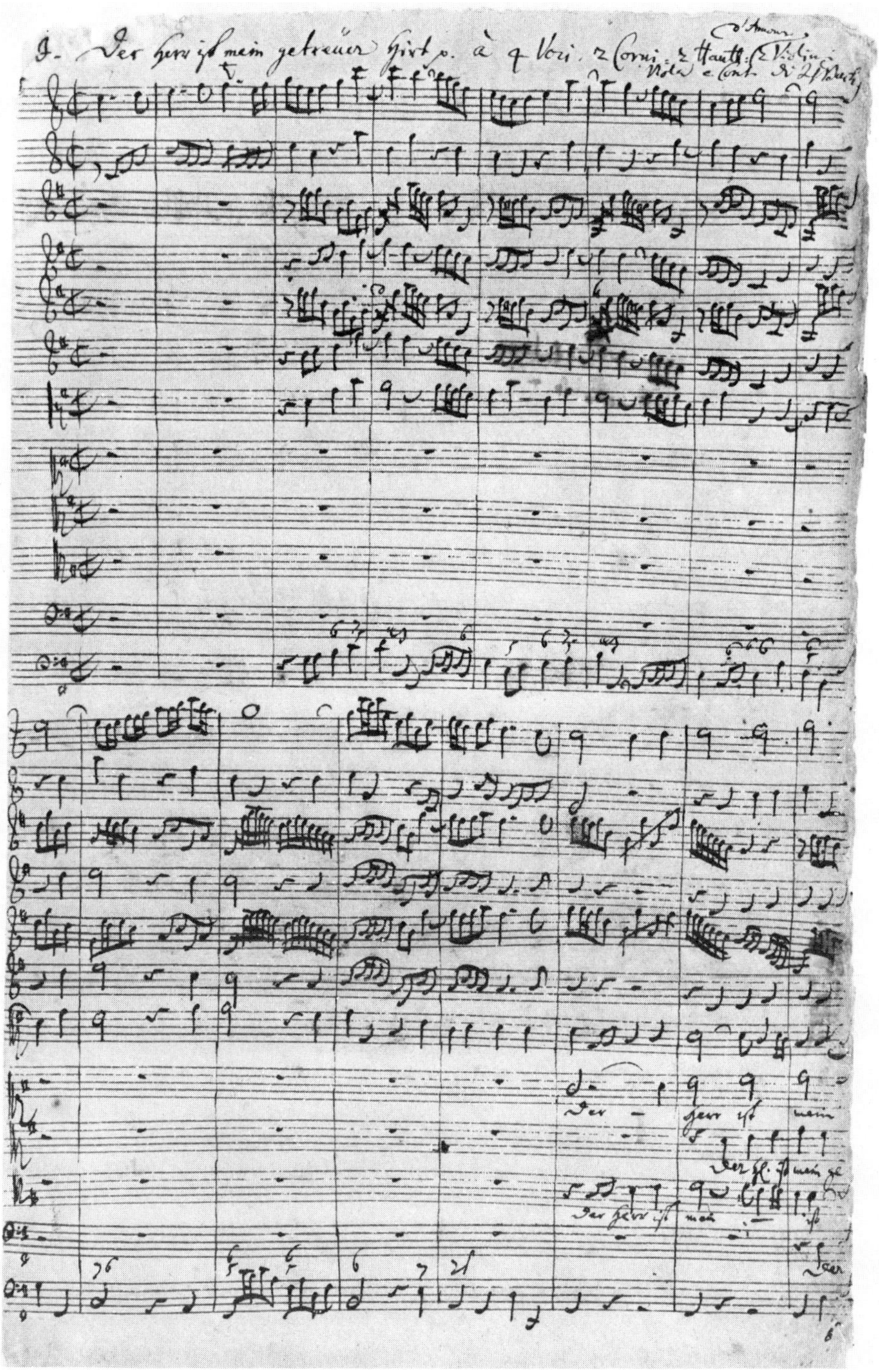

Johann Sebastian Bach's autograph manuscript of Cantata no. 112, "Der Herr is mein getreuer Hirt." Courtesy of the Mary Flagler Cary Music Collection, Pierpont Morgan Library.

van Beethoven, Vincenzo Bellini, Alban Berg, Georges Bizet, Johannes Brahms, Benjamin Britten, John Cage, Frédéric Chopin, Claude Debussy, Frederick Delius, Antonín Dvořák, Gabriel Fauré, Stephen Foster, César Franck, George Gershwin, Edvard Grieg, George Frederick Handel, Joseph Haydn, Franz Liszt, Gustav Mahler, Pietro Mascagni, Jules Massenet, Felix Mendelssohn, Wolfgang Mozart, Jacques Offenbach, Niccolò Paganini, John Howard Payne, Giacomo Puccini, Gioacchino Rossini, Erik Satie, Franz Schubert, Robert Schumann, Jean Sibelius, Johann Strauss (the younger), Richard Strauss, Igor Stravinsky, Sir Arthur Sullivan, Peter Ilich Tchaikovsky, Arturo Toscanini, Giuseppe Verdi, Richard Wagner, Carl Maria von Weber, Anton von Webern, and Hugo Wolf. The list contains one noncomposer, Toscanini. His name is included because the holograph of his orchestral arrangement of "The Star-spangled Banner," inscribed and dated, sold for $2,400 in 1953.

Here are some prices of characteristic autograph musical compositions by the "great composers," with the year in which these prices were realized: Bach, *Allein zu dir, Herr Jesu Christ* (140,000 DM, 1965); Bizet, *Djamileh* (50,000 DM, 1966); Brahms, *Ein deutsches Requiem* (80,000 DM, 1968); Foster, "Maggie by My Side" ($4,500, 1969); Franck, *Les Béatitudes* (75,000 DM, 1962); Gershwin, "By Strauss" ($1,150, 1964); Mahler, Symphony no. 4, second movement, 4½ pages ($2,600, 1972); Mascagni, *Cavalleria rusticana,* Intermezzo (£1,200, 1975); Massenet, *Thaïs* ($20,000, 1975); Mozart, String Quintet, K. 593 (170,000 DM, 1969); Payne, "Home! Sweet Home!" ($3,500, 1974); Puccini, *Madama Butterfly,* Act II, 4 pages ($3,000, 1972); Schubert, "Der Winterabend" (28,000 DM, 1964); Johann Strauss (the younger), *Die Fledermaus* (146,000 DM, 1962); Richard Strauss, *Don Juan, Reinschrift* ($12,000, 1975); Sullivan, *Trial by Jury* ($29,000, 1975); Weber, *Jubel-Cantate* ($5,500, 1972).

It is plain that the prices commanded by music manuscripts of the "great composers" place them out of reach of the average autograph collector, although sometimes dreams come true. Hermann Jung, in the *Ullstein Autographenbuch,* cites an instance where a knowledgeable employee of a Boston paper mill, while sorting through a batch of old wastepaper purchased from a German firm, came across a cache of rare musical manuscripts, among them portions of Weber's *Euryanthe,* Mozart's *Don Giovanni,* and other holographs of Beethoven, Haydn, and Daniel Auber. However, it is not wise to wait for such things to happen. It is no consolation to the average collector interested in music to realize that, in many instances, items such as those mentioned were bought by dealers, which means, in effect, that the prices listed are wholesale rather than retail. Either the top bidder already has a customer

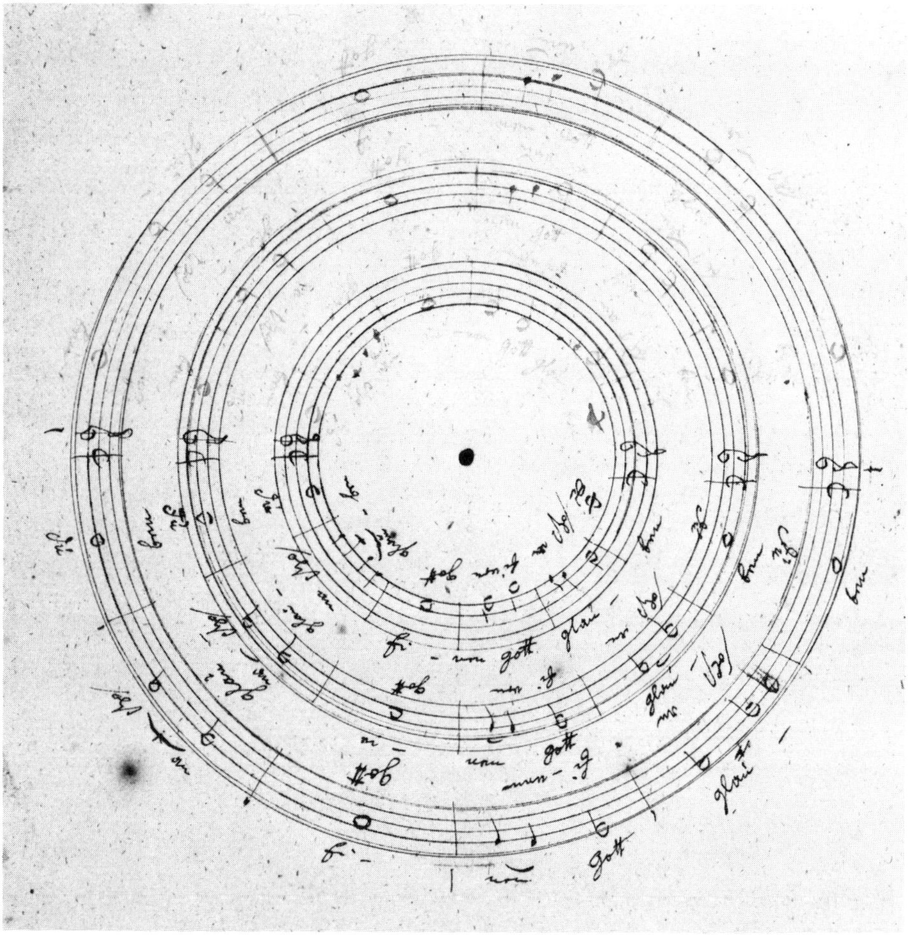

Franz Joseph Haydn's autograph manuscript of *Das erste Gebot,* a three-part canon, 1791. Courtesy of the Mary Flagler Cary Music Collection, Pierpont Morgan Library.

lined up for these items, or they will later appear in a catalog at considerably higher prices. It is estimated that the normal markup of "great composer" materials approximates double the cost to the dealer at an auction.

Good autograph music materials are experiencing an unprecedented boom—the prices, never really low in the twentieth century, have been skyrocketing in recent decades. This can be graphically illustrated by giving the lowest and the highest prices paid for autograph signed let-

Above: Hector Berlioz's autograph manuscript of *Le roi de Thulé*.
Courtesy of the Pierpont Morgan Library.

Left: Ludwig van Beethoven's autograph manuscript of Sonata for violin and piano, op. 96 in G major. Courtesy of the Pierpont Morgan Library.

ters of the "great composers" and the years in which these prices were realized, once again using 1951 and 1975 as the limiting years: Beethoven, $240 (1954) and £2,500 (1970); Brahms, $15 (1951) and £300 (1975); Chopin, £40 (1959) and £1,300 (1972); Debussy, £6 (1959) and $300 (1971); Grieg, $6 (1954) and $190 (1974); Liszt, $8 (1956) and $325 (1972); Mahler, £5 (1958) and $625 (1975); Mendelssohn, $20 (1956) and $400 (1968); Puccini, $9 (1960) and $350 (1972); Rossini, £5 (1959) and £400 (1975); Schubert, $80 (1956) and £1,900 (1967); Schumann, $13 (1951) and $700 (1972); Tchaikovsky, $75 (1954) and £500 (1964); Verdi, $8 (1951) and £380 (1975); Wagner, $16 (1954) and £400 (1973); Weber, $20 (1951) and $375 (1972). And the prices continue to zoom upward in the 1970's. The fact of the matter is that the "great composers" will remain the private preserve of the rich and knowledgeable collector.

Discouraging as this may seem, there remains considerable territory to be explored in the field of musical autographs if you are willing to concede that the "great composers" are priced out of the market for the average musically oriented collector. A careful examination of the list of "greats" will reveal several interesting facts and yield quite a few hints as to the directions the beginning collector should follow.

For one thing, the list shows that Americans are still plagued by an inferiority complex in regard to their own cultural heritage; of all the names mentioned, only four (Cage, Foster, Gershwin, and Payne) came from the United States. There are, of course, many other significant American composers of past and present. A check of *American Book Prices Current* reveals the names of Irving Berlin, Charles Cadman, George M. Cohan, Aaron Copland, Dan Emmett, Louis M. Gottschalk, W. C. Handy, Victor Herbert, Walter Kittredge, Calixa Lavallée, Jerome Kern, Oscar Levant, Edward MacDowell, Gian-Carlo Menotti, Ethelbert Nevin, Cole Porter, George F. Root, Samuel F. Smith, John Philip Sousa, and Samuel Woodworth, all selling for comparatively modest prices. Dealers' catalogs of the 1970's demonstrate that autographs of American musicians have not appreciated in value at anything like the explosive rate manifested by the traditional "great composers."

Another recent development of great interest to the collectors of musical autographs is the increasing availability of holographs by living composers, thanks in large part to a 1969 revision of the income tax law. Before that year it was customary for the most important American composers to donate their original manuscripts to a library or an institution of higher learning and then claim an income tax deduction equal to the "fair market value" of the work so donated. Such institutions as the Library of Congress, the public libraries, and the major universities were the beneficiaries of the pre-1969 law, and built up vast holdings of

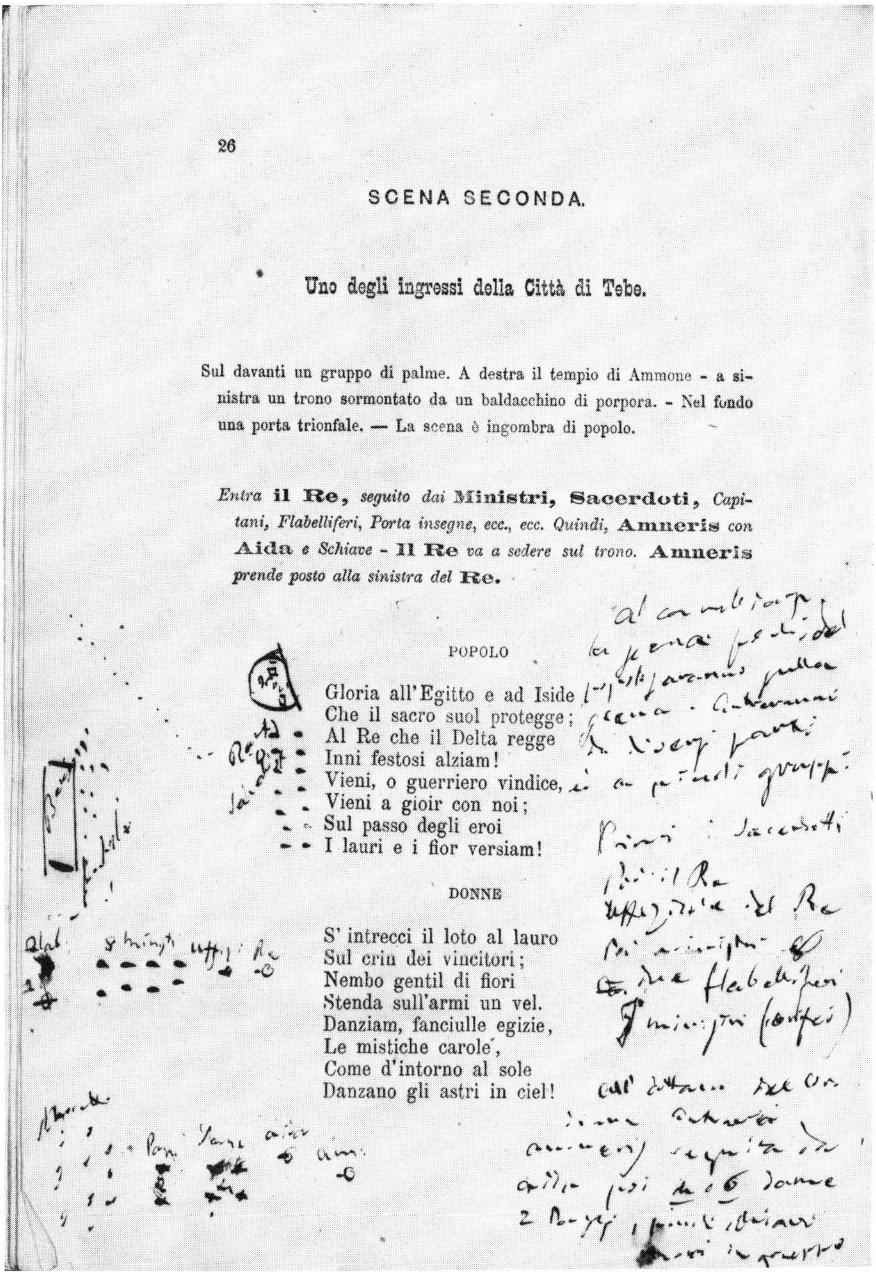
26

SCENA SECONDA.

Uno degli ingressi della Città di Tebe.

Sul davanti un gruppo di palme. A destra il tempio di Ammone - a sinistra un trono sormontato da un baldacchino di porpora. - Nel fondo una porta trionfale. — La scena è ingombra di popolo.

Entra **il Re,** *seguito dai* **Ministri, Sacerdoti,** *Capitani, Flabelliferi, Porta insegne, ecc., ecc. Quindi,* **Amneris** *con* **Aida** *e Schiave -* **Il Re** *va a sedere sul trono.* **Amneris** *prende posto alla sinistra del* **Re.**

POPOLO

Gloria all'Egitto e ad Iside
Che il sacro suol protegge;
Al Re che il Delta regge
Inni festosi alziam!
Vieni, o guerriero vindice,
Vieni a gioir con noi;
Sul passo degli eroi
I lauri e i fior versiam!

DONNE

S' intrecci il loto al lauro
Sul crin dei vincitori;
Nembo gentil di fiori
Stenda sull'armi un vel.
Danziam, fanciulle egizie,
Le mistiche carole,
Come d'intorno al sole
Danzano gli astri in ciel!

Giuseppe Verdi's *Aïda* (Milan: Ricordi, [*ca.* 1871–1872]), with autograph notes and diagrams. Courtesy of the Mary Flagler Cary Music Collection, Pierpont Morgan Library.

Arnold Schoenberg's autograph manuscript of the full orchestral score of *Gurrelieder,* 1911. Courtesy of the Mary Flagler Cary Music Collection, Pierpont Morgan Library.

manuscript materials at no cost. But in 1969, in a law directed not toward composers and other creators but, rather, toward politicians who would donate their papers to institutions and claim deductions based on "fair market value," this practice was halted. Composers were allowed to deduct only the actual cost of the materials (paper, ink, erasers, pens) they used in writing their manuscripts, and the gifts to institutions stopped coming.

The 1969 Tax Reform Act does not forbid a composer's family from claiming the "fair market value" of a manuscript after the composer's death, nor does it forbid such a claim on the part of a collector who wishes to make such a donation—only the composer is penalized. The result has been an increasing volume of music manuscripts by living composers on the open market, and thus increased opportunities for both collectors and dealers. Despite what appears to be a case of flagrant prejudice against composers (as well as creative workers in other arts), there seems to be no genuine possibility that this provision of the income tax statutes will be revised in the near future. One curious result of the 1969 act was Igor Stravinsky's offer, in 1970, to sell all his personal papers and manuscripts for $3.5 million, a price that included the corrected holograph score of *Le sacre du printemps,* put on the market earlier at $1 million. There were no takers, and the Stravinsky *Nachlass* (he died in 1971) came into the possession of his wife, who could legally give Stravinsky's manuscripts to appropriate institutions and claim an income tax deduction equal to their "fair market value." However, Mrs. Stravinsky was in greater need of cash than of large income tax deductions, and the bulk of Stravinsky's papers remain in her possession and on deposit in the Library of Congress and elsewhere.

Let us, however, talk of sums the average autograph collector can consider spending. Here is a list of autograph musical quotations written out and signed by the composers with the prices they brought between 1971 and 1975: Bartók, $100; Berg, $150; Brahms, $1,000; Copland, $75; Debussy, $325; Rudolf Friml, $100; Herbert, $25; Kern, $80; Zoltán Kodály, $250; Mascagni, £30; Massenet, $90; Ignace Paderewski, $100; Quincy Porter, $300; Francis Poulenc, $55; Sergei Prokofiev, $120; Puccini, $250; Sergei Rachmaninoff, $225; Nicolai Rimsky-Korsakov, $375; Sigmund Romberg, $90; Rossini, $200; Albert Roussel, $75; Anton Rubinstein, $150; Camille Saint-Saëns, $250; Sibelius, $200; Richard Strauss, $150; Tchaikovsky, £110; Ralph Vaughan Williams, $225; Verdi, £550; Wagner, $1,000. In order to arrive at a figure you can reasonably expect to pay by 1980, it would be safe to double these prices.

Another byway along which the collector will probably be in need of some guidance is that of photographs inscribed by the subject, some-

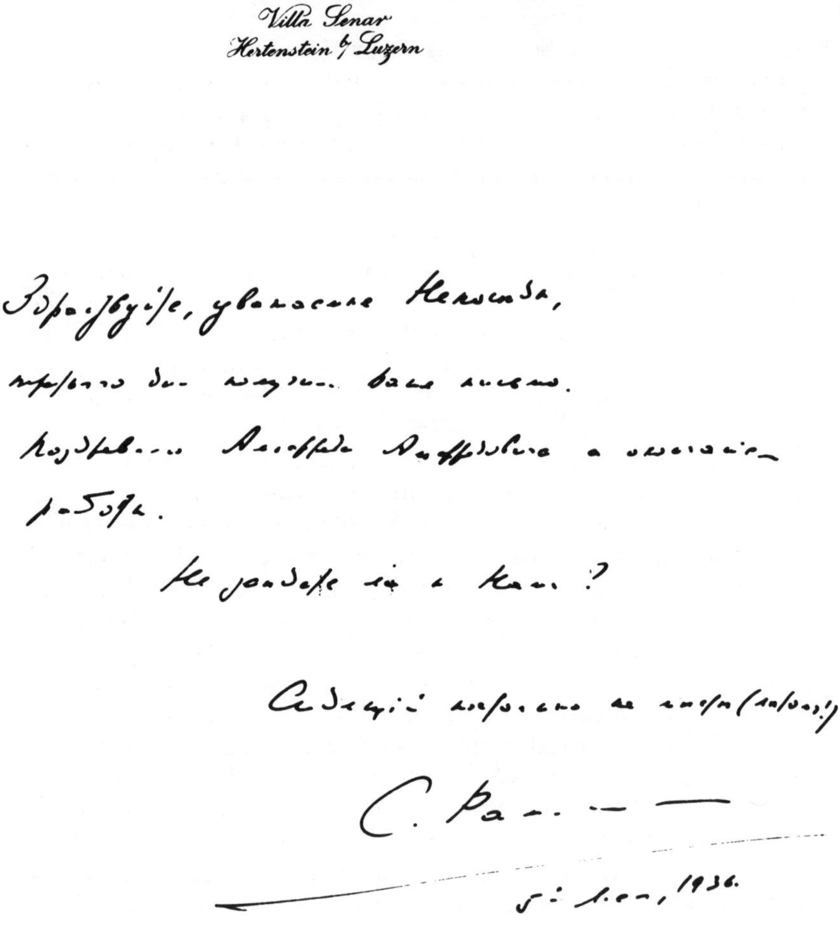

Letter of Sergei Rachmaninoff to Alfred Swan. From the Swan Music Collection, University of Virginia Library.

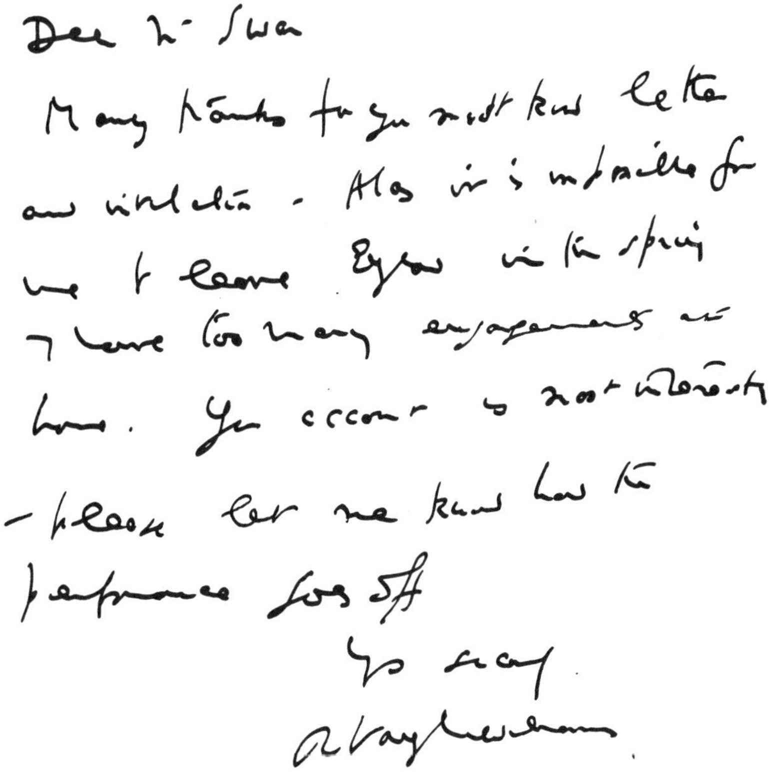

Dear Mr Swan

Many thanks for your most kind letter and invitation. Alas it is impossible for me to leave England in the spring as I have too many engagements at home. Your account is most interesting — please let me know how the performance goes off.

Yrs sincerely

R Vaughan Williams.

Letter of Ralph Vaughan Williams to Alfred Swan. From the Swan Music Collection, University of Virginia Library.

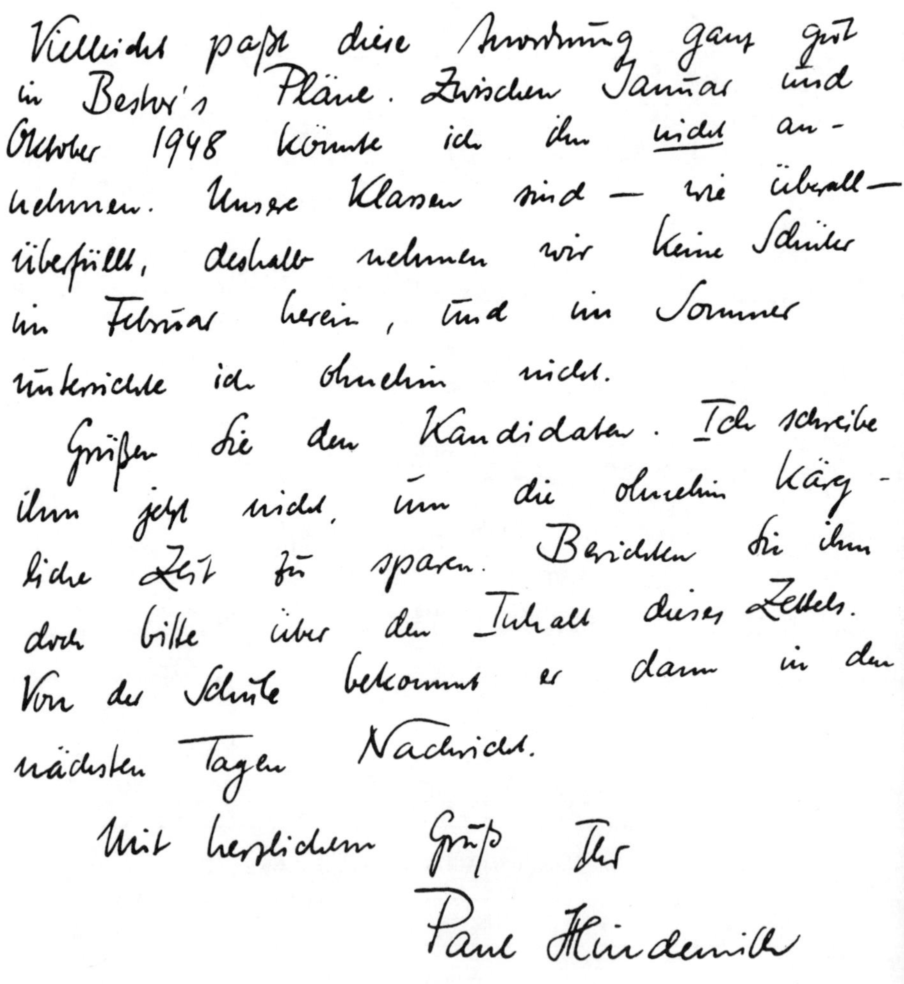

Vielleicht paßt diese Anordnung ganz gut in Bestor's Pläne. Zwischen Januar und Oktober 1948 könnte ich ihn nicht annehmen. Unsere Klassen sind — wie überall — überfüllt, deshalb nehmen wir keine Schüler im Februar herein, und im Sommer unterrichte ich ohnehin nicht.

Grüßen Sie den Kandidaten. Ich schreibe ihm jetzt nicht, um die ohnehin kärgliche Zeit zu sparen. Berichten Sie ihm doch bitte über den Inhalt dieses Zettels. Von der Schule bekommt er dann in den nächsten Tagen Nachricht.

Mit herzlichem Gruß Ihr

Paul Hindemith

Letter of Paul Hindemith to Alfred Swan. From the Swan Music Collection, University of Virginia Library.

times with a signature, sometimes with a dated signature, and sometimes with an autograph musical quotation signed and dated. Such photographs, together with an appropriate piece of paper on which there is the handwriting of the subject and perhaps a sample of his or her musical notation, frequently are used in framed ensembles. A list of signed photographs with the prices they brought between 1971 and 1975 includes Bartók, $130; Berlin, $70; Enrico Caruso, $110; Feodor Chaliapin, £25; Foster, $600; Gershwin, $600; Arthur Honegger, $45; Franz Lehár, $35; Liszt, $90; Mahler, $100; MacDowell, $250; Mascagni, £30; Massenet, $60; Paderewski, $90; Porter, $30; Puccini, £55; Rachmaninoff, $80; Rossini, £38; Saint-Saëns, $55; Dmitri Shostakovich, $80; Sibelius, £40; Sousa, $70; Johann Strauss (the younger), £60; Richard Strauss, $45; Stravinsky, $90; Tchaikovsky, £300; Toscanini, $140; Verdi, $300; Wagner, $500. Once again, it would be realistic in terms of the present-day autograph market to figure on spending close to double these sums to acquire comparable items.

Where are the great collections of music manuscripts in the United States? The largest is in the Library of Congress, and has been for many years; but the institution holding down the number-two spot is something of an interloper—the Pierpont Morgan Library in New York. Music was not one of this library's major fields of interest until 1968, when the Mary Flagler Cary Music Collection, one of the world's finest private collections, was willed to that institution. In the same year Robert Owen Lehman began to make annual gifts to the Morgan Library from his magnificent collection, as did Mrs. Janos Scholz from hers. In 1977, the library acquired the music manuscripts previously owned by the Heineman Foundation. Other institutions with major holdings in the field of musical autographs include the New York Public Library, the Memorial Library of Music at Stanford University, the Sibley Music Library at the Eastman School of Music in Rochester, New York, the Boston Public Library, and the Curtis Institute of Music in Philadelphia. From the prices cited in this brief overview of the field, it is not difficult to understand why there are few, if any, really great collections of musical autographs in the hands of private individuals.

COLLECTING SCIENTIFIC AND MEDICAL AUTOGRAPHS

RUDOLF F. KALLIR

COLLECTING in general demands two ingredients: talent and money. I have purposely put talent in first place because I have known rich people who did not have the sensitivity that is so indispensable to this activity. Frequently they discover, after many years, that they have backed the wrong horse. This does not mean that I endorse an investment psychology, but it is not possible to ignore the money angle completely. One of the greatest collectors of cultural and Renaissance material (very few autographs were in his collection), Albert Figdor of Vienna, said, about the turn of the twentieth century, "A collector who in a corner of his heart is not a dealer at the same time, is not a true collector." Only those who can combine a feeling for investment with a love for individual specimens are real collectors.

Collectors who engage exclusively in assembling scientific and medical material are not too common. Almost all of the great collections—and this would refer to the last century or century and a half—were quite comprehensive, science being only one of their components. The collectors of exclusively scientific autographs are, as a rule, scientists and medical men.

Science is a very rewarding field. It prevents the collector from becoming parochial. The range of historical items may be broadened ad libitum. A pioneer settler may be considered a historical figure, so that whatever he has written or signed, such as a land grant, has some historical importance for certain persons or territories, especially if it has some age. Science is more demanding. Great inventions and discoveries must be its backbone, and it is less easy to construe attractive circumstances and associations.

Mary Benjamin, in her well-known book on autographs, has written, "No popular demand for certain categories like foreign material

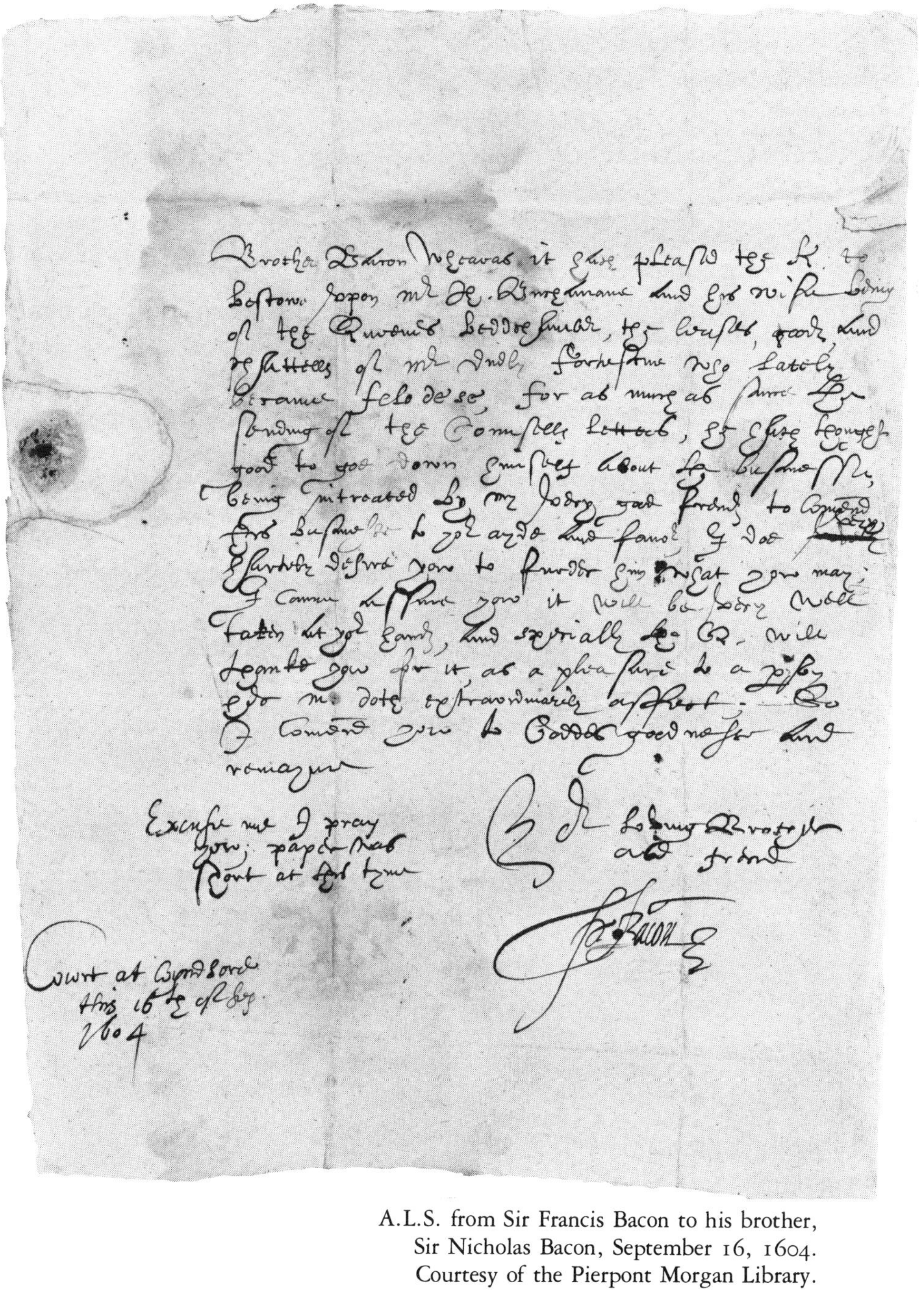

Brother Bacon whereas it hath pleased the K. to
bestowe upon Mr H. [illegible] and his wife being
of the Queenes beddchamber, the leases, goods and
chattells of Mr [illegible] Forteskue who lately
became felo de se, for as much as since the
sending of the Counsells letters, he hath thought it
good to goe down himself about the businesse,
being intreated by my very good frend to commend
his businesse to your ayde and favour I doe very
hartely desire you to further him what you may;
I can assure you it will be very well
taken at your hands, and specially the Q. will
thanke you for it as a pleasure to a person
who she doth extraordinarily affect. So
I commend you to Godds goodnesse and
remayne

Your loving brother and frend
Fr. Bacon

Excuse me I pray
you; paper was
short at this tyme

Court at Wyndsore
this 16th of Sep.
1604

A.L.S. from Sir Francis Bacon to his brother,
Sir Nicholas Bacon, September 16, 1604.
Courtesy of the Pierpont Morgan Library.

exists in America." She explains this by saying that Americans, for the most part, are not linguists. If, in the field of science, this tendency exists or ever was in existence, it has decreased conspicuously. Although scientific letters and documents originated mainly in Europe, with the French, Italian, and German languages in the forefront, the interest in America for these autographs and manuscripts is now quite pronounced.

Before the Revolutionary War, American scientific autographs worthy of being in a collection were practically nonexistent; and even during the first half of the nineteenth century, the range was limited. Two early names must nonetheless be mentioned: Benjamin Franklin and Benjamin Rush. Widely collected as Signers of the Declaration of Independence, they are equally entitled to prominent places in scientific collections, Franklin as inventor of the lightning rod and Rush as a physician from Philadelphia.

What, then, should a collector strive for? If he has a predilection for a special category within the scientific field, his path is prescribed. For instance, an ophthalmologist wishing to specialize in persons in his own profession would necessarily have limited possibilities. Albrecht von Graefe, Hermann von Helmholtz, and others, mostly German, are the leading figures, followed by lesser lights who would also have to be included in such a special collection. Frequently just a few enthusiasts are sufficient to boost prices, which go down as soon as one of the competitors stops collecting.

At the present time, the familiar names have almost disappeared from the market. Tycho Brahe, Galileo, René Descartes, Gottfried von Leibniz, Copernicus, Johannes Kepler, Isaac Newton, and Baruch Spinoza do appear from time to time at auctions, but less and less frequently. Such pieces are the remains of old, mainly French or Italian collections or repositories, and frequently are in poor condition or lack interesting content. Even such minor pieces, however, bring enormous prices. It is of great interest and highly instructive to look at the prices in old catalogs. The sale of the renowned collection of Count Ludwig Paar in 1893 was a sensation in its day. Let us mention a few figures for the purpose of illustration. An A.L.S. by Anders Celsius (extremely rare) sold for $5, and an A.L.S. of Descartes for $52. A fine letter by Kepler, all in his hand and written to the emperor about the illness of Prince Schwartzenberg, brought $90, but an album leaf of Kepler brought only $12. Two unsigned horoscopes in his hand fetched only $2 each. A letter signed by Emanuel Swedenborg (very rare) was sold for $21, a fine A.L.S. by Carolus Linnaeus for $7, and one of the very rare Franz Mesmer could have been had for $5. This was certainly the right time to start a collection, but the public was not attuned and the circle of interested people was limited.

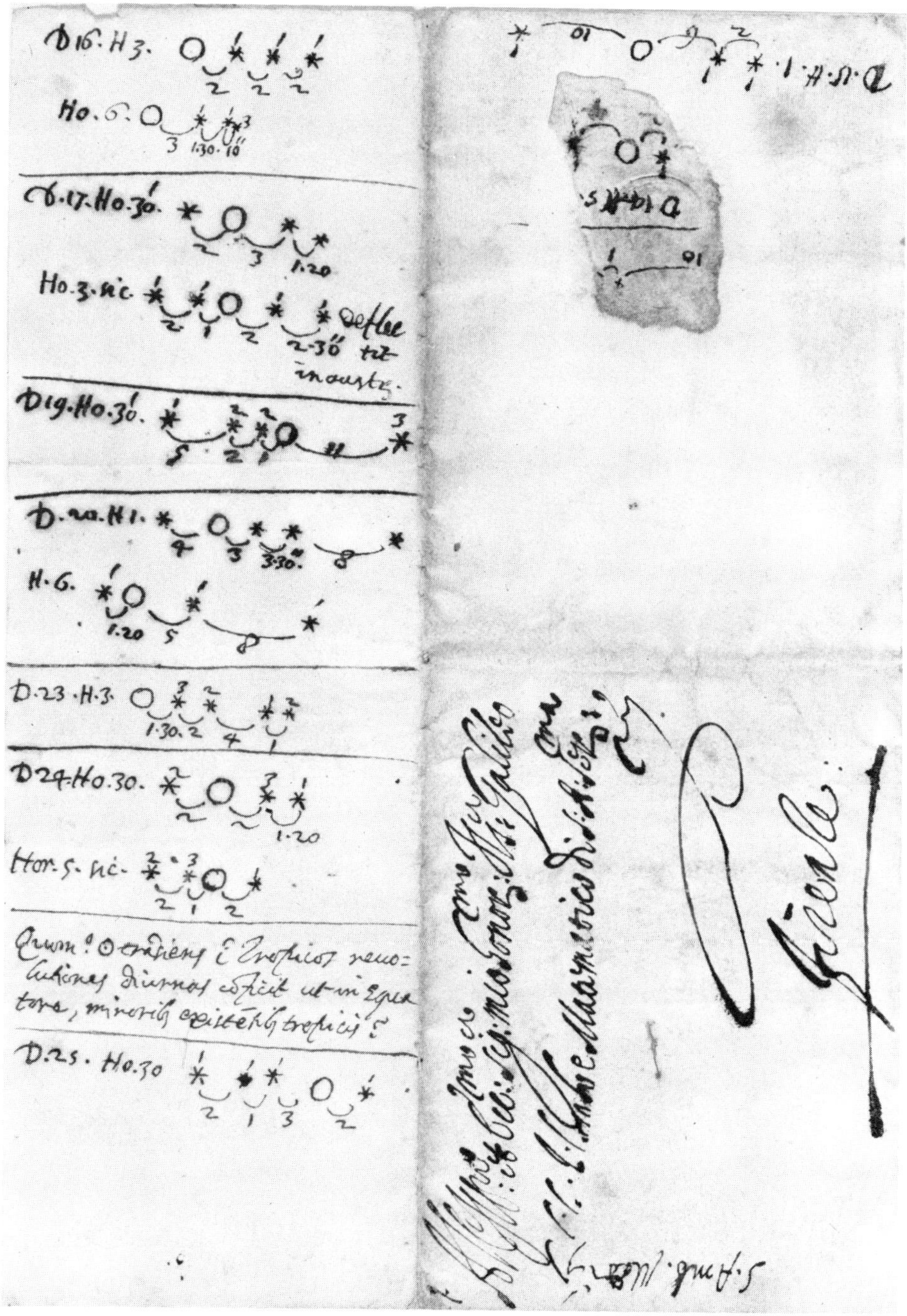

Autograph astronomical calculations of Galileo Galilei, 1611.
Courtesy of the Pierpont Morgan Library.

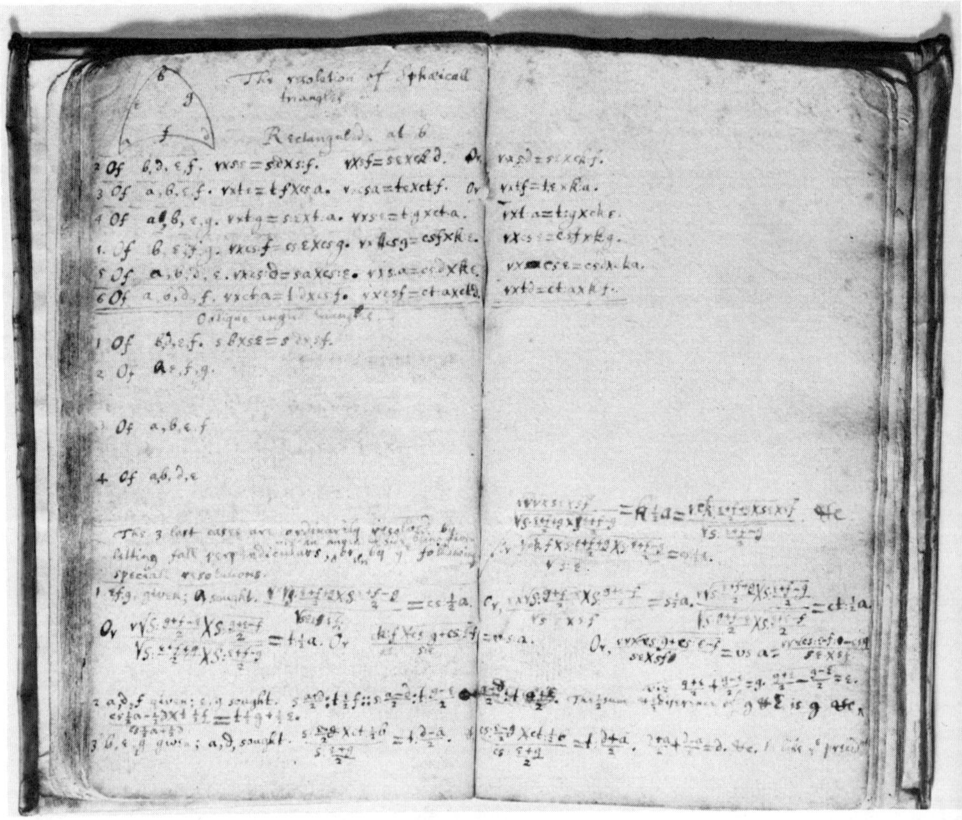

Autograph notebook of Sir Isaac Newton, *ca.* 1655–1662.
Courtesy of the Pierpont Morgan Library.

Right: An example of the handwriting of Alexander von Humboldt.
From the University of Virginia Library.

Goethe was an avid collector of autographs. Although there were no scientists included in the list of his collection, he did own a letter of George Washington. Autographs by Goethe himself may certainly be included in a scientific collection, for he made intensive scientific studies in the fields of chromatology, meteorology, and anatomy. I own a letter of Goethe to the Grand Duke of Weimar about weather forecasting, in which he expresses the opinion that it will never be possible to make precise weather forecasts.

In the years between the two world wars it was still possible to acquire desirable items at reasonable prices. Charavay in Paris, Madigan and Benjamin in New York, Liepmannssohn and Stargardt in Berlin, Maggs in London—to mention just a few prominent dealers—were places where the collector could browse to his heart's content. In those days letters of Alexander von Humboldt brought \$1 or \$2, a Johann Heinrich Pestalozzi letter \$9 (compared with a two-page A.L.S. sold at Stargardt in 1964 for \$500, and a similar letter, sold in February 1974 at Parke-Bernet for \$1,500). Rudolf Virchow was available for \$2 to \$3, and so the list could go on.

During World War II there was no dearth of material on the market, since it was, to a great extent, the property of refugees. The prices, compared with those of today, were very attractive. At Sotheby's a four-page manuscript (unsigned) of Isaac Newton fetched £5.10; and an A.L.S. of Charles Darwin, short but mentioning *On the Origin of Species,* changed hands for the same amount.

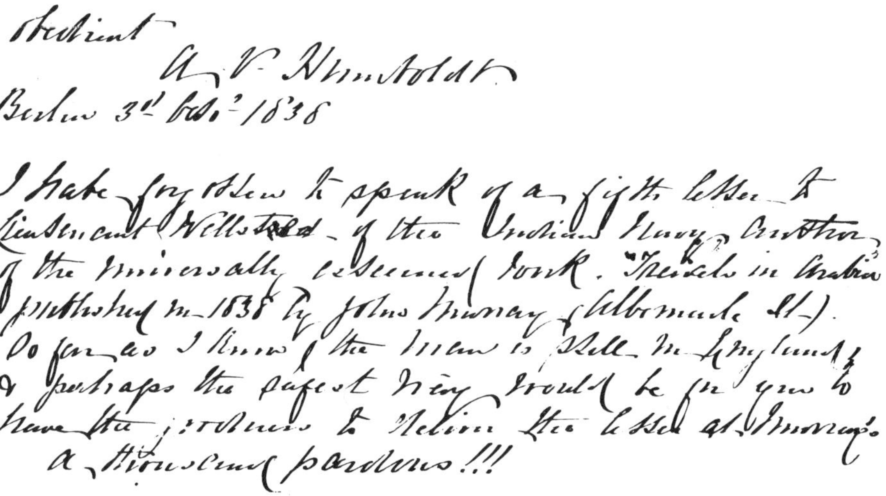
obedient
A. v. Humboldt
Berlin 3d Oct. 1838

I have forgotten to speak of a fifth letter to Lieutenant Wellsted of the Indian Navy, Author of the universally esteemed work. Travels in Arabia published in 1838 by John Murray (Albemarle St.). So far as I know the man is still in England & perhaps the safest way would be for you to have the goodness to return the letter at Murray's.
a thousand pardons!!!

Down Bromley Kent

Oct 27th

Dear Sir

I have heard from the Treasury, that they are ready to pay to you

£ s d
40 " 4 " 5. —

Dear Sir

Yours very faithfully

C. Darwin

I am dear Sir

yours very faithfully

Charles Darwin

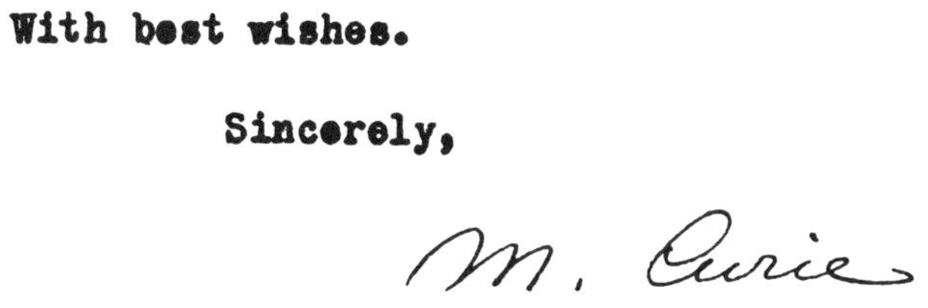
With best wishes.

Sincerely,

M. Curie

A signature of Marie Curie, codiscoverer of the properties of radium and polonium. From the Bacheller Collection, Clifton Waller Barrett Library, University of Virginia Library.

In the 1960's Sotheby in London, Drouot in Paris, and Parke-Bernet in New York were very active. In Switzerland, Rauch in Geneva and L'Art Ancien in Zurich had good material; but the steep rise in the level of prices had started.

Two of the greatest collections were sold by Stargardt: the Geigy collection in 1961 and the Ammann collection in 1962, both from Switzerland. Items of outstanding quality were still comparatively cheap. A few prices may serve as examples: a letter by Luigi Galvani, $200; Pierre Curie, $150; James Watt, $100; Heinrich Hertz, $400; Kepler, an album leaf, $850 (note the price of a similar item in the Paar sale mentioned above); Gregor Mendel, D.S., $65; and Alessandro Volta, $500. All of the prices quoted demonstrate the upward spiraling of values in recent years.

From my own experience I would consider the following names to be extremely rare, although the list is far from complete: Brahe, Celsius, Pierre Curie, Descartes, Sir Alexander Fleming, Benjamin Franklin (of scientific content), Galvani, William Harvey, Edward Jenner (especially if on vaccination), Kepler, H. A. Lorentz, Mendel, Georg Ohm, Wilhelm Roentgen, Ignaz Semmelweis, Swedenborg, and Wilbur Wright. Good letters of these personalities will undoubtedly increase in value.

Left: The example at the top shows a brief note in the hand of Charles Robert Darwin, October 27, [1843]; and the example at the bottom, his signature at a later period (May 16, 1865). From the Darwin-Evolution Collection, University of Virginia Library.

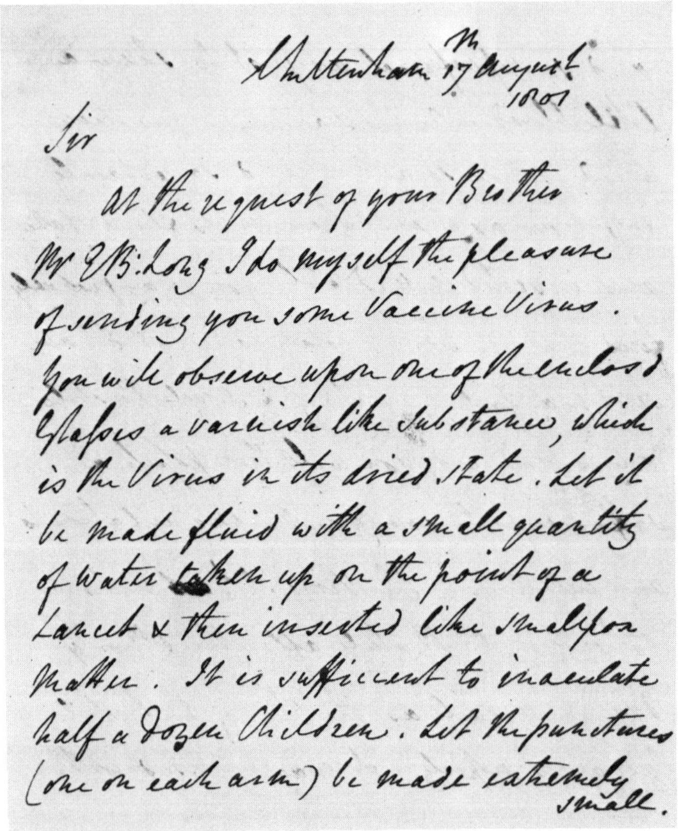

Cheltenham 17th August
1801

Sir

At the request of your Brother Mr E B: Long I do myself the pleasure of sending you some Vaccine Virus. You will observe upon one of the enclosd Glasses a varnish like Substance, which is the Virus in its dried State. Let it be made fluid with a small quantity of water taken up on the point of a Lancet & then inserted like smallpox Matter. It is sufficient to inoculate half a dozen Children. Let the punctures (one on each arm) be made extremely small.

Above and right: A letter by Edward Jenner concerning the shipment of "some Vaccine Virus." From the Tracy W. McGregor Library, University of Virginia Library.

and so superficial as just to shew a little blood. As the vaccine Virus when dried is not so active and so certainly infectious as when taken in its fluid state and inserted immediately, you may probably find that in some instances what I have sent may fail; but if a single Pustule only is produc'd, you will then possess a sufficiency to carry on the inoculation to any extent. The Virus shd. ~~not~~ never be taken from the Pustule after the 8th. or 9th day, & so early as the 5th. (if the Pustule advances properly) it may be used with full effect.

I remain, Sir,

Yr obt. humble St.

E Jenner

P.S. If it shd. so happen that you do not succeed with the enclos'd Glass, pray have the kindness to write & I will send another; how[ever] it is not likely to fail, as I have repeatedly sent it across the Atlantic in this way with the fullest effect.

15th. Embodying the results of our work in Cuba, so that he can put it in his last annual Report—

I do not share, Commandante Bueno, your hopefulness concerning finding some immunizing method—Protection & Prevention are far, far more important. The fundamental facts have been established—the others are of secondary importance. Hold on to Camp Lazear a while longer—Give my love to your dear wife & thank her so much for the offer of the room—Kiss Martha & T. Jefferson—Drink one to my health—Sincerely yours,
Walter Reed.

Additional scientific names that appear more frequently and that may be considered highly desirable if they have interesting content are James Watt, Volta, Louis Daguerre, Alexander Graham Bell, Robert Fulton, Robert Koch, Frederick Banting, Paul Ehrlich, and Samuel Hahnemann. Ten interesting letters of the last-named were appraised by Stargardt in 1962 for $400. In 1973 eight similar letters fetched $1,500 at Parke-Bernet. In addition, I would include Hertz, Louis Pasteur (on rabies), and Thomas Alva Edison.

Sigmund Freud and Albert Einstein share a special place in this hierarchy. Although not uncommon, they still command high prices if the documents refer to their own milieus of sex and relativity. A comprehensive letter written to me by Einstein concerning his relationship to Max Planck is most precious to me in light of a short remark in one corner of the letter, which reads, "I am sending you this scribble in its original as I know of your queer passion."

Collectors must bear in mind that even today there are new fields that have provided opportunities to persons with vision and imagination. Aviation, Nobel prize winners, the space age—with a certain amount of foresight, the proper pieces might be assembled that could prove of value in the future.

Below: Signature of the theoretical physicist Albert Einstein. From the University of Virginia Library.

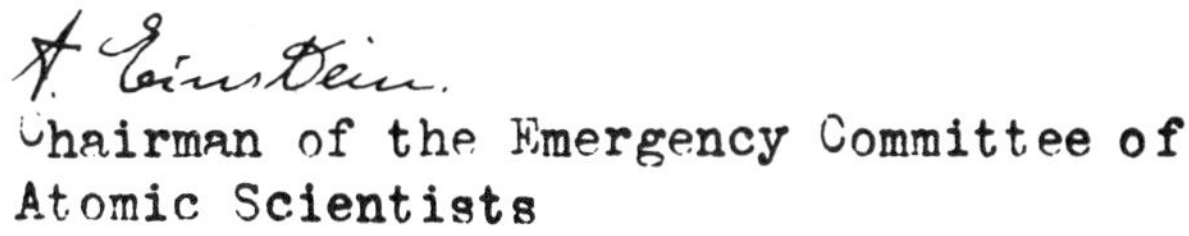
A. Einstein.
Chairman of the Emergency Committee of Atomic Scientists

Left: In this letter of Walter Reed to George M. Sterling, of June 5, 1901, Reed speaks of "our work in Cuba," and of the steps of "Protection & Prevention" that must be taken in the future to cut down on yellow fever. From the P. S. Hench–Yellow Fever Collection, University of Virginia Library.

In the field of aviation, Colonel Richard Gimbel of Yale concentrated his interest on the development of aeronautics from the time of Joseph and Jacques Montgolfier, Jean Pilâtre de Rozier, and Jean Pierre Blanchard. The collection of Otto Kallir of New York is wide-ranging as well and comprises Montgolfier, Vincenzo Lunardi, and Otto Lilienthal through Count Ferdinand von Zeppelin, the Wright brothers, and Charles Lindbergh. It is to be hoped that it will never be dispersed but will one day be settled in an institution for lasting residence.

Building a set of Nobel prize winners needs no guiding rules. Apart from the obvious great names, minor recipients would have to be included; the latter should be represented by first-class, scientifically important documents, preferably those referring to their prize-winning work. Minor items in this category appear as lots in catalogs.

Collections based on the space age have only begun. The names of the first astronauts will be of great interest in the coming years, but we are still too near these events to evaluate them accurately.

The collecting of scientific and medical autographs is most rewarding, and it is significant that the owners of the great Koch collection of musical manuscripts in Switzerland have been disposing of some of their priceless items and are now concentrating more on scientific pieces. This would almost seem to be a tradition, for the founder of the collection, Louis Koch of Frankfurt, had many years ago exchanged his collection of Napoleonica for the musical collection owned by the famous Siegfried Ochs, thus establishing one of the finest collections of musical autographs and manuscripts of the century.

COLLECTING THE DOCUMENTS OF ART

THOMAS B. BRUMBAUGH

"ARE YOU still collecting signatures?" I was asked by an acquaintance just the other day. I was scarcely able to take the kidding in good humor. It is, of course, a deeply serious matter to collect the signatures of the great and near-great on even the most indifferent of documents—an endeavor that, at times, by whatever chemistry, can move us to tears or laughter, lust, avarice, pride, euphoria, desolation, bankruptcy, and a number of other states and conditions. Abraham Lincoln, Robert E. Lee, Susan B. Anthony, Captain William Kidd, Maria Jeritza, Adolf Hitler, Pope John XXIII, Marie Antoinette, John Keats, Richard M. Nixon, Frédéric Chopin, Erasmus, Alexander Pope, Lenin, Marco Bozzaris, Harvey Cushing, and Paul Klee, reads the litany of our heroes and anti-heroes, the least scrap of whose handwriting represents a unique fragment of immortality.

And writing thus in praise of "mere signatures," what is no doubt one of the most marvelous and rare examples from any period has recently been discovered in western Greece. For a full century excavations had been carried out at Olympia, where, in ancient times, the athletic games were held amid superb monuments of architecture and sculpture. The German Archaeological Institute uncovered many treasures through its years of residence on the site, and in the 1950's was fortunate enough to locate the workshop of Phidias, the great sculptor of the colossal statue of Zeus, father of the gods, set up in the main sanctuary. The figure was made of gold plates attached to a wooden core, while the head, arms, and feet were covered with an ivory veneer. It was almost incredible news that molds for the gold plates, as well as bits of ivory, had been discovered.

In 1958 a rubbish heap left from the making of the legendary statue was finally uncovered and the rarest of artists' autographs was found, a unique example of Phidias himself. Across the bottom of a common black-glazed cup he had neatly incised "I belong to Phidias." Dr. Emil Kunze, director of the dig, suggested that the master must have been meticulous in all of his actions, for such proprietary statements are usually scratched in crude fashion. It was noted, too, that Phidias, born about 500 B.C., was quite an old man by the time his Olympian masterpiece was finished. Kunze confirmed this fact from the somewhat old-fashioned syntax employed by the artist. By 450 B.C. most people would have used the genitive form of their names to indicate ownership, rather than make the cup itself speak.

Be that as it may, the finest letters, much less signatures, of painters, sculptors, and architects, with a few notable exceptions, have seemed of peripheral interest to collectors in the United States and Canada. Too often their domain has been envisioned as lying somewhere south of musical material, and slightly north of opera singers and film stars of the 1930's. For nearly two centuries European auction houses and antiquarian booksellers have shown lively concern with artistic autographs, particularly in England, France, and Germany; thus the finest items are still to be discovered there. Americans remain content, it would seem, with the ubiquitous signed Auguste Rodin photographs, fragments of Sir Thomas Lawrence's unintelligible business correspondence, or those Marc Chagall and Salvador Dali signatures on museum cards, invariably priced at $50—Pablo Picasso at $100—as "ideal for framing." A John James Audubon, James McNeill Whistler, Pierre Bonnard, Claude Monet, Henri Matisse, or Maurice Utrillo manuscript might be expected in a very sophisticated offering.

Autograph of Maurice Utrillo. Courtesy of The Rendells, Inc.

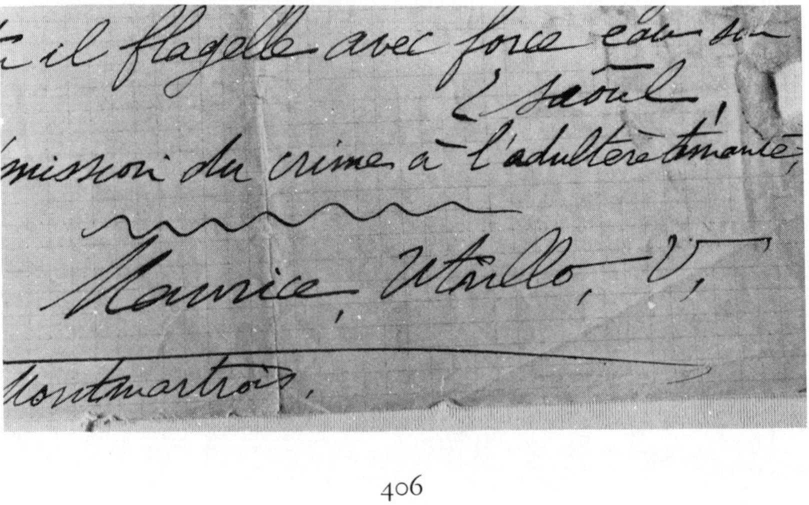

No doubt it is a factor in the matter that most letters of artists coming onto the market today are workaday things. Even the specialist, familiar with the aesthetics of their pages, is often surprised that such exquisite craftsmen as the French Impressionists can be so insensitive to the formal placement of sentences and paragraphs. Perhaps even before the twentieth century is gone, all of their surviving manuscripts will have been matted and framed with redemptive color reproductions, allowing us, if nothing else, to observe the close relationship between handwriting and artistic style.

Many times artists' calligraphy can be awkward, ill formed, and, above all else, expressive, unless, like Albrecht Dürer, Benvenuto Cellini, Eric Gill, or Maxfield Parrish, they were also trained calligraphers. Unless they were also literary figures such as William Blake, Washington Allston, William Morris, Dante Gabriel Rossetti, or Victor Hugo, the letter's content was not their primary concern; they used it first of all for communication. John Singer Sargent's notorious scrawl, on occasion totally illegible, if stylish and well arranged, immediately comes to mind. Almost too well-known are those tortuous Victorian letters with postscripts written in the opposite direction across already cramped pages. Sir Edward Burne-Jones, the late-blooming Pre-Raphaelite, was a master of the genre. I have a letter of his friend, the etcher Mortimer Menpes, written to Lillie Langtry, in which he mentions Whistler and Walter Crane; but relationships are lost amid the blotted verbs. Fortunately there is a tiny drawing of an easel and a phrase about being tied to it; and who could resist the embossed cameo of Cupid and Psyche and a self-conscious typeface heading the satiny, mauve-tinted quarto sheet? When but a mere shred of sense is salvaged, such manuscripts can be useful in the charting of an evasive career.

Admiration of the artist as cult hero and demigod has been a major aspect of collecting for some five centuries. A fair number of the four hundred or so Michelangelo letters survive, many in splendid condition, because they were preserved by his admiring contemporaries. The "Divine" Michelangelo, as his friend, "the father of art history," Giorgio Vasari, called him, and the Divine Raphael (described thus by the nineteenth-century master Jean Auguste Dominique Ingres) were recipients of almost unquestioning adulation by some fifteen generations of critics; paradoxically, they are revealed not as divinities, but as consummate human beings in the manuscripts. Can we ask more of old ink and paper, preserved and bequeathed to us despite the devastations of passing centuries?

In a world where great works of art are perhaps the most stable of commodities and the most valued of spiritual legacies from the past, the documents that authenticate and explicate them can be almost equally abode for the night: for there was a great hall there, wherein were fires made for folk.

Now that evening went Steingerd from her bower, and her handmaid with her, and they heard stranger folk in the hall, and the handmaid said; "Come, my Steingerd, let us look on the guests."

She said it needed not; and yet she went to the door, and stood up on the threshold, and looked over the wood-heap there: but there was a space betwixt the threshold and the wood-heap, and her feet showed thereby; and Kormak saw it, and sang:

Ah, how my heart now holdeth
hat heaven-bright land of gems!
Her light feet laid upon me
Great love in little space.
But those feet of the fair-coifed woman
Shall flit to bear me ruin
Full oft before all endeth,
If aught I know at all.

Now Steingerd finds that she is seen, so she turns away into a corner, and looks under the beard of Hagbard; for there was a pile of wood before the door, and an image of Hagbard was on the door-jamb: but the light smote on her face, and Tosti said:

"Lo there Kormak, the eyes beside Hagbard's head!"

Then sang Kormak a stave:

Fierce now upon me flame
The twin fires of her cheeks
Through the logs ready laid;
Nor may I laugh thereat.
The threshold gave me glimpses
Of her gloriously wrought ancles:
Through all the lapse of life
Young shall my longing be.

And yet again he sang:

The bright moon of the brow
Brake out from that light heaven
Of the goddess linen-girded
Eager glad to shine upon me:
But that beam of the goldbearer,
Bright cheeks moon-beam, bringeth surely
Henceforth harm enow upon me
Yea on her too, red rings' goddess.

Said Tosti: "Lo, how she stareth at thee!" Then Kormak sang:

he maiden might not move
er eyes from me. I, smitten
y hot flame, hid not anguish;
or her my prayers are ready.
She, the dark's deeds desiring,
Through the door's chink did peer;
With gold-hung neck laid hardby
Old Hagbard's neck she gazed.

Now the women come into the hall & sit down, and Kormak hears how they are talking about his looks. The handmaid said he was black and ugly; but Steingerd said that he was fair, and as goodly as might be: "But that one blemish he has, that his hair is swept over on to his brow."

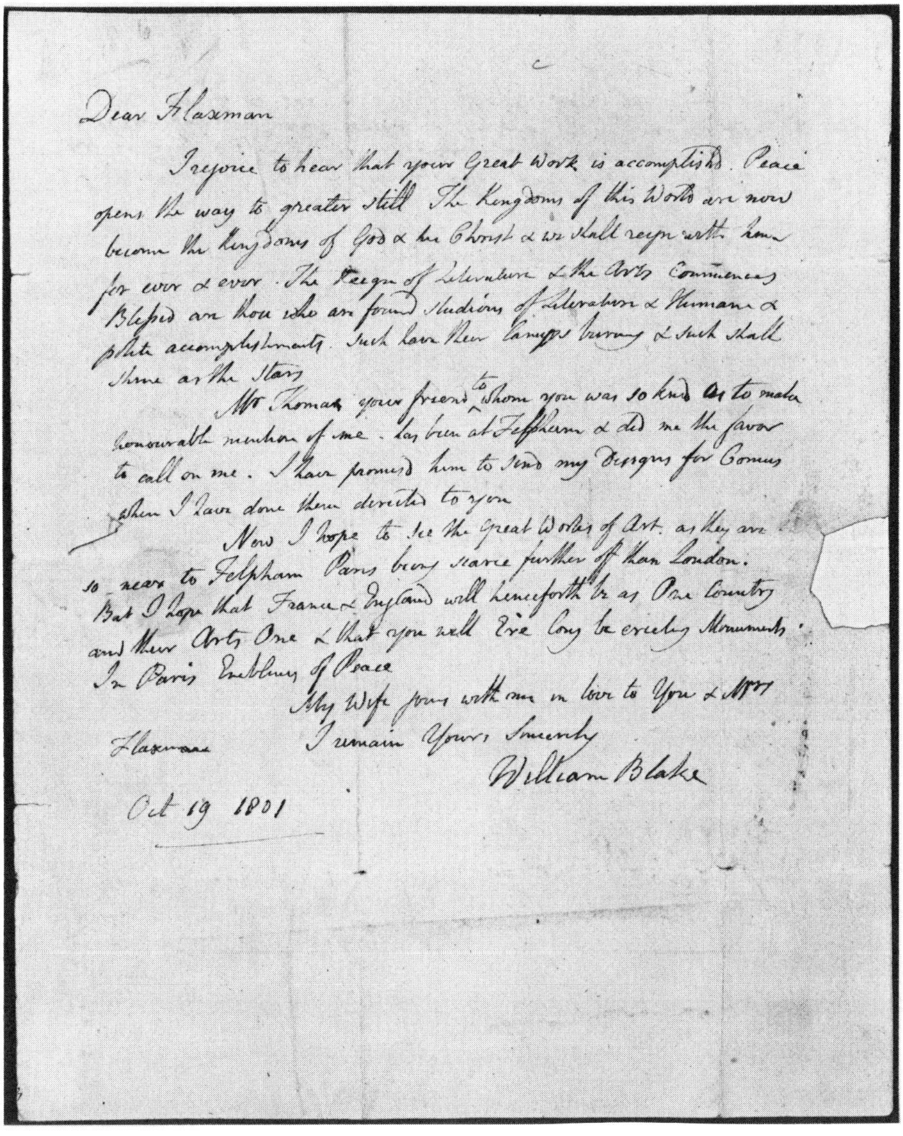

Dear Flaxman

I rejoice to hear that your Great Work is accomplishd. Peace opens the way to greater still The Kingdoms of this World are now become the Kingdoms of God & his Christ & we shall reign with him for ever & ever. The Reign of Literature & the Arts Commences Blessed are those who are found studious of Literature & Humane & polite accomplishments. Such have their Lamps burning & such shall shine as the Stars

Mr Thomas your friend to whom you was so kind as to make honourable mention of me. has been at Felpham & did me the favor to call on me. I have promisd him to send my Designs for Comus when I have done them directed to you

Now I hope to see the Great Works of Art. as they are so near to Felpham Paris being scarce further off than London. But I hope that France & England will henceforth be as One Country and their Arts One & that you will Ere long be erecting Monuments In Paris Emblems of Peace

My Wife joins with me in love to You & Mrs Flaxman

I remain Yours Sincerely

William Blake

Oct 19 1801

Above: A.L.S. from William Blake to John Flaxman, October 19, 1801.
Courtesy of the Pierpont Morgan Library.

Left: Page from a calligraphic M.S. of *Kormák's Saga,*
by William Morris, *ca.* 1871.
Courtesy of the Pierpont Morgan Library.

important. The art historian who labors in a museum or university library to re-create the life and times of even so humble a craftsman as the Scottish genre painter Sir David Wilkie must one day find my packet of letters linking him to the sculptor Patrick Park a boon to his project. Another scholar will be pleased to know that the youthful Élisabeth Vigée-Lebrun charged her portrait sitters at the court of Louis XVI according to a scale ranging from "un Buste sans main—50 Louis" to "une grande figure avec ses attributs—250 Louis." Still another will be concerned that in 1899 the great French symbolist painter-printmaker Odilon Redon was offering the American critic Sadakichi Hartmann a group of his lithographs as a means to introduce his work in New York. George Morland, eighteenth-century exponent of rustic genre scenes, has been the subject of a number of excellent monographs; but in my letter to his brother Henry, his next biographer will find a new account of the artist's return from France in 1785 to the chaos of his affairs at Margate.

As a teacher and enthusiastic collector of art history, I am sometimes asked how one begins to collect such things. I recount my own schoolboy purchase of letters of the Victorian portraitist Sir William Boxall, whose name meant nothing to me then, or a few others by Robert Lefèvre, first painter to Louis XVIII, from John Heise's lists issued in the 1930's and 1940's. Somehow I learned that, for a quarter or half a dollar, one might own such random fragments of the past; that there was a downright sensual pleasure in finding out that Boxall's correspondent, Dominic Colnaghi, was a leading London connoisseur and printseller in 1845; and that the artist was anxious to have a good engraving made of his portrait of the poet Walter Savage Landor. In 1823 Lefèvre was assuring Count La Rochefoucauld, beaux-arts minister in Paris, that he admired him as a faithful and fervent royalist, and would soon begin his portrait "in spite of the dampness of these dark winter afternoons." Appropriately, the finished picture as we see it in the Louvre might be described as aristocratic and rather melancholy in mood.

Today's novice collector will almost as easily and more pleasurably own a letter of some modern artist-hero, such as Wassily Kandinsky, for the price of theater tickets and supper at a good restaurant. He should, however, come to grips with the realities dictated by availability of other Kandinsky material. He should decide if this is to be a single gem in his collection or the beginning of an "archive." If the latter, will it discourage him to know that there are two or three Kandinsky archives already formed, and that there are a number of dedicated German and Austrian collectors of Kandinsky and his circle? And his letter bought in the New York market, he may learn, was something of a bargain compared with the costs of such letters in Berlin or Vienna, where most of the correspondence is likely to surface in future. Can he sustain interest and bear the anxieties and trials until new items appear on the market? Will he read widely in three languages, seeking information in specialized libraries, or hunt down those few Kandinsky relatives who still survive and perhaps own that crucial diary that is for sale at a certain price, and that explains the tantalizing reference in his letter to "the vicious lies of my so-called friends"? Finances aside, is he prepared psychologically to collect one of the greatest painters of the past century? He will soon have it made clear to him that such possessions are scarcely private, that scholars will (and must) insist upon having copies of his manuscripts, even demanding information about the sources of his purchases so that they too may write still more letters to libraries and pursue relatives in order to put together one more article or book on the master. The advanced collector will learn that heavy moral responsibilities come with the ownership of unique cultural property.

From 1965 to 1975 such diverse and legendary names as Michelangelo, Raphael, Lucas Cranach, Titian, Cellini, Giovanni da Bologna, Andrea Palladio, Inigo Jones, Hendrik Goltzius, Bartolomé Murillo, André Le Nôtre, Christopher Wren, Canaletto, Giovanni Piranesi, Pietro Longhi, William Hogarth, Thomas Gainsborough, Sir Joshua Reynolds, William Blake, and Francisco Goya were available, although usually in rare or unique examples, and in some cases at enormous cost. Those are the names to conjure with, the manuscripts worthy of the company of heroic items by Martin Luther, Charles V, Galileo, Niccolò Machiavelli, Sir Walter Ralegh, Saint Ignatius of Loyola, Isaac Newton, Voltaire, Richard Wagner, and Sigmund Freud. Theirs are the treasures we view in near disbelief in the cases at the British Library or the Library of Congress. Nonetheless, I was asked recently if I had "ever heard of collecting one of each," and learned that a former student had quietly put together an almost equally breathtaking group of fewer than a hundred names, including letters by painters, sculptors, and architects from Francesco Albani to Roy Lichtenstein. She had simply taken a standard text, Helen Gardner's *Art Through the Ages,* as a guide, and sought fine single specimens from the Renaissance to the present. At first glance very few of the great seventeenth-century masters appeared to be there, for Rembrandt, most desirable of all, is beyond hope; his seven known letters are in institutional collections. Jan Vermeer, Georges de La Tour, Diego Rodríguez de Silva y Velázquez, El Greco, and others were not present and are rarer still. In Holland and Spain the lower social status of the artist led to the neglect of his manuscripts, while in Italy and France a fascination with artistic "fame" made possible their preservation. Thus there were letters of Carlo Dolci, Salvator Rosa, Artemisia

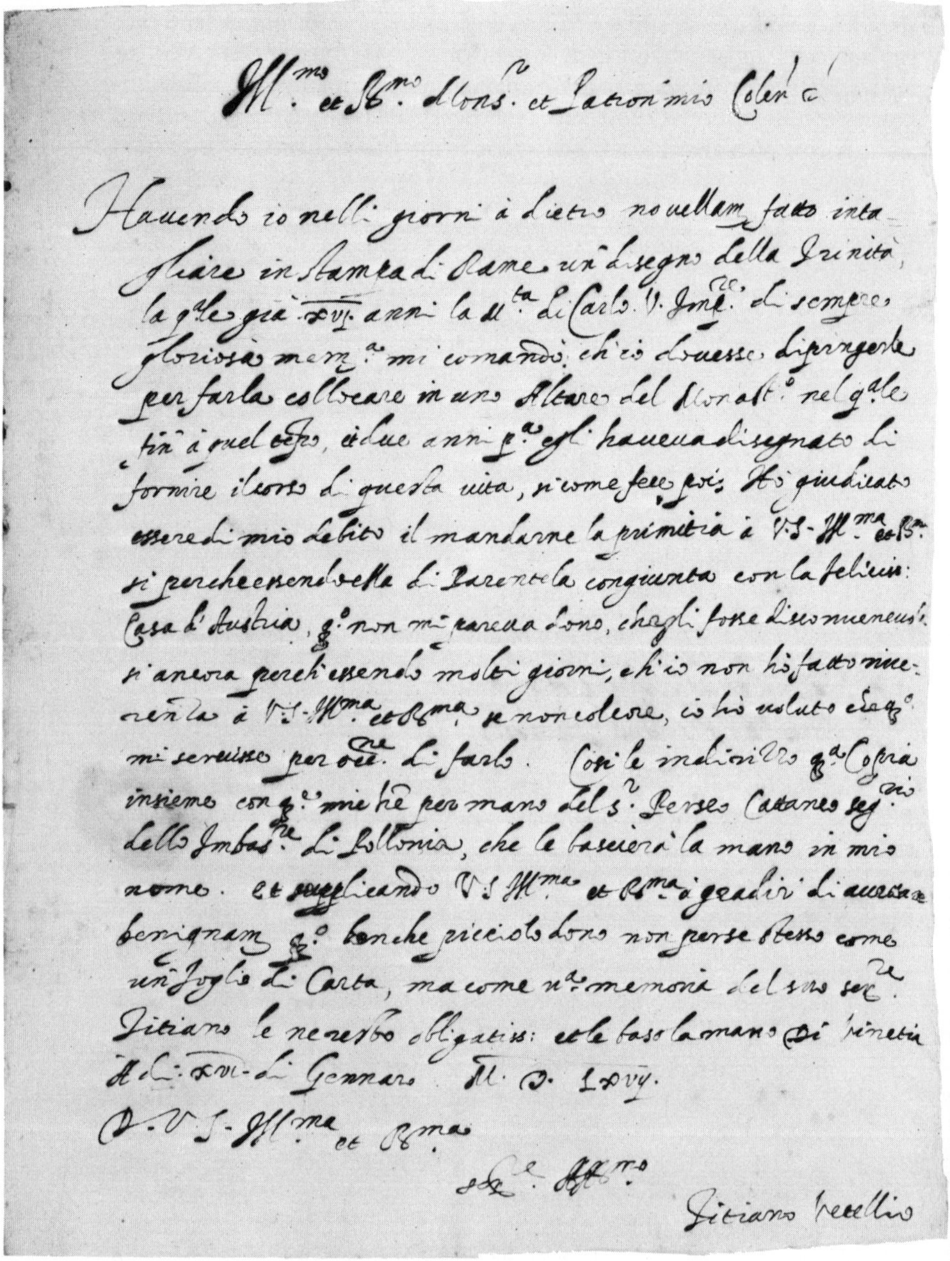

Ill.mo et R.mo Mons.r et Patron mio Coler.mo

Hauendo io nelli giorni à dietro nouellam.te fatto inta-
gliare in stampa di Rame un disegno della Trinità,
la q.le gia .XVI. anni la M.tà di Carlo V. Imp.re di sempre
gloriosa mem.a mi comandò, ch'io douesse dipingerle
per farla collocare in uno Altare del Monast.o nel q.le
fin' à quel tempo, i due anni q.a egli haueua disegnato di
fornire il corso di questa uita, si come fece poi: Ho giudicato
essere di mio debito il mandarne la primitia à V.S. Ill.ma et R.ma
si perche essendo della di Parentela congiunta con la felicis:
Casa d'Austria, q.o non mi pareua dono, che gli fosse disconueneuo-
le; si ancora perch'essendo molti giorni, ch'io non hò fatto riue-
renza à V.S. Ill.ma et R.ma, se non col cuore, io hò uoluto che q.o
mi seruisse per occ.ne di farlo. Con le inclusi ella q.a Copia
insieme con q.a mie hè per mano del S.r Perseo Cattaneo seg.rio
dello Imbas.re di Polonia, che le basciera la mano in mio
nome. Et supplicando V.S. Ill.ma et R.ma à gradir di accettare
benignam.te q.o benche picciolo dono non per se stesso come
un foglio di Carta, ma come un.a memoria del suo ser.re
Titiano le ne resto obligatis: et le baso la mano. Di Venetia
Alli .XVI. di Gennaro .M.D.LXVII.

D. V.S. Ill.ma et R.ma

Dev.mo Aff.mo

Titiano Vecellio

A.L.S. from Titian to Alessandro Farnese, January 16, 1567.
Courtesy of the Pierpont Morgan Library.

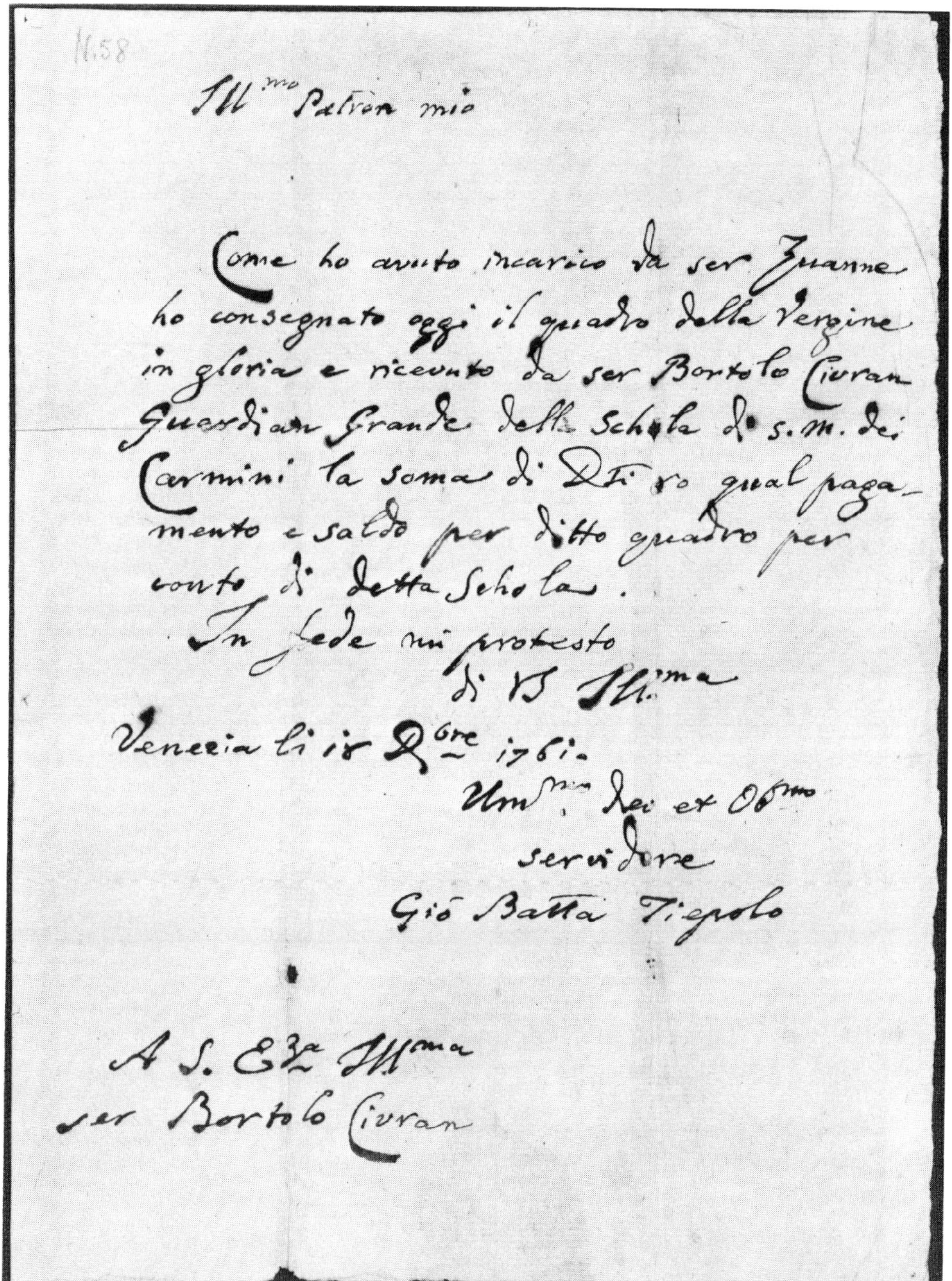

N.58

Ill.mo Patron mio

Come ho avuto incarico da ser Zuanne
ho consegnato oggi il quadro della Vergine
in gloria e ricevuto da ser Bortolo Civran
Guardian Grande della Schola di S. M. dei
Carmini la soma di D.ti 80 qual pagamento e saldo per ditto quadro per
conto di detta Schola.
In fede mi protesto
di V. S. Ill.ma
Venezia li 16 X.bre 1761.
Umil.mo Dev.o et Obb.mo
servidore
Giò Batta Tiepolo

A S. Ecc.za Ill.ma
ser Bortolo Civran

A.L.S. from Giovanni Battista Tiepolo to Bortolo Civran, December 16, 1761.
Courtesy of the Pierpont Morgan Library.

My Lord April 30 1761

We Artists, as we call ourselves are to have an Exhibition of our own in Spring Garden next week, for this purpose your Lordships Picture of my Painting is asked for, and I shall be extremely obliged to you if you can lend it me for a few days. it wants a little cleaning and fetching out which may be done at the same time, depend my lord upon the utmost care being taken of it. if your Lordship thinks proper to add this favour to the many great obligations you have bestowed on your Lordships

most devoted ~~[illegible]~~ most Obed^t Hum^ble Ser^t

Wm Hogarth

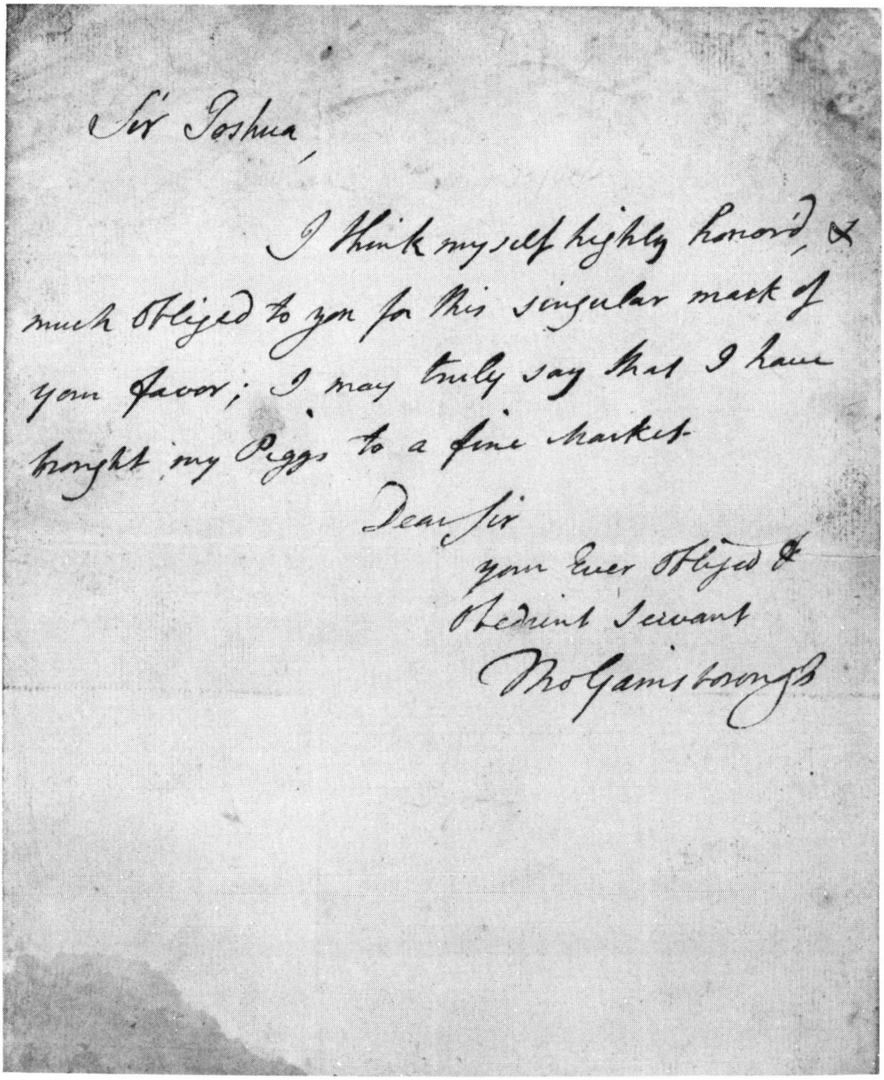

Sir Joshua,

I think myself highly honor'd, & much Obliged to you for this singular mark of your favor; I may truly say that I have brought my Piggs to a fine Market.

Dear Sir

your Ever Obliged & Obedient Servant

Thos Gainsborough

Above: A.L.S. from Thomas Gainsborough to Sir Joshua Reynolds, *ca.* April 1782.
Courtesy of the Pierpont Morgan Library.

Left: A.L.S. from William Hogarth to Lord Charlemont, April 30, 1761.
Courtesy of the Pierpont Morgan Library.

Gentileschi, Simon Vouet, Nicolas de Largillière, Louis Le Nain, Charles Le Brun, Jean-Antoine Houdon, and Jacques-Louis David. Anthony Van Dyck's initials on a receipt; a document of Baldassare Longhena, architect of Santa Maria della Salute in Venice, surely as desirable as others better known; and a beautiful letter of François Mansart, referring to the roofs of Versailles, were recent acquisitions. With a stamp collector's method and a relatively modest investment, it is apparent that a magnificent monument to quality and scholarship can still be built.

Belief in the charisma of such giants as Peter Paul Rubens, Bernini, Gustave Courbet, Edgar Degas, Edvard Munch, Picasso, or Kandinsky is now beyond question, and the making of books about them will never cease; but faith in the minor artist as a litmus, a true exemplar of his age, is equally important in our philosophy of history. The serious but less-affluent collector can serve himself, the past, and the future by conscientiously building a collection of such second-rank and moderately priced figures as E. M. Ward, Sir Francis Grant, Maurice Denis, Léon Lhermitte, Hans Thoma, Johannes Bosboom, Jules Dalou, or G. P. A. Healy. Even the finest paintings and drawings by a number of them may fetch less than letters of their more famous contemporaries. Soon the supply of once-despised Victorians from Sir Lawrence Alma-Tadema to Félix Ziem must be exhausted as those worthies are assigned new positions in the critical hierarchy. New York and Paris auctions that once sold, for a trifle, lots of fifty or a hundred letters by artists of modest reputation, now more often list them in twos and threes. The devastation of World War II, aided by disintegrating wood-pulp papers and compounded by casual disregard for the recent past, has taken its toll. Symptomatically, even the refusal of a dinner invitation from the monstrously prolific pen of Frederick, Lord Leighton, president of the Royal Academy, recently received a separate listing at £8 in a British catalog.

With all the current critical revaluation of forgotten reputations, and the compiling of catalogues raisonnés, it is difficult to believe that in the 1920's art historians and collectors were just beginning to recognize that Nicolas Poussin and Claude Lorrain were not the only painters of distinction in seventeenth-century France. In the eighteenth and nineteenth centuries, Italy was as profoundly art centered as it had been in the sixteenth; but research to that effect is just now beginning. And how many serious students of the baroque and rococo periods would not be hard pressed to name more than a handful of sculptors among the dozens of once-eminent masters then at work throughout Europe! The very phrase "American sculpture" seemed a contradiction in terms until Wayne Craven's study *Sculpture in America,* dealing with the achievements of three centuries, appeared in 1968 and finally opened our eyes. Meanwhile, American sculptors' letters continue to sell for small sums, even when they are offered on the inflated Americana market. Too many otherwise intelligent collectors continue to believe that art refers only to painting. Most of us will have to let the Pierpont Morgan Library or the Fondation Custodia in Paris make the high bid on that Watteau contract, the Albrecht Dürer letter with rebus drawings, or a new Leone Battista Alberti letter when it appears at auction, remembering that the time will come when the specialists must seek out our Ward, Denis, Thoma, Bosboom, or Healy archives in order to write a responsible account of their less and less accessible century.

Most collectors of artistic autographs are attracted first of all by famous names, but there are happy discoveries to be made in less obvious directions. One will rather often come across royal, ecclesiastical, presidential, or other official papers dealing with architectural matters, or contracts relating to interior decoration, tapestries, costumes, arms, numismatics, jewelry, and the like. Before me as I write is a document of the renowned Isabella of Spain, ordering payment to Fernando de Covarrubias (*fl. ca.* 1497–1503), a master embroiderer, for hangings to be used at the high altar of Seville Cathedral. Covarrubias also signed a receipt, dated 1500, on the same sheet for the promised sum of 20,000 maravedis. Isabella signed thousands of such papers, but the Covarrubias signature may be unique. In another document Henry IV of France arranged payments to the Gobelin family for services to the crown. Here is Marie de Medici ordering Spanish leather to decorate the walls of her apartments at Blois. Sir William Pepperrell, New England grandee and soldier, is signer of a remarkable contract specifying in detail the method for painting, "with Good Spanish brown and Linsut oyle," a new meetinghouse built in Kettery, Maine, in 1727. President Chester A. Arthur's "bargain-counter" letter to a Mr. Olmsted actually deals with an 1881 project of the great landscape architect Frederick Law Olmsted to redesign the White House lawn.

At this point the bargain hunter might be urged to practice caution, although at one time or another every collector will buy impulsively and fail to appraise or plan his purchases. Expensive decisions must often be made quickly, dependent upon inexpert information. Expertise often is developed in adversity. The brief but attractive John Singleton Copley letter that I traded for a dozen long letters of Copley Fielding, R.A., painter of marines and sky effects (I valued thirty as against two "Copley" pages), taught me, however painfully, the meaning of quality in art and autographs. The impulse to discard the evidence of a mistake was strong, yet I have resisted it long enough to realize that Fielding's letters to his brother Thales, mentioning a French friend Delacroix, must be among the most important ones he ever wrote. Moreover, I have lived to see a Victorian nonentity grow in importance throughout

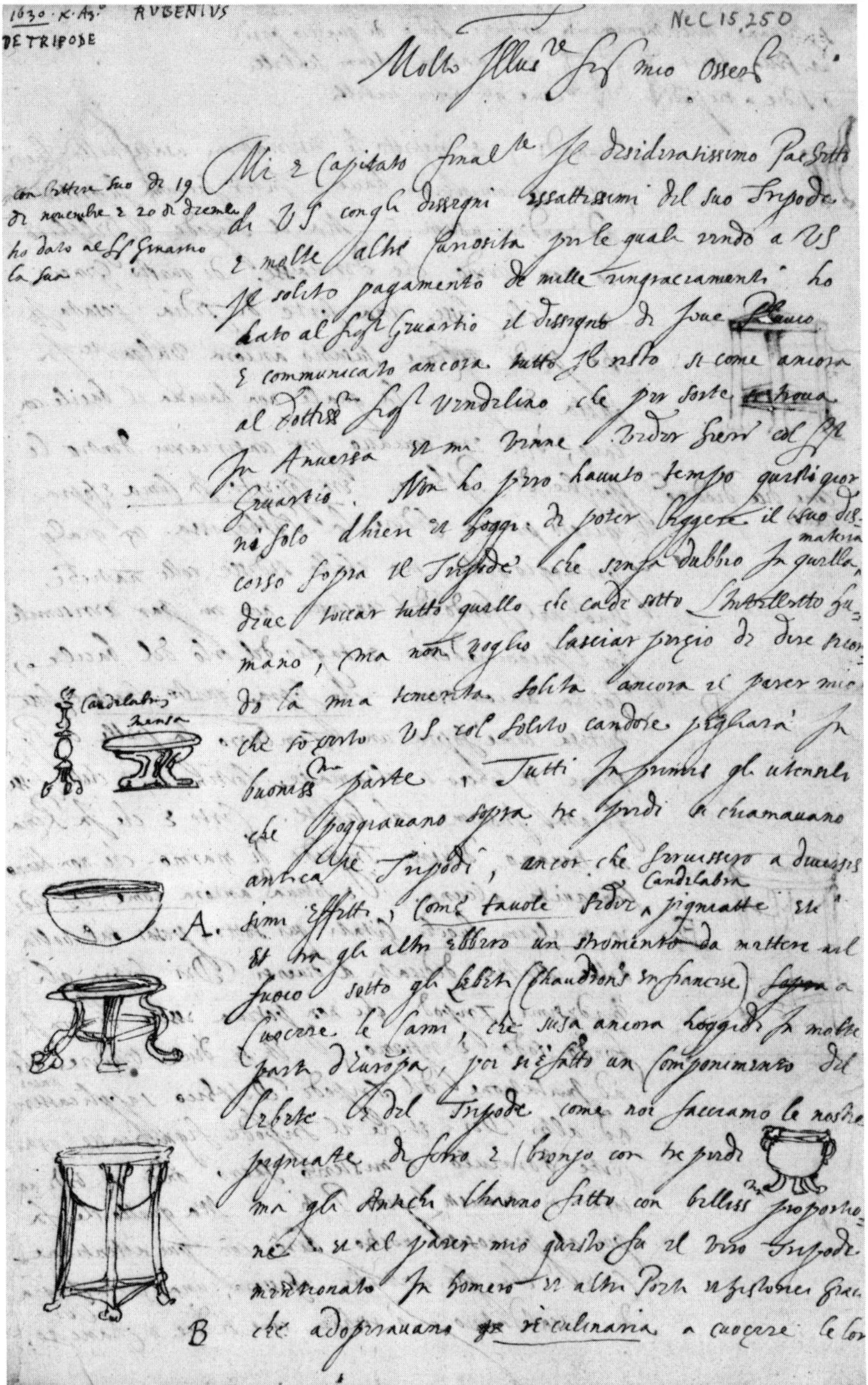

1630. X. Ag.o RUBENIUS

DE TRIPODE

NeC 15,250

Molto Ill.re Sig.r mio Oss.mo

con lettere suo di 19 di novembre e 20 di dicembre ho dato al Sig.r Guartio la sua

Mi è capitato finalmente il desideratissimo pacchetto di V.S. con gli dissegni essattissimi del suo Tripode e molte altre curiosità per le quali rendo a V.S. il solito pagamento di mille ringraciamenti. ho dato al Sig.r Guartio il dissegno di Gioue Pluuio e communicato ancora tutto il resto si come ancora al dottiss.mo Sig.r Vendelino che per sorte si troua in Anuersa e mi viene a veder spesso col Sig.r Guartio. Non ho pero hauuto tempo questi giorni solo d'hieri et hoggi di poter leggere il suo discorso sopra il Tripode che senza dubbio in questa materia diue toccar tutto quello che cade sotto l'intelletto humano, ma non voglio lasciar pero di dire secondo la mia temerità solita ancora il parer mio che son certo V.S. col solito candore pigliarà in buoniss.ma parte. Tutti in prima gli utensili che poggiauano sopra tre piedi si chiamauano alla antica Tripodi, ancor che seruissero a diuersissimi effetti, come tauole sedie candelabra pignatte etc. et tra gli altri ebbero un stromento da mettere nel fuoco sotto gli lebeti (chaudrons en francese) a cuocere le carni, che si usa ancora hoggidi in molte parti d'Europa, poi si è fatto un componimento del lebete et del Tripode come noi facciamo le nostre pignatte di ferro e bronzo con tre piedi ma gli Antichi l'hanno fatto con belliss.ma proportione et al parer mio questo fu il vero Tripode mentionato in Homero et altri Poeti et historici Greci che adopraruano in re culinaria a cuocere le lor

Above and right: Illustrated A.L.S. from Peter Paul Rubens to Nicholas Peiresc, August 1630. Courtesy of the Pierpont Morgan Library.

presenti che la istessa Venere con tutte le sue Gratie non potrebbe far meglio. Questi vagliono un Tesoro anzi sono inestimabili al parer mio. Si maravigliamo tutti che V.S. in tanta Calamità Publica stia col animo tanto riposato che possa col quello solito continuar la sua nobilissima curiosità nella osservatione rerum antiquarum. Specimen animi bene compositi et vera Philosophia imbuti. Spero però che al arrivo di questa haverà cessato il male e ch'ella sarà homai di ritorno nel suo Sacro museo, che piacerà al S. Iddio sia con ogni felicità e contentezza per molti anni come questo suo devotissimo servitore desidera con tutto il cuore et gli bacia le mani.

d'Agosto 1630

Si ha qui una gratiosissima nuova d'Italia che agli 22 di Luglio fu presa per assalto la Città di Mantoa con morte delle maggior parte delli habitanti che mi duole in estremo per haver servito molti anni la casa Gonzaga e goduto delle delicatezze di quel paese nella mia gioventù. Sic volu fatis. d'Anversa il

Di V.S. molto Ill.re

Questi dissegni sono squisitissimi et ben fatti e niuno in questo genere non si potrebbe far meglio. Sarà bene che V.S. tenga questo virtuoso giovane appresso di sè per esecutore delli suoi bellissimi concetti. Il ritratto di V.S. è stato gratissimo a me et a questi Signori che l'hanno veduto e restano intieramente sodisfatti della somiglianza ma io confesso non mi parere di ritrovare in questa faccia non so che di spiritoso et una certa emphasi nel sembiante che mi pare propria del Genio di V.S. Ill.ma la quale spero non si accerta facilmente per pittore da ognuno. Rendo a V.S. di nuovo mille gratie per tanti regali e la prego voler baciar le mani con tutto il cuore da mia parte al Gentilhuomo Sig. di Valavez Ill.mo suo fratello che me ha scritto di Lyone agli quattro di Julio dandomi nova d'haver ricevuto il mio ritratto che mi dubito sarà mal trattato per il longo viaggio et per tutti modi indegno del museo di V.S. ove non per qualità di pittore

Servitor Aff.mo

Pietro Paolo Rubens

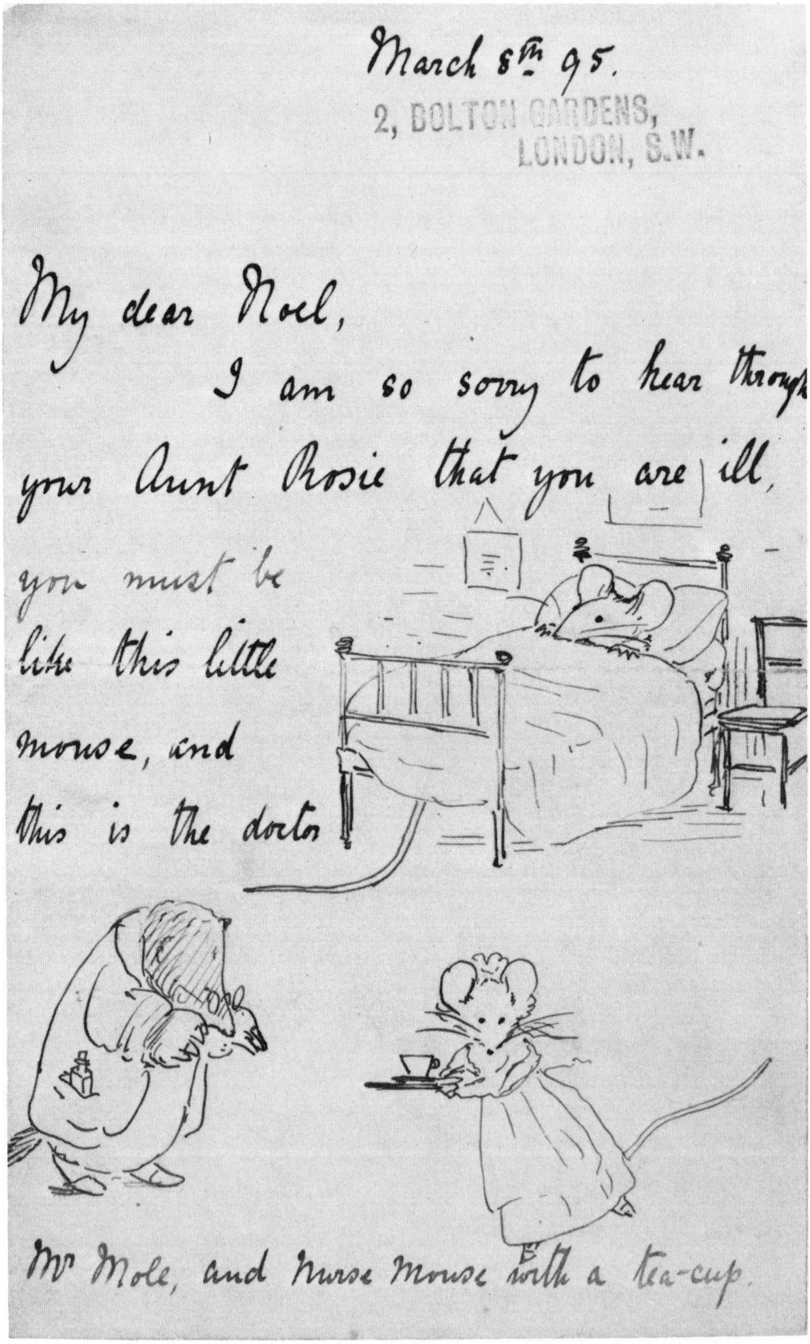

March 8th 95.

2, BOLTON GARDENS,
LONDON, S.W.

My dear Noel,
I am so sorry to hear throug
your Aunt Rosie that you are ill,
you must be
like this little
mouse, and
this is the doctor

Mr Mole, and Nurse Mouse with a tea-cup.

Above and right: Illustrated A.L.S. from Beatrix Potter to Noël Moore, March 8, 1895. Courtesy of the Pierpont Morgan Library.

I gave the elephant a lot of buns
out of a bag

but I did not give any to the ostriches
because people are not allowed to feed
them, since a naughty boy gave them old
gloves & made them ill.

I saw a black bear
rolling on its back.

I did not
know that
the old wolf
was so good
tempered. I remain yrs aff
Beatrix Potter.

some thirty years, and here in my acid-free folders is the means to help further in ranking him more closely with his namesake and his friend.

In every age the rich and powerful have spent part of their substance in the pursuit or the commission of extravagant and beautiful things. Fascinating documents of their association with artists have often made their names memorable when they might otherwise have been forgotten. Equally intriguing are the letters of those relatives, friends, enemies, collectors, students, and others who were able to observe the methods and personality of an important artist. A number of the finest items of this sort were gifts to my collection by dealers concerned only with the artist's holograph. With studious devotion to a period, a personage, an artistic theme or idea, one soon becomes aware of how much there is to be accumulated and learned, and how little the hurried catalogers really know about the subtleties involved.

In most cases only the collector will have the time to research an item with sufficient care. How rewarding for him to learn that the ten-dollar Clodion letter to an architect, glibly listed as "important," is very much so, for it deals with purchase of marble for the artist's statue of Charles de Montesquieu in the Institut de France. The Van de Velde letter was *not* that of Anton, the Dutch symphony conductor, as he guessed from the 1907 date, but is, rather, from Henri Van de Velde, the virtual creator of Art Nouveau, writing about a friend, the German impressionist Max Slevogt. The fact that a typed Norman Rockwell letter commands nearly as much as an autograph letter signed by the sculptor Aristide Maillol is simply an irony brought about by a failure of taste and the demand and supply of an American household name. The sensitive collector has every right—even an obligation—to take advantage of the situation. Coffee-table picture books make reputations at will, and Andrew Wyeth is rare and desirable for some; but the fact that there has been no modern monograph in English on the immortal Jacques-Louis David does not diminish the significance of his reasonably priced manuscripts. Letters of "Grandma" Moses and Le Corbusier may be similarly priced, but the serious collector should be concerned only that the architect is one of the movers and shapers of our age. He has, of course, a perfect right to collect the letters of any dear old lady for whatever sentimental reasons, just as the lover of drawings may choose a Hubert Robert confection for the price of a Rembrandt.

Let us venture a final word or two about illustrated letters, and a glance toward that huge band of nineteenth- and twentieth-century illustrators: Thomas Rowlandson, John Leech, George Cruikshank, Gavarni, Arthur Rackham, Cham, Alfred Rethel, Frederic Remington, Beatrix Potter, Randolph Caldecott, Walter Crane, Willy Pogány, Edmund Dulac, Howard Pyle, N. C. Wyeth, and the rest. Many of them

Sunday Morning May the 7th 1843

My Dear Father

What will we come to next! Wonders follow each other in such rapid succession that we have scarcely time to take breath between each. Scarcely had the "Aereal navigation Machine" struck wonder into the natives, than fresh astonishment was created by the fact of my not having committed suicide, on learning that the opening of the Royal Academy was put off for a week, and now the most astounding of all, has broken upon the World, in the shape of a gigantic pair of wings, by the aid of which, it is confidently asserted that man will be able to mount into the air and like the little "Richard" birds, "fly with the Zephyrs away, away." I take great interest in the invention, and fully expect in a year or two to witness the Military reviews in Hyde Park, with greater internal satisfaction than I have yet done, in consequence of being up in the air and able to see over the whole ground, without the slightest trouble

on Monday last of
Exhibition of the

A.L.S. from Richard Doyle to his father, May 8, 1843.
Courtesy of the Pierpont Morgan Library.

claim large sums from their devotees. The Victorian urge to tip an autograph into an illustrated first edition is still very much with us. Manuscripts with drawings are always appealing; and thus the illustrators, with their talent for the quick sketch, merged with the calligraphy itself, are much in demand. Even so, what serious student of Western culture would not rather have his pick of unembellished letters of modern masters from Pierre Auguste Renoir to Oskar Kokoschka (still very much alive and writing letters in 1977) for the same sums or less than what is often demanded for a decorated page by Sir William Russell Flint or H. K. Browne?

The occasional letter with a drawing more often than not is, first of all, a drawing, and thus it enters the realm of art. Those illuminated Edward Lear, Jean Louis Meissonier, Monet, Camille Pissarro, Paul Gauguin, or Van Gogh letters and album pages are usually cataloged and displayed in art collections. Every autograph hunter will inevitably own a few examples by lesser French or German masters, however. In folder B of my artists' file I prefer to seclude an overwrought Louis Boutet de Monvel letter beneath a plain postcard of Ernst Barlach that is much more beautiful in its holographic integrity. Would that the fates who hid away a communication from Phidias, allowing it to appear two and a half millennia later, might somehow preserve this poignant, youthful note from the great German sculptor as a reassuring letter to the world of 3477. Is it possible that only a signature of Emile Gallé, etched on a fragment of glass, or the names of David Smith or Alexander Calder, incised in steel, will survive from our time to greet that future age? Will even the signed bottoms of pots by Peter Voulkos and Bernard Leach survive to touch the hearts and minds of men born seventy-five generations hence?

RELIGIOUS MANUSCRIPTS

JAMES KRITZECK

SINCE WRITING BEGAN, as best we know, as a basically clerical invention and occupation of the Sumerian priesthood, it is somewhat surprising that the collection of religious manuscripts and autographs is no more widespread or specialized than it is. One has merely to peruse the catalogs, manuals, and annals of collecting in recent times to realize that this area seems of secondary or tertiary importance, and therefore invites some special consideration and recommendations.

Religion, most historians agree, is a major defining characteristic of civilization. Much depends, therefore, upon its definition as a term; and there has been constant effort over many centuries to make the definition more precise.* Because of the very nature of the effort, one tends to think, it can never be completed. That sort of thought is certainly not alien to manuscript collectors. Yet the common understanding of the term as a "binding" of the self to a set of beliefs and values, usually invoking the supernatural, will have to stand, for all practical purposes.

It remains exceedingly difficult to define a "religious" manuscript or autograph. In the course of gathering material for this article, the author sent out a rather extensive questionnaire to many persons. "What in the name of the seven Sutherland sisters is a religious manuscript, public or private?" asked one eminent collector. "Does the term include bibles? Letters from prelates? Lives of saints? Synodal decrees? Written material only? Published material?" One could argue, cogently enough, that all writing is religious, but again common sense must take over. Over millennia, scribes may have regarded their occupation as religious, but they have left us every indication from the quiet (and sometimes, we hear,

* On the overall question, the author prefers the balanced views of Wilfred Cantwell Smith, *The Meaning and End of Religion* (New York: Mentor, 1964), esp. pp. 7–74; and, *iuxta modum,* those of Arnold J. Toynbee, *A Study of History,* XII (London: Oxford University Press, 1961), pp. 68–102.

from the din) of their scriptoria that what they wrote was religious or not depending upon its subject matter and authority, not upon their own vocation.

So far as this author knows, there is not a single autograph of the founder of a major world religion, excepting, of course, their sects and relatively recent world religions claiming to be major. There is no autograph of Abraham or Moses, for example; or of Gautama Buddha; or of Jesus Christ (whose only recorded writing was a cryptic message in the sand); or of Mohammed, who has traditionally been regarded as illiterate by his followers.*

On stone, papyrus, parchment, various sorts of cloth, paper, and other materials, however, sundry early and later religious texts have been preserved. Most of them are, unsurprisingly, in the great museums and libraries of the world, and not infrequently in lesser museums, monasteries, and shrines. Sacred as they were and are, they were on the market even in ancient times; in medieval times they were fairly common prizes and articles for sale (egregiously during the disorders following the collapse of the Umayyad caliphate of Spain, and after the Fourth Crusade); in modern times they are even more plentiful. In 1452, as though it were a Romanov Fabergé Easter egg, Marguerite de Charny gave the Holy Shroud of Turin to Anne de Lusignan, the wife of the Duke of Savoy, in whose family's resolute possession this incomparable relic still resides.† Whole archives of religious groups, churches, synagogues, temples, madrasas, and (more often) insouciant or penurious noble families with popes and saints in their ancestry have been sold in lot and usually dispersed. It was still possible, when the author was a student residing at the American School of Oriental Research in Jerusalem, to be offered fragments of the Qumran (Dead Sea) Scrolls, at a reasonable price for an authentic crumbled fraction of one single letter of the alphabet—to the disgust of the scholar in him, the frustration of the collector in him, and the despair of the religious believer in him.‡

---

*Several objections might be lodged against these assertions, but note that it is not physical relics or disciples' writings that are referred to. The reference to Christ is John 8:06; cf. John 7:15. On Mohammed's alleged illiteracy, see R. Paret, "Ummī," *Encyclopaedia of Islam,* IV (Leiden: E. J. Brill, 1934), col. 1016.

†To the question "In the improbable event that you were offered a religious manuscript of undoubted authenticity and such value that it 'belonged' to a religion, would you give it to that religion?" the author received emphatically negative replies with the sole exception of one Roman cardinal. He was also informed that in most countries such a gift would be either forbidden or not tax-deductible. Granted that very few persons have the means to give such a gift, one wonders, then, how they would have the means to acquire or insure it.

‡It deserves to be said, however, that the entire scholarship and guardianship of the Qumran Scrolls is one of the most remarkable examples of good-willed, scientific, interfaith cooperation in our century. None of the many written accounts convey the sense of bridled exuberance that characterized it.

Apart from the Vatican, the British Library, the Bibliothèque Nationale, the Bodleian, the Ambrosiana, and other great national museums and libraries (Leningrad, Vienna, Munich, and the Escorial deserve special mention), most of the finest religious manuscripts are in university libraries and private collections throughout the world that are so well-known that it would be tedious to list them and perilous to evaluate or even categorize them.

In the United States one might begin by noting that J. P. Morgan's collection of letters of Methodist-Episcopal bishops started one of the greatest collections in the world. Beyond doubt, the finest collections of Catholic saints and popes outside the Vatican archives were assembled and are presently housed in the United States. America's collections of

Unquestionably among the most important of religious manuscripts are the Dead Sea Scrolls, discovered in 1947 by shepherd boys at Qumran, northwest of the Dead Sea. Associated with the Essene religious order, the scrolls are among the earliest biblical manuscripts, sacred to Jews, Christians, and Muslims. This is a section of the Isaiah "A" Scroll, opened to column 49, showing Isaiah 61:1. Jerusalem. Photograph courtesy of M. Trever and E. Nitowski.

Judaica are no less outstanding, and the arts (which so often include superb calligraphy) of religious significance from the Middle and Far East have been assiduously and imaginatively collected.

Yet, in 1930, Thomas F. Madigan's "Autograph Collector's Baedeker" of one hundred representative celebrities, fifty American and fifty European, "whose fame, in my humble opinion, is reasonably secure," contains a surprise. Many churchgoing personages grace the list; but the only two who could possibly be considered religious are, to one's embarrassment, Queen Elizabeth I of England and Armand, Cardinal de Richelieu, neither of whom made the list (which includes Voltaire and Thomas Jefferson), one suspects, on account of their outstanding or char-

A.L.S. from Bishop Samuel Seabury to Rev. Samuel Parker, August 18, 1785. Courtesy of the Pierpont Morgan Library.

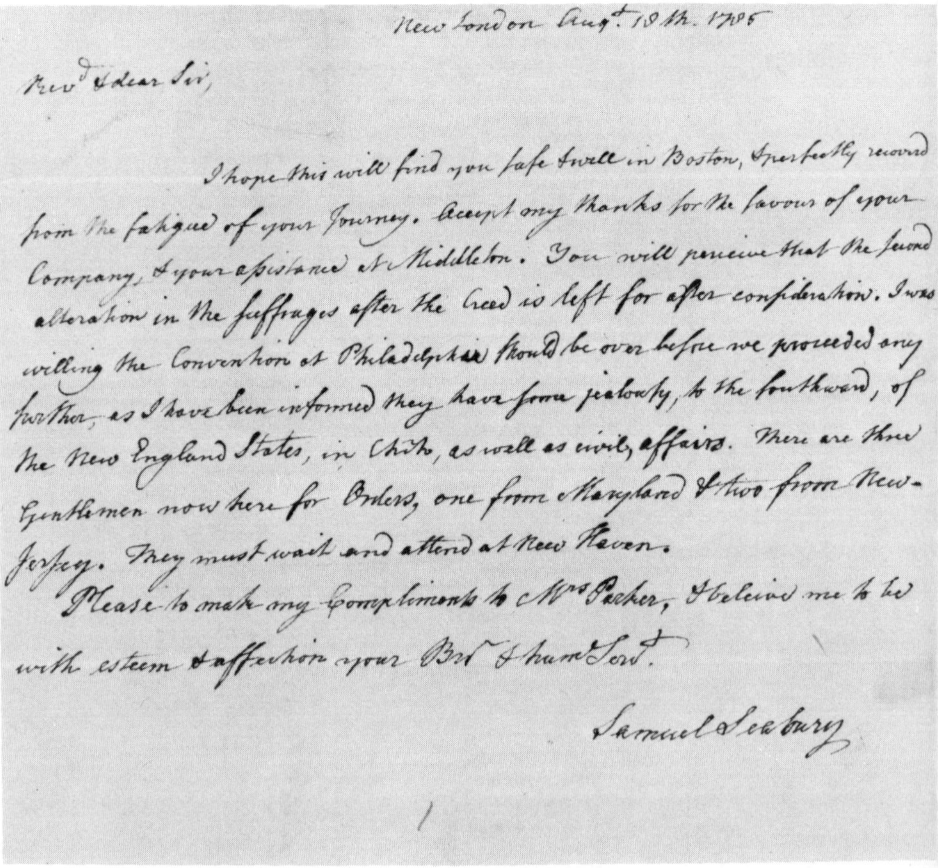

New London Augt. 18th. 1785

Revd & dear Sir,

I hope this will find you safe & well in Boston, & perfectly recovered from the fatigue of your Journey. Accept my thanks for the favour of your Company, & your assistance at Middleton. You will perceive that the second alteration in the suffrages after the Creed is left for after consideration. I was willing the Convention at Philadelphia should be over before we proceeded any further, as I have been informed they have some jealousy, to the southward, of the New England States, in Church, as well as civil, affairs. There are three Gentlemen now here for Orders, one from Maryland & two from New-Jersey. They must wait and attend at New Haven.

Please to make my Compliments to Mrs Parker, & believe me to be with esteem & affection your Br. & humble Servt.

Samuel Seabury

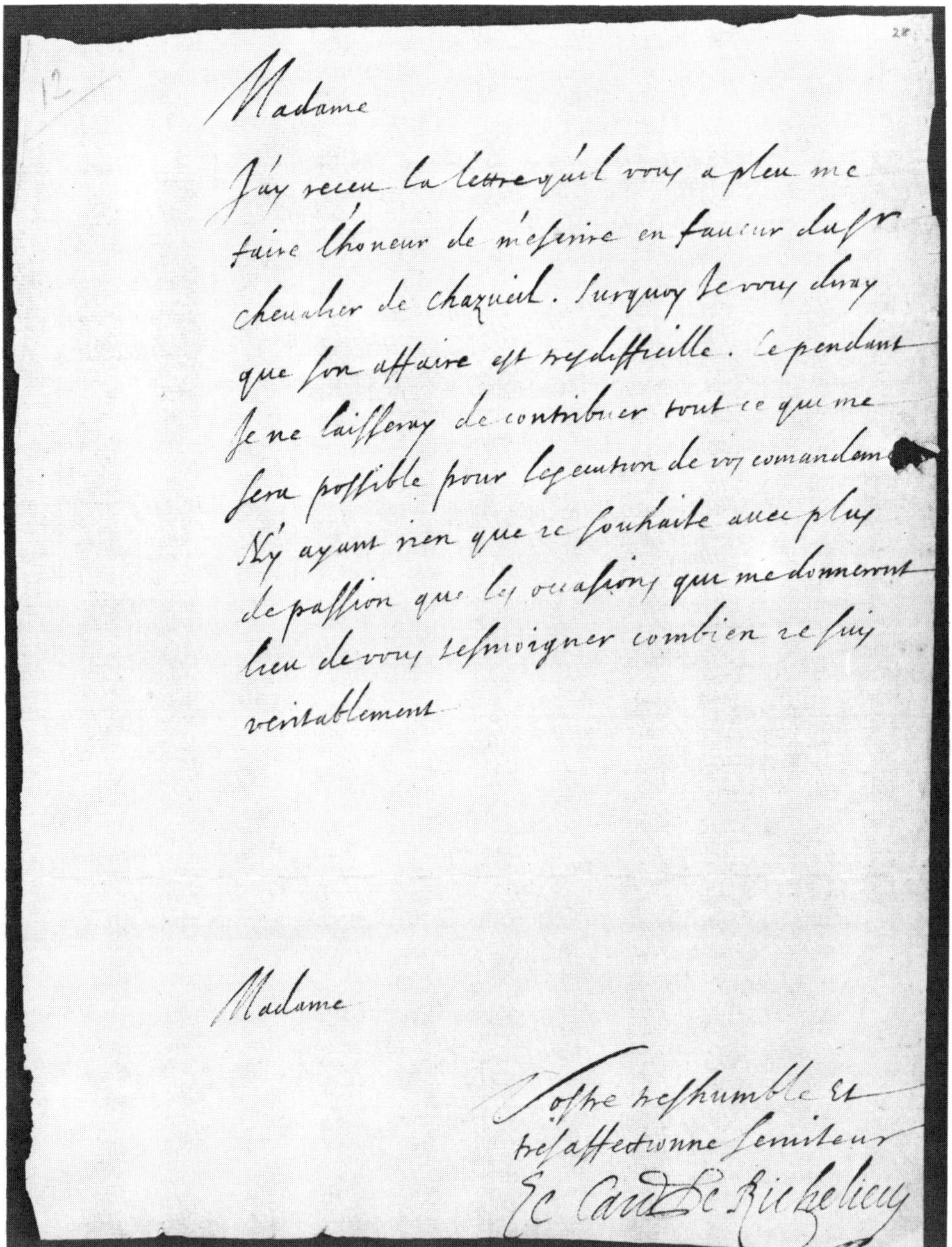

Madame

J'ay receu la lettre qu'il vous a pleu me
faire l'honeur de m'escrire en faveur du sr
chevalier de Chazueil. Surquoy je vous diray
que son affaire est tres difficille. Cependant
je ne laisseray de contribuer tout ce qui me
sera possible pour l'execution de vos comandem[ens]
N'y ayant rien que je souhaite avec plus
de passion que les occasions qui me donneront
lieu de vous tesmoigner combien je suis
veritablement

Madame

Vostre treshumble et
tresaffectionne serviteur
Le Card. de Richelieu

Armand Jean du Plessis, Cardinal, Duc de Richelieu,
to an unnamed "Madame" [n.d.].
Courtesy of the Pierpont Morgan Library.

acteristic piety. To make the point precisely, Madigan had himself assembled one of the truly great collections of Catholica and had been instrumental in assembling an even greater one for George Cardinal Mundelein of Chicago. He extols the latter, as it deserves, while placing his own tremendous achievement, forevermore unobtainable, in the context of the manner of protecting and displaying manuscripts.*

Paradoxically, therefore, religious manuscripts have been among the best bargains in the autograph and manuscript collecting world for many decades. An extraordinary number of them go unrecognized for what they are. Many of them have been underground, in all senses, for ages. Some, even those in the most venerable of surroundings, have been offered and accepted for sale. Significant materials from archaeological excavations are almost impossible to acquire by legitimate purchase, owing to agreements between the sponsoring expeditions and the governments involved. Nearly everything else under the sun is available and marketable.

Remarks from dealers are "It is a relatively unpopular field"; "Religious material is not often in any demand"; "Far less interest than in other fields"; "Everyone agrees religion rates last." Several dealers "do not handle them at all." The New York Public Library says "little or no effort" is expended in this area of collecting; "most of such manuscripts have been gifts, and most not in recent decades." Chicago replies that its public library does not have a history of manuscript collecting. The Smithsonian Institution says it is "pretty secular." The Library of Congress mentions that the acquisition of the "personal papers of eminent American theologians and religious leaders is of continuous and primary concern to the Library," and cites those of Henry Ward Beecher, Charles H. Brent, Titus Coan, John Haynes Holmes, Peter Marshall, Dwight Moody, Reinhold Niebuhr, and G. Bromley Oxnam. "We also have a large collection of Shaker manuscripts from the late 18th and 19th centuries." The National Archives is the crispest of all; it is "not authorized by law to collect religious manuscripts except for those that may by chance have been included with the official records."

Whether on account of the greater market for other materials, some distaste for religious materials that is a heritage of the Enlightenment, or the fact that the desiderata of collectors of religious autographs and manuscripts are so well-known that they never reach the catalogs or the auction rooms, religious manuscripts are simply not in vogue. Among all dealers and from all other evidence—from the buying patterns of Harvard, Yale, and Princeton and the collector with some hundreds or

*Thomas F. Madigan, *Word Shadows of the Great* (New York: F. A. Stokes, 1930), pp. 244–249, for the list; pp. 55–56, for Mundelein; pp. 237–242, on his own collection as a recommended example of "extra-illustration."

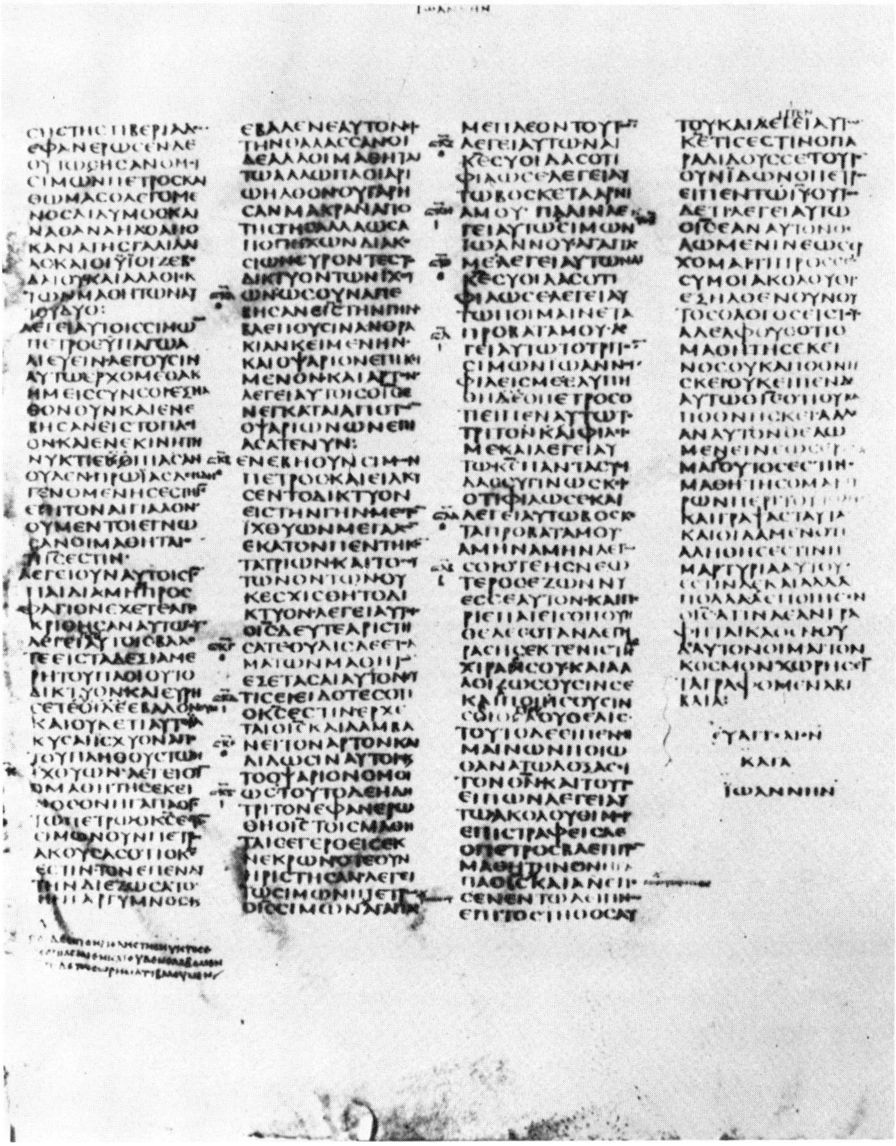

Codex Sinaiticus, an authoritative manuscript of the New Testament dating from the fourth century, was discovered at the monastery of St. Catherine on Mt. Sinai by Lobegott von Tischendorf in 1844, taken by him as gift for Czar Alexander II of Russia, and sold for £100,000 to the British Museum in 1933. This is the last folio of the Gospel of John. Photograph courtesy of B. Metzger and E. Nitowski.

thousands of dollars a year to spend on autographs—religious manuscripts do not rate at all. Political leaders, famous writers, musicians, artists, Bonapartes, Nazis—almost anything else—rates higher than religion. A penciled note from Jack Ruby in a jail cell fetched more than a letter of Pope Sixtus V to King Henry III of France begging for an end of the Catholic-Protestant wars. Examples could be endlessly multiplied. The Orient may or may not have something to teach us on this subject, too: Mahatma Gandhi rates higher than Indira Gandhi, and D. T. Suzuki higher than Yukio Mishima; Hirohito and Mao Tse-tung (a former deity and a new one, of approximately the same age) are a standoff at about even rarity.*

It is virtually impossible to obtain very rare or even particularly interesting religious manuscripts from India, Southeast Asia, East Asia, and (with some reservation) Japan. Those not preserved within the usually appropriate shrines and monasteries are usually in inaccessible Tibet or buried in impregnable vaults in Taiwan. Manuscripts from Japan are always carefully scrutinized and exorbitantly valued. Those from China, exiled through Hong Kong, are almost never offered for public sale. Indian religious manuscripts are in about the same position. Russian religious manuscripts occasionally appear in Vienna and Paris, or in Istanbul (an especially good market for icons, lectionaries, and other properties of dispossessed monasteries). African manuscripts are the rarest of all, and there is no need to mention pre-Columbian American or South Pacific manuscripts, which are generally even further beyond the range (or interest) of the average collector.

It is deucedly exasperating that within the Islamic world, from Islamic India all the way through the Persian, Arab, and Turkish world, rare manuscripts are being briskly sold and torn apart day after day; the walls of one large reception hall in Saudi Arabia, familiar to this author, are papered with them. Usually they fall into three distinct categories: (1) illuminated Koran leaves, the best, and even some of the worst, gold-illuminated; age and the fame of the calligrapher are the only criteria of value; (2) copies of the *Shah Namah* of Firdausi, the epic poet of Iran, mainly torn apart for the miniatures and seldom very important, let alone "religious" in the ordinary sense; and (3) annotated Korans, *Tafsirs* (commentaries that bridge exegesis and theology), and other Islamic religious works that may have considerable value because their owners and dealers have so scant an idea of these matters. If the un-

*These remarks are meant to be objective and helpful, not at all contemptuous. The subject of values lies at the very heart of the ethics of collecting, and is dealt with separately in this book and in those of Mary A. Benjamin, Charles Hamilton, and others. Dorothea Lady Charnwood has some choice and vintage remarks on the subject in her *An Autograph Collection* (New York: Henry Holt & Co., n.d.).

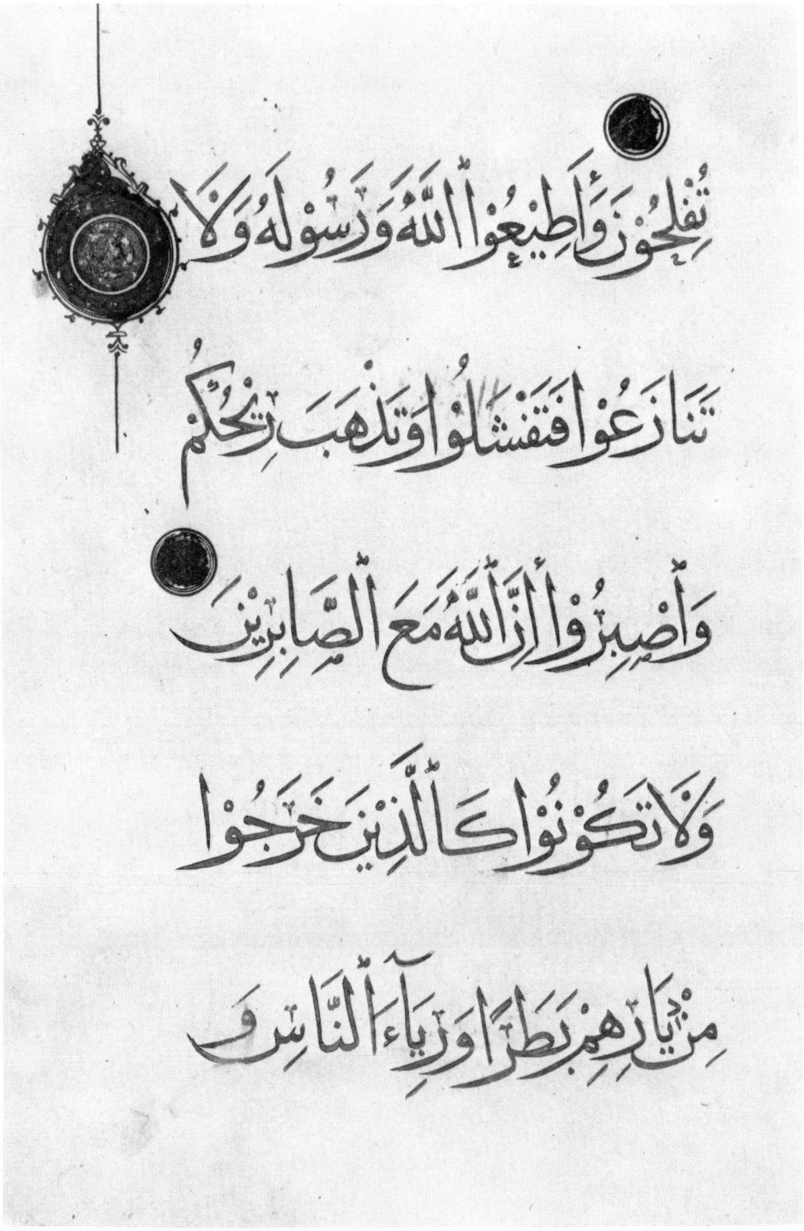
تفلحون وأطيعوا الله ورسوله ولا
تنازعوا فتفشلوا وتذهب ريحكم
واصبروا إن الله مع الصابرين
ولا تكونوا كالذين خرجوا
من ديارهم بطرا ورئاء الناس و

A fifteenth-century Persian manuscript of the Koran, the sacred book of Islam. The passage is Sura 8:45–47. From the Garrett Collection of Arabic Manuscripts, Princeton University Library.

Page from a fifteenth-century French book of hours. From the Edward L. Stone Collection, University of Virginia Library.

cataloged, loose manuscripts in Istanbul, Isfahan, and Tashkent were ever marketed, there would be a gold rush.*

Judaica, while somewhat infrequent in the catalogs and generally not of prime quality, is comparatively easy to collect, especially autographed rare books and inscribed religious objects (many synagogues have priceless collections, and in recent years some have been dispersed in Eastern Europe), though more and more against the higher bids of well-established professional collectors and their agents, as well as alert curators of formal collections. A distinguished European dealer reports that autographs of major Jewish personalities are eagerly collected. Easiest to collect are letters (rarely manuscripts) of early Zionist leaders, which are usually A.Ls.S. with considerable historical significance. Many of these collections, we are informed, are given, or intended to be given, to the state of Israel. However, some very fine collections of Judaica are also intended for retention and enrichment in other Jewish centers of learning. By and large, it is liturgical and scriptural manuscripts that engage the interest of major collectors of Judaica.

Every dealer whom the author queried replied that, as far as Protestant religious manuscripts are concerned, the letters of Martin Luther, John Calvin, John Wesley (who has many avid collectors), and other founders and their circles are most constantly in demand. However, since they are no longer in plentiful supply and letters are generally expensive, they are becoming out of the reach of collectors of more modest means. A second area has come into prominence, that of whole archives of congregations, or of churches, or of famous pastors and theologians who have, for one reason or another, been forced to sell or to dissolve their collections. Curiously enough, there is a notable market in some churches for the manuscripts of another; some archives are being carted out of the church on one side of the street and placed in those of the church on the other side of the street. For uniformity of collecting and excellence of descriptive cataloging, the Methodist and Mormon collections are outstanding, with certain collections of Luther and his circle not far behind, although seemingly deemed complete after the deaths of their donors. One very prominent expert in this field suggests that the pricing has "killed this collecting area" and suggests, as an example, the famous Phillips Brooks (1835–1893) as a fine candidate for collectors. He also cautions that the manuscripts of such figures as the late Martin Luther King, Jr., are likely to go outside religious collections al-

*By way of explanation: Turkish officials (who usually knew little if any Arabic) looted the Arab provinces of manuscripts that looked attractive on their shelves on the Bosporus. Isfahan was the sophisticated capital of Iran at the height of its modern cultural development; and Tashkent, now in Soviet Uzbekistan, the landlocked port for Bukhara and Samarkand, piles up the manuscripts in vigorous atheism.

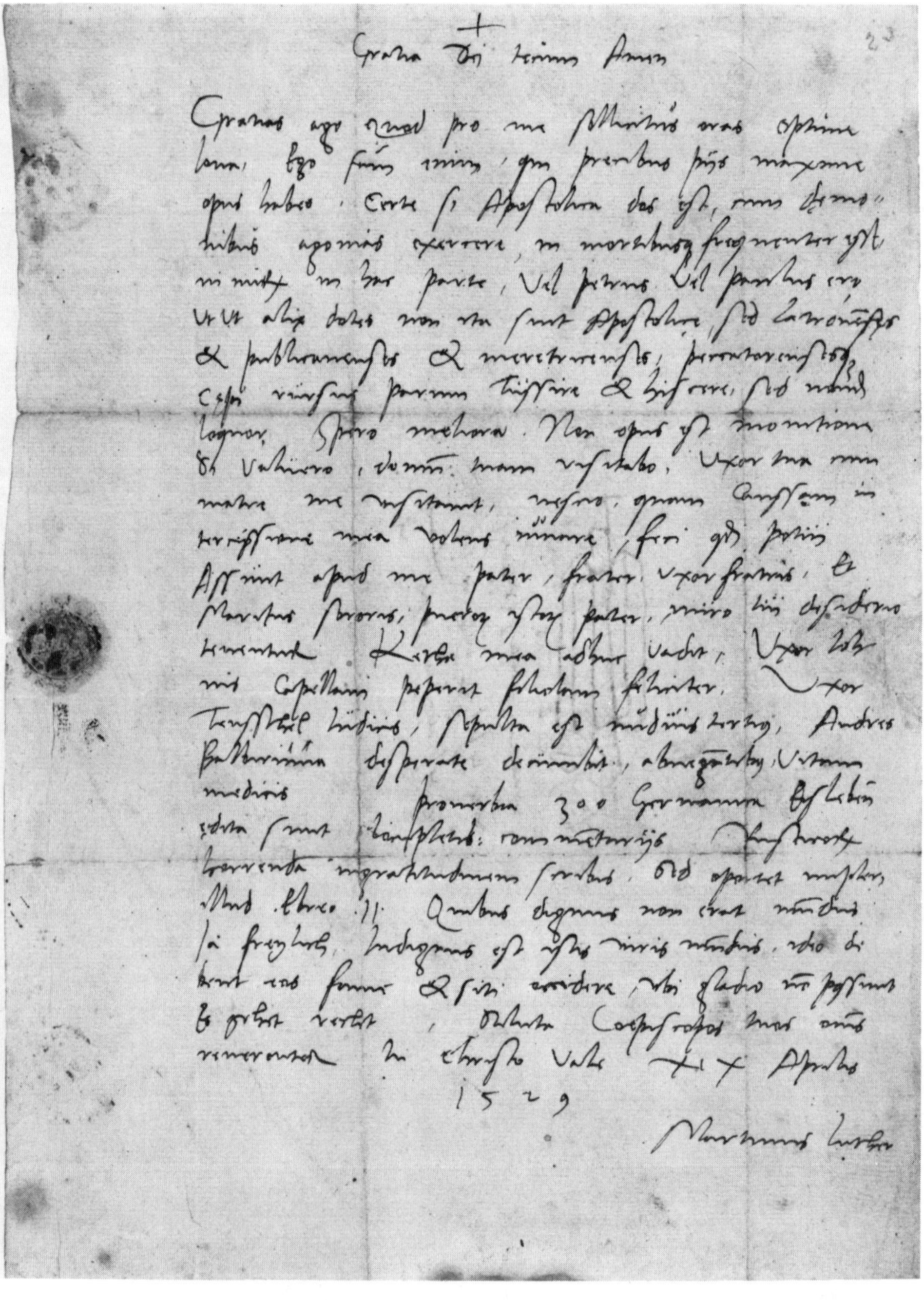

A.L.S. from Martin Luther to Archbishop Justus Jonas, April 19, 1529.
Courtesy of the Pierpont Morgan Library.

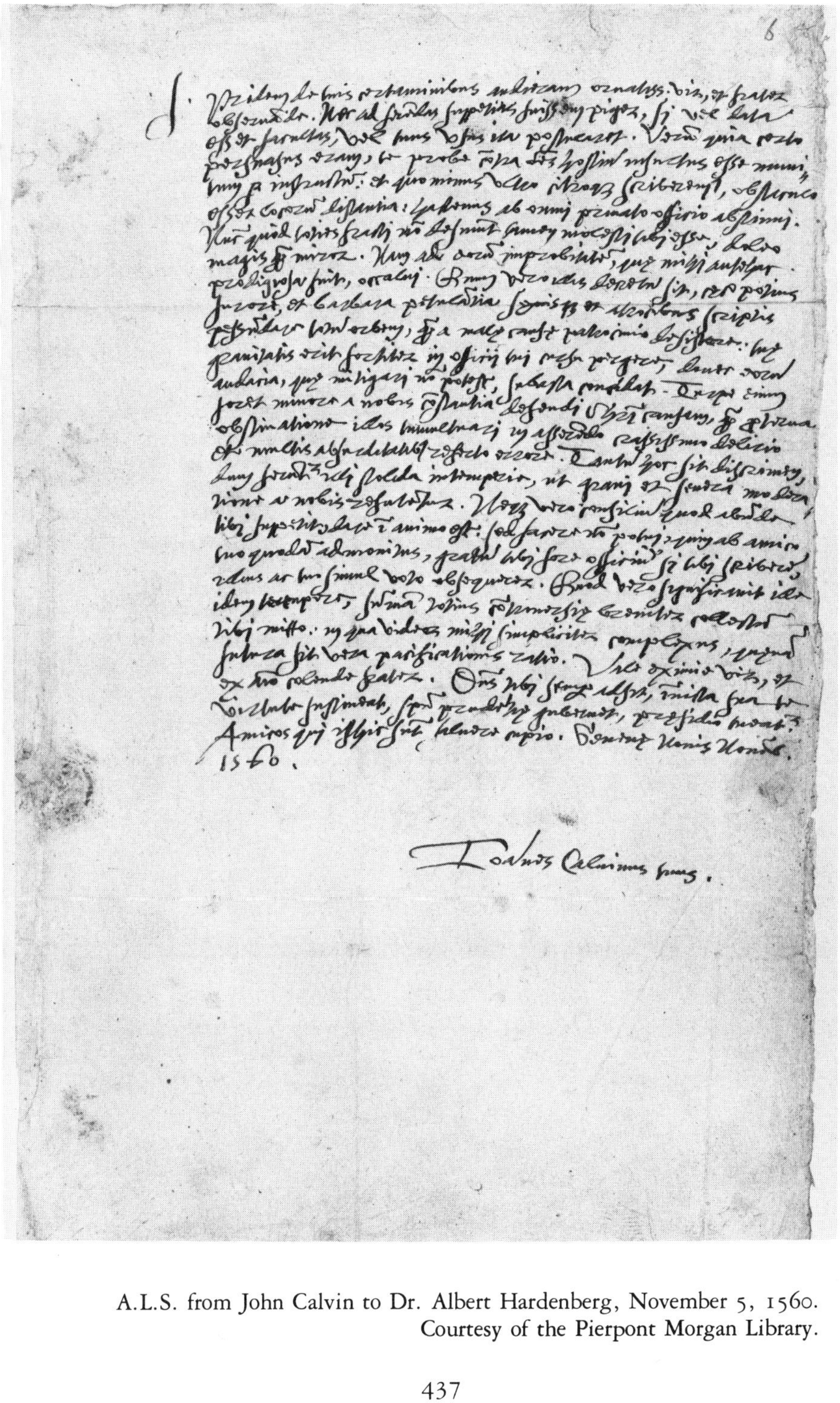

A.L.S. from John Calvin to Dr. Albert Hardenberg, November 5, 1560.
Courtesy of the Pierpont Morgan Library.

together, into those of collectors of "social movers" or of general "hall of famers."

The author should no more formulate an ecumenical principle on the basis of the last paragraph than he does while noticing that John Henry Cardinal Newman is invariably listed, in the replies to his questionnaire, with Luther and Calvin. That might have pained the cardinal even as a child. What it may say about the former and present state of the ecumenical movement is beyond the author's competence to speculate. The phenomenon may have more to do with Newman's superlative literary talents in any case, but there was certainly little in his life that was not religious in one sense or another. Newman collections abound, but it is still not difficult to begin one for fairly modest sums.*

Very likely, all things considered, Catholica is the best area in which to form substantial and meaningful collections. It is, by its very name, not difficult to collect. Letters of popes, saints, cardinals, and eminent Catholic personages are in great abundance, and usually are moderately priced. Nearly every catalog contains four or five of them, and that is the way to collect them. Some of the letters of popes as cardinals, or as holders of other offices, are far better items to own than official documents with simple "fiats," as pope, on routine clerical matters. Generally speaking, the Renaissance popes are most in demand, usually in connection with other sorts of collections. It is wise to know the history of the world well enough to know what it means when a pope writes to an Ottoman sultan or a Mauritanian "king," and when a mere cardinal nephew signs his uncle's now seemingly worthless name on a brief ordering Florence to pay dearly for the papal party on its way to Venice to launch the "Last" Crusade, aborted by the pope's death en route. It is also a good idea to know Pope Gregory X from Pope Gregory XI.†

The best sort of collections of religious autographs and manuscripts today, for intellectual challenge, realistic opportunity, investment value, and sheer achievement, would consist of letters and manuscripts of an ecumenical or transreligious nature. There is hardly a repository or dealer who would not be intrigued with and receptive to a collection of this type. With few exceptions, the prices have remained both reasonable and stable, based simply on the law of supply and demand. One dealer declares that this approach "is growing slowly, but slowly." Another says, in equally measured words, that it is "proportionate to the increase

*There are many fine Newman collections in England and the United States; the greatest of them, the Oratorian Collection at Brompton, has been microfilmed and is available at Memorial Library of the University of Notre Dame in Indiana.

†These are actual examples from the author's experience in collecting. It could be added that the science of paleography has been almost criminally neglected by many collectors and even dealers, thus subjecting facile guarantees to considerable reconsideration.

in collecting generally." The special delight in collecting religious manuscripts is, of course, as in collecting in general, *in ipso.* It is also *in genere.** One can still get a sultan's annotated golden Koran, the correspondence between two great rabbis, a Catholic saint's sermon notes, or a Zen master's secret diary for much less than one would have to pay for an early Picasso, a smudged Rembrandt lithograph, an indifferently reconstructed Grecian urn, a doubtful Aztec sundial, or a fine emerald bracelet at Tiffany's.

*The author's own collection, which has many component categories but is basically religious in nature, is housed in Alcuin Library at St. John's Abbey in Collegeville, Minnesota (a Benedictine monastery where he was a student as a young boy), which is best known in this field for its Monastic Microfilm Library, an enormously successful and ambitious initiative to preserve the great monastic collections of the world on film.

AUTOGRAPHS AND MANUSCRIPTS OF EXPLORATION AND TRAVEL

JOHN PARKER

THE LITERATURE of exploration and travel has a well-established place of prominence in Western culture. The story of the Argonauts' voyage and Homer's *Odyssey* rank among the most popular folktales of all time. Where is there an international hero equal to Columbus? Every corner of the earth has had its visitors and observers from afar. Often they have written down their impressions, and sometimes these have survived—in manuscript.

Among the earth's creatures man alone is driven from within to encounter the unfamiliar, seeking to place himself among the myriad cultures and, beyond that, to define his place in the larger structure of the universe. When the instinct to travel is curbed by the demands of life, reading and collecting the travel accounts of others is a highly enjoyable substitute, and an enlightening one, for the traveler tells not only what he sees but also what he is. He has nothing to observe with but his point of view; and his comments on what is strange to him give important insights into his culture, his personality, and his unquestioned assumptions.

It is the recognition of this intrinsic value of narratives showing man in a strange environment, surviving and observing and revealing himself, that has made travel literature so eminently collectible. The importance of geographical discoveries as historical events has also contributed to collectors' searches for accounts of exploration and travel. Yet a negative prejudice has proved a retarding factor, for "literary" scholars have seldom thought of travel literature as literature because it is largely factual in content rather than imaginative. Historians and scientists, on the other hand, have given travelers less than their due because of the amateurishness of their observations and the frequent inclusion of hearsay or imaginary materials in their writings.

What constitutes travel and exploration literature, what are its typical formats, and how do we measure its merits? Let us define it as any account of a journey to or residence in a place in which the author does not feel at home. His account may be recorded in any of a variety of forms: the report of a scientist on an expedition; the journal of a missionary; the diary of an immigrant; the letters of a soldier; a ship's log; the jottings of an itinerant merchant; the observations of an airplane pilot; and many others. Autograph signatures of important travelers, of course, belong in collections of travels in manuscript. The wise collector will cast a wide net where format is concerned—and will be ready to extend it.

Within these formats is a vast range in quality, with innumerable variations and limitations. One may choose ships' logs from one ocean or route; soldiers' letters and diaries from a particular war or campaign; missionary journals of a particular creed or place. In collecting manuscripts of travel, place will be dominant, for it is observations about a particular locale that will give cohesion to the collection. Immigrant diaries in general will not add up to much; but such diaries written about, say, the Ohio Valley or Australia will make a collection.

The merit of a travel narrative will, for the most part, be governed by three variables: the persons involved, the event, and the content of the manuscript. For example, who would not cherish a Marco Polo signature? The primacy of this traveler is enough. A Meriwether Lewis account of a casual visit to a relative would be something less than the best Lewis travel manuscript imaginable. A Lewis letter from *the* expedition that showed only his concern for family and friends at home would not be the top item either. The ultimate is the great explorer on his great expedition describing his great triumph—or defeat. Captain Robert Falcon Scott set the standards high when he wrote of his failure in Antarctica, a failure that led to his death, the approach of which he described graphically and stoically.

The world has been traveled and described by lesser figures than Polo, Lewis, and Scott. Still, where the traveler is obscure, the event and the content remain the dominant determinants of merit in the manuscript. Who would not settle for an anonymous companion of Ferdinand Magellan or Sir Francis Drake in holograph if he told the story well? And when both author and event are of minimal importance, the place can give merit to a manuscript. An eighteenth-century visit to Mt. Vernon, for example, on no particular occasion, would excite considerable demand, and rightly so. To each of us, of course, there are particu-

Above and right: Pages from a fifteenth-century copy of Jacobus de Verona, *Liber peregrinationis et indulgentie terre sancte,* with illustration of monasteries on Mt. Sinai. From the James Ford Bell Library, University of Minnesota.

d. m.

[D]e illo monte ubi portatum fuit corpus beate kathrine videtur tota arabia et totum desertum pharaonis in quo longo tempore steterunt filii israel et mare rubrum et mare de lamech et omnes montes propinqui et remoti videntur infimi ad altitudinem huius montis

[D]einde descendentes de monte cum magno labore et fatigati venimus ad Jardinum seu ortum qui est in valle qui irrigatur ab uno pulcherrimo fonte et ibidem aliqualiter refocillati assumpto nobiscum uno Calogero monacho dicti monasterii iter incepimus versus mare rubrum quod est ultra sanctam kathrinam per duas dietas et perambulavimus diebus duobus per illa deserta per rupes colles et planicies nostris pedibus cum ibi animalia vel Cameli vel asini non possunt ambulare propter viarum difficultatem tandem venimus ad mare rubrum in helym ubi populus dei ductus fuit a moyse dum transiret sicco pede per mare et pharao cum exercitu suo et curribus et equitatu fuit submersus

de mari rubro

[I]llud mare rubrum licet dicatur rubrum non habet aquam rubeam sed sicut aliud mare habet aquam claram et amaram sed quia montes circumstantes sunt rubei et terra est rubea ideo vocatur mare rubrum et habet arenam subtilissimam et bonos pisces de quibus ego ibidem comedi et non habet magnam profunditatem unde magnas naves non potest tolerare sicut naves grossas cochas vel galeas sed habet naves parvas euntes ad lamech et usque in civitatem sepulchri pessimi mahometi et usque in Indiam portantes piper gingiber Cinamomum sine[?] et alias preciosas species habet autem in una parte magnam latitudinem plus quam per quingenta miliaria et in alia parte plus quam per mille ut audivi a sarracenis a quibus per-

cancellum[?]

lar people, events, and places that have personal significance, and, therefore, a high emotional value that will not be reflected in the general manuscript market. The diary of an immigrant ancestor commenting on the new land of his choice would be a prime item for anyone with a feeling for travel manuscripts.

From Argonauts to astronauts is a vastness of time and space that invites the obvious question of what is available today for the collector. There are limits to our opportunities, and we may as well begin by recognizing them. Pre-Columbian travel materials are very rare, but not entirely unprocurable. Copies of important narratives such as the travels of Marco Polo and Sir John Mandeville do appear, but at prices in five figures. And these, of course, are copies. More readily available, but still very rare, is fourteenth- and fifteenth-century mercantile correspondence in which travel is secondary to the prices and quality of goods and other business concerns; but the awareness of distance, problems of conducting business in a strange country, and other manifestations of cultural differences give them a content to justify the travel collector's interest. The most typical genre of medieval travel narrative, the pilgrim's account of his visit to the Holy Land or to any of the numberless shrines in Europe, has all but disappeared. The number of them that were published indicates that they once were numerous. Their content is no longer considered very exciting, consisting largely of references to holy places visited; few contain more than a minimum of descriptive material.

Turning to the early phases of the age of discovery, one must not expect to find manuscripts from the great names—Christopher Columbus, Amerigo Vespucci, Ferdinand Magellan, Vasco Da Gama—showing up with any frequency. And when they do, the greatest caution should guide the collector. Such a time of heroes has been a temptation to the unscrupulous. In my judgment, more questionable travel and exploration manuscripts from the period 1450–1600 have come on the market since the 1950's than from any other comparable period. But there are authentic and collectible travel manuscripts from that time of great voyages and the beginning of empires. It was in the mid-sixteenth century that European missionaries established themselves abroad, reporting regularly to their superiors in Europe. Mercantile and colonial enterprises were taking hold in both America and Asia. The African trade served both. The stimulus of worldwide commerce headquartered in Europe resulted in increased travel for all sorts of reasons; and the accumulating wealth provided funds, especially in England, for young men seeking education to take the tour to Italy that became institutionalized in the succeeding two centuries, providing a special kind of travel narrative. But with all of this said, it must be repeated that travel narratives of any kind from the period 1450–1600 will be very rare.

In the next century and a half, 1600–1750, these types of travel accounts continued and increased. It was less a time of spectacular discovery than of empire building. The names are less well-known: administrators, churchmen, merchants, travelers for adventure, all journeying together in increased safety over established routes. The French artist Guillaume Gerlot in company with Ambrogio Bembo, an Italian aristocrat, toured the Middle East in 1672, leaving a finely illustrated description of their journey. The Jesuit Joachim Bouvet in 1698 sailed on the *Amphitrite,* the first French commercial ship to reach China, and told of the merchants' reception there. An Italian secretary, Giovanni Pietro Tasca, accompanying the French diplomat François Savary de Breves, reported hair-raising events of intrigue and assassination in Tunisia in 1606. The regularity of sailings from Europe to the far parts of the earth provides ships' logs in some number. These logs can vary from thin accounts of wind and weather to descriptions of life aboard ship and of

A.L.S. from Amerigo Vespucci to his father, October 19, 1476.
Courtesy of the Pierpont Morgan Library.

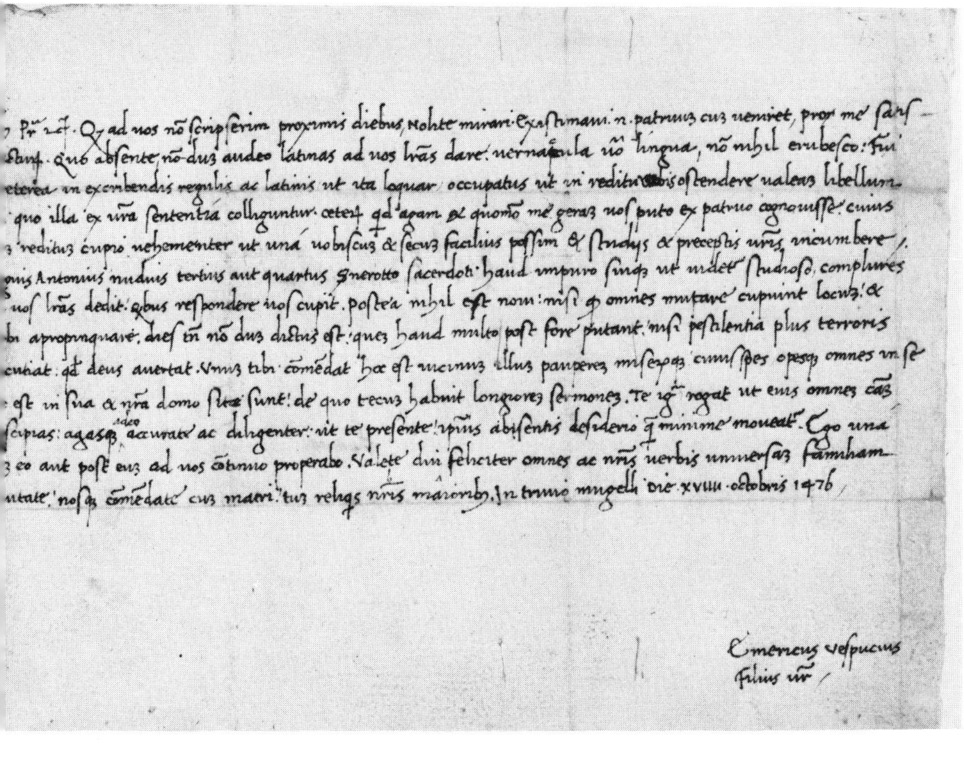

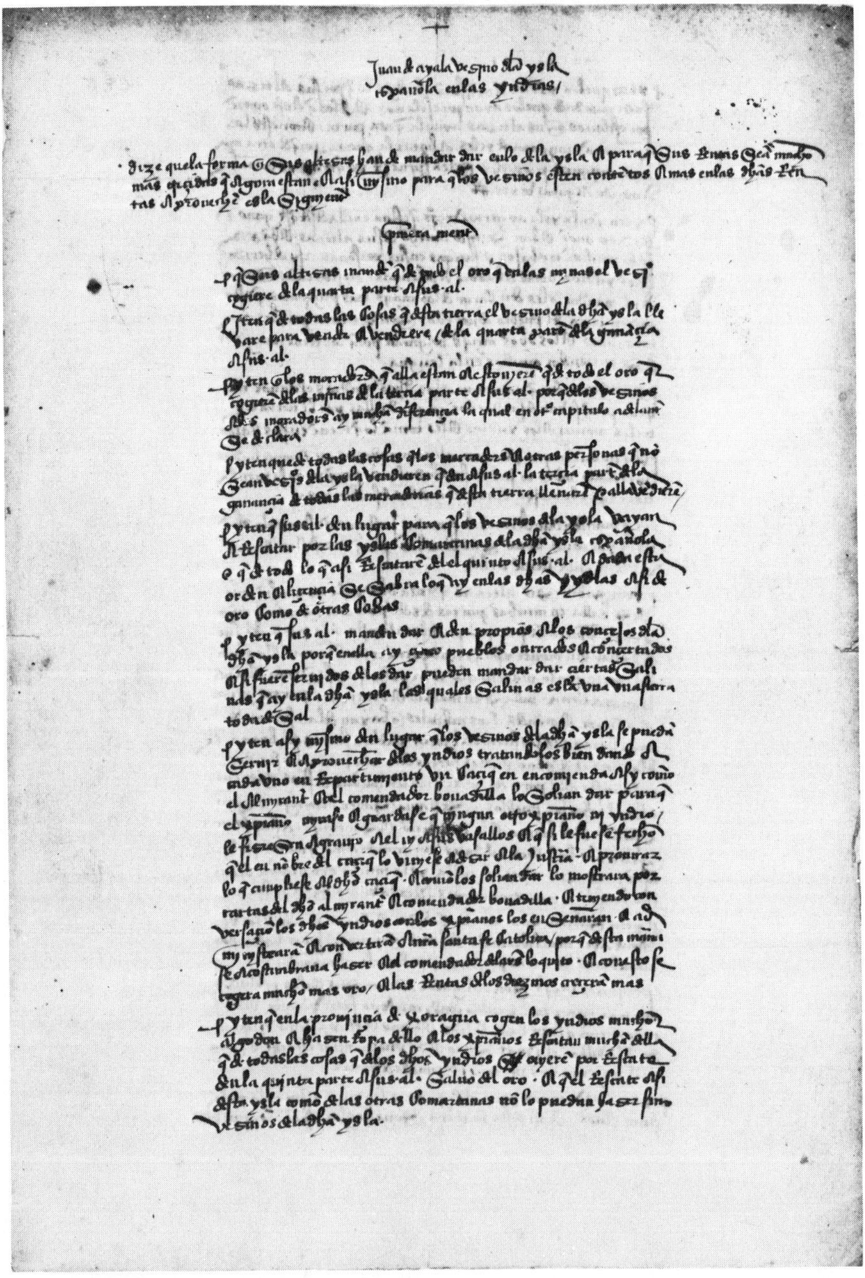

Letter from Juan de Ayala to Ferdinand and Isabella regarding conditions in Hispaniola, 1503. From the James Ford Bell Library, University of Minnesota.

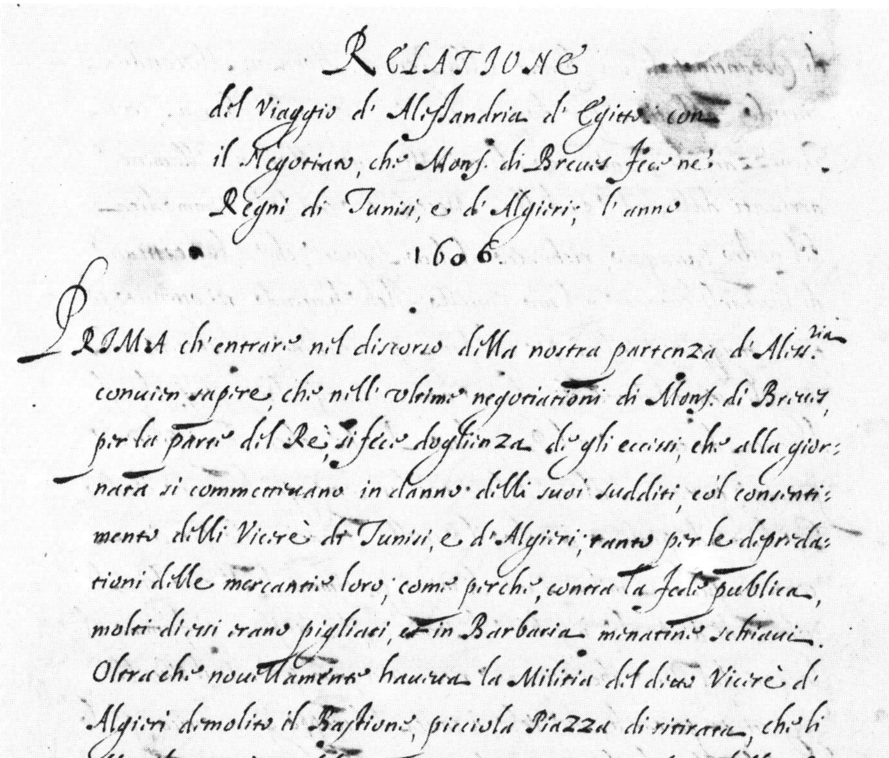

Relatione
del viaggio d'Alessandria d'Egitto con
il Negotiato, che Mons. di Breues fece ne'
Regni di Tunisi, e d'Algieri; l'anno
1606.

Prima ch'entrare nel discorso della nostra partenza d'Alessandria
conuien sapere, che nell'ultime negotiationi di Mons. di Breues,
per la parte del Re, si fece doglienza de gli eccessi, che alla gior-
nata si commetteuano in danno delli suoi sudditi, col consenti-
mento delli Vicerè di Tunisi, e d'Algieri, tanto per le depreda-
tioni delle mercantie loro, come perche, contra la fede publica,
molti di essi erano pigliati, et in Barbaria menatine schiaui.
Oltrache nouellamente haueua la Militia del detto Vicerè d'
Algieri demolito il Bastione, picciola Piazza di ritirata, che li
Marsiliesi, già qualch'anni, teneuano per commodità della Pe-
sca, e traffico del Corallo. Et hauendo il Signor di Breues dal
Gran Signore ottenuto molti ordini fauoreuoli, così per la libera-
tione de gli detti schiaui, et restitutione delle mercantie, come
per la riedificatione del detto Bastione; stimò, che, per operar
qualche buona cosa in honore del seruitio del Re, et beneficio
delli suoi sudditi, fosse necessario di passare in Barbaria, et
condurui seco un' autoreuole Personaggio, che li buoni ordini
potesse mandare ad essecutione. Menò dunque al suo partir

Title page of Giovanni Pietro Tasca's *Relatione del viaggio d'Alessandria d'Egitto* (1606). From the James Ford Bell Library, University of Minnesota.

May it please your Maj.^tie

My Necessities requiring me to go to Sea in a Merchant man, and not knowing what accidents may happen in the world; (with humble Submission) I presume (in Duty and Service to your Matie and my Country) to give your Maj.^tie the following information, with hopes my boldness therein will be pardoned.

If there should happen any Warr betwixt England and Spaine; The Citty of Sancta Phee is exceeding Rich, and lyes near the Heart of that part of the Empire of Peru, in America which the Spaniard Enjoyes, and by the best Accounts I have had they are fourty dayes Rydeing to it from Carthagena, by reason of the many Mountaines, that are in the way; And Carthagena is only a Port for the Landing of Goods, and receiving Treasure on Board, that come from that Citty, and other Inland parts there.

I beleive the Spaniard little thinks it is known in England that there is a River runs up to that Citty; And I beleive my selfe to be the first man, that ever brought Intelligence thereof to England; And that it may be of Service to your Maties; I would give an Account, what River this is, at what times of the year, and with what Craft, it may be Passed; with some other remarkable passages, that must be used by any such as undertake to go up the said River, but for what Strength may be needfull is Submitted to your Maties wisdome.

When I was in Darien, the Indian Prince or Governo^r (whose name was Diago, and who was very ready to discover the Country to me) was the first that told me, that the Maine Branch of the Great River of Darien went to the said Citty of Sancta Phee, which I never had heard of before, though I had used the Seas of America at times, as Master and Pylott twenty odd years: Upon which information given me, I began to make a further inquiry into the truth of it, which was affirmed to me; The said Indian Governo^r

having

mercantile activity in distant ports. The firm establishment of overseas trading companies produces an occasional bundle of correspondence or an archive of a mercantile family that will yield interesting travel observations.

And, of course, for the Americana collector, this period provides accounts of migration and settlement, the beginnings of the movement inland that continued unabated through the eighteenth century, producing the occasional manuscript by or about such major figures as Daniel Boone, George Rogers Clark, and Jonathan Carver. The comparative rarity of such accounts should not deter the collector from seeking traces of those who followed after them, unknowns whose descriptions of travels and settlings in the new west are not less interesting.

After 1750 a new ingredient appears. This is the scientist systematically seeking the plants, animals, and minerals of the earth, and fishes of the sea. Royal scientific societies in many countries sponsored expeditions that included specialists in many fields. They wrote formal reports on their findings, and they also wrote letters to their colleagues. For the history of science collector, such reports and letters can be the foundation stones of a collection. They represent an instance, no less than the pilgrimage, where travel was an essential part of the undertaking. One needs to cite such figures as Sir Joseph Banks, Carolus Linnaeus, Peter Simon Pallas, and Thomas Pennant among late eighteenth-century figures to demonstrate the close relationship between science and travel. The three scientifically motivated voyages of Captain James Cook, equipped with the best instruments and accompanied by some of England's best scientists, are early milestones that show the growing importance of science and the diminishing of commercial motivation in the age of discovery.

For the North American collector, the nineteenth century is probably of greatest appeal, for manuscripts are more readily available that relate to American and Canadian history and to family histories. An ancestor's diary recording the voyage to America, the journey upriver to better land, the overland trek to more freedom, the return east for more company and comfort—these are the riches of home-grown American travel narratives. If they bring less money in the sales than do the accounts of the rush to the gold fields, they are, nevertheless, enduring as sources of history—national, state, local, and family. Such tales as these have been heard from our grandparents who usually, but not always, thought them too commonplace to write down.

Left: Captain Richard Long informs his sovereign, William III, of his travels in the isthmus of Darien, 1700. From the James Ford Bell Library, University of Minnesota.

Another nineteenth-century episode in American history that has produced a substantial volume of travel narratives is the Civil War. The soldier making his way from his home to Vicksburg, to Charleston, or whatever, writes not just of war. He is aware of his travels, of cultural differences within the United States. He has adventures unrelated to the war. He unwittingly tells much of his own origins as he comments on what he sees. Civil War diaries and correspondence are not unusual documents in family papers, and will undoubtedly continue to be available to collectors of American travels for years to come.

The last half of the nineteenth century in North American history, of course, was a time of magnificent mobility that must have produced many still undiscovered travel narratives. The covered wagons that went west, the cowboys on the cattle drive, the railroads being built, and the sailing voyages around Cape Horn to California have produced more movies and television shows than their actual importance might justify. Yet this was North America putting itself together, and the abundance of books on this aspect of American history suggests more manuscripts

Pages from the 1850 journal of Edward Wortley Wharncliffe, an English buffalo hunter in the Dakotas. From the Division of Archives and Manuscripts, Minnesota Historical Society.

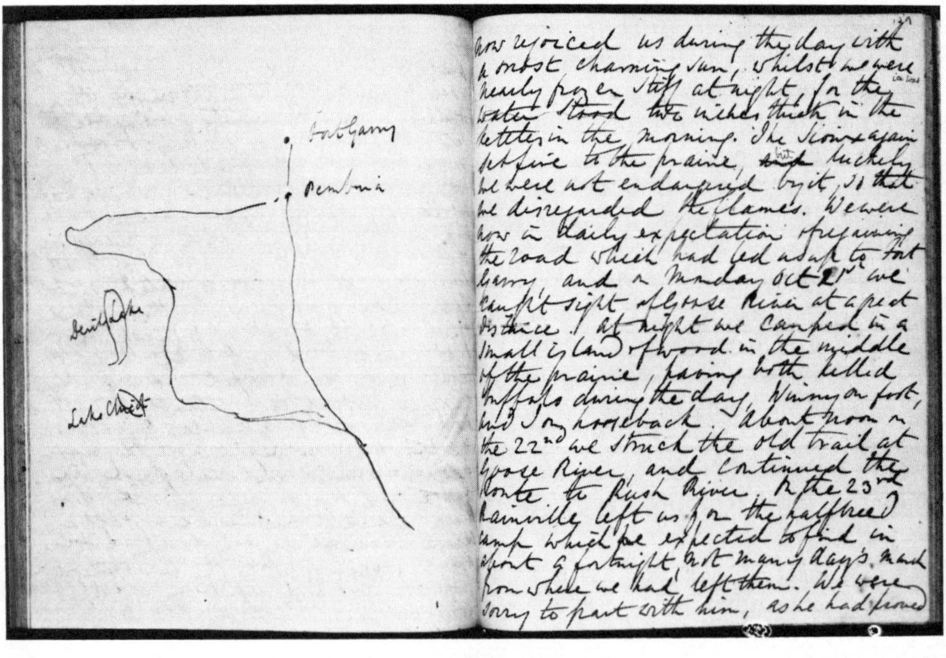

now rejoiced us during the day with
a most charming sun, whilst we were
nearly frozen stiff at night, for the
water stood two inches thick in the
kettles in the morning. The Sioux again
set fire to the prairie, ~~and~~ but luckily
we were not endangered by it, so that
we disregarded the flames. We were
now in daily expectation of regaining
the road which had led us up to Fort
Garry and on Monday Oct 21st we
caught sight of Goose River at a great
distance. At night we camped in a
small island of wood in the middle
of the prairie, having both killed
buffalo during the day, Wenning on foot,
and I on horseback. About noon on
the 22nd we struck the old trail at
Goose River, and continued the
route to Rush River. On the 23rd
Rainville left us for the halfbreed
camp which we expected to find in
about a fortnight, not many days' march
from where we had left them. We were
sorry to part with him, as he had proved

than have been collected systematically thus far. Perhaps the Buffalo Bills and Annie Oakleys have diverted our attention from the average traveler of this period whose experience, recorded in diaries and letters home, was less spectacular but the real stuff of which history is made. The era of the passenger train is about over. Who has the letters and diaries that tell what it was like to be a passenger on the Rock Island or the Northern Pacific when they were new and the land was unsettled? Such an experience must have been recorded frequently, for travelers were aware that they were participants in an exciting, nation-building enterprise. Railroad builders we have collected. Railroad riders we have yet to seek.

And where there were no rails, people rode horseback and walked. Sometimes they told what it was like. One of them wrote of making his way westward through a south-flowing herd of buffalo some fifty miles wide—a graphic word picture of man invading the animals' world on the northern plains.

If one would find the narratives of western travel that laid the foundations for communities and economic development, it is not primarily the historically important figures who must be sought out. The American west was traversed, settled, hunted, and mined by unknowns, many of whom must have written home to family and friends, for loneliness was abundant in that empty land.

If there is one major difference between travel narratives and most other types of collectible manuscripts, it is in this importance of the lesser figures. There is a distinction that needs to be made between travel and exploration. The former has generally been overshadowed by the latter because it has been easier for us to seek out the great milestones of geographical progress, the events of obvious importance, and the personalities associated with them. There continued to be great discoverers in the nineteenth and twentieth centuries, particularly in polar explorations; and the big names are still available to collectors: Charles Wilkes, Robert F. Scott, Ernest Shackleton, Roald Amundsen, Robert Peary, Richard Byrd, and others. Correspondence about their expeditions continues to turn up—some of it, alas, from typewriters—as do occasional signed photographs. New technology has changed the format, but the content is no less interesting or less important for that. And, of course, the modern expedition, in contrast with those of two centuries earlier, has a much higher percentage of literate members, thus expanding the number of manuscripts that may emerge from a single expedition.

If the generation of giants, the explorers, has come to an end, the age of the common man as traveler is only well begun. This brings me to some thoughts on new opportunities in the field of collecting.

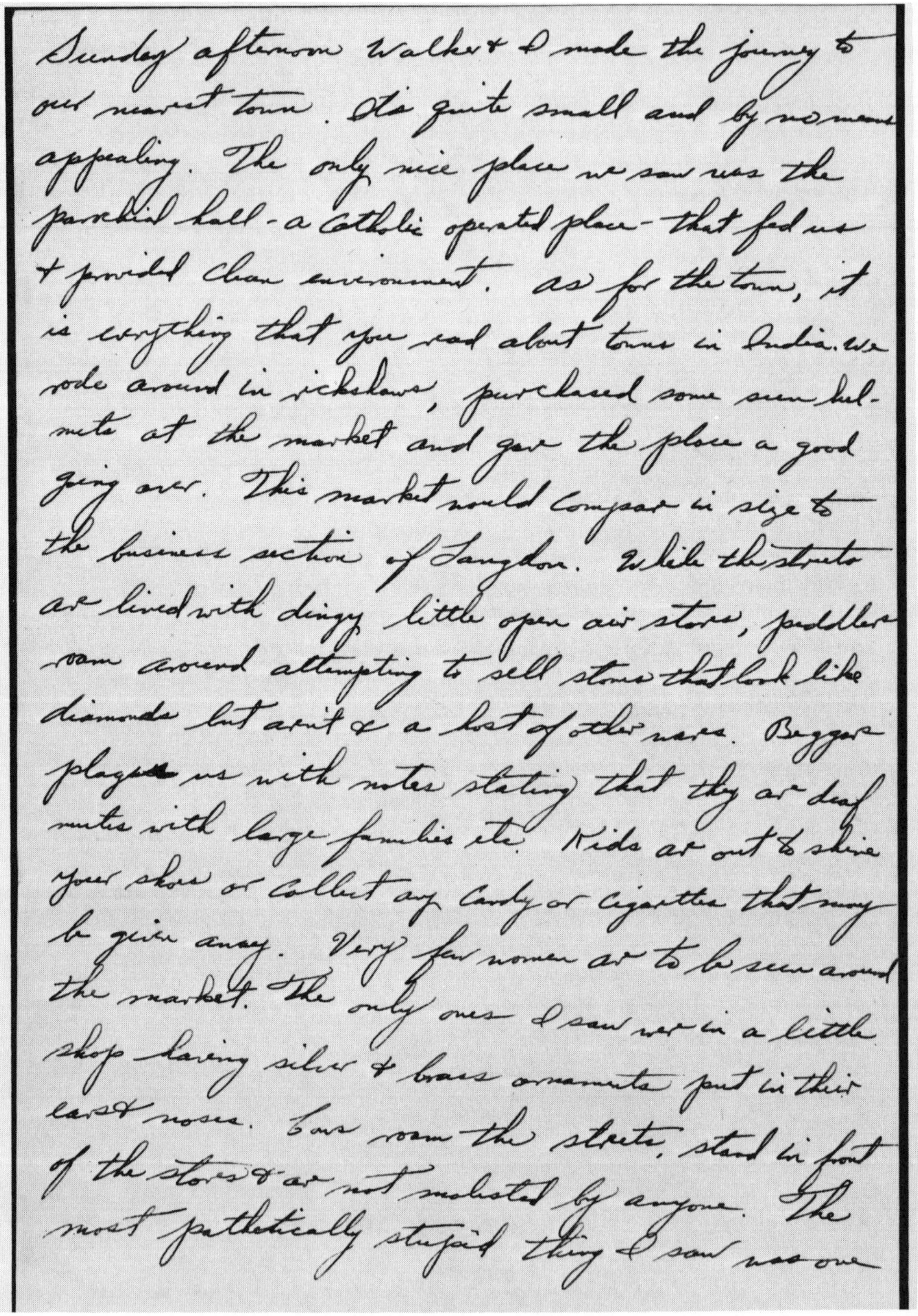
Sunday afternoon Walker & I made the journey to
our nearest town. It's quite small and by no means
appealing. The only nice place we saw was the
parochial hall - a Catholic operated place - that fed us
& provided clean environment. As for the town, it
is everything that you read about towns in India. We
rode around in rickshaws, purchased some sun hel-
mets at the market and gave the place a good
going over. This market would compare in size to
the business section of Langdon. While the streets
are lined with dingy little open air stores, peddlers
roam around attempting to sell stones that look like
diamonds but aren't & a lost of other wares. Beggars
plagued us with notes stating that they are deaf
mutes with large families etc. Kids are out to shine
your shoes or collect any candy or cigarettes that may
be given away. Very few women are to be seen around
the market. The only ones I saw were in a little
shop having silver & brass ornaments put in their
ears & noses. Cows roam the streets, stand in front
of the stores & are not molested by anyone. The
most pathetically stupid thing I saw was one

A World War II soldier writes home from India in 1944.

Within the past two generations, travel has become commonplace. Economically, diplomatically, and culturally the world has become ever more closely integrated. How did it get that way? People going from here to there. I recall my grandfather telling of his first extended automobile trip: one hundred miles over treeless, trackless prairie. He did not write it down, of course, but such narratives must exist; and they will surely surface in family correspondence and diaries. We are an automobile-dominated culture, and manuscripts from the first two decades of the twentieth century will tell a lot about the building of that culture.

And in the same way we should be looking to the generation of barnstorming pilots who proved the airplane a dependable mode of transportation to provide us with a scattering of logs and letters and other memorabilia that will tell us how the air age began. Could anything be more collectible?

Forces other than technology have been at work in the twentieth century to give mobility to the average person and thereby increase the potential volume of travel narratives for collectors. In the coming years, the attics of the Western world will yield letters and diaries no less interesting than those of the Civil War; and they will contain comments on such places as Murmansk, Bougainville, and Saipan. Young men and women discovering the world, often quite against their wishes, tell of their great adventure, their part in America's emergence as a military colossus, while Britons abroad sense the end of their imperial mission. The letters home and the diaries will be much closer to the truth about little pockets of war than are contemporary published accounts, for there is no need for propaganda. And more interesting than the mere truth of a narrative will be the honest expression of feelings: of wonder, shock, fear, admiration, disgust, homesickness. These, too, are the ingredients of conquest and empire, small parts of a great story; but more than that, they are fragments of lives. Is that not the heartbeat of manuscript collecting, after all?

AUTOGRAPHS AND MANUSCRIPTS OF RADICALS AND REFORMERS

WALTER GOLDWATER

THE COLLECTOR of autographs and manuscripts of radicals and reformers is fortunate in that, aside from those of the most obvious people—Karl Marx and V. I. Lenin, let us say—there has not been an overwhelming demand and prices are still within the sights of the less-pecunious enthusiast. Of course, the trite saying that content is everything must hold in this field as well as anywhere else. I shall digress enough here to tell briefly of my first encounter with an autograph collector in the 1930's.

Edwin Bachmann was a fine violinist and an avid, though rather parsimonious, autograph collector. He visited my shop when I was just starting in business, and told me he wanted to buy Dickens letters. In due course I located a modest letter, and offered it to him for $50. His reply has stuck with me through the years: "Mr. Goldwater, the only Dickens letter for which I would pay $50 would have to read this way, 'My dear wife, On my deathbed I wish to make this final confession. All the novels and other writings which have been published under my name were actually written by my dear friend and colleague, William Makepeace Thackeray.' " Of course, I decided to set myself the task of finding that letter for him, so I could get the $50 he had promised, but he died before I found it. I have, in fact, not located it yet.

So, in the case of radical material, it seems to me fruitless, perhaps even juvenile, to collect simple signatures of Petr Kropotkin, Mikhail Bakunin, Leon Trotsky, or Eugene Debs, when these are of no more interest than stamps or coins. What one really wants to find is the letter from Harvard's John Reed stating his reasons for breaking with the Communists; or the diary of Norman Thomas (now at the New York Public Library) searching his soul during the period in 1940–1941 when he found himself opposing help to Great Britain and, hence, on the same side as Al Smith and the Liberty League, and the record of his deep sense of relief, after Pearl Harbor, when he no longer had to keep up his "principled" position of opposing all wars, for which he had suffered so much twenty-odd years earlier. One wants to find material that is not generally known and is unpublished, but that does, or must, or—we feel—should exist.

A borderline type of case is the letter or article that has been published but has some content of importance to the writer, the movement, or the world. In the early 1920's Lenin wrote "Letter to American Workingmen," which was published in pamphlet form and is not too scarce. But the way that letter reached the United States was unique. It was typed on a piece of cloth and brought to the United States by someone in whom Lenin had confidence (rumor always had it that it was Armand Hammer, art collector and tycoon), sewn inside the sleeve of his coat. This item was for sale during my early days in the trade and I actually handled it, though I did not make the final sale and do not remember where it went.

Alexander Berkman, in his book *Prison Memoirs of an Anarchist,* tells something of the difficulty he had in communicating with the outside world. It was largely owing to this difficulty, no doubt, that his attempt to tunnel his way out of prison failed, though some people think this fiasco was due simply to the normal ineptness of radicals in the United States. During his incarceration (fourteen years, for the attempted assassination of the millionaire Henry Clay Frick) for some time, I believe, he was permitted to write only one letter a week, on one sheet eight and one-half by eleven inches. Since he had a vast number of things he wanted to say, and a great many people to whom he wanted to write, he developed and perfected a handwriting so small that it could be read only with a magnifying glass. He would thus write five or six letters on the two sides of the sheet, and these would later be copied and sent to their proper destinations. My father had one of these when I was a child; I would like to have it now, and would think it worth having.

I remember, too—again when I was quite young—that my father told me I ought to write to political prisoners, to keep their spirits up. I entered into a correspondence, mostly consisting of a chess game, with Warren K. Billings. At that time Billings was in prison in California following his conviction for involvement in the bombing of a Preparedness Day parade in San Francisco in 1916, for which he and Tom

Mooney had been condemned to death (they were later given reprieves and were finally freed). During that long correspondence he would sometimes unburden himself to me; and one letter, while not admitting any participation in the actual 1916 bombing, indicated very strongly that he had been involved in others, and that he was penitent. Such a letter would certainly be nice to have, for it would modify all accounts of the story and the whole Mooney case.

How would one begin to collect radical autographs and manuscripts? First, I suppose, one would have to decide exactly what he meant by the term and when to start: with Wat Tyler, Louis de Saint-Just, Denmark Vesey, or the Chicago Anarchists? In my own field of interest, "radical" means socialist, anarchist, or communist; its period begins about 1870, perhaps a little earlier to allow for items connected with Karl Marx, Friedrich Engels, Louis Blanqui, and the Communards, and extends to the present time. For peripheral material there would be the Utopians: John Humphrey Noyes and Edward Bellamy; and the thinkers: Thorstein Veblen and John Dewey; but generally, I think I would stick to the doers: Albert Parsons, Bill Haywood, Eugene Debs, Leon Trotsky; and the politically important people such as Josef Stalin, Karl Liebknecht, Rosa Luxemburg, Jean Jaurès, Norman Thomas, let us say. Then there are the writers—Karl Kautsky, Nikolai Bukharin, Sidney Webb (it is a little harder to think of an American in this category; who would, for instance, want to collect Alexander Bittelman or even Scott Nearing?)—who made some contribution to radical theory. The number of possibilities, however, is almost endless; at present I have a few autograph letters from certain "Anarchists of the deed," written from prison in France where they were being held before their executions for the deaths resulting from their throwing bombs into cafés in the 1880's; a letter from Friedrich Adler, who assassinated Count von Stuerckh during World War I; a few letters from Trotsky to members of the Socialist Workers Party in the United States; books inscribed by Kropotkin to his daughter; Robert Minor's Communist Party card; and a number of similar things that interest me. At this point I must note that I am not a collector and that I think keeping such items, unless they have original content, is juvenile; but I find myself utterly unwilling to part with them!

What, then, should the collector look for?

First, and least important, any autograph or inscription or brief note by anyone he considers to be a radical.

Second, any original manuscript or typescript by any such person; or original typescripts or possibly mimeographed material produced by the political parties or groups themselves, even without the name of the writer; or a letter from such a source, whether published or unpublished. I realize that as soon as the dirty word "duplicated" is used, I may be going afield; but I would not reject a carbon copy of a letter from Lenin that came from his archives (suppose he made three carbons!) or a letter from such a source, whether published or unpublished.

Third, any manuscript that is known to exist or that is assumed to exist, containing unpublished material.

And fourth, and most important, if not the only important category: material that may or may not exist but that would, if found, clarify or somehow change (or confirm, but that would be less exciting) what is generally accepted as fact. This, I feel, is the significance of the conversation about the Dickens letter mentioned earlier, after its absurdity is discounted. Typical of existing material in this category is the Norman Thomas diary. Another exciting example comes from the period just after the United States entered World War II. The Communist Party, which at that time was one of the most strongly patriotic groups (having changed its antiwar position abruptly the previous June, when Germany attacked Russia), was anxious to have the Trotskyist groups (which still, although halfheartedly, kept an anti-imperialist war position) convicted and imprisoned under the Smith Act. This act, which made it a crime to advocate the overthrow of the government by force and violence, had actually been promulgated in order to curb the activities of the Communist Party and was later used for that purpose. However, in 1942 the only group it might have fit was the Socialist Workers Party, the "official" Trotskyists. The act was invoked, and eighteen members of the party were indicted.

There was a persistent rumor that the Communist Party had sent an *amicus curiae* letter to the prosecuting attorney and the attorney general's office, as well as to the court, detailing reasons why the Trotskyists should be convicted. The Communist Party and its friends denied this, and at that time it was not established as true. The eighteen Trotskyists were convicted, and served substantial prison sentences. After the death of Earl Browder, long-time head of the Communist Party, there was found among his papers a copy of a detailed brief sent to the court pointing out in minute detail just how the Trotskyists were Marxists, and giving date, place, and line of every subversive quotation in their press, thus proving they were indeed trying to overthrow the government by force and violence. This brief is a treasure, and the autograph collector who unearths any such thing will have found at least a figurative pot of gold.

I have a detailed letter from a black scholar who tells me of his visit to Paul Robeson. He says that Robeson started to speak about his disillusionment with the Communist Party, but was physically prevented from doing so. It is only conjecture, but one feels that somewhere within the archives of the Communist Party there must exist at least one letter expressing this disillusionment or worse. Will this ever come to light? We must keep an eye out for it. And then there is the Alger Hiss case: Will there ever be found a manuscript of his, perhaps kept in a vault until after his death, or possibly in the hands of some trusted friend, that will tell the whole story?

Some of the truths will come out, and others will not; but the true autograph collector will make it his business to keep seeking. In my opinion, this is the way he will be able to justify his existence.

BRITISH THEATER AND DANCE

C. A. KYRLE FLETCHER

THE COLLECTING of theatrical autograph material has gathered momentum during recent years and presents an interesting and varied field of research for the collector who turns to entertainment as an expression of social life in the present as well as the past. There are many areas in theater history that remain uncharted and might well arouse the curiosity of a new collector. The scope of this essay is limited to the British theater and to dance.

The first and most obvious form of collecting is that of letters of famous actors and actresses—personalities who, by their very presence on the stage, attract the imagination of the audience. The names are legion from the days of Shakespeare to the present, and the collector may well consider making a representative collection of single letters beginning in the eighteenth century, with David Garrick as the most important actor. A study of contemporary playbills will present other names in his group: Spranger Barry, Samuel Foote, Charles Macklin, Catherine (Kitty) Clive, and Colley Cibber and his family. Their letters are not easy to find, but they come on the market from time to time and their rarity makes them expensive.

The turn of the eighteenth and nineteenth centuries produced another group of famous players: Edmund Kean, John Philip Kemble, Sarah Siddons, and Dorothy Jordan. Like the actors of the earlier period their letters are scarce, but a collector making a representative collection should make the effort to acquire an example of each even if the letters are not important. Kean signed many theater admission tickets, and his vigorous signature is a tangible record of his flashing personality. As the century moves on, the task of the collector eases and he will have no difficulty in finding letters of famous actors and actresses from a time when the theater moved away from classical influences to the more romantic.

A few names in this group would include Charles Kemble, brother of Mrs. Siddons, and his daughter, Fanny Kemble; Charles Kean, remembered for his pioneer work in Shakespearean production; William Charles Macready, a famous tragedian; Charles Mathews and his son Charles James Mathews, both comedians; and Lucia Mathews, known as "Madame Vestris," who demanded extra salary when she played "breeches" parts such as Macheath in *The Beggar's Opera.*

The theater of the late nineteenth century is generally thought dull, and little work has been done on this period; but names like Samuel Phelps, who produced Shakespeare at Sadler's Wells Theatre, and John Lawrence Toole, a genial and much-loved comedian, are well worth the collector's consideration; along these lines he may well find that he can work in depth, building up a group of letters centered around one actor and his circle.

At the end of the century the theater blossomed again with the careers of Henry Irving and Ellen Terry. It is not difficult to find their letters, but much research has already been done on their lives and works; however, an example of each would grace a collection. Ellen Terry's spontaneous letters, whose words exactly identify her thoughts and emotions, and Irving's, with a rigid and undemonstrative approach, present two very different personalities when placed side by side.

From the twentieth century there is abundant choice for the collector, and a real harvest may be gathered from a time when the actor-manager and the matinee idol flourished. Sir Herbert Beerbohm Tree and Sir Frank Benson are remembered for their Shakespearean productions, Sir George Alexander for his productions of plays by Sir Arthur Wing Pinero and Oscar Wilde, and Sir John Martin-Harvey for his romantic productions of *The Only Way* and *The Corsican Brothers.* But the twentieth century has also seen the fading out of the "star" actor and the emergence of the team theater exemplified in La Compagnie des

The handwriting of Edmund Kean.

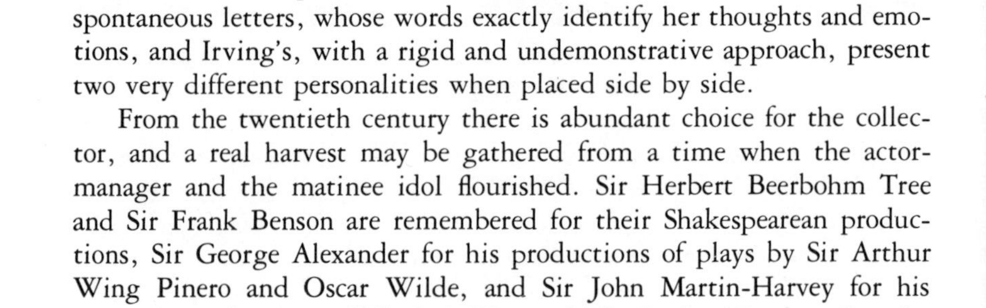

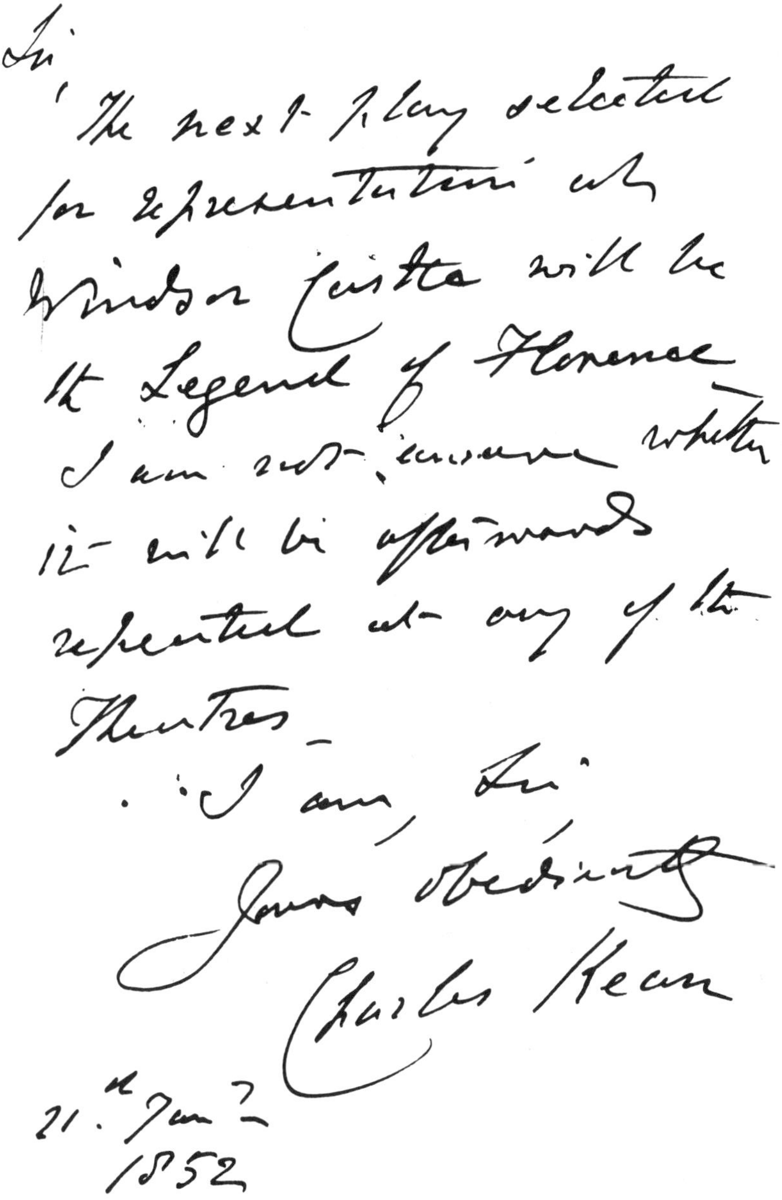

Sir,

The next play selected for representation at Windsor Castle will be the Legend of Florence — I am not aware whether it will be afterwards represented at any of the Theatres —

I am, Sir,

Yours obediently

Charles Kean

21st Jany

1852

A.L.S. of Charles Kean, January 21, 1852. By permission, Folger Shakespeare Library, Washington, D.C.

Quinze that visited London in the 1930's; and it is for the collector to back his judgment on what he believes to be good and worth preserving, recalling names like George Devine, Jacques Copeau, Michel St.-Denis, and André Obey.

Having briefly outlined possible avenues of collecting among the great stage personalities, it is important to stress the type of material the collector should aim to possess. The most interesting letters are those containing information about the place and date of production; the conditions of engagement between actor and manager; the actor's method of interpretation, for instance, in costume and makeup; and the reaction of the audience to his performance. One or two examples will serve to illustrate these points. Dion Boucicault as a very young man wrote to his mother describing his success when *London Assurance* was first produced in 1841. Janet Achurch agreed with Richard Mansfield to play Candida in 1895; she was also the first actress in England to play Nora in *A Doll's House.* Ellen Terry wrote to Sir James Matthew Barrie about her sis-

Letters of Ellen Terry and Sir Henry Irving.

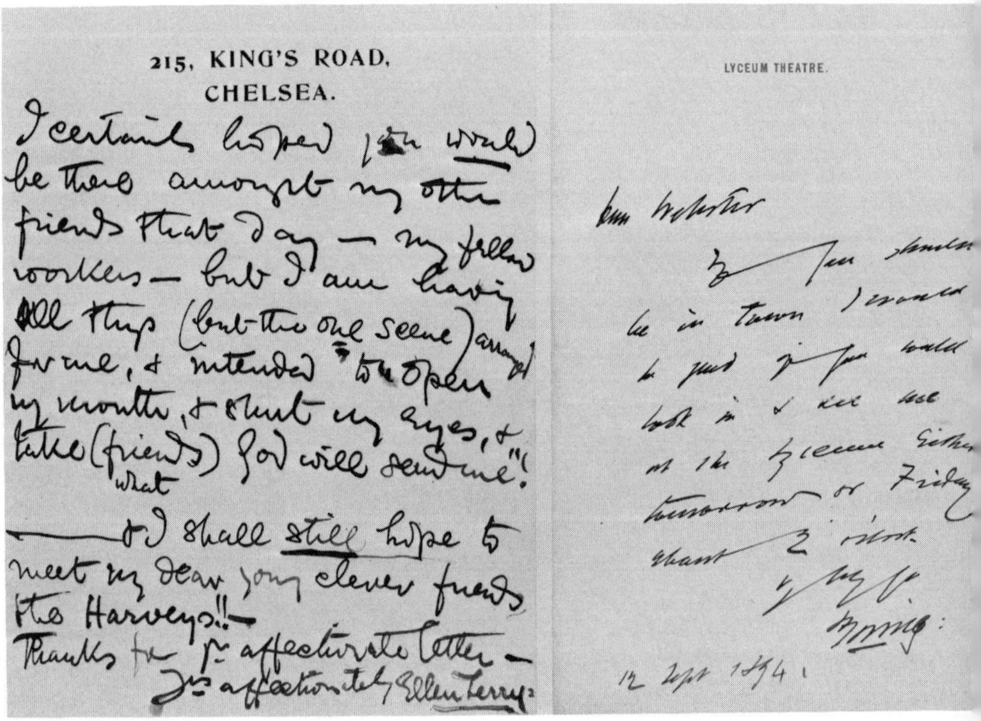
215, KING'S ROAD,
CHELSEA.

I certainly hoped you would be there amongst my other friends that day — my fellow workers — but I am having all things (but the one scene) arranged for me, & intended to open my mouth, & shut my eyes, & take (friends) what God will send me"! — & I shall still hope to meet my dear young clever friends the Harveys!! — Thanks for yr affectionate letter — Yrs affectionately Ellen Terry.

LYCEUM THEATRE.

ter Marion, who played Susan Throssel in *Quality Street.* And W. C. Macready wrote a letter of welcome to the American actor Edwin Forrest on his arrival in England, commending him on his "distinguished talent." Later their personalities clashed and a feud developed, culminating in a riot in New York.

A popular and inexpensive form of collecting is that of signed photographs of famous performers, which can be useful to the research worker if they portray the actor in costume and makeup. Almost every actor-manager at the turn of the nineteenth century and later played the part of Hamlet, as did Sarah Bernhardt, and a collection of "Hamlet" photographs would be interesting for its variety of interpretation.

The European theater presents a line of approach similar to that of the British theater; and with the exception of François Joseph Talma and Eleonora Duse, the collector will have little difficulty in finding letters of important performers such as Sarah Bernhardt, Henri-Louis Lekain, Rachel (Élisa Félix), Anne-Françoise Mars, Louis Delaunay, and Tommaso Salvini.

Having considered the players, the collector might turn his attention to the happenings backstage, where he will find still more creative activity in the realms of literature and art. As with the actors, it is difficult to find manuscript material of playwrights up to the end of the eighteenth century, and the early nineteenth century did not produce any of outstanding quality; but there are a few who still arouse interest. For instance, James Sheridan Knowles wrote several popular plays, including *Virginius* and *The Hunchback;* and James Robinson Planché was a prolific writer of burlesques, extravaganzas, and pantomimes who also advocated accuracy of costume in historical productions.

Throughout the century many adaptations of famous novels were made, and this might prove a rewarding subject for the research worker. Charles Dickens' Christmas story *The Cricket on the Hearth* was adapted and produced over and over again. Wilkie Collins' novel *Armadale* was produced under the title of *Miss Gwilt,* and interleaved copies of both these exist with the author's or adapter's manuscript alterations. Other novelists whose work was similarly used are Sir Walter Scott, Edward Bulwer-Lytton, Charles Reade, and George Du Maurier.

As the twentieth century approached, many new dramatists started to write, using contemporary social life and problems as their themes. George Bernard Shaw, Sir James Barrie, and Oscar Wilde have been avidly collected. Good unpublished letters of Wilde are scarce, but it is still comparatively easy to find those of Shaw and Barrie. Shaw's letters can be superb, for he knew exactly how he wanted his plays produced and could give practical suggestions. In writing to Paul Shelving about a dress for Miss Chatwyn in *Back to Methuselah,* he insists, "There must be no horizontal lines and no contours, only straight lines of supernatural length and fleshless slenderness, like those of a tenth century mosaic virgin." There are many other dramatists of this period, not so ardently collected, such as Sir Arthur Wing Pinero, Henry Arthur Jones, T. W. Robertson, James Bridie, John Drinkwater, and Stephen Phillips.

The play is only of academic interest until it has been brought to life by the players; and the role of the director, like the conductor of an orchestra, is to interpret the play and present his interpretation to the audience. His work coordinates not only the individual work of the actors and actresses, their grouping and movement, but also that of the scene and costume designers and the stage staff responsible for lighting, sound effects, and properties. With the advance of new mechanical techniques, direction has become more complex and the role of the director more important. There are many famous directors worthy of consideration, among them Edward Gordon Craig, Max Reinhardt, Harley Granville-Barker, Charles Dullin, Sergei Diaghilev, William Poel, and Louis Jouvet. With the exception of Reinhardt, most of whose work has already been preserved, the collector should be able to find manuscript material of these men; but if he is adventurous, he might well look to some of the more contemporary directors.

The work of scene and costume designers is obviously perpetuated in their original drawings; but in addition it is possible to find autograph letters of artists such as Charles Ricketts, Rex Whistler, George Sheringham, Léon Bakst, Adolphe Appia, and many others. As an example, Charles Ricketts wrote to Lillah McCarthy about her costume in *Arms and the Man,* "This was the first occasion when the bustle was revived on the stage, to-day no Cochraine [sic] review [sic] can do without it."

In the context of the director and his team of workers, the prompt book that is essential to their work can provide an interesting record of stage direction. This is usually an interleaved copy of the play to which the director or his stage manager adds his notes and instructions. Prompt copies are much in demand today by the research worker who wishes to reconstruct the way in which a play was produced. Recently the stage manager's copy of *Madame Sans-Gêne* by Victorien Sardou, produced by Sir Henry Irving, became available. It is annotated in great detail, for Sir Henry worked out his productions in advance with meticulous care. In addition to plans of the stage sets, lists of properties, signals for lighting changes, diagrams showing the movements of actors and stage crowds, directions for offstage noises of tramping soldiers, drums, and pistol shots, there are instructions for the makeup of each actor and the correct pronunciation of the characters' names spelled out in phonetics. An interesting fact about this production was that Sir Henry, who was a tall man, had the stage furniture built in large

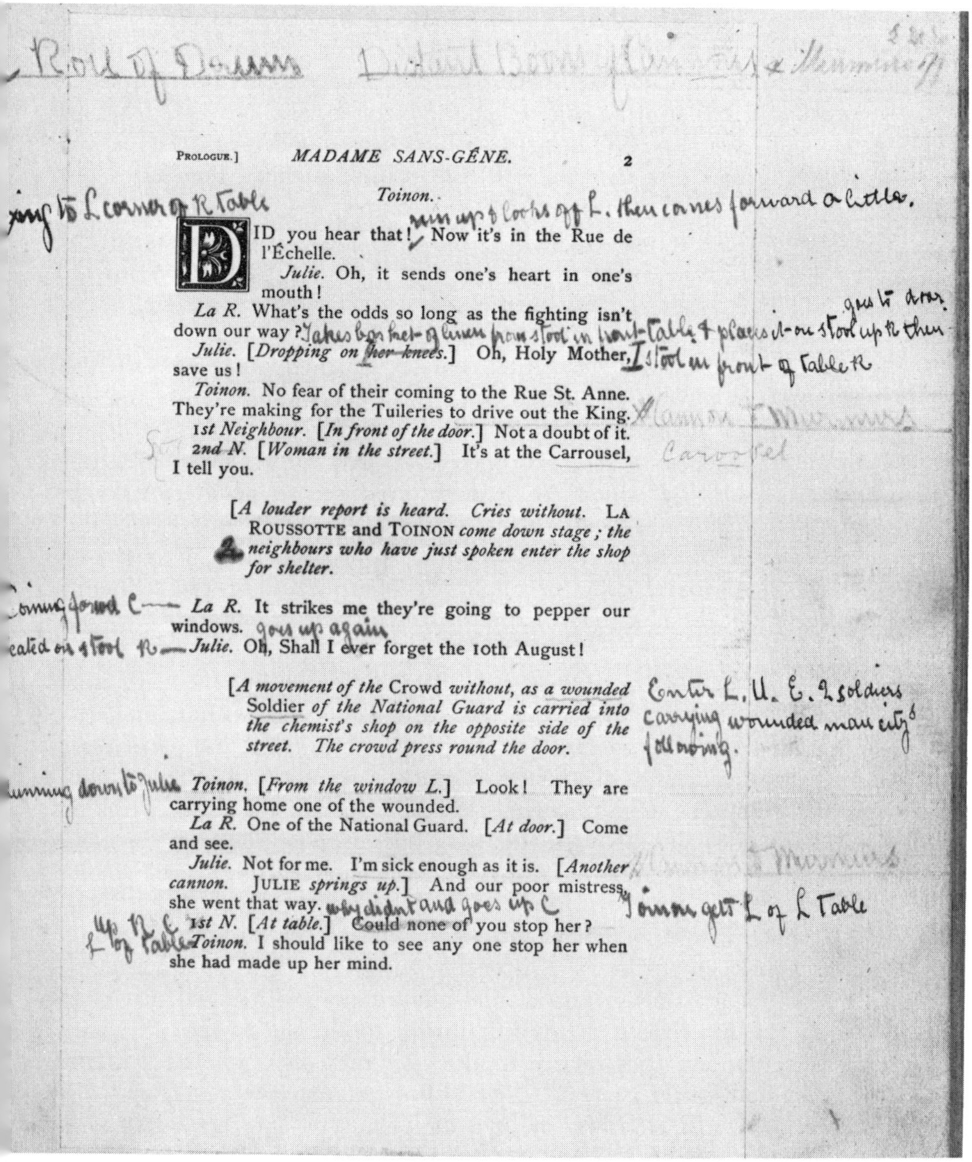

PROLOGUE.] *MADAME SANS-GÊNE.* 2

Toinon.

DID you hear that! Now it's in the Rue de l'Échelle.

Julie. Oh, it sends one's heart in one's mouth!

La R. What's the odds so long as the fighting isn't down our way?

Julie. [*Dropping on her knees.*] Oh, Holy Mother, save us!

Toinon. No fear of their coming to the Rue St. Anne. They're making for the Tuileries to drive out the King.

1st Neighbour. [*In front of the door.*] Not a doubt of it.

2nd N. [*Woman in the street.*] It's at the Carrousel, I tell you.

[*A louder report is heard. Cries without.* LA ROUSSOTTE and TOINON *come down stage; the neighbours who have just spoken enter the shop for shelter.*

La R. It strikes me they're going to pepper our windows.

Julie. Oh, Shall I ever forget the 10th August!

[*A movement of the* Crowd *without, as a wounded* Soldier *of the National Guard is carried into the chemist's shop on the opposite side of the street. The crowd press round the door.*

Toinon. [*From the window L.*] Look! They are carrying home one of the wounded.

La R. One of the National Guard. [*At door.*] Come and see.

Julie. Not for me. I'm sick enough as it is. [*Another cannon.* JULIE *springs up.*] And our poor mistress she went that way.

1st N. [*At table.*] Could none of you stop her?

Toinon. I should like to see any one stop her when she had made up her mind.

Page from the prompt book of *Madame Sans-Gêne.*

proportions so that his own height would appear diminished because the part he was playing was that of a short man, Napoleon.

The theater as a building, and its administration and finance, is another aspect of theater history. Much has been written about the two royal theaters, Covent Garden and Drury Lane, that operated under letters patent from 1662 to 1843. Their records, however, have not remained intact and it is still possible to acquire material that has been dispersed over the years. Recently documents have been found giving lists of acting companies with their salaries; lists of plays with the number of performances; lists of doorkeepers and messengers; and interesting information about the music porter's duty to call musicians to rehearsal and the presence of an attendant in the painting room to grind colors for the scene painters.

Other items that the collector might find are printed share certificates, a way by which the theater could be financed, sometimes with an attractive engraving of the ground plan of the theater, completed and signed by the manager and shareholder; and box office returns, recording the number of seats sold and their cost. Not to be forgotten is the benefit system by which the actor received the whole or part of the proceeds for a night's performance during a season. This is often mentioned in agreements between actor and manager and advertised on playbills; a pioneer collector might well be puzzled by the colloquial phrase "half a ben" [benefit] that actors used in communicating with one another.

So far the legitimate theater has been discussed; but there are other branches of entertainment, such as music hall, dance, pantomime, circus, puppetry, and cinema. The story of the music hall is a particularly interesting subject with its roots in the eighteenth century; but during Queen Victoria's reign it became a popular part of the theater, linking up with the colorful Victorian song sheets, now collected for their lithograph covers. Among many famous names in music hall are Sir George Robey, Sir Harry Lauder, Dan Leno, Marie Lloyd, "Little Tich" (Harry Relph), Vesta Tilley, and Nellie Wallace. It is easy to find their signed photographs in costume and makeup, as well as brief autograph letters; but it is not so easy to find more important material that gives an insight into their work. Worth looking for are the sketches they used in their performances. Harry Lauder, for instance, employed a master painter and writer of verse, Neil M'Fadyen, to write his "gags" and "patter." Lauder gave him the idea for a character and theme he had in mind—for instance, "If I ever marry again" or "The Boss o' the Hoose"—and M'Fadyen would write the appropriate words. Fortunately, he preserved Lauder's letters. Gus Elen, famous for his presentation of cockney life, also kept a manuscript commonplace book that contained

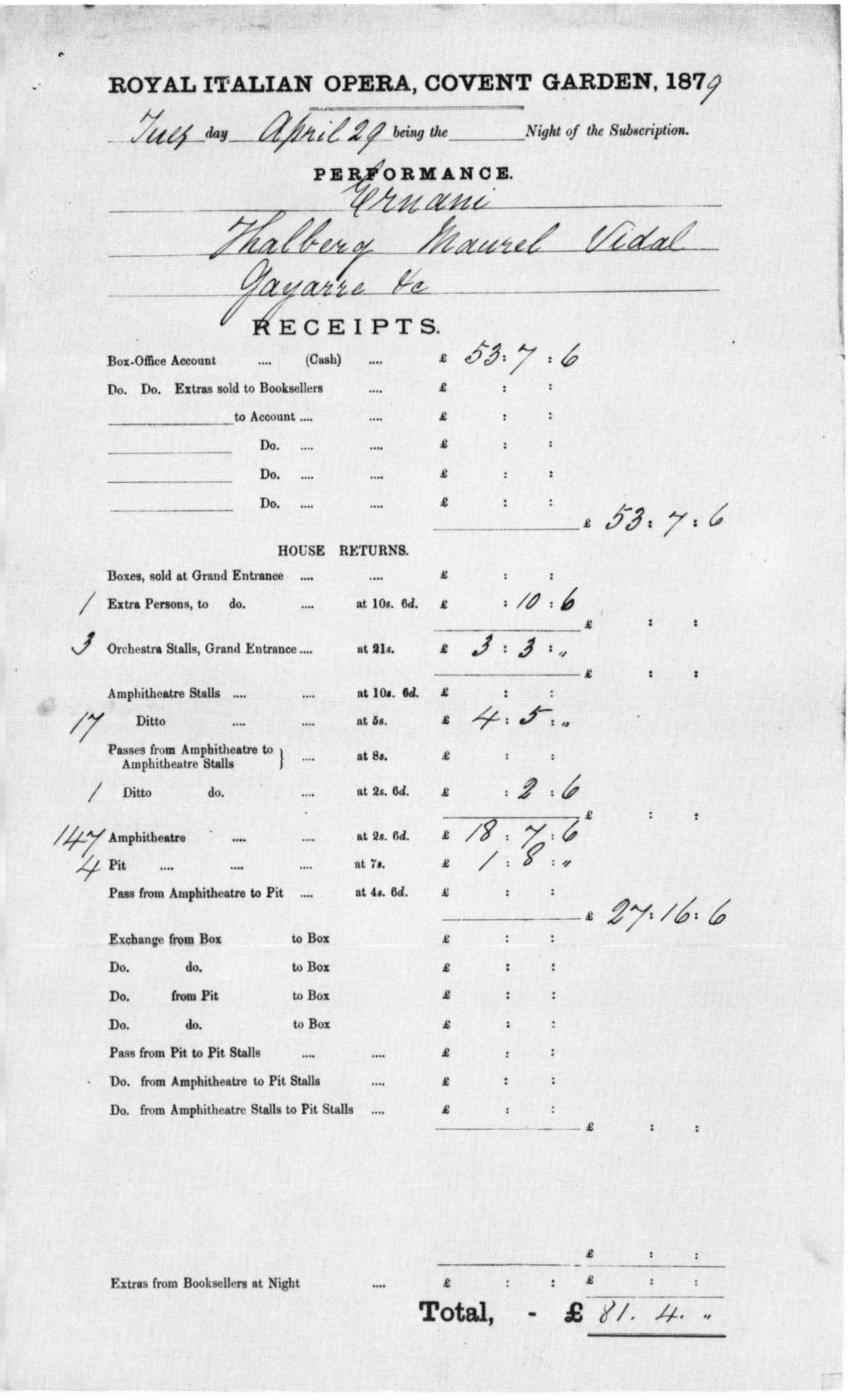

ROYAL ITALIAN OPERA, COVENT GARDEN, 1879

Tues day April 29 being the ______ Night of the Subscription.

PERFORMANCE.

Ernani

Thalberg Maurel Vidal

Gayarre &c

RECEIPTS.

Box-Office Account .... (Cash)		£ 53 : 7 : 6		
Do. Do. Extras sold to Booksellers		£ : :		
______ to Account		£ : :		
______ Do.		£ : :		
______ Do.		£ : :		
______ Do.		£ : :	£ 53 : 7 : 6	

HOUSE RETURNS.

	Boxes, sold at Grand Entrance		£ : :	
1	Extra Persons, to do.	at 10s. 6d.	£ : 10 : 6	£ : :
3	Orchestra Stalls, Grand Entrance	at 21s.	£ 3 : 3 : "	£ : :
	Amphitheatre Stalls	at 10s. 6d.	£ : :	
17	Ditto	at 5s.	£ 4 : 5 : "	
	Passes from Amphitheatre to Amphitheatre Stalls	at 8s.	£ : :	
1	Ditto do.	at 2s. 6d.	£ : 2 : 6	£ : :
147	Amphitheatre	at 2s. 6d.	£ 18 : 7 : 6	
4	Pit	at 7s.	£ 1 : 8 : "	
	Pass from Amphitheatre to Pit	at 4s. 6d.	£ : :	£ 27 : 16 : 6
	Exchange from Box to Box		£ : :	
	Do. do. to Box		£ : :	
	Do. from Pit to Box		£ : :	
	Do. do. to Box		£ : :	
	Pass from Pit to Pit Stalls		£ : :	
	Do. from Amphitheatre to Pit Stalls		£ : :	
	Do. from Amphitheatre Stalls to Pit Stalls		£ : :	£ : :
				£ : :
	Extras from Booksellers at Night		£ : :	£ : :

Total, - £ 81. 4. "

A box office return from Covent Garden, April 29, 1879.

the words of about fifty music hall songs with his notes about the "business" he introduced to accompany them.

Dance is another fascinating subject; and provided the collector does not seek material of famous dancers like Vaslav Nijinsky or Anna Pavlova, his task is not too difficult. Much more than any other branch of the theater, its scope is international. Nowadays, for example, it is almost impossible to find anything relating to the court ballet of Renaissance Italy from which the professional ballet developed in the eighteenth century, producing the famous dancers Marie Camargo and Marie

A caricature of Harry Lauder, by the noted English music hall star. From the Tracy W. McGregor Library, University of Virginia Library.

Sallé. This period is virtually out of bounds to the collector, but treasures of the romantic ballet, which came into being during the nineteenth century, may be within his reach. It is still possible to find autograph material of Gaetano Vestris and the Vestris family, occasionally a Maria Taglioni letter, likewise one of Carlotta Grisi or Fanny Cerrito, and perhaps fewer of Lucile Grahn. These four women are immortalized in the beautiful lithograph of the *Pas de Quatre* that was produced in London in 1845. Letters of Fanny Elssler, Taglioni's rival, are also to be found. In England the romantic ballet reached the height of its popularity under the management of Benjamin Lumley at the King's Theatre in the Haymarket, with Jules Perrot as ballet master. The two great

Signed photograph of Harry Lauder.

choreographers of the period were Jean Coralli and Auguste Bournonville; letters of the former are sometimes available.

After the triumphs of the romantic ballet, a reaction set in and it was not until the foundation of the Imperial Russian Ballet, for which the great ballet master Marius Petipa choreographed, that the ballet once more flourished. The Ballets Russes, under the direction of Sergei Diaghilev, was the premier ballet company from 1909 to 1929. Much has been written about this movement and much has been collected; but a persistent collector may still find letters of some of the dancers and choreographers such as Tamara Karsavina, Léonide Massine, Serge Lifar, and Michel Fokine. Although Diaghilev conducted his negotiations by telegram or through agents, written or typed agreements for engaging dancers and musicians with his signature are still available. It is not easy to find letters of Enrico Cecchetti, a great teacher who trained Pavlova, and of Nikolai Serghiev, who kept records in dance notation of many Russian ballets; this serves to remind the collector that acquiring dance material is not limited to the dancer alone. Occasionally it is possible to find autograph material of Léon Bakst, Alexandre Benois, and Mikhail Larionov, some of the important scene and costume designers of Russian ballet.

If the collector will turn to the less-spectacular revival of Russian ballet in the 1930's by Colonel W. De Basil and René Blum, he might find records that have not yet been explored. The names of Léonide Massine, George Balanchine, Tatiana Riabouchinska, and Irina Baronova come within this period.

During the twentieth century there has been a movement away from the classical ballet that has found expression in the work of Isadora Duncan, Martha Graham, Émile Jaques-Dalcroze, Ruth St. Denis, and Mary Wigman (the founder of the modern European style). Apart from Isadora Duncan, the collector's search should not be too difficult.

It becomes clear that a collector of theatrical autograph material should avoid the eighteenth century except for acquiring a few representative names, and should look to the many other areas of endeavor that come later. For example, very little attention has been paid to the British provincial theater and the circuit system, although many letters of less-known actors, actresses, and managers exist that provide source material on this subject. There is also the interchange of British and European visiting companies. Many English actors took their productions abroad; for instance, Charles Kean visited Europe, Australia, and the United States; and Sir John Martin-Harvey made tours in Canada.

Another subject that might appeal is the function of the drama critic; apart from Bernard Shaw and Sir Max Beerbohm, the critic has not received very much attention, although his power to influence audience opinion is important in setting standards of production. Now that censorship has come to an end in Britain, its history and the relations between theater management and the Lord Chamberlain's Office deserve examination. There are also interesting links between royalty and the theater: command performances at Windsor Castle; visits of royalty to the theater; associations that, for example, existed between Mrs. Jordan and the Duke of Clarence (later William IV) and between Mary ("Perdita") Robinson and the Prince Regent (later George IV).

For the imaginative collector the possibilities are wide-ranging. He should not neglect the period of change in the nineteenth century, when many new theaters were erected and when the study of archaeology and new-found knowledge influenced stage presentation, especially of the plays by Shakespeare. Although theater history has long been thought of as the Cinderella of the collecting world, the quest into its source material will unfold patterns of human activity and achievement that will bring the collector an ever-increasing satisfaction and endless amusement.

AMERICAN THEATER

FRANKLYN LENTHALL

IN COMPARISON with that of other countries, American theater history is brief; it is probably for that reason that there are so few public collections in the United States. One also assumes that there are relatively few private collections but cannot be certain because, as Sacha Guitry, a most catholic collector, remarked, the private collector is too frequently the closet collector and unless private collections suddenly appear on the market, one often is not aware of their existence. From time to time, superb material is offered for sale because of the death of individuals who had intense pleasure bringing it all together; then, too, for financial reasons the closet collector is sometimes prematurely pressured into selling. Because a very small percentage of the population of the United States buys tickets to the performing arts, it seems only logical that an even smaller percentage would be interested in the collecting and preservation of theater-related autograph and manuscript material.

In an age of audiovisual aids, the staff of most museums and theater collections have learned that the success of an exhibition (as judged by numbers in attendance and an enthusiastic press) is determined by the number of three-dimensional theater items that can be borrowed or acquired to enhance choice or rare autograph and manuscript material. For example, a copy of the last theatrical contract signed on September 22, 1890, by the great actor Edwin Booth and his distinguished partner-actor Lawrence Barrett will attract only specialists in Booth autograph material; but should articles of costuming used by these brilliant artists in their last theatrical engagements appear in the same exhibition, the average layman will view both with interest. The layman does not know that the contract is a one-of-a-kind rarity in itself and that, though comparatively rare, articles of costuming are much easier to acquire.

The Theatre Museum, Boothbay, Maine, recently acquired a stunning portrait of Edwin Booth; exhibition of this painting will be enhanced because we have the provenance provided by Blanche DeBar Booth, niece of the actor. Locating autograph material pertaining to the artist Hugo Svensen and additional manuscript material of Blanche DeBar Booth's creates a challenge. We know, of course, that Blanche was the daughter of Junius Brutus Booth, Jr., and Clementine DeBar, and that she was adopted by Ben DeBar, actor-manager brother of Clementine. He was a British subject and violent secessionist at the time of the Civil War. Manuscript material of Blanche and Ben DeBar's should be relatively inexpensive, letters selling for as little as $25.

Photograph of actors Edwin Booth and Lawrence Barrett.

Scripts used by actors in actual productions of plays are very desirable and frequently appear on the market; if directions or other comments are annotated in the actor's or director's hand, one expects to pay more for this material. The collector should keep in mind that the greater the reputation of the actor, the more one will have to pay; play scripts annotated by lesser stars of the past can be purchased for considerably less. It has been our experience that the latter group frequently provides the more exciting information for the theater historian. Henry Irving's prompt copy of *Madame Sans-Gêne* with his holograph annotations for his role of Napoleon recently sold for $150. Plays produced by Junius Brutus Booth, Jr., in which his wife, Agnes, played leading roles, copied in longhand with her annotations, were very briefly on the market and sold for $200. Of fascination for the scenic designer and theater historian are the small, simply executed, colored designs for the sets for the various acts of these plays. Sold separately for $100 was the exquisitely jeweled crown worn by Agnes when she had a leading role in *Cleopatra.*

Collecting autographs and manuscript material in the field of American theater, like all collecting, requires the skill of a Sherlock Holmes, the devotion of a fanatic, and the patience of a saint. Sacha Guitry summed it up beautifully when he wrote:

> If I could count up all the hours, days, months, years that I've spent in choosing the items in my collection, in waiting for them, hunting for them, pursuing and finding them. . . . I'm prepared to agree that you have to be a bit crazy to be a collector. Greed soon enters into it —insatiableness appears in its turn. . . .

Interestingly, Edwin Booth, a collector in his own right, expressed the preference for more "visual" items for judging the talents of actors. Writing in 1866, he said, "I have often sat down until dawn, alternating reading memoirs of the great actors of the past, and contemplating their portraits and death-masks which hang upon the walls; and somehow I seem to derive a more satisfactory idea of their capabilities from their counterfeit presentments than from the records of their lives." I would assume that "records of their lives" includes autograph and manuscript material. I doubt if many collectors of manuscript material would agree with Edwin Booth.

There is one pertinent question that concerns all Guitry's "crazy collectors"—where does one find autograph and manuscript material? Excellent material can still be obtained in unexpected places. Just recently an extra-illustrated two-volume life of Edwin Forrest by Lawrence Barrett came into the Theatre Museum. Rare playbills and superb prints are "tipped in" with an artistry that would have impressed Rev. James Granger.* Included with the playbills and engravings are letters of great rarity and, of even more exciting importance, there are ten pages from the diary of John B. Wright entitled "Last Theatrical Star Season of Edwin Forrest." Wright was Forrest's stage manager and prompter for Forrest's final tour.

Some of the best autograph and manuscript material has been used for extra-illustration in one-of-a-kind volumes. Frequently, for display purposes the collector or museum curator must offend the bibliophile by removing rare material from one of these treasured volumes.

Of equal interest are letters of agreement to contracts written by both Forrest and Wright, letters of contract that surprise the reader because of their seeming naiveté and expressed trust, especially after reviewing the last lengthy theatrical contract signed by Edwin Booth and Lawrence Barrett.

Macabre tales of rare materials being rescued from burning pyres and heaps of discarded refuse are too numerous to be reviewed with humor. I literally snatched from the flames an ancient cigar box containing all the letters that actor Joseph Proctor had written to his family while treading the boards in the fall of 1859 in an England hostile to American actors. Little is known of Proctor, but he was one of the best and most versatile actors of his period. He was what would be called today "an actor's actor"—the actor upon whom all the so-called stars call for supporting roles of major importance. These letters indicate that he resented his cool reception in England and cited as proof that his criticisms were justified the fact that the distinguished American actress Matilda Heron (of *Camille* notoriety) "paid one hundred dollars for her opening night and did not appear a second time."

The Theatre Museum was recently alerted to the fact that a local person was hauling to the dump attic rubbish including manuscript material and personal memorabilia of the famous actress Julia Arthur. Much rare material was lost, but we managed to salvage the rest. Astoundingly, the gentleman in question had been associated with Miss Arthur professionally; in fact, he had been best man at her wedding. Yet he could not imagine that her effects would be of interest to anyone. Unfortunately, American actors, with rare exception, have little feeling for preserving the theatrical past.

In recent years one of the institutions in New York City operated under the auspices of the Society for the Prevention of Cruelty to Chil-

* A vicar of Shiplake in the eighteenth century, by reputation one of the poorest theologians and preachers of his age. Little did he dream that he would be remembered for his idea of illustrating a dictionary of national biography; thus the term "grangerizing" is known to bibliophiles the world over.

Engraving of Rev. James Granger, whose biographical dictionary of England was increased to six volumes by adding illustrations and biographies taken from other books. Books that contain illustrations collected from other books are known as grangerized volumes.

dren was taken over by the Welfare Department of that city; in the process, files maintained by the S.P.C.C. were being destroyed. This society regularly employed officers who visited all New York City theaters to make certain that child labor laws were being enforced by the managers. These inspectors were a constant threat to overeager stage mothers, for their visits ensured that underage children were not appearing in theatrical productions and that those of age to appear were not exceeding the legal time limit for actual work on stage. These files, containing a veritable treasure trove of playbills with notations by the officers in charge, were rescued by a young actor who happened to be making a movie at the old Pathé studios nearby. Some of the officers were marvelously inventive and quite obviously theater buffs; not only did they follow through on their duties by reporting the required statistics of the S.P.C.C., but they also commented on the quality of the production. Of especial interest to the theater historian, they made excellent critical comments about the juvenile performances. Quite obviously the appearances of the celebrated Gypsy Rose Lee and her equally famous sister, June Havoc, came under this rigid scrutiny.

Gifts are the most satisfying source for any collector but, needless to say, they are rare. The effects of Roland Young, gifted actor, artist, and author, recently came into the Theatre Museum. His correspondence with the artistic elite of his period, plus the illustrative and manuscript material for articles and books of his creation, have proved to be the gift par excellence. Of particular interest is Young's guest book with holograph material in the form of inscriptions, poetry, and works of art by the coterie of artists with whom he surrounded himself. Exquisite drawings by Everett Shinn, Jo Davidson, and Charles Addams, interspersed with bars of music written by leading composers of the day, make of this guest book a veritable feast for the eyes. On today's market this book would sell for not less than $1,000.

Ultimately the serious collector must turn to the professional dealers in autograph and manuscript material. The choicest items in the Theatre Museum collection have derived from such reputable dealers. More and more the individual or estate selling the best material relies on the marketing expertise and contacts of the professional dealer; quite obviously the best dealers are the leading bidders for the most desirable items at auctions. Personally, I insist on indubitable authentication with, if possible, a provenance of clarity and interest. It is not unusual to see exhibited autograph and manuscript material of questionable and dubious provenance. It is more likely that the best provenance will come from the reputable dealer, as opposed to those merchants of questionable integrity or from the original source of the material. The private individual who passes on such material to the dealer or collector too frequently relies on failing memory and embroidered stories passed down with added color from generation to generation.

Unfortunately and frequently, the reputable dealer is forbidden to disclose the source of his material. Several years ago we were offered for purchase forty-five letters written by Edwin Booth to a very close friend, a less-known artist of the Hudson River School, Jervis McEntee; we had to purchase sight unseen and with the knowledge that the source would forever remain a mystery. Even more frustrating, when Edwin Booth's love poems, written to Mary Devlin in 1857, three years before their marriage (she was his first wife), were sold, the transaction was consummated with the stipulation that the source remain a mystery to the buyer. Incidentally, these poems prove conclusively that Edwin Booth did not always play the melancholy Dane.

Neophyte collectors will wonder if the most desirable material of rarity is already buried in institutional or private collections. This is an honest concern; but one must keep in mind the settling of estates, the accident of gift or discovery, and the fact that reputable dealers have the uncanny talent for unearthing new and exciting manuscript material. It is not uncommon for the dealer who has helped the collector realize the definitive assemblage of manuscript material to be instrumental in the resale of that material. Thus the neophyte with the zest for collecting will have the reward of discovering and acquiring fabulous materials.

A word of advice to the tyro collector: Avoid what could be referred to as the "overcollected" theater personalities—for example, the elder Booth and his sons Edwin (America's most famous actor) and John Wilkes of assassin fame; add to the rarity of the latter's memorabilia the rather keen competition one encounters with the multitude of Lincoln collectors, and one sees the impracticality. Letters of the elder Booth and those of Edwin Booth sell for between $100 and $200, depending on content. Because of the paucity of John Wilkes Booth holograph material and because he is overcollected by theater historians and Lincoln buffs, his letters would bring more than $1,500; it is not uncommon for an autographed carte de visite or cabinet photograph of this actor to carry a price tag of $600 to $1,000.

Add to the list of overcollected personalities the names of Edwin Forrest and Charlotte Cushman, American actors of great fame and fortune, and English actors David Garrick, Edmund Kean, Sarah Siddons, and all the Kembles, Edwin Forrest and Charlotte Cushman letters sell for an average of $65, but it has been this collector's experience that Forrest holograph material is relatively rare. Letters of Garrick, Kean, and Siddons are of great rarity and seldom sell for less than $100 if they are of meritorious content; letters of all the Kembles appear more frequently, and one should expect to pay from $75 to $100 for them.

Right: An engraving and autograph of actress Charlotte Cushman.

Below left: Cabinet photograph of Henry Irving, signed by him.

Below right: Cabinet photograph of actress Ellen Terry, signed by her in 1888.

Also to be included would be Italy's realistic and sensuous Eleonora Duse, France's Sarah Bernhardt of "farewell-tour" fame, and the fantastic Rachel. Two of these great artists gave their final performances in the United States, and the other was an outstanding favorite. Duse and Rachel manuscript material in any form is extremely rare, and $100 for letters of either of these geniuses is reasonable; for Duse a more realistic price would be $150. Lovely Ellen Terry and the enigmatic Sir Henry Irving, the famous acting team, acquired fame and fortune because of their many tours in this country and, because of their extreme popularity, are too much collected. Interestingly, until recently, though very collectible, manuscript material of Irving and Terry could be obtained by reasonable expenditure; it was not uncommon to find their letters selling for less than $50. Slowly but surely the market on these two stars is creeping up to three figures.

Of course, the fact that the artists mentioned are so "overcollected" does not preclude adding your name to existing lists; the professional dealer usually avoids partiality.

Many of America's greatest actors remain "unsung" by today's collectors; as is true in the commercial theater today, many of these artists did not achieve fame as we know it, but were good enough to cause concern and create jealous feelings in the so-called stars of their respective periods. Frequently they were called upon to support the acclaimed artists whose manuscript material we seek today. Collectors should seek out items relating to actors like Joseph Jefferson, Francesca Romana Madalena Janauschek, Lawrence Barrett, Helena Modjeska, Edward Loomis Davenport and his daughter Fanny, Tommaso Salvini, Sol Smith Russell, James O'Neill (by far a greater artist than his playwright son Eugene imagined him), Mr. and Mrs. William Jermyn Florence, and all of the Wallacks. With the exception of James O'Neill (because of the continued and growing interest in his playwright son and the Italian genius Salvini, manuscript material of the above-mentioned artists is available for prices ranging from $25 to $75. I name but a few of the many who shared their artistry and talent with American audiences.

Challenges for the novice collector are many. One of the rarest playbills is the Booth benefit for the Shakespeare Fund, held on November 25, 1864, at the Winter Garden Theater in New York City. The play presented was *Julius Caesar,* with the three Booth brothers appearing for the only time in the same performance: Junius B. Booth, Jr., as Cassius; Edwin Booth as Brutus; and John Wilkes Booth as Marc Antony. What a challenge for the collector to locate autograph or manuscript material for all twenty-four artists listed on this playbill; material relative to the production of the play; and eventually to locate an autographed program of the ceremony that took place in Central Park,

Cabinet photograph of actress Helena Modjeska,
signed by her in 1897.

Caricatures by actor Roland Young of Eugene O'Neill and his wife,
Carlotta Monterey, signed by the artist
and by the subject of each drawing.

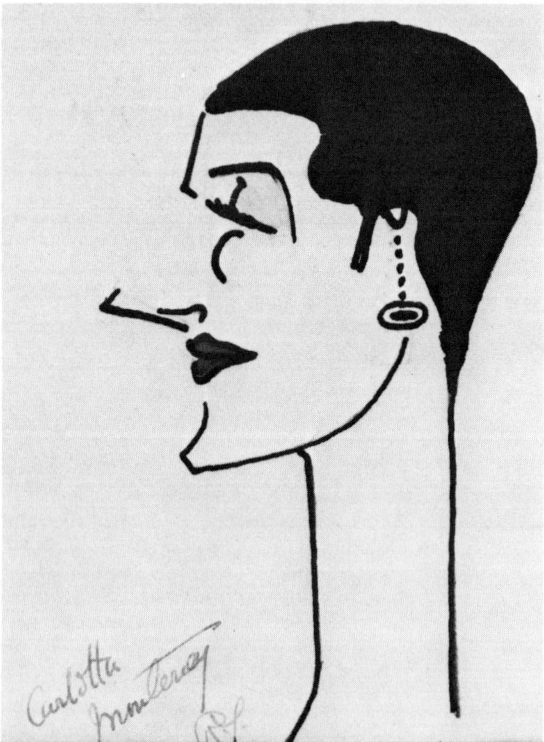

New York City, the day the statue of Shakespeare was dedicated. There is extant, for example, a long letter of Edwin Booth's offering advice to the sculptor who created the celebrated statue. The statue stands today as a further challenge to the artists of graffiti.

Though not as rare a playbill, the collector could track down one of the original playbills used the night of Lincoln's assassination and collect manuscript material involving that historic performance, beginning with Tom Taylor's original manuscript of the program for *Our American Cousin.* A warning to the collector: Beware of facsimiles of this playbill, further complicated by the fact that two different playbills were printed and used that evening of April 14, 1865.

Few people are aware that Elizabeth Arnold Poe, mother of the poet Edgar Allan Poe, was an actress of stature. Anticipate the excitement of locating a playbill of her first American performance, in Portland, Maine, on January 17, 1797, or the original manuscript of the poem she recited that evening, a poem written by a Portland gentleman:

> Tho' now like a bird of passage fly
> Where Phoebus' rays with stronger ardor burn,
> With still stronger ardor shall I seek return.
> Then I may hope at a maturer age,
> Indulged by you, to tread the Portland stage.

Mary Anne Duff (née Dyke) (1794–1857), an American actress born in London and an artist of excellence, shared the focus of the tallow with actors of great fame like Junius Brutus Booth the elder. Her appearances generated an unparalleled excitement in her time; she retired into obscurity but eventually returned to the stage in 1835. After final retirement she renounced the Catholic faith in which she had been born and educated, then entered with "great zeal" the humbler communion of the Methodist Church. She died September 5, 1857, in her sixty-third year. From that time until 1874 her grave was unknown; she had completely isolated herself from most of her contemporaries and the world of make-believe. Somewhere manuscript material relative to her theatrical and religious life awaits the diligent collector.

As a final challenge to the would-be collector, the search for manuscript material pertaining to the brief stage career and personal life of Priscilla Elizabeth Cooper could uncover a wealth of information relative to the theater of that period and, more important still, further illuminate the presidency of John Tyler. Priscilla Cooper was the daughter of Thomas Abthorpe Cooper (1776–1849), a great tragic actor of English birth who became a firm favorite with the American public shortly after his arrival; he was known for the tragic roles of Shakespeare, his best interpretation being that of Macbeth. With the decline of his popularity and fortune, as an added inducement for the increase of box office receipts he introduced his beautiful and interesting daughter, Priscilla, to the American public on February 17, 1834, in *Virginius* with Edwin Forrest as Dentatus. In the gentler line of tragic heroines she won well-merited applause from the audience and appreciation by the critics.

She continued on the stage until her marriage to Robert Tyler, son of the president-to-be, on September 12, 1839. Because President Tyler's first wife was an invalid, Priscilla was for three years the presiding lady of the White House until President Tyler married again. Her graceful dignity and courteous urbanity won universal approval; her levees were more than favorably compared with those of the great courts of Europe, and though almost totally ignored by historians, she was without a doubt one of the most popular White House hostesses. In 1843 President Tyler appointed Thomas Cooper superintendent for the United States branch mint at Dahlonega, Georgia, where he served for six years; he was afterward superintendent or chief engineer of several Southern railroads. The collector with the skill of a Sherlock Holmes, the devotion of a fanatic, and the patience of a saint could make a manuscript-autograph coup with yet undiscovered material of this fascinating father-daughter relationship; the effect of this acting duo on the presidency of our nation should prove very enlightening.

Because of the very nature of the beast, the diversity of material available to the collector of the American theater boggles the imagination. The wealth of such memorabilia needs but be synchronized with fascinating chirograph material. As, for example, bibliophilic material tempts and teases the serious collector. In September 1976 a beautifully tooled slipcased volume of Francis Wilson's *Joseph Jefferson* sold for $200. This book is unique, in that this special copy was bound in fabric from the breeches worn by Joseph Jefferson in his superb portrayal of Bob Acres in *The Rivals.* The volume carries Wilson's bookplate and his autograph inscription attesting to the authenticity of the fabric. Loosely inserted into the book are two letters, one from Jefferson to Wilson thanking him for sending a copy of the same book; the other letter is one of praise by Charles W. Stearne, who pleasantly questions one of Wilson's quotes attributed to Auguste Friedrich Ferdinand von Kotzebue in Kotzebue's play *The Stranger.* Stearne feels certain the line is Colonel Dumas's in Edward Bulwer-Lytton's *The Lady of Lyons.* Quite obviously the holograph material makes this a volume of great rarity.

One of the more reputable West Coast dealers in autographs announced in spring 1976 an extraordinary three-volume William Winter edition of *The Plays of Edwin Booth.** Extraordinary because Winter's an-

*Vols. I–II of this work are titled *The Shakespearean Plays of Edwin Booth,* while vol. III bears the title *The Miscellaneous Plays of Edwin Booth.*

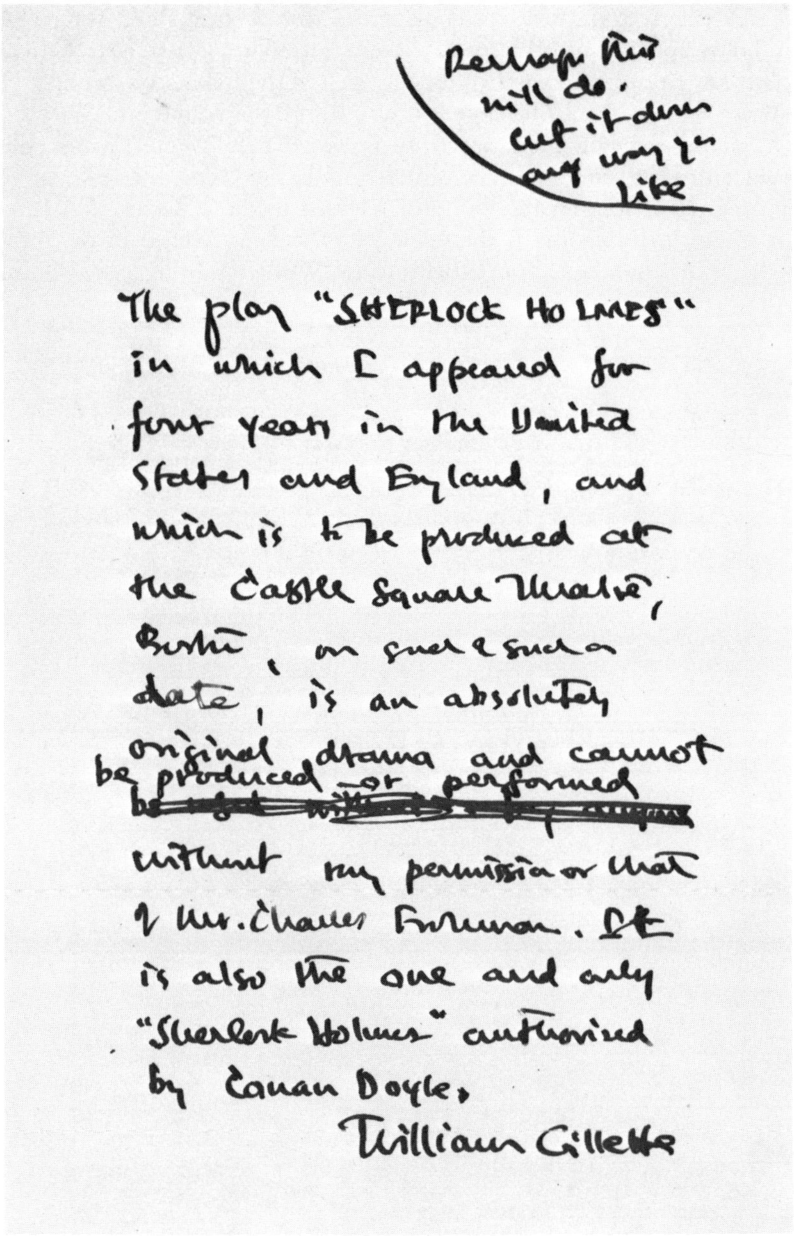

Perhaps this will do. Cut it down any way you like

The play "SHERLOCK HOLMES" in which I appeared for four years in the United States and England, and which is to be produced at the Castle Square Theatre, Boston, on such & such a date, is an absolutely original drama and cannot be produced or performed ~~[illegible]~~ without my permission or that of Mr. Charles Frohman. It is also the one and only "Sherlock Holmes" authorized by Conan Doyle.

William Gillette

A document in the hand of and signed by actor William Gillette. From the Clem D. Johnston Collection, University of Virginia Library.

notations correct the text throughout the three volumes and several of his holograph poems add special interest; important letters of Edwin Booth are tipped into each volume as well. David Belasco's bookplates indicate that the books belonged to him before they came into Winter's possession, and holograph inscriptions prove that Winter passed the books on to his son.

More esoteric, perhaps, but still relevant to the collector of American theater memorabilia is the existence of what is defined in the glass world as actress glass. The LaBelle Glass Works of Bridgeport, Ohio,

Playbill for the final performance given by actor Edwin Booth.

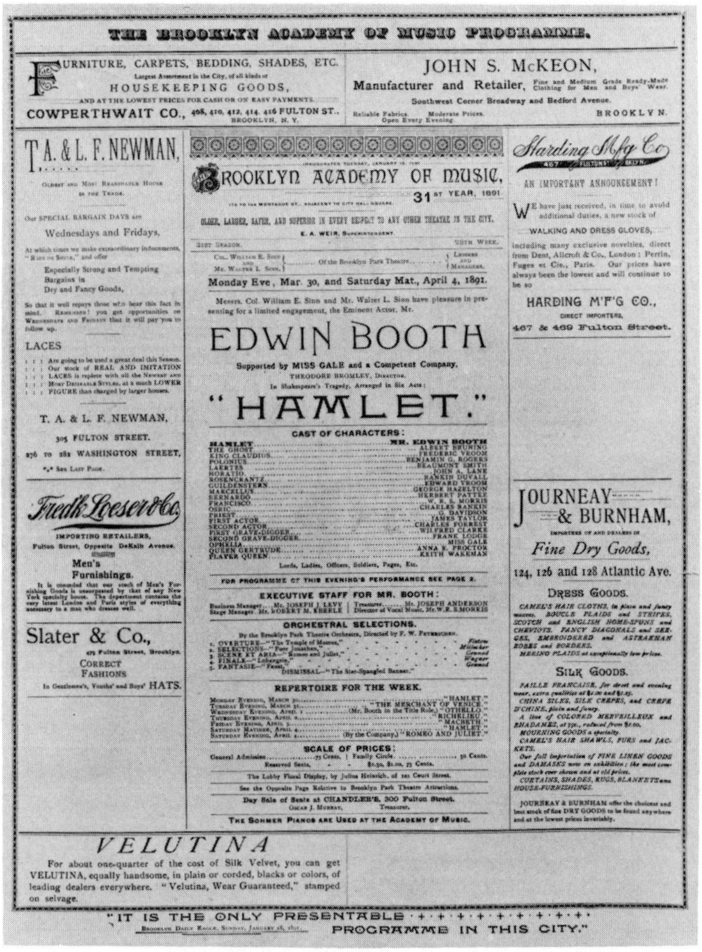

THE BROOKLYN ACADEMY OF MUSIC PROGRAMME.

FURNITURE, CARPETS, BEDDING, SHADES, ETC.
Largest Assortment in the City, of all kinds of
HOUSEKEEPING GOODS,
AND AT THE LOWEST PRICES FOR CASH OR ON EASY PAYMENTS.
COWPERTHWAIT CO., 408, 410, 412, 414, 416 FULTON ST., BROOKLYN, N. Y.

JOHN S. McKEON,
Manufacturer and Retailer, Fine and Medium Grade Ready-Made Clothing for Men and Boys' Wear.
Southwest Corner Broadway and Bedford Avenue.
Reliable Fabrics. Moderate Prices. Open Every Evening. BROOKLYN.

T. A. & L. F. NEWMAN,
Oldest and Most Reasonable House in the Trade.
Our SPECIAL BARGAIN DAYS are
Wednesdays and Fridays,
At which times we make extraordinary inducements, "Rain or Shine," and offer
Especially Strong and Tempting Bargains in Dry and Fancy Goods,
So that it well repays those who bear this fact in mind. Remember! you get opportunities on Wednesdays and Fridays that it will pay you to follow up.

LACES
Are going to be used a great deal this Season. Our stock of REAL AND IMITATION LACES is replete with all the Newest and Most Desirable Styles, at a much LOWER FIGURE than charged by larger houses.

T. A. & L. F. NEWMAN,
305 FULTON STREET.
276 TO 282 WASHINGTON STREET.
*** See Last Page.

Fred'k Loeser & Co.
IMPORTING RETAILERS,
Fulton Street, Opposite DeKalb Avenue.
Men's Furnishings.
It is conceded that our stock of Men's Furnishing Goods is unsurpassed by that of any New York specialty house. The department contains the very latest London and Paris styles of everything necessary to a man who dresses well.

Slater & Co.,
475 Fulton Street, Brooklyn.
CORRECT FASHIONS
In Gentlemen's, Youths' and Boys' HATS.

BROOKLYN ACADEMY OF MUSIC,
31ST YEAR, 1891
OLDER, LARGER, SAFER, AND SUPERIOR IN EVERY RESPECT TO ANY OTHER THEATRE IN THE CITY.
E. A. WEIR, Superintendent.
31ST SEASON. 25TH WEEK.
Col. William E. Sinn and Mr. Walter L. Sinn, Of the Brooklyn Park Theatre, Lessees and Managers.
Monday Eve, Mar. 30, and Saturday Mat., April 4, 1891.
Messrs. Col. William E. Sinn and Mr. Walter L. Sinn have pleasure in presenting for a limited engagement, the Eminent Actor, Mr.

EDWIN BOOTH
Supported by MISS GALE and a Competent Company,
THEODORE BROMLEY, Director.
In Shakespeare's Tragedy, Arranged in Six Acts:

"HAMLET."

CAST OF CHARACTERS:

HAMLET	MR. EDWIN BOOTH
THE GHOST	ALBERT BRUNING
KING CLAUDIUS	FREDERIC VROOM
POLONIUS	BENJAMIN G. ROGERS
LAERTES	BEAUMONT SMITH
HORATIO	JOHN A. LANE
ROSENCRANTZ	RANKIN DUVALL
GUILDENSTERN	EDWARD VROOM
MARCELLUS	GEORGE HAZELTON
BERNARDO	HERBERT PATTEE
FRANCISCO	W. R. S. MORRIS
OSRIC	CHARLES RANKIN
PRIEST	G. DAVIDSON
FIRST ACTOR	JAMES TAYLOR
SECOND ACTOR	CHARLES FORREST
FIRST GRAVE-DIGGER	WILFRED CLARKE
SECOND GRAVE-DIGGER	FRANK LODGE
OPHELIA	MISS GALE
QUEEN GERTRUDE	ANNA R. PROCTOR
PLAYER QUEEN	KEITH WAKEMAN

Lords, Ladies, Officers, Soldiers, Pages, Etc.

FOR PROGRAMME OF THIS EVENING'S PERFORMANCE SEE PAGE 2.

EXECUTIVE STAFF FOR MR. BOOTH:
Business Manager ... Mr. JOSEPH J. LEVY | Treasurer ... Mr. JOSEPH ANDERSON
Stage Manager ... Mr. ROBERT M. EBERLE | Director of Vocal Music, Mr. W. R. S. MORRIS

ORCHESTRAL SELECTIONS.
By the Brooklyn Park Theatre Orchestra, Directed by F. W. Petersichen.
1. OVERTURE—"The Temple of Momus," - Flotow
2. SELECTIONS—"Poor Jonathan," - Millöcker
3. SCENE ET ARIA—"Romeo and Juliet," - Gounod
4. FINALE—"Lohengrin," - Wagner
5. FANTASIE—"Faust," - Gounod
DISMISSAL—"The Star-Spangled Banner."

REPERTOIRE FOR THE WEEK.
Monday Evening, March 30 ... "HAMLET."
Tuesday Evening, March 31 ... "THE MERCHANT OF VENICE."
Wednesday Evening, April 1 ... (Mr. Booth in the Title Role) "OTHELLO."
Thursday Evening, April 2 ... "RICHELIEU."
Friday Evening, April 3 ... "MACBETH."
Saturday Matinee, April 4 ... "HAMLET."
Saturday Evening, April 4 ... (By the Company) "ROMEO AND JULIET."

SCALE OF PRICES:
General Admission ... 75 Cents. | Family Circle ... 50 Cents.
Reserved Seats, - - $1.50, $1.00, 75 Cents.

The Lobby Floral Display, by Julius Heinrich, of 121 Court Street.
See the Opposite Page Relative to Brooklyn Park Theatre Attractions.
Day Sale of Seats at CHANDLER'S, 300 Fulton Street.
Oscar J. Murray, Treasurer.
THE SOHMER PIANOS ARE USED AT THE ACADEMY OF MUSIC.

Harding Mfg Co
467 Fulton St. B'klyn.
AN IMPORTANT ANNOUNCEMENT!
WE have just received, in time to avoid additional duties, a new stock of
WALKING AND DRESS GLOVES,
including many exclusive novelties, direct from Dent, Allcroft & Co., London; Perrin, Fuges et Cie., Paris. Our prices have always been the lowest and will continue to be so.
HARDING M'F'G CO.,
DIRECT IMPORTERS,
467 & 469 Fulton Street.

JOURNEAY & BURNHAM,
Importers of and Dealers in
Fine Dry Goods,
124, 126 and 128 Atlantic Ave.

DRESS GOODS.
CAMEL'S HAIR CLOTHS, in plain and fancy weaves, BOUCLE PLAIDS and STRIPES, SCOTCH and ENGLISH HOME-SPUNS and CHEVIOTS. FANCY DIAGONALS and SERGES, EMBROIDERED and ASTRAKHAN ROBES and BORDERS.
MERINO PLAIDS at exceptionally low prices.

SILK GOODS.
FAILLE FRANCAISE, for street and evening wear, extra qualities at $1.00 and $1.25.
CHINA SILKS, SILK CREPES, and CREPE D'CHINE, plain and fancy.
A line of COLORED MERVEILLEUX and RHADAMES, at 75c., reduced from $1.00.
MOURNING GOODS a specialty.
CAMEL'S HAIR SHAWLS, FURS and JACKETS.
Our fall importation of FINE LINEN GOODS and DAMASKS now on exhibition; the most complete stock ever shown and at old prices.
CURTAINS, SHADES, RUGS, BLANKETS and HOUSE-FURNISHINGS.
JOURNEAY & BURNHAM offer the choicest and best stock of fine DRY GOODS to be found anywhere and at the lowest prices invariably.

VELUTINA
For about one-quarter of the cost of Silk Velvet, you can get VELUTINA, equally handsome, in plain or corded, blacks or colors, of leading dealers everywhere. "Velutina, Wear Guaranteed," stamped on selvage.

"IT IS THE ONLY PRESENTABLE PROGRAMME IN THIS CITY."
Brooklyn Daily Eagle, Sunday, January 18, 1891.

designed and produced this rare pattern in the 1870's. This was the golden era of the American theater, and it was during this period that many stage favorites took to the road, playing one-night stands in local opera houses. Thus it was not unusual for many of these stars to be immortalized in glass, some in roles for which they were famous and others as themselves. The LaBelle Glass Works burned in 1879. Only three actors are represented in this glass: Stuart Robson, William H. Crane, and James S. Maffit—depicted on the covered cheese dish. Eight actresses are presented on the other pieces.

Were contracts drawn up between the managers of the LaBelle Glass Works and the artists depicted on the glass? Was there any exchange of letters regarding this lively immortalizing of the stars of the golden era? Surely with diligent pursuit the interested collector could locate some intriguing manuscript material. In 1971, through the perusal of holograph material and autographed cabinet photographs in the Theatre Museum, the true identity of one of the actors portrayed on the cheese dish was established. Erroneously all books and articles on actress glass identified this man as Sanderson Moffatt in a curtain raiser entitled *The Lone Fisherman;* actually, it is James S. Maffit as The Lone Fisherman in Edward Everett Rice's *Evangeline.* Our research proved that the term "musical comedy" was used for the first time to describe this outlandish, rowdy takeoff of Longfellow's poem.

John Rogers was the first American artist to give popular appeal to sculpture. Like Currier and Ives, he was concerned with illustrating the daily life of America. He broke away from the classical style that then prevailed, believing that people would appreciate seeing sculpture of their own time. A self-taught artist, he fashioned his original models in clay and passed them on to artisans who, by means of molds, reproduced the groups in plaster. Between 1860 and 1893 he made a successful career by reproducing 100,000 copies of his eighty statuette groups. Most people are not aware that Edwin Booth posed for the Iago, Lear, and Shylock Shakespearean groups; three different Rip Van Winkle groups were posed for by Joseph Jefferson, who also posed as Bob Acres in *The Rivals.* Dion Boucicault posed for his own play *The Shaughraun.* Holograph material in the form of letters between sculptor and actor arranging time and costuming exists today, and surely a wealth of additional material awaits discovery.

Knowing the diversity of material available on the American theater, one cannot exhaust the subject in an article as brief as this. It seems worthwhile to mention the souvenirs occasionally given out in the more affluent days of the late 1800's. These diminutive gifts usually marked special days in the run of a production and were presented by the management to audiences to celebrate these anniversaries. These dated mementos make fascinating collectors' items and range in price from $25 to $100. Manuscript material exists in the form of an exchange of letters between J. and J. G. Low, of art tile fame, and the producers of *Esmeralda,* arranging for the design and manufacture of a souvenir tile celebrating the 150th performance of the play in 1891. The play's star, Annie Russell, is depicted in costume on the face of the tile with the other pertinent information. It seems reasonable to assume that other holograph material exists regarding the manufacture, design, and distribution of these souvenirs. Did the stars themselves consent to this type of portraiture?

For the seasoned or the neophyte collector, limitations usually are imposed not from without but from within. The sky is the limit; be adventuresome, be bold, and above all, be imaginative. Be prepared to spend hours, days, months, and years in choosing, waiting, hunting, pursuing, and finding. Watch out for greed and the frightening state of insatiability. You will probably be judged a bit crazy, but the enjoyment and knowledge derived are your reward.

JUSTICES OF THE SUPREME COURT OF THE UNITED STATES

GERHARD A. GESELL

COLLECTING AUTOGRAPHS AND MANUSCRIPTS of justices of the Supreme Court of the United States presents some almost insurmountable obstacles and, frequently, unexpected rewards. The ultimate is to assemble signed material on official stationery of the court, preferably on a legal subject, for each of the more than one hundred justices who have served since 1796. There is as yet apparently no collection of this kind that is complete.

Specialties are obvious. The most common is a collection covering the thirteen chief justices. Collections concentrating upon a particular justice or a particular subject that has continuously required the court's consideration, such as civil rights, should also be mentioned. Some collectors will undoubtedly show special interest in autographs of men nominated to the court who failed to be confirmed, and there is also a wealth of documentation relating to the confirmation battles over the relatively few justices whose nominations were hotly opposed but eventually approved.

Many justices have had no prior judicial experience, while others served with distinction on state or lower federal courts. Some justices had significant public careers, usually prior to appointment to the court. Thus opportunities exist for the collector to assemble manuscripts and autographs that "fill out" the justice's activities during his life. Because there were justices who were governors, candidates for president, attorney general, solicitor general, senator, and one who also served as president (William H. Taft), the possibilities are numerous once the collector moves away from items specifically attributable to the period of the justice's tenure on the court.

Autographs of early justices are particularly interesting. At the outset the justices rode circuit, sitting as trial judges; and legal material

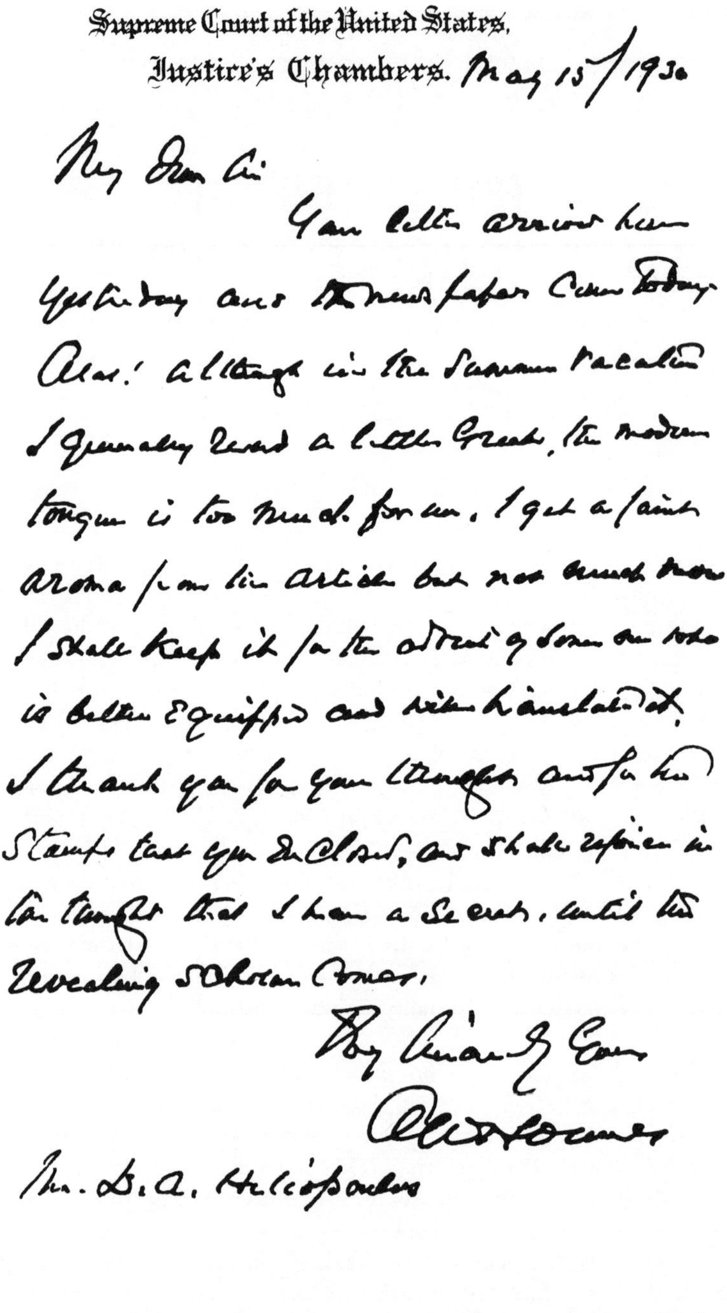
Supreme Court of the United States,
Justice's Chambers. May 15/1930

My dear Sir

Your letter arrived here yesterday and the newspaper came today. Alas! although in the summer vacation I generally read a little Greek, the modern tongue is too much for me. I get a faint aroma from the article but not much more. I shall keep it for the advent of some one who is better equipped and will translate it. I thank you for your thoughts and for the stamps that you enclosed, and shall rejoice in the thought that I have a secret, until the revealing shadow comes.

Very sincerely yours
O W Holmes

Mr. D. A. Helicopoulos

Letters of justices of the Supreme Court written on the letterhead of the court, like this example by Oliver Wendell Holmes, are the most sought-after examples for collectors in this field. From the University of Virginia Library.

over signature exists in handwritten letters to lawyers, clerks of court, and occasionally a colleague. From these early times bank drafts and letters of recommendation or introduction exist, along with purely social notes. The available material of more recent vintage, while of the same general character, is usually more self-conscious and formal. Letters to applicants for clerkships and responses to comments from citizens on particular opinions occasionally appear.

Special value attaches to material from the estates of the official reporters of the court. This takes the form of proof corrections, comments on literary style, and editorial changes of formal opinions. Occasionally an example is more amusing and highly prized, as the item below suggests:

March 13, 1935

Dear Mr. Butler,

I think you make sufficient proof of your good will toward the Court when you visit us Monday mornings and listen with such patience to the wording of opinions.

Today, however, you submitted cumulative proof when you left a fine apple for each of us, from the Chief Justice at the top to the junior associate at the bottom.

If I had to choose between the opinions and the apples, I know where my choice would fall.

Many thanks and cordial greetings.

Faithfully yours,
Benjamin N. Cardozo

Perhaps a collector's most prized items are notes sent by a justice from the bench to someone in the audience during argument. Justices often use a messenger-page to say "hello" in this delightful and sometimes revealing, informal way. These chits are very rare; and since the justice usually is on a first-name basis with the addressee, purists among us autograph collectors may not be inclined to acquire such an item.

Photographs of the full court signed by each member sitting, first-day covers, and autographed cards or notes solicited by collectors are numerous, particularly in the period since 1900. Surprisingly, some justices have recently also been willing to autograph a reproduction of an important opinion sent in with a request for signature, perhaps not realizing that this type of material is soon offered for sale. These items, of course, are not genuine manuscripts.

It must be remembered that traditionally the justices, by the very nature of their responsibilities, have lived a confined life and usually

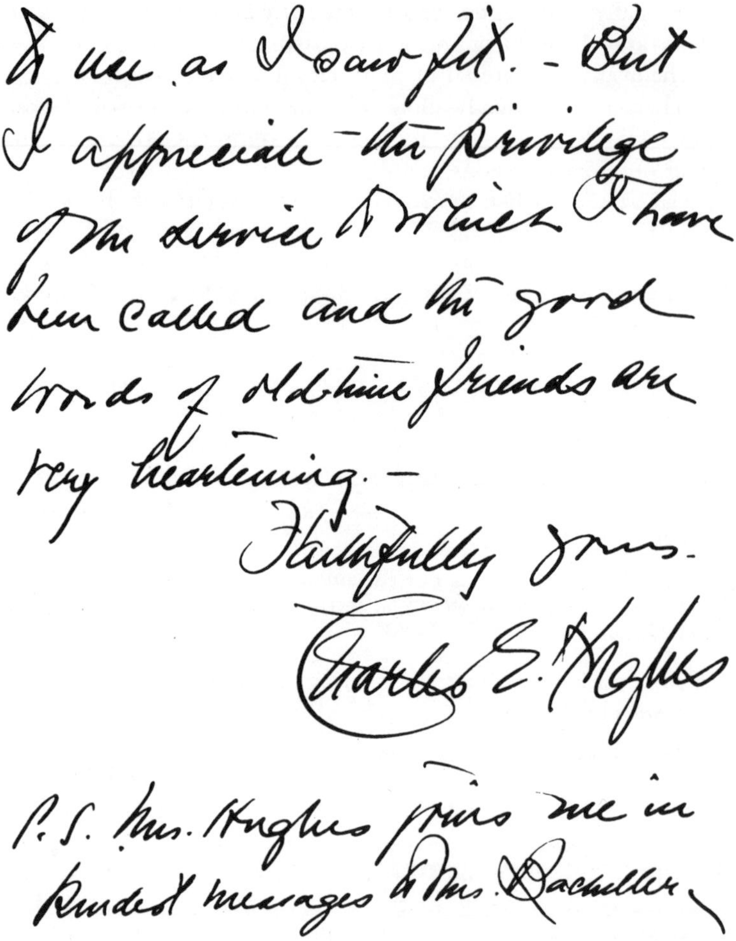

to use as I saw fit. — But I appreciate the privilege of the service to which I have been called and the good words of old time friends are very heartening. —

Faithfully yours.

Charles E. Hughes

P.S. Mrs. Hughes joins me in kindest messages to Mrs. Batcheller.

Newly appointed justice Charles Evans Hughes thanks a friend who had congratulated him on his appointment. From the Batcheller Collection, Clifton Waller Barrett Library, University of Virginia Library.

have avoided involvement in nonjudicial activities while serving as justices. Their work is done in private, and their contacts with their brethren rarely are disclosed. Their official actions remain of record only with the clerk of court. Judicial papers are often intentionally destroyed upon death or termination of service, in order to preserve the confidentiality of the court's deliberations and thought processes. Law clerks who have access to papers of this type respect their confidential relationship. If such papers are preserved, the most revealing material is passed by gift to an appropriate institution and usually does not come into general circulation.

Some justices have maintained a running correspondence with men of affairs or special acquaintances, and often the material is highly revealing. The published exchanges between Mr. Justice Felix Frankfurter and President Franklin D. Roosevelt are a recent example.

Under the leadership of Chief Justice Warren Burger, a Supreme Court Historical Society is taking shape under distinguished sponsorship. Manuscripts of the court's activity and correspondence of this type will undoubtedly gravitate more and more to this society.

In attempting to complete a full set of autographs, the collector finds the pickings very sparse as he passes back toward the early days of the court. It sometimes seems that a few justices could not write. Others had short terms and vanished with little to reflect their judicial activity. Some of the most difficult items (items that may not even exist) are of early justices who were on the bench but a short time, such as James Iredell and Howell E. Jackson, or who were nominees, such as Robert H. Harrison. Prized early items include signatures of Alfred Moore and Thomas Todd, and there are others.

As others of us who collect appreciate, however, there is always the unsettling feeling that useful items exist. They are difficult to come upon, however, and those who find a hidden possibility of course tell no one else.

This is not an area where the collector need be unduly alert for forgery or dubious authenticity. By and large the justices are private men, given to personal writing; and of course their official signatures are never but by their own hands.

In short, this is a field that will more and more challenge collectors, particularly those trained in the law.

SECTION IV

BIBLIOGRAPHY

NOTES ABOUT THE CONTRIBUTORS

GLOSSARY

INDEX

BIBLIOGRAPHY

WORKS OF GENERAL OR SPECIFIC USEFULNESS

Baker, Jay Newton. *The Law of Disputed and Forged Documents.* Charlottesville, Virginia: Michie, 1955.

Benjamin, Mary A. *The Presidents: A Survey of Autograph Values.* New York: Walter R. Benjamin Autographs, Inc., 1965. Analyses of the quality, demand, and availability of presidential material through Lyndon Johnson, but now quite out-of-date.

Binns, Norman E. *An Introduction to Historical Bibliography.* London: Association of Assistant Librarians, 1962.

Bordin, Ruth B., and Robert M. Warner. *The Modern Manuscript Library.* New York: Scarecrow Press, 1966. A short manual intended as an introductory text for professionals entering the field, but also containing useful information for the collector as well as a view of how professionals handle manuscripts.

Briquet, Charles Moise. *Les filigranes.* Amsterdam: Paper Publications Society, 1968. Facsimile of the 1907 edition with supplementary material; the standard work on watermarks.

Brumbaugh, Thomas B. "Pursuing the Documents of Art." *Auction,* 2, no. 6 (February 1969): 10–13.

Carvalho, David N. *Forty Centuries of Ink, or a Chronological Narrative Concerning Ink and Its Background.* New York: Banks Law Publishing Co., 1904. Includes the history of ink and writing instruments as well as modern (1904) inks, their uses, and other information; still cited as the standard work.

Charavay, Étienne. *Faux autographes; affaire Vrain-Lucas; étude critique sur la collection vendue à M. Michel Chasles et observations sur les moyens de reconnaître les faux autographes.* Paris: J. Charavay aîné, 1870. The noted French dealer's exposé of the forgeries of Vrain-Lucas.

Chu, Petra Ten-Doesschate. "Unsuspected Pleasures in Artists' Letters." *Apollo: A Journal of the Arts,* 104 (October 1976): 298–305.

William L. Clements Library. *Facsimiles & Forgeries: A Guide to a Timely Exhibition. . . .* Ann Arbor, Michigan: [Clements Library], 1950. This catalog lists many of the better-known facsimiles.

Deuel, Leo. *Testaments of Time: The Search for Lost Manuscripts and Records.* New

York: Knopf, 1965. Extremely interesting history of the search for and translations of papyrus scrolls, clay tablets, and other early writings in Europe, Asia, and the Americas. Contains many small facsimiles of early manuscripts as well as an excellent bibliography on this subject.

Diringer, David. *Writing.* New York: Praeger, 1962.

Duckett, Kenneth W. *Modern Manuscripts: A Practical Manual for Their Management, Care, and Use.* Nashville, Tennessee: American Association for State and Local History, 1975. While intended for the manuscript professional, this volume contains much of interest to the collector, including a bibliography, list of common facsimiles, and a list of appraisers.

Elsevier's Lexicon of Archive Terminology. Amsterdam–London–New York: Elsevier, 1964. One hundred seventy-five archival terms in six languages, defined in French.

Farrer, James Anson. *Literary Forgeries.* London–New York: Longmans, Green and Co., 1907. The standard work on these interesting frauds.

Freidel, Frank, and Richard K. Shoman, eds. *Harvard Guide to American History.* 2 volumes. Cambridge, Massachusetts: The Belknap Press of Harvard University Press, 1974. A bibliographical guide to American history; very useful in determining where to look for information on any aspect of American history.

Grebanier, Bernard D. N. *The Great Shakespeare Forgery.* New York: Norton, 1965. Concerns the forgeries of William Henry Ireland.

Greg, Walter Wilson. *English Literary Autographs, 1550–1650.* 3 volumes. Oxford: Oxford University Press, 1925–1932; reprinted Nendeln, Liechtenstein: Kraus Reprint, 1968.

Harrison, Wilson R. *Suspect Documents: Their Scientific Examination.* London: Sweet and Maxwell, 1958. A textbook for criminology students by a noted English document examiner that contains useful information for the collector interested in the detection of forgeries.

———. *Forgery Detection: A Practical Guide.* New York: Praeger, 1963. A slim guide directed to the layman who is not equipped with scientific instruments beyond a good magnifying glass.

Haselden, Reginald Berti. *Scientific Aids for the Study of Manuscripts.* Oxford: Oxford University Press for the Bibliographical Society, 1935. A standard guide to the use of ultraviolet and infrared lamps, microscopes, microphotography, and other techniques.

Heawood, Edward. *Watermarks, Mainly of the 17th and 18th Centuries.* Hilversum, Netherlands: Paper Publications Society, 1950.

Hunter, Dard. *Old Papermaking.* [Chillicothe, Ohio: the author], 1923.

———. *Papermaking: The History and Technique of an Ancient Craft.* New York: Knopf, 1943.

———. *Papermaking by Hand in America.* Chillicothe, Ohio: Mountain House Press, 1950.

Jahans, Gordon A. "A Brief History of Paper." *Book Collectors' Quarterly,* 15 (July–September 1934): 43–58.

Jensen, Hans. *Die Schrift in Vergangenheit und Gegenwart.* Berlin: Veb Deutscher Verlag der Wissenschaften, 1958.

Johnson, Allen, *et al.*, eds. *Dictionary of American Biography.* 11 volumes and

5 supplements. New York: Scribners, 1928–1977. The standard reference work for information about prominent, deceased citizens of the United States; known as the *DAB*.

Jung, Hermann. *Ullstein Autographenbuch. Vom Sammeln handschriftlicher Kostbarkeiten.* Frankfurt-am-Main, 1971. Contains much information on the history of autograph collecting as well as an indication of market values at the time of its publication.

Labarre, E. J. *Dictionary and Encyclopedia of Paper and Papermaking.* 2nd ed., revised and enlarged. Amsterdam: Swets & Zeitlinger, 1952.

Leisinger, A. H., Jr. "The Exhibit of Documents." *American Archivist,* 26 (January 1963): 75–86.

McNeil, Donald R. *The American Collector.* Madison, Wisconsin: State Historical Society of Wisconsin, 1955.

Mitchell, Charles Ainsworth. *Inks, Their Composition and Manufacture.* 4th ed., revised. London: C. Griffin, [1937?].

Moran, Hugh A. *The Alphabet and the Ancient Calendar Signs: Astrological Signs in the Origin of the Alphabet.* Palo Alto, California: Pacific Books, [1953].

Nash, Ray. *American Penmanship 1800–1850: A History of Writing and a Bibliography of Copybooks From Jenkins to Spencer.* Worcester, Massachusetts: American Antiquarian Society, 1969.

Reed, Ronald. *The Nature and Making of Parchment.* Leeds, England: Elmete Press, 1976.

Rembrandt Harmenszoon van Rijn. *Seven Letters.* Edited by J. Gerson. The Hague: L. J. C. Boucher, 1961.

Shorter, Alfred H. *Paper Mills and Paper Makers in England, 1495–1800.* Hilversum, Holland: Paper Publications Society, 1957.

Sowards, Neil. *The Handbook of Check Collecting.* Fort Wayne, Indiana: the author, 1976.

Stephen, Leslie, and Sidney Lee, eds. *The Dictionary of National Biography.* 22 volumes and 6 supplements. London: Smith, Elder & Co., 1908. The standard biographical dictionary of deceased Britons; known as the *DNB*.

Stevenson, Allan Henry. *Paper as Bibliographical Evidence.* London: The Bibliographical Society, 1962.

Strutz, Henry. "Autograph Cataloguer, Save That Album." *Hobbies,* 80 (May 1975): 154–155. Discusses many prominent European autographs and famous compendia of them, such as the *Pax Mundi* collection.

———. "Autographs and Foreign Languages." *Hobbies,* 80 (September 1975): 154–155. Points up the importance of foreign languages and parallels between language learning and autograph collecting. Its points are illustrated with facsimile signatures by many European literary personalities.

Sutherland, James, ed. *Oxford Book of Literary Anecdotes.* Oxford: Clarendon Press, 1975.

Waters, C. E. *Inks.* Circular C426 of the National Bureau of Standards, U.S. Department of Commerce. Washington, D.C.: U.S. Government Printing Office, 1940. Old but standard treatment.

Weeks, Lyman Horace. *A History of Paper-Manufacturing in the United States, 1690–1916.* New York: Lockwood Trade Journal Company, 1916.

Wilson, James Grant, and John Fiske, eds. *Appleton's Cyclopaedia of American*

Biography. 6 volumes. New York: D. Appleton, 1887–1889. Many facsimiles; though its biographical data are not always accurate, information may be found here about persons not readily locatable elsewhere.

GENERAL GUIDES TO COLLECTING

Benjamin, Mary A. *Autographs: A Key to Collecting.* New York: R. R. Bowker, 1946; rev. ed., 1963. This volume has been for many years the best and most practical introduction to the field.

Bresslau, Harry. *Handbuch der Urkundenlehre.* 3rd ed. 3 volumes. Berlin: Walter de Gruyter & Co., 1958. Originally published in 1911 and still the best work on early German and Italian official documents.

Draper, Lyman Copeland. *An Essay on the Autograph Collections of the Signers of the Declaration of Independence and of the Constitution.* New York: Burns & Son, 1889. Old but interesting commentary on early collecting efforts in these fields of specialty, but with few modern applications.

Gerigk, Herbert. *Neue Liebe zu alten Schriften. Vom Autogrammjäger zum Autographensammler.* Stuttgart: Deutsche Verlags-Anstalt, GmbH., 1974. Useful, practical handbook on all areas of autographic interest.

Hamilton, Charles. *Collecting Autographs and Manuscripts.* Norman, Oklahoma: University of Oklahoma Press, 1961. Contains useful information about autographs, combined with numerous anecdotes and personal experiences of one of the more colorful autograph dealers and auctioneers; there are also many facsimiles.

———. *Scribblers and Scoundrels.* New York: Paul S. Eriksson, Inc., 1968. A compendium of experiences and reminiscences about autographs and their forgers by the noted New York dealer and auctioneer.

Hamilton, Charles, and Diane Hamilton. *Big Name Hunting: A Beginner's Guide to Autograph Collecting.* New York: Simon & Schuster, 1973.

The Manuscript Society. *What Is Autograph Collecting?* [Somerville, Massachusetts]: the Society,[1969]. Brief pamphlet introduction to the craft.

Mecklenburg, Günther. *Vom Autographensammeln: Versuch einer Darstellung seines Wesens und seiner Geschichte im deutschen Sprachgebiet.* Marburg: J. A. Stargardt, 1963. The author is the most prominent German manuscript dealer and auctioneer; the work is a comprehensive survey of major autograph collections and activity in Germany, Austria, and Switzerland.

Munby, Alan Noel Latimer. *The Cult of the Autograph Letter in England.* London: Athlone, 1962. A survey of English collectors and collections.

Notlep, Robert. *The Autograph Collector: A New Guide.* New York: Crown, 1968. A general introduction to the craft, but not at all accurate.

Patterson, Jerry E. *Autographs: A Collector's Guide.* New York: Crown, 1973. General guide but not entirely reliable on availability, prices, and values; a good many facsimiles.

Rawlins, Ray. *Four Hundred Years of British Autographs.* London: J. M. Dent, 1970. Contains a thirty-five-page introduction to autograph collecting followed by some 120 pages of facsimiles of signatures of collectible English and British persons, plus a three-page bibliography of books containing facsimiles; the standard and very good guide to British autographs.

Rendell, Diana J., and Kenneth W. Rendell. *Fundamentals of Autograph Collecting.* Somerville, Massachusetts: Kenneth W. Rendell, Inc., 1972. A brief beginner's guide to collecting issued by a leading dealer.

Ricci, Seymour de. *English Collectors of Books and Manuscripts (1530–1930) and Their Marks of Ownership.* Cambridge, England: Cambridge University Press, 1930, 1960.

Scott, Henry T., and Samuel Davey. *A Guide to the Collector of Historical Documents, Literary Manuscripts and Autograph Letters.* London: S. J. Davey, 1891. Contains an "index of valuable books of reference, where several thousand facsimiles of handwriting may be found. . . ." as well as other interesting material.

———. *Autograph Collecting: A Practical Manual for Amateurs and Historical Students.* London: L. U. Gill, 1894. Old, but interesting for the picture it shows of the period.

Stevens, Robley D. *Enjoy Your Leisure Time: Autograph Collecting Guide.* Ann Arbor, Michigan: Edwards Bros., [1955].

Storm, Colton, and Howard Peckham. *Invitation to Book Collecting: Its Pleasures and Practices With Kindred Discussion of Manuscripts, Maps, and Prints.* New York: Bowker, 1947. A gracefully written volume that will introduce the autograph collector to fields of interest closely allied to his own.

Sullivan, George. *The Complete Book of Autograph Collecting.* New York: Dodd, Mead, 1971. A general manual of about 150 pages apparently intended for the younger person entering the field; a good many facsimiles; addresses of celebrities.

Tessier, Georges. *Diplomatique royale française.* Paris: Editions Picard & Co., 1962. The best work on French royal documents, with many facsimiles.

Williams, Robert. *Adventures of an Autograph Collector.* New York: Exposition, 1952. Forty-five pages of text are followed by fifteen pages of plates and thirty-five pages of appendices of values, association items, and so on. Unfortunately, a Robert Spring forgery, reproduced as a genuine autograph, has caused some problems.

Wolbe, Eugen. *Handbuch für Autographensammler.* Berlin: R. C. Schmidt, 1923. Considerably out of date, but contains much information that is still useful.

FACSIMILES AND HANDWRITING

See also the titles included in the "Memoirs and Reminiscences," "Musical Autographs," and "Works of General or Specific Usefulness" sections, for many contain facsimiles.

Ammann, R. *Die Handschrift der Künstler.* Bern: H. Huben, [1953].

Autographs of Prominent Men of the Southern Confederacy and Historical Documents. Houston, Texas: Cumming & Son, 1900.

Bérard, Auguste Simon Louis, *et al. Isographie des hommes célèbres, ou collection de facsimile de lettres autographes et de signatures.* 4 volumes. Paris: 1828–1843;

Supplément by Étienne Charavay, 1880. Perhaps the most useful book of facsimiles of European figures.

Brotherhead, William, ed. *The Book of the Signers: Containing Fac-simile Letters of the Signers of the Declaration of Independence.* Philadelphia: W. Brotherhead, 1861.

Cahoon, Herbert, Thomas V. Lange, and Charles A. Ryskamp. *American Literary Autographs From Washington Irving to Henry James.* New York: Dover Publications, Inc., in association with the Pierpont Morgan Library, 1977.

Carr, Paul K. *The Autographs of President Gerald R. Ford.* New York: Universal Autograph Collectors' Club, 1974. Contains reproductions of known handwriting, as well as secretarial and Autopen signatures.

Charavay, Étienne. *Catalogue de la précieuse collection d'autographes composant le cabinet de M. Alfred Bovet. La vente aura a Paris. . . .* 3 volumes. Paris: É. Charavay, 1884–1885. Many facsimiles unobtainable elsewhere.

Croft, Peter J. *Autograph Poetry in the English Language.* 2 volumes. New York: McGraw-Hill, 1973. A chronological exposition of facsimiles from William Herbert to Dylan Thomas.

Dawson, Giles Edwin, and Laetitia Kennedy-Skipton. *Elizabethan Handwriting.* New York: Norton, [1966].

Fairbank, Alfred John, and Berthold Wolpe. *Renaissance Handwriting.* London: Faber and Faber, [1960].

Friendenthall, Richard. *Letters of the Great Artists From Ghiberti to Gainsborough* and *Letters of the Great Artists From Blake to Pollock.* London: Thames and Hudson, 1963. Portraits and facsimiles, some in color.

Geigy-Hagenback, Karl. *Album von Handschriften berühmter Persönlichkeiten vom Mittelalter bis zur Neuzeit.* 1925. Contains more than thirteen hundred facsimiles and is invaluable for the great German and some European literary figures.

Grieve, Hilda Elizabeth Poole. *Examples of English Handwriting, 1150–1750 . . . .* [Essex, England]: Essex Education Committee, 1974.

Hamilton, Charles. *The Robot That Helped to Make a President.* New York: [Charles Hamilton?], 1965. Describes the Autopen and provides a guide to the recognition of secretarial and Autopen signatures of John F. Kennedy, especially through the use of clear plastic overlays bearing examples of the machine signatures; the standard guide.

———. *The Book of Autographs.* New York: Simon & Schuster, 1978. Contains more than 5,000 prices and 1,000 illustrations, with information on how and what to collect.

Hardy, William John. *The Handwriting of the Kings and Queens of England.* [London]: Religious Tract Society, 1893.

Hector, Leonard Charles. *Paleography and Forgery.* York, England: St. Anthony's Press, 1959.

———. *The Handwriting of English Documents.* 2nd ed. London: E. Arnold, 1966. A standard and accepted reference work.

Jenkinson, Hilary. *Paleography and the Practical Study of the Court Hand.* Cambridge, England: Cambridge University Press, 1915.

Johnson, Charles. *English Court Hand, A.D. 1066 to 1500.* Oxford: Clarendon Press, 1915.

Lescure, M. de. *Les autographes et le goût des autographes en France et à l'etranger.* Paris: V. Gay, 1865.

Netherclift, Joseph. *Autograph Letters, Characteristic Extracts, and Signatures, From the Correspondence of Illustrious and Distinguished Women of Great Britain, From the XIVth to the XIXth Century.* [London: J. Netherclift], 1838. Many other volumes of facsimiles of autographs were published in later years by this Englishman.

Nichols, John G. *Autographs of Royal, Noble, Learned, and Remarkable Personages Conspicuous in English History.* London: J. B. Nichols and Son, 1829.

Petti, Anthony G. *English Literary Hands From Chaucer to Dryden.* London: Edward Arnold, 1977.

Poetry. Famous Verse Manuscripts. Facsimiles of Original Manuscripts as Submitted to Poetry. [Chicago]: *Poetry,* 1954.

Quaritch, Bernard. *Facsimiles of Choice Examples Selected From Illuminated Manuscripts, Unpublished Drawings, and Illustrated Books of Early Date.* 4 volumes. London: B. Quaritch, 1890.

Rawlins, Ray. *The Guinness Book of World Autographs.* Enfield, Middlesex, England: Guinness Superlatives, Ltd., 1977. Contains 1,400 facsimiles of signatures of prominent persons in many fields of endeavor.

The Rendells, Inc. *Autograph Letters, Manuscripts, Drawings—French Artists & Authors.* Newton, Mass.: The Rendells, Inc., 1977. Contains facsimiles of the signatures of nearly all the prominent French authors and artists as well as many facsimiles of manuscripts.

Stevens, Benjamin Franklin. *Facsimiles of Manuscripts in European Archives Relating to America, 1773–1783.* 24 volumes. London: Malby & Sons, 1889–1895; reprinted in 25 volumes. Wilmington, Delaware: Mellifont Press, 1970. Contains 2,107 facsimiles.

Taylor, John M. *From the White House Inkwell: American Presidential Autographs.* Rutland, Vermont: Charles E. Tuttle Co., 1968. General characteristics of what is available; includes fine facsimiles of the signatures and handwritings of all of the presidents to the date of its publication.

Thomas, George C. *Autograph Letters and Autographs of the Signers of the Declaration of Independence.* Philadelphia: privately printed, 1908. An interesting and revealing private collection of letters and documents of the Signers.

Thompson, H. Keith, and Henry Strutz. *Doenitz at Nuremberg: A Re-appraisal.* New York: Ambler, 1977. This volume is made up of contributions from more than four hundred persons who have commented on the trial; it includes more than three hundred photographs and facsimiles of the contributors.

Warner, Sir George Frederick, ed. *Facsimiles of Royal, Historical, Literary and Other Autographs in the Department of Manuscripts, British Museum.* London: British Museum, 1899.

———. *Universal Classic Manuscripts.* London–Washington, D.C.: M. W. Dunne, 1901. Contains 150 facsimiles from originals in the Department of Manuscripts, British Museum.

William, Henry Smith. *The History of the Art of Writing.* London: Hooper & Jackson, [1902?]. Four portfolios of facsimiles, some in color—portfolio no. 1, Oriental; no. 2, classical; no. 3, medieval; and no. 4, modern—two hundred facsimiles per portfolio.

Winsor, Justin. *Narrative and Critical History of America.* 8 volumes. Boston–New York: Houghton Mifflin, 1884–1889. Contains a good many facsimiles.

Wright, C. E. *English Vernacular Hands From the Twelfth to the Fifteenth Centuries.* Oxford: Clarendon Press, 1960. Brief but sound descriptions of the change in vernacular handwriting; well illustrated by twenty-four full-page illustrations.

MEMOIRS AND REMINISCENCES

Broadley, Alexander Myrick. *Chats on Autographs.* New York: Frederick A. Stokes Co., [1910]. Reminiscences of an English dealer containing general advice to the collector.

Charnwood, [Dorothea Mary Roby (Thorpe)], Lady. *An Autograph Collection and the Making of It.* New York: Henry Holt, [1930]. In this and other volumes, a great English collector relates some of her experiences.

Goodspeed, Charles. *Yankee Bookseller.* Boston: Houghton Mifflin, 1937. Memoirs of the noted Boston bookseller who also handled autographs.

Gratz, Simon. *A Book About Autographs.* Philadelphia: William J. Campbell, 1920. A general book about collecting, including considerable information about European and American collections, both private and public, and about forgers; concludes with a useful dialogue between Mr. Old and Mr. Young on rarities and other subjects.

Hill, George Birckbeck. *Talks About Autographs.* Boston–New York: Houghton Mifflin, 1896. General description of the collection of this English gentleman, accompanied by a few facsimiles; few American autographs mentioned.

Joline, Adrian H. *Meditations of an Autograph Collector.* New York: Harper & Bros., 1902. Another collector's memoirs.

Madigan, Thomas F. *Word Shadows of the Great.* New York: Frederick A. Stokes, 1930. Interesting reminiscences of an early twentieth-century manuscript dealer.

Muir, Percival Horace. *Minding My Own Business.* London: Chatto & Windus, 1956. Memoirs of a book dealer who searched the Continent for musical manuscripts and rare printed items in the 1930's.

Osborn, James M. *Neo-philobiblon: Ruminations on Manuscript Collecting.* Austin, Texas: Humanities Research Center of the University of Texas, 1973. Memoirs of the great collector whose collection of pre-1815 British material, including manuscripts, is now at Yale.

Rosenbach, Abraham S. Wolf. *Books and Bidders.* Boston: Little Brown, 1927.

———. *A Book Hunter's Holiday: Adventures With Books and Manuscripts.* Boston–New York: Houghton Mifflin, 1936. This book, and the one immediately above, contain the reminiscences of one of the greatest collectors and dealers of modern times.

Sims, George Robert. *Among My Autographs.* London: Chatto & Windus, 1904. A collector's memoirs with seventy facsimiles.

MUSICAL AUTOGRAPHS

Albrecht, Otto Edwin. *A Census of Autograph Music Manuscripts of European Composers in American Libraries.* Philadelphia: University of Pennsylvania Press, 1953. Lists 2,017 manuscripts now in the United States by 571 European composers, with current and former owners indicated. A new edition is expected to appear shortly.

———, Herbert Cahoon, and Douglas C. Ewing. *The Mary Flagler Cary Music Collection: Printed Books and Music, Manuscripts, Autograph Letters, Documents, Portraits.* New York: Pierpont Morgan Library, 1970. Collection comprises 152 manuscripts as well as an impressive number of autograph letters. Copiously illustrated with facsimiles.

———. "Musical Treasures in the Morgan Library." *Notes,* 18 (June 1972): 643–651. A comprehensive description of the Morgan Library's holdings.

Barksdale, A. Beverly. *Composer Portraits and Autograph Scores.* Toledo, Ohio: Toledo Museum of Art, 1954. Catalog of a comprehensive exhibition held October 3–November 7, 1954.

Books and Manuscripts From the Heineman Collection. New York: Pierpont Morgan Library, 1963.

Catalogue of the Famous Music Library . . . of the Late W. H. Cummings. [London: Sotheby, Wilkinson & Hodge, 1917.] An auction catalog of one of the great private collections of music autographs, sold in 1918. Much of the material was acquired by the Nanki Music Library in Tokyo, which issued a catalog of the Cummings material in 1925.

Deutsch, Otto Erich. "Collections, Private." *Grove's Dictionary of Music and Musicians.* 5th ed. New York: St. Martin's Press, 1954. II, 373–375. A pioneering survey, through 1950, of the history of private music collections in Great Britain and Ireland dispersed or acquired by public libraries.

The Elizabeth Sprague Coolidge Foundation Autograph Musical Scores. Washington, D.C.: U.S. Government Printing Office, 1950. A catalog of the Coolidge Foundation autographs in the Music Division, Library of Congress, as of 1950.

An Exhibit of Music Including Manuscripts . . . Held in Washington, D.C. on December 28, 29 and 30, 1938. Washington, D.C.: U.S. Government Printing Office, 1939. An exhibition in the Library of Congress prepared for the sixtieth annual convention of the Music Teachers National Association.

Gerstenberg, Walter, and Martin Hürlimann. *Musikerhandschriften von Palestrina bis Beethoven.* Zurich: Atlantis Verlag, 1960. Contains 159 facsimile plates, with brief descriptive commentaries and identification of sources.

———. *Musikerhandschriften von Schubert bis Stravinsky.* Zurich: Atlantis Verlag, 1961. English ed., *Composers' Autographs,* Ernst Roth, trans. 2 vols. Teaneck, N.J.: Fairleigh Dickinson University Press, 1968. Contains 140 plates with brief descriptive commentaries and identification of sources. Both editions are based on the earlier work by Georg Schünemann (see below).

Goldbeck, Frederik, and A. Fehr. *Bibliothèque Alfred Cortot . . . catalogue.* [Argenteuil: R. Coulouma, 1936.] One of the great private collections, now widely dispersed. Unfortunately, only the first volume of the catalog was published.

Gombosi, Marilyn, ed. *Catalog of the Johannes Herbst Collection.* Chapel Hill: University of North Carolina Press, 1970. A comprehensive catalog of eighteenth- and early nineteenth-century manuscripts in the archives of the Moravian Music Foundation of Winston-Salem, N.C.

Grasberger, Franz. *Die Handschriften der Meister: Berühmte Werke der Tonkunst im Autograph.* Vienna: Gesellschaft der Musikfreunde, 1966. A catalog of six exhibitions devoted to the holograph scores of great masters from Bach down to the present held in the Gesellschaft der Musikfreunde, May 22–June 20, 1966. Richly illustrated with facsimiles.

———. *Kostbarkeiten der Musik.* I: *Das Lied.* Tutzing, Germany: Hans Schneider, 1968. A lavish production illustrated with many facsimiles of holograph songs; no further volumes have appeared.

Hürlimann, Martin. *Musiker-Handschriften: Zeugniss des Zurcher Musiklebens.* Zurich: Atlantis Verlag, 1969. Catalog of an exhibition held in Zurich's Helmhaus, June 1–22, 1969; lavishly illustrated with facsimiles.

Jans, Hans Jörg, ed. *Musiker-Handschriften: Originalpartituren aus der Sammlung Dr. h. c. Paul Sacher.* Lucerne: Bärtschi & Hasler, 1973. Catalog of an exhibition in the Kunstmuseum in Lucerne, August 19–September 8, 1973; lavishly illustrated with facsimiles.

Jung, Hermann. See comments on this author's book in the section of this bibliography headed "Works of General or Specific Usefulness."

King, A. Hyatt. *Some British Collectors of Music.* Cambridge: Cambridge University Press, 1963. The activity of private collectors of music in England, with an appendix containing classified lists of collectors from the mid-seventeenth century to the present.

Kinsky, Georg. *Musikhistorisches Museum von Wilhelm Heyer in Cöln.* Katalog IV: *Musik-autographen.* 4 parts in 3 volumes. Leipzig: Breitkopf & Härtel, 1910–1916. Describes 1,673 items; one of the finest collections of musical autographs ever assembled; dispersed and sold at auction in 1926. The catalog is considered a model of bibliographical scholarship.

———. *Katalog der Musikautographen Sammlung Louis Koch . . . von Scarlatti bis Stravinsky.* Stuttgart: Hoffmannsche Buchdruckerei F. Krais, 1953. An important collection of musical autographs in which the music of the classic and Romantic periods in Germany is strongly represented.

The Koussevitzky Music Foundation, 1942–1967. Washington, D.C.: Serge Koussevitzky Foundation in the Library of Congress, 1967. A catalog of works commissioned by the Koussevitzky Foundation, the holographs of which are in the Music Division, Library of Congress.

Lesure, François, and Nanie Bridgman. *Collection musicale André Meyer: Manu-*

scrits, autographes, musique imprimée et manuscrit. . . . Abbéville: F. Paillart, [1960]. Beautifully illustrated with 292 plates.

Mecklenburg, Günther. *Vom Autographensammeln. . . .* See comments on this author's book in the section of this bibliography headed "General Guides to Collecting."

Pfudel, Ernst. *Die Musik-Handschriften der Konigl. Ritter-Akademie zu Liegnitz.* ("Monatshefte für Musikgeschichte. Beilage. Jahrgang 18 & 21"). Leipzig: Breitkopf & Härtel, 1886–1889. An interesting early work.

Schmieder, Wolfgang. *Musiker-Handschriften in Drei Jahrhunderten.* Leipzig: Breitkopf & Härtel, 1939.

Schünemann, Georg. *Musikerhandschriften von Bach bis Schumann.* Berlin–Zurich: Atlantis Verlag, 1936. The precursor of the Gerstenberg-Hürlimann anthologies. Contains many facsimiles from the musical manuscripts in the Berlin State Library.

Van Patten, Nathan. *A Memorial Library of Music at Stanford University.* Stanford: Stanford University Press, 1950. A collection of 1,226 entries; the emphasis of the collection is on "association items."

Versteigerung der Musikbibliothek des Herrn Dr. Werner Wolffheim. 2 volumes in 4 parts. Berlin: M. Breslauer & L. Liepmannssohn, 1928–1929. Classified catalog of one of the finest collections ever assembled.

Waters, Edward N. "The Music Collection of the Heineman Foundation." *Notes,* 7 (March 1950): 181–216. A detailed description.

———. *Autograph Musical Scores and Autograph Letters in the Whittall Foundation Collection.* Washington, D.C.: U.S. Government Printing Office, 1951. A descriptive catalog of items in the Music Division, Library of Congress, as of 1951.

Winternitz, Emanuel. *Musical Autographs From Monteverdi to Hindemith.* 2 volumes. Princeton: Princeton University Press, 1955. An extremely lavish production reissued by Dover Publications in a paperbound edition in 1965. The first volume is devoted to commentary on the plates; the second contains 196 full-page facsimiles of musical autographs.

PERIODICALS

L'amateur d'autographes. Jacques-Étienne Noel Charavay *et al.,* eds. Paris: Charavay, 1840's to date. The catalogs of this autograph firm, founded in 1838, contain numerous facsimiles. Especially notable is the catalog of the Alfred Bovet collection (1884), which contained more than eight hundred facsimiles.

American Antiquarian. Charles De F. Burns, ed. New York: C. De F. Burns, 1869–1880. A dealer's catalogs containing lists of autographs, reminiscences, texts of letters, and other material.

American Archivist. Chicago: Society of American Archivists, 1938 to date. Occasionally contains articles of interest to collectors.

American Book Prices Current. New York: Bowker, 1895 to date. Annual publication compiled from auction records. Contains a section on prices of autographs. Cumulative indexes.

American Clipper Monthly Catalogue of American Historical and Literary Material. Elenore Bruno, ed. Merion Station, Pennsylvania: American Autograph Shop, 1934–1943. Contains excellent reminiscences of collectors and dealers, and also texts of many fine letters, news notes of the autograph world, and other items.

Autograph News. Huntsville, Alabama: Jeff Marsh, 1972 to date. The only monthly publication in the autograph field. Brief articles on various aspects; profiles and addresses of prominent persons; classified ads; photo-offset reproduction. $8.00 per year. Address: *Autograph News,* 7606 Charlotte Avenue, Huntsville, Alabama 35802.

The Book Collector. London: *The Collector,* 1952 to present. Carries articles of interest to the autograph collector fairly regularly, because many book collectors also collect autographs. $24.00 per year. Address: *The Collector,* Ltd., 3 Bloomsbury Place, London WCIA 2QA.

Cohasco Report: A Newsletter of Interest to the Autograph and Historical Document Investor and Collector. New York: Cohasco, Inc., 1977 to present. Begun in 1977, this single-sheet publication by a dealer contains news about the investment possibilities in autographs. Free. Address: Cohasco, Inc., 321 Broadway, New York, New York 10007.

The Collector. A Magazine for Autograph and Historical Collectors. New York City–Hunter, New York: Walter R. Benjamin Autographs, Inc., 1887 to present. A sales catalog of an old and respected dealer that also contains useful essays and advice on many aspects of collecting. Free to customers in good standing; others, $10.00 per year. Address: Walter R. Benjamin Autographs, Inc., Post Office Box 255, Scribner Hollow Road, Hunter, New York 12422.

History News. Nashville, Tennessee: American Association for State and Local History, 1941 to date. A slick-paper, monthly publication, almost a newsletter, that contains occasional articles and technical leaflets of interest to the collector of autographs. Cost depends on category of membership. Address: American Association for State and Local History, 1315 Eighth Avenue South, Nashville, Tennessee 37203.

Manuscripts. [New York]: Manuscript Society, 1948 to date (begun as *Autograph Collectors' Journal*). This quarterly publication of the largest organization of collectors, dealers, and professionals contains articles on all aspects of collecting and collectors. Regular sections on areas of collecting and auction reports. Photographs and facsimiles; news notes; autograph of the quarter. Sent to members of the society, membership in which is $15.00 per year. Address: Executive Secretary, The Manuscript Society, 1206 N. Stoneman Avenue #15, Alhambra, California 91801.

The Month at Goodspeed's. Boston: Goodspeed's Book Shop, 1929–1969. For forty years the house publication of the great Boston firm. Contains a vast treasury of material on autographs and autographed books, excellent editorial material, and many facsimiles.

Pen and Quill. Brooklyn, New York: Universal Autograph Collectors' Club, published bimonthly, 1967 to date. Brief articles on various aspects of collecting; addresses of prominent and collectible persons; question-and-answer column; photo-offset reproduction. Sent to members of the club, dues for which are $6.00 per year. Address: Universal Autograph Collectors' Club, Post Office Box 102, Midlands, Brooklyn, New York 11230.

PRESERVATION AND RESTORATION

Banks, Paul N. "Matting and Framing Documents and Art Objects on Papers." Technical Leaflet. Chicago: The Newberry Library, 1968.

Barrow, William J. *The Barrow Method of Restoring Deteriorated Documents.* Richmond, Virginia: W. J. Barrow, 1966. An explanation of the Barrow process of deacidification and lamination, the latter process not favored by collectors and somewhat controversial among archivists and conservators.

Clapp, Anne F. *Curatorial Care of Works of Art on Paper.* Oberlin, Ohio: Intermuseum Conservation Association, 1973. Aimed at the curator; discusses problems that lie within curatorial control; warns of problems best left to conservators; includes formulas for paste, lists of supplies and their sources.

Cunha, George Martin, and Dorothy Grant Cunha. *Conservation of Library Materials: A Manual and Bibliography on the Care, Repair and Restoration of Library Materials.* 2 volumes. Metuchen, New Jersey: Scarecrow Press, 1972. Especially valuable for its bibliography volume.

Doloff, Francis W., and Roy L. Perkinson. *How to Care for Works of Art on Paper.* Boston: Museum of Fine Arts, 1971. A forty-six-page pamphlet for the nonspecialist; contains practical advice on framing and simple repairs, as well as some sources of supplies.

Guldbeck, Per E. *The Care of Historical Collections: A Conservation Handbook for the Nonspecialist.* Nashville, Tennessee: American Association for State and Local History, 1972. Contains a brief section on the care of paper and gives instruction for repair of simple problems.

Horton, Carolyn. *Cleaning and Preserving Bindings and Related Materials.* Chicago: American Library Association, [1969]. Primarily directed at books, but contains valuable comments on paper care and handling.

Kathpalia, Yash Pal. *Conservation and Restoration of Archive Materials.* Paris: UNESCO, 1973. An excellent paperbound manual covering all aspects of the work of the conservator, and written in layman's language. It includes formulas for various processes, and addresses of suppliers.

Minogue, Adelaide E. "The Repair and Preservation of Records." *Bulletin of the National Archives,* no. 5. Washington, D.C.: U.S. Government Printing Office, 1943. Old but standard treatment.

Time-Life Books. *Caring for Photographs: Display, Storage, Restoration.* New York: Time-Life Books, [1972]. A very useful book containing formulas for solutions for cleaning daguerreotypes and other items, as well as much other valuable advice.

THEATER AND DANCE

Beaumont, Cyril William. *Complete Book of Ballets: A Guide to the Principal Ballets of the Nineteenth and Twentieth Centuries.* Garden City, New York: Garden City Publishing Co., 1941, 1949.

———. *Supplement to the Complete Book of Ballets.* Garden City, New York: Garden City Publishing Company, 1942.

Chujoy, Anatole, and P. W. Manchester. *The Dance Encyclopaedia.* Revised ed. New York: Simon and Schuster, [1967].

Clarence, Reginald, comp. *"The Stage" Cyclopedia. A Bibliography of Plays.* London: "The Stage," 1909.

Enciclopedia dello spettacolo. 9 volumes. Roma: Casa Editrice Le Maschere, [1954–1962].

Guest, Ivor Forbes. *The Romantic Ballet in England: Its Development, Fulfilment, and Decline.* London: Phoenix House, [1959].

———. *The Romantic Ballet in Paris.* London: Pitman, 1966.

Harding, James. *Sacha Guitry: The Last Boulevardier.* New York: Scribners, 1968.

Hartnoll, Phyllis, ed. *The Oxford Companion to the Theatre.* New York: Oxford, 1967.

The London Stage, 1660–1800. A Calendar of Plays, Entertainments & After Pieces, Together With Casts, Box-receipts and Contemporary Comment. 11 volumes. Carbondale, Illinois: Southern Illinois University Press, 1960–1968.

National Portrait Gallery. *Portraits of the American Stage, 1771–1971.* Washington, D.C.: Smithsonian Institution, 1971.

Nicoll, Allardyce. *A History of English Drama, 1660–1900.* 6 volumes. Cambridge, England: Cambridge University Press, 1952–1959.

Samuels, Charles, and Louise Samuels. *Once Upon a Stage: The Merry World of Vaudeville.* New York: Dodd, Mead, 1974.

Society for Theatre Research. *Theatre Notebook.* London: the Society, 1945 to date.

CHANGING HANDWRITING

Eastburn, Walter N. "The Problem of Aging Signatures." *Manuscripts,* 9, no. 4 (Fall 1957): 258–260.

———. "John Morton, Changeable Signer." *Manuscripts,* 12, no. 1 (Winter 1960): 12–19.

Eaton, Dorothy S., and Vincent L. Eaton. "George Washington's Handwriting." *Autograph Collectors' Journal,* 4, no. 1 (Fall 1951): 20–22.

Eaton, Vincent L. " 'Abraham Lincoln His Hand and Pen.' " *Manuscripts,* 11, no. 1 (Winter 1959): 5–12.

Fields, Joseph Edward. "Thomas Lynch, Jr., and His Autographs." *Autograph Collectors' Journal,* 4, no. 1 (Fall 1951): 6–10.

———. "The Autographs of Arthur Middleton." *Autograph Collectors' Journal,* 4, no. 2 (Winter 1952): 2–18.

Lingelbach, William E. "B. Franklin and the Art of Writing." *Autograph Collectors' Journal,* 4, no. 3 (Spring 1952): 3–9.

Nash, Ray. "The Handwriting of the Founding Fathers." *Manuscripts,* 7, no. 4 (Summer 1955): 208–213.

Reed, John F. "Questions and Answers." *Manuscripts,* 16, no. 4 (Summer 1964): 53–54. Concerns George Washington's handwriting.

NOTES ABOUT THE CONTRIBUTORS

GORDON T. BANKS was for many years head of the autograph department of Goodspeed's Bookshop, Boston, and is generally considered the doyen of manuscript dealers in the United States. He has been active in the affairs of the Manuscript Society, serving as its president.

CLIFTON WALLER BARRETT entered the shipping business in 1920 and was cofounder, in 1932, of the North Atlantic and Gulf Steam Ship Corporation. He served in New York as vice-president and director until 1952, when he became president. His knowledge of, interest in, and collecting of American literature brought him membership and an active role in many organizations: chairman, Fellows of the Pierpont Morgan Library; and trustee of the McGregor Library at the University of Virginia, of the New York Public Library, of the Thomas Jefferson Memorial Foundation, and of the John Carter Brown Library. Mr. Barrett was chairman of the Friends of the Columbia Libraries, and has served as president of the Grolier Club, the Bibliographical Society of America, and of the American Antiquarian Society. His numerous publications include *Bibliographical Adventures in Americana* (1950), *American Fiction: The First Seventy-five Years* (1954), *John Greenleaf Whittier: Politician, Antiquarian* (1958), and *The American Writer in England* (1969). His great collection of American literature—manuscripts, books, photographs, paintings—is now at the University of Virginia, where it is formally known as the Clifton Waller Barrett Library of American Literature. Mr. Barrett, who has retired to Charlottesville, is able to remain active in the operation of the library, and it benefits from his unparalleled knowledge of its materials.

MARY A. BENJAMIN (Mrs. Harold G. Henderson) joined her father in the autograph business in 1925, and from 1937 to 1943 was the manager of the firm and editor of *The Collector* (established in 1887), the firm's highly respected autograph catalog and journal. Upon her father's death, she became owner of the firm and publisher, as well as editor, of *The Collector*. In 1971, when her nephew joined the firm, it was incorporated as Walter R. Benjamin Autographs, Inc. Miss Benjamin is a life member of the New-York Historical Society, and a member of the International League of Antiquarian Booksellers, the Manuscript Society, and the Grolier Club. She also has served on the governing board of the Antiquarian Booksellers' Association of America. She is the author of *Autographs: A Key to Collecting* (1946) and *The Presidents: A Survey of Autograph Values* (1965), and has contributed articles to magazines and journals. Profiles of Miss Benjamin appeared in the *Saturday Evening Post* in 1946, and in the *New Yorker* in 1959. Her private collection consists of letters and documents of the saints of the Roman Catholic Church, which she has presented to Georgetown University as a memorial to Rev. Francis X. Talbot, S.J., a family friend, for whom the collection is named.

EDMUND BERKELEY, JR., curator of manuscripts, university archivist, and associate professor at the University of Virginia, holds degrees from the University of the South and from the University of Virginia. He began his archival career at the Virginia State Library in 1963, and moved to the University of Virginia in 1965. He is a fellow and council member of the Society of American Archivists, and is a writer and editor whose articles have appeared in *American Archivist, Virginia Magazine of History and Biography, Georgia Archive,* and *Manuscripts.* Mr. Berkeley has spoken before the American Library Association, the Society of American Archivists, and the Manuscript Society.

THOMAS B. BRUMBAUGH is professor of fine arts at Vanderbilt University, Nashville, Tennessee, where he teaches courses in the history of art. His specialty is American and French painting of the nineteenth century. Prof. Brumbaugh is the editor of *Architecture of Middle Tennessee* (1974), and has published articles on autographs and the arts in *American Book Collector, Manuscripts, Art Journal,* and *Art News.*

MICHEL CASTAING is director of the noted French autographs firm of Charavay, founded in 1830.

DAVID HERR COBLENTZ is a Presbyterian minister. A native of Ohio, he is a graduate of Davidson College in North Carolina and of Union Theological Seminary in Virginia. His pastorates have been in the Carolinas and Virginia. He is a director and past president of the Manuscript Society, and is a subeditor of *Manuscripts,* to which he has contributed numerous articles. Rev. Coblentz' personal autograph collection includes a set of the signers of the Constitution; letters of Nathanael Greene, Thomas Jefferson, James Monroe, Robert E. Lee, Thornton Wilder, and Felix Mendelssohn; and colonial Virginia and Revolutionary War manuscripts.

CHARLES F. COONEY is currently the managing editor of *Civil War Times Illustrated.* Formerly a manuscript librarian in the Manuscripts Division of the Library of Congress, he has written on the Civil War for *Manuscripts, Civil War Times Illustrated, American Heritage,* and other publications.

JOHN C. DANN was born in Wilmington, Delaware, and graduated from Dickinson College, Carlisle, Pennsylvania. He received M.A. and Ph.D. degrees from the College of William and Mary, and is a member of the history department faculty at the University of Michigan, where he is also director of the William L. Clements Library. Prof. Dann is editor of *The Revolution Remembered* (1977), a collection of Revolutionary War soldiers' reminiscences, and is coeditor of a guide to the manuscript holdings of the Clements Library.

ROY L. DAVIDS is a director and head of the manuscripts department for Sotheby Parke-Bernet & Co., London.

JOSEPH E. FIELDS, a physician and a noted collector, was a founder and first president of the Manuscript Society. He has been a frequent contributor to *Manuscripts,* and is a member of the editorial board of this book.

C. A. KYRLE FLETCHER and her husband, the late Ifan Kyrle Fletcher, were directors of C. & I. K. Fletcher, Ltd. He was an antiquarian bookseller specializing in the history of theater and entertainment. Mr. Fletcher sold not only books but all the relics that bring theatrical history to life, including original scene and costume designs, portraits and prints of actresses and actors, and the properties they used. Since her husband's death in 1969, Mrs. Fletcher has continued the business but has dealt only in autograph material, in which she has always specialized. Many of the firm's catalogs, prepared by Mrs. Fletcher, are collector's pieces; and the archives and correspondence of the business have been accepted for preservation by the Greater London Record Office.

GERHARD A. GESELL, a native of Los Angeles, holds A.B. and LL.B. degrees from Yale. He began his legal career in Washington with the Securities and Exchange Commission in 1935, and entered private practice in Washington in 1941. His practice continued until 1967, and in 1968 he was appointed judge of the United States District Court for the District of Columbia. Judge Gesell belongs to various legal groups and associations. A hobby of many years has been the collecting of autographs of members of the United States Supreme Court.

WALTER GOLDWATER is the owner of the University Place Book Shop in New York City, which he established in 1932. For most of the intervening period the shop has specialized in books on chess, radical literature, Africa, blacks, and the West Indies. In these last categories he has maintained what is probably the largest and best stock in the country; more than 200 catalogs have been issued in these fields of specialization. Mr. Goldwater was the nominal owner and publisher of the magazine *Dissent* for the first fifteen years of its publication. He recently gave a series of lectures at the Columbia School of Library Service on acquisitions librarianship, and has spoken widely on radical literature, chess, black literature, and incunabula. His published monographs include *Radical Periodicals in America, 1890–1950* (1964), a bibliography that is the definitive work; *The Second Annual Goldwater-Marshall Chess Tournament* (1969); and *Shashki: How to Read Books in Russian on Spanish Pool Checkers* (1969). Mr. Goldwater has written a great many book reviews that have appeared in the *Times Literary Supplement* (London), *Antiquarian Bookman,* and *Papers of the Bibliographical Society of America.* He has one of the largest personal collections of incunabula in the country, and the four Shakespeare Folios; but he thinks "book-collecting is juvenile."

CHRISTOPHER C. JAECKEL has been an associate of his aunt, Mary A. Benjamin, and an officer in the firm of Walter R. Benjamin Autographs, Inc., since 1971. His background is similar to that of the founder of the firm, since his grandfather, Walter R. Benjamin, spent a number of years as a newspaper reporter before venturing into autographs in 1887, while Mr. Jaeckel was for several years a television director, news reporter, and newscaster. His particular interest is western Americana, and he also collects signed photographs. A member of the Manuscript Society, an associate member of the Antiquarian Booksellers' Association of America, and a member of local historical societies, Mr. Jaeckel occasionally lectures on various phases of autograph collecting.

RUDOLF F. KALLIR, born in Vienna, left his native country after receiving a law degree. From 1946 he was executive vice-president of the German Mannesmann Company in New York. He has collected autographs since childhood, and became, after his retirement, a *marchand amateur.* Mr. Kallir frequently has been retained by institutions such as Harvard, the Library of Congress, and the Bartók Archives for expert appraisals. His memoirs, *Autographensammler-Lebenslanenglich,* were published in 1977 in Zurich with a foreword by composer Gottfried von Einem.

HERBERT E. KLINGELHOFER, a former president of the Manuscript Society, is chairman of its book committee and a coeditor of this book. A private collector specializing in historical autographs, he has lectured on various aspects of autograph collecting. He is the author of numerous articles in *Manuscripts, Maryland Historical Magazine,* and *William and Mary Quarterly,* chiefly treating of autographs and literary and historical subjects, as well as the arrangement of manuscript collections and family archives.

JAMES KRITZECK, professor of Oriental languages and history at the University of Notre Dame, has collected manuscripts, chiefly of religious significance, since his boyhood. His personal collection is housed in a special room designed by Marcel Breuer in the Alcuin Library of St. John's Abbey in Collegeville, Minnesota. Dr. Kritzeck was educated at Princeton and Harvard, and has published many books and articles in his academic field of Islamic studies. He has also been a consultant to various international and ecumenical religious organizations, including the Papal Secretariat for Non-Christians. He has an honorary doctorate in letters in addition to his earned doctorate in philosophy, and has been knighted twice.

WALTER G. LANGLOIS is professor of French literature and chairman of the French department at the University of Wyoming in Laramie. He collects books, manuscripts, and autographs in a number of areas but specializes in French writers of the nineteenth and twentieth centuries, with particular emphasis on André Malraux. He has published several books and numerous articles and reviews in journals such as *Publications of the Modern Language Association, French Review, Magazine littéraire,* and *Manuscripts.* Prof. Langlois is editor of the semiannual journal *Malraux Miscellany* and of the yearly volumes of Série André Malraux. He is an active member of professional organizations, including the Société d'Étude du XXe Siècle (board of directors) and the Manuscript Society (vice-president).

FRANKLYN LENTHALL is a theater historian and an avid collector of all theater memorabilia. He is curator of the Boothbay Theatre Museum in Boothbay, Maine, one of the very few—if not the only—theater museums in America (founded 1957). He has published articles on theater and the collecting of theater memorabilia in leading magazines and newspapers, and is in great demand as a lecturer on the history of theater and the birth of a theater museum. Mr. Lenthall has taught at two schools of acting in New York City, and at the Katharine Long School under the sponsorship of the Metropolitan Opera. For eighteen years he was co-owner–producer of the Boothbay Playhouse, a summer theater, and directed more than 172 of its productions.

IRVING LOWENS holds a B.S. from Columbia and an M.A. from the University of Maryland. Since 1961 he has been chief music critic of the *Washington Star.* He has held positions in the Music Division of the Library of Congress, and has received the Moramus Award (1960) for distinguished service to American music, and the ASCAP–Deems Taylor Award for the excellence of his music criticism in 1973 and 1977. The recipient of numerous grants for travel and study abroad, Mr. Lowens has found time to be active in many organizations in his field, and to publish *Music and Musicians in Early America,* and an extensive bibliography of American songsters published before 1821, as well as numerous articles. His collection of musical autographs is one of the most extensive in the United States.

RICHARD MAASS has been a collector since the mid-1940's, specializing in American colonial and revolutionary autographs of New York State and in material relating to the battles of Lexington, Concord, and Bunker Hill. He has an additional interest in seventeenth-century English Restoration autographs, although he admits that he sometimes strays beyond these fields. He has published in *Manuscripts,* the *Journal of the American Library Association,* and in historical journals, and is a member of the Grolier Club, a former president of the Manuscript Society, and is currently president of the American Jewish Committee.

MICHAEL PAPANTONIO started his career in the rare book business in the mid-1920's with the Brick Row Book Shop in New York. His own business was founded in 1936 and continued to 1943. In 1946 he was cofounder, with John S. Van E. Kohn, of the Seven Gables Bookshop, Inc., a firm that continues to operate in New York City; it specializes in American and English literature, autographs, letters, and manuscripts. Mr. Papantonio's personal collection included early American bindings, catalogs, literature, and autograph material dealing with the early American book trade and publishing, and early American posters. An illustrated catalog of a traveling exhibition of his bindings was issued in 1972; the books were displayed in eight American institutions. Mr. Papantonio died while this book was in press.

JOHN PARKER is a graduate of the University of Michigan, having received a Ph.D. in library science there in 1960. He is curator of the James Ford Bell Library at the University of Minnesota, a position he has held since 1953. His publications include *Van Meteren's Virginia, 1607–1612* (1961), *Books to Build an Empire* (1966), *Discovery: Developing Views of the Earth From Ancient Times to the Voyages of Captain Cook* (1972), *The Journals of Jonathan Carver and Related Documents, 1766–1770* (1976), and an article in *Manuscripts.*

JOHN F. REED, a collector of historical manuscripts for more than thirty years, has since 1960 specialized in the American Revolution. He retired from business to turn author, and has produced two books—*Campaign to Valley Forge* (1965) and *Valley Forge, Crucible of Victory* (1969)—as well as numerous articles, many of them in *Manuscripts.* He is a former vice-president of the Manuscript Society, and is a director of the Valley Forge Historical Society, and trustee and historian of Freedoms Foundation at Valley Forge.

DIANA J. RENDELL is a cofounder of the autograph and manuscript firm of The Rendells, Inc., and specializes in forming and developing collections for private individuals and institutional collectors. She is coauthor of *Fundamentals of Autograph Collecting* (1972). Her personal collection includes ancient writings and classical antiquities, old master drawings, and manuscripts and books relating to philosophy, psychology, and art.

KENNETH W. RENDELL has been a partner in the firm of The Rendells, Inc., since its founding in 1961. This company deals in all types of autograph material. His personal collection concentrates on immigration and exploration as well as modern art, with a particular emphasis on surrealism. He has published a number of articles in *Manuscripts,* and has spoken at annual meetings of the American Library Association, the Manuscript Society, and the Society of American Archivists. Mr. Rendell also has served as president of the Manuscript Society and of the International Association of Autograph Dealers. He is a member of the editorial board and a coeditor of this book, and coauthor of *Fundamentals of Autograph Collecting* (1972).

LESLIE J. SCHREYER is an attorney specializing in tax and estate planning with the firm of Chadbourne, Parke, Whiteside & Wolff in New York City. He is an autograph collector and a member of the Manuscript Society.

HENRY STRUTZ holds an M.A. from Brown University and has been a college teacher of English, foreign languages, and history for more than twenty years. He has taught at Columbia, City College of New York, Rutgers, Yeshiva, and Skidmore, and is currently on the faculty of the State University of New York at Alfred. A skilled translator and editor who is qualified in five languages, Mr. Strutz has made translations of manuscript collections for donation to the archival collections of major American universities. The recipient of several awards, including the Ward Medal, he has written a volume of verse and several books. His articles have appeared in scholarly journals and national magazines, and he is currently under contract to write three books. Mr. Strutz is coeditor of *Doenitz at Nuremberg: A Re-appraisal* (1977). He is a member of the Manuscript Society, and is listed in *Contemporary Authors.*

CAROLYN HOOVER SUNG is a native of South Carolina and is a graduate of Winthrop College; she holds an M.A. from the University of Maryland, and is completing her doctorate in American studies. She is presently assistant chief for bibliographic service, photographic service, Library of Congress. Her main research interests are nineteenth-century American and British collectors of Americana, the history of Washington, D.C., women's history, and the history of the Carolina Piedmont region.

H. KEITH THOMPSON, a Yale graduate in naval science and history, is a consultant, appraiser, and cataloger in the field of manuscripts and rare books with the Charles Hamilton Galleries, Inc., in New York. He is the coeditor of *Doenitz at Nuremberg: A Re-appraisal* (1977), has edited a biography of Hermann Goering, and has written extensively for periodicals.

ROBERT L. VOLZ is the custodian of the Chapin Library at Williams College. He holds a B.A. from Marquette University, and an M.A. in L.S. from the University of Wisconsin-Madison. Former positions held by Mr. Volz include that of head of special collections at Bowdoin College, and seven years as head of the Rare Book Department of the Rush Rhees Library at the University of Rochester.

ROBERT C. WIEST is the manager of the graphic conservation department of R. R. Donnelley & Sons Company, Chicago, which he joined in 1971 after several years during which he owned and operated the Bark River Press, "a private press with commercial overtones." While operating the press, he studied bookbinding, printing, and calligraphy. Previously, he had worked for General Electric for nineteen years, serving in manufacturing divisions in Schenectady, New York, Lynchburg, Virginia, and Milwaukee, Wisconsin.

JOHN WILSON is a noted British autograph dealer specializing in British historical autographs. Born in Manchester, he came into the autograph business "via the rare book trade"; he started his own firm in 1967.

GLOSSARY

ABBREVIATIONS: Following is a list of abbreviations in common use by collectors, dealers, and professionals. Frequently they appear without periods, though they have been written with periods in this book.

A.	Autograph
A.D.	Autograph Document
A.D.S.	Autograph Document Signed
A.L.	Autograph Letter
A.L.S.	Autograph Letter Signed
A.Ls.S.	Autograph Letters Signed
A.Ms.	Autograph Manuscript
A.Ms.S.	Autograph Manuscript Signed
A.Mss.S.	Autograph Manuscripts Signed
A.N.	Autograph Note
A.N.S.	Autograph Note Signed
A.P.C.	Autograph Postcard
A.P.C.S.	Autograph Postcard Signed
ca.	*Circa*
D.	Document
Hs.	*Handschrift* (handwritten)
L.	Letter
M.O.C	Member of the Old Congress (the one that existed from September 1774 until March 1789)
Ms.	Manuscript
Ms(s).	*Maschinenschrift* (typewritten)
N.	Note
n.d.	No Date
n.p.	No Place
P.C.	Postcard
S.	Signed
T.	Typed
T.L.	Typed Letter
T.L.S.	Typed Letter Signed
T.Ms.	Typed Manuscript
T.Ms.S.	Typed Manuscript Signed
Vol(s).	Volume(s)

ADDRESS LEAF: a leaf of a letter joined to that on which the message is written; the address is written on this leaf after it is folded around the message leaf to protect it in passage.

ARCHIVES: (1) the noncurrent RECORDS, in any medium, of an organization or institution preserved because of their continuing administrative, legal, or historical value; (2) the agency responsible for selecting, preserving, and making available archival materials; (3) the building or part of a building where such materials are kept.

ARCHIVIST: a person engaged in professional-level work in an ARCHIVES. See also MANUSCRIPT CURATOR.

AUTHENTICATION: determination that a record, manuscript, letter, document, or other item is what it purports to be.

AUTOGRAPH: (1) traditionally, a SIGNATURE; (2) a writing, signed or unsigned, in the hand of the author. See also HOLOGRAPH.

AUTOGRAPH DOCUMENT: a handwritten, unsigned DOCUMENT.

AUTOGRAPH DOCUMENT SIGNED: a DOCUMENT entirely in the hand of the person signing it.

AUTOGRAPH LETTER: a handwritten, unsigned LETTER.

AUTOGRAPH LETTER SIGNED: a LETTER entirely in the hand of the person signing it.

AUTOGRAPH MANUSCRIPT: any writing, other than a LETTER, NOTE, or DOCUMENT, that is unsigned.

AUTOGRAPH MANUSCRIPT SIGNED: any writing, other than a LETTER, NOTE, or DOCUMENT, entirely in the hand of the person signing it.

AUTOGRAPH NOTE: (1) a short, informal, handwritten message or LETTER, usually lacking a salutation or complimentary close; (2) a brief writing intended to assist the memory or to serve as the basis for a fuller statement.

AUTOGRAPH NOTE SIGNED: a short, informal writing or a handwritten message or LETTER, usually lacking a salutation or complimentary close, entirely in the hand of the person signing it.

AUTOGRAPH POSTCARD SIGNED: a POSTCARD on which the writing is entirely in the hand of the person signing it.

AUTOGRAPH QUOTATION SIGNED: a quotation, generally from an author's literary works, written out and signed, usually in response to a request for an autograph.

BID: at an auction sale, the amount of money one is willing to spend to purchase the material constituting a particular LOT.

BROADSIDE: a piece of printing on one side of the sheet only, often of FOLIO size.

CABINET PHOTOGRAPH: a photographic style popular in the nineteenth century in which the photographic image, which is about five and one-half by three and three-quarters inches, is mounted on a card that provides narrow margins at the top and sides but a wider margin at the bottom, where the name of the photographer or the autograph (often a facsimile) of the subject may appear.

CACHET: a special design printed on an envelope, usually to the left of the address space, honoring an event or person; often found on FIRST DAY COVERS.

CARTE DE VISITE PHOTOGRAPH: a photographic style very popular in the nineteenth century and similar to the CABINET PHOTOGRAPH, except that the photographic image is smaller, *ca.* three and one-half by two and one-quarter inches.

CONTEMPORARY COPY: a copy of a LETTER, DOCUMENT, or MANUSCRIPT made soon after the composition of the original, but written by someone other than the author of the original.

CORRESPONDENCE: (1) LETTERS, POSTCARDS, MEMORANDA, NOTES, TELEGRAMS, and any other form of addressed, written communication sent and received; (2) a series containing both incoming and outgoing letters.

COVER: see LETTER.

DEACIDIFICATION: the chemical process by which the acid-alkaline chemical balance of a paper document is brought to a minimum pH of 7.0 to assist in its preservation.

DEED: a writing containing some transfer, bargain, or contract, bearing signatures and seals. By the end of the nineteenth century in the United States, genuine seals rarely appeared on documents; but the word "seal" surrounded by square brackets or a circle must appear. Generally, deeds appearing in autograph collections or on the autograph market are those used to convey land. They are frequently referred to as INDENTURES, from the early practice of making two copies of the deed, laying one on top of the other, and cutting the edges of both at the same time in a wavy line, so that their genuineness would be readily established.

DEED OF GIFT: a signed, written legal instrument containing a voluntary transfer of title to real or personal property without a monetary consideration. This type of instrument is commonly used to transfer manuscripts to a repository, and often takes the form of a contract establishing conditions governing the transfer of title and specifying any restrictions on access or use.

DEPOSIT: manuscripts loaned to a repository without transfer of title.

DOCKET: filing information written on the VERSO of a communication received, usually giving its author, date, and (sometimes) a note about the contents.

DOCUMENT: (1) recorded information, regardless of medium or characteristics, but usually taken to mean a single writing, typing, or printed instrument for the communication of information; (2) an original or official paper, which is not a letter, substantiating a fact, event, or transaction.

ELECTROSTATIC COPY: a reproduction made by a copying machine that uses an electrically charged plate and powdered graphite or other substance in its operation; sometimes called a "dry" copier, since no liquids are used in the process. The copy produced is normally a positive copy and the same size as the original, but there are machines available that will enlarge or reduce during the copying process. Frequently the trade name "Xerox" is incorrectly used as a generic term to designate all such dry-process copies, whether produced on the machines of the Xerox Corporation or not.

ENDORSEMENT: (1) comment, acknowledgment, or notation written upon a document or a letter by the recipient. It may be in the margin, on the reverse, or on an accompanying sheet. Nineteenth-century documents filed after folding were often provided with a headed space for endorsements on the folded face that presented itself when the document was filed; (2) a reply, comment, of forwarding statement added to a military letter, as contrasted with a separate reply.

EXECUTIVE MANSION/WHITE HOUSE CARD: small cards, first used by Ulysses S. Grant, bearing the signature of the president in the center, and with an Executive Mansion imprint in the upper right (*ca.* two and three-quarters by four and one-quarter inches). Slightly larger cards (*ca.* six by eight inches) have been used, bearing a small VIGNETTE of the White House in the upper center, below which the president signs.

FAIR COPY: a clean copy, bearing few, if any, corrections or additions, of a literary work in the hand of its author.

FIRST DAY COVER: an envelope, often bearing a special design or imprint (called a CACHET) in honor of the occasion, and bearing a stamp canceled on the first day it was available for sale.

FOLIO: see SIZES.

FOXING: the light-brown stains, apparently thought to resemble the paw prints of a fox, left on paper by the action of certain molds.

FRANK: a signature placed on an envelope, usually where the stamp would be, which allows the letter to be carried without charge by the postal service. The word "free" is often added after the signature, and occasionally between the first and last name.

FRENCH REPUBLICAN CALENDAR: during the French Revolution, a calendar for the new state was devised in 1793. The year 1792 was chosen as year I. There were twelve months (Vendémiaire, Brumaire, Frimaire, Nivôse, Pluviôse, Ventôse, Germinal, Floréal, Prairial, Messidor, Thermidor, and Fructidor), each containing thirty days, with the addition of five supplementary days in ordinary years and six in leap years. This calendar was in use until 1805.

HOLOGRAPH: a writing entirely in the hand of the author, which may or may not be signed. Synonymous in most contexts with AUTOGRAPH, but especially useful when it is necessary to emphasize that the whole manuscript is in the hand of the author.

INDENTURE: see DEED.

INLAID: the preservation and display technique of gluing a manuscript, letter, or other item into an opening in a stronger sheet.

LAMINATION: a mechanically assisted process, generally preceded by DEACIDIFICATION, of reinforcing weak or damaged paper documents by enclosing them between two sheets of plastic foil (usually cellulose acetate) and two sheets of tissue that, through the application of heat and pressure, become thermoplastic and impregnate the original. More properly referred to as the thermoplastic lamination process. See also SILKING.

LEAF: a single piece of material that may be folded before use for writing or after printing. An unfolded leaf may bear one or two PAGES of writing or printing only; a folded leaf may bear many pages, depending upon the number of folds.

LEGAL SIZE: (1) a standard paper size, eight and one-half by fourteen inches (U.S. government, eight by twelve and one-half inches); (2) capable of holding legal-size documents. See also LETTER SIZE.

LETTER: a handwritten or typed message intended for the perusal only of the person or organization to whom it is addressed, distinguished from other messages by a formal salutation and complimentary close. Normally, letters are enclosed in addressed envelopes that are usually sealed; before about 1840, separate envelopes were rare, and the letter was usually folded to reveal a blank portion (called the LETTER COVER) on which the address was written.

LETTER BOOK: (1) a book of unlined or lined pages on which letters have been written. The letters may be drafts written by their author or fair copies made by the author or clerks; (2) copies of letters, originally on loose sheets and most frequently carbon copies, bound together, usually in chronological order. Sometimes written as one word.

LETTER COVER: see LETTER.

LETTERPRESS COPY: a copy of a document or a letter transferred from the original to tissue paper through direct contact with the original by means of pressure and moisture in a copying press. The tissue is usually very flimsy and must be handled with great care; the ink tends to run when such copies are made, and they are frequently difficult to read.

LETTER SIZE: (1) a standard paper size, eight and one-half by eleven inches (U.S. government, eight by ten and one-half inches); (2) capable of holding letter-size papers or documents. See also LEGAL SIZE.

LITERARY MANUSCRIPTS: manuscripts, including drafts and proofs, of literary compositions such as novels, essays, plays, or poetry.

LITERARY PROPERTY RIGHT: the common-law right under which the author of a letter, manuscript, or literary composition (or his heirs) retains the right of first publication of the text regardless of the ownership or location of the original document. Unlike statutory copyright, common-law copyright exists in perpetuity and is terminated only by general publication or dedication to the public. Literary property rights disappeared when the Copyright Act of 1976 took effect on January 1, 1978.

LOT: in an auction sale, the group of material sold at one time. See also BID.

MANUSCRIPT: a piece of writing (typed pieces are sometimes included) other than a letter, note, or document. Frequently used synonymously with AUTOGRAPH.

MANUSCRIPT CURATOR: a person engaged in professional-level work in an institution preserving manuscripts. Frequently the title used is "manuscript librarian," especially if the institution is a library and the person's training was received in a library school. See also ARCHIVIST.

MEMORANDUM: (1) a brief, informal communication typically written for interoffice communication, frequently on paper headed "Memorandum"; (2) a brief or informal note of some transaction or an outline of an intended instrument; (3) an informal diplomatic communication.

MONOGRAM: a SIGNATURE consisting of a number of letters arranged in a square, connected by vertical, diagonal, and horizontal lines, drawn largely by a scribe but always with a few letters added personally by the individual whose signature it is.

MOUNTED: a preservation process by which the manuscript is glued to a larger, sturdier sheet for protection.

MUSTER ROLL: a list of the men belonging to a military unit, giving the status of each.

NOTE: (1) a short informal message or LETTER, usually lacking a salutation or complimentary close; (2) a brief writing intended to assist the memory or to serve as the basis for a fuller statement.

OCTAVO: see SIZES.

PAGE: one side of a leaf bearing writing or printing.

PAPERS: (1) a natural accumulation of personal and family materials, as distinct from RECORDS; (2) a general term used by professionals to designate more than one type of manuscript material.

PARAPH: an addition to a signature in the form of a flourish or swirl below or behind the SIGNATURE, frequently accomplished by extending the tail of a descending letter.

PARCHMENT: an animal skin, usually sheep, goat, lamb, or calf, especially prepared to receive writing. The finer varieties, from young animals, are called VELLUM.

PATRIOTIC COVER: an envelope used during the American Civil War bearing a CACHET with a patriotic theme.

PENDANT SEAL: the seal required on a legal document; it is attached to the foot of the paper by a ribbon, braided cord, or a parchment strip. Used chiefly in Europe, these seals are often large, handsome, and heavy.

PICTOGRAM: a pictorial design adopted and used as a SIGNATURE, as James McNeill Whistler's butterfly.

POSTCARD: a card on which a message may be written for mailing without an envelope.

PROVENANCE: the record of ownership of a MANUSCRIPT or collection of PAPERS.

PUBLIC RECORDS: (1) in general usage, RECORDS accumulated by government agencies at all levels; ARCHIVES; (2) RECORDS open to public inspection by law or custom.

QUARTO: see SIZES.

RECORDS: all recorded information, regardless of medium or characteristics, made or received and maintained by an organization or institution in pursuit of its legal obligations or in the transaction of its business. See also ARCHIVES.

RECTO: the right-hand page of a book, and the front of a separate LEAF. The left-hand page of a book, and the back of a separate LEAF, are called the VERSO.

REPLEVIN: (1) recovery of property through legal means by an individual or organization; (2) the writ and legal act by which an institution or person takes over such property.

RESERVE: in an auction, the minimum BID that will be accepted for a LOT.

SEA LETTER: a document in four languages—English, French, Spanish, and Dutch—signed by the president and secretary of state of the United States, identifying to anyone concerned that the vessel to which it was issued was from the United States, and giving details about the proposed voyage. Sea letters were carried by all vessels sailing from the United States except those sailing into the Mediterranean, where a special passport was required by the 1795 treaty between the United States and the dey of Algiers.

SEAL TEAR: before the invention of envelopes, letters were folded and held closed with sealing wax, which, when the letter was opened, sometimes tore away a portion of the letter.

SIGNATURE: the name of a person written in his own hand in the fashion in which he habitually writes it, often incorporating flourishes or other distinctive features; sometimes called an AUTOGRAPH.

SIGNER: a Signer of the Declaration of Independence; the word is always capitalized in autographic usage.

SIGN MANUAL: a SIGNATURE consisting of the initials of the names, and often of titles, combined and connected by loops. Commonly used by monarchs of the fifteenth and sixteenth centuries and always penned by the monarch himself.

SIGNUM: a sign used in place of a SIGNATURE, originally often in the shape of a cross but taking other forms. A signum is used today by an illiterate person when he makes "his mark."

SILKING: a process of preservation in which thin sheets of silk gauze are fastened, using wheat or rice paste, to one or both sides of a manuscript, letter, or other item.

SIXTEENMO: see SIZES.

SIZES: the measurements of autographs, derived from printers' and booksellers' sizes; determined by the number of times the single sheet, or LEAF, is folded to produce the pages of a book. If the sheet was folded once to produce two leaves (each of which bears two pages, for a total of four), the book is a FOLIO; if folded to produce eight pages, it is a QUARTO; and so on. Today these terms imply to an autograph collector a manuscript roughly comparable in size to a book described by these terms. Thus a FOLIO is roughly twelve by nineteen inches; a QUARTO (4to), about nine by twelve inches; an OCTAVO (8vo), about six by nine inches; a TWELVEMO (12mo), sometimes called a small octavo, about five by seven inches; and a SIXTEENMO, about four by seven inches.

SLEEPER: an item whose true value or identification is missing by the person offering it for sale, allowing a fortunate person to purchase the item well below its true value.

TELEGRAM: the typed or manuscript record of a message transmitted electronically by telegraphic equipment.

TWELVEMO: see SIZES.

VELLUM: see PARCHMENT.

VERSO: see RECTO.

VIGNETTE: a small design, picture, or portrait, without a definite border, that shades off into the paper on which it is printed.

INDEX

Page numbers in boldface refer to illustrations.

Abbott, Charles D., 259
Abbreviations, systems of, 22–23, 27, 55, 61
Abolition and abolitionists, collections on, 207
Abraham, 426
Académie Française, 291
Acetate folders, use of, 135, 139
Achebe, Chinua, 329
Achurch, Janet, 462
Acid-free filing folders, 135, 147, 422
Acid-free slip sheets and papers, 144, 146
Acidic papers, 144
Acid salts, paper containing, 146
Acoustical systems, 5
Acquisition, methods of, 66–73, 470
Actors and actresses, 459–460, 464, 466, 470, 474
Actress glass, 486–487
Adams, Abigail Smith, 256
Adams, John, 254; contemporaries with the same name, 121–122; forgeries of, 96; handwriting of, 119–122, **123**, 124–125, 215, **217**; original letters of, 121
Adams, John Quincy, **221**, 227, 254, 306
Adams, Luisa Johnson, 256
Adams, Maude, 307
Adams, Samuel, 96
Addams, Charles, 477
Addison, Joseph, 288
Address, forms of, 82
Address leaf, 192
Adenauer, Konrad, 361
Adhesives: proprietary, 144; water-based, 149
Adler, Friedrich, 456
Admirals, 354
Admission tickets, theater, 459
Adolphus, Gustavus. *See* Gustavus II (king of Sweden)
Adventure and adventurers, 445
Adventures of Tom Sawyer, The (Twain), 32
Aeronautics, development of, 403–404
Africa, 43; black writers in, 328; countries in, emerging, 304, 328; language and literature of, 328–329; manuscripts of, 432; oral literary traditions of, 329; trade in, 444
Age: as factor in handwriting, 74, 76; as factor in value of item, 180
Agents, 70
Agnon, Shmuel Yosef (Samuel Josef Czaczkes), 327
Ahnung und Gegenwart (Eichendorff), 307
Aïda (Verdi), **385**
Air: dry and freely moving, desirability of, 146; washing devices for, 146
Airborne pollutants, 143
Air conditioning, need for, 143
Airplane and the air age, 441, 453
Akkadians (Semitic), 8
Alaska, 188
Albani, Francesco, 411
Albert (prime consort of Victoria of Great Britain), 44
Albert II (Holy Roman emperor), **367**
Alberti, Leone Battista, 417
Alberti, Count Mariano, 95
Albums, scrap, 129, 424
Alcott, Louisa May, 267
Alcuin Library, St. John's Abbey, Collegeville, Minnesota, 439 n

Aleichem, Sholom (Soloman Rabinowitz), 327
Alembert, Jean Le Rond d', 291, 293
Alexander, Sir George, 460
Alexander I (czar of Russia), 361, 373
Alexander II (czar of Russia), 431
Alexander III (Alexander the Great, king of Macedonia), 13; forgeries of, 94
Alexandria, great library of, 42
Algonquian Indians, 4
Allein zu dir, Herr Jesu Christ (Bach), 380
Allen, Eliza, 46
Allen, Grant [pseud. Olive Pratt Rayner], *The Typewriter Girl,* 32
Allston, Washington, 407
Alma-Tadema, Sir Lawrence, 416
Alphabet system of writing, 5, 9, 19, 123
Amado, Jorge, 318
Ambrosiana library, 427
American Antiquarian, The, 48
American Antiquarian Society, 336, 342
American Art Association, 50, 259
American Art Association–Anderson Galleries, 50
American Association for State and Local History, 167
American Autograph Shop, 335
American Book Prices Current, 186, 384
American dealers buying in Europe, 375
American First Editions (Johnson), 269
American Historical Association, 167
American Library Directory, 167
American Literary Autographs From Washington Irving to Henry James (Cahoon *et al.*), 259 n
American Penmanship 1800–1850: A History of Writing and a Bibliography of Copybooks From Jenkins to Spencer (Nash), 30 n
American Revolution: autograph material of, 63, 205, 216, 334, 394; bicentennial of, 179; European and English sources of, 335; letters from leaders of, 333; 1776 as magic date of, 181; manuscript markets, 332–337; pseudonyms used during, 110; records of, 337
American School of Oriental Research in Jerusalem, 426
Amherst, Lord Jeffrey, archive of, 334
Ammann collection, 399
Amundsen, Roald, 451
Analytic scripts, pictorial, 9
Anand, Mulk Raj, 329
Anarchists, 456
Ancestors, diaries of, 444, 449
Anderdon, John L., 44
Andersen, Hans Christian, 320; "Christian Winther (After Having Read His 'The Flight of the Hart')," 321
Anderson, Sherwood, 265
Anderson Galleries of New York, 50, 209
André, John, 206
Andreyev, Leonid, 325
Anglo-Norman legal documents, 290
Anglo-Saxon semiuncial script, development of, 24
Animals: markings on, 4; skins of, used as writing surfaces, 28, 35, 78
Anne (queen of England), 44, 352, 354
Anouilh, Jean, 302
Anthony, Susan B., 405
Anthropology, museums for, 329
Anthroposophical Society, 310
Anti-imperialists, war position of, 457
Antiqua: cursive form of, 23, 24; development of humanistic style of, 23, 27
Antiquarian booksellers, 406; in Germany, 377
Antiquarian Booksellers' Association of America, 179
Antique: auctions, 346; dealers, 71; shops, 67, 179
Apachamoul, account of martyrdom of, 14
Apollinaire, Guillaume, 299
Appia, Adolphe, 464
Appleton's Cyclopedia of American Biography, 114
Appointments, military and naval, 212
Appraisals and appraisers, 187, 194–196
Arab book of etiquette, 434
Arabic script, 13
Arab world: authors of, 328; ink developed in, 28; language formation in, 328; manuscripts in, 330, 432; papermaking spread to, 43
Aragon, Louis, 299
Aragon and Castile, kings of, 371
Aramaic nomads, 9
Archaeology, study of, 405, 471
Architecture and architects, 406, 411, 417, 422
Archives: beginnings of, 176, 192, 410; church, 426, 435; of Communist Party, 458; family, 43; German, 305; Healy, 417; long-term survival of, 62; of madrasas, 426; mercantile, 449; national, 140, 157, 168, 430; public and private, 193, 196, 305; state, 336; storage areas for, 142; of synagogues, 426; Vatican, 43, 427; of writers, 262, 265
Archivists, 50, 191, 194, 198
Argonauts, voyages of, 440, 444
Ariel (Rodó), 318

Aristotle, 41
Armadale (Collins), 463
Arms and the Man, 464
Arnold, Benedict, 337
Arnold, William Harris, 259
Arrabal, Fernando, 303
Arrangement and housing of manuscripts, 134, 142, 146–147, 179, 210
Art: centers, 50, 331; collecting documents of, 405–424; decorative, 4; historians, 410, 416; market, 331
Artaud, Antonin, 303
Arthur, Chester Alan, 215, 235, 255, 417
Arthur, Ellen Herndon, 256
Arthur, Julia, 475
Artifacts, 64, 156; Pre-Columbian, 318
Artists, 188, 370–371, 432; autographs of, 406, 417, 464; calligraphy of, 407; holographs of, 422; letters of, 407, 464; personalities of, 422; reputations of, 416
Art nouveau, creator of, 422
Arts: interest in, 63; knowledge of, 181, 190; performing, 472
Art Through the Ages (Gardner), 411
Ascenders and descenders, gradual emergence of, 18
Asia: East, 432; religious manuscripts in, 432; Southeast, 432
Assis, Joaquim Maria Machado de. *See* Machado de Assis, Joaquim Maria
Assyria, 3; cuneiform adopted by, 5; dictionaries of, 8; kings of, 8
Astronauts, 404, 444
Astronomy texts, 9
Atheism, 435 n
Atmospheric pollution, 143
Attics: hot and dry, 143; old trunks in, 71; source materials found in, 147, 162, 179, 335
Auber, Daniel, 380
Auction(s): bidders at, 70, 197, 477; buying and selling at, 50, 117, 161, 191, 196, 317, 333, 416, 430; catalogs, 60, 70–71, 116, 135, 159, 175, 272, 335, 347, 361, 375; guidelines at, 69–71; houses, 70–71, 174–175, 179, 186–187, 192, 197, 272, 359, 373–377, 406; prices, 49–50, 67, 69, 136; public, 178–180, 190
Auctioneers, 111, 347
Audiovisual aids, age of, 472
Audubon, John James, 406
Austen, Jane, 285; *Volume the Second,* 274–275; *Volume the Third,* 272, 273
Australia, 36, 441
Austria, 307, 370, 373; collectors in, 410
Authenticity and authentication: of autographs, 73, 91; dubious, 493; guarantee of, 197; of ink, 73; knowledge of, 98, 178; of paper, 73; warranty of, 175
Autobiography (Franklin), 262
Autocrat of the Breakfast-Table, The (Holmes), 259
Autograph Collection, An (Charnwood), 432 n
"Autograph Collector's Baedeker" (Madigan), 428
Autograph Collectors' Journal, 50, 119
Autographs: A Key to Collecting (Benjamin), 160
Autographs and manuscripts, 50, 89, 191, 406, 480; abbreviations for, 53–55, 180, 183–185, 376; acquisition of and bidding for, 66–73; African and Arabic, 330, 432; on the American Revolution, 203, 332–342; artistic, 406, 417; auctions for, 50, 175, 185, 208; authentication of, 73, 91, 98; bargains and competition for, 362, 430; catalogs of, 371; Civil War, 343–346; colonial, 332–335, 340–342; control over, 163; curators of, 164, 335, 342; dealers in, 48, 49, 119, 344, 373; display of, 134, 137–138, 141, 147; dual nature of, 170, 178; English, 270–288, 347–360; European, 304–331, 361–376; examination and evaluation of, 74, 187; of explorers, 440–453; forged, 73, 174–175; gifts of, 196; historical, 270, 332–335, 343, 346; history of collecting, 40–50; inlaid on paper, 136; as intellectual and physical property, 170; as investments, 171–172; of justices of the Supreme Court, 489; language of, 53–62; legal ramifications of collecting of, 170–177; literary, 258–303; loss or destruction of, 191; market for, 60, 162, 191, 334, 424, 444; medical, 392–404; of music and musicians, 64, 135, 182, 377–391, 404; ownership or title to, 192; philosophy of collecting, 63–65, 129; preservation and repair of, 142–155; prices for, 69, 196, 270, 430; protection and identification of, 61, 136–137; provenance of, 60, 194; published and unpublished, 54, 162, 168, 175–176; of radicals, 454–458; of reformers, 454–458; religious, 425–439; reproduction of, 86, 135, 163, 191, 266; research and history of, 40–50, 54, 266; royal, 348–349, 370–371; scholarly research

Autographs and manuscripts (*continued*) uses of, 156–169, 266; of science and scientists, 392–404; sets of, 44, 63, 65; Shaker, 430; size and measurements of, 56, 134–135; stolen, 174–175; swapping of, 72; theater-related, 459, 470, 472; theft of, 191, 194; on travel, 440–453; values of, 178; vocabulary and terminology used in collecting of, 53–55, 180, 183–185, 376
Automatic writing devices, use of, 55, 103
Autopen: collectors shun, 103; deception with, 103; legality of, 105; political figures use, 67, 103, 214; presidential use of, 248–253; use and operation of, 50, 58, 91, 100–105
Aviation, field of, 403–404, 441, 453
Ayala, Juan de, **446**
Ayres, Philip, 288
Aztec sundial, 439

"B" (signature of Earl of Beaconsfield), 358
Babylonia: cuneiform adopted by, 5; influence of, 3, 8
Bach, Johann Sebastian, 207, 377–378; *Allein zu dir, Herr Jesu Christ,* 380; "Der Herr is mein getreuer Hirt," **379**
Bacheller Collection, Clifton Waller Barrett Library, University of Virginia Library, 399, 492
Bachmann, Edwin, 454
Back to Methuselah, 463
Bacon, Sir Francis, 347, **393**; forgeries of, 96
Bacon, Sir Nicholas, letter to, **393**
Baghdad, early paper mills established in, 36
Bakst, Léon, 464, 470
Bakunin, Mikhail, 454
Balanchine, George, 470
Baldwin, James, 311
Balkan royalty, 304
Ballet: classical, 470; masters of, 469–470; professional, 468; of Renaissance Italy, 468; revival of, 470; romantic, 469–470; Russian, 470
Ballets Russes, 470
Ball-point pens: and multiple copies, 30–31; U.S. Army adopted, 30
Baltimore, Lord. *See* Calvert, George
Balzac, Honoré de, 189, 289, 297
Bamberger, Louis, 48
Bangs and Company auction sales, 50
Bank checks, 204, 344
Bank drafts, 491
Banks, Gordon T., 49, 119, 342; "John Adams—His Handwriting," 120–125
Banks, Sir Joseph, 449
Banting, Frederick, 403
Bantu language, 328
Barbier, Jules, 307
Barbusse, Henri, 126, 302
Barca, Pedro Calderón de la. *See* Calderón de la Barca, Pedro
Bargains in collecting, 334, 340, 417, 430
Bark of trees used for writing surfaces, 28
Barlach, Ernst, 424
Barnum, P. T., 100
Barojay Nessi, Pío, 317
Baronova, Irina, 470
Baroque period, 315, 317, 327, 416
Barrett, Clifton Waller, 259, 266; library of, at University of Virginia, 33, 262, 265, 323, 399, 492
Barrett, Lawrence, 472, **473**, 474–475, 480
Barrett, Oliver R., 48, 178
Barrie, Sir James Matthew, 462–463
Barry, Spranger, 459
Bartók, Béla, 207, 378, 387, 391
Baseball players, 184
Basements, dangers of damp, 143
Basler, Roy P., ed., *The Collected Works of Abraham Lincoln,* 166 n
Bastard script styles, 24, **26**, 27
Batchelder, John, Autograph Collection, Library of Congress, 308, 316, 321
Baudelaire, Charles, 190, **297**
Beaconsfield, Earl of (Benjamin Disraeli), 108, 355, **356**, 358, 359
Béatitudes, Les (Franck), 380
Beaumarchais, Pierre Augustin Caron de, 295
Beauvoir, Simone de, 302
Beckett, Samuel, 298, 311
Beckford, William, *Dreams, Waking Thoughts, and Incidents,* **271**
Becque, Henri, 298
Bécquer, Gustavo, 318
Bedell, Grace, 343
Beecher, Henry Ward, 430
Beerbohm, Sir Max, 470
Beethoven, Ludwig van, 63, 188, 377–378, 380, 384; Sonata for violin and piano, op. 96 in G major, **382**
Beggar's Opera, The (Gay), 460
Belasco, David, 486
Belgium and the Belgians, 190, 327
Bell, Alexander Graham, 403
Bellamy, Edward, 456
Bellamy, Francis, 129
Bellini, Vincenzo, 380
Belorussian language, 326
Bembo, Ambrogio, 445

Bembo, Pietro, 371
Benavente y Martínez, Jacinto, 317
Benefit system, 126, 466
Benevento, writing school of, 21
Bengali language, 329
Ben-Gurion, David, 327
Benjamin, Mary A., 138, 178–188, 342, 392, 432 n; *Autographs: A Key to Collecting,* 160; "Values," 68, 178–188
Benjamin, Walter R., Autographs, Inc., 213, 342
Benjamin brothers, 48, 397
Bennett, Arnold, 270
Benois, Alexandre, 470
Benson, Sir Frank, 460
Beppo (Byron), 285
Bequests to charities, 173
Berchet, Giovanni, 315
Berg, Alban, 380, 387
Berg Collection at New York Public Library, 259, 262
Bergson, Henri, 298
Berkeley, Edmund, Jr., 342; "Changing Handwriting," 117–119; "The Language of Autograph Collecting," 53–62; "Writing Instruments and Materials," 28–39
Berkman, Alexander, *Prison Memoirs of an Anarchist,* 455
Berlin, Irving, 126, 129, 377, 384, 391, 411
Berlioz, Hector, 98; *Le roi de Thulé,* 383
Bernanos, Georges, 302
Bernhardt, Sarah, 463, 480
Bernini, Giovanni Lorenzo, 416
Berry juice used for writing, 28
Bertram, Ernst, 314
Besterman, Theodore, archives in Geneva, Switzerland, 294
Béthune, Philippe de, 43
Beyle, Marie Henri [pseud. Stendhal], 297
Bhalo, Ahman Hassir bin Juma, 328
Bibliothek des Domkapitels, 21
Bible, references to, 28, 42
Bibliothèque Nationale, 43, 427
Bids, bidding, and bidders, 69, 71, 197–198, 477
Bielson, James, 265
Bierce, Ambrose, 267; *Tales of Soldiers and Civilians,* 262
Biermann, Wolf, 314
Big Name Hunting (Hamilton), 104
Bildungsroman (developmental novel), 307
Billings, Warren K., 455
Bill of exchange, 342
Bill of lading, 342
Bindings of books, 56
Binns, Norman E., 34–36; *An Introduction to Historical Bibliography,* 34 n
Biographies and biographers, 111
Birch, Thomas, 50
Bismarck, Prince Otto von, 361, 370
Bittelman, Alexander, 456
Bizet, Georges: *Carmen,* 307; *Djamileh,* 380
Bjørnson, Bjørnstjerne, 320
Black African writers, 328
Blackwell's of Oxford, 271
Blake, William, 283, 407, 409, 411
Blanchard, Jean Pierre, 404
Blanqui, Louis, 456
Blasco Ibáñez, Vincente, 317
Bleaches, use of, 152
Blithedale Romance, The (Hawthorne), 259
Bliven, Bruce, Jr., *The Wonderful Writing Machine,* 32 n
Blixen, Baroness Karen. *See* Dinesen, Isak
Bloch, Jean Richard, 302
Blok, Aleksandr, 325
Bloomfield, Ben, 49
Bloy, Léon, 298
Blum, René, 470
Blunk, Hans Friedrich, 314
Boccaccio, Giovanni, 315
Bodleian Library at Oxford University, 44, 279, 427
Bodley, Sir Thomas, 44
Boer War in South Africa, 355
Bogotá, 320
Bohemia, 326
Boileau-Despréaux, Nicolas, 290
Bukhara, port of, 435 n
Böll, Heinrich, 312
Bologna, Giovanni da, 411
Bolton, Rev. Robert, 44
Bonaparte. *See* Napoleon I
Bonaparte family, 362, 432
Bonet, Alfred, 44
Bonnard, Pierre, 406
Book Collectors Quarterly, The, 37 n
Book of the Dead, 11
Book of Gates, 10
Book of hours, 434
Bookplates, 486
Books: auctions of, 50; capitals of, 20; coffee-table, 422; collectors of, 258; dealers in, 66, 153, 179, 373; dimensions and sizes of, 56–57, 64; friendship and sentiment types of, 127, 129; letterpress, 131; lice in, 143; looseleaf, 134–136; octavo, 56; orderly, 160, 332, 334; picture, 422; public buying habits and industry growth, 38, 317; rare, 172,

Books (*continued*)
337, 435; reference, 135. *See also* Libraries
Booksellers: antiquarian, 179, 377, 406; early, 336; German, 377
Book of Sir Thomas More, The, 285
Book of Snobs (Thackeray), **109**
Bookstores, 67; in Buenos Aires, 320; in Italy, 315; secondhand, 71
Boone, Daniel, 449
Booth, Agnes, 474
Booth, Blanche DeBar, 473
Booth, Edwin, 472, **473,** 474–475, 478, 480, 483, **486,** 487
Booth, John Wilkes, 478, 480
Booth, Junius Brutus, Sr., 483
Booth, Junius Brutus, Jr., 473–474, 480
Boothbay, Maine, Theatre Museum in, 472
Booth benefit for the Shakespeare Fund, 480
Borgia, Cesare, 371
Borgia, Lucrezia, 371
Borgia family, 371
Bormann, Martin, 370
Borrowdale, Cumberland, England, 34
Bosboom, Johannes, 416–417
Bosporus, manuscript shelves looted in, 435 n
Bossuet, Jacques Bénigne, 290
Boston Public Library, 46, 391
Boswell, James, 270
Boucicault, Dion, *London Assurance; The Shaugraun,* 487, 462
Bougainville, Louis Antoine de, 453
Boundaries, chronological, 3
Bourbon family, 362
Bournonville, Auguste, 470
Boutet de Monvel, Louis, 424
Bouvet, Joachim, 445
Bovet, Alfred, 44
Bowen, Catherine Drinker, *John Adams and the American Revolution,* 120
Box office returns, theatrical, 466
Boxall, Sir William, 410
Boyle, Robert, 94
Bozzaris, Marco, 405
Bracebridge Hall (Irving), 262
Brahe, Tycho, 394, 399
Brahms, Johannes, 384, 387; *Ein deutsches Requiem,* 380
Bramah, Joseph, 30
Brazil, 318, 326
Brecht, Bertolt, 305, 308, 312
Brent, Charles H., 430
Brent, Daniel, 221
Breton, André, 289, 299, **300,** 327
Brezhnev, Leonid, 99, 190
Bridie, James, 464
"Brief History of Paper, A" (Jahans), 37 n, 38 n, 39 n
Brienne, Antoine Loménie de. *See* Loménie de Brienne, Antoine
Briquet, C. M., *Les filigranes,* 78
British Library, 12, 19, 25, 44, 93, 133, 140, 274, 411, 427
Britten, Benjamin, 207, 380
Broadsides, description of, 56, 64, 157
Broderick, John C., 342
Brompton, Oratorian Collection at, 438 n
Brontë, Charlotte, 283
Brontë, Duke of (Horatio Nelson), 358
Brooks, Phillips, 435
Brothers Karamazov, The (Dostoyevsky), 323
Browder, Earl, 457
Brown, Charles Armitage, 280
Brown, John, 116
Brown, J. Stanley, 234
Browne, H. K. [pseud. Phiz], 424
Browning, Elizabeth Barrett, 283
Browning, Robert, 281
Brumbaugh, Thomas B., "Collecting the Documents of Art," 405–424
Bruno, Guido, and his daughter Elenore (autograph dealers), 49
Brush and brush pens, 13, 16, 42
Bryant, William Cullen, "Thanatopsis," 129
Buchanan, James, **113, 229,** 254
Buck, Pearl, 330
Bucke, Richard M., 266
Buddha, Gautama, 330–331, 426
Buell, Don Carlos, 344
Buenos Aires, bookstores in, 320
Buffalo, University of, 259
Buffered or "permanent" papers, 146, 148
Buffon, Georges, 291
Bukharin, Nikolai, 456
Bulgaria, Greek influence in, 326
Bulwer-Lytton, Edward, 463, 484
Bunker Hill, as source for collecting, 205–207
Burden of proof, 175
Burger, Warren, 493
Burgess, Hugh, 38
Burghley, Lord (William Cecil), 347
Burgoyne, General John, 206
Burke, Edmund, 94
Burne-Jones, Sir Edward, 407
Burnett, Edmund S., *Letters of Members of the Continental Congress, 1774–1789,* 158 n
Burney collection of manuscripts, 44
Burns, Charles De F., 48
Burns, Robert, 66, 94, 277; final page of letter by, 276
Burnside, General Ambrose, 344, 346

Burr, Aaron, 96
Burroughs, Edgar Rice, 328
Burroughs, William, 331
Burt, William Austin, 31
Busch, Wilhelm, *Max und Moritz,* 307
Business correspondence, 13, 27, 56, 86, 334, 344, 406
Business Land, 24, **25**
Bute, Earl of (John Stuart), 355
Butler, Samuel: letterpress of, 132; *Notebooks,* 131
Butor, Michel, 302
Buying and buyers, 70–72, 174
Byrd, Richard, 451
Byrd, William (1674–1744), *Journal,* 262
Byron, Lord, 280, 306–307; *Beppo,* 285, **286**; dog's collar belonging to, **286**
Byron, Major George Gordon De Luna, 93–94, 281
"By Strauss" (Gershwin), 380

Cabell, James Branch, 267; *Jurgen,* 265
Cabell Memorial Foundation, Charlottesville, Virginia, 216
Cabinets: display and storage in, 146; fireproof and legal size of, 134–135; for photographs, 344
Cadman, Charles, 384
Caesar, Julius, 94, 329
Cage, John, 380, 384
Cahoon, Herbert, *et al., American Literary Autographs From Washington Irving to Henry James,* 259 n
Cain, Henri Louis. *See* Lekain
Caldecott, Randolph, 422
Calder, Alexander, 424
Calderón de la Barca, Pedro, 317
Calendar, New Style or Gregorian, 356, 358
Caliphate of Spain, 426
Calligraphy, ornate art of, 43, 94, 216, 330, 407, 428
Calvert, George (Lord Baltimore), 334
Calvin, John, **437**, 438; letters of, 435
Camargo, Marie, 468
Camels' hair brushes, invention of, 42
Cameras for copying purposes, 163–164
Camerorius, Ludwig, 43
Camoẽs, Vaz de, 317
Campana, Dino, 315
Camus, Albert, 298, **301**, 302
Canada: collectors in, 406; history of, 449
Canadian fur trade, as a source for collecting, 63
Canaletto (Antonio Canal), 411
Čapek, Karel, *R.U.R. (Rossum's Universal Robots),* 326–327
Capital gains tax, 171
Capitals: book, lapidary, and rustic, 20
Capital script, development and then replacement of, 20
Capodistrias, Joannes (Giovanni Capo d'Istria), 373
Carbon copies, 130–131
Cardinals, Roman, 426, 438
Cardozo, Benjamin N., 491
Carducci, Giosuè, 315
Carew, Thomas, 288
Carey, Mary Flagler, 391
Caribbean area, writers from, 328
Carleton, Sir Dudley, 288
Carlisle, Earl of (Charles Howard), 355
Carlyle, Thomas, **87**
Carmen (Bizet), 307
Carnegie Book Shop, 49, 160, 342
Caroline (queen of England), 360
Carolingian script, **21**, 22–24
Carradine, John, 99
Carré, Michel, 307
Carte de visite, signed, 344
Carter, James Earl (Jimmy), **252, 253,** 255; machine signatures of, 104
Carter, Rosalynn Smith, 257
Caruso, Enrico, 391
Carvalho, David N., 32 n, 34; *Forty Centuries of Ink, or a Chronological Narrative Concerning Ink and Its Background,* 28 n, 29
Carver, George Washington, 188
Carver, Jonathan, 449
Carvings in stone, 3, 20
Cases, flat-topped, 139
Casoni, Fred, 104
Castaing, Michel, "The Market for Autographs: The European Scene," 189–190
Castile, kings of, 110, 371
Catalogs: auction, 60, 70–71, 116, 135, 159, 175, 272, 335, 347, 361, 375; British, 416; dealers', 57, 60, 67–68, 135, 189, 272, 291, 298, 302, 333–334, 344, 361, 384; descriptions in, 61, 69–70, 114, 134–136; European, 371; French, 189, 299, 302; German, 307; Italian, 315; scholars use of, 159; Swiss, 307; terms of sale in, 305
"Catherine, or the Bower" (Austen), **273**
Catherine II (Catherine the Great, czarina of Russia), 373
Catholicism and Catholics: church history of, 203; collections of, 430, 438; personages, 302, 427, 438–439; and Protestant wars, 432

Cavafy, C. P., 325
Cavalleria Rusticana (Mascagni), 380
Caveat emptor, theory of, 72, 179, 192, 195
Cave walls as writing surfaces, 28
Cavour, Camillo di, 373
Cecchetti, Enrico, 470
Cecil, family name of, 358
Cela, Camilo, 318
Céline, Ferdinand, 302
Cellini, Benvenuto, 407, 411
Cellulose acetate sheets, 62, 153
Celsius, Anders, 394, 399
Cendrars, Blaise, 299
Centennial Exposition of 1876, 32
Center for Editions of American Authors, 266
Central America, Indians in, 318
Cerrito, Fanny, 469
Certificates, 36, 103, 466
Cervantes, Miguel de, 317
Césaire, Aimé, 328
Cézanne, Paul, 188
Chagall, Marc, 406
Chaliapin, Feodor, 391
Cham (Amédée de Noé), 422
Chamberlain, Jacob Chester, 258–259
Chamberlain, Mellen, 46, 333
Chambry, Étienne Pierre Louis, 44
Chamfort, Sébastien, 294
Chamisso, Adelbert von, *Peter Schlemihls wundersame Geschichte,* 312
Channey, Lon, Jr., 99
Chanson de Roland, 290
Chapin Library of Williams College, 131, 132, 309, 372, 374
Chaplin, Charlie (Sir Charles Spencer Chaplin), 99
Char, René, 299
Charavay, Étienne, *Faux autographes: affaire Vrain-Lucas: étude critique sur la collection vendue à M. Michel Chasles et observations sur les moyens de reconnaître les faux autographes,* 94 n
Charavay in Paris (dealers), 397
Charcoal, use of, in drawings, 28, 148
Charity and charitable contributions, 171–173
Charlemont, Lord, letter to, **414**
Charles I (king of England), 94, **351,** 354
Charles II (king of England), 94, **351,** 354
Charles V (Holy Roman emperor), 362, **367,** 371, 411
Charles VI (Holy Roman emperor), **368**
Charles VI (king of France), **363**
Charles VII (Holy Roman emperor), **369**
Charles VII (king of France), **363,** 366
Charles VIII (king of France), **363,** 366
Charles IX (king of France), 362, **364**
Charles X (king of France), **365**
Charles XII (king of Sweden), 373
Charles Hamilton Galleries, Inc., 336, 342
Charwood, Dorothea, Lady, *An Autograph Collection,* 432 n
Charny, Marguerite de, 426
Charters, royal, 348, 371
Chasles, Michel, 94
Chateaubriand, François de, 295
Chatham, Earl of (William Pitt), 94, 108, 355
Chatterton, Thomas, 92, 281
Chatwyn, Miss, 463
Check Collectors' Round Table, 50 n
Chekhov, Anton, 323
Chemicals and chemical migration, 30, 79, 143–144
Chénier, André, 295
Chevalier, Sulpice Guillaume [pseud. Gavarni], 422
Chiang Yee, 330
Chicago Public Library, 430
China, 432, 445; literature of, 304, 330; paper invention in, 36; pictography of, 4; rare autographs of, 330–331; writings of, on woven cloth, 42
Chivers, Thomas Holley, 267
Chopin, Frédéric, 380, 384, 405
Choreography and choreographers, 470
Chou En-lai, 330
Christian, George B., Jr., 242
Christian names or initials, 359
"Christian Winther (After Having Read His 'The Flight of the Hart')" (Andersen), **321**
Christie's Auction House, 50, 377
Church: archives, 426, 435; history, 203; leaders, 203–204, 445; libraries, 44
Church of England, 203
Churchill, family name of, 358
Churchill, John (Duke of Marlborough), 108, 35
Churchill, Sarah (Duchess of Marlborough), 354
Churchill, Sir Winston, 355
Church of St. Michael the Archangel, letter discussing work on, **15**
Cibber, Colley, 459
Cicero, 42
Cinema, 184, 406, 460, 466
Cioran, Emil M., 326
Circus, 466
Cist, Lewis J., 46, 111, 333
Civil rights, 489
Civil War, American, 63, 138, 179, 181, 343–346, 450

Civil War, English, 63, 354
Civran, Bortolo, letter to, 413
Clapp, Jane, *International Dictionary of Literary Awards,* 299 n
Clarence, Duke of (William IV, king of England), 353, 471
Clark, Abraham, 157–158
Clark, George Rogers, 449
Claudel, Paul, 299
Claude Lorrain (Claude Gelée), 416
Clay tablets or cones, recordings on, 3, 6, 7, 8, 28–29, 41
Cleaning agents, use of, 149
Clemens, Samuel Langhorne. *See* Twain, Mark
Clements, William L., 48
Clements Library at University of Michigan, 337
Cleomenes II (king of Pergamum), 36
Cleopatra, 94
Clerks, law, 493
Cleveland, Frances Folsom, 256
Cleveland, Grover, 76, 215, 236, 238, 255
Clients, ethics of, 70
Clipped signatures, 344, 346
Clive, Catherine (Kitty), 459
Clodion (Claude Michel), 422
Closings, 82, 86
Cloth, various uses for, 28, 426
Coan, Titus, 430
Coblentz, David Herr, "Organizing and Displaying Your Collection," 134–141
Cockling (an irregular waviness), 149
Cocteau, Jean, 299, 312
Codex Sinaiticus, 431
Coffee-table picture books, 422
Cohan, George M., 384
Cohen, Joshua J., 46
Cohn, Alexander Meyer, 46
Colbert, Jean B., 366
Cole, Howson C., 342
Cole, Robert, 44
Coleridge, Samuel Taylor, 93, 283, 306, 308
Colette, 302
Collected Works of Abraham Lincoln, The (Basler, ed.), 166
Collections and collecting: Americana, 449; art history, 410; assets of, 209; of autographs, 63–65; building of, 337–342; Canadian, 406; displaying of, 134–141; eclectic, 65; fads in, 184; family, 179; history of, 40–50; institutional, 64–65, 170, 347, 411, 478; inventory and inspection of, 143–144, 163; language and vocabulary used with, 53–62; of libraries, 41; manuscript, 129, 270; opportunities for, 332–336; organization of, 134–141; private, 64–65, 136–137, 157, 159, 161–162, 170–171, 178, 180, 185, 194, 267, 335–337, 347, 391, 427, 472; research value of, 54; security of, 163; specialized, 65, 67–68, 181, 203–210; subjects of, 64–65; thematic approach to, 342. *See also* specific collections
Collector, The, 49, 137
Collectors: 111, 191–194, 387; book, 66, 258; closet, 472; disappointments in, 348; disposition of, 209; ethical, 72, 432; experienced, 66, 72, 271; guidelines for, 69; neophyte, 410, 478, 488; nonspecialist, 181; private, 64–65, 136–137, 157–162, 170–171, 178, 180, 185, 194, 267, 335–337, 347, 391, 427, 472; professional, 435; public, 159; and publishing rights, 198; shun autopen signatures, 103
Collins, Wilkie, *Armadale,* 463
Collins, William, 285
Colnaghi, Dominic, 410
Colonial administrators and governors, 205, 334, 341
Colonial manuscripts, 334–337, 340–341
Colonial period, material and records of, 332–342
Colors and coloring matter, factor of, 4, 78–80, 84, 139–140
Columbia University, 214
Columbus, Christopher, 440, 444
Comedians and musical comedy, 460, 487
Commissions, 71, 153; military, 55, 135, 215, 231, 348, 354
Common-law copyright, 175–176
Common-law tradition, 162
Communist Party, 318, 455–458
Compagnie des Quinze, La, 460
Composers, 175, 182, 188, 207, 378, 380–381, 384, 387, 477
Condorcet, Marie Jean de, 291
Conductors, musical, 378
Confederate States of America, material concerning, 343–345. *See also* Civil War
Confessions of an English Opium-Eater, The (De Quincey), 277
Congress and congressmen, 135, 176, 325, 345–346
Conkling, Roscoe, 162
Conquistadors, Spanish, 108
Conrad, Joseph, 325, 328
Conservation workshops, 143, 146, 153–154
Conservators, need for, 144, 148–154
Constant, Benjamin, 295

Constitution of the United States, signers of, 135, 333
Conté, Nicholas, 34
Continental Congress, members of, 157–158, 162, 333
Cook, James, 449
Coolidge, Calvin, **243**, 255
Coolidge, Grace Goodhue, 257
Cooney, Charles F., "Autographs of the American Civil War," 343–346
Cooper, James Fenimore, *The Deerslayer,* 265; *The Pathfinder,* 262, 266
Cooper, Priscilla Elizabeth, 483–484
Cooper, Thomas Abthorpe, 483–484
Copeau, Jacques, 462
Copernicus, Nicholas, 325, 394
Copland, Aaron, 207, 384, 387
Copley, John Singleton, 417
Coptic form of writing, 13, **14**, **15**
Coptos, bishop of, letter to, **15**
Copy(ies): ball-point pen, 30–31; carbon, 130–131; contemporary, 57; electrostatic, 89, 130–131, 163; fair, 126–133; illegal, 191; letterpress, 60, 131; moral right to make, 196; multiple, 30–31; and tracing, 76; types and methods of making, 57–60, 126; working, 126–133; Xerox, 135, 163
Copyright, 162–163; common-law, 175–176; protection of, 175–176
Copyright Revision Act, 176
Coralli, Jean, 470
Corneille, Pierre, 290
Correspondence: business, 24, 27, 56, 86, 334, 344, 406; family, 453; mercantile, 444; military, 332, 450; private, 13, 27, 106, 110, 477
Corsican Brothers, The, 460
Corso, Gregory, 331
Cosey, Joseph, 82, **83**, **96–97**, 179, 216, 346
Costumes and costume designers, 417, 464, 470
Cotton, Sir Robert Bruce, 44; manuscripts of, in the British Library, 133
Courbet, Gustave, 416
Courten, William, 44
Court hand prevailing in England, 107
Courts of justice, 107, 491, 493; records of, 334
Covarrubias, Fernando de, 417
Covarrubias, Miguel, 318
Covent Garden, 466; box office return from, **467**
Cowboys, 450
Cowley, Abraham, 288
Cowper, William, 285, **287**
Cox, Richard J., 342
Cox, Samuel H., 127
Craig, Edward Gordon, 464
Cranach, Lucas, 411
Crane, Hart, 269
Crane, Stephen, 267; *The Red Badge of Courage,* 262, **264**, 265–266
Crane, Walter, 407, 422
Crane, William H., 487
Craven, Wayne, *Sculpture in America,* 416
Credibility of purchaser, 192
Crete and Cretans, 4–5
Crevel, René, 299
Cricket on the Hearth, The (Dickens), 463
Crimean War, 355, 358
Critics and criticism, 378
Crocker-Tennyson Collection, University of Virginia Library, 282
Cromwell, Oliver (lord protector of England), 94, 284, 288, **351**, 359
Cromwell, Richard (lord protector of England), **351**
Crowley, Christine Guyonneau, 189 n
Cruikshank, George, 422
Crusades, 366, 426
Cryptic designs, 108
Culture: influences of, 5; Western, 315, 327, 384, 424
Cuneiform inscriptions and writing, 5, **6**, 8–9, 40–41
Curators, 111, 435; book, 66; manuscript, 164, 335, 342; museum, 475; print, 153
Curie, Marie, **399**
Curie, Pierre, 399
Currency: depreciation of, 187, 190; signed, 332
Current market values, knowledge of, 136, 185, 196
Cursive: forms of hieroglyphics, 13; minuscule script, 16, **17**, 18, **20**, **21**, 23; types of antiqua, 23–24
Curtis Institute of Music in Philadelphia, 391
Cushing, Harvey, 405
Cushman, Charlotte, 478, **479**
Custer, George Armstrong, 99
Customhouses, contents of, 179
Customs manifests, 342
Cuttlefish, ink of, 28
Cyrillic alphabet, 107, 378
Czaczkes, Samuel Josef. *See* Agnon, Shmuel Yosef
Czechoslovakia, 374; German-Austrian influence in, 326

Dabit, Eugène, 302
Dabney, Richard Heath, 119

Daguerre, Louis, 403
Dalcroze, Émile Jacques. *See* Jaques-Dalcroze, Émile
Dali, Salvador, 406
Dalou, Jules, 416
Daly, Augustin, 48
"Damp-stained," definition of, 61
Dance material and dancers, 459, 466, 468, 470
Dandy roll, invention of, 38
Danforth, Elliott, 46
Dann, John C., "American Colonial and Revolutionary Autographs," 332–342
D'Annunzio, Gabriele, *Le martyre de St.-Sébastien,* 316; postcard by, **316**
Dante Alighieri, 315
Danton, Georges Jacques, 366
Darío, Rubén, 318, **319**
Darnley, Henry Stewart, 348
Dartford, England, paper mill at, 43
Darwin, Charles Robert, **398,** 399; *On the Origin of Species,* 397
Darwin-Evolution Collection, University of Virginia Library, 399
"Das erste Gebot" (Haydn), **381**
Dates, datelines, and dated signatures, 86, 181, 183, 391
Daudet, Alphonse, 298
Davenport, Edward, 480
Davenport, Fanny, 480
David, Jacques-Louis, 416, 422
Davids, Roy L., "English Literary Autographs," 270–288
Davidson, Jo, 477
Davies, Scrope, 285
Davis, Jefferson, 344–346
Davis, Richard Harding, 265
Davis, Varina, 346
Daybooks, 342
Dayton, Elias, 157
Deacidification, process of, 62, 146, 149
Dead Sea Scrolls, 328, 426, **427**
Dealers, 53, 111, 185, 191, 387; antique, 71; book, 66, 153, 179, 373; catalogs of, 57, 60, 67–68, 135, 189, 272, 291, 298–299, 302, 333–336, 344, 361, 384; and clients, 70; foreign, 68, 189, 299, 302, 375, 435; guidelines for, 69; lists, 67–68, 71, 116, 136; professional and experienced, 194, 477, 480; reputable, 67, 174, 194–195; rivalry among, 48–50; specialist, 48–49, 179, 373, 397; stamp, 179
Dearborn, Dr. Frederick M., 48
DeBar, Ben, 473
DeBar, Clementine, 473
De Basil, Colonel W., 470
Debs, Eugene, 454, 456
Debts, tallies recording of, 4
Debussy, Claude, 316, 380, 384, 387
Declaration of Independence (Israel), 327
Declaration of Independence (U.S.), Signers of, 46, 64, 112, 114, 133, 156–158, 180–181, 203–204, 332, 340, 355, 394
Decomposition of photochemicals, 145
Deeds: Indian, 206; land, 180; vellum, 135
Deerslayer, The (Cooper), 265
Deframing, process of, 152
Degas, Edgar, 416
De Gaulle, Charles, 189, 361, 366
De Gibler. *See* Byron, Major George Gordon De Luna
D'Egmont, Count Lamoral, 373
Dehmel, Richard, **311**
Delaunay, Louis, 463
Delius, Frederick, 380; *Fennimore and Gerda,* 320
Delivery schedules, 152, 154
Demotic writing, **12,** 13
Denis, Maurice, 416–417
Denmark, 320
Depressions, and effects on collecting, 50, 183, 315, 331, 334, 340
De Quincey, Thomas, 285; *The Confessions of an English Opium-Eater,* 277
"Der Herr is mein getreuer Hirt" (Bach), **379**
"Der Winterabend" (Schubert), 380
Descartes, René, 394, 399
Descenders, gradual emergence of, 18
Designs and designers, 108, 474
Desnos, Robert, 299
Destouches, Louis Ferdinand, 302
Deterioration and destruction of autographs, principal causes of: atmospheric pollution, 143; chemicals, 144; heat and humidity, 144, 147; insects, 143; light, 145; mankind, 143; self-destructive characteristics of paper and images, 146
Deuel, Leo, 34; *Testaments of Time: The Search for Lost Manuscripts and Records,* 35 n
Devine, George, 462
Devlin, Mary, 478
Devonshire, Duke of (1720–1764), 355
Dewey, John, 456
Dhammapada, 330
Diaghilev, Sergei, 464, 470
Diary(ies), 160, 455, 457; of the Civil War era, 168, 450–451; family, 453; of immigrants, 441, 444, 449; Zen master's, 439
Dibble, John, 206

Dickens, Charles, 68, **75**, 108, 272, 283, 288, 463; letters of, 280, 454, 457; paraph of, **108**
Dickinson, Emily, 262, 330; portion of letter of, **261**
Dickinson, John, 156
Dictation of letters, 212
Dictionary, Assyrian, 8
Dictionary of American Biography (DAB), 114, 166, 168
Dictionary of National Biography (DNB), 358
Diderot, Denis, 291, 293
Dillon, John, 44
Dinesen, Isak (Baroness Karen Blixen), 328–329
Diplomas, signed, 36
Dip pen, 30
Directors, stage and screen, 464
Directory of Historical Societies and Agencies in the United States and Canada, 167
Discovery, age of, 392, 440, 444, 449
Disney, Walt, 99
Display and displays: cases of collections, 134–141; colors used in, 139–140; purpose of, 65, 147, 210
Disraeli, Benjamin (Earl of Beaconsfield), 108, 355, **356**, 358, 359
Division of Archives and Manuscripts, Minnesota Historical Society, 450
"Dixie" (Emmett), 129
Dixon, Elizabeth, 180
Dixon, James, 180
Dixon Pencil Company, 34
Djamileh (Bizet), 380
Dockets, 76, 212
Dr. Grimshawe's Secret (Hawthorne), 259
Document(s), 18, 74, 370, 394; Anglo-Norman, 290; business, 13; collections of, 65, 405–424; definition of, 54–55; display and arrangement of, 86, 140; Dutch, 327; government, 56, 58; holes in, 84; legal, 55, 290, 347–348, 356; material written on, 16, 39, 78; signed, designated by "D.S.," 55, 180; source of, 164; storage of, 147; value of, 162
Documentary minuscule, Greek, **18**
Documents Famous and Infamous, Selected From the Henry W. and Albert A. Berg Collection of English and American Literature (Szladits), 281 n, 284 n
Doenitz, Karl, 371
Doges of Venice, 371
Doheny, Estelle Betzold, 48
Dolci, Carlo, 411
Dolliver Romance, The (Hawthorne), 259
Doll's House, A, 462
Donations, 336. *See also* Gifts
Donelson, Andrew Jackson, 223
Don Giovanni (Mozart), 380
Don Juan (Strauss), 380
Donkin, Brian, 38
Donnadieu, A., 44
Donne, John, 280, 284, 285, 288; verse letter of, **278**
"Donne discovery," much-vaunted, 284
Donnelley, R. R., and Sons, 150, 151
Dorian Islands, 16
Dos Passos, John, 265
Dostoyevsky, Feodor, *The Brothers Karamazov,* 323
Doucet, Jacques, 299
Douglass, Frederick, 188
Dowson, Ernest, 288
Doyle, Sir Arthur Conan, 182, 284
Doyle, Richard, **423**
Drafts of materials, 57, 340
Drake, Sir Francis, 441
Drama and dramatists, 463–464
Drawings, 210, 416; rebus, 417
Dreams, Waking Thoughts, and Incidents (Beckford), **271**
Dreer, Ferdinand Julius, 46, 158, 333
Dreiser, Theodore, 265, 267
Drinkwater, John, 464
Driscoll, Emily, 49
Drouot (dealer in Paris), 399
Drury Lane Theatre in London, 466
Dryden, John, 285
Dryness, as necessary condition for manuscripts, 145
Dudevant, Amandine Aurore Lucie Dupin [pseud. George Sand], 297
Duff, Mary Anne Dyke, 483
Du Gard, Roger Martin, 298
Duhamel, Georges, 302
Duke University, 342
Dulac, Edmund, 422
Dullin, Charles, 464
Dumas Alexandre (Dumas père), 295
Dumas, Alexandre (Dumas fils), 295, 317
Duncan, Isadora, 470
Dunois, Jean de, 366
Dupin-Dudevant, Aurore Lucie [pseud. George Sand], 297
Durand, P. M., 100
Duras, Marguerite, 302
Dürer, Albrecht, 407, 417
Duse, Eleonora, 316, 480
Dutch: administration, 205; autographs and documents, 327; war of independence, 373
Dvořák, Antonín, 207, 380
Dyes, use of, 28

East Asia, religious manuscripts from, 432
East Europe, 325–326, 435
Eastman School of Music, 391
Economic conditions, as factor in collecting, 50, 183, 315, 331, 334, 340
Edgehill-Randolph Papers, University of Virginia Library, 113
Edgeworth, Maria, 283
Eddy, Mary Baker, 96
Edison, Thomas Alva, 32, 403
Educational institutions, 137, 176
Edward (Earl of Oxford), 44
Edward IV (king of England), 348, **349**
Edward V (king of England), 348, **349**
Edward VI (king of England), 347, **351**
Edward VII (king of England), **353**
Edward VIII (king of England), **353**
Egerton, Sir Thomas, 288
Egypt: hieroglyphic inscriptions of, **9–12**; ideographics in, 5; ligature, popularity of, 13; pictography of, 4; Ptolemaic rulers of, 92; writings in, 3, 13, 41
Ehrenburg, Ilya, 325
Ehrlich, Paul, 403
Eichendorff, Joseph von, 306; *Ahnung und Gegenwart,* 307
Ein deutsches Requiem (Brahms), 380
Einstein, Albert, **403**
Eisenhower, Dwight David, 99, 138, 182, **247**, 249, 255
Eisenhower, Mamie Doud, 257
"Elaine" (Tennyson), **282**
Electronic signature-signing devices, 100, 102
Electrostatic copiers, 57–58, 89, 130–131, 163
Elen, Gus, 466
Elima, 328
Eliot, George, 280
Eliot, T. S., 265–266, 306; *The Waste Land,* 266
Elitism, aversion to, 312, 330, 378
Elizabeth (queen of Rumania [pseud. Carmen Sylva]), 326
Elizabeth I (queen of England), 43, 347, 348, **351**, 428; Privy Council of, 108
Elizabeth II (queen of England), **353**
Elizabethan era, 314
Ellesmere, Sir Thomas Egerton. *See* Egerton, Sir Thomas
Elliott, Arthur, 48
Elssler, Fanny, 469
Éluard, Paul, 299
Emecheta, Buchi, 329
Emerson, Ralph Waldo, 180, 259, 262, 265, 306, 308; "Good Bye," 126
Emigré German writers, 312
Emmanuel, Pierre, 299
Emmet, Thomas Addis, 46, 333
Emmett, Dan, 384; "Dixie," 129
Encapsulation (protective process), 62, 135, 147
Encyclopédie, 291, 293
Endorsements, 76, 212
Engels, Friedrich, 373, 456
England, 23, 188, 270, 304, 315, 356–359, 406, 416, 444; auctions in, 71; Christianity and the church in, 24, 203; civil war in, 63, 354; colonial administration in, 205; court and round hand of, 27, 107; first paper mill in, 43; historical autographs of, 347–360; language of, 328–330; libraries in, 93, 133, 140, 427; literary autographs of, 64, 270–288; monarchs of, 43, 108, 135, 347–348, 428, 471; museum collections in, 44, 411; postal handstamps first used in, 83; prime ministers of, 355; religious leaders of, 203; Restoration in, 205; revolutions and wars of, 349, 354; scientists in, 449; the theater in, 459, 463, 470; translations in, 327
English Literary Hands From Chaucer to Dryden (Petti), 36 n, 37 n,
English secretary hand, **26**
Engravings, 135, 210, 333
Enlightenment, age of, 291, 430
Envelopes, 103; mylar, 147
Environment, sterile control of, 143–147
Epic poets, 304
Episcopal bishops, 427
Erasmus, Desiderius, 405
Erasures uncommon in forgeries, 84
Erech (Uruk), stratum of, 8
Escorial library, 427
Espronceda, José de, 318
Essays, 41, 281
Essex, Lord (favorite of Queen Elizabeth I), 347
Estate(s): appraisals of, 187; planning of, 174; settling of, 209, 477–478; tax laws on, 170–173, 335
Este family, 371
Esterbrook, Richard, 30
Ethics: agent's, 70; of collecting, 70, 195, 432 n; as moral standards, 191–199
Ethylene oxide, 145
Etruscans, alphabet and language of, 19
Etting, Frank, 46
Etude, 377
Eumenes II (king of Pergamum), 42
Euphrates valley and river, 5, 9
Europe: auction houses in, 70–71, 317, 406; catalogs in, 371; dealers in, 375,

Europe (*continued*)
435; Eastern, 325–326, 435; handwriting used in, 375; historical autographs in, 361–376; literature in, 304–322; manuscripts in, 54, 394; missionaries of, 444; the theater in, 463. *See also* individual countries of Europe
Euryanthe (Weber), 380
Evaluations, range of, 189–190
Evangeline (Rice), 487
Evans, Mary Ann. *See* Eliot, George
Evarts, William, 48
Evelyn, John, 284
"Excelsior" (Longfellow), 126
Executive Mansion cards: introduced by Grant, 232, 235; use of, **213**, 239
Exhibitions, 111, 137–141
Existentialism, 289, 302
Explorations and explorers: autographs and manuscripts of, 440–453; literature on, 440–441; Portuguese and Spanish, 371; as source for collecting, 334, 451
Export-licensing regulations, 359

Faber, Kaspar, 34
Fabergé, Romanov, 426
Fables, 41
Fabric conservator, 152
Facsimile(s), 114, 253, 284; commonness of, 58; definition of, 57; detection of, 73; ink density in, 58; in manuscripts, 86, 266; of political figures, 57, 67, 249, 252; of signatures, 213; and work copies, 131
Fading due to light, 145
Fadyen, Neil M., 466
Fair copies, 126–133, 266, 277, 280; definition of, 57; sentimental value of, 129; signed, 182
Fair market value, 384, 387
"Fair use," doctrine of, 176
Falla, Manuel de, 310
Family: archives, 43; correspondence, 341, 453; history, 449; papers, 335
Far East, 29; literature of, 329
Farnese, Alessandro, letter to, **412**
Farnese family, 371
Farrer, James Anson, *Literary Forgeries,* 92 n, 93 n
Fascism in Italy, 362
Faulkner, William, 269; *The Marionettes,* 265; *The Reivers,* 133
Fauré, Gabriel, 380
Faust (Goethe), 310
Faux autographes: affaire Vrain-Lucas: étude critique sur la collection vendue à M. Michel Chasles et observations sur les moyens de reconnaître les faux autographes (Charavay), 94 n
Federal taxes: estate, 173–174; income, 170–173
Feinstone, Sol, 157
Fennimore and Gerda (Delius), 320
Ferber, Edna, 267
Ferdinand I (Holy Roman emperor), **367**
Ferdinand II (Holy Roman emperor), **368**
Ferdinand II (king of Spain), 334, 371; letter to, **446**
Ferdinand III (Holy Roman emperor), **368**
Fersen, Count Hans, 373
Fesch, Joseph Cardinal, 44
Feuchtwanger, Lion, 305
Field, Eugene, 267
Fields, Dr. Joseph E., 122; "Confused Identities," 111–116; "The History of Autograph Collecting," 40–50
Fields, W. C., 99
Figdor, Albert, 392
Filigranes, Les (Briquet), 78
Filing and filing folders, 134–135
Fillmore, Abigail Powers, 256
Fillmore, Caroline McIntosh, 256
Fillmore, Millard, **227**, 254
Fillon, Benjamin, 44, 290
Film stars, 406
Filtration materials, 145
Finland, 304, 320, 373
Firdausi, *Shah Namah,* 432
Fireproof storage facilities, 134–135
Fisher, Dr. Otto, 48
Fitzgerald, F. Scott, 262, 265, 269; *The Great Gatsby,* 266
Fitzpatrick, John C., ed., *The Writings of George Washington,* 161 n
Flat-top cases and filing, 134–135, 139
Flaubert, Gustave, 298
Flaxman, John, letter to, **409**
Flea markets, 117, 346
Fledermaus, Die (Strauss), 380
Fleming, Alexander, 399
Fleming, John F., 49
Fletcher, C. A. Kyrle, "British Theater and Dance," 459–471
Flint, Sir William Russell, 424
Florence, Mr. and Mrs. William Jermyn, 480
Fluorescent lights and lighting, 140–141, 145, 147
Flynn, Errol, 99
Fogg, Dr. John S. A., 46
Fokine, Michel, 470
Folders: acetate, 135, 139; acid-free, 135, 147, 422; clear plastic, 135; manila, 134–135; mylar, 135, 139

Folger Shakespeare Library, Washington, D.C., 461
Folio items, large, 56, 135
"Folk conscious" literature, 312
Following the Equator (Twain), 262
Fondation Custodia in Paris, 417
Fontane, Theodor, 312
Foote, Charles B., 259
Foote, Samuel, 459
Forbes, General John, 334
Ford, Allyn K., 48
Ford, Elizabeth Bloomer, 257
Ford, Gerald Rudolph, **251**, 255; machine signatures of, 104
Ford, Worthington Chauncey, ed., *The Writings of George Washington,* 161 n
Forgers and forgeries: amateur, 82; characteristics of, 74–78; detection of, 73–91; early, 92; erasures uncommon in, 84; nib marks in, 80; problems of, 95–96, 98, 174–175, 253, 281, 346, 493; professional, 245; purchase of, at auctions, 39, 179; successes and downfalls of, 92–99; and unethical practices, 196
Formal business hand, 25
Forrest, Edwin, 463, 474–475, 478, 484
Forrest, Nathan Bedford, 344
"Forsyte Saga" (television series), 306
Forty Centuries of Ink, or a Chronological Narrative Concerning Ink and Its Background (Carvalho), 28 n, 29
Foscolo, Ugo, 315
Foster, Stephen, 384, 391; "Maggie by My Side," 380
Fountain pens, use of, 30–31, 39
Fouqué, Friedrich de La Motte-, 312
Fourdrinier, Henry, 38
Fourdrinier, Sealy, and papermaking machine, 38
Foxing (reddish-brown spots), 61, 145
Fraktur script, 24
Framing and frame shops, 137, 144, 147, 153
France, Anatole, 298
France: auctions in, 71; cabinet ministers of, 366; catalogs from, 188–189, 299, 302, 375; collecting in, 21, 23, 27, 304, 315, 317, 406, 411, 416, 424; concern in, for property rights, 290; dealers in, 189, 299, 302, 373; impressionism in, 63, 407; influence of, in Rumania, 326; intellectual history of, 289, 291, 366; language of, 323, 326–328, 394; literary traditions and literature in, 189, 289–303; monarchs of, 43, 182, 290, 314, 362, 366, 376, 410; spoliation claims in, 162; steel pen point produced in, 30
Francis I (Holy Roman emperor), **369**
Francis I (king of France), 362, **363**
Francis II (Holy Roman emperor), **369**
Francis II (king of France), 362, **363**
Franck, César, *Les Béatitudes,* 380
Franco, Francisco, 373
Franco-Prussian War, 362
Frankfurter, Felix, 493
Frankish Empire, 21
Franklin, Benjamin, 120, 332, 337, 341, 394, 399; *Autobiography,* 262
Franz Joseph (emperor of Austria), 326
Frauenliebe und -leben (Schumann), 312
Freeman, Mary E. Wilkins, 267
Freeman's auction sales, 50
Frederick, Lord Leighton, 416
Frederick II (Frederick the Great, king of Prussia), 361
Frederick III (Holy Roman emperor), 110, 366, 367
Frederick III (emperor of Germany), **369**
Freidel, Frank B., *The Harvard Guide to American History,* 167 n
French Academy, 291, 294, 298
French Revolution, 361–362, 366
Freon solvent, 149
Freud, Sigmund, 64, 306, 323, 326, 403, 411
Frick, Henry Clay, 455
"Friends of the library" organizations, 337
Friendship and sentiment books, 127, 129
Friml, Rudolf, 387
Fromentin, Eugène, 297
From the Tablets of Sumer (Kramer), 40 n
Frontenac, Count Louis, 334
Frontier in Ohio Valley, 337
Frost, Robert, 98, 265–266, 269
Fugard, Athol, *The Island,* 329; *Sizwe Bansi Is Dead,* 329
Fulda, Ludwig, 311
Fulton, Robert, 403
Funerary texts, 13

Gage, General Thomas, 207
Gaignières, Roger de, 43
Gainsborough, Thomas, 411, **415**
Galilei, Galileo, 315, 394, **395**, 411
Gallé, Emile, 424
Galleries, 153
Gall nuts, use of, in ink, 29
Galsworthy, John, 306
Galvani, Luigi, 399
Gama, Vasco da, 444

Gandhi, Indira, 432
Gandhi, Mahatma, 432
García Lorca, Federico, 317
Gard, Roger Martin du, 298, 302
Gardner, Helen, *Art Through the Ages,* 411
Garfield, James Abram, 204, 234, 254
Garfield, Lucretia Rudolph, 256
Gargantua, 290
Garibaldi, Giuseppe, 373
Garland, Judy, 99
Garrett, John Work, 48
Garrett Collection of Arabic Manuscripts, Princeton University Library, 433
Garrick, David, 459, 478
Garrison, William Lloyd, 207
Garro, A., 316
Gaskell, Elizabeth Cleghorn, 283
Gauguin, Paul, 188, 424
Gautier, Théophile, 295
Gavarni. *See* Chevalier, Sulpice Guillaume
Gay, John, 288; *The Beggar's Opera,* 460
Geibel, Dr. Carol, 46
Geibel, Emanuel von, 311
Geigy, Charles, 399
Geigy-Hagenbach, Karl, 46
Gelée, Claude. *See* Claude Lorrain
Genealogy and genealogists, 4, 111
General Assembly of the Church of Scotland, 284
"Generation of '98," 318
Generic similarities in handwritings, 284
Genet, Jean, 303
Geneva, Switzerland, 294, 399
Gentileschi, Orazio, 411
Genuineness, paramount importance of, 70, 73, 104, 179
Geography, factor of, 3, 5, 340, 440
George, Stefan, 310
George I (king of England), 352
George II (king of England), 44, 352
George III (king of England), 352
George IV (king of England), 352, 471
George V (king of England), 353
George VI (king of England), 353
George Perkins Papers, Rare Book and Manuscript Library, Columbia University, 214
Georgia Department of Archives and History, 253
Gerald R. Ford Presidential Materials Project, 251
Gerbel, Dr. Carol, 46
Gerlot, Guillaume, 445
German Archaeological Institute, 405
Germantown, Pennsylvania, paper mill in, 36
Germany: antiqua script of, 24; antiquarian booksellers in, 377; archives of, 305; collectors and collections in, 21, 32, 70–71, 83, 188, 307, 315, 373, 375, 406, 410, 424; emigré writers of, 312; Fraktur script of, 24; language of, 305, 307, 323, 325–326, 394; literature and literary traditions of, 304–314, 320; nationalism in, 314; political situations in, 306,310, 312, 362; princely houses in, 304, 366; Protestant Reformation in, 370; reunification of, 370; signatures of emperors of, 369
Gerry, Elbridge (vice-president of the United States), 206
Gershwin, George, 207, 384, 391; "By Strauss," 380
Gerstenbergk, Baron Georg Heinrich von, 95
Gesell, Gerhard A., "Justices of the Supreme Court of the United States," 489–493
Gesetz, Das, 313
Giambologna. *See* Bologna, Giovanni da
Gibran, Kahlil, 328
Gide, André, 289, 298–299, 328
Gifts, 172–173, 192, 196, 387
Gilbert, Sir William S., *The Mikado,* 331
Gill, Eric, 407
Gillette, William, 485
Gillott, Joseph, 30
Gilmor, Robert, 46, 333
Gimbel, Colonel Richard, 404
Ginsberg, Allen, 331
Giono, Jean, 302
Giraudoux, Jean, 302
Girsu, 6
Giscard d'Estaing, Valéry, 190
Giusti, Giuseppe, 315
Gladstone, Herbert, 357
Gladstone, William E., 85, 347, 355
Glasgow, Ellen, 265, 267
Glass, actress, 486–487
Glazing of prints, 144–145
Glidden, Carlos, 31
Gnostic scriptures, 328
Goatskins, used as parchment, 42
Gobelin family, 417
Godolphin, Sidney, 355
Goebbels, Paul Joseph, 370; *Michael,* 314
Goering, Hermann, 370
Goethe, Johann Wolfgang von, 63, 188, 306–307, 308–309, 314, 317, 397; *Faust,* 310; *Wanderers Sturmlied,* 308; *Wilhelm Meister,* 307
Gogh, Vincent Van. *See* Van Gogh, Vincent

Gogol, Nikolai, 323
Golden Age (*Siglo de oro*) of Spain, 317
Golden Tradition, The (anthology of Urdu poetry), 329
Goldsmith, Oliver, 283, 285
Goldwater, Walter, "Autographs and Manuscripts of Radicals and Reformers," 454–458
Goltzius, Hendrik, 411
Goncourt, Edmond de, 209, 298
Goncourt, Jules de, 298
Gonzaga family, 371
"Good Bye" (Emerson), 126
Good Soldier Schweik, The (Hašek), 326
Goodspeed, C. E., 49
Goodspeed's Book Shop, Inc., 342
Goose quills for writing, 29–30, 39, 80
Gordimer, Nadine, 329
Gorki, Maxim, **322**, 323, 325
Gorki Papers, Library of Congress, 322
Gospel According to Saint John, 431
Gosse, Sir Edmund, *The Works of Thomas Gray,* 272
Gothic script, **22**, 23, 107
Gottfried von Strassburg, 304
Gottlieb, Frederick, 38
Gottschalk, Louis M., 384
Gounod, Charles, 307
Government documents, 56, 58
Governors, colonial, 334, 341
Goya, Francisco, 411
Gozzi, Count Carlo, 317
Grabbe, Christian, 311
Grable, Betty, 99
Graefe, Albrecht von, 394
Graham, Martha, 470
Grahn, Lucile, 469
"Grandfather clause," 173
"Grandma" Moses, letters of, 422
Granger, Rev. James, 475, **476**
Grant, Sir Francis, 416
Grant, Julia Dent, 256
Grant, Ulysses Simpson, 213, 215, **232**, 254; introduced Executive Mansion cards, 232, 235; letter to, **345**
Granville-Barker, Harley, 464
Graphite, 34
Grass, Günter, 312
Gratz, Simon, 46
Graves, R. P., 128, 130
Gravitt, Alan T., 104–105
Gray, Arthur, 280, 288
Great Gatsby, The (Fitzgerald), 266
Greco, El, 411
Greece, 325, 373; alphabet developed in, 16; cursive script of, **17**; documentary script of, **18**; forgers flourished in, 92; language of, 13, 378; library in, 41; monumental script of, **16**; papyrus used in, 16, 41; printing types in, 18; Roman conquest of, 19; script styles of, 3, **12**, 14, 16, 18; uncial script of, **17**
Greeley, Horace, 106
Green, Julien, 302
Greene, Nathanael, 205, 337, **338**, **339**
Gregorian (New Style) calendar, 356, 358
Gregory X (pope), 438
Gregory XI (pope), 438
Greville collection of manuscripts, 44
Grid-pattern watermarks, 78
Grieg, Edvard, 310, 380, 384
Grillparzer, Franz, 306–307
Grimmelshausen, Hans Jakob von, *Simplicissimus,* 307
Grisi, Carlotta, 469
Groth, Klaus, 310
Grüne Heinrich, Der (Keller), 307
Guards, security, 141
Gudea, 6
Guerrillas, Confederate, records of, 344, 345
Guest books, 477
Guide to Manuscripts and Archives in the United States (Hamer), 168 n
Guide to the Study of the United States of America, A (Mugridge and McCrum), 167 n
Guitry, Sacha, 472, 474
Guizot, François, 361
Gunther, Charles F., 46
Gurrelieder (Schoenberg), 320, **386**
Gustavus II (Gustavus Adolphus, king of Sweden), 361
Gutiérrez, Antonio Garcia, 317–318
Gwinnett, Button, **88**, 116; A.L.S. from, **115**; forgeries of, 96

Haggard, Sir Henry Rider, 328
Hahnemann, Samuel, 403
Hale, John M., 46
Halévy, Jacques, 307
Half-uncials, Anglo-Saxon, **25**
Halifax, Earl of (Charles Montagu), 355
Hallam, Arthur Henry, 128, 130
Halleck, Henry W., 344
"Hall of Famers," 438
Halpern, Irving, 342
Hamburg, autograph market in, 329
Hamer, Philip M., *Guide to Manuscripts and Archives in the United States,* 168 n
Hamilton, Charles, 49, 70, 91, 98–99, 120, 432 n; *Big Name Hunting,* 104; *The Robot That Helped to Make a President,*

Hamilton, Charles (*continued*) 104, 248 n; *Scribblers and Scoundrels,* 104. *See also* Charles Hamilton Galleries, Inc.
Hamilton, George, 104
Hamlet (Shakespeare), 93, 463
Hammer, Armand, 455
Hammurabi, code of, 8, 41
Hamsun, Knut, 320
Hancock, John, 114, 120, 124, 206
Handel, George Frederick, 380
Handstamps, postal, 83
Handwriting: age revealed in, 74; comparison of, 73–75, 86; development of, 3–27; evolutionary changes in, 117–119; generic similarities in, 284; illness revealed in, 74; types and styles of, 21, 30, 54–55, 86, 212, 246, 248, 375
Handy, W. C., 384
Hardenberg, Dr. Albert, letter to, **437**
Hardenberg, Friederich von [pseud. Novalis], 306
Harding, Florence de Wolfe, 257
Harding, Warren Gamaliel, **242,** 255; used professional forger, 245
Hargrave collection of manuscripts, 44
Harleian manuscripts, 44
Harley, Edward, 44
Harley, Robert (Earl of Oxford and Mortimer), 44, 355
Harris, Doris, 327, 342
Harris, Joel Chandler, 267
Harrison, Anna Symmes, 256
Harrison, Benjamin (1833–1901), **237,** 255; used typewriter, 238
Harrison, Caroline Scott, 257
Harrison, Mary Dimmick, 257
Harrison, Robert H., 493
Harrison, William Henry, 68, **79,** 212, **224,** 254
"Hartington" [pseudonym of the Duke of Devonshire], 355
Hartmann, Arthur, 126
Hartmann, Sadakichi, 410
Harvard Guide to American History, The (Freidel and Showman), 167 n
Harvard University, 262, 430; graduates of, 341
Harvey, William, 399
Hašek, Jaroslav, *The Good Soldier Schweik,* 326
Hastings, Warren, impeachment of, 360
Hauptmann, Gerhart, 308; *The Weavers,* 314
Havoc, June, 477
Hawthorne, Nathaniel, 262, 265; *The Blithedale Romance,* 259; *Dr. Grimshawe's Secret,* 259; *The Dolliver Romance,* 259; *The Scarlet Letter,* 258; *Septimius Felton,* 259
Haydn, Franz Joseph, 326, 380; "Das erste Gebot," **381**
Hayes, Lucy Webb, 256
Hayes, Rutherford Birchard, **233,** 254
Haywood, William Dudley "Big Bill," 456
Hazlitt, William, essays of, 272
Healy, G. P. A., 416–417
Hearn, Lafcadio, 259, 331
Hearst, Phoebe Apperson, 48
Hearst, William Randolph, 48
Heat and preservation of documents, 4, 143, 145, 147
Heath, Baron, 44
Heath, William, 340
Heathcote family, 206
Hebel, Johann Peter, 310
Hebrew scholars, 28, 42
Heine, Heinrich, 96, 188, 311–312
Heineman Foundation, 391
Heise, E. V., 224
Heise, John, 410
Helmholtz, Hermann von, 394
Hemans, Felicia, 128, 130
Hemingway, Ernest, 265, 269, 311, 317, 328
Henderson, Benjamin, 48
Henkels, Stan V., 50
Henrietta Maria (queen consort of King Charles I of England), 288
Henry, Patrick, 96
Henry II (king of France), 363
Henry III (king of France), 364, 432
Henry IV (king of France), **364,** 417
Henry V (king of England), **349**
Henry VI (king of England), **349**
Henry VII (king of England), **350**
Henry VIII (king of England), 44, 347–348, **350**
Henze, Hans Werner, 330
Herbert, Victor, 384, 387
Herder, Johann von, *Stimmen der Völker in Liedern,* 326
Heredia, José María, 311
Heredia, José María de, 298
Hérédia, José-Maria de, 298, 311
Heron, Matilda, 475
Herrick, Robert, 285
Hertz, Heinrich, 399, 403
Herzl, Theodor, 327
Hess, Rudolf, 370
Hesse, Hermann, *Steppenwolf,* 312
Hettenried, Carl Herz von, 46
Heydrich, Reinhard, **371**
Hidden signatures, 106–110

Hieratic script, 11, 13
Hieroglyphics: cursive form of, 13; earliest extant, 12; Egyptian, 9–12, 41; oral reading of, 13; sacredness of, 9, 13
Hill, A. P., 344
Hill, Walter H., 259
Himmler, Heinrich, 370
Hindemith, Paul, 390
Hirohito (emperor of Japan), 99, 432
Hiss, Alger, 458
Historical libraries, 333, 335, 342
Historical societies, 146, 157, 208–209; local, 167, 336; Pennsylvania, 158; state, 335–337; Virginia, 342
History and historians: art, 410, 416; and autograph collecting, 40–50, 54, 347–360; British, 347–360; Canadian, 449; church, 203; European, 304–331, 361–376; family, 449; French, 291, 366; highlights of, 361–362; interest in, 63, 111, 190, 270, 361, 375, 440; military, 354; North American, 450; philosophy of, 180–181, 416; Russian, 373; sources of, 449; theater, 459, 466, 472, 474, 477–478. *See also* specific historical subjects
History of America in Documents, 375
Hitler, Adolf, 99, 312, 370, 405
Hittites, 5
Hoaxes, literary, 92
Ho Chi Minh, 330
Hoffmann, E. T. A., 307
Hogarth, Georgina, 283
Hogarth, William, 411, 414
Holberg, Baron Ludvig, 320
Hölderlin, Friedrich, 306; *Hyperion,* 307
Holland, 327, 373, 411
Hollingsworth, Zackary T., 46
Holmes, John Haynes, 430
Holmes, Oliver Wendell (American author and physician), 259, 262, 265; *The Autocrat of the Breakfast-Table,* 259
Holmes, Oliver Wendell (American jurist), 490
Holographs, 54–55, 67, 131, 207, 312, 361, 380, 384, 422
Holy Land, pilgrim's account of, 444
Holy Roman Empire, rulers of, 366–369
Holy Shroud of Turin, 426
Homer, *Odyssey,* 440
"Home Sweet Home" (Payne), 380
Homonyms, 5
Homophones, 12
Honegger, Arthur, 391
Honesty, basic rules of, 191–192
Hong Kong, 432
Hooft, Pieter, 327
Hooker, Joseph, 344
Hoover, Herbert Clark, 212, 244, 255
Hoover, Lou Henry, 257
Hopkins, Gerard Manley, 288
Hostick, King V., 49
Hôtel Drouot in Paris, 190
Houdon, Jean-Antoine, 416
Houston, John, A.L.S. to, 115
Howard, Charles (Earl of Carlisle), 355
Howe, William T. H., 259, 262
Howells, William Dean, 267
Hubbard, Mrs. John, 48
Hudson River School, 478
Hudson Valley landholders, 341
Huger, Lt. Col., A.L.S. to, 115
Hughes, Charles Evans, 492
Hugo, Victor, 289, 295, 296, 407
Humanistic antiqua, development of, 23, 27
Humboldt, Alexander von, 397
Hunchback, The (Knowles), 463
Hundred Years War, 361, 366
Hungary, 373
Huntington, Henry E., 48; library and art gallery of, 48, 262, 337, 342
Huston, Harvey L., 102
Huysmans, Camille, 298
Hviezdoslav. *See* Pavol Országh
Hyde, family name of, 358
Hygroscopic qualities of vellum, 152
Hyperion (Knowles), 307

Ibáñez, Vincente Blasco. *See* Blasco Ibáñez, Vincente
Ibsen, Henrik, 320, 321
Iceland, 320
I Ching, 320
Identification and identities: confusing or mistaken, 86, 111–116; ownership marks of, 106, 136–137, 194; problem of, 337; proof of, 91
Ideograms and ideographs, 4–5, 8, 12, 40
Ignatius of Loyola, Saint, 411
Illegal copying, 191
Illig, Moritz, 39
Illinois State Historical Library, 345
Illiteracy, 107
Images, characteristics of, 74, 146, 149
Immigrant ancestors, diaries of, 441, 444
Imperial Russian Ballet, 470
Impressionism, French, 63, 407
Inca: ancient, 3; oral tradition of, 318
Incandescent lights and lighting, 145, 147
Income taxes, 170, 173, 384

Index files and material, 136
Index to the Abraham Lincoln Papers, 168
India: Britain's conquest of, 359; epics of, 330; literature of, 304, 329–330; religious manuscripts of, 432
India ink, type of, 80
Indiana University, 265
Indian Ocean, 328
Indians (American): Algonquian, 4; of Central America, 318; culture of, 318; deed by, 206; pictograms of, 108; used notched sticks, 4
Infirmities, physical affect of, on writing ability, 76
Inflation, as factor on market values, 183, 187, 340, 344
Infrared lights, use of, 74
Ingres, Jean Auguste Dominique, 407
Inheritance: autographs by, 173, 192; lawsuits over, 290; taxes, 196, 209
Initials: monarchs used, 110; used as signatures, 245, 359
Ink(s): absorption of, 80; aniline, 79; Arabs evolved, 28–29; authentication of, 73; bottles, 30; chemical testing of, 79; coloring matter found in, 78–80, 84; durable, 29; erasures and eradication of, 74, 84; faded, 31, 183, 185, 337; flow of, 76, 89; indigo added to, 79; iron-nut gall, 29, 39, 78–79, 81; logwood added to, 79; Old Testament references to, 28; primitive, 29; restoration of, 185; uniform density of, 58, 76
Inlaying, practice of, 61
"In Memoriam" (Tennyson), 280
Inquiry Into the Authenticity of Certain Miscellaneous Papers (Malone), 93
Inscribed religious objects, 435
Inscriptions, cuneiform, 8
Insects and insecticides, dangers of, to manuscripts, 143–144
Inspections, regular system of, for collections, 143–144
Institut de France, 422
Institutions: activities of, 138, 267, 336–337; collections of, 63, 170, 347, 411, 478; educational, 137, 176; gifts to, 387; libraries of, 259; private and public, 153, 209
Insurance, 141, 187
Internal Revenue Service (IRS), 196
International Autopen Company, 100, 103–104
International Business Machines Corporation (IBM), 32
International Dictionary of Literary Awards (Clapp), 299 n
Introduction to Historical Bibliography, An (Binns), 34 n
Inventions and inventors, 36, 370, 392
Inventory of collections, 163
Investment possibilities of collecting, 65, 171, 187–188, 211, 253, 340, 438
Invitation to Book Collecting (Storm and Peckham), 54 n
Ionesco, Eugène, 303, 326
Ionic alphabet of Miletus, 16
I promessi sposi (Manzoni), 315
Iredell, James, 493
Ireland, Samuel, 93
Ireland, William Henry, 93, 270, 281
Ireland and the Irish, 24, 204, 327, 358
Iron-nut gall ink, 29, 39, 78–79, 81
Iroquois Indians, 4
Irving, Sir Henry, 460, 474, 480; cabinet photograph of, **479**; letter to, **462**
Irving, Washington, 266; *Bracebridge Hall,* 262; "Rip Van Winkle," first page of, **263**; *The Sketch Book of Geoffrey Crayon, Gent.,* 262
Isabella I (Isabella the Catholic, queen of Castile and Léon), 334, 371, 417; letter to, 446
Iscariot, Judas. *See* Judas Iscariot
Isfahan, loose manuscripts in, 435
Islamic world, religious works in, 432
Israel, State of, 304, 435; Declaration of Independence of, 327
Istanbul: good market for icons and lectionaries, 432; loose manuscripts in, 435
Italy, 21, 23, 83, 188, 373, 411, 416; bookstores in, 315; culture of, 315, 317, 468; history of, 362, 371; language of, 394; literature of, 204, 315–317, 327; noble houses of, 371; script in, 19, 27; tour to, 444
Ivan IV (Ivan the Terrible, czar of Russia), 373

Jackson, Andrew, 212, **222**, 254
Jackson, Howell E., 493
Jackson, Rachel Robards, 256
Jackson, Thomas J. ("Stonewall"), 344
Jacob, Max, 299
Jacobus de Verona, *Liber peregrinationis et indulgentie terre sancte,* **442–443**
Jaeckel, Christopher C., "Autographs of American Presidents," 211–257
Jahans, Gordon A., "A Brief History of Paper," 37 n, 38 n, 39 n; on papermaking, 36–37, 39
James, Charles Thomas Clement, 283–284
James, Henry, 262

James I (king of England), 94, 108, 285, **351**
James II (king of England), **352,** 358
James Ford Bell Library, University of Minnesota, 442, 446, 447, 449
Jamestown, settlement at, 332, 334
Janauschek, Francesca Romana Madalena, 480
Japan, 148; economic market of, 331; literature of, 331; manuscripts of, 432; paper and tissues of, 61, 153; pen development in, 31; translated works of, 331
Jaques-Dalcroze, Émile, 470
Jarrett, Miss, 321
Játiva in Valencia, Spain, 43
Jaurès, Jean, 456
Jay, John, 206
Jean II (king of France), 362
Jean Paul (Johann Paul Friedrich Richter), 307
Jefferson, Joseph, 480, 484, 487
Jefferson, Martha Skelton, 256
Jefferson, Thomas, 60, 120, 160, 254, 332, 428; and Declaration of Independence, 133, 156; facsimile of signature of, 57; letters of, **59,** 117, **218;** notes of, 156–157; polygraph of, 100, **101**
Jeffress Collection, University of Virginia Library, 345, 356
Jenkins, Charles Francis, 48
Jenner, Edward, 399, **400–401**
Jensen, Hans, *Die Schrift in Vergangenheit und Gegenwart,* 18, 20, 24
Jeritza, Maria, 405
Jermyn, Henry, 288
Jesus Christ, 14, 426
Jewett, Sarah Orne, 267; letter of, **268**
Jewish personalities and centers of learning, 435
Jiménez, Juan Ramón, 318; letter to, **319**
Jiménez Papers, Library of Congress, 319
Joan of Arc, 94, 366
Jodl, Alfred, 370
John III (king of Poland). *See* Sobieski, John
John XXIII (pope), 405
John Adams and the American Revolution (Bowen), 120
John of Austria (half brother of Philip II), 371
Johnson, Andrew, 178, **231,** 254
Johnson, Claudia Taylor "Lady Bird," 257
Johnson, Eliza McCardle, 256
Johnson, Lyndon B., 182, **249,** 255; forgery of, 99; library of, in Austin, 140; machine signatures of, 104
Johnson, Merle, *American First Editions,* 269
Johnson, Reverdy, 106
Johnson, Samuel, 280, 283
Johnson, Uwe, 314
Johnston, Albert Sidney, 344
Johnston, Clem D., Collection, University of Virginia Library, 109, 277, 356, 365, 485
Johst, Hanns, 314
Jolson, Al, 99
Jonas, Justus (archbishop), letter to, **436**
Jones, Charles Colcock, 46
Jones, Henry Arthur, 464
Jones, Inigo, 411
Jones, James (American author), 311
Jonson, Ben, 283, 285
Jordan, Dorothy, 459
Jordan, Mrs., 471
Joseph I (Holy Roman emperor), 366, **368**
Joseph II (Holy Roman emperor), **369**
Journal (Byrd), 262
Journals, 160, 441
Journals (Thoreau), 259
Jouvet, Louis, 464
Joyce, William L., 342
József, Laszlo, 30
Jubel-Cantate (Weber), 380
Judaica, collections of, 327, 428, 435
Judas Iscariot, 94
Judges, justices, and judicial papers, 64, 489, 492
Julius Caesar, 480
Juma Bhalo, Ahman Hassir bin, 328
Jung, Hermann, *Ullstein Autographenbuch,* 380
Jurgen (Cabell), 265
Justice: courts of, 107, 491, 493; records of, 334

Kabuki Theater in Japan, 331
Kafka, Franz, 312, 326
Kalb, Johann, 205
Kalevala (Finnish national epic), 320
Kallir, Otto, 404
Kallir, Rudolf F., 305; "Collecting Scientific and Medical Autographs," 392–404
Kamante, *Longing for Darkness,* 329
Kandinsky, Wassily, 410–411, 416
Kani, John, *The Island,* 329; *Sizwe Bansi Is Dead,* 329
Kant, Immanuel, 188
Kanteletar, 320
Karlfeldt, Erik, 320
Karloff, Boris, 99

Karsavina, Tamara, 470
Kautsky, Karl, 456
Kawabata, Yasunari, 331
Kazantzakis, Nikos, 325
Kean, Charles, 460, **461,** 470
Kean Edmund, 459, **460,** 478
Kearney, Phillip, 344
Keats, John, 93, 272, 280, 285, 405; letter by, **279;** "Ode to a Nightingale," 280
Keitel, Wilhelm, 370
Keller, Gottfried, 306; *Der grüne Heinrich,* 307
Kemble, Charles, 460
Kemble, Fanny, 460
Kemble, John Philip, 93, 459
Kennedy, Jacqueline Bouvier. *See* Onassis, Jacqueline Bouvier
Kennedy, John Fitzgerald, 97, 99, 184, **248,** 255, 314; and Autopen, 214; handwritten letters of, 248; signature of, 91
Kennedy, Robert F., 99
Kenya, 328
Kepler, Johannes, 394, 399
Kern, Jerome, 384, 387
Kesselring, Albert, 371
Key, Francis Scott, 207
Khafre (king of ancient Egypt), 42
Khrushchev, Nikita, 314
Khodasevich, Vladislav, letter of Maxim Gorki to, **322**
Khufu (king of ancient Egypt), 42
Kidd, William, 405
King, Martin Luther, Jr., 435
King Lear (Shakespeare), 93
Kings, queens, and monarchs, 8, 43–44, 64, 94, 108, 110, 135, 285, 304, 314, 334, 347–348, 355, 358, 362, 366, 370–371, 376, 417, 428, 432, 469
King's Theatre, 469
Kipling, Rudyard, 283, 329
Kirschenbaum, David, 49
Kitton, Frederick George, 283
Kittredge, Walter, 384
Klee, Paul, 405
Kleist, Heinrich von, 306–307
Klingelhofer, Herbert E., 311; "Acquiring Autographs and Manuscripts," 66–72; "Hidden Signatures," 106–110
Klopstock, Friedrich, 306
Knaus, Friedrich von, 100
Knowles, James Sheridan, 463
Koch, Louis, 404
Koch, Robert, 403–404
Kodály, Zoltán, 387
Koester, William H., 259
Kokoschka, Oskar, 424
Kolbenheyer, Erwin, 314
Königinhof manuscript forgery, 326
Koran, The, 432, **433,** 439
Kormák's Saga, **408**
Kosciusko, Thaddeus, 337
Kossuth, Ferenc, 373
Kotzebue, Auguste Friedrich Ferdinand von, 484
Kramer, Dr. Samuel Noah, *From the Tablets of Sumer,* 40 n; "Sumerian Literature—Man's Oldest Manuscripts in Clay," 40 n
Kritzeck, James, "Religious Manuscripts," 425–439
Kropotkin, Petr, 454, 456
Kunze, Dr. Emil, 406

LaBelle Glass Works of Bridgeport, Ohio, 486–487
Lafayette, Marie Joseph Paul Yves Roch Gilbert du Motier, Marquis de, 332, 340
Laforgue, Jules, 298
Lagerkvist, Pär, 320
Lagerlöf, Selma, 320
Lamartine, Alphonse de, 189, 289, 295, 375
Lamb, Charles, 270
Laminating material, process of, 61–62, 153
La Motte-Fouqué, Friedrich de. *See* Fouqué, Friedrich de La Motte-
Lampblack, invention of, 28
Land grants, 212, 218, 220–221, 223, 334
Landor, Walter Savage, 410
Landsdowne collection of manuscripts, 44
Langlois, Walter G., "French Literary Autographs," 289–303
Langtry, Lillie, 407
Language(s): African, 328–329; Arabic, 328; of collectors, 53–62; English, 328–330; Etruscan, 19; foreign, 305, 318, 375; French, 323, 326–328, 394; German, 305, 307, 323, 325–326, 394; Greek, 13; Italian, 394; South African, 328–330; written and spoken, 5, 305, 375
Lao-tzu, *Tao Te Ching,* 330
Lapidary capitals and script, 16, 20
Largillière, Nicolas de, 416
Larionov, Mikhail, 470
La Rochefoucauld, François de, 291
L'Art Ancien in Zurich, 399
La Salle, Robert de, 334
Latin: alphabet, 19–20; script and writings, 20, 24

Latin American authors, 317–320
La Tour, Georges de, 411
Laube, Heinrich, 311
Lauder, Sir Harry, 466; caricature of, **468**; photograph of, **469**
Laurel, Stan, 99
Lautreamont, Isidore Ducasse de, 189
Lavallée, Calixa, 384
Lawrence, Sir Thomas, 406
Laws and lawsuits, 41, 290
Laxness, Halldór, 320
Layouts, general, 82, 86
Lazarus, 94
Le Brun, Charles, 416
Le Nain, Louis, 416
Leach, Bernard, 424
Leaf foldings, 56
Lear, Edward, 283, 424
Leather, use of, 143
Leaves of Grass (Whitman), 262
Lebold, Foreman M., 48
LeConte de Lisle, Charles, 295
Lederer, Richard M., 48
Ledgers, 342
Lee, C. F., Jr., 161
Lee, Charles, 161, 205, 340
Lee, Christopher, 99
Lee, Gypsy Rose, 477
Lee, Richard Henry, 96
Lee, Robert E., 344, 405
Leech, John, 422
Lefèvre, Robert, 410
Leffingwell, Edward H., 111
Legal documents: legality of, 55, 105, 290, 347–348, 356; ramifications of collecting, 170–177
Léger, Alexis Saint-Léger [pseud. St.-John Perse], 298
Lehár, Franz, 391
Lehman, Robert Owen, 391
Leibniz, Gottfried von, 394
Lekain (Henri Louis Cain), 463
L'Enfer, 126
Lenin, V. I., 373, 405, 454–455, 457
Leningrad, library of, 427
Leno, Dan, 466
Le Nôtre, André, 411
Lenox, James, 46
Lenthall, Franklyn, "American Theater," 472–488
Leonardo da Vinci, 133
Leopardi, Giacomo, 315
Leopold I (Holy Roman emperor), **368**
Leopold II (Holy Roman emperor), **369**
Leopold II (king of the Belgians), 366
Lermontov, Mikhail, 323
Lessing, Gotthold Ephraim, 306, 308, 312
Letterpress copies and books, 60, 131, 156
Letters: auction prices of, 161; condition and contents of, 86, 175–177, 185–186; copies of, 340; dictated, 212; general layout of, 82, 86, 345; handwritten, 212; as means of communication, 18, 54, 65, 84, 121, 266, 377, 422, 438, 475; published and unpublished, 175, 456–457; rarity of, 183–185; of recommendation, 491; repair of, 185; salutations of, 82; scientific, 394; Victorian, 407; wartime, 161, 333–334, 343, 346, 441
Letters of Delegates to Congress, 1774–1789 (Smith, ed.), 156
Letters of Members of the Continental Congress, 1774–1789 (Burnett), 158 n
Levant, Oscar, 384
Levi, Carlo, 317
Lewis, Laurence, 46
Lewis, Meriwether, 441
Lewis, Sinclair, 267
Lhermitte, Léon, 416
Libbie, C. F., 50
Liber peregrinationis et indulgentie terre sancte (Jacobus de Verona), **442–443**
Liberty League, 455
Libraries and librarians: British, 93, 133, 427; church and monastic, 44; established, 8, 62; French, 43; historical, 333, 335, 342; institutional, 259; national and city, 140, 266, 328, 427; need and use of, 50, 111, 137, 160, 176, 179, 181, 191–192, 194, 198, 208, 211, 270, 272, 337, 411; private and public, 41–42, 166, 384; rare book, 172, 337; state, 336; university, 167, 209, 410, 427. *See also* specific names of libraries
Library of Congress, 136, 147, 156, 169, 308, 313, 316, 319, 322, 324, 336–337, 342, 384, 387, 411, 430; Manuscript Division of, 157, 164, 172, 391
Libreria L. Gonelli & Figli, 315
Librettos, 307
Lichtenstein, Roy, 411
Liebknecht, Karl, 456
Liepmannssohn and Stargardt (dealers in Berlin), 397
Lifar, Serge, 470
Life on the Mississippi (Twain), 32, 265
Ligatures: characteristics of, 21–22, 27; popularity of, in Egypt, 13
Lights and lighting: and displays, 140–141; fluorescent, 140–141, 145, 147; incandescent, 145, 147; indirect, 141; in-

Lights and lighting (*continued*)
frared, 74; ultraviolet, 74, 84, 145, 147–148
"Like-kind" property, definition of, 171–172
Lilienthal, Otto, 404
Lilly, Josiah K., 48
Lincoln, Abraham, 254; cabinet of, 345; collections on, 160, 164–166, 178, 215, 310, 344, 405, 478; forgeries of, 82, 96, 346; last hours of, 180; letters of, **165**, 168, 343; secretarial signature of, 346; signatures of, **77**, 104, **230**
Lincoln, Mary Todd, 96, 180, 256
Lincoln, Mordecai, 178
Lincoln Day by Day: A Chronology (Miers), 168 n
"Lincoln, Welles, and the Public Service" (McDonough), 164 n
Lindbergh, Charles Augustus (American aviator), 404
Lindisfarne Gospels, **25**
Lindsay, Vachel, 265
Linnaeus, Carolus, 394, 449
Lin Yutang, 330
Lists, dealers', 67–68, 71, 116, 136
Liszt, Franz, 380, 384, 391
Literary Forgeries (Farrer), 92 n, 93 n
Literature and literary traditions: African, 329; American, 258–269; Babylonian, 8; Chinese, 304, 330; English, 64, 270–288; European, 304–322; of exploration and travel, 440; Far East, 329; "folk conscious," 312; French, 289–303; German, 304–314; hoaxes in, 92; Indian, 304, 329–330; interest in, 13, 63, 181, 371, 373, 375, 463; Italian, 315–317; Japanese, 331; Latin American, 317–318; political, 310; romantic and classical circles, 8, 295; vernacular, 27
Livingston, Robert R., 157
Livingston family, 206
Llosa, Mario Vargas, 318
Lloyd, Marie, 466
Lloyd George, David, 355
Loesser, Frank, *Most Happy Fella,* 315
Logbook entries, 358
Logwood added to ink, 79
Lombardic script, 21
Loménie de Brienne, Antoine, 43
London, Jack, 262
London, England, 190, 373; libraries in, 140, 266; market advantages in, 329, 399
London Assurance (Boucicault), 462
London Magazine, 277
Long, Captain Richard, **448**
Longfellow, Henry Wadsworth, 259, 262, 265, 306; "Excelsior," 126
Longhena, Baldassare, 416
Longhi, Pietro, 411
Longing for Darkness (Kamante), 329
Looseleaf book system, 134–136
Lope de Vega Carpio, Félix, 317
Lorca, Federico García. *See* García Lorca, Federico
Lord Chamberlain's Office, 471
Lorentz, H. A., 399
Lorenzo the Magnificent (Lorenzo de' Medici), 371
Lorrain, Claude. *See* Claude Lorrain
Lorre, Peter, 99
Loti, Pierre (Julian Viaud), 298
Loud, John, 30
Louis XI (king of France), 362, **363**
Louis XII (king of France), **363**
Louis XIII (king of France), **364**
Louis XIV (king of France), 43, 290, 314, **364**, 366, 375
Louis XV (king of France), **364**, 366
Louis XVI (king of France), 182, **364**, 366, 410
Louis XVII (king of France), 362, **364**
Louis XVIII (king of France), **365**, 366, 410
Louis Napoleon Bonaparte, **365**
Louis Philippe, **365**, 376
Louvre Museum, 410
Louÿs, Pierre, 298
Low, J. and J. G., 488
Lowell, James Russell, 265
Lowens, Irving, "Musical Autographs and Manuscripts," 377–391
Lucas, Denis Vrain-, 94
Lugosi, Bela, 99
Lumley, Benjamin, 469
Lunardi, Vincenzo, 404
Lusignan, Anne de, 426
Luther, Martin, 183, 411, 435, **436**, 438
Luxemburg, Rosa, 456
Luzi, Mario, 316
Lynch, Thomas, Jr., 96, 112, 180; A.L.S. from, **115**
Lyon, Nathaniel, 344
Lytton, Edward, 463

Maass, Richard, "Specialized Collecting," 203–210
McCardle, Eliza, 178
McCarthy, Lillah, 464
McClellan, George, 344
McCrum, Blanche P., *A Guide to the Study of the United States of America,* 167 n

McDonough, John, 166; "Lincoln, Welles, and the Public Service," 164 n
McDougall, Alexander, 340
MacDowell, Edward, 384, 391
McDowell, Irvin, 344
McDowell, Turner, 224
McEntee, Jervis, 478
M'Fadyen, Neil, 466
McGregor, Tracy W., Library, of University of Virginia Library, 279, 400, 468
Machado, Antonio, 318
Machado de Assis, Joaquim Maria, 318
McHenry, James, 205, 336
Machiavelli, Niccolò, 411
McKinley, Ida Saxton, 257
McKinley, William, **238**, 255
Macklin, Charles, 459
Macpherson, James, 281
McPherson, James B., 344
Macready, William Charles, 460, 463
Madama Butterfly (Puccini), 380
Madame Sans-Gêne (Sardou), 474; page from prompt book of, **465**
"Madame Vestris" (Lucia Mathews), 460
Madigan, Patrick F., 49
Madigan, Thomas F., 49, 161, 397, 428, 430; "Autograph Collector's Baedeker," 428; *Word Shadows of the Great,* 430 n
Madison, James (bishop), letter written by, **113**
Madison, Dorothea Todd, 219, 256
Madison, James, **45**, **219**, 254
Madrasas, archives of, 426
Maeterlinck, Maurice, 298, 327
Maffit, James S., 487
Magellan, Ferdinand, 441, 444
"Maggie by My Side" (Foster), 380
Maggs in London, 397
Magna Carta, 347
Magnesium carbonate, aqueous solution of, 149
Mahabharata, 330
Mahler, Gustav, 311, 326, 380, 384, 391; Symphony no. 1 in D major (*Titan*), 307
Maillol, Aristide, 422
Maintenon, Mme de, 182
Mallarmé, Stéphane, 298
Malone, Edmund, *Inquiry Into The Authenticity of Certain Miscellaneous Papers,* 93
Malraux, André, 302
Management and managers, theater, 470–471
Manchester, bishop of, 359
Manchester, Duke of, 359
Mandelstam, Osip, 325
Mandeville, Sir John, 444
Manifests, customs, 342
Manila folders for filing, 134–135
Mann, Thomas, 305, 310, 312, 314, 323; *Das Gesetz,* **313**; *Der Zauberberg,* 307
Mannerheim, Carl von, 320, 373
Manning, James H., 48
Mansart, François, 416
Mansfield, Richard, 307, 462
Manuscript Society, The, 49, 119, 141, 162, 164
Manuscripts. *See* Autographs and manuscripts
Manuscripts, 50, 119
Manzoni, Alessandro, *I promessi sposi,* 315
Maoris of New Zealand, 4
Mao Tse-tung, 330, 432
Maps, United States, 334
Marburg, Germany, 190, 329
Margaret of Parma, 371
Maria Theresa, 373
Marie Antoinette, 405
Marion, Francis, 337
Marionettes, The (Faulkner), 265
Marivaux, Pierre de, 295
Markets: autograph and manuscript, 50, 60, 162, 189–190, 191, 334–337, 444; open, 335, 377. *See also* specific markets by name
Market values, 136, 185, 187, 196, 337, 362
Marks and markers for identifying legal ownership, 31, 193–194
Marlborough, Duchess of (Sarah Churchill), 354
Marlborough, Duke of (John Churchill), 108, 354, 361
Marlowe, Christopher, 285
Marmontel, Jean, 291
Marriage contracts, 290
Mars, Anne-Françoise, 463
Marshall, John, 96
Marshall, Peter, 430
Martin, A. Bradley, 259
Martin, H. B., 260
Martin, Mary H., 166, 168
Martin-Harvey, Sir John, 460, 470
Martyre de St.-Sébastien, Le (D'Annunzio), 316
Marvell, Andrew, 288
Marx, Karl, 373, 454, 456; and Marxists, 457
Mary I (Mary Tudor, queen of England), 348, **351**
Mary II (queen of England), 348, **352**
Mary Flagler Cary Music Collection, Pierpont Morgan Library, 379, 381, 385, 386

Maryland Historical Society, 342
Mary Magdalene, 94
Mary Queen of Scots, 94, 183, 348
Masaryk, Thomas G., **374**
Mascagni, Pietro, 317, 387, 391; *Cavalleria Rusticana,* 380
Masonry, 221
Massachusetts Historical Society, 168
Massenet, Jules, 387, 391; *Thaïs*, 380
Massey, Linton R., 265
Massine, Léonide, 470
Masters, Edgar Lee, 265; *Spoon River Anthology,* 266
Matchmaker, The (Wilder), 310
Mathews, Charles James, 460
Mathews, Lucia ("Madame Vestris"), 460
Matisse, Henri, 406
Matthias (Holy Roman emperor), **368**
Maupassant, Guy de, 298
Maurepas papers, catalog of, 130
Mauriac, François, 298, 302
Maximilian I (Holy Roman emperor), 110, **367**
Maximilian II (Holy Roman emperor), **367**
Max und Moritz (Busch), 307
Mayakovsky, Vladimir, 325
Mayer, Brantz, 46
Mazarin, Jules (cardinal), 366
Meade, George G., 344
Meaning and End of Religion, The (Smith), 425 n
Mearns, David C., 164
Measurements and sizes of books and manuscripts, 56–57, 134–135
Mechanical signing devices and robots, 100, 103–105, 251
Mecklenburg (auction house), 190
Mecklenburg, Klaus, 305
Medici, Catherine de', 23
Medici, Lorenzo de'. *See* Lorenzo the Magnificent
Medici, Marie de', **372**, 417
Medici family, 371
Medicine and medical men, 188, 392–404
Mediterranean cultures, 5
Meilhac, Henri, 307
Meissonier, Jean Louis, 424
Meistersinger, Die (Wagner), 310
Melville, Herman, 179, 259, 262, 265, 267, 269; letter of, **260**
Melville, Lord, impeachment of, 360
Memorial Library of University of Notre Dame, 438 n
Mendel, Gregor, 399
Mendelssohn, Felix, 380, 384
Meng Tien, 42
Menotti, Gian-Carlo, 207, 384
Menpes, Mortimer, 407
Merchants and mercantile operations, 441, 444–445, 449
Mérimée, Prosper, 297
Mesmer, Franz, 394
Mesopotamia, 4–5, 9
Metal pens and signature stamps, 29, 60
Methanol, use of, 149
Methodist Church leaders, 427, 435
Metternich, Clemens Wenzel Nepomuk Lothar, Fürst von, 361
Metzdorf, Robert F., 130
Mexico, 108, 320, 344
Meyer, Conrad Ferdinand, 306
Michael (Goebbels), 314
Michel, Claude [pseud. Clodion], 422
Michelangelo Buonarroti, 315, 407, 411
Michelet, Jules, 295
Michigan, University of, 337
Microscope, examination by, 73, 84, **150**; stereoscopic, 73–74
Middle Ages, 18, 20, 304, 356, 444
Middle East, 445. *See also* individual countries
Middle Kingdom, sarcophagus of, 9
Middleton, Arthur, 112
Miers, Earl Schenck, *Lincoln Day by Day: A Chronology,* 168 n
Migration: chemical, 144; and settlement accounts, 449
Mikado, The (Gilbert and Sullivan), 331
Milan, Italy, autograph market of, 329
Miletus, Ionic alphabet in, 16
Milhaud, Darius, 207
Military: appointments, 212; arms, 417; commissions, 215, 348; correspondence, 332, 450; history and historians, 354; personnel, 332–335, 340, 343, 346; reports, 344
Mill, Henry, 31
Millay, Edna St. Vincent, 269
Miller, Arthur, *A View From the Bridge,* 315
Miller, Henry, 311
Milton, John, 285, 288
Ministers of state, 362
Minnesota, University of, 442, 446, 447, 449
Minnesota Historical Society, 450
Minor, Robert, 456
Minuscule scripts, **18**, 20, 22, 24
Mirabeau, Honoré de, 294
Mishima, Yukio, 331, 432
Miscellaneous Plays of Edwin Booth, The, 484 n
Miss Gwilt, 463
Missionaries: European, 44; journals of, 441
Mistral, Frédéric, 298

Mistral, Gabriela, 318
Mit Goethe durch das Jahr, 310
Mobuto, 328
Modern Language Association, 266
Modjeska, Helena, 480; cabinet photograph of, **481**
Moffatt, Sanderson, 487
Mohammed, 426
Molière, Jean Baptiste, 188, 290
Molina, Tirso de. *See* Tirso de Molina
Monasteries and shrines, 44, 432
Monet, Claude, 406, 424
Money and monetary appreciation, 180–181, 337–338, 341
Monks, copies of manuscripts made by, 305
Monmerqué, M., 44
Monmouth, Duchess of, 288
Monnier's 1851 watermarked paper, 96
Monograms, 106, 108, **109**
Monroe, Elizabeth Kortright, 256
Monroe, James, 219, **220,** 254
Monroe, Marilyn, 99
Monsieur Memoir. *See* Byron, Major George Gordon De Luna
Montagu, Charles (Earl of Halifax), 355
Montaigne, Michel de, 290
Montale, Eugenio, 316
Monte Cassino, writing school of, 21
Monterey, Carlotta, caricature of, **482**
Montesquieu, Charles de, 291, 422
Montgolfier, Jacques, 404
Montgolfier, Joseph, 404
Month and day abbreviation, 61
Montherlant, Henri de, 302
Montigny, Lucas de, 44
Monumental script, **16, 19,** 20
Monuments, sacred, 9
Monvel, Louis Boutet de. *See* Boutet de Monvel, Louis
Moody, Dwight, 430
Mooney, Thomas, 455–456
Moore, Alfred, 493
Moore, Nöel, letter to, **420–421**
Moors, paper manufacturing by, 43
Moral standards, 191–199
Moravia, Alberto, 317
More, Sir Thomas, 285
Moréas, Jean, 311
Morgan, John Hunt, 344
Morgan, J. Pierpont (1837–1913), 48, 427
Morgan, J. Pierpont (1867–1943), 48, 258
Morgan, Junius S., 48
Morgan Library. *See* Pierpont Morgan Library
Morgenstern, Christian, 307
Mörike, Eduard, 307
Morland, George
Morland, Henry, 410
Mormon Church, collections of, 435
Morocco, 43
Morris, Arthur J., Law Library of the University of Virginia, 104
Morris, Lewis, 336
Morris, Robert, 340
Morris, William, 407, **408**
Morrison, Alfred, 44, 46
Morris Plan Bank, 59
Mosby, John Singleton, 344, **345**
Moses, 426
Most Happy Fella (Loesser), 315
Motus-proprii, signing of, 110
Mounting and framing procedures, 144, 153
Mount Vernon, Virginia, 441
Moussorgsky, Modest, 310
Movie idols, 184, 406, 460, 466
Mozart, Wolfgang A., 183, 207, 377; *Don Giovanni,* 380
Mugridge, Donald H., *A Guide to the Study of the United States of America,* 167 n
Munch, Edvard, 416
Mundelein, George Cardinal, 48, 430
Munich, Germany, 329, 427
Murillo, Bartolomé, 411
Murmansk, 453
Museum of Fine Art, Moscow, 17
Museums, 146, 211, 328, 406, 426, 472; anthropological, 329; British, 44, 411; conservators, 153; curators, 475; French, 410; national, 427; personnel of, 144; theatre, 474–475, 477, 487. *See also* specific names of museums
Music and musical scores: autographs of, 377–391, 404; collections of, 127, 181, 188, 190, 207, 317, 328, 373, 375; manuscripts of, 64, 135, 182, 377–391
Musical comedies and farces, 93, 487
Music halls, 466, 468
Musicians and musicologists, 182, 190, 207, 370, 378, 384, 432
Musset, Alfred de, 295
Mussolini, Benito, 312, 316, 376
Myers, Bailey, 46
My Grandmother, 93
Mylar, various uses for, 62, 135, 139, 147
Myths, 41

Nabokov, Vladimir, **324,** 325
Nabokov Papers, Library of Congress, 324
Nachlass (Stravinsky), 387
Nag Hammadi codices, 328
Names: changes in, 110, 358; identical, 111–112; signatures of, 106

Napoleon I, 63, 110, 188–189, 361–362, **365**, 366, 404; marshals of, 65
Napoleon II (Duke of Reichstadt), 362, 375
Napoleon III (Louis Napoleon Bonaparte), 295, 362, **365**
Napoleonic Wars, 362
Narayan, R. K., 329
Naropa Institute, 331
Narratives, travel, 41, 441, 444, 449–451
Nash, Ray, 30; *American Penmanship, 1800–1850: A History of Writing and a Bibliography of Copybooks From Jenkins to Spencer,* 30 n
National Archives, United States, 140, 157, 168, 430
Nationalism, 326; German, 314; Scottish, 327
National script, emergence of, 21
National Society of Autograph Collectors, 50, 120
National Union Catalogue of Manuscript Collections, The, 168
Naturalism, 295, 298
Nature, transreligious, 438
Naval appointments and records, 164, 166, 168, 212
Naval Historical Foundation Manuscript Collection: A Catalog, 168 n
Nazi leaders and Nazism, 188, 312, 314, 370–371, 432
Nearing, Scott, 456
Nebuchadnezzar II (king of Babylonia), inscription of, 7
Nelson, Lord Horatio, 117, 347, 354, 358, 361
"Nelson and Brontë" (signature of Lord Nelson), 358
Neruda, Pablo, 318
Nestroy, Johann Nepomuk, 310
Netherlands, The, Spanish regents of, 371
Nevin, Ethelbert, 384
New Amsterdam, Dutch autographs of, 327
Newberry Library, 265
New England: seventeenth-century, 334; writers of, 64–65, 259, 262, 265
New England Document Conservation Center, 153
New Jersey, 34
New Jersey Historical Society, 342
Newman, Barry, 315
Newman, John Henry Cardinal, 438
Newman, Julia Sweet, 49, 342
Newton, Sir Isaac, 394, 397, 411; autograph notebook of, **396**
New York, New York, 329, 334, 410, 477
New-York Historical Society, 342
New York Public Library, 262, 391, 430, 455; Berg Collection in, 259, 262
New York Times, 160
New Zealand, 4
Nib marks of pen, 76, 80, 89
Nicaragua, 318
Nicholas II (czar of Russia), 373
Nicholson, James William Augustus, 164, 166, 168–169
Niebuhr, Reinhold, 430
Nietzsche, Friedrich, 310
Nigeria, 328–329
Nijinsky, Vaslav, 468
Nile River, papyrus thickets along, 35
Nineveh, excavations at, 8
Nitowski, E., 427
Nixon, Richard Milhouse, **250**, 255, 405; forgery of, 99; machine signature of, 104
Nixon, Thelma Ryan, 257
Nobel prize, 64, 298, 315, 317, 325, 327, 331; winners of, 318, 320, 403–404
Noé, Amédée de. *See* Cham
Norman Conquest in England, 24
North Carolina, 104–105
North Carolina, 193 n; University of, 336, 342
Northern Pacific Railroad, 451
Norton, Robert C., 48
Norway, 320
No Surrender: My Thirty-Year War (Onoda), 331
Notched sticks used by Indians, 3–4
Notebooks (Butler), 131
Notes: promissory, 342; social, 491
Notre Dame, University of, Memorial Library of, 438 n
Novalis (Friederich von Hardenberg), 306
Noyes, John Humphrey, 456
Ntshona, Winston, *The Island,* 329; *Sizwe Bansi Is Dead,* 329
Numismatics, 417
Nutcracker, The (Tchaikovsky), 307
Nyerere, Julius, 328

Oberon (Wieland), 306
Obey, André, 462
O'Casey, Sean, 327
Ocho, Siegfried, 404
Octavo size, 56
"Ode to a Nightingale" (Keats), 280
Odyssey (Homer), 440
Oehlenschläger, Adam, 320
Offenbach, Jacques, 307, 380
Ohio Valley frontier, 337, 441

Ohrn, Georg, 399
Old Testament, references to ink in, 28
"Oliver P." (signature of Cromwell), 359
Olmsted, Frederick Law, 417
"On approval" order for autographs, 69
Onassis, Jacqueline Bouvier, 99, 184, 257, 329
O'Neill, Eugene, 262, 265, 269, 480; caricature of, **482**
O'Neill, James, 480
Only Way, The, 460
Onoda, Lt. Hiroo, *No Surrender: My Thirty-Year War,* 331
Open market, letters on, 335, 337
Operas: Italian, 317; singers in, 188, 406
Opportunities for collecting in United States, 332–336
Oratorian Collection at Brompton, 438 n
Orderly books, use of, 160, 332, 334
Organizing of collections, 134–141
Oriental: manuscripts, 204; religions, 312, 330
Origin of Species, On the (Darwin), 397
Országh, Pavol [pseud. Hviezdoslav], 326
Ortega y Gasset, Josí, 317
Ottoman Empire, sultan of, 438
Our American Cousin, playbill of, 483
Ovid, 131, 133
Owen, Wilfred, 288
Ownership: decedent's, 173; legal, 192–193; private, 199; and provenance, 60; public, 199; statement of, 163
Oxford and Mortimer, Earl of (Robert Harley), 44, 355
Oxford University, Bodleian Library at, 44, 427
Oxnam, G. Bromley, 430
Ozone, effects of, 143, 146

Paar, Count Ludwig, 46, 394, 399
Paderewski, Ignace Jan, 328, 373, 387, 391
Paganini, Niccolò, 380
Page, Thomas Nelson, 265
Pages, sizes of, 56
Paine, Thomas, 124, 206
Paintings and painters, 9, 188, 406, 411, 416–417
Paleography, 16, 375, 438
Paleolithic period in history, 4
Palestine, 5
Palladio, Andrea, 411
Pallas, Peter Simon, 449
Palmerston, Lord (Henry John Temple), 347
Pamphlets, 64
Panama, 318
Pantagruel (Rabelais), 290
Pantomime, 466
Papadiamantopoulos, Iannis, 311
Papal Curia, 21
Papantonio, Michael, "American Literary Autographs," 258–269
Paper: acidic and acid-free, 144–146; aging of, 84; authentication of, 73, 77, 84; autographs inlaid on, 136; chemically treated, 30; conservators, 152–153; deterioration of, 39; development of, 36–39, 43, 78, 155; handmade, 38–39; Japanese, 153; laid lines in, 38, 78; machine-made, 38–39; manufacture of, 36, 38, 73, 78; "permanent" or buffered, 146; preservation of, 150; pulp, 38–39, 78, 416; rag, 38, 78; self-destructive characteristics of, 143, 146, 416; sensitized, 58; vellum replaced by, 43; watermarks in, 78; woven wire frame for, 37–38, 78; yellowed, 337
Paper mills: England, 43; Germantown, 36; Samarkand, 36; Toledo, 36
Papillons (Schumann), 307
Papyrus: early Greek documents on, 16, **17**, 41; fragment of, **10**, **17**; rarity of, 39; thickets on Nile River, 35; use of, 3, 9, 13, 20, 34, 426
Paraguay, 318
Paraph, 106, **108**, 119, 182
Parchment, early use of, 20, 35–36, 39, 42, 78, 84, 426
Pardons, signatures on, 231
Paret, R., "Ummī," 426 n
Paris, France, 190, 329, 373, 399, 416–417, 432
Paris, Treaty of, 362
Park, Patrick, 410
Parke-Bernet Galleries, 160, 397, 399, 403; catalog of the Maurepas Papers, 130; guarantees given by, 70; sales by, 161, 336
Parker, John, "Autographs and Manuscripts of Exploration and Travel," 440–453
Parker, Peter J., 342
Parker, Rev. Samuel, letter to, **428**
Parrish, Maxfield, 407
Parsons, Albert, 456
Partisan rangers, Confederate, records of, 344
Pascal, Blaise, 94, 188
Pascoli, Giovanni, 315
Pas de Quatre, 469
Pasternak, Boris, 325
Pasteur, Louis, 190, 403

Pastors and clergymen, 341, 435
Pathfinder, The (Cooper), 262, 266
Patmore, Coventry, 280
Paton, Alan, 329
Patriotic groups, 457
Pavese, Cesare, 317
Pavlova, Anna, 468, 470
Payne, John Howard, 384; "Home Sweet Home," 380
Pay receipts, 332
Peace negotiations and treaties, 4, 362
Peary, Robert, 451
Peck, Frederick S., 48
Peckham, Howard, *Invitation to Book Collecting,* 54 n
Peel, Sir Robert, 347
Péguy, Charles, 299
Peiresc, Nicholas, letter to, **418–419**
Pell family, 206
Pen(s): dip, 30; first company for, 30; fountain, 30–31, 39; Japanese, 31; metal, 29; movement of, 87–89; nib, depth of, 76, 80, 89; pressure of, 87–89; quill, 29–30, 39, 80; reed, 16, 29; shading of strokes of, 87–89; steel, 30, 80. *See also* Autopen
Pen-and-ink drawings, 138
Pencils, use of, 34, 82
Penn, John, 112, 114
Penn, William, 334
Pennant, Thomas, 449
Pennsylvania, University of, 265
Pennsylvania Historical Society, 158, 342
Pepperrell, Sir William, 417
Perceval, Spencer, 284
Peretz, Isaac, 327
Pergamum, 36, 42
Period collections, 362
Periodicals, 64
Perrot, Jules, 469
Perry, Matthew C., 166, 331
Perse, St.-John (Alexis Saint-Léger Léger), 298
Persia, 328, 330; renaissance in, 9
Personality cults, 318, 330
Pessoa, Fernando, 318
Pestalozzi, Johann Heinrich, 397
Peter I (Peter the Great, czar of Russia), 373
Peter Schlemihls wundersame Geschichte (Chamisso), 312
Petipa, Marius, 470
Petrarch, 315
Petroglyphs, 4
Petrograms, 4
Petti, Anthony G., *English Literary Hands From Chaucer to Dryden,* 36 n, 37 n
Peyton, Craven, 58, 218
Phatudi, Cedric Makepeace, 329
Phelps, Samuel, 460
Phidias, 405–406, 424
Philip II (king of Spain), 371
Philipse family, 206
Phillipps, Sir Thomas, 44, 46, 204, 271
Phillips, Stephen, 464
Phiz. *See* Browne, H. K.
Phoenicia, 4
Phonetic system of writing, 5, 8, 12, 40
Phonograms, 12
Photochemical decomposition, 145
Photography and photographs, 58, 135, 188, 344, 346, 406, 451, 463, 491
Photoreproduced copies, 58, 114, 131, 163
Picasso, Pablo, 99, 188, 406, 416, 439
Pictograms, 9, 106, 108–**109**
Pictography and pictographic writings, 4, 8–19, 12, 40
Picture books, coffee-table, 422
Picture writing, modifications of, 4, 40, 135, 422
Pierce, Franklin, **228,** 254
Pierce, Jane Appleton, 256
Pierpont Morgan Library, 48, 115, 233, 259, 265, 351, 379, 381, 383, 385, 386, 391, 393, 395, 396, 409, 412, 413, 415, 417, 418, 420, 423, 428, 429, 436, 437, 445
Pilots, barnstorming, 453
Pinero, Sir Arthur Wing, 460, 464
Pirandello, Luigi, 316
Piranesi, Giovanni, 411
Pissarro, Camille, 424
Piston, Walter, 127
Pitt, William, 94, 108, 355
Pizarro, Francisco, 108
Planché, James Robinson, 463
Planck, Max, 403
Plastics, tinted, 144
Plato, 328
Playbills, 459, 466, 474–477, 483
Plays, production of, 471, 474
Plays of Edwin Booth, The (Winter), 484
Playwrights, 320, 463
Pleadwell, Dr. Frank L., 48
Pledge of Allegiance to the Flag, 129
Plexiglass UF-3, 145, 147–148
Pocahontas (ship), 166
Poe, Edgar Allan, 96–97, 179, 265, 267, 483; *Tamerlane,* 259
Poe, Elizabeth Arnold, 483
Poel, William, 464
Poems, poets, and poetry, 98, 182, 277, 280, 285, 371; courses in, 331; dialect, 310–311; epic, 304; German, 307, 320; Italian, 315; New England, 64–65

Pogány, Willy, 422
Pointed sticks for writing instruments, 29
Poland, 328, 373; history of, 325, 376; literary names of, 325
Politics and politicians, 63, 67, 387, 432, 455–456; German, 306, 310, 312; in Great Britain, 334–335, 340–341; Roman Catholic, 371
Polk, James Knox, **225**, 254; paraph of, 108
Polk, Sarah Childress, 256
Polo, Marco, 441, 444
Polygraph, 100, **101**
Pompeii, ruins of, 29
Ponge, Francis, 299
Pontius Pilate, 94
Pope, Alexander, **277**, 405
Popes and saints, 371, 426–427, 432, 438
Porter, Cole, 384
Porter, Katherine Anne, 267
Porter, Quincy, 387
Portugal: explorations of, 371; literature of, 317–318
Postal history, knowledge of, 83
Postcards, 424
Postmedieval manuscripts, prices for, 270
Potter, Beatrix, **420–421**, 422
Poulenc, Francis, 387
Pound, Ezra, 262, 265, 269, 288
Poussin, Nicolas, 416
Pratt, Herbert L., 48
Pre-Columbian explorations, 432, 444
Premachine papermaking, 37
Pre-Raphaelites, 407
Preservation, methods of, 61, 142–155
Presidents of the United States: autographed signature sets of, 64–65, 103, 135–136, 183–184, 211–213, 253–255, 327, 417; wives of, 64, 184, 256–257
Preston, Jean F., 342
Prévost, Abbé (Antoine François Prévost d'Exiles), 294
Prices and costs of collecting, 68–69, 136, 179–180, 183–184, 187, 198, 270, 340–341, 430
Prime ministers, 64, 355
Prince Albert autograph collections, 44
Princeton University, 262, 430; library of, 433
Prints and printing, 58, 210, 410; curators of, 153; invention of, 18, 42–43, 54–55
Prisoners, political, 455
Prison Memoirs of an Anarchist (Berkman), 455
Prix Fémina, 299
Prix Goncourt, 298
Prix Interallié, 299
Prix Théophraste-Renaudot, 299
Proctor, Joseph, 475
Proctor, Redfield, 48
Professionalism, 152, 245, 435, 477, 480
Prokofiev, Sergei, 387
Promissory notes, 332, 342
Proof, burden of, 175
Propaganda, 306
Property: rights, 290; stolen, 193; transfers of, 171, 290
Proprietary marks, 4
Protection of autographs and documents, 61–62, 136–137
Protestantism, 370, 432, 435
Proust, Marcel, 299
Provenance, 60, 67, 129, 162, 166, 194, 281, 477
Proverbs, 41
Provincial Congress, 206
Pseudonyms and pen names, use of, 32, 106, 111
P. S. Hench–Yellow Fever Collection, University of Virginia Library, 403
Ptolemy, 13, 42, 92
Publication and publishing rights, 160–162, 175–176, 196, 198, 456–457
Public domain, 159, 162, 176
Public Records Office, London, 25, 26
Puccini, Giacomo, 106, 384, 387, 391; *Madama Butterfly,* 380; *Turandot,* 317
Pulitzer prize, 269, 298
Puppetry, 466
Pupus Torguatianus, inscription of, **21**
Pushkin, Aleksandr, 323
Pyle, Howard, 422

Quality Street, 463
Quarterly Journal of the Library of Congress, 156, 164
Quarto sheets, 56, 407
Quasimodo, Salvatore, 317
Questionnaires to dealers, 342
Quill pens, 29–30, 39, 80
Quipu, 4
Quisling, Vidkun, 320
Qumran Scrolls. *See* Dead Sea Scrolls

Rabelais, François, *Gargantua,* 290; *Pantagruel,* 290
Rabinowitz, Solomon (Sholom Aleichem), 327
Rachel (Élisa Félix), 463, 480

Rachmaninoff, Sergei Vasilyevich, 387, **388,** 391
Racine, Jean, 188, 290
Rackham, Arthur, 422
Radiation, ultraviolet, 147
Radicals and radical material, 454–458
Raffles, Sir T. Stamford, 44
Raftor, Catherine. *See* Clive, Catherine (Kitty)
Raglan, Baron (Lord Fitzroy Somerset), 358
Railroads, 360, 450–451
Rakau whakapapa, genealogical information on, 4
Ralegh, Sir Walter, 285, 347, 411
Ramayana (Sanskrit epic of India), 330
Rampel, H., 377
Ramses II, private library of, 42
Rao, Santha Rama, 329
Raphael, 407, 411
Rare-book dealers, 172, 179, 337
Rathbone, Basil, 99
Rau, Santha Rama, 329
Rauch (dealer in Geneva), 399
Ravel, Maurice, example from typewriter of, **90**
Ravenna script, 21
Rayner, Olive Pratt. *See* Allen, Grant
Re, invocation from, **9**
Reade, Charles, 463
Realism, 295; socialist, 314, 318, 326
Rebellions, 354, 362
Rebus drawings, 417
Receipts, pay, 332
Recommendation, letters of, 491
Recording devices, 146
Records and record keeping, 27, 136
Recto, right-hand side of page, 56
Red Badge of Courage, The (Crane), 262, **264,** 265, 266
Redon, Odilon, 410
Reed, John, 455
Reed, John F., "Ethics," 70, 191–199
Reed, Walter, **402**
Reed stylus and pens, 8, 16, 29, 31
Reference books on autographs, 135
Reformation, Protestant, 361, 370
Reforms and reformers, 454–458
Refugee authors, 314
Regional material, 336
Regnal years, 356
Régnier, Henri de, 298
Rehdiger, Thomas, 43
Reichstadt, Duke of. *See* Napoleon II
Reinhardt, Max, 464
Reivers, The (Faulkner), 133
Relatione del viaggio d'Alessandria d'Egitto (Tasca), **447**
Religion and religious systems, 430, 438; Catholic, 371, 427, 432, 438–439; concepts of, 4, 435; councils, 371; East Asian, 432; and hieroglyphics, 9, 13; Indian, 432; Islamic, 432; leaders of, 203–204, 430; manuscripts on, 425–439; Oriental, 312, 330; Protestant, 370, 432, 435; Russian, 432; Sumerian, 8
Relph, Harry ("Little Tich"), 466
Rembrandt Harmenszoon van Rijn, 411, 422
Remington, E., and Sons, 31
Remington, Frederic, 422
Renaissance period, 23, 315, 317, 327, 392, 411, 438; authors of, 290; Italian, 468; Persian, 9; princes of, 371
Renan, Ernest, 297
Rendell, Diana J., "The Development of Writing," 3–37
Rendell, Kenneth W., 297, 305, 342; "The Detection of Forgeries," 73–91; "Famous Forgers: Their Successes and Downfalls," 92–99; "Who Collects Autographs and Manuscripts, and Why: The Philosophy of Collecting," 63–65
Rendells, The, Inc., 17, 22, 23, 406
Renoir, Pierre Auguste, 188, 424
Rental agreements, 290
Repairs of tears and voids, 142–155, 185
Reports and reporters: court, 491; military, 344
Reputation, importance of, 67, 174, 191, 194–195, 416
Resale values, 71, 160–161, 195
Research and researchers, 54, 64, 164, 191, 198, 203, 266, 422
Restoration period, in England, 205, 354
Retained copy, definitions of, 57
Rethel, Alfred, 422
Reuter, Fritz, 310
Reverdy, Pierre, 299
Revolutions, European, 349, 361–362
Revolution, American. *See* American Revolution
Reynolds, Sir Joshua, 188, 411; letter to, **415**
Rhode Island Historical Society, 342
Riabouchinska, Tatiana, 470
Rice, Edward Everett, *Evangeline,* 487
Rice-starch paste, 148
Rich, Nathaniel, 284
Richard III (king of England), 348, **349**
Richelieu, Armand, Cardinal de, 291, 366, 428, **429**
Richter, Johann Paul Friedrich [pseud. Jean Paul], 307

Ricketts, Charles, 464
Riley, James Whitcomb, 265
Rilke, Rainer Maria, 311, 326
Rimbaud, Arthur, 189, 297
Rimsky-Korsakov, Nicolai, 387
"Rip Van Winkle" (Irving), first page of, 263
Risorgimento, 315
Rittenhouse, William, 43
Rivas, Ángel de, 317–318
Robbe-Grillet, Alain, 302
Robert, Hubert, 422
Robert, Nicholas Louis, 38
Roberts, Charles, 46
Robertson, T. W., 464
Robeson, Paul, 457
Robespierre, Maximilien, 366
Robey, Sir George, 466
Robinson, E. A., 269
Robinson, Mary ("Perdita"), 471
Robot That Helped to Make a President, The (Hamilton), 104, 248 n
Robson, Stuart, 487
Rochester, University of, 127, 128
Rock drawings, 4
Rockwell, Norman, 422
Rococo period, 416
Rodenbach, Georges, 327
Rodin, Auguste, 311, 406
Rodó, José Enrique, *Ariel,* 318
Roentgen, Wilhelm, 399
Rogers, John (American sculptor), 487
Roi de Thulé, Le (Berlioz), **383**
Rolland, Romain, 298–299
Romains, Jules, 302
Roman Catholicism, 203, 371, 426–427, 432, 438–439
Roman conquest of Greece, 19, 20
Roman cursive script, **21**
Roman monumental script, **19**
Romantic age, 63, 295, 312, 333
Romantic ballet, 469–470
Roman uncial script, **20**
Romberg, Sigmund, 387
Ronsard, Pierre de, 290
Roosevelt, Alice Lee, 257
Roosevelt, Anna Eleanor, 99, 257
Roosevelt, Edith Carow, 257
Roosevelt, Franklin Delano, 185, 239, **245,** 255, 493
Roosevelt, Theodore, 185, 213, **239,** 255, 318
Roosevelt family, 206
Root, George F., 384
Rorem, Ned, 207
Rosa, Salvator, 411
Rosegger, Peter, 310
Rosenbach, Philip, 49
Rosenbach Company of Philadelphia, 49, 375
Rosenbach Foundation, 49
Rose Tattoo, The (Williams), 315
Rosetta stone, **12**
Rossetti, Dante Gabriel, 93, 407
Rossini, Gioacchino, 380, 384, 387, 391
Rousseau, Jean Jacques, 291, **292,** 294
Roussel, Albert, 387
Rovere family, 371
Rowlandson, Thomas, 422
Rowley (imaginary fifteenth-century monk invented by Thomas Chatterton), 92
Roxborough Township (first paper mill in Pennsylvania), 43
Royal Academy, 416
Royal charters, 348, 371
Royal Society, 44, 449
Royalty and royal functions, 304, 348–349, 354, 370–371, 417, 466, 471
Rozier, Jean Pilâtre de, 404
R. R. Donnelley and Sons, 150, 151
Rubber signature stamps, 60
Rubens, Peter Paul, 416, **418–419**
Rubinfine, Joseph, 342
Rubinstein, Anton, 387
Ruby, Jack, 432
Rudolf II (Holy Roman emperor), **368**
Rufus, C. Antonius, dedication to, **19**
Rumania, 326
R.U.R. (*Rossum's Universal Robots*) (Čapek), 326–327
Rush, Benjamin, 124, 182, 394
Rush Rhees Library, University of Rochester, 127, 128
Russell, Annie, 488
Russell, Bertrand, 325
Russell, Mattie, 342
Russell, Sol Smith, 480
Russia: ballet in, 470; collecting in, 304–305, 314, 317, 323; history of, 320, 373; literature of, 323–325; minority-language writers in, 326; music in, 378; religion of, 432
Rust, Richard, 266
Rustic capitals, 20

Sacher-Masoch, Leopold von, 306
Sachs, Hans, 310
Sackville, Thomas, 285
Sacre du printemps, Le (Stravinsky), 387
Sade, Marquis de, 294, 306
Sadler's Wells Theatre, 460
Saggiori, Renato, 315

Sailing voyages, 450
Saint Catherine monastery, 431
St.-Denis, Michel, 462
St. Denis, Ruth, 470
Saint Exupéry, Antoine de, 302
St. John's Abbey, 439 n
St. John's College, Cambridge, 131
Saint-Just, Louis de, 456
Saint-Pierre, Jacques H. B. de, 291, **294**
Sainte-Beuve, Charles Augustin, 297
Ste. Geneviève library in Paris, 299
Saints, letters and lives of, 425–426, 438
Saint-Saëns, Camille, 387, 391
Saipan, 453
Salerno, writing school of, 21
Sales, terms of, 50, 175, 197
Sallé, Marie, 468–469
Salvini, Tommaso, 463, 480
Samarkand, 435 n; papermaking in, 36, 43
Sand, George (Amandine Aurore Lucie Dupin Dudevant), 297
Sanders, Ed, 331
Sang, Philip D., 48
Santa Maria della Salute in Venice, 416
Sapiat emptor theory, 72
Sardou, Victorien, 307, 464; *Madame Sans-Gêne,* page from prompt book of, **465**
Sargent, John Singer, 407
Sarraute, Nathalie, 302
Sartre, Jean-Paul, 289, 298, 302
Satie, Erik, 380
Savoy, Duke of, 426
Scammell, Alexander, 340
Scandinavian literature, 320
Scarcity, standards and degrees of, 183–184, 189–190
Scarlet Letter, The (Hawthorne), 258
Scene designers, 474
Schakovskoy, Princess Zinaida, letter of Vladimir Nabokov to, **324**
Schiller, Johann C. F. von, 95, 188, 306–308, 312, 314, 317
Schmidt, Franz, 310–311
Schnitzler, Arthur, 306
Schoenberg, Arnold, 320; *Gurrelieder,* **386**
Scholars and scholarship, contributions to, 156–169, 440; Hebrew, 42; world of, 156–169
Scholz, Mrs. Janos, 391
Schools: foreign language, 318; writing, 21
Schopenhauer, Arthur, 188
Schreyer, Leslie J., "Legal Ramifications of Manuscript Collecting," 170–177
Schubert, Franz, 108, 377, 384; "Der Winterabend," 380
Schultze, Carl E., 108
Schumann, Robert, 307, 380, 384; *Frauenlicke und-leben,* 312; *Papillons,* 307
Scientific materials: collecting of, 41, 370, 373, 392–404; history of, 449; interest in, 8, 41, 63, 190
Scientists, 182, 440–441, 449
Scott, Robert Falcon, 441, 451
Scott, Sir Walter, 94, 106, 283, 289, 317, 463
Scottish history, 327, 354, 358
Scribblers and Scoundrels (Hamilton), 104
Scribe, Augustin Eugène, 307, 317
Script: Anglo-Saxon semiuncial, 24; Arabic, 13; bastard, 24, 27; Beneventan, 21; cursive, 16, 18; demotic, 13; Fraktur, 24; German, 24; Gothic, 22–23, 107; Greek, 3, 14, 18; hieratic, 13; ideographic, 40; Italian, 19; lapidary, 16; Latin, 20, 24; minuscule, 18, 20–24, 107; national emergence of, 21; phonetic, 5, 8, 12, 40; Ptolemaic, 13; of Ravenna, 21; Roman capital, 20; rounded, 16, 27; Semitic, 14
Sculptors, 406, 410–411, 416, 487
Sculpture in America (Craven), 416
Seabury, Bishop Samuel, letter from, **428**
Secondhand book stores, 71
Secretaries and secretarial signatures, 27, 184, 253, 346
Secretary hand, English, **26**
Security measures, 139, 163–164
Seferis, George, 325
Semites, script from, 14
Semitic Akkadians, 8
Semiuncial script, 24
Semmelweis, Ignaz, 399
Senancour, Etienne Pivert de, 295
Senators, 343
Senegal, 328
Senghor, Léopold Sédar, 328
Sensitized paper, 58
Sentiment books, 127, 129
Sepia and ink color, 28
Septimius Felton (Hawthorne), 259
Serghiev, Nikolai, 470
Seton, Ernest Thompson, 108
Sévigné, Madame de, 290
Seward, William Henry, 130–131
Sforza family, 371
Shackleton, Sir Ernest Henry, 451; example from typewriter of, **90**
Shahar, David, 327
Shah Namah (Firdausi), 432
Shaker manuscripts, 430
Shakespeare, William, 93, 285, 317, 471
Shakespearean Plays of Edwin Booth, The, 484 n

Shaughraun, The (Boucicault), 487
Shaw, George Bernard, 136, 283, 463, 470
Shelley, Percy Bysshe, 63, 94, 280, 285
Shelving, Paul, 463
Sheridan, Richard Brinsley, 93
Sheringham, George, 464
Sherman, William Tecumseh, 344
Shevchenko, Taras, 326
Shinn, Everett, 477
Ships': logs, 441, 445; papers, 55, 218, 327, 426
Sholes, Christopher Latham, 31
Sholokhov, Mikhail, 325
Shops: antique, 67, 71, 179; dealer's, 68
Shostakovich, Dmitri, 391
Showman, Richard K., *The Harvard Guide to American History,* 167 n
Shrewsbury, Duke of (Charles Talbot), 355
Sibelius, Jean, 207, 320, 380, 387, 391
Sibelius, Ralph, 387
Sibley Music Library, 391
Siddons, Sarah, 459–460, 478
Sidney, Sir Philip, 280, 285
Sienkiewicz, Henryk, 325
Sign manuals, 106–**107**
Signa-Signer (electromechanical device): capabilities of, 58, 91, 100–105; invented by Harvey L. Huston, **102**; legality of, 105
Signers of the Declaration of Independence, 46, 64, 112, 114, 133, 156–158, 180–181, 203–204, 332, 340, 355, 394
Signers of the U.S. Constitution, 135, 333
Sign manual, **107**
Signo (machine invented by P. M. Durand), 100, 106
Signum, **107**
Silent Traveller in London (Chiang Yee), 330
Silking, protective method of, 61–62, 153
Silva, Diego de, 411
Simms, William Gilmore, 267
Simon, Claude, 302
Simplicissimus (Grimmelshausen), 307
Singer, Isaac Bashevis, 327
Singers, 378; opera, 188, 406
Singh, Khushwant, 329
Sin-Kashid (king of Uruk), 7
Sitting Bull, 99
Sixtus V (pope), 432
Size and measurements of books and manuscripts, 56–57, 134–135
Sizuki, D. T., 432
Sizwe Bansi Is Dead (Kani, Ntshona, and Fugard), 329
Sketch Book of Geoffrey Crayon Gent., The (Irving), 262
Skin of animals, 28, 35, 42, 78
Skorzeny, Otto, 99
Slavery, history of, 188
Slevogt, Max, 422
Slip sheets, use of, 146
Sloane, Sir Hans, 44
Smathers, James, 32
Smetana, Bedřich, 326
Smith, Alexander Howland, 94, 281
Smith, Alfred E., 455
Smith, David, 424
Smith, Isaac, 164, 166
Smith, Paul H., 157; *Letters of Delegates to Congress, 1774–1789,* 156; "Time and Temperature: Philadelphia, July 4, 1776," 156 n
Smith, Samuel F., 384
Smith, Wilfred Cantwell, *The Meaning and End of Religion,* 425 n
Smith Act, 457
Smithsonian Institution, 430
Sobieski, John (king of Poland), 376
Socialist countries, 314
Socialist realism, 314, 318, 326
Socialist Workers Party, 456–457
"Social movers," 438
Society for the Prevention of Cruelty to Children, 475–477
Soldiers, letters and diaries of, 161, 333–334, 343, 346, 441
Solvents, use of, 148–149, 152
Solzhenitsyn, Aleksandr, 325
Somerset, Lord Fitzroy (Baron Raglan), 358
Sonata for violin and piano, op. 96 in G major (Beethoven), **382**
Songs: colorful Victorian sheets of, 466; music hall, 468
Sotheby's (London auction house), 50, 277, 280, 285, 397, 399
Soulé, Samuel W., 31
Sousa, John Philip, 384, 391
South African War. *See* Boer War
South African writers, 329
Southam, B. C., 285
South Caroliniana Library, 342
Southern Historical Collection at University of North Carolina, 336, 342
Southey, Robert, **128,** 328
South Sea Bubble, 354
Souvenirs, theatrical, 487–488
Soviet Uzbekistan, 435 n
Soyinka, Wole, 328
Space age, 403–404, 444
Spain, 27, 188, 373, 411; Anglo-Saxon attitude toward, 317; explorations of, 371; "Generation of '98" in, 318; literature of, 317–318, 327; monarchy and

Spain (*continued*)
rulers of, 110, 334, 371, 417, 426; music in, 317; paper mills of, 36; pictography of, 4
Spanish Armada, 349
Specialized fields of collecting, 53, 64–68, 134–135, 181, 203–210. *See also* individual fields
Speer, Albert, 371
Spencer, Robert (Earl of Sunderland), 355
Spenser, Edmund, 285, 288
Spilman, John, 43
Spinoza, Baruch, 394
Spoliation claims of the French, 162
Spoon River Anthology (Masters), 266
Sprague, Rev. William Buell, 46, 203–204, 333; letter to, 47
Spring, Robert, 95–96, 179, 216
Staël, Mme de, 182, 295
Stage personalities and staff, 462, 464
Stain removal, 149–150
Stalin, Josef, 373, 456
Stamped signatures, 58, 60
Stamps: collection of, 84, 179
Standards, ethical and moral, 191–199
Stanford University, 391
Stanhope, James (Earl of Stanhope), 355
Stanley, family name of, 358
Stargardt, J. A., 305, 375, 399, 403
"Star-spangled Banner, The," 380
Statesmen of all periods, 343, 347. *See also* individual statesmen
State University of New York, 259
State v. *Watts*, 289 N.C. 445, 222 S.E. 2d 389 (1976), 104
Statute of limitations, factor of, 175
Stauffer, David McNeely, 46, 116
Stearne, Charles W., 484
Steel: engravings, 333; pens, 30, 80
Stein, Gertrude, 262
Steinbeck, John, 269
Stendhal (Marie Henri Beyle), 297
Steppenwolf (Hesse), 312
Stereoscopic microscope, 73–74
Sterling, George M., letter of Walter Reed to, 402
Steuben, Baron Friedrich von, 205, 337
Stevens, Henry, 49
Stevens, Wallace, 262, 265
Stevenson, Robert Louis, 284, 285
Stewart, family name of, 358
Sticks, notched, 3–4
Stifter, Adalbert, 306
Stimmen der Völker in Liedern (Herder), 326
Stokes, Allen H., 342
Stokowski, Leopold, 106
Stolen property, 191, 193–194
Stone, carvings in, 3, 16, 20, 28, 426
Stone, Edward L., Collection, University of Virginia Library, 434
Storage facilities, 142, 146–147, 179, 210
Storm, Colton, *Invitation to Book Collecting*, 54 n
Storm, Theodor, 306
Strabo, 41
Strauss, Johann, 391; *Don Juan*, 380; *Die Fledermaus*, 380
Strauss, Richard, 380, 387, 391
Stravinsky, Igor, 207, 380, 391; *Nachlass*, 387; *Le sacre du printemps*, 387
Strindberg, Johan August, 311, 320
Strutz, Henry, "European and World Literatures," 304–331
Stuart, Gilbert, 188
Stuart, J. E. B., 344
Stuart, John (Earl of Bute), 355
Study of History, A (Toynbee), 425 n
Stuerckh, Count von, 456
Sturgis, Russell, 283
Stutler, Boyd B., 116
Stylus, use of, 8, 41
Sulfur dioxide, 143, 146
Sulfuric acid, 143
Sullivan, Sir Arthur, 380; *The Mikado*, 331
Sully-Prudhomme, René, 298
Sultan of Ottoman Empire, 438
"Sumerian Literature—Man's Oldest Manuscripts on Clay" (Kramer), 40 n
Sumer and Sumerian period: administrative system of, 8; civilization in, 8; clay tablets of, 6–7; collectors of, 3, 41; cuneiform writing in, 5 6, 7, 40; legal system of, 8; protoliterate era of, 40; religion of, 8, 425
Sunderland, Earl of (Robert Spencer), 355
Sung, Carolyn Hoover, "Your Manuscripts and The Scholarly World," 156–169
Supervielle, Jules, 299
Supply and demand, law of, 69, 178, 183, 190, 306, 438
Supreme Court Historical Society, 493
Supreme Court justices, 64, 489
Surrealism movement, 299
Sutherland sisters, 425
Sutton, Arthur, 98–99
Suzuki, D. T., 432
Svensen, Hugo 473
Svevo, Italo, 317
Swahili language, 328
Swan, Alfred, letters to, **388, 389, 390**
Swan, Arthur, 50
Swan Music Collection, University of Virginia Library, 388, 389, 390
Swann Galleries, 169

Sweden, 320, 373
Swedenborg, Emanuel, 394, 399
Sweet, Forest G. ("Pop"), 49, 335
Swift, Jonathan, 288
Swinburne, Algernon, 162, 311
Switzerland, 190, 399; dealers in, 307, 373
Syllabic writing, development of, 5
Sylva, Carmen. *See* Elizabeth (queen of Rumania)
Symbolist movement, 295, 298, 326
Symbols, use of, 5, 8
Synagogues, archives of, 426, 435
Synge, J. M., 327
Synodal decrees, 425
Syria, 5, 328
Szladits, Lola L., *Documents Famous and Infamous, Selected From the Henry W. and Albert A. Berg Collection of English and American Literature,* 281 n, 284 n

Tablets, clay, recordings on, 3, 8, 28–29, 41
Table-type cases, 140
Taft, Helen Herron, 257
Taft, William Howard, **240,** 255, 489
Taglioni, Maria, 469
Tagore, Sir Rabindranath, 329
Taine, Hippolyte, 297
Talbot, Charles (Duke of Shrewsbury), 355
Tales of Soldiers and Civilians (Bierce), 262
Talleyrand, Prince Charles Maurice de, 366
Tallies, 3
Tallmadge, Colonel Benjamin, 206
Talma, François Joseph, 463
Tamerlane (Poe), 259
Tao Te Ching (Lao-tzu), 330
Tarkington, Booth, 262
Tasca, Giovanni Pietro, 445; *Relatione del viaggio d'Alessandria d'Egitto,* **447**
Tashkent, manuscripts in, 435
Tasso, Torquato, 95, 315
Tate, Allen, 262
Tate, John, 43
Taxes and taxation: after-, 171; capital gains, 171; deferral treatment, 171; estate, 170–174, 335; gift, 173; income, 170–173, 384; inheritance, 196, 209; planning, 170–172; savings, 171
Tax Reform Act of 1969, 171–172, 265, 387
Taylor, John, 277
Taylor, Margaret Smith, 256
Taylor, Robert H., 260, 268
Taylor, Tom, 483
Taylor, Zachary, **226,** 254, 344
Tchaikovsky, Peter I., 380, 384, 387, 391; *The Nutcracker,* 307
Tefft, Israel K., 46, 333
Temple, family name of, 358
Temple, Henry John (Lord Palmerston), 347
Temple, Sir William, 288
Temple Eanna, 7
Temple walls, 9
Tennyson, Alfred Lord, 94, **127,** 283; "Elaine," **282;** "In Memoriam," 280
Termites, 143
Terra-cotta cone, **11**
Terry, Dame Ellen Alicia, 460, **462,** 480; cabinet photograph of, **479**
Terry, Marion, 463
Terry, Roderick, 48
Testaments of Time: The Search for Lost Manuscripts and Records (Deuel), 35 n
Test plates, as measuring devices for comparing handwritings, 74
Texas, University of, 259
Thackeray, William Makepeace, 94, 120, 283, 312, 454; *Book of Snobs,* drawing from, **109**
Thaïs (Massenet), 380
"Thanatopsis" (Bryant), 129
Thatcher, John Boyd, 46
Thatcher, John Boyd, 46
Theater: admission tickets for, 459; American, 472, 484, 486–487; British, 459–471; collections, 64, 459–460, 470, 472, 475; commercial, 480; European, 463; history, 303, 459–460, 466, 471–478; Japanese, 331; legitimate, 466; New York City, 477; personalities, 462, 464, 478; royal, 466, 471; souvenirs, 487–488; Yiddish, 327
Theft of manuscripts, 141, 163, 191, 193–194
Thematic approach to collecting, 342
Thibault, Jacques Anatole. *See* France, Anatole
Thiers, Louis Adolphe, 366
Thirteen Author Collections (Wilson), 258
Thirty Years War, 370
Thoma, Hans, 416–417
Thoma, Ludwig, 310
Thomas, Edward, 288
Thomas, M., 50
Thomas, Norman, 456; diary of, 455, 457
Thomas Mann Papers, Library of Congress, 313
Thompson, H. Keith, Jr., 342; "The Autopen and the Signa-Signer," 100–105
Thoreau, Henry David, 179, 262, 265, 267; *Journals,* 259

Thornton, John, 287
Thrale, Mrs. Hester L., 280
Thurloe, John, 288
Tibet, 432; literature of, 331
Ticknor, William D., 267
Tiepolo, Giovanni Battista, 413
Tigris River and Valley, 5, 9
Tiles, souvenir, 488
Tilley, Vesta, 466
"Time and Temperature: Philadelphia, July 4, 1776" (Smith), 156 n
Tirso de Molina, 317
Tischendorf, Lobegott von, 431
Titan, The (Mahler), 307
Titian, 411, 412
Titles, 106, 358–359
Tocqueville, Alexis de, 297
Todd, Thomas, 493
Toledo, Spain, paper mill in, 36
Tolstoy, Leo, 190, 323
Toole, John Lawrence, 460
Toscanini, Arturo, 380, 391
Touch-typing, appearance of, 32
Toynbee, Arnold, *A Study of History,* 425 n
Tracing of writing, 76
Tracy W. McGregor Library, University of Virginia Library, 279, 400, 468
Trading companies and trade, 359, 444, 449
Tradition and traditionalists, 162, 302, 330
Tragedians, 460
Tragedy of Pudd'nhead Wilson, The (Twain), 265
Transcripts, definition of, 57, 163
Translations of foreign materials, 305, 327–331
Transportation, mode of, 453
Transreligious nature, 438
Travel: accounts, 440, 445; adventures, 445; importance of, 441, 453; literature, 440–441; manuscripts of, 440–453; medieval, 444; narrative, 41, 441, 444, 449–451; observations, 449; pre-Columbian, 444
Tree, Sir Herbert Beerbohm, 460
Tree bark, as writing surface, 28
Trever, M., 427
Trichlorethylene, 148
Troas, Alexandria, dedication from, 19
Tromp, Admiral Maarten, 373
Tronchin, François, 291
Trotsky, Leon, 373, 454, 456–457
Truman, Bess Wallace, 257
Truman, Harry S., 182, 213, 246, 255
Trunks, attic, 162
Ts'ai Lun, 36
Tunisia, 445
Turandot (Puccini), 317
Turgenev, Ivan, 323
Turgot, Anne Robert Jacques, 366
Turkey, 325, 376, 432, 435
Turner, Dawson, 44
Turner, Frederick Jackson, 305
Twain, Mark, 110, 265; *The Adventure of Tom Sawyer,* 32; *Following the Equator,* 262; forgeries of, 96; *Life on the Mississippi,* 32, 65; *The Tragedy of Pudd'nhead Wilson,* 265; typed letter of, 33
Tyler, John, 47, 225, 254, 483–484
Tyler, Julia Gardiner, 256
Tyler, Letitia Christian, 256
Tyler, Robert, 484
Tyler, Wat, 456
Typed letter signed (T.L.S.), 55
Typewriter and typing services, 31–33, 39, 57, 74, 89–90, 163, 238, 241, 288
Typewriter Girl, The (Allen), 32
Tyutchev, Feodor I., 323
Tzara, Tristan, 326

Ukrainian poetry, 326
Ullstein Autographenbuch (Jung), 380
Ultraviolet light, 74, 84, 145, 147–148
Umayyad caliphate of Spain, 426
"Ummī" (Paret), 426 n
Unamuno, Miguel de, 317
Uncial script, 13, 14, 16, 17, 18, 20
Undset, Sigrid, 320
Unethical practices, 191, 196
Ungaretti, Giuseppe, 316
Union of African Writers, 328
Universal Autograph Collectors' Club, 50 n
Universities, libraries of, 167, 209, 410, 427; major, 208, 384. *See also* specific universities
Unpublished letters and manuscripts, 168, 175, 266–267, 340, 456–457
Upcott, William, 44
Ur, clay tablets of third dynasty of, 6
Urdu poetry, anthology of, 329
Uruguay, 318
Uruk, king of, 7
Utah Supreme Court, 105
Utrecht, Peace of, 362
Utrillo, Maurice, 406
Uzbekistan, 435 n

Valencia, Spain, paper manufacturing in, 43
Valéry, Paul, 298
Valois kings of France, 362

Value: awareness of, 178–188; current, 185, 196; emotional, 444; fair market, 384, 387; investment, 438; market, 185, 187, 196; resale, 160–169, 195; sentimental, 129; upward spiraling, 399
"Vampire" letter, facsimile of, 285
Van Buren, Hannah Hoes, 256
Van Buren, Martin, **223,** 254
Van Cortlandt family, 206
Vandalism, 141
Van Dyck, Sir Anthony, 416
Van Gogh, Vincent, 327, 424
Vasari, Giorgio, 407
Vatican: archives, 43, 427; library, 203
Vatican Museum, 16, 21
Vaughan Williams, Ralph, 387, **389**
Vaults: airless, 143; impregnable, 432
Veblen, Thorstein, 456
Velázquez, Diego Rodríguez de Silva y, 411
Velde, van de (Dutch family of artists), 422
"Vellomaniac," self-styled, 271
Vellum, 35–36; from animal skins, 78; deeds on, 135; destruction of, 143; documents on, 39; holes in, 84; hygroscopic, 152; replaced by paper, 43
Venice, 416; doges of, 371
Verdi, Giuseppe, 315, 380, 384, 387, 391; *Aïda,* **385**
Verga, Giovanni, 317
Vergennes, Charles G. de., 366
Verhaeren, Émile, 298, 327
Verlaine, Paul, 297
Vermeer, Jan, 411
Vernacular literature, 27
Verso pages, 56
Vertical dimensions and filing, 57, 134–135
Vesey, Denmark, 456
Vespucci, Amerigo, 444, **445**
Vestris, Gaetano, 469
Viaud, Julien [pseud. Pierre Loti], 298
Victoria (queen of Great Britain), 44, 110, 183, 349, **353,** 361, 466; letter to, **45**
Victorian age, 314, 407, 410, 416–417
Victory, H.M.S., 358
Vienna: autograph market of, 329, 373, 376, 411, 432; library in, 427
Vietnam, 330
View From the Bridge, A (Miller), 315
Vigée-Lebrun, Élisabeth, 410
Vigny, Alfred de, 295
Violinists, 188
Virchow, Rudolf, 397
Virginia, University of, 259, 262, 265, 266, 342; library of, 33, 45, 47, 58, 59, 97, 101, 104, 108, 109, 113, 119, 262, 265, 277, 279, 323, 345, 356, 365, 388, 389, 390, 396, 399, 400, 403, 434, 468, 485, 490, 492. *See also* specific libraries within University of Virginia Library
Virginia Historical Society, 342
Virginius (Knowles), 463
Vocabulary and terminology of collecting, 54, 82
Volta, Alessandro, 399, 403
Voltaire, François Marie Arouet de, 188, 291, 294, 330, 411, 428
Volume the Second (Austen), **274–275**
Volume the Third (Austen), 272, **273**
Volz, Robert L., "Fair Copies and Working Copies," 126–133
Vondel, Joost van den, 327
Vortigern and Rowena, 93
Vouet, Simon, 411, 416
Voulkos, Peter, 424
Vowel sounds, 13, 19

Wagner, Richard, 181–182, 380, 384, 387, 391, 411; *Die Meistersinger,* 310
Wakeman, Stephen H., 258
Waldegrave, Earl, 355
Wales, history of, 204
Wallace, Nellie, 466
Wallack family, 480
Walpole, Horace, 92, 280
Walpole, Sir Robert, 355
Walter R. Benjamin Autographs, Inc., 213, 342
Wampum belts, 3–4
Wanderers Sturmlied (Goethe), 308
Ward, General Artemas, 161
Ward, E. M., 416–417
Warren, Robert Penn, 177
Wars and war services, 344, 349, 354–355, 362, 367, 370, 373
Washington, Booker T., 188
Washington, Judge Bushrod, 46
Washington, George, 46, 95, 215, **216,** 229, 254, 310, 332, 337, 341; forgeries of, **95–96,** 216; letters of, 160–161, 205, 230, 397; prices paid for autography by, 161; script of, 120, 216
Washington, Lund, 161
Washington, Martha Custis, 256
Washington Post, 377
Wassermann, Jakob, 311
Waste Land, The (Eliot), 266
Watergate scandal, 184
Waterhouse, Benjamin, 124
Waterman, L. E., 30
Watermarks on paper, 37–38, 78
Water-stained, definition of, 61

Watt, James, 38, 399, 403
Watteau contract, 417
Wax-covered woodblocks, use of, 28
Weavers, The (Hauptmann), 314
Webb, Sidney, 456
Weber, Carl Maria von, 384; *Euryanthe,* 380; *Jubel-Cantate,* 380
Webern, Anton von, 380
Webster, Daniel, 180
Weill, Kurt, 207
Weimar, grand duke of, 397
Weinheber, Josef, 314
Weisberg, Charles, 96
Welk, Lawrence, 305
Welles, Gideon, 164–166, 168–169
Wellesley, Arthur (Duke of Wellington), 358
Wellesley, family name of, 358
Wellington, Duke of, 347, 354–355, 358
Werfel, Franz, 305, 326
Werner, Abraham G., 34
Wesley, Arthur (Duke of Wellington), 358
Wesley, John, 435
West, B. C., 193 n
West, Benjamin, 112
Westphalia, Peace of, 362
Wharncliffe, Edward Wortley, **450**
Wharton, Edith, 262, 267
Wharton, Thomas, 288
Whistler, James McNeill, 406–407; butterfly pictogram of, 108–**109**
Whistler, Rex, 464
White, Henry Kirke, 288
White House cards, 213, **214**, 246, 247, 249–250
Whitman, Walt, 96, 259, 289; *Leaves of Grass,* 262
Whittier, John Greenleaf, 265
Wieland, Christoph Martin, *Oberon,* 306
Wiest, Robert C., "Nothing Is Forever: Preservation, Reapirs and Your Responsibility," 142–155
Wigman, Mary, 470
Wilberforce, William, 207
Wilde, Oscar, 283, 311, 460, 463
Wildenbruch, Ernst von, 311
Wilder, Thornton, 267; *The Matchmaker,* 310
Wilhelm Meister (Goethe), 307
Wilkes, Charles, 451
Wilkie, Sir David, 410
William, Walter R., 48
William I (king of Prussia and emperor of Germany), **369**
William II (king of Prussia and emperor of Germany), **369**
William III (king of England), 348, **352**; letter to, **448**
William IV (king of England), **353**, 471
William the Silent (William I, prince of Orange), 373
Williams, Dr. George C., 48
Williams, Mary A., 48
Williams, Ralph Vaughan. *See* Vaughan Williams, Ralph
Williams, Roger, 183
Williams, Tennessee, 269; *The Rose Tattoo,* 315
Williams, William Carlos, 262, 265
Williams College, Chapin Library at, 131, 132, 309, 372, 374
Wills and inheritance, 290
Wilson, Carroll A., 259; *Thirteen Author Collections,* 258
Wilson, Edith Galt, 257
Wilson, Ellen Axon, 257
Wilson, Francis, 484
Wilson, John, "British Historical Autographs," 347–360
Wilson, Woodrow, 90, **118–119**, **241**, 255, 262
Wilson Cary Nicholas Papers, University of Virginia Library, 113
Wilson-Dabney Correspondence, University of Virginia Library, 119
Windsor Castle, collection housed at, 44; command performances at, 471
Winter, William, 486; *The Plays of Edwin Booth,* 484
Winter Garden Theatre, 480
Wire frames and papermaking, 37–38, 42, 78
Wisdom, William B., 262
Wolf, Hugo, 307
Wolfe, James, 334
Wolfe, Thomas, 262, 265
Wonderful Writing Machine, The (Bliven), 32 n
Woodhull, Nathaniel, 206
Woodworth, Samuel, 384
Word Shadows of the Great (Madigan), 430 n
Wordsworth, Dorothy (Dora), 284
Wordsworth, Mary, 284
Wordsworth, Sara, 284
Wordsworth, William, 280, 284, 285, 289
Work copies, 126–133
Working papers of authors, 277
Workshops, conservation, 143, 146, 153–154, 331
Works of Thomas Gray, The (Gosse, ed.), 272
"Worn along folds" description, 61
Wray, Fay, 99
Wren, Christopher, 411

Wright, John B., diary of, 475
Wright, Richard, 311
Wright, Wilbur, 399, 404
Writing: ancient, 3, 9; Coptic, 13; cuneiform, 9; development of, 3–37; Egyptian, 13; erotic, 330; examination of, 73, 77; Greek, 16, 21; ideographic, 4, 8; instruments and devices for, 28–39, 55, 103; phonetic, 5; pictographic, 4, 8–9, 12, 28, 40; schools, 21, 27; style and skills, 27–28, 75–77
Writings on American History, 167
Writings of George Washington, The (Fitzpatrick), 161 n
Writings of George Washington, The (Ford), 161 n
Wyeth, Andrew, 422
Wyeth, N. C., 99, 422

Xerox copies of manuscripts, 135, 163

Yale University, 262, 341, 430
Yankee soldiers, letters from, 343
Yee, Chiang, *Silent Traveller in London,* 330
Yellow River Concerto, 330
Yevtushenko, Yevgeny, 325
Yiddish culture and linguistic amalgam, 327
Yoga, 329
Young, John, 44
Young, Owen D., 262
Young, Roland, 477, 482

Zaïre, 328
Zauberberg, Der (Mann), 307
Zen Buddhism, vogue of, 331
Zen master's secret diary, 439
Zeppelin, Count Ferdinand von, 404
Ziem, Felix, 416
Zionism, leaders of, 435
Zola, Émile, 298
Zurich, Switzerland, 399

U.S. PRES 211